The Cambridge Handbook of Psychology and Economic Behaviour

Psychologists have been observing and interpreting economic behaviour for at least fifty years, and the last decade, in particular, has seen an escalated interest in the interface between psychology and economics. *The Cambridge Handbook of Psychology and Economic Behaviour* is a valuable reference resource dedicated to improving our understanding of the economic mind and economic behaviour. Employing empirical methods – including laboratory experiments, field experiments, observations, questionnaires and interviews – the *Handbook* covers aspects of theory and method, financial and consumer behaviour, the environment and biological perspectives. With contributions from distinguished scholars from a variety of countries and backgrounds, the *Handbook* is an important step forward in the improvement of communications between the disciplines of psychology and economics. It will appeal to academic researchers and graduates in economic psychology and behavioural economics.

Alan Lewis is Professor of Economic Psychology in the Department of Psychology at the University of Bath. He is a former editor of the *Journal of Economic Psychology* and his books include *Morals, Markets and Money: Ethical, Green and Socially Responsible Investing* (2002) and *The New Economic Mind: The Social Psychology of Economic Behaviour* (with Paul Webley and Adrian Furnham, 1995).

The Cambridge Handbook of Psychology and Economic Behaviour

Edited by

ALAN LEWIS

CAMBRIDGE
UNIVERSITY PRESS

CAMBRIDGE UNIVERSITY PRESS
Cambridge, New York, Melbourne, Madrid, Cape Town, Singapore, São Paulo, Delhi

Cambridge University Press
The Edinburgh Building, Cambridge CB2 8RU, UK

Published in the United States of America by Cambridge University Press, New York

www.cambridge.org
Information on this title: www.cambridge.org/9780521856652

First published 2008

Printed in the United Kingdom at the University Press, Cambridge

A catalogue record for this publication is available from the British Library

ISBN 978-0-521-85665-2 hardback

This book is first and foremost dedicated to my wife Sandie Lewis. I would also like to dedicate it to all my past, current and future economic psychology students.

Contents

Part I Introduction, theory and method

Part II Finance

Part III Consumer behaviour in the private sector

vii

Figures

Tables

Notes on the contributors

Aaron Ahuvia is an Associate Professor of Marketing at the University of Michigan-Dearborn School of Management. Professor Ahuvia served as Vice-President for Academic Affairs for the International Society for Quality of Life Studies, is a former Associate Editor for the *Journal of Economic Psychology*, and is the 2007 winner of the University of Michigan-Dearborn Annual Research Award. His research looks at the nature of contemporary consumer culture with a special focus on how people can build successful lives within this environment.

Gerrit Antonides is Professor of Economics of Consumers and Households at Wageningen University, the Netherlands. He is (co-)editor of the *Journal of Economic Psychology*. His research topics are behavioural economics, financial decision making and consumer behaviour.

Russell Belk is Kraft Foods Canada Chair in Marketing at York University. He is past president of several professional associations and a fellow in the Association for Consumer Research. His work involves the meanings of possessions, collecting, gift giving and materialism, and is often cultural, visual, qualitative and interpretive. He has authored or edited a number of journal articles and books including *Handbook of Qualitative Research Methods in Marketing* (2006) and *Consumer Culture Theory* (with John Sherry Jr, forthcoming). He is also editor of *Research in Consumer Behavior*.

Valerie Braithwaite is Head of the Regulatory Institutions Network (RegNet) Program in the College of Asia and the Pacific at the Australian National University (ANU), and former Director of the Centre for Tax System Integrity at the ANU. She is editor of *Taxing Democracy: Understanding Tax Avoidance and Evasion* (2003) and of a special issue on responsive regulation and taxation in the journal *Law and Policy*. She is the author of a forthcoming research monograph, *Defiance in Taxation and Governance*.

Carole Burgoyne is an economic psychologist at the University of Exeter, UK. Her main research interests include the psychology of money, the material aspects of intimate relationships and gift giving. She is a co-author of

The Economic Psychology of Everyday Life (2001) and is currently investigating the financial and legal aspects of non-married heterosexual cohabitation.

John G. Cullis is Reader in Economics at the Department of Economics and International Development, University of Bath. Most of his research has been concerned with the application of microeconomic theory to non-market contexts. His work has appeared in a number of leading academic journals including the *Journal of Economic Psychology* and the *Journal of Socio Economics*. He is co-author (with Philip Jones) of *Micro-economics and the Public Economy: A Defence of Leviathan* (1987).

Werner F. M. De Bondt is Richard H. Driehaus Professor in Behavioral Finance at DePaul University, Chicago. He has published widely in economics and finance journals including the *American Economic Review* and the *Journal of Finance*. He is editor of the *Journal of Behavioral Finance*.

Bruno S. Frey is Professor of Economics at the University of Zurich. He received an honorary doctorate in economics from the Universities of St Gallen (Switzerland, 1998) and Göteborg (Sweden, 1998). He is the author of numerous articles in professional journals and books, including *Not Just for the Money* (1997*), Economics as a Science of Human Behaviour* (1999*), Arts and Economics* (2000), *Inspiring Economics* (2001), *Successful Management by Motivation* (with Margit Osterloh, 2001), *Happiness and Economics* (with Alois Stutzer, 2002) and *Dealing with Terrorism – Stick or Carrot?* (2004).

Tommy Gärling is Professor of Psychology at the Department of Psychology, and an associate of the Center for Consumption Science, Göteborg University, Sweden. He is also an associate of the Center of Excellence in Public Transport Services (SAMOT), Karlstad University, Sweden, and the Umeå School of Business, Umeå University, Sweden. He has published extensively in leading transportation journals such as *Transportation Research* and *Transportation* and is the editor or co-editor of eight books including, most recently, *Threats from Car Traffic to Urban Life Quality* (2007).

Danyelle Guyatt holds a PhD in Economic Psychology and is a Visiting Fellow at the University of Bath. Her research has focused on institutional investor behaviour and the impediments to long-term responsible investing. She is currently undertaking a research project for the Rotman International Centre of Pension Management on collaboration amongst pension funds and the evolution of conventions.

Denis Hilton is Professor of Social Psychology at the University of Toulouse-II. His research interests centre on social cognition, reasoning, judgement and decision-making, and experimental economics. During 2001–3 he was a CNRS research fellow in the Department of Economics at the University of Toulouse-I.

Tim Jackson is Professor of Sustainable Development at the University of Surrey, England and Director of the ESRC Research Group on Lifestyles, Values and Environment. He sits on the UK Sustainable Development Commission and was academic representative on the UK Sustainable Consumption Round Table. He is editor of the *Earthscan Reader on Sustainable Consumption* (2006).

Philip R. Jones is Professor of Economics at the Department of Economics and International Development, University of Bath. He has published extensively on public finance and public choice in leading economics and political science journals, e.g. *American Economic Review*, *Economics Journal*, *Journal of Public Economics*, *British Journal of Political Science* and *Political Studies*. He is co-author (with John Cullis) of *Public Finance and Public Choice* (2nd edn, 1998).

Simon Kemp is Professor of Psychology at the University of Canterbury, New Zealand. He was co-editor of the *Journal of Economic Psychology* from 2000 to 2005, and has authored or co-authored two books on economic psychology, most recently *Public Goods and Private Wants: A Psychological Approach to Government Spending* (2002). His current research projects include the psychology of government decision-making and the nature of psychological measures.

Erich Kirchler is University Professor at the Institute for Restaurant Economics, Education Psychology and Evaluation at the University of Vienna, Austria. He has published widely, especially in the fields of tax compliance and household consumption patterns. He is co-author of *Conflict and Decision Making in Close Relationships* (2001).

Stephen E. G. Lea is Professor of Psychology at the University of Exeter, UK. He was editor-in-chief of the *Journal of Economic Psychology* from 1991 to 1995, and has co-authored or edited a number of books in economic psychology, including *The Individual in the Economy* (1987) and *The Economic Psychology of Everyday Life* (2001). He has wide research interests in economic psychology, with a current emphasis on the psychology of money, poverty and debt. His other research interests include animal cognition and behavioural ecology, and ways in which different disciplines interact over common subject matter.

Alan Lewis is Professor of Economic Psychology at the University of Bath. He was editor-in-chief of the *Journal of Economic Psychology* from 1996 to 2000. He is currently working on two research projects: sustainable and socially responsible investment, and cultural differences in tax evasion. His most recent book is *Morals, Markets and Money* (2002).

Terry Lohrenz is a Research Instructor in the Human Neuroimaging Laboratory, Department of Neuroscience, Baylor College of Medicine in Houston, Texas. His work focuses on neuroeconomics and neuroimaging.

Peter Loukopoulos is currently a researcher at the Swedish National Road and Transport Research Institute. He completed his PhD at Göteborg University as a social psychologist specializing in people's adaptation to travel demand management measures. His current research examines traffic safety campaigns. He has published in various transportation and social psychological journals such as *Transportation Research* and *Journal of Applied Social Psychology*.

P. Read Montague is the Brown Foundation Professor of Neuroscience and Professor of Psychiatry at Baylor College of Medicine in Houston, Texas, where he also directs the Human Neuroimaging Lab, the Center for Theoretical Neuroscience and the newly formed Computational Psychiatry Unit. He has been a member of the Institute for Advanced Study in Princeton, NJ, a fellow at Rockefeller University in New York, and a fellow at the Salk Institute in San Diego, CA. His work focuses on computational neuroscience, neuroeconomics and neuroimaging.

Ellen K. Nyhus is Associate Professor of Marketing at the Faculty of Eonomics at the University of Agder, Norway. She completed her PhD at the Norwegian School of Economics and Business Administration, specializing in household saving and borrowing behaviour. Most of her research concerns household economic decisions such as saving, investments, labour supply and economic socialization. Her current research focuses on the effect of psychological variables on wages. She has published in various psychology journals such as the *Journal of Economic Psychology* and the *British Journal of Psychology*.

Clive L. Spash is an Economics Professor and Science Leader within the Sustainable Ecosystems Division of CSIRO, Canberra, Australia. He is Editor-in-Chief of *Environmental Values*, and has over a hundred publications, including *Greenhouse Economics: Value and Ethics* (2002) and (with Michael Getzner and Sigrid Stagl, eds.) *Alternatives for Environmental Valuation* (2005). He was Vice-President and then President of the European Society for Ecological Economics from 1996 to 2006.

Paul C. Stern is director of the Committee on the Human Dimensions of Global Change at the US National Research Council. He is co-author of *Environmental Problems and Human Behavior* (2nd edn, 2002) and co-editor of *Understanding Risk: Informing Decisions in a Democratic Society* (1996), among other works. His primary research interests are the human dimensions of environmental problems, particularly individual and household behaviour and the development of governance institutions. His co-authored article 'The Struggle to Govern the Commons' won the 2005 Sustainability Science Award from the Ecological Society of America.

Alois Stutzer is Assistant Professor of Economics at the University of Basel. His research interests range from economics and psychology to political economics. He has co-authored the book *Happiness and Economics* (2002) and co-edited the volume *Economics and Psychology. A Promising New Cross-Disciplinary Field* (2007) (both with Bruno S. Frey).

Karl-Erik Wärneryd is Professor Emeritus of Economic Psychology at the Stockholm School of Economics, Sweden. Most of his research has been related to consumer behaviour and household financial management. His most recent books include *The Psychology of Saving*: *A Study on Economic Psychology* (1999) and *Stock-Market Psychology*: *How People Value and Trade Stocks* (2001).

Paul Webley is Director and Principal of the School of Oriental and African Studies and Professor of Economic Psychology at the University of London. He has co-authored four books on economic psychology, most recently *The Economic Psychology of Everyday Life* (2001). His current research focuses on children's economic behaviour and tax compliance.

Michael Wenzel is Senior Lecturer at the School of Psychology at Flinders University, Adelaide, Australia. He is a social psychologist with a particular interest in justice, social identity, inter-group relations and compliance. A current research project investigates retributive and restorative responses to transgressions.

Ulrich Witt is Professor of Economics and Director at the Max Planck Institute of Economics in Jena, Germany. He has published extensively on evolutionary economics in general and on economic behaviour from an evolutionary perspective in particular. His most recent book is *The Evolving Economy* (2003).

PART I

Introduction, theory and method

1 Introduction

ALAN LEWIS

I was very pleased to be asked to edit this volume for Cambridge University Press, not least because I have been in the economic psychology business for over twenty-five years. A quarter-century of publication of the *Journal of Economic Psychology* was notched up in 2005 (Kirchler and Holzl, 2006). It is a good time to take stock as well as look to the future.

Psychology has become one of the most popular degree subjects in industrialized countries and is continuing to spread its net. Pure and applied forms have become blurred as the relevance of the subject both theoretically and in everyday life has become apparent. With these developments, it was only a matter of time before psychologists turned their attention to economic behaviour.

Psychology has been described as a synthetic science and economics as analytic: psychology has aped the empirical approaches of the natural sciences while economics has much more in common with mathematics. The synthetic route requires observation of economic behaviour, the testing of hypotheses and the construction of generalizations based on those observations. Psychology's quest to understand mind and behaviour is now directed in this context to building an appreciation of the economic mind and economic behaviour.

The contributors to this volume reflect the breadth and depth of this undertaking, covering aspects of theory and method, consumer behaviour, the environment and, finally, biological perspectives. The contributors are distinguished scholars from the USA, France, Sweden, Norway, the UK, Austria, the Netherlands, Australia, New Zealand, Switzerland, Germany and Canada. The majority of authors have first degrees in psychology or economics but there are also contributors with backgrounds in finance, management science and mathematics: all, in their various ways, are committed to the study of psychology *and* economics.

The title *The Cambridge Handbook of Psychology and Economic Behaviour* was chosen with care. The title is an inclusive one where essays employ a range of methods: laboratory experiments, field experiments, questionnaire studies, observations, interviews; the list is a long one. In short, both qualitative and quantitative methods are deemed acceptable and no one single area of psychology is given precedence. This broader remit is in contrast to handbooks in behavioural economics (Camerer, Loewenstein and Rabin, 2004) and experimental economics (Kagel and Roth, 1995). Behavioural economics has been heavily influenced by a single area, namely cognitive psychology, and the work of Daniel Kahneman and Amos Tversky among others. The award of the 2002 Nobel Prize in economics to the psychologist Daniel Kahneman (in the same year that the work of Vernon Smith on experimental economics was honoured) gave the field considerable legitimacy within the economics profession. Behavioural economics is almost entirely driven by an economics-led research programme, with some convenient findings from cognitive psychology tagged on: for example, Prospect Theory. Experimental economics employs even less psychology, except in the sense of using the experimental method, which has a long tradition in psychology, to explore economic behaviour. Both behavioural economics and experimental economics maintain as a central theme the model of rational economic man: for the majority of behavioural economists heuristic decision making is viewed as encompassing interesting and consistent exceptions to rationality; while in experimental economics 'subjects' almost always make repeated decisions in experimental settings where real money can be lost or won as a result. The introductory chapter of the *Handbook of Experimental Economics* (Roth, 1995) records that one of the pioneering experiments was conducted by the psychologist L. L. Thurstone but from then on psychology barely gets a mention.[1]

The developments in behavioural economics and experimental economics are both to be welcomed: the current *Handbook* is accessible to psychologists as well as economists, providing economists can continue this trend of expanding their economic imagination.

In the chapter that immediately follows, 'Theory and method in economics and psychology', Denis Hilton is in an optimistic mood, believing that economists are indeed becoming more interested in human thought and behaviour. There are still, however, serious methodological misunderstandings between the two disciplines which are traced in a historical analysis. Economics is depicted as being driven by prediction rather than explanation, and as having a view of the person as a learning organism swayed by reinforcement in the behaviourist tradition; that rational economic man may share some of the characteristics of a laboratory white rat. The main thrust of the chapter is that the current enthusiasm among some contemporary economists for 'objective' evidence of economic rationality in brain functioning (neuroeconomics) is a kind of reductionism which side-steps the psychological level of analysis: we need to illuminate the 'black box' between economic antecedents (stimuli) and economic responses. For Hilton, not all the intellectual traffic is one way, that

---

[1] I overstate the case. Roth (1995) says 'a question we frequently hear from some of our psychologist colleagues, and one we can reasonably ask ourselves, is "what accounts for economists' reluctance to abandon the rationality model, despite considerable contradictory evidence?"' (p. 76). Roth argues that approximations of human behaviour can live with counter-examples, even if there are a lot of them. The gap between the two disciplines may not be as wide as it first appears, as psychologists do not object to a broader interpretation of rationality: psychologists certainly do not see their subject as the study of irrationality. Roth finishes on a positive note, writing that experimental economics should 'avoid establishing rigid orthodoxies on questions of methodology' (p. 86).

is from psychology to economics, and he concludes that there are instances when a psychologist should be more like an economist.

The chapters in part II are all concerned with finance. In the first chapter, 'The economic psychology of the stock market' by Karl-Erik Wärneryd, the author draws on evidence from cognitive psychology and the study of the emotions to develop a model of expectation formation. The chapter makes it clear that not all investors are the same and that financial experts are in some cases as flawed as the rest of us. Next, De Bondt, in a comprehensive essay, 'Stock prices: insights from behavioral finance', shows how investor psychology can influence the dynamics of world equity markets. This author believes that behavioural finance can provide the groundwork for an alternative theory to the theory of rational and efficient markets. Webley and Nyhus in their contribution, 'Inter-temporal choice and self-control: saving and borrowing', empirically examine how people make choices over time. There appear to be many exceptions to the standard economic model of inter-temporal choice: for example, many people, even intelligent ones, are myopic and want good things now, not later. The merits of experimental studies of inter-temporal choice have already been appreciated by some influential economists; the authors argue that questionnaire studies of saving and borrowing behaviour and insights from social as well as cognitive psychology deserve attention.

In economics, choices are modelled as being made by individuals with little or no reference to the social context in which those choices are made.[2] Some cognitive psychologists take a similar view. Social psychologists see things rather differently, attesting that most (and perhaps all) choices are dependent on the social milieu. In Burgoyne and Kirchler's chapter, 'Financial decisions in the household', the social nature of choice and decision making is the central frame of reference not only where choices are made with respect to another person but also where choices are negotiated and in some cases disputed within the confines of close relationships and partnerships.

In the last chapter of part II, Danyelle Guyatt's 'Corporate social responsibility: the case of long-term and responsible investment', the social nature of economic choice is broadened further to take into account the welfare of society as a whole. Is the sole responsibility of business to make as much money as possible for stockholders, or are there wider concerns dependent in part on the values, preferences and moral commitments of participants? This contribution examines the choices that institutional investors face and how they might change in the future.

Part III on consumer behaviour in the private sector starts with two chapters which are closely related. In the first, 'Consumption and identity', Belk asks us to consider whether 'who we are' is becoming increasingly dependent

---

[2] In contrast, work in behavioural economics has consistently shown that in social dilemma games people gain non-pecuniary benefit from mutual cooperation and will punish unfair behaviour, i.e. social preferences frequently predominate (Fehr and Fischbacher, 2003).

on what we consume and display, creating a superficiality at the expense of a deeper appreciation of life and spirituality. In the second, the myth of a simple relationship between wealth and happiness is debunked by Ahuvia in his comprehensive review 'Wealth, consumption and happiness'. The chapter concludes that perhaps a culture less obsessed with economic growth could be a happier one.

Antonides' 'Comparing models of consumer behaviour' announces a change of key. In this contribution, the author dispassionately assesses the strengths and weaknesses of intuitive, heuristic and emotion-based models compared to rule-based, systematic and analytic models variously constructed by marketing experts, consumer psychologists and economists. He concludes that economic models do not do justice to the complexity of contemporary consumer environments.

The chapters in part IV are dedicated to the study of consumer behaviour in the public sector. In the introductory essay by Kemp, 'Lay perceptions of government economic activity', the author opines that psychology can help us unravel whether public policy really improves well-being and whether governments provide services that citizens want. In a more ambitious essay by Cullis and Jones, 'How big should government be?', *Homo economicus* is compared to their concept of *Homo realitus*. Both are seen as having implications for government 'intervention' in markets: if the assumptions underlying *Homo economicus* reign then there is little need for consumer protection or corrections for market failure; *Homo realitus* on the other hand needs the government to take on the role of 'corrective government'. The part ends with an extensive review of the empirical literature on the tax gap by Braithwaite and Wenzel, 'Integrating explanations of tax evasion and avoidance'. The question is posed, 'if the deterrence models favoured by economists are accurate, why is there so much voluntary compliance?' The authors develop a consumer–citizen perspective where individuals not only weigh up the costs and benefits of compliance in a narrow sense but also assess the benefits, justice and fairness of fiscal policy both for themselves and for society as a whole.

Part V comprises five chapters devoted to environmental issues, with the first being Jackson's contribution on 'Sustainable consumption and lifestyle change'. The themes of consumer behaviour and the role of government are revisited as the author feels we are entering a new era: an era where policy makers will attempt to influence our everyday consumption, threatening 'freedom of choice'. The chapter underlines how sustainable consumption has deep-seated psychological dimensions, making the passage of lifestyle change a rough one. The following chapter focuses this discussion on household consumption in Stern's 'Environmentally significant behavior in the home'. This essay is centred on 'private sphere' behaviour conducted largely behind closed doors. Stern believes there are blind spots in the approaches taken by psychologists and economists in this field and that interdisciplinary work must be the priority for the future.

The motor car is very important to us and not just in an instrumental sense, as Gärling and Loukopoulos point out in their chapter on 'Economic and psychological determinants of car ownership and use'. The chapter assesses which policy interventions are likely to work. Continuing this theme of environmental policy making, Frey and Stutzer's chapter, 'Environmental morale and motivation', makes the important point that heavy-handed intervention can result in a reduction in the implicit motivation and goodwill of citizens. Environmental morale and motivation must be sustained if cooperation problems in this realm are to be overcome.

The last chapter in part V is Spash's 'Contingent valuation as a research method: environmental values and human behaviour'. The author shows that the contingent valuation method is a flawed one, that the search for the holy grail of a perfect survey instrument is pointless, but that insights from psychology can help in the interpretation of results where behavioural motives are taken into account.

The final part (part VI) comprises biological perspectives. Psychology as a discipline is hard to define, yet many are relatively happy with a description of psychology as the study of 'mind, brain and behaviour'. Psychologists have been involved in, among other things, locating the seats of emotion in the brain, the interpretation of language and the production of speech and the varying functions of the two hemispheres. In recent years economists and psychologists have become interested in which parts of the brain are responsible for economic decision making, and comprehensive reviews of neuroeconomics already exist (Camerer, Loewenstein and Prelec, 2005). The chapter by Lohrenz and Montague, 'Neuroeconomics: what neuroscience can learn from economics', achieves something different, as it assumes that evolutionary efficiency is an inherently economic mechanism and is built into the brain. These building blocks are examined using functional magnetic resonating imaging (fMRI), paying special attention to the processing of rewards and social exchange.

The evolutionary theme is also pursued in the penultimate chapter, 'Evolutionary economics and psychology', where Witt explores, in particular, the influence of innate learning mechanisms on behavioural adaptations during the course of economic transformations. While Witt is concerned with economic transformations in recorded history, the final chapter, 'Evolutionary psychology and economic psychology', goes back much further, as for Lea our economic minds to some extent reflect Stone Age selection pressures. In this context, fast and frugal heuristics, for example, can be viewed as an adaptive toolbox rather than as exceptions to rationality and, perhaps controversially, much of our economic behaviour relies on processes that we share with other animals.

I commend this collection to you and take the opportunity to thank all of the contributors for their efforts in improving communications between the two disciplines of psychology and economics.

1.1 References

Camerer, C., G. Loewenstein and D. Prelec. 2005. Neuroeconomics: How neuroscience can inform economics. *Journal of Economic Literature* 43, pp. 9–64.

Camerer, C., G. Loewenstein and M. Rabin. 2004. *Advances in Behavioral Economics*. New York: Russell Sage.

Fehr, E. and U. Fischbacher. 2003. The nature of human altruism. *Nature* 425, pp. 785–91.

Kagel, J. and A. Roth (eds.). 1995. *The Handbook of Experimental Economics*. Princeton, NJ: Princeton University Press.

Kirchler, E. and E. Holzl. 2006. Twenty-five years of the *Journal of Economic Psychology* (1981–2005): A report on the development of an interdisciplinary field of research. *Journal of Economic Psychology* 27(6), pp. 793–804.

Roth, A. 1995. Introduction to experimental economics. In J. Kagel and A. Roth (eds.) *The Handbook of Experimental Economics*. Princeton, NJ: Princeton University Press.

2 Theory and method in economics and psychology

DENIS HILTON

2.1 Introduction

Economics is increasingly looking to psychology and neuroscience in order to revise its assumptions about how people process information and make choices. New subdisciplines of economics have sprung up, such as behavioural economics, psychological economics, cognitive economics and neuroeconomics, which draw extensively on findings in psychology and neuroscience. In addition, the new field of experimental economics enables economists to test theories about human choice behaviour directly in controlled conditions. Economists are increasingly abandoning the assumption that people are fully rational in their choices, and are becoming increasingly interested in constructing models which incorporate realistic assumptions about human thought and behaviour.

This chapter will take a psychologist's point of view on these developments. Despite the fact that economists and psychologists are often addressing the same fundamental question – why humans make the choices they do – there is often puzzlement about the other side's theory and methodology. These kinds of misunderstanding may reflect lack of knowledge not only of the background and aims of the other's discipline, but also of the historical context of the social sciences.

I will try to explain the aims and methods of economics in a way that will make their theoretical orientations seem more understandable to psychologists. I will first try to chart the various ways that economists are seeking to use psychology in their work. I will then suggest that economics – even of the new psychological kind – is still strongly rooted in a metatheoretical perspective that many psychologists would recognize as behaviourist. I will accordingly

I would like to acknowledge the unstinting hospitality of the economics department at the University of Toulouse, which has given me remarkable opportunities to talk with economists, and to listen to them discussing their work amongst themselves. This was greatly facilitated by a research fellowship from the French CNRS between 2001 and 2003. In particular I would like to thank Laure Cabantous, Bruno Frey, Rom Harré, Robin Hogarth, John McClure, Steven Sloman and Bernard Walliser for helpful comments on previous drafts, and Bruno Biais, Guido Friebel, Bruno Jullien, Sébastien Pouget, Paul Seabright, Marcela Tarazona and Jean Tirole for many helpful and instructive discussions concerning economics and psychology.

address two major questions about theoretical frameworks and scientific explanation. The first is to do with the issue of levels of explanation, and whether and how psychological-level explanations can inform economic questions, and in turn whether and how neuroscience can inform economics. The second is to do with depth of explanation, which contrasts psychology's more realist approach to constructing and testing socio-cognitive theories in scientific explanations of behaviour to the more instrumental perspective of economics. I argue that this realist approach can lead not only to improved explanation of the facts, but to greater opportunities for modification of economic behaviour at both the individual and societal level.

This chapter therefore pays attention to differences in how theories are constructed and evaluated in the two disciplines. In my view, this perspective can shed light on the recent debate about methods in economics and psychology, which has focused on experimentation (e.g. Croson, 2005; Hertwig and Ortmann, 2001, 2003; Sugden, 2005b). I will suggest, for example, that much of the heat in this debate has been generated by differences in theoretical orientations (cognitivist and realist in the case of psychology, behaviourist and instrumentalist in the case of economics). While written from a psychologist's point of view, this chapter may still be useful to economists. Through throwing a different light on their assumptions and practices, it may help economists to reflect on their own professional identity and epistemological approach, in much the same way that spending a period abroad teaches us about our own national identities, through observing what raises foreigners' eyebrows.

2.2   Rational behaviourism in economics

At the beginning of the twentieth century economics and psychology (like philosophy and linguistics) were confronted with the success of the natural sciences. Both attempted to adopt the methods of the natural sciences through taking behaviourist approaches (measuring observables, such as behaviours rather than thoughts and feelings, in psychology, prices and market share rather than experienced value, etc., in economics). While psychology primarily adopted the experimental methods of the natural sciences, economists retained the eighteenth-century model of *Homo economicus* as motivated by rational self-interest, but adopted mathematical formalisms to render their theories more precise and 'scientific'. In addition, they adopted the revealed preference axiom which assumes that preferences will be revealed in objectively measurable phenomena such as prices and market share (Lewin, 1996).

Below I identify some behaviourist characteristics of economics. This can be done by measuring economics up against Lyons' (1977) checklist for identifying behaviourist theories, namely: a rejection of internal states of the organism as scientific explanations of behaviour; a tendency to see no essential difference between the behaviour of humans and other animals; an emphasis on the importance of learning and reinforcement (positive and negative) in explaining behaviour; and a penchant for instrumentalist (i.e. predictive) rather than realist (i.e. explanatory) theories of behaviour.

2.2.1 Rational behaviourism

The 'revealed preference' assumption embodies what might be called a 'rational behaviourist' approach, as it combines the rational self-interest model of choice with a behaviourist approach to measurement. To know an agent's preferences, one does not have to ask her; one simply observes what choices she makes. In addition, there are some important symmetries between economists' models of the rational calculation of self-interest and psychologists' models of how stimulus–response (S–R) associations are formed: both assume that with experience, the organism (or agent) will learn the costs and benefits associated with actions that it (she) takes. Both approaches emphasize the importance of learning and incentives for understanding behaviour.

The rational self-interest model effectively makes the same predictions as Thorndike's (1911) Law of Effect that links reward to response – any response that leads to a reward is likely to be repeated. In the language of 'rational behaviourism' this can be expressed as the price effect in economics – an activity can be encouraged by raising the price. Neoclassical economics – like behaviourist psychology – assumes that human behaviour will be explained by situational costs and benefits (gain–loss matrices, reward–punishment schedules). Economics assumed that no curiosity need be expressed about the intervening cognitive processes that led from stimulus to response (it was assumed that gain–loss matrices would be calculated correctly by rational choice processes), while radical behaviourism in psychology argued that no attention should be paid to intervening cognitive processes, as they were unobservable.

Although it may seem paradoxical that the economists' model of *Homo economicus* drawn from the eighteenth-century Enlightenment should yield essentially the same method of analysing behaviour as the early twentieth-century psychologists' model of *Rattus norvegicus*, that is indeed what happened. Values and preferences of decision-makers are to be inferred from observing them make choices under varying conditions. Economists, like behaviourist psychologists, abhorred finding out people's values and preferences just by asking them disinterested questions. Indeed, a striking illustration of the convergence of economics and behaviourism comes from the use of revealed preference theory to infer demand curves for animal preferences (Kagel *et al.*, 1981).

2.2.2 Experimental procedures in economics and psychology: the debate over learning and incentives

Tellingly, the first line of defence that economists put up against the implications of psychologists' experimental findings on bias and error was that they were based on questionnaire research with no payoffs for correct responses. Experimental economists were sceptical about whether these findings would be reproduced with experienced, financially motivated participants who fully understood their task, and who had opportunities to learn. This position is a variant of the *tabula rasa* theory that underpins behaviourism, in that it assumes that cognitive biases are 'malleable' rather than being inherently structured, and thus can be eliminated by appropriate market conditions. And indeed markets sometimes do eliminate biases: for example, List (2004) found that the procedure devised by Kahneman, Knetsch and Thaler (1986) to demonstrate the endowment effect (involving exchanging mugs for chocolate bars) works with normal consumers but not with expert dealers in picture cards of sports stars whose behaviour approximates to that predicted by the standard neoclassical model.

Nevertheless, the major result of economists' research on human bias and error has been to demonstrate how often biases in judgement and choice observed in experimental settings generalize to both real-world economic settings (Camerer, 2000; Hilton, 2001) and to experimental settings with financial incentives (Camerer and Hogarth, 1999; Hertwig and Ortmann, 2001). These reviews show that while incentives reduce (but do not eliminate) bias and error in approximately 55% of cases, they have no effect in approximately 30% of cases, and have paradoxical effects (i.e. actually *increase* bias and error) in approximately 15% of cases. On the whole then, these results vindicate the cognitive programme of research of psychology, since they show that the way cognitive processes frame how people perceive reality will indeed affect their behaviour independent of learning and incentives.

2.2.3 The costs and benefits of the behaviourist stance: instrumentalism vs. realism in explanation

A common puzzle for psychologists is to understand how economists can hold on to the rational self-interest model of human choice and behaviour. After all, it has been so clearly discredited by innumerable experimental studies. The clue to this puzzle may be that psychologists' aims in developing models of choice are different from those of economists. Whereas psychologists aim to develop *realist* models of cognitive processes that are accurate and testable descriptions of how the human mind works, economists' aims in building models are often much more pragmatic. In particular, economists seek models of choice that are useful in helping them understand and explain economic questions at the

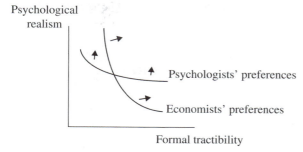

Figure 2.1 Indifference curves for theory preferences in economists and psychologists. Reprinted from *European Economic Review*, 46, Rabin, M. 'A perspective on psychology and economics', pp. 657–85, Copyright 2002, with permission from Elsevier

collective level, concerning market behaviour, prices, laws, institutions and so on. So if many economists hold on to the rational choice model despite its evident falsity as an exact descriptive model of individual human choice, it may be for other reasons, such as its simplicity and elegance in generating more-or-less correct implications for understanding these higher-level economic questions. This *instrumentalist* position means that these economists are likely to give up the standard expected utility (SEU) model of choice only if a more psychologically plausible model enables them to make significantly better predictions about economic questions such as market share and prices, or helps them write more effective contracts and legislation (see Sugden, 2005b).

Rabin (2002) cleverly models these different orientations of economists and psychologists with indifference curves (see figure 2.1). Economists' preference for models is strongly influenced by their formal properties (elegance, tractibility), and less so by their realism and descriptive accuracy. For psychologists the inverse is true.

2.3 Levels and kinds of explanation

We have seen that despite the diversity of ways (behavioural, psychological, cognitive, neuroeconomic and experimental) in which economists have been integrating psychology, each of these subdisciplines possesses significant assumptions that differentiates it from experimental psychology. This is no bad thing, as all can enrich (and in my view some already have enriched) psychology in significant ways (see, for example, the discussion of social cognitive neuroscience below). However, I will argue that economists' use of psychology and neuroscience is likely to profit from careful attention to two questions.

The first, which I term the 'levels of explanation' question, concerns distinguishing between economic (social), psychological and neuroscientific levels of explanation, and the ways in which these levels of explanation interrelate. I will argue for a hierarchical model of scientific questions and explanation, where explanations are constrained but not determined by explanations at a lower level. I first illustrate this generative model of explanation by showing how properties of collectives (e.g. markets) may emerge from (and be explained by) lower-level properties of their components (agents). In turn I consider how properties of agents may emerge from (and be explained by) properties of their brains. However, I conclude that economics cannot be reduced directly to neuroscience: an intermediate level of psychological explanation is necessary.

Having established the need for an autonomous psychological level of explanation, I then turn to the second 'depth of explanation' question. Here I address the need at the cognitive (psychological) level of explanation to develop theories that are explanatory in nature, and which thus offer greater power for prediction and control than 'shallow' behaviourist-style explanation, which I will show to still be often favoured in psychologically inspired economics.

2.3.1   Levels of scientific questions: economics, psychology and neuroscience

Economics, psychology and neuroscience have different objects of study, and pose their scientific questions at different levels. Economics typically studies the behaviour of collective phenomena such as firms, markets and prices, and asks questions like: How can markets achieve efficient allocation of goods? What causes markets to fail? Psychology typically studies the individual, their personality, the way they perceive, remember, and make judgements and choices, and asks questions like: What causes depression in an individual? Why do people make irrational choices? Neuroscience typically studies brains, mapping brain anatomy and circuits, and relating this to functional processes such as vision, hearing and decision-making. So far, neuroscience seems to focus more on mapping what parts of the brain or brain circuits are associated with different psychological functions (e.g. short- vs. long-term memory; emotional vs. 'rational' decision-making) than on answering theoretically driven questions (see table 2.1).

Of course, the picture given above is something of an oversimplification, as it is easy to see points of overlap. For example, while economists following in the tradition of Hayek see economies as 'brains' that transmit information (see Forsyth et al., 1992), the social psychology of group processes examines how information flows around groups in a way that is close in spirit to this kind of economic analysis (e.g. Nowak, Szamrej and Latané, 1990). But the important point is to see that different levels of scientific question exist, and to understand how questions at one level can be answered by facts, assumptions or hypotheses that draw on another level.

Table 2.1 *Three levels of scientific question and associated scientific disciplines*

Domains of study (Level of question)	Level of explanation	Kinds of science
Market behaviour	Human collectives	Economics
Small group decision-making		Social psychology of groups
Cognitive processes in judgement- and decision-making	Human individuals	Cognitive psychology
		Social cognition
Individual values and preferences		Artificial intelligence
Brain and body function	Brain and body parts and systems	Neuroscience

2.3.2 Generative explanation: how economic phenomena can emerge from psychological characteristics

A cornerstone of classical economics has been to explain a seemingly paradoxical result: how socially desirable equilibrium states can emerge from a society of uniquely self-interested actors (Smith, 1776/1993; Turgot, 1761). This can be explained in the following way. If there is a lack of grain at Toulouse due to crop failure but a surplus at Limoges where the harvest was good, prices will rise in Toulouse and drop in Limoges. This will have two advantages. First, the high prices in Toulouse will discourage people there from hoarding grain because it will be too expensive, thus encouraging grain to be distributed to more people. And second, the higher prices in Toulouse will attract grain from Limoges through encouraging an entrepreneur to buy low in Limoges, and accept the cost (and risk) of shipping grain to Toulouse in order to sell high there. These classic market mechanisms make some hypotheses about human nature: namely, that some people are smart enough to spot opportunities, and greedy enough to take the risks necessary to exploit them.

In science as in common sense, questions typically arise when we need to know how something surprising or undesirable has come about (Weiner, 1985). We can see that Smith's famous example of the 'hidden hand' that redistributes goods to where they are needed is so powerful because it shows how surprising properties (e.g. a socially desirable distribution mechanism) can emerge from a self-organizing system based on actors whose sole motive is rational self-interest. The point of the example is that market success occurs *because* (not *in spite*) of a psychological property of its agents – their self-interest. Smith's equilibrium model is a paradigm case of generative explanation (Harré, 1988) which shows how an effect (social welfare in the distribution of goods) can be produced by a mechanism (prices) built of components that possess specified (but unexplained) causal powers (selfish agents). The kind of explanation involved here thus seems to consist in building a model which *can* generate the effects of interest (see Sugden, 2000).

2.3.3　Questions about deviations: the logic of contrastive explanation

Following Smith, neoclassical economics established efficient market theory as an ideal mechanism for the distribution of goods. Subsequent theories in economics have taken *Homo economicus* and efficient market theory as a foil, and have sought to explain deviations from this 'norm' (e.g. Sugden, 2005a). Such 'contrastive explanation' (Hesslow, 1983, 1988; Lipton, 1991) identifies as a cause the property in the deviation model which 'makes the difference' between the effect observed (a market anomaly) and what should be expected according to efficient market theory. The kind of explanation involved here seems to involve counterfactual reasoning about what will happen if we *modify* a certain characteristic of the SEU/efficient market model. Deviation models can focus either on market failures or on psychological 'irrationality' for explanations of market anomalies.

2.3.3.1　Within-level explanation: explaining market anomalies through market failure

In a classical form of explanation in economics, questions will be resolved by explanations which stay at the same level of analysis. For example, a market anomaly will be explained by a market failure (e.g. failure of buyers and sellers to have access to the same information about the quality of the product). For example, Akerlof's (1970) analysis of 'lemons' shows that in markets of rational actors where there is asymmetric information (e.g. sellers of used cars know more about the quality of the car than potential buyers), the price of used cars will drop dramatically as buyers assume that sellers will only offer low-quality cars (lemons) and refuse to pay high prices. So sellers will in turn not be motivated to sell high-quality cars, and only low-quality cars will be offered for sale. This leads to 'adverse selection' in the market, as bad products drive out good products, leading the example to be presented as showing how 'asymmetric information can result in market failure' (Pindyck and Rubinfield, 1998, p. 620; see also Sugden, 2000, for a more detailed exposition of Akerlof's argument). Here the explanation for market failure is found in terms of market characteristics (distribution of information in the market), rather than in terms of psychological characteristics of individuals.

Similarly, typical explanations in psychology stay 'in house' at the same level. For example, decisions to choose a certain diet can be predicted by a weighted combination of our beliefs that the diet will work, the desirability of being thinner for us, the desirability of being thinner for important others, and our desire to please those others (Ajzen and Fishbein, 1980). However, with the advent of neurosciences, much thought has gone into how psychological-level explanations (in terms of beliefs, desires, rules of inference, etc.) can be constrained by what is known about the components of the system (serial or parallel computer, brain) on which these algorithms run (Marr, 1982). Consequently, interesting properties at one level of explanation can emerge from the properties of the components at a lower level.

2.3.3.2 Cross-level explanation: explaining market failure through psychological characteristics

In cross-level explanation, the underlying psychological properties of market agents can also be used to explain market failure. Efficient market theory assumes that under the right market conditions (e.g. informational symmetry between buyers and sellers), markets composed of fully rational agents will allow goods to be exchanged to the benefit of both parties. However, change the nature of the component parts of the system and new properties will emerge in the system itself. For example, if we assume – following Kahneman and Tversky's (1979) prospect theory – that losses loom larger than gains in the minds of market agents, then markets can lose liquidity because of the 'disposition effect' (Shefrin and Statman, 1985), as agents refuse to trade goods of equivalent value because the experienced loss has higher disutility than the experienced gain has utility for them.

This 'disposition effect' could explain anomalies such as that observed in the British housing market in the early 1990s when a dramatic fall in house prices meant that many owners would have to sell houses at a loss compared to what they had paid before the market collapsed. Of course, because of the market collapse they could also buy other houses more cheaply. But loss aversion would explain why many would continue to live for months and even years in a house in one city (say Manchester), while commuting for hours to another (such as Edinburgh) where they had taken a job, with all the attendant commuting costs and dislocation of personal and family life. The psychological hurt that would be caused by selling a house at a loss would outweigh the gain incurred by buying one in their new place of work.

2.4 Explanation across two levels: is neuroeconomics possible?

A question that merits consideration is whether intelligible explanations can be achieved by going down *two* levels (e.g. from economics through psychology to neuroscience). Scientific explanation often proceeds by attributing a phenomenon to some disposition of another entity, which serves as the end-point in an explanatory chain. In turn the explanation can be expanded by attributing this disposition to the disposition of another entity at a lower level, which is attributed with an unexplained 'causal power' to produce the effects it does. As Harré (1988, p. 142) writes:

> the chemical behaviour of liquids, solids and gases is explained by the behaviour of unobservables, molecules and chemical atoms . . . But one might well ask for an explanation of the behaviour of chemical atoms, for example why do they chum up in the proportions they do? The next level of explanation simply repeats the pattern of the level above. Drawing on the behaviour of positively and negatively electrically charged bodies as a source-model, a further step is taken, in which electrically charged electrons and protons are invoked, the story being filled out with neutral neutrons. The electrical properties of these structures explain the differences in behaviour of chemical atoms.

As we shall see below, this kind of reductionism across levels of explanations seems to be a pattern of explanation envisaged in what has come to be called 'neuroeconomics'.

Economists seem to be in two brains (minds) about how neuroscience will inform economics: as Camerer, Loewenstein and Prelec (2005, p. 9) write:

> Some important insights will surely come from neuroscience, either directly or because neuroscience will reshape what is believed about psychology which in turn informs economics.

Other economists clearly write as if they favour the direct route. For example, Fehr, Fischbacher and Kosfeld (in press) assert that:

> Neuroeconomics merges methods from neuroscience and economics to better understand how the human brain generates decisions in economic and social contexts . . . Neuroeconomic studies . . . enable us to go beyond the prevailing 'as if' approach in economics by uncovering the neural mechanisms behind individual decisions.

The psychological level of explanation appears to be overlooked in this merger (see Rusticini, 2005). This is all the more surprising as the seminal 'neuro-economic' studies that Fehr *et al.* cite (Breiter *et al.*, 2001; Rilling *et al.*, 2004; Sanfey *et al.*, 2003) are in fact due to collaborations between psychologists, ethologists and neuroscientists.

Nevertheless, it is easy to see that Fehr *et al.*'s theoretical argumentation requires a psychological level of description (tastes, preferences) and is supported by psychological observations (questionnaire and behavioural evidence). They begin by reviewing experimental evidence that shows that people possess 'other-dependent preferences' that are inconsistent with the rational self-interest model. For example, they establish the accuracy of this psychological-level description of human nature through reviewing relevant experimental evidence which persistently shows that people have 'a taste for revenge', that is they will forgo personal rewards in order to punish people who transgress social norms in experimental games. They then ask the question:

> Why do we observe these strong deviations from the predictions of the standard model? What are the driving decisions behind the decision to trust, to reciprocate trust, and to punish non-reciprocation?

They then describe a study by Dequervain *et al.* (2004) in which one participant (player A) was given the opportunity to punish a partner (player B) who had abused her in a previous round of a sequential social dilemma game, even though this would incur financial cost. Noting that 'questionnaire and behavioural evidence indicates that player A indeed had a strong desire to punish the defector', they argue that punishment of the defector has intrinsic utility for her because it is associated with activation in the dorsal striatum, a zone associated with pleasure and reward in the primate brain. Neuroscience evidence is thus used to support the psychological-level assertion that people have a taste for revenge on those who have wronged them.

2.4.1 The autonomy of levels of explanation

The Dequervain *et al.* study is thus informative about the origin of a psychological taste for revenge. It does not support the idea, for example, that people learn to take revenge for reputational reasons, and may therefore be relevant to economic theories about how people come to acquire this taste (see Fehr and Schmidt, in press, for a review). But it does not obviate the necessity of a psychological-level explanation, as I show below.

To answer the question of whether a neuroscientific fact can elucidate an economic one without recourse to a psychological level of explanation, the appropriate test requires counterfactual reasoning. If experiments on social control had turned out differently (say people were not prepared to pay to punish transgressions of social norms), we could not conclude that people had a taste for revenge, and we would not be able to use this concept to explain economic phenomena. However, if Dequervain *et al.*'s (2004) results had turned out differently (no difference was found in brain functioning in the dorsal striatum as a function of opportunities to take revenge), this result would of course necessitate a new theory of how taste for revenge comes to be a human characteristic. However, it would have no implication for the first link in the chain of explanation: economic anomalies could still be explained by a psychological taste for revenge. This example shows that the psychological level of explanation is autonomous, and cannot be reduced to (i.e. be substituted by) a neuroscientific one.

It is easy to see that a similar intransitivity of causation will arise in other examples. For example, we have seen above how asymmetric reaction to gains and losses modelled by prospect theory can explain the disposition effect, thus illustrating how economic phenomena at the market level can be explained through reference to the psychological properties of the agents in that market. In turn, we might seek to explain this asymmetry in valuing gains and losses in terms of the differential reaction of the fronto-median area of the cortex, which shows twice as much brain activity in reaction to losses as compared to gains (Gehring and Willoughby, 2002). One may speculate that if fronto-median activity vehicles experienced utility, then this may explain why losses loom larger than gains. But once again, even if Gehring and Willoughby's results had turned out differently, this would not invalidate prospect theory, which could still explain the disposition effect in market behaviour. Indeed the fact that prospect theory has been developed in psychology and applied to economics before the relevant neuroscience studies had been performed serves to illustrate the limitations of neuroscientific-level theories for economic theories *per se*.

2.4.2   Neuroeconomics as social cognitive neuroscience

While neuroeconomics offers the promise of many important insights, its import for economics will not bypass the need for a psychological level of explanation. Its importance for economists will be to buttress explanations of economic behaviour motivated by psychological assumptions.

For psychologists, neuroeconomics might best be thought of as a sub-branch of social cognitive neuroscience, with a particular interest in economic questions and use of experimental economic techniques (such as experimental games) to induce emotional states such as envy, guilt and desire for revenge. In contrast, social psychologists have studied emotions such as shame, regret and guilt through asking participants to imagine such scenarios (e.g. Smith *et al.*, 2002), and neuroscience studies have used similar scenario techniques (Berthoz *et al.*, 2002). However, experimental games of the kind devised by economists allow researchers to generate real emotional states in controlled conditions. In this sense the more behavioural orientation of economists has opened up an exciting line of inquiry for psychologists interested in the study of emotion.

2.5   Depth of explanation: on creating and testing cognitive theories in economics

Having proposed a hierarchical structure that may help understand the scope of economic, psychological and neuroscientific levels of explanation, and how they may fruitfully be demarcated from and interact with each other, I will now concentrate on the cognitive level of explanation. I will first attempt to explain why economists and psychologists formulate and test cognitive theories in systematically different ways. I begin by setting the present dialogue between economists and psychologists in a historical context, notably the rise of behaviourism in the twentieth century which I will argue is still more influential in contemporary economics than in psychology. I then attempt to clarify what each discipline's fundamental 'paradigms' (in a Kuhnian sense, i.e. preferred research questions, frameworks and techniques) are.

Economics has been essentially a deductive science (if that is possible), which works from axioms to deduce 'results' (e.g. about what a market equilibrium price should be, etc.). For economists, a 'result' is very often a theoretical prediction about what behaviour should be expected given a set of assumptions, and which is mathematically derived from a set of axioms. For example, Biais and Pouget (1999) prove that in the trading game devised by Plott and Sunder (1988) there should be no trading at all if all actors in the game are fully rational (Bayesian), as all rational actors will recognize that in these markets with asymmetric information, only offers that lose the agent money will be accepted by a rational counter-party. For Biais and Pouget (1999) this constitutes a 'result', even though they knew full well that it was quite wrong as a descriptive model of how humans behave (there is in fact considerable trading in these markets). The mathematical formalization characteristic of economic theories helps spell out how the prediction must follow from the theory's presuppositions.

On the other hand, psychology (like physics, chemistry, biology, etc.) is essentially inductive in nature, using experimental results to validate theories. For psychologists, a 'result' is obtained when the predictions of a theory have withstood experimental test better than the predictions of other rival theories. Although psychological theories are rarely expressed in mathematical form, psychologists generally follow the procedure of 'strong inference' (Platt, 1964) in which successive explanations are generated and eliminated by a programme of experimental research.[1]

It is only recently that economics has come to adopt the method of strong inference that is characteristic of mature experimental sciences. To gauge this, it suffices to read the way Fehr and Schmidt (in press) introduce their experimental research programme on other-dependent preferences. Having described the existence of various alternatives to choice models that depend purely on rational self-interest, they write:

> One of the exciting aspects of this development is that the newly developed theories of other-regarding preferences were tested in a new wave of experiments, sometimes before they were published . . . These experiments . . . show that it is possible to discriminate between different motivational assumptions . . . There has always been a strong convention in economics of not explaining changing puzzling observations by changing assumptions on preferences. Changing preferences is said to open Pandora's Box because everything can be explained by assuming the 'right'

---

[1] The sense of induction that I use here is essentially the hypothetico-deductive method as described by Mill (1872/1973). Mill regarded induction as a 'method of proof' of theories that had already been generated, and provided canons for the elimination of hypotheses, principally based on the methods of agreement and difference that are still used in strong inference to this day.

preferences. We believe that this convention made sense in the past when economists did not have the tools to examine the nature of preferences in a scientifically rigorous way. However, due to the development of experimental techniques these tools are now available.

No contemporary psychologist would feel it necessary to write such a passage for his peers. Indeed, many psychologists would find it hard to believe that theories could be published in respectable scientific journals without accompanying experimental tests. In fairness to economics, it should be noted that deriving predictions about market behaviour from assumptions about the characteristics of agents is often not a trivial affair, and often a significant scientific contribution in its own right. Indeed, the programme of research described by Fehr and Schmidt (in press) combines the best of both worlds: mathematical rigour in deriving non-trivial predictions from theories, and experimental rigour in seeking the observations that will discriminate between those theories.

2.6 Depth of explanation: the cognitive revolution in psychology

While economics still adopted a behaviourist position, psychology increasingly drew on analogies with computer science that demonstrated the reality of cognitive processes, and, inspired by Broadbent, Bruner, Chomsky, Piaget, Simon and others, the discipline underwent a cognitive revolution. Psychology at this point sought inspiration from artificial intelligence and formal linguistics to create cognitive theories with a strong structuralist flavour that typically distinguish information-processing systems (automatic vs. controlled; short- vs. long-term memory systems; visual vs. auditory vs. articulatory short-term memory stores; 'modules' for language, social cognition, etc.). This was accompanied by a distinctive kind of theory-building and testing, which aims at 'deep' explanations that posit unobservable entities which *generate* the observed phenomena in question. I attempt to describe how such deep explanation using hypothesized causal models that generate behaviour differs from 'shallow' behaviourist explanation below.

The story I am about to tell is apocryphal. Whether or not it is true does not matter, as it will still serve to illustrate why psychologists abandoned behaviourist theories for the kind of cognitive theories that enable explanatory models of the kind they build and test today. According to the story, psychologists discovered that Welsh-speaking children were poorer at mental arithmetic than English-speaking children. A behaviourist should be satisfied with this discovery, for he could specify a set of externally observable stimulus conditions (S, speaking Welsh vs. speaking English) which would predict how well a child would respond (R) on an externally observable task (problems requiring mental arithmetic). The explanation would satisfy the classic schema of behaviourism:

$$S \rightarrow R$$

There were however some problems with this explanation. Although predictive, it lacks explanatory power: we do not know *why* Welsh children are worse at mental arithmetic than English children. Another problem is one of coherence: since mental arithmetic is taken as a sign of mental ability, difference in performance would seem to imply that Welsh children have less ability than English ones, which seems implausible (even though I am English).

The puzzle can however be easily resolved by a cognitive theory in terms of limited working memory capacity. The Welsh words for numbers are longer than the English ones (which are generally monosyllabic), and therefore take up more space in verbal working memory, causing fewer items of information to be rehearsed, thus leading to less effective performance on the mental arithmetic tasks. The explanation now includes an O term that represents mental operations that intervene between stimulus and response and takes the form:

$$S \rightarrow O \rightarrow R$$

The explanation is more satisfying: it explains why performance is different in Welsh and English children in positing a *mechanism* that shows *how* the difference can be produced. It also resolves the question of coherence: the worse performance of the Welsh-speaking children is attributed to their language not to their intelligence. The cognitive explanation is in this sense 'deeper' as it *explains how* the phenomenon comes about. The behaviourist explanation is 'shallow', since it only *predicts* when the phenomenon should be observed.

In addition, the hypothesized mechanism suggests some simple experiments to test the theory: find a group of bilingual children and, using a counterbalanced experimental design, ask them to solve matched sets of problems in Welsh and English. Here, according to the theory, differences in performance should be expected in the same children. Another experiment would be to suppress verbal rehearsal in both Welsh- and English-speaking children, for example by asking them to perform a concurrent verbal task while doing the arithmetic. Here, according to the theory, differences in performance should be eliminated.

This is how psychologists typically use strong inference to test a theory. They use the theory to generate hypotheses that are tested through controlled experimentation, allowing causal induction through application of Mill's (1872/1973) method of difference, the fundamental canon of scientific induction. They therefore vary the presence and absence of the putative cause (speaking Welsh vs. speaking English while doing mental arithmetic) to see if it has the expected effects on the effect of interest (performance on the mental arithmetic task). They also use techniques to interfere with the operation of the cause when present (e.g. distraction to block mental rehearsal). This is because they believe short-term memory buffers to be *real* entities, which can be knocked out by appropriate procedures. In this they seem no different to physicists who believe in the reality of atoms, nuclei and electrons, but who infer their existence through theory-laden experimental observation techniques because they cannot observe them directly (Hacking, 1983).

This has led psychology to a blend of cognitive theorizing and experimental validation which favours 'mini-models' which can explain a set of experimentally controlled observations. Models are tested by manipulating the presence and absence of hypothesized causal factors (and disablers) that the theory predicts should have an effect. In this way, psychologists seek to demonstrate their understanding of a phenomenon by constructing experiments in which they can make a phenomenon appear and disappear as the result of appropriate manipulations predicted by the theory being tested. As an example of this 'now you see it, now you don't' approach to explaining a phenomenon, framing effects support prospect theory because presenting a gamble in terms of gains induces risk aversion whereas framing it in terms of losses produces risk seeking. For psychologists, it is usually far more important to publish 'experimental results' that are predicted by a theory, than to show how predictions can be deduced from that theory. Mathematics rarely comes into play, being usually considered an inessential distraction.

2.7 The need for cognitive explanation: incentives, overconfidence and statistical methodology

In this section I review two cases in detail where I argue that psychologically inspired economics could benefit from 'deeper' cognitive theories in two domains that have attracted substantial attention from psychologically inspired economists: incentives and overconfidence. Finally, I discuss how the disciplines appear to favour statistical tests that favour their metatheoretical orientations.

2.7.1 The behaviourist economics of incentives: rediscovering the need for cognitive theories

Psychology cast off the mantle of behaviourism in the 1950s, in part due to demonstrations that Thorndike's Law of Effect cannot explain significant parts of human behaviour. A notable example is Festinger and Carlsmith's (1959) work on the paradoxical effects of reward, which showed that increasing payment for a boring task could actually lead to *less* motivation to perform it, which they interpreted in terms of reduction of cognitive dissonance. Later research in psychology has pointed to the importance of 'intrinsic motivation' in performing many tasks, and the fact that external incentives can undermine this intrinsic motivation (a phenomenon called 'crowding out' by economists).

An economist who has done much to call the attention of his colleagues to the implications of relevant work in psychology on the 'crowding out' of motivation is Frey (1997). But even here – in an economist who is both very knowledgeable about and sympathetic to psychology – the theoretical statements have a distinctly behaviourist feel in the way they detail a set of conditions in which crowding out should or should not occur. Following his review of the literature, Frey suggests that incentives 'crowd out' intrinsic motivation when there is:

– intrinsic interest of the task
– personal relationship of principal and agent
– participation of agent in principal's decisions

and when employees

– are only rewarded for doing the work specified (no promotions, honours, prizes, etc.)
– perceive rewards as 'controlling' rather than 'supportive'.

Although this is a very useful summary of when intrinsic motivation is crowded out, it gives little in the way of specifying psychological mechanisms that bind these conditions into a single, coherent explanation that explains *how* and *why* crowding occurs. Four of the five conditions given specify situational characteristics, and only one refers to cognition (perception of the intention behind the reward).

An experimental field study on incentives gives an even clearer example of how a behaviourist orientation still appears to guide psychologically inspired economic theorizing and research. For example, Gneezy and Rusticini (2000) have shown that fining parents for coming late to collect their kids from school actually causes them to come late even more often than a control group who were not fined. This is a classic demonstration of a paradoxical effect of a (dis)incentive, of the kind identified by Festinger and Carlsmith (1959). But while Festinger and Carlsmith used their data to sound the death knell of behaviourism in psychology, arguing that cognitive processes (e.g. dissonance reduction) have to be invoked, Gneezy and Rusticini do not go beyond their demonstration to develop and test rival cognitive theories that explain *why* they get their effect.[2]

Gneezy and Rusticini are quite aware of the kinds of cognitive theories that could explain the paradoxical effects of incentives in their study. One hypothesis that they evoke (but do not test) is that offering money changes the participants' perception of the exchange relationship. For example, one can predict,

---

[2] Indeed, Gneezy cheerfully sees this as a job for psychologists (Gneezy, personal communication)!

following the Durkheimian analysis proposed by Tetlock *et al.* (2000), that in *sacred* domains (e.g. giving blood, giving time to help immigrant children), offering money for a greater engagement would be perceived as insulting, as it would call into question the actor's generosity. However, in *profane* domains (e.g. working overtime for an accountancy firm, taking on more responsibilities in an office), offering an incentive for more work would be perceived as a compliment by the employee because it confirms the perceived competence of the worker. These hypotheses were confirmed in a questionnaire study using hypothetical scenarios (Buscato *et al.*, 2004). The fact that offering money can be perceived negatively by the intended recipient has been documented by Burgoyne and Routh (1991) in their study of the unacceptability of money as a gift, for example at Christmas.

2.7.1.1 Explanation, prediction and control

Based on economic research on incentives, we would have some predictive statements we can make. Based on a simple induction from empirical studies (Camerer and Hogarth, 1999; Hertwig and Ortmann, 2001), we could predict (say) that incentives work 55% of the time, have no effect 30% of the time, and have paradoxical effects 15% of the time. We could be still more specific and note that paradoxical effects are obtained only in tasks using judgements and decisions, and never in games and markets (see Hertwig and Ortmann, 2003). Or we could use Frey's (1997) typology to specify when we would expect incentives to work, and when we should get paradoxical effects. But we would be still lacking a theory about an underlying mechanism that explains why we should get normal incentive effects in some cases, and paradoxical effects in others. For example, Bénabou and Tirole (2003) suggest that parents' decisions about when to propose incentives to their children will be based on experience about when they work. However, this 'explanation' still seems to fall short for a cognitive theorist – it is a bit like explaining language learning through 'experience' – but what exactly would this tell us about the grammatical rules that are being learned here?

Whether or not the predictions made by the sacred–profane distinction are confirmed by further research, it seems to me that this kind of socio-cognitive model should be useful in designing effective use of incentives. By obtaining a theoretical clarification of how incentives and disincentives are *perceived* and *interpreted*, we will surely be in a better position to predict their effects and to propose ways of framing them such that they will be perceived in a way that will make them work. All this should be useful information to managers, yet so long as economists do not engage in experimental and empirical research on cognitive processes, they will not be able to address these issues directly (see McKenzie, 1997, for a related critique of the weak level of evidence provided by Thaler, 1991 to support his claim that endowment effects explain market anomalies). Of course, psychologists do exactly this kind of research, and this no doubt helps explain why textbooks on organizational behaviour abound with policy recommendations based on psychological research, just as consumer behaviour textbooks make extensive use of cognitive models of persuasion to make recommendations about how to design messages.

2.7.2 From overconfidence to kinds of overconfidence

A cognitive hypothesis that has received much attention from behavioural economists is that overconfidence leads investors to lose money on financial markets. Using theoretical arguments, Odean (1998; see also Benos, 1998; Daniel, Hirshleifer and Subrahmanyam, 1998) showed that overconfidence (in two distinct senses: (a) considering oneself to have better information than other market players; and (b) overestimating the precision of one's information) should lead to poor performance in financial markets. In addition, Barber and Odean (2001) produced a behavioural 'demonstration' of overconfidence using a database on private investors obtained from a large bank. They found that men tend to trade more than women and incur greater losses due to failure to make profits that offset transaction costs. Using gender as a proxy for overconfidence, they argued that this result demonstrates that men are more overconfident than women, and that this overconfidence leads to lower trading profits (see the chapters by De Bondt and Wärneryd in this volume).

Let us consider the logic of these demonstrations. First, while the theoretical demonstrations that the two kinds of overconfidence (in oneself compared to others, or in the precision of one's information) will lead to suboptimal performance provide two sufficient causes for the losses observed by Barber and Odean (2001), there is no independent evidence that they were indeed the effective causes. Second, Barber and Odean obtained no direct measure of overconfidence (in either sense) in their market participants, but used gender as a proxy for overconfidence. As research has persistently failed to find gender differences in miscalibration (Gigerenzer, Hoffrage and Kleinbölting, 1991), miscalibration (overestimating the precision of one's information) cannot explain the difference in male and female trading behaviour. Either it is overconfidence in the second sense (in oneself compared to others) that explains this effect, or it is something else yet again. The theoretical demonstrations that suboptimal performance should result from overconfidence in either sense are only demonstrations that these *can* be causes of a particular effect; they are not demonstrations that these processes *are* the *actual* causes in a particular observed case.

To obtain evidence that these processes actually are causes of the effect in question, we need to use experimental methods combined with scientific realism to verify the presence of the hypothesized underlying processes. Using an experimental financial market with asymmetric information, Biais *et al.* (2005) replicated Barber and Odean's finding that men trade more than women. However, Biais *et al.* (2005) found no correlation between gender and overconfidence in judgement. Biais *et al.* (2005) used a quasi-experimental method to study the effect of overconfidence, which they operationalized using a questionnaire test of miscalibration, where participants were required to answer general knowledge questions through setting 90 per cent confidence intervals on their responses (Alpert and Raiffa, 1982). This gave them an independent means to classify participants as high or low in miscalibration (i.e. the tendency to overestimate the precision of one's judgements), and thus allowed them to show that miscalibration did not explain overall differences in male and female earnings. Finally, Biais *et al.* (2005) sought to pass the 'now you see it, now you don't' test by showing that miscalibration (as predicted) hurt traders in 'winner's curse traps' (situations where the stated price was a poor indicator of real asset value) but not when prices were good signals of real asset value.

To summarise: while gender affects trading behaviour, and overconfidence in judgement leads to lower profits in an experimental financial market, there is no evidence (*pace* Barber and Odean) that gender produces lower profits in men due to their greater miscalibration of judgement. It is of course possible that gender causes lower profits in men through another *kind* of overconfidence than miscalibration in judgement. In fact, Odean's (1998) theoretical model contains two parameters for overconfidence: one representing overconfidence in the precision of one's knowledge (i.e. underestimating conditional uncertainty); and another representing a belief that one has better information than other agents. Miscalibration of judgement appears to correspond to the first kind of overconfidence, whereas 'positive illusions' (Taylor and Brown, 1988) that the self is superior to others, has high control over outcomes, etc., appear to correspond to the second kind of overconfidence. In fact, Hilton *et al.* (2007) show that the tendency to make miscalibrated judgements is not correlated with the tendency to entertain positive illusions such as the better-than-average effect, unrealistic optimism and high perceptions of personal control.

Distinguishing kinds of overconfidence and careful operationalization of these constructs will allow research questions to be generated and experimentally tested. For example, does positive self-evaluation lead people to trade more often (thus explaining why men are more active in financial markets than women), whereas accuracy in judgement may lead people to make better, more perspicacious and profitable trades? The prospect of experimental and other kinds of empirical tests may provide a new kind of constraint when building their models (see Hilton, 2007b, for further discussion).

2.7.3   Statistical methods for testing causal models: interacting and mediating variables

Finally, economists' and psychologists' different theoretical orientations seem to show up in the preferences for statistical tests shown by editors in the respective fields, which Croson (2005) calls 'surprisingly parochial'. She notes that economists prefer regression analyses whereas psychologists prefer analysis of variance (ANOVA) despite the close formal similarity of these techniques. Psychologists probably favour ANOVA because, for example, the different levels of a variable can reflect the levels of experimental manipulations. In addition, ANOVA automatically calculates interaction terms which reveal the 'now you see it, now you don't' nature of causal production/prevention of an effect (e.g. risk aversion vs. risk seeking) depending on facilitating/blocking conditions (e.g. gain vs. loss framing).

On the other hand, experimental economists prefer regressions, probably because this is the preferred method for expressing predictions in the field. Croson (2005) notes correctly that they steer away from interaction terms, an observation confirmed by our own experience. In Biais *et al.* (2005), we originally used an interaction term in our regression analysis to show that miscalibration hurt traders' earnings in winner's curse traps but not in other market situations. However, the editor supported a reviewer who requested that we calculate two separate regressions for winner's curse traps and other market situations.

Finally, a statistical method that has spread like wildfire in social psychology and organizational behaviour in the last twenty years is causal path analysis (Baron and Kenny, 1986). Psychologists have adopted path analysis in droves because it allows them to make strong tests of S–> O–> R causal chains. Specifically, it allows them to test whether the hypothesized intervening variables (Os) may mediate the effect of independent variables (Ss) on dependent variables (Rs). For example, Valenzuela, Srivastava and Lee (2005) show that the kind of (personality vs. situational constraint) attributions made for an opponent's behaviour seems to mediate the effects of different cultural orientation (US vs. Korea) in accepting hypothetical offers in an ultimatum bargaining game. Despite its widespread use in psychology, I have yet to see this technique used to test hypotheses by experimental economists. No doubt this will come, as economists build, operationalize and test theories about the intervening effect of cognitive variables (such as attributions, perceptions of fairness, etc.) on economic behaviour.

2.8 Conclusions

I have a confession to make. I started professional life as an attribution theorist in social psychology, and indeed, old habits die hard, as the previous handbook chapter I was asked to write was on this very topic (Hilton, 2007a). Attribution theory describes the way we explain others' behaviour, and shows that we typically search for explanations when we are surprised by others' behaviour. In addition, these explanations tend to be *contrastive* in nature: they focus on *abnormal conditions* – causal factors that differentiate the target case being explained from the normal case of our experience. So while an important part of science in both disciplines is mastering the key literature, going to conferences and asking questions about human choice processes, these cannot explain the difference between the disciplines as both do it. Contrastive explanations are achieved by focusing on what is different between the two.

So it is that I have spent much of my time in recent years asking the ethnocentric but (for me) natural question: *Why can't an economist be more like a psychologist?* The chapter you have read gives my current answer. In part the differences are due to situational constraints, namely the different kinds and levels of questions that economists and psychologists address. But I cannot escape the feeling that there are deeply ingrained subcultural traditions about what constitutes 'good work' in the fields, and that economists will continue to take an instrumentalist tack when modelling choice processes, whereas psychologists will take a realist one. This will not change overnight. Interesting work will continue to have occasional difficulties in crossing disciplinary barriers. Editors with behaviourist orientations in economics may continue to reject psychological work that does not incentivize subjects. Conversely, it is easy to imagine that editors with cognitive orientations in psychology would reject much experimental economics as being 'mere' demonstrations that lack strong inference tests of rival models of underlying cognitive processes.

2.8.1 *Homo economicus*: now you see him – now you don't

The other feature of economics that differentiates it from psychology is the dominance of a single theoretical model – *Homo economicus*. This makes economics essentially deductive in nature, as its principal theoretical challenge is either: (a) to make interesting new deductions from this rational model (e.g. about what should follow from it in certain specified market conditions); or (b) to show how minor changes in assumptions will lead to different deductive consequences. Economists will find these 'deviation' models (Sugden, 2005b) attractive if they are able to use simple assumptions to offer a wide range of new predictions in domains that interest them. A paradigm case of explanatory power combined with theoretical parsimony is prospect theory (Kahneman and Tversky, 1979), and this no doubt helps explain its success in economics. Part of the reason for the success of prospect theory in economics is that it makes a simple additional assumption (it is changes of state that matter, not final wealth) which explains a widespread phenomenon – the differences in reactions to gains and losses.

The continuing erosion of the dominance of *Homo economicus* may nevertheless necessitate a change of theoretical strategy for economists. No longer will it be possible to adhere to the grand project of applying a single kind of economic analysis based on *Homo economicus* to all domains of life (see Becker, 1993). This audacious project seems to have gone as far as it can (and further), and may have to beat a well-organized retreat. For example, if economists accept that people are *sometimes* self-interested, and *sometimes* sensitive to others' welfare (see Fehr and Schmidt, in press), then they may begin to build causal models that tell us *when* and *why* we expect them to be one or the other. Similarly, we will need causal models to tell us when and why incentives work or backfire, when optimism is likely to be productive rather than counterproductive, and so on. Economics will thus need 'contingent' theories that specify how situational characteristics interact with cognitive mechanisms to produce (or prevent) the effects in question. These models will probably look quite like some of the cognitive psychology models that I have reviewed. In this vein, it is worth noting the related trend in psychology to contingent models of decision-making, where task characteristics and informational environments 'select' optimal strategies (Gigerenzer, Hoffrage and Kleinbölting, 1991; Payne, Bettman and Johnson, 1993).

2.8.2 Opportunities for psychology

I wish to conclude by identifying two major opportunities for psychology that emerge from the recent interest that economics has shown in psychology. The first is practical, the second theoretical.

2.8.2.1 Interventions on economic behaviour

Psychologically inspired economists have shown the relevance of psychological research to a wide range of questions of social importance, such as the quality of decision-making, the experience of happiness, and so on. However, while economists will focus on economic instruments to deal with these problems, psychologists can propose other solutions. For example, Landier and Thesmar (2005) recommend certain kinds of debt structuring for banks that will enable them to deal with over-optimistic entrepreneurs. However, psychologists can propose courses on decision-making to managers and entrepreneurs aimed at averting them from well-known decision traps. Similarly, while economists may propose (dis)incentive schemes to promote behaviours that are desirable (e.g. recycling) or undesirable (e.g. smoking), social psychologists are well placed to design communication strategies that are likely to persuade people to engage in (or disengage from) these activities of their own accord. It seems to be up to psychologists to step forward to do this kind of work, as we have seen that even psychologically inspired economists tend to go blurry and shy away when it comes down to the nitty-gritty of modelling and influencing cognitive processes.

2.8.2.2 Why should a psychologist be more like an economist?

So far most of the intellectual traffic has been from psychology to economics. This is no doubt because psychology does not depend on economic assumptions in the way that economics depends on psychological assumptions, and therefore will not be affected by economic theories in the same way. But economics deals with social structures and processes in which the individual operates, and may help psychology capture and model important aspects of human social environments. For example, Frey and Stutzer (2002) give an insightful review of how socio-economic and political factors can influence reports of subjective well-being and happiness.

At the level of methodology, we have seen how experimental economic games have provided new procedures for psychologists to capture key aspects of social interactions, and to study topics such as social emotions and cultural effects on behaviour in a controlled way. And at the level of theory, economists may be able to provide psychologists with the tools that can help them model the way social processes modify psychological ones, in the way described by Adam Smith in *The Theory of Moral Sentiments* (1759/2002), where he describes how our emotional reactions are regulated by social interactions with others, until they come into a state of equilibrium. Bénabou and Tirole (2003) show how the kind of concepts that Smith used (equilibrium, the regard of others) can be translated into terms familiar to both contemporary economists (signalling, principal–agent theory) and social psychologists (self-perception, attribution, etc.). Much remains to be done to work out the details of how this kind of theoretical integration can be operationalized and tested in ways that would be meaningful to psychologists. But its very existence suggests that the tools of economics may yet help psychologists address a question that has been largely neglected in recent social cognition research – the social regulation of thought and emotion.

2.9 References

Ajzen, I. and Fishbein, M. 1980. *Understanding Attitudes and Predicting Social Behavior*, Englewood Cliffs, NJ: Prentice-Hall.

Akerlof, G. A. 1970. 'The market for "lemons": Quality uncertainty and the market mechanism', *Quarterly Journal of Economics* 84: 488–500.

Alpert, M. and Raiffa, H. 1982. 'A progress report on the training of probability assessors', in D. Kahneman, P. Slovic and A. Tversky (eds.), *Judgement Under Uncertainty: Heuristics and Biases*, Cambridge: Cambridge University Press, pp. 294–305.

Barber, B. M. and Odean, T. 2001. 'Boys will be boys: Gender, overconfidence, and common stock investment', *Quarterly Journal of Economics* 116: 261–92.

Baron, R. M. and Kenny, D. A. 1986. 'The moderator–mediator variable distinction in social psychological research: Conceptual, strategic and statistical considerations', *Journal of Personality and Social Psychology* 51: 1173–82.

Becker, G. 1993. 'Nobel lecture: The economic way of looking at behavior', *Journal of Political Economy* 101: 385–409.

Bénabou, R. and Tirole, J. 2003. 'Self-knowledge and self-regulation: An economic approach', in I. Brocas and J. D. Carrillo (eds.), *The Psychology of Economic Decisions*: vol. I: *Rationality and Well-being*, Oxford: Oxford University Press, pp. 137–68.

Benos, A. 1998. 'Aggressiveness and survival of overconfident traders', *Journal of Financial Markets* 1: 353–83.

Berthoz, S., Armony, J. L., Blair, R. J. and Dolan, R. J. 2002. 'An fMRI study of intentional and unintentional (embarrassing) violations of social norms', *Brain* 125: 1696–1708.

Biais, B., Hilton, D., Pouget, S. and Mazurier, K. 2005. 'Judgmental overconfidence, self-monitoring and trading performance in an experimental financial market', *Review of Economic Studies* 72: 297–312.

Biais, B. and Pouget, S. 1999. 'Microstructure, incentives and convergence to equilibrium in experimental financial markets', Working paper, University of Toulouse.

Breiter, H. C., Aharon, I., Kahneman, D., Dale, A. and Shizgal, P. 2001. 'Functional imaging of neural responses to expectancy and experience of monetary gains and losses', *Neuron* 30: 619–39.

Burgoyne, C. B. and Routh, D. A. 1991. 'Constraints on the use of money as a gift at Christmas: The role of status and intimacy', *Journal of Economic Psychology* 12: 47–69.

Buscato, T., Noury, F., Raynaud, M. and Rocher, A. 2004. 'Effets des incitations financières sur la motivation dans les domaines sacrés et profanes', Mémoire de recherche, University of Toulouse-II.

Camerer, C. 2000. 'Prospect theory in the wild: Evidence from the field', in D. Kahneman and A. Tversky (eds.), *Choices, Values and Frames*, Cambridge: Cambridge University Press, pp. 288–300.

Camerer, C. and Hogarth, R. M. 1999. 'The effects of financial incentives in experiments: A review and capital–labor–production framework', *Journal of Risk and Uncertainty* 19: 7–42.

Camerer, C., Loewenstein, G. and Prelec, D. 2005. 'Neuroeconomics: How neuroscience can inform economics', *Journal of Economic Literature* 43: 9–64.

Croson, R. 2005. 'The method of experimental economics', *International Negotiations: Research Methods in Negotiation and Social Conflict* 10: 131–48 (special issue edited by P. Carnevale and C. W. de Dreu).

Daniel, K., Hirshleifer, D. and Subrahmanyam, A. 1998. 'Investor psychology and security market under- and overreactions', *Journal of Finance* 53: 1839–85.

De Bondt, W. and Thaler, R. 1985. 'Does the stock market overreact?' *Journal of Finance* 40(3): 793–808.

Dequervain, D., Fischbacher, U., Treyer, V., Schelhammer, M., Schnyder, U., Buck, A. and Fehr, E. 2004. 'The neural basis of altruistic punishment', *Science* 305: 1254–8.

Fehr, Fischbacher and Kosfeld (in press). 'Neuroeconomic foundations of trust and social preferences', *American Economic Review*.

Fehr, E. and Schmidt, K. (in press). 'The economics of fairness, reciprocity and altruism: Experimental evidence and new theories', in S.-C. Kolm and J. M. Ythier (eds.), *Handbook on the Economics of Giving, Reciprocity and Altruism*.

Festinger, L. and Carlsmith, J. M. 1959. 'Cognitive consequences of forced compliance', *Journal of Abnormal and Social Psychology* 58: 203–10.

Forsyth, R., Nelson, F., Neumann, G. R. and Wright, J. 1992. 'Anatomy of an experimental stock market', *American Economic Review* 82: 1142–61.

Frey, B. S. 1997. *Not Just for the Money: An Economic Theory of Personal Motivation*, Cheltenham: Edward Elgar.

Frey, B. S. and Stutzer, A. 2002. *Happiness and Economics: How the Economy and Institutions Affect Human Well-being*, Princeton: Princeton University Press.

Gehring, W. J. and Willoughby, A. R. 2002. 'The medial frontal cortex and the rapid processing of monetary gains and losses', *Science* 295: 2279–82.

Gigerenzer, G., Hoffrage, U. and Kleinbölting, H. 1991. 'Probabilistic mental models: A Brunswikian theory of confidence', *Psychological Review* 98: 506–28.

Gneezy, U. and Rusticini, A. 2000. 'Pay enough or don't pay at all', *Quarterly Journal of Economics* 115(3): 797–810.

Hacking, I. 1983. *Representing and Intervening: Introductory Topics in the Philosophy of Natural Science*, Cambridge: Cambridge University Press.

Harré, R. 1988. 'Modes of explanation', in D. J. Hilton (ed.), *Contemporary Science and Natural Explanation: Commonsense Conceptions of Causality*, Brighton: Harvester Press, pp. 129–44.

Hertwig, R. and Ortmann, A. 2001. 'Experimental practices in economics: A methodological challenge for psychologists', *Behavioral and Brain Sciences* 24: 383–451.

2003. 'Economists' and psychologists' experimental practices: How they differ, why they differ, and how they could converge', in I. Brocas and J. D. Carrillo (eds.), *The Psychology of Economic Decisions*: vol. I: *Rationality and Well-being*, Oxford: Oxford University Press, pp. 253–72.

Hesslow, G. 1983. 'Explaining differences and weighting causes', *Theoria* 49: 87–111.

1988. 'The problem of causal selection', in D. J. Hilton (ed.), *Contemporary Science and Natural Explanation: Commonsense Conceptions of Causality*, Brighton: Harvester Press, pp. 11–32.

Hilton, D. J. 2001. 'Psychology and the financial markets: Applications to trading, dealing and investment analysis', *Journal of Psychology and Financial Markets* 2: 37–53.

2007a. 'Causal explanation: From social perception to knowledge-based attribution', in A. Kruglanski and E. T. Higgins (eds.), *Social Psychology: Handbook of Basic Principles*, 2nd edn, New York: Guilford Press.

2007b. 'Overconfidence, trading and entrepreneurship: Cognitive and cultural processes in risk-taking', in R. Topol and B. Walliser (eds.), *Cognitive Economics: New Trends (Contributions to Economic Analysis)*, vol. 280.

Hilton, D. J., Régner, I., Cabantous, L. and Vautier, S. 2007. 'Judgmental overconfidence: Cognitive bias or positive illusion?' Working paper, University of Toulouse.

Kagel, J. H., Battalio, R. C., Rachlin, H. and Green, L. 1981. 'Demand curves for animal consumers', *Quarterly Journal of Economics* 96: 1–13.

Kahneman, D. E., Knetsch, J. L. and Thaler, R. E. 1986. 'Experimental tests of the endowment effect and the Coase theorem', *Journal of Political Economy* 98: 25–48.

Kahneman, D. E. and Tversky, A. 1979. 'Prospect theory: An analysis of decision under risk', *Econometrica* 47: 263–91.

Landier, A. and Thesmar, D. 2005. 'Financial contracting with optimistic entrepreneurs: Theory and evidence', unpublished working paper, University of Chicago.

Lewin, S. B. 1996. 'Economics and psychology: Lessons for our own day from the early twentieth century', *Journal of Economic Literature* 34: 1293–1323.

Lipton, P. 1991. *Inference to the Best Explanation*, London: Routledge.

List, J. A. 2004. 'Neoclassical theory vs. prospect theory: Evidence from the marketplace', *Econometrica* 72: 615–25.

Lyons, J. 1977. *Semantics*, vol. I, Cambridge: Cambridge University Press.

Marr, D. 1982. *Vision: A Computational Investigation into the Human Representation and Processing of Visual Information*, San Francisco: W. H. Freeman.

McKenzie, C. 1997. 'What are the motives? A problem with evidence in the work of Richard Thaler', *Journal of Economic Psychology* 18: 123–35.

Mill, J. S. 1872/1973. 'A system of logic ratiocinative and inductive' (8th edn), in J. M. Robson (ed.), *Collected Works of John Stuart Mill*, vols. VII and VIII, Toronto: University of Toronto Press.

Nowak, A., Szamrej, J. and Latané, B. 1990. 'From private attitude to public opinion: A dynamic theory of social impact', *Psychological Review* 97: 362–76.

Odean, T. 1998. 'Volume, volatility, price and profit when all traders are above average', *Journal of Finance* 53: 1887–1934.

Payne, J., Bettman, J. W. and Johnson, E. J. 1993. *The Adaptive Decision Maker*, Cambridge: Cambridge University Press.

Pindyck, R. S. and Rubinfield, D. L. 1998. *Microeconomics*, 4th edn, Upper Saddle River, NJ: Prentice-Hall.

Platt, J. 1964. 'Science, strong inference – Proper scientific method (the New Baconians)', *Science* 146: 347–53.

Plott, C. and Sunder, S. 1988. 'Rational expectations and the aggregation of diverse information in laboratory security markets', *Econometrica* 20: 1085–1118.

Rabin, M. 2002. 'A perspective on psychology and economics', *European Economic Review* 46: 657–85.

Rilling, J. K., Sanfey, A. G., Aronson, J. A., Nystrom, L. E. and Cohen, J. D. 2004. 'Opposing BOLD responses to reciprocated and unreciprocated altruism in putative reward pathways', *Neuroreport* 15(16): 239–43.

Rusticini, A. 2005. 'Introduction. Neuroeconomics: Present and future', *Games and Economic Behavior* 52: 201–12.

Sanfey, A. G., Rilling, J. K., Aronson, J. A., Nystrom, L. E. and Cohen, J. D. 2003. 'The neural basis of economic decision-making in the ultimatum game', *Science* 300: 1755–8.

Shefrin, H. and Statman, M. 1985. 'The disposition to sell winners too early and ride losers too long: Theory and evidence', *Journal of Finance* 40: 777–90.

Smith, A. 1759/2002. *The Theory of Moral Sentiments*, 6th edn, K. Haakonssen (ed.), Cambridge: Cambridge University Press.

   1776/1993. *An Inquiry into the Nature and Causes of the Wealth of Nations*, K. Sutherland (ed.), Oxford: Oxford University Press.

Smith, R. H., Parrott, W. G. and Eyre, H. L. 2002. 'The role of public exposure in moral and nonmoral shame and guilt', *Journal of Personality and Social Psychology* 83(1): 138–59.

Sugden, R. 2000. 'Credible worlds: The status of theoretical models in economics', *Journal of Economic Methodology* 7: 1–31.

2005a. 'Experiments as exhibits and experiments as tests', *Journal of Economic Methodology* 12(2): 291–312.

2005b. 'Experiment, theory, world: A symposium on the role of experiments in economics', *Journal of Economic Methodology* 12(2): 177–84.

Taylor, S. and Brown, J. 1988. 'Illusion and well being: A social psychological perspective on mental health', *Psychological Bulletin* 103: 193–210.

Tetlock, P. E., Krisel, O. V., Elson, S. B., Green, M. C. and Lerner, J. S. 2000. 'The psychology of the unthinkable: Taboo trade-offs, forbidden base-rates, and heretical counterfactuals', *Journal of Personality and Social Psychology* 78: 853–70.

Thaler, R. H. 1991. *The Winner's Curse: Paradoxes and Anomalies of Economic Life*, New York: Free Press.

Thorndike, E. L. 1911. *Animal Intelligence*, New York: Macmillan.

Turgot. 1761. *Le commerce des grains*. Reprinted in P. Vigreux (ed., 1947), *Turgot: Textes choisis*, Paris: Dalloz.

Valenzuela, A., Srivastava, J. and Lee, S. 2005. 'The role of cultural orientation in bargaining under incomplete information: Differences in causal attributions', *Organizational Behavior and Human Decision Processes* 96: 72–88.

Weiner, B. 1985. '"Spontaneous" causal thinking', *Psychological Bulletin* 109: 74–84.

PART II

Finance

3 The economic psychology of the stock market

KARL-ERIK WÄRNERYD

3.1 Introduction

In his memoirs, former US president Bill Clinton (2004) says: "All elections are about the future." In the same vein, it can be said that all decisions are about the future and people tend to neglect relevant aspects of the future. Perfect knowledge about the future is of course not possible. More or less well-founded expectations serve instead. Psychologically, expectations are formed on the basis of earlier, personal experience, other people's experiences, and information from many other sources. Expectations may amount to firm convictions, strong hopes or fears, or, at the other extreme, mere conjectures that are made with little confidence. In any case, they are more or less colored by emotions, and are associated with moods, hopes, and fears.

The economic theory of financial markets is based on the concept of expectation. While originally used by economists as a presumably psychological concept, it now stands for mathematical expectation and hardly has any connection to psychology. Although cognitive psychology rests on thinking that arose in Gestalt psychology in which expectation played an important role, too little research attention has been directed to the study of financial expectations that would seem pertinent to the developments in stock markets. In this chapter, an attempt is made to facilitate understanding of stock-market psychology by employing expectation as a unifying concept and relating cognitive and emotional findings to a simple model of expectation formation.

3.2 The perspective: the individual investor and the financial market

Like in consumer behavior studies, in the chapter the attention is directed towards the characteristics of individuals or households and what influences their decision making. The professionals who deal with financial investment usually focus on aggregate data or curves that reflect what has recently or earlier happened in the marketplace. Their aim is typically to search explanations for developments in market trends for the whole market, for leading industries, or for individual business firms. The behavior of individual investors is of secondary, if any, interest, except perhaps that of potential brokerage customers.

In the chapter, the concept of expectation is based on a psychological model of expectation formation and it deals with some of the implications of this model. Economic theories of financial behavior may recognize differences in risk aversion, but no other personality differences. All investors are assumed to have the same expectations, with some spread around the mean, and to act rationally. With attention trained on individual behavior, the researcher inevitably faces the question of the possibility and extent of individual differences. This in its turn leads to the idea that there may be segments of investors who are in some important respect similar to other investors in the same segment, but characteristically different from investors placed in other segments. Certainly recent financial theory recognizes two categories or segments of investors: (a) the informed, rational investors and (b) the noise traders. The latter are laymen while the informed traders are professionals (at least in some interpretations).

The view taken here is that there are essential differences among investors and that there are segments of buyers and sellers in financial markets. Investors exhibit varying psychological characteristics that influence their expectations and financial behavior. These disparities among investors influence developments in markets and the study of them is likely to improve explanation and prediction. Furthermore, investors and investment behavior can be studied with hypotheses and methods from modern psychology.

3.3 The use of psychology in the study of financial markets

John Stuart Mill (1843) saw the aim of science as explanation with as few laws as possible ("to diminish as much as possible the catalogue of ultimate truths"). The ideal was that every phenomenon could be seen as a special case of one general law under which all other laws could be subsumed as special cases; this thinking was behind his idea of the economic man who was equipped with the single motive of maximizing economic utility. While with its fundamental reliance on the concept of rationality, economic theory strives to live up to the goal set by Mill, psychology is more of a cafeteria offering choices among behavioral laws that are subject to contingencies ("it all depends"). In fact, economists looking for psychological explanations of economic behavior have a too rich assortment of empirical laws to choose among and as a rule do not appreciate the contingent conditions. The most popular loan from psychology is prospect theory that is beautifully simple and comprehensive (Kahneman and Tversky, 1979). This has given it an extra appeal to many economists. Later, other developments in cognitive psychology have attracted adherents among economists in the field called *behavioral finance* (see De Bondt's chapter in the current volume), maybe because in cognitive heuristics they have sensed the possibility of finding laws regulating irrational behavior.

In an effort somewhat to control the cafeteria choices from psychology, I propose to relate selected psychological hypotheses to a framework or model that encapsulates the formation of expectations.

3.4 Psychological expectations

To a cognitive psychologist, expectations are subjective, belong to people, and can be studied as characteristics of people. While both economists and psychologists dealt with expectations in the nineteenth century when both disciplines grew into sciences, the concept was mostly neglected and even rejected by both professions from the early 1900s. The most notable exception was Gestalt psychology in which experimental researchers studied the formation of expectations. They observed perceptual phenomena and formulated laws of perceptual organization. Essentially, the laws concerned how humans formed expectations through completing trends and tendencies. Basing themselves on earlier experience, humans tended to fill in gaps in incomplete perceptions. The Gestalt psychologists emphasized wholes rather than details or parts which was common in behaviorist psychology.

Based on experience, we fill in gaps in information because we are led to expect completeness (closure), or things are close together or are similar and thus are perceived as belonging together, and we expect good continuation rather than abrupt changes in trends (which makes us inclined to use momentum strategies in handling stocks). We learn three things from the Gestalt psychologists (Katona, 1975):

(a) past experience tends to dominate our expectations (habitual or routine behavior)
(b) new experience may overcome these tendencies if strong enough (new information)
(c) habitual behavior may be upgraded through new learning (insight, problem solving).

3.5 A model of expectation formation

Based on economic and psychological theories of expectations, three sets of beliefs are assumed to constitute expectations. The three sets have different importance in different contexts, indicated by weights. Here is the model (Wärneryd, 1997):

$$EXP_{t+1} = w_1 B_{Pt} + w_2 B_{At} + w_3 B_{It}$$

where

$EXP_{t+1} =$ expectation about period $t + 1$ stated at time t_0
B_{Pt} $=$ beliefs based on extrapolation of past experience
B_{At} $=$ beliefs due to discrepancies between expectations and outcomes
B_{It} $=$ beliefs based on new information

w_1, w_2, w_3 are (empirical) weights varying from 0 to 1 and sum to 1.

The basic idea is that expectations are formed and revised on the basis of *past experience* of a phenomenon (or similar phenomena, involving generalization), *learning* from how successful earlier, in particular intentional, expectations were, and finally, on *new information* in the individual's immediate or more distant environment. If the weight of one set of beliefs equals zero, the other sets are the basis for forming an expectation. Most expectations are simply founded on past experience. In terms of the model this means that the other two sets of beliefs have weights close or equal to zero. Normally, earlier experience has the greatest weight (often $=1$). For example, momentum strategies which derive from the idea of good continuation of the trend tend to dominate among private investors. People prefer to expect "more of the same." Economists talk about *extrapolative expectations*. Keynes (1936, p. 51) stressed the significance of earlier experience: "[A] large part of the circumstances usually continue substantially unchanged from one day to the next. Accordingly it is sensible for producers to base their expectations on the assumption that the most recently realized results will continue except in so far as there are definite reasons for expecting a change." If there is no earlier experience, information in the environment will serve to form expectations. New information has to be dramatic to get more weight than earlier experience (Katona, 1975). Speculating investors seem to be on a continuous lookout for new information indicating changes or turning points in stock prices and may be inclined to pursue contrarian strategies, going against the current trend.

B_{At} represents "error-learning." This set of beliefs operates primarily when the expectation is similar to a goal or plan, an *intentional* expectation. The expectation is *contingent* when the outcome cannot be affected by anything the holder of the expectation does. This distinction had already been noted by James Mill (1829) in his book on psychology:

> In contemplating pains and pleasures as future; in other words, anticipating them, or believing in their future existence; we observe, that, in certain cases, they are independent of our actions; in other cases, that they are consequent upon something which may be done, or left undone by us.
> (James Mill, 1829, vol. II, p. 256)

He also noted the difference between interpretations of the past and expectation of the future. Expectation was not singly based on past experience.

The model encompasses the fact that an investor may learn from earlier mistakes in expectation formation and tries to adjust what direct extrapolation of earlier experience suggests. In times of rapid developments up or down, underestimates resulting from interpolations of earlier experience tend to be corrected or adjusted and expectations become *adaptive*. They may still remain underestimates since humans are not capable of handling exponential developments. Impressive but more moderate price changes may be overcompensated for and the learning component may reinforce and hasten the development, especially if important investors are influenced by it and try to compensate for earlier underestimates. What happens when expectations are confronted with later outcomes is no doubt important and some of it has been studied under the label of surprise (Teigen and Keren, 2003).

B_{It} are beliefs based on available new information. They can be divided into two sets of beliefs, one pertaining to the individual/household, the other to economy-wide information. In some, presumably rare, cases the new information will have such dominance that other sets of beliefs get zero weights. Over-optimism or, at the other extreme, panic reactions and stock-market crashes following certain new information are examples of such situations. For stock-rate developments, it is essential on which components investor expectations are formed. A vital question is when a bear market will turn into a bull market and vice versa. Stock-market transactions are affected by the turning points when expectations based on earlier experience change into something else on the basis of dramatic new information which is not necessarily directly related to the stock exchange, such as the effects of the 9/11 event in 2001.

In the following, findings from cognitive and motivational psychology are related to the three components of the expectation formation model. This involves presentation of some characteristic ways of simplifying information processing which are referred to as *heuristics*.

> The term *judgmental heuristic* refers to a strategy – whether deliberate or not – that relies on a natural assessment to produce estimation or a prediction. One of the manifestations of a heuristic is the relative neglect of other considerations.   (Tversky and Kahneman, 1983, p. 294)

A heuristic is essentially a procedure for problem solving that functions by reducing the number of possible alternatives and solutions and thereby increases the chance of a solution. Many authors in the field of finance use the concept of *cognitive bias* to explain decisions in financial markets. While cognitive bias generally refers to limited cognitive capacity, use of the term in behavioral finance often concentrates on the fact that people utilize heuristics to facilitate their decision making. Since financial economists, even those with an inclination towards behavioral finance, tend to relate their hypotheses to the rationality postulate, they see the utilization of such heuristics as deviations from rationality and they call those "cognitive errors" rather than using the psychologists' more positive word, "heuristics" (cf. Shefrin, 2000).

3.6 What is past experience?

An individual's past experience is subjective. Memories are known to be fallible because they are selective and unconsciously manipulated. Information processing starts with selective attention to phenomena in the world and the continued process includes many possibilities for storing and retrieving information that create deviations from more objective data. Looking back at earlier developments of, say, stock prices, a person may well recall something that is pretty close to objective data over how the stock market or a single stock has developed. This is probably the case if the person is inclined to follow market information in the mass media and in other sources. Still, even if there is agreement between objective data and the person's stored information, the interpretation of the data may be highly personal and something quite different than when expectations derive from mere extrapolation of trends. Economists dealing with extrapolative expectations, that is, expectations based on data on past developments, have realized that and usually put extra weight on the most recent developments.

When the role of past experience is discussed it helps to look at the use of some psychological heuristics that have consequences for retrieving memories: *availability*, *representativeness*, and *conservatism*.

3.6.1 Availability

The *availability* heuristic is often cited and explains a large number of everyday experiences. A person is said to employ the availability heuristic whenever s/he estimates probability or frequency by the ease with which instances or associations can be brought to mind. More recent things are easy to recall, instances of large classes are recalled better and faster than instances of less frequent classes, likely occurrences are easier to imagine than unlikely ones, and associative connections are strengthened when two events frequently occur together (Tversky and Kahneman, 1982c, pp. 163–4; Rothman and Hardin, 1997).

Stephan (1999, p. 108) distinguished between (1) experience-based, (2) memory-based, and (3) imagination-based availability. *Experience-based* availability means that people rely on what they have seen or heard. They neglect the fact that their samples probably have been small and biased. If unemployed workers answer a question about how many workers are unemployed, or social workers about how many families need social relief, they tend to overestimate the numbers according to the availability heuristic. They derive their estimates from their own experience, which involves frequent contacts with the relevant groups, and they are likely to exaggerate the actual number. Ask a stock owner how many households own stocks and you can expect that the answer will be an overstatement or at least be higher than what a non-owner of stocks would estimate. *Memory-based* availability depends on the ease with which memories are available and can be brought to mind. It is related to well-known memory factors such as: (a) how intense the attention was, (b) the salience of the impression, (c) the vivacity of the impression, (d) the familiarity of the object or event, and (e) spatial and temporal propinquity. The higher the values on these factors, the stronger the memory trace and the higher the availability is.

Stephan (1999) discusses how the advertising for stocks in the privatization of German Telekom played on these factors to create availability among private investors, who were the prime target group for the campaign. He notes that the average German had earlier been very skeptical about investing money in stocks, but that many of the purchasers were persuaded to believe in the value of the company and its future development. He also demonstrates the effect of the availability heuristic in an experiment that dealt with German companies. Well-known companies were more available and tended to dominate the impression.

Imagination-based availability arises as a consequence of how easy it is to imagine something. If it is easier to imagine a certain situation than another, the former will tend to dominate the thinking. The stock price seems, for example, apt to go up when a firm announces a new sales contract, even though the value of the contract is insignificant in relation to total sales volume. Investors may not evaluate the risk of different investments based solely on the historical standard deviation of returns. They may impute extra "risk" to foreign investments because they know less about foreign markets, institutions, and firms (French and Poterba, 1991, p. 225).

A person may see the addition of something familiar to an uncertain event as raising the probability of the event happening when it actually decreases it. Experiments show that a scenario that includes a possible cause and an outcome could appear more probable than the outcome on its own (Tversky and Kahneman, 1983, p. 307). Such techniques have, for example, been exploited in publicity about an event that is favorable to a company. It should be noted that the use of the availability heuristic does not always lead to incorrect estimates of frequencies (Stephan, 1999, p. 119). Some correct data may be easy to recollect.

3.6.2 The base-rate fallacy and representativeness

Kahneman and Tversky (1973) demonstrated that people had a tendency to neglect base-rate or statistical information in favor of similarity judgments. In a typical study, the participants were asked to predict the field of study of a graduate student or the profession of somebody on the basis of a brief description. The description contained some personality traits that were similar to the stereotype of a profession, for example, of lawyers or engineers. The participants' judgments turned out to be determined by the degree of similarity between the description and the stereotype of the profession. This happened even when the participants were made familiar with the base rates, that is, the frequencies of law and engineering students and professionals in the population. This is known as the *base-rate fallacy*.

This heuristic is often equated with the heuristic of *representativeness*: an event is judged probable to the extent that it represents the essential features of its parent population or of its generating process. It means, among other things, that people in situations of uncertainty tend to look for familiar patterns and are apt to believe that the pattern will repeat itself. The neglect of base rates seems more general than representativeness and cannot always be explained by this heuristic.

Gigerenzer and Hoffrage (1995, pp. 699–700) suggest some reasons why base rates are neglected and intimate that in many inference problems base rates are uninteresting. It is not always wrong to neglect the base rates. They state that people find it more natural to handle frequencies than probabilities. The participants in their studies were asked what the probability was that a woman with a positive mammogram actually had breast cancer. They did better with data on mammograms and breast cancer presented as frequencies than with data presented as probabilities. Despite the frequencies and the fact that all necessary information was offered in the tasks, only slightly less than half of the algorithms used by the participants were classified as being Bayesian reasoning.

Cosmides and Tooby (1996) investigated whether inductive reasoning performance changed depending on whether the participating college students were asked to judge a frequency or the probability of an event. The participants completed a frequentist medical diagnosis problem. The results were interpreted as indicating that frequentist representations caused various cognitive biases to disappear, including overconfidence, the conjunction fallacy, and base-rate neglect.

Fiedler *et al.* (2000) also found that frequencies were better handled in some situations. They explain the problem in terms of the *sampling hypothesis*. When making a judgment, people sample information from memory and from the environment and then make inferences on the basis of the information represented in the sample, using rather simple methods. The requested probability is referred to as the "criterion" and the conditional probability as the "predictor." According to the results, a sample that is focused on the criterion leads to more neglect of base rates than a sample focused on the predictor. The authors stress that the neglect of base rates is primarily associated with low base-rate probabilities. They also find that in addition to focusing on criterion or predictor, the size of the cognitive sample is important.

In Shefrin and Statman's (1994) Behavioral Capital Asset Pricing Model (CAPM) noise traders are assumed to underweight base-rate information. They make forecasts by overweighting recent events and by underweighting more distant events that form the base rate. Noise traders look at the most recent patterns and believe that those will be repeated in the future.

The base-rate fallacy no doubt occurs, but may be less common than has been assumed in behavioral finance. Some findings may have suffered from methodological lack of clarity (see Fiedler, 2000; Fiedler *et al.*, 2000). Gigerenzer and Hoffrage (1995) as well as Fiedler *et al.* (2000) talk of natural rather than probabilistic situations and assert that people are not inclined towards logical inference and deductive reasoning. Investors, like most other people, may not construe situations in the way the experimental designs presume.

While the neglected use of base-rate data has been amply studied and discussed, less attention has been bestowed on the likely case that, when the base-rate probability is high, there could be a tendency to overlook the specific symptoms. Judging from newspaper stories, a patient with indistinct symptoms of pneumonia may sometimes be misclassified as having the flu at times when almost everyone else seems to be affected by it. In finance, undue attention to the base rate may occur when the majority of stocks go up. Details about a specific firm are neglected and investors may believe in its stock without grounds. When, say, hi-tech stocks fall, other stocks, including those for which there is good news, tend to join. When the majority of stocks go up, a positive effect spreads to stocks that may not deserve it because of bad news. The sudden cascades of information that some economists have propounded may be cases of undue attention given to base rates: investors at first do not heed the information from their own experience and immediate environment, but concentrate on earlier developments, that is, on the base rates of stock prices. This may be seen as the reverse of the base-rate fallacy. The base rate dominates the specifics.

The phenomenon is well known in the psychology of learning and is called "generalization" or in experimental psychology often "stimulus generalization." Generalization is a kind of inference about the unknown and normally means that what is known to be true about all known members of a class of objects is true of all members including those not yet observed. Observations that emanate from a large group or a majority in a population are extended to include all. The converse is "discrimination," which means that differences, especially minor ones, are attended to. An interesting finding is that when people are anxious they tend to generalize more, that is, include more stimuli and discriminate less. Exuberance may have similar effects. Irrational exuberance may thus be explained as being caused by failures to discriminate due to strong positive or negative emotions (Shiller, 2000b).

3.6.3 Conservatism

Delays in reactions to information have been attributed to various factors in behavioral finance, one of which is *conservatism*. The concept was suggested by the psychologist Ward Edwards (1982) and involves slow updating of models in the face of new evidence. People's behavior is not Bayesian, but may get closer to it by repeated trials. Edwards points to "human misaggregation of data" as the major cause of conservatism.

The use of the concept in finance was rejected by, among others, Fama (1998), who was critical of its use (and the use of other psychological concepts in finance). Other authors apply conservatism to explain underreaction to economic news. Financial analysts are, according to Shefrin (2000), inclined to make only partial adjustments at first and are slow to arrive at the correct estimation of new probabilities. Barberis *et al.* (1998) and Shleifer (2000) suggest that under- and overreactions of stock prices can be explained by conservatism and representativeness.

The representativeness heuristic has been held to be inconsistent with conservatism. Conservatism (which is sometimes labeled underconfidence) and overconfidence are not compatible in the sense that they cannot occur at the same time for one individual. The question then arises under what circumstances overconfidence occurs and under what circumstances conservatism prevails. Griffin and Tversky (1992) tried to reconcile overconfidence, which is close to representativeness, and underconfidence, which is similar to conservatism. The hypothesis they tested was that people focus on the strength or extremeness of the available evidence with insufficient regard for its weight or credence. This mode of judgment yields overconfidence when strength is high and weight is low, and underconfidence when strength is low and weight is high. The assumption is that people update their beliefs depending on the strength and weight of new evidence. The strength of the evidence is inferred from aspects like salience and extremity whereas weight has to do with such factors as sample size.

3.7 Learning from past experience

Expectations of outcomes may differ more or less from what actually happens and the person who had the expectations will be surprised, negatively or positively as the case may be. Since expectations seem mostly based on past experience such surprise may lead to adaptations of future expectations of the same kind – the learning factor in the model. Surprises are usually classified as emotions and are not always evaluated in a purely rational way. It is thus possible that a smaller gain is a more pleasant surprise than a larger gain if the former derives from an unexpectedly high rise in price and the latter arose from a smaller gain than expected. Similarly, a loss can involve a pleasant surprise if the loss is lower than expected.

In cognitive psychology, expectations have often been quantified in terms of probabilities. According to this interpretation, unexpected events can simply be described as low-probability outcomes and the surprise follows when they occur (Teigen and Keren, 2003). In financial economics, surprise is used to describe unexpected turns in firms' earnings and it is often explained as a result of shock. Business firms are more or less forced to state their expectations of future earnings in their quarterly and annual reports. Studies indicate that firms try carefully to avoid negative surprises and therefore have a tendency to understate their expected earnings and get the advantage of a positive surprise (Brown and Higgins, 2005).

3.7.1 Hindsight bias

It is not always easy to learn from experience since *hindsight bias* is a possible threat to real insight. Hindsight bias is described as follows:

> In hindsight, people consistently exaggerate what could have been anticipated in foresight. They not only tend to view what has happened as having been inevitable, but also to view it as having appeared "relatively inevitable" before it happened. People believe that others should have been able to anticipate events much better than was actually the case. They even misremember their own predictions so as to exaggerate in hindsight what they knew in foresight.   (Fischhoff, 1982, p. 428)

Hindsight depends on memory and memory is fallible. Retrieving memories is a constructive process. Memory traces are deficient because of errors in impressions, limitations in storage capacity, and interference in recall processes. While this does not mean that memories are always incorrect, it points to the need to be somewhat cautious in using one's memories. Looking back, one tends to find patterns in random events, clear trends, and explanations that may seem useful for future use. Recent research has focused on the relationship between confidence and hindsight, the "knew-it-all-along effect."

> [E]vents that the best-informed experts did not anticipate often appear almost inevitable after they occur. Financial punditry provides an unending source of examples. Within an hour of the market closing every day, experts can be heard on the radio explaining with high confidence why the market acted as it did. A listener could well draw the incorrect inference that the behavior of the market is so reasonable that it could have been predicted earlier in the day.   (Kahneman and Riepe, 1998, p. 55)

Hoffrage and Hertwig (1999, pp. 191–2) argued that hindsight should not be seen as an error in information processing. It is "a by-product of two generally adaptive processes: first, updating knowledge after receiving new information; and second, drawing fast and frugal inferences from this updated knowledge." Three views of hindsight bias are reviewed. The first, in the literature the most common view, focuses on the potential harmful effects. A second view stresses the adaptive aspects since hindsight bias may contribute to the esteem we enjoy from others and from ourselves. The third view, which is the main point, maintains that memory must be selective and that recall when memory has sorted out certain traces is a constructive, adaptive process. The process is the updating of information, which as a by-product may have hindsight bias.

Forming memories of earlier decision situations may involve leaving out trivial details and pulling out the essential factors in the situation, which can then be used for future decision making. Like any other type of learning, hindsight can lead to better preparation for the future. Hindsight is necessary since "perception of a surprise-free past may portend a surpriseful [*sic*] future" (Fischhoff, 1982, p. 428). In this view, despite the fact that unsatisfactory outcomes may occur, the hindsight bias, like other heuristics, implies adaptive behavior that should not be classified as flaws or errors. Hindsight may be useful to the individual or it may be harmful depending upon the circumstances. Even hindsight bias may serve some purpose for the individual, such as useful self-confidence (which may not please fellow humans).

Hindsight usually outperforms foresight, since events tend to become clear and causal structures appear disentangled when one is looking back. Part of the superiority may be specious due to hindsight bias. Ostensibly successful decisions in the past may lead an investor to believe in her/his own ability and serve as a guide for future decisions. It should not surprise anyone that stories about how successes were achieved or failures avoided in the stock market may be far from objective accounts, even with no intention to lie on the part of the storyteller. Hindsight bias is rarely fully conscious. Hindsight, with or without bias, may give rise to strong feelings such as pride or regret. Such emotional hindsight, though often biased, may influence the disposition to act in future situations and, if inducing pride, perhaps lead to buying or, if producing regret, to selling at the wrong moment.

3.8 Treatment of new information and influences on information processing

New information, if attended to at all, is interpreted and treated using simplifying heuristics, since reality is too complex to handle with perfect rationality. Many types of heuristics are applicable to information processing. Here I would like to draw attention to *anchoring and adjustment* and *illusion of control*. In a later section, the focus will be on the *affect heuristic* and other affective influences on information processing.

3.8.1 Anchoring and adjustment

Anchoring bias means that people make estimates by starting from an initial value that is subjected to *adjustment* before the final answer is arrived at. The initial value may be given by the formulation of the problem or partial calculation. Due to anchoring in the first place, later adjustments are usually insufficient. Consequently, different starting points yield different estimates that are biased towards the initial values (Tversky and Kahneman, 1982a). The first figure apparently serves as an anchor and later adjustments are insufficient, especially when the anchor is low. When investors make forecasts of future stock values, their forecasts may be affected by the value that they use as a starting point even if they do not believe in it and make adjustments. Studies show that when investors are asked to give confidence intervals for probability estimates, the intervals are often too narrow, and this is ascribed to the effect of anchoring (Stephan and Kiell, 2000).

If there are anchoring effects, financial analysts could be expected to be slow to upgrade their evaluations when there are sudden increases in earnings. An American investment fund is said to be based on the idea that the stocks of a firm may be mispriced because of anchoring effects. Stephan (1999) suggested that this heuristic can create overconfidence, meaning that investors have a tendency to believe too much in their well-considered estimates. The mere fact that the judgments are anchored and then adjusted inspires confidence. He demonstrated clear anchoring effects in experiments carried out by himself and co-authors.

Stephan (1999) also found that there were anchoring effects from tasks that were unrelated to the crucial forecasts. People who had worked on discriminating a certain number in a series of numbers flashed on a screen showed anchoring effects when they, with a different experimenter and in a different setting, were asked to forecast a future stock exchange value. Stephan warns that overestimation of the probability of favorable environmental conditions may lie behind many individual failures in financial markets. The anchors have in such cases been too high, especially for young investors who grew up in a predominantly bull market.

Knowledge about anchoring effects may protect an investor from too easily accepting an offer to buy stocks. It happens that a less serious broker offers a client stocks that the broker knows are above the financial capacity of the client. When the client says "no," an offer of a more reasonably priced bundle of stocks is made. In relation to the anchor that the first offer established, the second offer will appear favorable. There will also, according to Cialdini (1988), be strong pressure on the client to accept the new offer because of the demands of reciprocity. The broker has made a concession when dropping the first offer in favor of the second, lower-price offer and this calls for an appropriate concession on the part of the client, who is more likely to buy than if there had been no high-price offer.

3.8.2 Illusion of control

Perceived control is an important factor in Ajzen's Theory of Planned Behavior (Ajzen, 1991). If a person perceives that there is no control of means to achieve a desired purpose, a positive attitude towards the act does not produce the commensurate behavior. Perceived control can produce self-confidence although it may be an illusion. Langer (1982) hypothesized that perceived skill in chance situations would cause people to feel inappropriately confident.

Illusion of control refers to "an expectancy of a personal success probability inappropriately higher than the objective probability would warrant." People behave as though chance events are subject to control. The illusion may have some basis in fact, but generally the label is used when there is some form of obvious superstition behind a certain act.

Langer noted that dice players clearly behaved as if they were controlling the outcome of the toss. They tended to throw the dice softly if they wanted low numbers or to throw hard for high numbers. They believed that effort and concentration would pay off. Indicators of confidence in Langer's studies showed that people would not distinguish chance- from skill-determined events even if they were aware of chance factors.

Why is it that people who are ordinarily reasonably rational in their decision making hesitate to make bets after a die has been thrown, but not yet read, while they are willing to place bets before the die is thrown? It cannot just be overconfidence in one's own ability. Such results were obtained in a study by Tversky and Heath (1991). They let the participants choose between two alternatives: (1) A stock is selected at random from the *Wall Street Journal*. You guess whether it will go up or down tomorrow. If you're right, you win $5. (2) A stock is selected at random from the *Wall Street Journal*. You guess whether it went up or down yesterday. You cannot check the paper. If you're right, you win $5.

It turned out that 67 percent of the participants selected the first alternative. The authors suggest that relative ignorance was lower for this alternative since nobody could know the outcome then. Illusion of control makes people believe that they can influence future events even if they have no such power and have to rely on some magic of good or bad luck. Illusion of control and overconfidence in ability coincide to some extent, but not completely. A recent simulation study of stock traders found that there was illusion of control to a varying degree among traders and that it was maladaptive in this context (Fenton-O'Creevy *et al.*, 2003). *Illusion of prediction* and *illusion of knowledge* are other phenomena of overconfidence. In fact, people's perception of their ability to predict outcomes may surpass their perceived ability to control outcomes.

3.9 Affective influences on expectation formation

3.9.1 Feelings, emotions, and investment in the stock market

"The stock market was optimistic yesterday." Do stock markets then have feelings? Judging from many newspaper headlines, a stock market can be moody, sad, optimistic, pessimistic, and display many other characteristics of human behavior. Developments at the stock exchange are often described in terms that are taken from psychology, notably everyday psychology. Still, the answer should from a psychologist's standpoint be "no, stock markets do not have feelings or moods." Do investors have feelings and moods? Here the answer is a definite "yes, investors have more feelings than they think." This also holds for professional investors and experts on stock-market intricacies.

When used on stock markets, labels indicating emotions are mere metaphors and they originate from examination of aggregate curve behaviors in the financial markets. The use of such labels summarizes developments, usually in a striking way, and, for good or for bad, consign curve behaviors into categories that appeal to earlier experiences and are felt to constitute knowledge. The danger is that stock market feelings are taken to be the feelings of the individuals participating in the transactions. Even when most stock prices plummet and the market is said to be pessimistic, transactions are made, implying that there are buyers and sellers with differing expectations.

Do emotions featured by investors influence transactions or are they mostly irrelevant, even though they may be a good topic for discussion? On October 19, 1987, the stock market in New York crashed as the Dow Jones Industrial Average plunged 508 points, or 22.6 percent in value – its biggest-ever percentage drop. On April 13, 2000, the Nasdaq index dropped 9.7 percent and the Dow Jones almost 6 percent. Commentators on TV, in several countries, used almost the same expression: "Now it is all psychology." What did they mean? They were certainly not thinking of the psychology that dominated the incipient behavioral finance and which was primarily based on cognitive issues. While cognitive psychology has informed behavioral finance, the psychology of emotions and motivation has received much less attention in finance. The main reason is probably that despite recent advances, research in these areas has yielded less stable and impressive results than those in cognitive psychology.

Feelings and motivation include emotions, affects, and moods. *Mood* is often referred to in reviews of financial markets. Maybe something can be learned from psychological studies of an individual's mood. Gasper (2004) investigated how mood influenced information processing. She dealt with three problems: (1) the fastness of the processing, (2) the role of stimuli or the circumstances (ambiguous vs. unambiguous), and (3) individuals' ability to decrease mood effects. The results indicated that judgments of unambiguous situations were less influenced by mood differences. Increases in affect intensity were associated with faster reaction times. When feelings were not relevant to the task a sad mood had less effect, in particular if the irrelevance was pointed out to the participants in the study. These results seem to have some implications for stock market behaviors. Information with some ambiguity may lead to serious overreaction when sad moods prevail.

In recent years, research on emotions has made progress and both positive and negative effects of emotions are now distinguished (see, for example, McGraw *et al.*, 2004). The *affect heuristic* and *affective forecasting* are two recent innovations in the study of the effects of emotions. Even though the research on both is still sparse, they seem worth looking at.

3.9.2 The affect heuristic

The *affect heuristic* concept emanates from the debate in psychology as to what extent there can be an affective reaction that consistently precedes cognitive evaluation of a (strong) stimulus. The question is whether an affective reaction can precede and rule out cognitive evaluation altogether or delay it. If there is *a primary affective reaction*, people may be much more ruled by emotions than is generally assumed in rationality discussions.

Zajonc (1980) maintained that there is a primary affective reaction that evaluates the stimulus as good or bad before the stimulus is cognitively checked. He rejected the idea of most contemporary theories that affect was post-cognitive, that it occurred only after considerable cognitive operations had been accomplished. Experimental evidence demonstrates that reliable affective discriminations (like/dislike ratings) can be made in the total absence of recognition memory (old/new judgments). Zajonc pointed out differences between judgments based on affect and those based on perceptual and cognitive processes. He concluded that affect and cognition are under the control of separate and partially independent systems that can influence each other in a variety of ways, and that both constitute independent sources of effects in information processing. Some reactions that may be important for our survival may no doubt be guided by primary affects with little or no deliberation. This may be true for certain reactions following events in the stock market. A strongly threatening stimulus leads to attempts to distance oneself as quickly as possible without really thinking until it is too late. The economists' discussion of herd behavior is reminiscent of primary affective reactions without conscious evaluation.

The ideas about a primary affective reaction have met with opposition, but they have recently been further explored by a group of decision theorists led by Paul Slovic (Slovic *et al.*, 2002) who launched the affect heuristic. These authors suggest that affect may serve as a cue for many important judgments. An overall, readily available affective impression is an easy escape from weighing the pros and cons or retrieving from memory any relevant examples. This holds especially when the required judgment or decision is complex or the recourse to mental resources is limited. The affect heuristic is a mental shortcut similar to availability and representativeness.

There is accordingly a human tendency for primary affective reactions and subsequent cognitive handling of the stimulus information. The affect heuristic warns the investor to be on her/his guard when analyzing information about stocks and stock events. The first reaction may be emotional and color the continued information processing. If the reaction is extremely strong there is no cognitive elaboration, rather panic or exuberance.

3.9.3 Affective forecasting

"Foreseeing the future is one of the most appealing of all psychic powers" (Wilson and Gilbert, 2003, p. 345). Like other choices, selecting stocks involves forecasts. It is generally assumed that the forecasts have to do with utility in terms of economic value. It is well known and accepted, although little considered, that emotions, including mood at the time of the decision, affect the estimates of value. It is less recognized that prediction of the feelings that will follow after a certain outcome may affect the decision:

> Anyone who has ever made an important decision knows that emotions play a role. Not only do immediate emotions, or those experienced while making a choice, shape decisions but also anticipated emotions about future consequences. Anticipated feelings of guilt, dread, and excitement allow people to simulate what life would be like if they made one choice or another.   (Mellers, 2000, p. 910)

People apparently base many decisions on affective forecasts: predictions about their emotional reactions to future events influence their choices.

Recent research on affective forecasting has focussed on the accuracy of affective predictions. There is a tendency to overestimate the enduring impact that future events will have on one's emotional reactions. Affective forecasts often display an *impact bias*, meaning that people overestimate the intensity and duration of their emotional reactions to future events. One cause of the impact bias is *focalism*, the tendency to underestimate the extent to which other events will influence one's thoughts and feelings. When thinking about how happy they will be if they win a major award, for example, and how long they will feel that way, people might not anticipate the speed with which they will make sense of their achievement, creating new knowledge structures to understand it. If so, they will overestimate the duration of the pleasure it will bring and may be at a disadvantage in managing their emotional lives. There are sad newspaper stories about the emotional quandary of the young man who got the highest prize ever in the Swedish Lotto!

A new dimension is added to this by the hypothesis of a pleasure paradox (Wilson *et al.*, 2005). The basic premise is that people make sense of their world in a way that speeds recovery from emotional events and that this sense-making process is largely automatic and nonconscious. These processes are described by the acronym *AREA*: attend, react, explain, adapt. People *attend* or orient to novel, relevant events; they *react* emotionally to the events; they *explain* or make sense of the events; and as a result they *adapt* to them, in that they think about them less and have a less intense emotional reaction when they do.

Sense-making is very similar to hindsight, which is known to create biases (Wilson *et al.*, 2005). People fail to anticipate how quickly they will make sense of things that happen to them in a way that speeds emotional recovery. This is especially true when predicting reactions to negative events.

This research raises two things for investor consideration in connection with stock market transactions: (1) imagining the feelings that would accompany a great gain will probably lead to overestimation of the degree of happiness, and (2) loss aversion embodies an overestimation of the negative effects of a loss.

In both cases, people tend later to make sense of what happened, a process that is governed by other events.

3.10   The prediction of stock-market developments and the measurement of expectations

In principle, it is possible to assess values of the three components in the expectation formation model through interview surveys. In a way reminiscent of surveys of consumer confidence, people can be asked about their investments and factors influencing them, such as expectations regarding stock market developments. Many investors search for indicators that will reveal something about future stock prices. The use of technical analysis is a case in point. A novel approach is the attempt to get indicators from measuring investor expectations in a way similar to consumer confidence indexes. After having been coldly received by most economists, the Index of Consumer Sentiment, which was launched by George Katona at the University of Michigan, is now broadly accepted and has a good standing as a predictor of consumer purchases in the short run ("consumer optimism"). There are a few similar attempts to assess investor expectations through regular surveys.

A special difficulty with forecasts of stock market developments should be noted: if the forecasts are believed, they can be suspected of being self-fulfilling. If the forecast predicts that prices will rise, investors will have fewer doubts, sell less and buy more, thereby implementing the prediction. If falling prices are predicted, there will be more sellers and more hesitant buyers and prices will fall, all on the proviso that investors believe in the forecast results. For good reasons, regular forecasts of stock markets as a whole are rare whereas forecasts for individual firms are made and to some extent published. In their quarterly reports, firms report their expected developments over the next six months and perhaps longer. Financial analysts scrutinize such reports, make their own predictions of the earnings, and may figure out the proper price of the stock which in its turn leads to recommendations to buy or sell.

The longest series of data on *investor expectations* is provided by the Yale School of Management Stock Market Confidence Indexes. Professor Robert Shiller has been collecting data on expectations since 1984, using question-naires that cover a number of aspects: (a) the one-year Confidence Index (the percentage of the population expecting an increase in the Dow in the coming year), (b) the Buy-On-Dips Confidence Index (the expectation that the stock exchange index will go up the next day after a fall of more than 3 percent one day), (c) the Crash Confidence Index (the percentage of the population who attach little probability to a stock market crash in the next six months), (d) the Valuation Confidence Index (the percentage of the population who think that the market is not too high). The explanatory value of these indexes seems good, but the predictive capacity is open to some doubts. Shiller (2000a), who analyzed stock-market bubbles, concluded that there was evidence that while bubbles and investor confidence among institutional investors varied over time, the variations were often significant though not enormous.

The University of Michigan Investor Survey is based on representative samples of US households. To be eligible, a household must have at least $25,000 in stocks or stock mutual funds, including stocks held in retirement-related accounts. The survey answers are used to compute two indexes of investor confidence. While the Indexes of Investor Sentiment and Investor Expectations produced by the University of Michigan are calculated on the basis of the same questions about the national economy and the respondent's own financial situation, there are also questions directly aimed at assessing stock market expectations. The following question which originates from the Survey of Economic Expectations of the University of Wisconsin is used by the University of Michigan and by, for example, the DNB surveys at CentER, Tilburg University:

> Suppose that tomorrow someone were to invest one thousand dollars in such a mutual fund. Please think about how much money this investment would be worth one year from now. What do you think is the per cent chance that this one thousand dollar investment will increase in value in the year ahead, so that it is worth more than one thousand dollars one year from now?

One question (not included in the calculation of the Indexes) asks for new information: "During the last few months have you heard of any favorable or unfavorable changes in business conditions. What did you hear?" The answers which are reported in separate tables match the "new information" component of the expectation formation model presented earlier.

Manski (2004) has made a thorough review of the economists' use of subjective expectations data from surveys and, together with Dominitz (Dominitz and Manski, 2005), analyzed investor expectations from the University of Michigan and similar survey data from the University of Wisconsin. They looked for the co-variation between the indexes and actual stock-price development. I fully agree with their conclusion:

> We think that even rich longitudinal data measuring expectations in detail will not suffice to understand expectations formation fully. Considering the general problem, without specific reference to equity expectations, Manski (2004) argues that understanding expectations formation will also require intensive probing of persons to learn how they perceive their environments and how they process such new information as they may receive.
> Large-scale population surveys . . . are not amenable to investigations of this type, the time available to query respondents is too limited and the standardized question–response format of interviews is too confining. To learn how people process information and form expectations, economists may need to engage small samples of respondents in lengthy interviews.

Another attempt at elucidating the usefulness of measures of subjective financial expectations was made by Vissing-Jorgensen (2004). She analyzed new data from UBS/Gallup on investor expectations and stockholdings for 1998–2002. Here are some of the variables she looked at: (1) one-year own past return, (2) expected one-year own return, (3) expected one-year market return ("Thinking about the stock market more generally, what overall rate of return do you think the stock market will provide investors during the coming twelve months?"), and (4) expected ten-year market return ("And, what annual rate of return do you think the stock market will provide investors over the next ten years?"). More specific questions concerned: (1) overvaluation perception ("Do you think the stock market is overvalued/valued about right/undervalued, or are you unsure?"), (2) expected three-month market change, (3) expected one-year market change ("A year from now, do you think the stock market will be higher than it is now, lower, or about the same?").

The evidence suggested that, even for wealthy investors, (1) expected returns were high at the peak of the market, (2) many investors thought the market was overvalued but would not correct quickly, (3) investors' beliefs depended on their own investment experience (the author calls it a version of the law of small numbers), (4) the dependence of beliefs on own past portfolio performance is asymmetric, consistent with theories of biased self-attribution – believing that profits are caused by one's own skill and losses are due to unfortunate circumstances. The author concludes that investor beliefs affect their stockholdings and she suggests that understanding beliefs is in fact useful for understanding stock prices.

Another sign of the increasing interest in predicting the stock market is the Dutch Postbank Investor Barometer (PIB) which started in 2002. It asks, among other things, whether the Amsterdam stock market index (AEX) will increase/decrease during the next three months, whether it is a good time for risky investments or for less risky investments, whether the value of the respondent's investment portfolio increased/decreased during the last three/six months, and whether the respondent expects that the value of her/his investment portfolio will increase/decrease during the next three months.

Van Raaij (2005), who contributed to the design of the Barometer, has analyzed some of the results so far. He found a correlation of 0.777 between a lagged index and the AEX and drew the conclusion that the PIB index predicted the AEX better than the latter predicted the former.

In sum, there is now some evidence that measures of expectations can help explain what happens to stock market rates. It must be admitted that there is still some uncertainty about the possibilities of using the data for predicting turning points in total financial markets. The use of the measures may as yet only be supplementary to the use of other, equally fallible indicators.

3.11 Individual differences and segments of investors

A number of studies show that there are large differences among private investors (see, for example, De Bondt, 2004). A fundamental tenet of economic psychology is that there may be critical differences among consumers. By and large, financial economists recognize two categories of investors: those who are informed and rational and the others, often called noise traders, who disturb the predictive value of efficient market theory. After having gone through many empirical studies of investors (including my own studies), I propose the following four segments (based on Wärneryd, 2001):

1. *Well-to-do investors* who invest part, but never all, of their wealth in risky securities and who are not very active, with only a few transactions each year. They prefer to buy rather than to sell, and keep adding to their financial wealth; together they own a considerable part of total stocks. They have long-term goals and expectations. They have a persistent interest in the implications of new information which they carefully weigh before making any transactions. In turbulent times, they seem to have a stabilizing influence on the financial market.

2. *Really wealthy investors* who systematically invest in securities and who try to compose asset portfolios. They often employ the services of brokers and expert traders. They have greater profit-orientation than the first group and make more frequent transactions (so that deposit costs are paid by commissions). They have both short- and long-term goals, more volatile expectations, and may be more easily shaken than the first group.

3. *Speculating investors* who make frequent transactions in the stock market and who have few other assets than stocks and derivatives. They are often willing to borrow money to exploit what they think of as opportunities. Their expectations are short term and they may tend to form those on the basis of scanty information. They can be suspected of combining information, intuition, and feelings into "instant scenarios" of the future. Day-traders seem to belong to this category. A few are successful while others perish.

4. *Naive investors* who are enticed by stories of high potential profits in the stock market. Some of them may be lured by the marketing efforts accompanying privatization sales of stocks in government-owned companies. Their expectations are similar to preferences and hopes and are based on little information and strong feelings.

The importance of these segments varies between financial markets and is correlated with how widespread stock ownership is in a country. Consideration of the segments and their sizes seems essential when stock market reactions and developments are discussed.

In many ways, professional investors seem to use similar heuristics and yield to the same type of social factors as ordinary investors. Given that humans are far from perfect information processors as psychological theory suggests, the question arises: are there people who consistently do better than others and, if so, under what circumstances? Research has shown that experts may not do too well on a task although they are seen as experts and believe in themselves as experts on the basis of their knowledge and experience

(Ericsson and Lehmann, 1996). Many studies indicate that financial experts have difficulties outperforming private investors in the stock market (see Wärneryd, 2001, pp. 284–7; Andersson, 2004). At any rate, they do not consistently make better predictions or outperform ordinary investors, but some may do it sometimes (see Porter, 2004; Stotz and von Nitzsch, 2005).

3.12 Concluding remarks

The approach to the study of financial behavior advocated in the chapter focuses on individual expectations and proposes close attention to the process of expectation formation. It utilizes recent findings in cognitive psychology and suggests further use of research on feelings and emotions. It recognizes differences among individuals, but maintains that they can be brought together in segments with similar characteristics.

The economic psychology of the stock market encompasses studies that are of great potential interest not only to researchers in psychology and finance, but also to observers and actors in financial markets who want to understand what goes on and lies behind the shifts in the aggregate market curves. The psychology of market changes then refers to individuals with human characteristics and not to aggregate curves for individual stocks or the total market. The purpose of financial economic psychology is to study the optimism or pessimism of the investors rather than of the market.

3.13 References

Ajzen, I. (1991), "The theory of planned behavior," *Organizational Behavior and Human Decision Processes*, 50, 179–211.

Andersson, P. (2004), "How well do financial experts perform? A review of empirical research on performance of analysts, day-traders, forecasters, fund managers, investors, and stockbrokers" (EFI report 2004: 9), Stockholm: Stockholm School of Economics.

Barberis, N., A. Shleifer, and R. Vishny (1998), "A model of investor sentiment," *Journal of Financial Economics*, 49, 307–43.

Brown, L. D. and H. N. Higgins (2005), "Managers' forecast guidance of analysts: International evidence," *Journal of Accounting and Public Policy*, 24, 280–99.

Cialdini, R. B. (1988), *Influence: Science and Practice*, 2nd edn, Glenview, IL: Scott, Foresman and Co.

Clinton, B. (2004), *My Life*, New York, NY: Alfred A. Knopf.

Cosmides, L. and J. Tooby (1996), "Are humans good intuitive statisticians after all? Rethinking some conclusions from the literature on judgment under uncertainty," *Cognition*, 58(1), 1–73.

De Bondt, W. (2004), "The values and beliefs of European investors," downloaded from, http://fac.comtech.depaul.edu/wdebondt /Publications.

Dominitz, J. and C. F. Manski (2005), "Measuring and interpreting expectations of equity returns," draft: February 2005 (www.ssrn.com).

Edwards, W. (1982), "Conservatism in human information processing," in D. Kahneman, P. Slovic, and A. Tversky (eds.), *Judgment under Uncertainty: Heuristics and Biases*, Cambridge: Cambridge University Press, 359–69.

Ericsson, K. A. and A. C. Lehmann (1996), "Expert and exceptional performance: Evidence of maximal adaptation to task constraints," *Annual Review of Psychology*, 47, 273–305.

Fama, E. F. (1998), "Market efficiency, long-term returns, and behavioral finance," *Journal of Financial Economics*, 49(3), 283–306.

Fenton-O'Creevy, M., N. Nicholson, E. Soane, and P. Willman (2003), "Trading on illusions: Unrealistic perceptions of control and trading performance," *Journal of Occupational and Organizational Psychology* 76, 53–68.

Fiedler, K. (2000), "Beware of samples! Cognitive-ecological sampling approach to judgment biases," *Psychological Review*, 107(4), 659–76.

Fiedler, K., B. Brinkmann, T. Betsch, and B. Wild (2000), "A sampling approach to biases in conditional probability judgments: Beyond baserate neglect and statistical format," *Journal of Experimental Psychology: General*, 129, 399–418.

Fischhoff, B. (1982), "Debiasing," in D. Kahneman, P. Slovic, and A. Tversky (eds.), *Judgment under Uncertainty: Heuristics and Biases*, Cambridge: Cambridge University Press, 422–44.

French, K. R. and J. M. Poterba (1991), "Investor diversification and international equity markets," *American Economic Review*, 81(2), 222–6.

Gasper, K. (2004), "Do you see what I see? Affect and visual information processing," *Cognition and Emotion*, 18(3), 405–21.

Gigerenzer, G. and U. Hoffrage (1995), "How to improve Bayesian reasoning without instruction: Frequency formats," *Psychological Review*, 102, 684–704.

Griffin, D. and A. Tversky (1992), "The weighing of evidence and the determinants of confidence," *Cognitive Psychology*, 24(3), 411–35.

Hoffrage, U. and R. Hertwig (1999), "Hindsight bias: A price worth paying for fast and frugal memory," in G. Gigerenzer, P. M. Todd, and the ABC Research Group (eds.), *Simple Heuristics that Make Us Smart*, Oxford: Oxford University Press, 191–208.

Kahneman, D. and W. Riepe (1998), "Aspects of investor psychology," *Journal of Portfolio Management*, 24(4), Summer, 52–65.

Kahneman, D. and A. Tversky (1973), "On the psychology of prediction," *Psychological Review*, 80, 237–51.

(1979), "Prospect theory: An analysis of decision under risk," *Econometrica*, 47, 263–91.

Katona, G. (1975), *Psychological Economics*, New York: Elsevier.

Keynes, J. M. (1936), *The General Theory of Employment, Interest and Money*, London: Macmillan.

Langer, E. J. (1982), "The illusion of control," in D. Kahneman, P. Slovic, and A. Tversky (eds.), *Judgment under Uncertainty: Heuristics and Biases*, Cambridge: Cambridge University Press, 231–8.

Manski, C. F. (2004), "Measuring expectations," *Econometrica*, 72(5), 1329–76.

McGraw, A. P., B. A. Mellers, and I. Ritov (2004), "The affective costs of overconfidence," *Journal of Behavioral Decision Making*, 17(4), 281–95.

Mellers, B. A. (2000), "Choice and the relative pleasure of consequences," *Psychological Bulletin*, 126(6), 910–24.

Mill, J. ([1829] 1869), *Analysis of the Phenomena of the Human Mind*. 2 vols. 2nd edn, edited by J. S. Mill, London: Longmans, Green, Reader, and Dyer. Downloaded February 25, 2005 from: http://gallica.bnf.fr.

Mill, J. S. ([1843] 1925), "The logic of the moral sciences," in *A System of Logic, Ratiocinative and Inductive* (Book VI), 8th edn, London: Longman, Green, & Co.

Porter, G. E. (2004), "The long-term value of analysts' advice in the *Wall Street Journal*'s investment dartboard contest," *Journal of Applied Finance*, 14(2), 52–65.

Rothman, A. J. and C. D. Hardin (1997), "Differential use of the availability heuristic in social judgment," *Personality and Social Psychology Bulletin*, 23(2), 123–38.

Shefrin, H. (2000), *Beyond Greed and Fear: Understanding Behavioral Finance and the Psychology of Investing*, Boston, MA: Harvard Business School Press.

Shefrin, H. and M. Statman (1994), "Behavioral Capital Asset Pricing Theory," *Journal of Financial and Quantitative Analysis*, 29(3), 323–49.

Shiller, R. J. (2000a), "Measuring bubble expectations and investor confidence," *Journal of Psychology and Financial Markets*, 1(1), 49–60.

(2000b), *Irrational Exuberance*, Princeton, NJ: Princeton University Press.

Shleifer, A. (2000), *Inefficient Markets*, Oxford: Oxford University Press.

Slovic, P., M. Finucane, E. Peters, and D. C. MacGregor (2002), "The affect heuristic," in T. Gilovich, D. Griffin, and D. Kahneman (eds.), *Heuristics and Biases: The Psychology of Intuitive Judgment*, Cambridge: Cambridge University Press, 397–420.

Stephan, E. (1999), "Die Rolle von Urteilsheuristiken bei Finanzentscheidungen: Ankereffekte und kognitive Verfügbarkeit" [The role of judgmental heuristics in financial decisions: Anchoring and availability effects], in L. Fischer, T. Kutsch, and E. Stephan (eds.), *Finanzpsychologie*, Munich and Vienna: R. Oldenbourg Verlag, 101–34.

Stephan, E. and G. Kiell (2000), "Decision processes in professional investors: Does expertise moderate judgmental biases?" in E. Hölzl (ed.), *IAREP/SABE Conference Proceedings: Fairness and Competition*, Vienna: WUV, Universitätsverlag, 416–20.

Stotz, O. and R. von Nitzsch (2005), "The perception of control and the level of overconfidence: Evidence from analyst earnings estimates and price targets," *Journal of Behavioral Finance*, 6(3), 121–8.

Teigen, K. H. and G. Keren (2003), "Surprises: Low probabilities or high contrasts?" *Cognition*, 87, 55–71.

Tversky, A. and C. Heath (1991), "Preferences and beliefs: Ambiguity and competence in choice under uncertainty," *Journal of Risk and Uncertainty*, 4, 5–28.

Tversky, A. and D. Kahneman (1982a), "Judgment under uncertainty: Heuristics and biases," in D. Kahneman, P. Slovic, and A. Tversky (eds.), *Judgment under Uncertainty: Heuristics and Biases*, Cambridge: Cambridge University Press, 3–20.

(1982b), "Evidential impact of base rates," in D. Kahneman, P. Slovic, and A. Tversky (eds.), *Judgment under Uncertainty: Heuristics and Biases*, Cambridge: Cambridge University Press, 153–60.

(1982c), "Availability: A heuristic for judging frequency and probability," in D. Kahneman, P. Slovic, and A. Tversky (eds.), *Judgment under Uncertainty: Heuristics and Biases*, Cambridge: Cambridge University Press, 163–78.

(1983) "Extensional versus intuitive reasoning: The conjunction fallacy in probability judgment," *Psychological Review*, 90(4), 293–315.

Van Raaij, W. F. (2005), "Investor confidence," paper presented at the IAREP Colloquium, Prague, September 22, 2005.

Vissing-Jorgensen, A. (2004), "Perspectives on behavioral finance: Does 'irrationality' disappear with wealth? Evidence from expectations and actions," *NBER Macro Annual 2003*, Cambridge, MA: MIT Press.

Wärneryd, K.-E. (1997), "Demystifying rational expectations theory through an economic–psychological model," in G. Antonides, W. F. van Raaij, and S. Maital (eds.), *Advances in Economic Psychology*, Chichester: Wiley & Sons, 211–36.

(2001), *Stock-Market Psychology. How People Value and Trade Stocks*, Cheltenham, UK and Northampton, MA: Elgar.

Wilson, T. D., D. B. Centerbar, D. A. Kermer, and D. T. Gilbert (2005), "The pleasures of uncertainty: Prolonging positive moods in ways people do not anticipate," *Journal of Personality and Social Psychology*, 88(1), 5–21.

Wilson, T. D. and D. T. Gilbert (2003), "Affective forecasting," in M. P. Zanna (ed.), *Advances in Experimental Social Psychology*, 35, New York: Academic Press, 346–411.

Zajonc, R. B. (1980), "Feeling and thinking: Preferences need no inferences," *American Psychologist*, 35(2), 151–75.

4 Stock prices: insights from behavioral finance

WERNER F. M. DE BONDT

Modern finance postulates that the capital markets of the leading industrialized nations are rational and efficient. This survey assesses the theory and evidence regarding investor psychology as a determinant of stock prices. In particular, I review (i) the concept of efficient markets and (ii) what is known about the structure and dynamics of equity prices. I examine the origins of behavioral finance, why it modifies standard asset pricing theory, and how it contributes to our practical understanding of stock market bubbles and investor under- and overreaction to news.

In recent decades, hardly any topic in finance has been investigated in as much detail as the behavior of stock prices. Economists are interested because of the role of security prices in guiding resource allocation. The ideal is a competitive capital market in which rational prices instantaneously and accurately reflect all available information and sustain economic efficiency. In contrast, the attention of amateur and expert investors is more practical. They seek early access to news, develop trading rules, or carry out fundamental analysis in hopes of attaining superior investment performance. The aim of their labor is a portfolio of assets that earns a higher return than a portfolio of arbitrarily selected securities with comparable risk, liquidity, tax burden, etc. Empirical research in modern finance – exemplified by the seminal contributions of Fama (1965a and b, 1970, 1976) – focused on the futility of these efforts, especially if search and trading costs are taken into account. Stock prices were shown to be responsive to news and to approximately follow a random walk.[1]

Parts of this chapter were presented at the University of Bath, the University of Durham, the University of Glasgow, Erasmus University Rotterdam, the Chicago-Kent School of Law, the Federal Reserve Bank of Chicago, California State University-Fullerton, the University of Stellenbosch, the 2004 annual meeting of the Midwest Finance Association in Chicago, the 2006 meeting of the Portuguese Finance Association in Porto, the Investment Analysts' Society of Chicago, the Investment Analysts' Society of Omaha-Nebraska, and public events, organized by LGT Capital Management, open to investors in Frankfurt and Zurich. I thank Richard Dowen, William Forbes, Claire Hill, Alan Lewis, Thierry Post, John McKernan, Zak Nel, Ana Paula Sera, Mark Stohs and Rob Watson for encouragement, comments and conversations, and Veronica Simms for administrative assistance. Some ideas and facts discussed here first appeared in my 1983 working paper.

[1] The random walk is approximate since expected price changes are non-zero if there is an equilibrium positive trade-off between risk and return. Since genuine news is unpredictable, the random walk evidence is often presented in support of the hypothesis of rational markets.

4.1 The challenge

Our present-day understanding of these issues, it is fair to say, leaves considerably more room for dispute than the precise conclusions put forward in the 1960s and 1970s indicate. First, the analytical models of Stiglitz, Grossman, and others emphasize the limits of arbitrage and the strictness of the conditions under which efficient capital markets may generate Pareto-optimal resource allocations (Grossman and Stiglitz [1980]; Stiglitz [1981]). Second, since the late 1970s when modern finance reached its highpoint, financial economists have compiled many empirical anomalies that baffle the mind and that go against the traditional theory. For example, Ball and Brown (1968), Latane and Jones (1977), and Watts (1978) were among the first scholars to document a systematic drift in returns after earnings announcements – an observation that keeps researchers puzzled to this day (see, e.g., Chordia and Shivakumar [2006]). Around the same time, Charest (1978) noticed how it can take months before the full impact of changes in dividends is impounded in prices. (This finding is confirmed by Michaely *et al.* [1995].) Analogous observations were made by Givoly and Lakonishok (1979, 1980) with respect to analyst forecast revisions of earnings per share. Over the years, the list of abnormalities has expanded greatly. Some patterns in security prices are related to the calendar, for example the month (Rozeff and Kinney [1976]), the turn of the year (Givoly and Ovadia [1983]; Roll [1983]), and the day of the week (Gibbons and Hess [1981]; French [1983]). Other anomalies come into view in the cross-section of companies. Small firms earn unusually large returns (Banz [1981]; Reinganum [1981]), as do firms with low price–earnings (PE) ratios (Basu [1977]), or firms that are neglected by investors (Arbel and Strebel [1983]).[2]

Modern finance has responded to the challenge of return predictability in different ways. For instance, it questions the pervasiveness and robustness of the new facts (Fama [1998]) or it reinterprets them as non-anomalous (e.g., Timmerman [1993] and Brav and Heaton [2002]). A routine maneuver that plays down the significance of the findings is to cast doubt on the valuation models that must unavoidably be part of every test of the efficient markets hypothesis. This is the position taken by, for example, Jensen (1978) and Ball

---

(However, as Shiller [1984] emphasizes, it is also consistent with inefficient markets.) Lorie and Hamilton (1973) describe the history of modern finance and its theories of the stock market. Mandelbrot and Hudson (2004) assess the random walk evidence.

[2] Other perplexing findings initially recorded in the 1970s and 1980s include: (1) investment advice offered by *Value Line* may be the basis for exceptional returns (Copeland and Mayers [1982]); (2) the secondary dissemination of analyst recommendations in the *Wall Street Journal* affects stock prices (Lloyd-Davies and Canes [1978]); (3) changes in the *NBER Index of Leading Indicators* predict changes in stock prices, and assets appear to be overvalued during economic expansions and undervalued during contractions (Umstead [1977]); (4) long-term non-linear dependence in stock returns (Greene and Fielitz [1977]). Keim and Ziemba (2000) survey the worldwide stock market anomaly evidence.

(1978). The Sharpe–Lintner Capital Asset Pricing Model (CAPM) states that the expected return for any stock (in excess of the risk-free rate) equals beta times the expected market risk premium. Skepticism about this model runs deep. It stems from unfavorable empirical tests as well as from hesitation about the model's testability (Roll [1977]). The theoretical studies of Merton (1973) and Ross (1976) laid the groundwork for multifactor models. These authors propose that the compensation for bearing risk is comprised of several risk premia rather than one. However, the consumption-CAPM (Breeden [1979]) and the arbitrage pricing theory (APT) do not a priori specify the relevant state variables.[3] Based on an extensive analysis of US data, Fama and French (1992, 1996) add two factors (for size and value) to the market risk premium.[4] Whether multifactor models greatly enhance our practical understanding of the determination of stock prices is a matter of debate. However, once the Fama–French factors are taken into account, some of the stock price anomalies lose strength, and the "excess" returns that are earned may be fair payment for (time-varying) risk.

Some researchers have taken a different approach and have asked whether price levels (rather than rates of return) can be reconciled with valuation models built on the joint assumptions of rational utility-maximizing agents and frictionless markets. Prominent among the expectations models of asset prices is the Miller–Modigliani (1961) view of stock prices as the appropriately discounted present values of expected future cash flows (LeRoy [1982]). Shiller (1981, 1989, 2000) finds that stock price fluctuations cannot be solely attributed to movements in dividends around the historical trend. Over the last century, he says, dividends simply did not vary enough to rationally justify the price movements (see also LeRoy and Porter [1981]). There is excess volatility or, as Federal Reserve chairman Alan Greenspan put it years afterward, "irrational exuberance."

Yet, the extraordinary variability of stock prices may also reflect changes in the rates of return that investors require. The consumption variability associated with expected fluctuations in economic activity induces stock price variability, the magnitude of which depends on the level of risk-aversion of the representative investor. Grossman and Shiller (1981) estimate the degree of risk-aversion that would validate the observed stock price volatility. The postwar data imply implausibly high estimates. Also, the historical price movements in bonds, land, or housing do not match those of stocks (Shiller [1989]). Still, that is what should happen if asset price fluctuations chiefly reflect changes in discount rates.

---

[3] This is a problem: for example, Shanken (1982) argues that the APT is no more testable than the CAPM.

[4] Contemporary asset-pricing research may also add a momentum factor. Cochrane (2000) presents a survey of modern asset-pricing theory.

Shiller's findings of excess stock price volatility cast doubt on the assumption of rational expectations.[5] Changes in stock prices are strongly correlated with changes in corporate earnings that follow about one or two years later. Maybe investors perceive short-term developments to be of great consequence for the long-term outlook of the economy. The trouble is that the argument is in conflict with the tendency of dividends to follow trends for over a century. So, it implies that investors grossly overreact to new information or, alternatively, that they are myopic.[6]

The concept of stock market overreaction may appear radical but it is not a complete departure from past belief. In *The General Theory*, John Maynard Keynes argued that "day-to-day fluctuations in the profits of existing investments, which are obviously of an ephemeral and non-significant character, tend to have an altogether excessive, and even an absurd, influence on the market" ([1936], pp. 153–4). In various forms, the hypothesis is also found in Taussig (1921), Macauley (1938), Williams (1938), and Working (1949, 1958). With the prosperity of the 1920s, the crash and the depression in mind, Williams (1938) notes that security prices "have been based too much on current earning power, too little on long-run dividend paying power" (p. 19).[7]

Over its history, economics has produced many scholars – ranging from Thorstein Veblen, Vilfredo Pareto, Wesley Mitchell, or George Katona to Herbert Simon, George Akerlof, and Daniel Kahneman – who sought to introduce behavioral assumptions. Still, a good number of economists keep their distance. For instance, the search for rational micro-foundations of macro-economics that originated in the 1970s was a shift that is 180 degrees in the opposite direction. In 1976, Barro and Fischer (p. 163) stated that

> . . . the rational expectations assumption may be excessively strong . . . but it is more persuasive . . . than the alternative of using a rule of thumb for expectations formation that is independent of the stochastic properties of the time path of the variable about which expectations are formed. A fundamental difficulty with theories of expectations that are not based on the predictions of the relevant economic model . . . is that they require a theory of systematic mistakes.

The purpose of this chapter is twofold. First, I appraise the theory of rational and efficient markets, and I support tests of efficiency that compare stock

---

[5] In different ways, Friedman (1980) and Lovell (1986) also ask whether the cumulative empirical evidence supports the doctrine of rational expectations.

[6] Competing hypotheses are that the market is rightfully concerned with a low-probability, high-loss event (e.g. war or nationalization) or that the historical standard deviation of dividends (around the trend) is a poor measure of the subjective uncertainty about dividends. Note that both of these arguments inherently depend on unobservables.

[7] In a marvelously absorbing story, Allen (1931) gives a detailed account of the great bull market of the 1920s and its aftermath. Klein (2001) critically reviews all major studies of the 1929 crash. Kindleberger (1978) develops a general model of financial crises (including stock market bubbles) and confronts it with history.

prices with "intrinsic values" of companies as in Graham and Dodd (1934). Against Barro and Fisher, I contend that at this moment in time the groundwork for a theory of systematic bias exists. Indeed, the failure of rationality as a descriptive model matches the findings of behavioral science. Much of this breakdown may be understood in terms of a limited number of psychological mechanisms, for example mental frames and heuristics, that shape human cognition, emotion, and social interaction. Thus, behavioral finance gives positive content to concepts like investor sentiment, crowd opinion or animal spirits that, by themselves, look inoperative and hollow. The rise of behavioral finance does not mean, however, that we must abandon economic man *in toto*. Since the behavioral model is one of bias, the rational approach retains some of its normative allure.[8] Economic agents are seen as boundedly rational, i.e., they are thought to act sensibly within the decision-making context and within the limits of their cognitive and emotional abilities.

Next, I turn to the empirical evidence. I discuss how investor psychology influences the structure and dynamics of world equity markets. In particular, I emphasize investor over- and underreaction, and the remarkable performance of value stocks compared to glamour stocks. The overreaction effect was discovered in the context of the study of the price–earnings ratio anomaly. In the cross-section of securities, stocks with low PE ratios earn significantly higher risk-adjusted returns than high PE stocks.[9] The overreaction hypothesis says that this happens because, relative to their intrinsic value, many high PE stocks are temporarily overpriced. Investors, the contention is, get inappropriately optimistic about the business prospects of these firms. Similarly, low PE stocks are underpriced because the market is inappropriately pessimistic. Once false beliefs take hold, however, only a great deal of opposing news (e.g., a series of negative earnings surprises) succeeds in turning prices around, and this behavior generates drifts in stock prices. (Investors do not easily change attitude. They tend to discount any news report that opposes "what they know to be true," and they give extra weight to confirming information.) Thus, trends and reversals in share price are dissimilar but connected aspects of the same phenomenon. Both the initial overreaction and the later underreaction differ from the reaction which Bayes' theorem defines as best. What is decisive is that deviations from optimality can be detected and predicted by statistics (such as past return performance) that are correlated with investor sentiment. Below, I develop the overreaction hypothesis in more detail, and I review many empirical studies. A large majority of them use data for the United States and other

---

[8] How much of its normative status the rational model can hang on to is a matter of intense discussion in decision theory and philosophy. See, for example, the work of Elster (1979), Nozick (1993), Simon (1983), and Searle (2001).

[9] Likewise, firms with low market value-to-book value (MB) ratios beat stocks with high MB ratios, and firms that greatly underperformed the market index over the previous three to five years, i.e. past losers, beat past winners. Other commonly used sorting variables that appear to capture the same effect include the price-to-sales ratio, the cash flow yield, and dividend yield.

G-7 countries. On balance, the evidence indicates that investor psychology is a significant determinant of security prices. In sum, I conclude that the stock markets of the world's leading industrialized nations are not rational and efficient, i.e., there are systematic and measurable disparities between the stock prices and fundamental values of large publicly traded corporations.[10] The concept of overreaction may well embody a pervasive trait of human conduct that applies under general, identifiable circumstances – in market as well as non-market contexts.[11]

4.2 What are rational and efficient markets?

While the notion of rational and efficient capital markets is a cornerstone of modern finance, significant ambiguities are associated with its meaning. The concept may be analyzed from the perspective of economic outcomes, investor beliefs, or equilibrium prices free from arbitrage opportunities. That many individual investors act in ways that are less than fully rational does not create controversy. Some researchers closely associated with the rational expectations (RE) approach, for example Muth (1961) or Mishkin (1981), plainly state that RE is not a descriptive assumption.[12] In spite of this, they stress that as long as arbitrageurs eliminate profit opportunities, market behavior corresponds to

[10] The survey of Daniel *et al.* (2002) also finds that there is "fairly definitive proof" (p. 141) that equity markets are subject to mispricing, and Shleifer (2000) chooses "inefficient markets" as the title of his book on the subject. Other surveys of behavioral finance and various aspects of investor psychology include De Bondt (1989, 2000, 2002, 2005b), De Bondt and Thaler (1995), Shefrin (1999, 2001, 2005), and Hirshleifer (2001). Fama (1998) and Rubinstein (2001) present a critique of behavioral finance. They also offer an orthodox analysis of the empirical evidence – in favor of stock market rationality. According to Rubinstein, "the belief in rational markets stems from a long cultural and scientific heritage probably dating back to the Greeks, who elevated 'reason' as the guide to life."

[11] For example, overreaction agrees with (1) findings in the market for government bonds: when long-term interest rates are high relative to short rates they move down in the next period (Shiller [1979]); (2) findings in the market for corporate bonds: low-grade (high-yield) (junk) bonds outperform high-grade bonds (Hickman [1958]); (3) the rewards of investing in distressed or bankrupt companies with illiquid debt (Rosenberg [1992]; Gilson [1995]); (4) the steep fall and later steep recovery of the prices of low-mileage used cars during the 1973–4 energy crisis (Daly and Mayor [1983]); (5) journalists' observations on the fickleness of public opinion and political reporting: "British political reporters can be as mercurial as American ones. After a by-election in a South London district, the press here began to write off Labour and prophesy the disappearance of its leader, Michael Foot. Then a few weeks later Labour retained its seat in another by-election. The political writers thereupon resurrected both the party and Mr. Foot. This inconstancy in reading tea-leaves illustrates a constant tendency in human nature from which journalists, British or American, don't escape. That's a tendency to overvalue the latest in a series of events, particularly if it is unexpected or dramatic" (Royster [1983]).

[12] Nonetheless, RE is often interpreted as a behavioral assumption. For example, Lucas (1975) assumes in his illustrious model of the business cycle that economic agents form their individual forecasts by minimizing the expectation of the forecast error (based on the equilibrium probability distribution), conditional on the information available to them. See also the discussion in Lovell (1986) and Conlisk (1996).

the concept of economic man. So, it is not investor folly *per se* that drives the conclusion that actual market prices often differ from rational prices.[13] We need to argue additionally that in the price formation process there are significant institutional and economic limits on the degree to which experts can offset the actions taken by less sophisticated investors. A well-known paradox of full informational efficiency is that it destroys any incentive to spend resources on costly information (Grossman and Stiglitz [1980]).[14]

If the market is inefficient, false security prices impinge on traders' wealth positions, and episodes of mispricing have systemic welfare implications that extend far beyond the boundaries of any specific market.[15] From this angle, the standard definitions put forward by Fama (1970) – which distinguish between weak, semi-strong and strong form market efficiency and which encourage the study of price movements in reaction to historical, publicly and privately available information – are problematic. Fama's taxonomy hints that more information is better than less, but this is contradicted by welfare economics.[16]

The Miller–Modigliani (1961) characterization of market efficiency, which defines rational stock prices as the sums of the discounted values of subsequent cash flows (and which is the starting point for Shiller's volatility tests), can be defended in a variety of ways. One justification weighs the true value received *ex post* by long-term buy-and-hold investors who collect dividends against the prices paid and received *ex ante* by short-term speculators. History teaches us that there have been times when the market index put a price of $2 on $1 of true value, and that there have been times when the price was only 50 cents. If there is a persistent pattern in the deviations from value (e.g., excess

---

[13] Hayek (1948) also takes "the antirationalistic approach which regards man not as a highly rational and intelligent but as a very irrational and fallible being" (p. 8). But Hayek further believes that "human Reason, with a capital R, does not exist in the singular, as given or available to any particular person, . . . but must be conceived as an interpersonal process in which anyone's contribution is tested and corrected by others" (p. 15). Thus, the market process transcends the bounded rationality of the individual participants.

[14] Verrecchia (1982) presents a model in which optimal information acquisition and equilibrium prices are determined simultaneously. Traders' conjectures about how much information prices reveal are fulfilled by their own acquisition activities. Hellwig (1982) shows that the Grossman–Stiglitz paradox can be overcome if investors learn only from prices at which transactions have actually been completed. In this case, the return to being informed is non-zero.

[15] How does a boundedly rational resource allocation compare to an allocation that obtains if all agents are fully informed and fully rational? It is unclear. Both equilibria may be subjectively Pareto-optimal. However, Pareto-optima for different configurations of information and decision expertise cannot be ordered in a simple way (Easley and Jarrow [1982]). Presumably, amateur investors are better off if they make portfolio choices free from cognitive error; fully rational agents are worse off, however, since they can no longer gain wealth at the expense of amateurs. In a fascinating paper, De Franco *et al.* (2007) offer dollar estimates of the wealth transfers between individual investors, institutional investors, and others that are related to misleading analyst reports during the recent stock market bubble.

[16] The analysis in Grossman (1989, chapter 3) is similar to Fama. Within the context of a revealing rational expectations equilibrium, traders condition their beliefs on prices and thereby infer the information available to other traders. Hellwig (1980) stresses that rational agents will neglect their own private information and look at price only. In equilibrium, investors' beliefs are homogeneous and they represent the best possible assessment of an asset's worth.

price volatility) that cannot be traced to evolving risk attitudes or Bayesian learning, a blend of investor foolishness and market frictions may be the cause. A second rationalization for the model refers to Tobin's q. Corporate investment is powerfully influenced by the ratio of the market value of the capital stock to its replacement cost.

The Miller–Modigliani model has been criticized, however, for its restrictive emphasis on business fundamentals, for example its disregard of the "greater fool theory." Some authors hold as rational any investor beliefs that if generally acted upon are self-confirming (Azariadis [1981]; Froot and Obstfeld [1991]). In their view, the market may rationally launch itself onto an arbitrary self-fulfilling price bubble. Non-uniqueness is a general feature of dynamic models involving expectations (McCallum [1983]). While there is no choice-theoretic rationale for singling out solutions that do not suffer from extrinsic uncertainty ("sunspots"), these are the only Pareto-optimal allocations (Cass and Shell [1983]).

Another critique of the Miller–Modigliani view of stock prices says that the question of market efficiency cannot be solved by reference to the price and cash flows of individual assets but only by examining whether there are identifiable arbitrage opportunities – i.e., violations of the law of one price – between securities (Long [1981]). However, in a stock market bubble many assets may be overpriced all at once. Therefore, the absence of arbitrage opportunities does not imply efficiency in the Miller–Modigliani sense. Also, the definition of a pure arbitrage opportunity has nothing to do with the particular content of the information reflected in prices. Therefore, the successful or unsuccessful search for such opportunities is not a test of the efficiency of market prices with respect to diverse sets of data.

In sum, Miller–Modigliani market efficiency is not implied by a lack of arbitrage opportunities. Neither does it follow from the assumptions of rational behavior and rational expectations. The wealth allocations to which rational prices lead are no more and no less desirable than most other allocations. Still, the Miller–Modigliani view of market efficiency corresponds to an intuitive notion shared by investment professionals around the world, namely that stock prices should reflect intrinsic values.

4.3 How is rationality in markets achieved?

A key question in finance is how rational and efficient markets can possibly come about. What are the dynamics of the price formation process? I now want to examine briefly the micro-foundations of rational expectations (RE) models from a theoretical perspective.[17] Blume et al. (1982) provide a useful

---

[17] An alternative approach is to set up experimental (laboratory) markets, as pioneered by Vernon Smith. For instance, Smith et al. (1988) study bubbles, crashes, and the evolution of subjects'

overview of some relevant literature. As may be expected, equilibrium is the
starting point. From there, the models work backwards to the restrictions that
the existence, uniqueness, and stability of equilibrium put on the behavior
of individual economic agents. Nearly every analysis investigates the internal consistency of the rational expectations hypothesis with other informational assumptions. Typically, the authors search for forecast rules which
lead to convergence to a self-fulfilling equilibrium. For example, Cyert and
DeGroot (1974) show how a Bayesian learning process can generate rational
expectations. (Other models include Grossman [1989, chapter 2], Townsend
[1978], DeCanio [1979], Friedman [1979], Bray [1982], and Frydman [1982].)
In general, the search is disappointing. Not only are the models extremely
demanding in terms of the information processing capacity of agents, there
is no guarantee that, even if traders revise their expectations in an appropriate way, prices rapidly, if at all, converge to a revealing rational expectations
equilibrium.

A much weaker characterization of market efficiency (that guides us to a
partial answer in response to the key question) is the notion of consensus beliefs
(CB) (Rubinstein [1975]; Beaver [1981]). A market is efficient with respect to
an information set A if the prices it generates are identical to the prices of an
otherwise identical economy in which A describes the information available
to every investor. The consensus belief is the homogeneous belief induced by
knowledge of A. Provided that A is the union of all private information sets
and that traders have CB, the market reaches full information efficiency even
if traders do not condition their actual beliefs on equilibrium prices.[18]

The concept of consensus beliefs resembles the theory of market efficiency
in Verrecchia (1979). This paper offers sufficient conditions so that prices
achieve full informational efficiency and vary as if all investors knew the
objective return distributions. The analysis requires neither revealing rational
expectations nor costless information. Verrecchia's main theorem states that
the dispersion of prices converges to the true underlying dispersion function as
the number of market participants becomes large.[19] The theorem stirs interest
in part because, in the author's words, it is based upon "a relatively weak set of
assumptions" (p. 79). The set is weak since no economic or institutional constraints on market participation will produce prices that are biased. Apart from
technicalities, there are five assumptions: (1) all traders are expected-utility

---

price expectations. Their aim is to characterize the price process and its convergence to
fundamental value. Smith *et al.* find expectations to be adaptive but prices do converge towards
levels consistent with rational expectations, mainly when all traders are experienced. The most
common outcome is a market characterized by a price bubble.

[18] For details, I refer the reader to Verrecchia (1980). This author studies the conditions under
which (i) each investor acquires what he perceives to be an optimal amount of information
and (ii) the degree of precision implicit in CB is no less than the precision in any individual
assessment, i.e., no informed investor can earn excess returns. Easley and Jarrow (1983) show
that an efficient CB equilibrium generically fails to exist.

[19] Figlewski (1982) derives a similar "law of large numbers" result in a more restrictive setting.

(EU) maximizers; (2) they are risk-averse; (3) they are Bayesian decision-makers; (4) their assessments of uncertain future prospects are unbiased; (5) their assessments are pairwise independent. As a group, the first four of Verrecchia's assumptions add up to a convenient definition of rational economic man. Suppose I concede to Verrecchia that the assumptions listed above may suffice to motivate a theory of efficient markets: are they plausible descriptions of individual behavior?

4.4 "Rational economic man" re-examined

Many economists will be inclined to answer in the affirmative. However, behavioral science advises otherwise.[20] Nisbett and Ross (1980), Kahneman *et al.* (1982), Tversky and Kahneman (1986), Baron (1988), Gilovich (1991), Plous (1993), Conlisk (1996), Schwartz (1998), Rabin (1998), Hastie and Dawes (2001), and Gilovich *et al.* (2002) offer easily readable surveys of the vast experimental literature.

Numerous studies question the descriptive validity of the EU axioms. For instance, Kahneman and Tversky's (1979) prospect theory includes a certainty effect: people overweigh outcomes that are certain relative to outcomes that are merely probable. This effect helps to explain the Allais paradox. As a second example, Tversky (1969) documents systematic violations of transitivity. According to Schoemaker (1982), the failure of the EU model stems from "an inadequate recognition of various psychological principles of judgment and choice" (p. 548).[21]

In general, behavioral theories stress the limits of people's computational abilities and knowledge. Man seeks cognitive simplification. A central insight is that the nature of a decision task is a prime determinant of behavior. Problem-solving is not easily understood by studying final choices without consideration of the decision process (Payne [1976]). It is often modeled as a selective search based on rules-of-thumb and a variety of cognitive schemata ("mental frames"). Three widely known rules-of-thumb are the availability, representativeness, and anchoring-and-adjustment heuristics (Tversky and Kahneman [1974]). On the whole, heuristics and knowledge structures are extremely useful; mental

---

[20] Hereafter, I acknowledge but I do not return to the argument that Verrecchia's assumptions are only meant to be "as if" representations of individual behavior, i.e., rationality is truly an equilibrium concept. Neither do I discuss the normative status of the assumptions of rationality, their practical utility in building simple models that may be predictive, or the tautological claim that, if it is modeled appropriately, all behavior is rational (Becker [1976]).

[21] The failure of the EU model is also easily seen outside the laboratory. Consider, for example, the extraordinary business success of the gaming industry in the United States (state lotteries, sports betting, etc.). Field studies produce more puzzling evidence. For example, in an investigation of flood and earthquake insurance, Kunreuther *et al.* (1978) find that almost half of the respondents (who are well informed about the availability of government-subsidized insurance) act contrary to subjective expected utility maximization. Eisner and Strotz (1961) discuss perplexing facts relating to flight insurance.

life could scarcely be managed without them. Sometimes, however, they produce misunderstanding and illogical behavior: for example, alternative frames
of what is objectively one and the same problem can produce reversals in preference (Grether and Plott [1979]). Hogarth (1980) lists thirty-seven sources
of bias. Nisbett and Ross (1980) mention even more. The biases touch both
experts and non-experts. They have some bearing on every stage of the decision
process – be it attention, perception, memory, analysis, simulation, output, or
feedback.

Framing effects highlight the pivotal role of reference points and aspiration
levels in evaluating outcomes and risk-taking (Kahneman and Tversky [1984]).
Targets are related to the notions of satisficing (Simon [1945, 1957]), disappointment, and regret (Loomes and Sugden [1982]). Whereas in EU theory
various actions are assessed in terms of their impact on final wealth, prospect
theory defines the value function over gains and losses relative to a reference point that depends on the structure of the task. The value function is
concave for gains and convex for losses, implying risk-seeking preferences
for below-target outcomes. The empirical evidence on risk preferences of
financial professionals and executives (Libby and Fishburn [1977]; Laughhunn
et al. [1980]; MacCrimmon and Wehrung [1986]; March and Shapira [1987])
confirms that risk perception may be related to the failure to obtain a target return. Note that in EU theory risk preference is viewed as a personality
characteristic. However, the data suggest that risk-taking is partly situationally
determined (Vlek and Stallen [1980]). A dozen studies reviewed by Slovic
(1972a) indicate little correlation, from one setting to another, in a person's
preferred level of risk-taking. Schoemaker (1993) and Weber and Milliman
(1997) review alternative conceptualizations of decision-making under risk.

It may be thought that in view of the fallibility of judgment people often lack
decision confidence. Yet, many studies show the opposite (Einhorn and Hogarth [1978]; Langer [1975]). This contradiction focuses our attention on the
link between learning and experience, and the validity of Bayes' theorem as a
descriptive model. Why do mistakes persist in the face of contrary experience?
In some circumstances, new information has too little influence on opinions
already formed ("conservatism"). In other circumstances – where the representativeness heuristic is at work – individuals nearly ignore base-rate knowledge
(Tversky and Kahneman [1974]; Grether [1980]). Other factors restrict our
ability to learn. Because of hindsight bias, outcomes often fail to surprise people as much as they should (Fischhoff [1975]). People also tend to attribute
success to skill and failure to chance. Finally, in some decision situations,
poor heuristic decision rules are reinforced with positive outcome-feedback
(Einhorn [1980]).

The biases relating to forecasting and subjective probability assessment are
of special interest since they bear on the issue of the rationality of expectations.
To repeat, experimental studies leave little doubt that man is mediocre as an

intuitive statistician.[22] Hence, the actual forecasting performance of economic agents merits examination. Hogarth and Makridakis (1981) provide a wide-ranging survey that draws on more than forty studies. There is ample evidence of habitual miscalculation. Over a wide range of problems, mechanistic time series models are more accurate than intuitive procedures. Some studies examine predictions made by economic and financial experts (e.g., Friedman [1980]; Lakonishok [1980]; Brown and Maital [1980]; Ahlers and Lakonishok [1983]; De Bondt and Thaler [1990]; De Bondt [1991]). The data typically show large and systematic forecast errors. Once again, many individual forecasts do not improve upon the predictions of naïve models.

Group mean (consensus) forecasts are on average more exact than individual predictions – through the cancellation of errors of opposite sign, it would seem (Hogarth [1975]; Zarnowitz [1984]). This result matters because it is easy to think of the market price as a weighted average of traders' expectations. However, much inaccuracy remains after aggregation. The likely explanation is that, contrary to Verrecchia's fifth assumption, people's predictions are highly correlated. Forecasters often base their opinions on shared information. In addition, many fall victim to the same decision errors. Finally, if people worry how they come across to others, there is pressure towards conformism (see e.g. Asch [1955] or Janis [1972]). Social pressures may force people to conform to popular thinking ("compliance") even when they privately disagree. The more problematical the decision to be made (e.g., when there are few objective guidelines, and/or the potential losses are large), the more dangerous bad outcomes can be for reputation.[23] Classic works in sociology that explore some of these phenomena are LeBon (1895), Canetti (1962), and Smelser (1963).[24]

---

[22] To cite but a few of many judgment biases documented in the laboratory: insensitivity of probability estimation to sample size; the belief that small samples are highly representative of the population from which they are drawn; the overestimation of small probabilities and underestimation of large probabilities; poor calibration; unrealistic optimism and wishful thinking; misconception of random sequences and regression towards the mean.

[23] That money managers never stop worrying about their image is illustrated by the following two quotes from the *Wall Street Journal*. The first (November 30, 1982) illustrates compliance in a bull market: "When the market surged in August, [money] managers feared being left behind. 'Whether you were bullish or bearish, you couldn't stay out', Mr. Ehrlich says." (Ehrlich was the chairman of Bernstein-Macauley, a well-known money management firm.) The second quote (March 26, 1982) shows the same idea in a bear market: "Once a stock starts to collapse, it collapses completely, because no institutional manager can afford to show it in his portfolio at the end of the quarter. As long as the stock isn't there on April 1, you don't know whether he sold it January 2 or March 30. At some point in the slide, the managers sell the stock because they know the other managers are selling the stock because nobody wants to show it in the portfolio at the end of the quarter. Now, you may say this isn't rational, but the quarterly report is the time horizon we have to work with."

[24] There is a great deal of related research in political science and economics. For example, Devenow and Welch (1996) survey rational herding models in financial economics. Mutz (1998) studies how perceptions of mass opinion affect individual political judgment, for example, when a candidate for US President gains momentum in the primaries because of favorable pre-election polls.

With few exceptions, economists and psychologists alike have looked upon risky decision-making as a cognitive activity. The survey papers of Loewenstein *et al.* (2001) and Slovic (2002) evaluate recent evidence that the emotional reactions to risk often conflict with their cognitive assessments. Consider, for example, fear of flying. Emotions can distort cognitive appraisals, and appraisals can give rise to emotion. The risk-as-feelings hypothesis emphasizes "gut feelings," that is, what is felt at the moment of decision.[25] The findings tie in with the work of brain scientists like Damasio (1994) or LeDoux (1996). Loewenstein *et al.* list many phenomena that resist easy explanation in cognitive-consequentialist terms. (For example, sudden loud noise can cause fear well before we uncover the source of the noise.) Notably, a series of studies suggests that differences in emotional responsiveness, associated with age and gender, are linked to differences in the willingness to take risks.

In summary, I have evaluated the premises underlying many (but not all) models of stock market efficiency. My examination lays emphasis on the experimental literature.[26] In addition, numerous archival and field studies (based on interviews and trading records) reveal that people's shortcomings in judgment and choice matter for the financial behavior of households and institutions "in the real world." For instance, investors often ignore basic principles when they build investment portfolios. In her study of asset allocation, Bange (2000) finds that many people buy and sell stocks as if they extrapolate recent market movements into the future. In this sense, they are so-called positive feedback traders. Huberman (2001) shows that people overinvest in what is familiar to them and do not diversify as much as they should. The familiarity bias reflects in part the imagined exploitation of informational advantage. It implies comfort with what is well known and discomfort with what is foreign. As a final point, De Bondt (2005a) illustrates how, among European investors, differences in cultural values and beliefs help to explain differences in asset allocation. (Evidently, self-interest is modeled after the conduct of reference groups.) Wärneryd's (2001) survey details many non-logical practices and idiosyncrasies in real world investment behavior. Kahneman and Riepe (1998) and De Bondt (1998) offer checklists of classic illusions and errors "that every investor and financial advisor should know about." For now, I conclude that models of stock prices have to acknowledge (1) the likely impact of

---

[25] Slovic (2002) gives many examples from business: for example, how firms market consumer products by attaching emotional tags such as "new," "improved," "100% natural," and so on. Perhaps the same psychological mechanism was at work during the internet bubble when many US firms changed their name to a "dotcom" name. Cooper *et al.* (2001) find that investors earned as much as 53 percent in abnormal stock returns for the five days around the announcement date. The value increase was not transitory and its magnitude was unrelated to the fraction of the firms' business derived from the internet.

[26] Note that, while empirical studies may examine investor and market behavior, well-designed experiments have the benefit that they allow us to analyze people's motives as well as their decisions. The cost of experiments is that they may lack external validity and/or that they induce demand effects, i.e., subjects try to please the experimenter.

non-rational traders on prices, and (2) the essential role and the limits of arbitrage activity.[27]

4.5 Limits to arbitrage

What are the limits to arbitrage? Below, I list several reasons why the trading behavior of professional arbitrageurs does not nullify the price impact of unsophisticated traders. First, as investors with superior forecasting ability or inside information purchase (or sell) undervalued (overvalued) stock, they assume increasing amounts of diversifiable business risk (Levy [1978]). In addition, arbitrageurs with short investment horizons must worry about the unpredictability of "noise trader" sentiment and of future resale prices (Shleifer and Vishny [1997]; Shleifer [2000]). Abreu and Brunnermeier (2002, 2003) discuss a related problem: synchronization risk. Since any rational trader cannot remedy mispricing alone, he has to guess when a critical proportion of his peers will attempt to exploit an arbitrage opportunity and cause a price correction. Competition pushes the arbitrageur not to wait too long to act, but holding costs stop him from acting too early. This leads to delayed arbitrage.

Secondly, institutional factors also impede full price adjustment. For example, the sale of stock can force a trader to incur capital gains taxes, and restrictions on short-sales have an asymmetric impact on investors with favorable and unfavorable information. As stated by Miller (1977), the net result is that, among individual traders, the optimists sway a company's stock price more than the pessimists. Specifically, strong heterogeneity of investor beliefs is associated with high prices and low expected returns in the cross-section of firms. (Jarrow [1980] dissects Miller's arguments.) The empirical work of Figlewski (1981), Diether *et al.* (2002), Chen *et al.* (2002), Ofek and Richardson (2003), and others is consistent with Miller's position.[28] The prices of stocks for which there is more negative information – measured by short interest – tend to be too high. Note that, in theory, a full price correction not only fails to happen, it is unachievable. Arbitrageurs cannot take into account what is known by those

---

[27] Hayek (1948) mutters in agreement: "The statement that, if people knew everything, they are in equilibrium is true simply because that is how we define equilibrium. The assumption of a perfect market in this sense . . . does not get us any nearer an explanation of when and how [an equilibrium] will come about . . . we must explain by what process [people] will acquire the necessary knowledge . . . We have to deal here with assumptions about causation, so that what we assume must not only be regarded as possible (which is certainly not the case if we just regard people as omniscient) but must also be regarded as likely to be true . . . these apparently subsidiary hypotheses . . . that people do learn from experience, and about how they acquire knowledge, . . . constitute the empirical content of our propositions . . . economists frequently do not seem to be aware that the nature of these hypotheses is in many respects rather different from the more general assumptions from which the Pure Logic of Choice starts" (p. 46).

[28] For instance, in their discussion of the internet bubble, Ofek and Richardson (2003) document both (i) diversity of opinion between institutional and retail investors and (ii) significant market frictions. The authors link the bursting of the bubble to an unparalleled level of insider selling and lockup expirations (which correspond to the loosening of short-sales constraints).

who do not trade. The heart of the matter is that, in a world with non-trivial trading costs and disagreement, every individual not only chooses the size of his holdings in each asset, but also in which assets to invest (Mayshar [1983]). As a general rule, prices depend in a complex manner on the structure of transaction costs and beliefs across investors. Under some circumstances, it may turn out that only information held by marginal investors matters. Full information efficient prices, however, ought to be independent of the distribution of private information among investors.

The previous line of reasoning presupposes that arbitrageurs take an investment stance opposite to the position taken by less skilled traders. However, it may be sensible for investors with superior talent to ride the trend rather than to go against it (Keynes [1936]). Harrison and Kreps (1978) show that, with short-sales restrictions, some investors may logically bid up the price of a stock in anticipation of selling it at a higher price than they themselves think it is worth. Surprisingly, it follows that, if an equilibrium price is to be found, it must exceed what any investor is willing to pay for the asset if obliged to hold it forever. In sum, arbitrage does not prevent rational speculative bubbles (see also Tirole [1982]).

Lastly, we may hope that noise traders will somehow learn over time and stop stumbling.[29] This is a psychological argument, not an economic one. As we have seen, the evidence for it is weak. Its weight is further diminished by the fact that, in markets (as in the rest of life), there is a continual inflow of youngsters and an outflow of older – presumably, wiser – folks. A related justification for efficient markets is a Darwinian natural selection process by which, over time, wealth is gradually redistributed from investors with poor forecasting ability to those with superior information or competence: "Only the fit survive." Among others, Figlewski (1978, 1982) and Blume and Easley (1992) show that such weeding-out does not lead to full information efficiency, in the short or in the long run. Blume and Easley show that fit investment rules need not be rational, and that rational investment rules need not be fit.

4.6 The price–earnings ratio anomaly

As long as security analysis has been a profession, i.e., since the days of Graham and Dodd (1934), many investment advisors have counseled their clients to invest in low PE (value) stocks and to avoid high PE (glamour) stocks.[30]

---

[29] Timmerman (1993), Lewellen and Shanken (2002), Markov and Tamayo (2006), and Brav and Heaton (2002) are prominent examples of this type of argument. Brav and Heaton rationalize trends and reversals in stock prices. They assume that the representative investor is a rational Bayesian information processor but that he does not have full knowledge of the fundamental structure of the economy. In my comments on Brav and Heaton (De Bondt [2002]), I discuss in more detail why the rational learning approach is inadequate.

[30] PE multiples continue to be used extensively by financial practitioners to value companies, and explain stock prices remarkably well. See, for example, recent research by Liu *et al.* (2002). The PE multiple is the ratio of the price paid per share of stock (P) to the earnings

Evidently, this approach embodies nonconformist, contrarian thinking that runs against mass sentiment.[31] Oppenheimer and Schlarbaum (1981) report the returns earned by a so-called defensive investor who follows the specific rules recommended by Benjamin Graham in his book *The Intelligent Investor* (1949). Corrected for trading costs, the strategy earns an average risk-adjusted rate of return that is 2 to $2\frac{1}{2}$ percent per annum higher than the market return. Basu (1977) examines the PE strategy for about 1,400 firms listed on the New York Stock Exchange (NYSE) between 1956 and 1971, and obtains similar results. Reinganum (1981) forms high and low PE portfolios with identical CAPM-beta risk. The portfolios are updated both annually and quarterly. Using quarterly PE ratios for NYSE and Amex stocks between 1955 and 1977, he finds a mean difference in annualized returns in the order of 30 percent. With annual PEs for the period 1962–75, the discrepancy is roughly 7 percent. Other studies include McWilliams (1966), Nicholson (1968), Peavy and Goodman (1983), Basu (1983), Dreman (1977; 1982), Jaffe *et al.* (1989), Fuller *et al.* (1993), Lakonishok *et al.* (1994), and Dreman and Berry (1995).[32]

Why does the PE strategy work? There are at least two explanations. They are not mutually exclusive. One explanation is that the excess returns and the risk of the strategy are measured wrongly because of misspecification of the capital asset pricing model. Ball (1978) points to the effect of omitted risk factors. PE ratios may proxy for such variables and seemingly explain differences in securities' rates of return.[33] The trouble with Ball's argument is that it is untestable as long as one does not spell out which variables are omitted.

---

per share (EPS) over a fiscal year or quarter. EPS are measured in various ways. Some studies use proxies for "normalized" earnings that would obtain "if the company were experiencing normal operations" (Malkiel and Cragg [1970], p. 605). Some studies present descriptive statistics and look into the determinants of PE ratios (e.g., Benishay [1961]; Bell [1974]; Beaver and Morse [1978]). Usually, they start from the Gordon growth model. This model is similar but not identical to the Miller–Modigliani model (Gordon [1994]). In its simplest form, the model asserts that – in a world of certainty and perfect markets – the price of a security is the sum of the present values of a dividend stream that grows at a constant rate g over an infinite horizon, $P/E = D/(r - g)$, where D symbolizes a constant dividend payout rate, and r is the risk-free discount rate. The Gordon model is not easily extended to uncertainty. Only under restrictive assumptions may one replace D, r, and g by their respective mathematical expectations (LeRoy [1982]).

[31] Humphrey Neill (1954), a business journalist of the 1930s and 1940s sometimes referred to as "America's No. 1 Contrarian," justifies contrarian investing with references to the writings of William Stanley Jevons, Gustave LeBon, Gabriel Tarde, and Jean-Jacques Rousseau, among others.

[32] Fuller *et al.* (1993) and Dreman (1998) divide the sample universe of stocks into industries. Within each industry, they judge the later returns of high PE stocks against the returns of low PE stocks. In most cases, low PE stocks do better – regardless of industry and market performance.

[33] For instance, Reinganum (1981) makes the case that the size effect discovered by Banz (1981) subsumes the PE effect, and that both are related to the same missing factor. This is surprising since the cross-sectional rank of the PE ratio of a typical firm varies a great deal over time whereas the rank of its market value does not. Basu (1983) disputes Reinganum's findings. Cook and Rozeff (1984) and Jaffe *et al.* (1989) re-examine the problem but do not reach definitive conclusions.

The next explanation is behavioral. It is due to, among others, Graham (1949) and Dreman (1977, 1982). The explanation has three parts. First, it is assumed that waves of investor optimism and pessimism have an effect on the stock market as well as the price movements of individual stocks. The profitability of the contrarian strategy is believed to be attributable to transitory blips in (relative) PE ratios. Many naive investors systematically over- or underestimate the growth prospects of individual firms – either because they extrapolate current earnings trends, or because they extend the latest price trends, or for other reasons. For instance, over a short period of time, masses of investors may become aware of (and fall in love with) an investment theme that promises immense future profits even though there is no demonstrated past record of sales and earnings growth. (See, for example, the story of ENMD detailed in Huberman and Regev [2001].)[34] Barth *et al.* (1999) demonstrate that firms with patterns of increasing (or non-decreasing) earnings, lasting five years or longer, have higher PEs than other firms, and that the PEs fall significantly when the pattern is broken. In sum, to the extent that the motives to trade are security-specific, investor overreaction can raise or lower the price and the PE ratio of one stock relative to other stocks.

Second, sophisticated traders who grasp what is going on either are not powerful enough to change the price drastically (say, because of short-sales constraints or other institutional frictions) or they prefer to bet on the continuation rather than on the reversal of past trends. For instance, in a historical study of the South Sea Bubble and the trading records of Hoare's Bank in London, Temin and Voth (2004) show that the bank greatly benefited from riding the bubble. Likewise, Brunnermeier and Nagel (2003) report that the exposure of hedge funds to technology stocks peaked in September 1999, approximately six months before the peak of the internet bubble.[35] Further,

---

[34] Andreassen (1987) examines the key role played by attributional processes ("story telling") in the stock market. Causal attributions first made by journalists lead many investors to detect trends in earnings or prices that they would not see otherwise. Stock market rumors have a similar sense-making function (Rose [1951]). Related experimental research appears in Schmalensee (1976), Eggleton (1976, 1982), De Bondt (1993), and Maines and Hand (1996). Bloomfield and Hales (2002) present subjects with time-series graphs for company earnings. The subjects behave as if the earnings process shifts between a mean-reverting and a trending regime. They underreact to changes that are preceded by a lot of reversals and they overreact to changes preceded by few reversals.

[35] To repeat, such destabilizing speculative behavior may be quite rational: for example, because of synchronization risk. Another argument often encountered in the business press refers to financial incentives in delegated portfolio management. It says that many money managers feel pressured by clients to generate fast gains. With quarterly performance reviews, there is a constant threat of dismissal (or removal of a portion of the money under management). On the other hand, the operation of investment management firms involves high fixed and low variable costs. Once the break-even point is reached, new business improves profitability rapidly. All these factors shorten the manager's time frame. Independent thinking is discouraged. Also, by law and business custom certain standards of prudent behavior are to be maintained. Portfolio managers buy recent winners because they are "fearful of looking silly if they missed a big bull market" (*Wall Street Journal*, October 7, 1982). Similarly, in a bear market, the pressure is intense to sell recent losers.

sophisticated agents may also stoke the fire (or keep quiet) because bullish (or bearish) market sentiment affects their personal interests indirectly, say, as brokers, analysts, corporate insiders, venture capitalists, auditors, etc.[36]

The third and final part of the hypothesis is that, sooner or later, competitive market forces take over. Success invites rivalry in the product markets. Failure causes internal pressure to hire new management and to restructure the business. It also induces mergers and acquisitions. As a result, the realized growth in corporate earnings per share (EPS) diverges from the false beliefs impounded in security prices. Changes in EPS larger or smaller than the median change, history shows, do not persist over time beyond what is predicted by chance (Chan *et al.* [2003]). Therefore there is no valid pretext for movements in PEs that assume many years of extraordinarily large or small earnings growth. Investments in high PE stocks are disappointing because actual earnings trail projected earnings. The reverse is true for low PE stocks. A large segment of the investing public is surprised – it did not anticipate the competitive push towards average returns – and various price corrections ensue. Depending on the scale of the initial euphoria or hysteria and other factors, the price correction process may take just months or several years.[37]

4.7 Price and value on Wall Street

The evidence that relative stock returns can be forecasted by factors that seem incompatible with rational asset pricing theory has been mounting for years. The PE, book-to-market, and size factors discussed before are simply among the statistical factors that are most well known. Haugen and Baker (1996) fit a model to the returns of the firms in the Russell 3000 stock index (1979–93) that uses twelve key factors.[38] Equity returns are surprisingly predictable over short horizons. Similar results apply to the United Kingdom, Japan, Germany, and France. There is a startling commonality in the key factors worldwide. On the other hand, there is no sign that the differences in realized returns are

---

[36] Perkins and Perkins (1999) take a compelling, behind-the-scenes look at the investment bankers who created the IPO mania of the late 1990s. The book offers extensive bubble value calculations for 133 internet companies. The authors advised the shareholders of these 133 companies "to get out now" (p. 231). They predicted accurately that a "shakeout" of the internet stock market was "imminent" (p. 9).

[37] Also in agreement with the behavioral view, PE ratios change how earnings surprises influence share prices (Basu [1978]). Over the twelve months that lead up to the date of the annual earnings announcement, positive earnings surprises boost the prices of stocks with low PEs more than the prices of stocks with high PEs. In the same way, negative surprises depress the prices of high PE stocks more than the prices of low PE stocks. Subsequent to earnings announcements (either of positive or negative sign), low PE stocks once again beat high PE stocks (Basu [1975]).

[38] In actuality, Haugen and Baker start their analysis with nearly fifty factors, but they quickly focus on the ones that are most important. Evidently, the various statistical factors are correlated with one another. There is no reason to think that each factor represents a different economic determinant of stock returns.

risk related. Haugen and Baker believe that the return differentials come as a surprise to investors and that they are evidence of systematic mispricing.

In contrast to Haugen and Baker's statistical approach, De Bondt and Thaler (1985) motivate their tests for mispricing with the representativeness heuristic of Tversky and Kahneman (1974). De Bondt and Thaler assume that many investors, in violation of Bayes' rule, overreact to news and that as a result the stock market also overreacts. They look for predictable price reversals over two- to five-year horizons. For instance, in a typical analysis, they rank the returns of extreme past winner and loser stocks listed on the New York Stock Exchange at the end of 1930 and every year thereafter. Next, they use a five-year test period to compare the performance of the fifty NYSE stocks that did the worst during the previous five years (the rank period) and the fifty stocks that did the best. When risk is controlled for, the difference in test period return is on average about 8 percent a year.[39] Much of the price correction happens in the first three years after portfolio formation, but the drift in prices continues for as long as five years.[40]

What is noteworthy about De Bondt and Thaler's 1985 paper is that it was the first rejection of the efficient markets hypothesis clearly predicted by a behavioral theory. The empirical methods (i.e., comparing the returns, and other variables of interest, of winner and loser stocks for several years before and after portfolio formation) are now standard in asset pricing research. Interestingly, the 1985 paper not only documents price reversals but also finds price momentum (in table I) and momentum followed by predictable reversals (in table I and figure II): facts that Thaler and I did not emphasize and that were rediscovered afterward by Jegadeesh and Titman (1993, 2001) and others.

Jegadeesh and Titman (1993) find price momentum, i.e. over three- to twelve-month horizons, firms with high past returns (winners) continue to outperform firms with low past returns (losers).[41] A significant part of the

---

[39] Numerous articles have discussed the methods to measure the risk of winner and loser stocks. Some of this literature is reviewed in De Bondt and Thaler (1987, 1989) and in Lakonishok *et al.* (1994). Much of the evidence indicates the risk of long-term losers is less than the risk of long-term winners, and that the contrarian strategy is profitable in bear as well as in bull markets. A rationalization of the book-to-market premium suggested by Fama and French (1992) is that high book-to-market (BM) firms have a greater chance of financial distress. Griffin and Lemmon (2002) find, however, that among firms with high distress risk the difference in returns between high and low BM firms is too large to be explained by the Fama–French model. Firms with high distress risk also experience large price reversals around earnings announcements.

[40] In an early study with UK data for 1967–72, Jones *et al.* (1976) investigate a model based on two stylized facts emphasized by Little (1962) and Whittington (1971). These are the tendency of company profitability to be mean-reverting to an industry-wide mean and, secondly, that PE ratios do not predict earnings growth in a reliable way. Jones *et al.* suggest a strategy of selling companies with a history of above-average profitability and high PE ratios and using the proceeds to buy shares in corporations with a history of below-average profitability and low PE ratios. While the strategy is profitable, "there was no fortune to be made" (p. 89).

[41] The debate about price momentum (or "relative strength") goes back to Levy (1967) and Jensen and Benington (1970). In more recent research, Moskowitz and Grinblatt (1999) find industry momentum, i.e., industries that performed well over the recent past (three to twelve months) continue to beat industries that performed poorly. In addition, Chen and De Bondt (2004) find

puzzle is the further evidence that supports underreaction to earnings news. If companies are ranked on the basis of earnings surprises (surrounding the day of their earnings announcements), companies with positive earnings news are much better subsequent investments than are companies that report bad news. The effect lasts for several months, possibly as long as a year. Part of the explanation is that both analyst earnings forecasts and stock prices are "functionally fixated," i.e. they fail to reflect the implications of current earnings news for future earnings (Abarbanell and Bernard [1992]; Bernard and Thomas [1990]).[42] Surprisingly, the strategy has reliably paid off for more than twenty-five years (Latane and Jones [1977]; Rendleman *et al.* [1982]; Bernard [1993]). Chordia and Shivakumar [2006] demonstrate that earnings momentum subsumes price momentum.

How do we reconcile overreaction with underreaction, and price reversals with earnings and price momentum? Perhaps many people initially share a cognitive frame that is wrong. Between 1998 and 2002, for example, the prices of Amazon, Yahoo!, and eBay were highly correlated because traders classified all three firms as internet firms even though they had very different business models (Cornell [2004]). Investors and their advisors freely talk about "growth firms" and "declining industries" even though statistical analysis provides little evidence of reliable time-series patterns in annual earnings changes (except in the tails of the distribution). In other words, all too often, labels and categories that are wrong "stick," i.e. they persuade. No wonder, then, that when an earnings surprise hits, many investors refuse to believe it. Mental frames take time to adjust, and this slow correction process is reflected in prices.[43] Consistent with this analysis of the data, long-term past stock market losers are found to experience an unusually large number of positive earnings surprises. Past market winners go through an unusually large number of negative surprises (Chopra *et al.* [1992]). Also, compared to growth stocks, value stocks experience more good earnings news (LaPorta *et al.* [1997]).

How do security prices respond to news? The answer depends in part on how investors' simple psychological models are influenced by new information. There are two effects. The first has to do with the short-term impact of the news – say, an earnings surprise – in light of the consensus forecast of the future that is already built into prices. The second effect depends on how the news changes the perceived odds that one future scenario rather than another will come true. At times, minor pieces of news trigger a change in consensus

---

style momentum for stocks that are part of the S&P-500 Index. For instance, small-cap value stocks may go on to outperform large-cap growth stocks over three- to twelve-month horizons if they did so in the past.

[42] Sloan (1996) looks at a different type of earnings fixation. Based on US data for 1962–91, he finds that stock prices behave as if investors do not differentiate between the cash and accrual components of current earnings. The accrual component of earnings exhibits lower persistence over time, however. Hence, stock prices overreact. Companies with high (low) levels of accruals experience negative (positive) abnormal stock returns around subsequent earnings announcements.

[43] Security analysts' earnings forecasts, discussed below, are a good example.

opinion and lead to a big price reaction. In agreement with this point of view, Dreman and Berry (1995) find that positive and negative earnings surprises affect high PE and low PE stocks in an asymmetric manner. Good news for low PE stocks and bad news for high PE stocks (so-called event triggers) generate much bigger (absolute) price reactions than good news for high PE stocks and bad news for low PE stocks. Substantially similar findings but for a larger sample of US firms appear in Skinner and Sloan (2002).

What causes the winner/loser price reversals? A likely explanation is that many traders naively extrapolate past earnings trends.[44] "Overreaction to earnings" is a broad concept that appears in a variety of studies and that has been tested in different ways. De Bondt and Thaler (1987) find that past three- to five-year price movements predict reversals in earnings growth. In other words, past loser firms see their profits grow much faster than past winners. This finding strongly suggests that many investors fail to recognize mean reversion in earnings. Lakonishok *et al.* (1994) use past sales growth (separately or combined with the book-to-market ratio, the earnings yield, and the cash flow-to-price ratio) to rank stock into portfolios. The fact that this strategy has some success (i.e., low growth stocks beat high growth stocks) again supports extrapolation bias.[45]

Still one more test of the extrapolation theory is to bet against security analysts' forecasts of earnings growth. This would be lucrative if analyst earnings forecasts are too extreme, and if their forecasts capture market sentiment.[46] Apparently, an arbitrage strategy that buys the 20 percent of firms for which security analysts' predictions of earnings growth are most pessimistic, and that finances the purchases by selling short the 20 percent of firms for which analysts' forecasts are most optimistic, earns consistent profits. The abnormal returns grow with the length of the forecast period: for example, they are much greater for five-year forecasts than for one-year forecasts (De Bondt [1992]). Analogous results appear in Bauman and Dowen (1988), LaPorta

---

[44] Thus, stock market overreaction is thought to be linked to foreseeable errors in investor and market forecasts of future cash flows that are corrected afterward. (A broader version of the same hypothesis says that the market is sometimes too optimistic and sometimes too pessimistic, but that the extreme beliefs are not linked to cash flows in the recent past or in the near future.) There are, however, two other behavioral interpretations of the overreaction evidence. The first theory stresses irrational risk perceptions. Many stocks with low PEs certainly look more risky than high PE stocks. The second theory puts the accent on herding behavior. At times, the market takes on a life of its own, when many traders jump on or off the bandwagon in reaction to what they believe other traders are doing. Prices aggregate information. If news disseminates slowly, it may be beneficial to look for patterns in prices (Hirshleifer [1994]). Note that all three behavioral theories may be true to some degree. (The theories are not mutually exclusive.) Finally, it may be that there is also some variation over time in risk premiums that is rationally justified.

[45] The evidence is supportive but relatively weak. See Dechow and Sloan (1997) and Zarowin (1989).

[46] Both assumptions are correct. However, it is not the case that analyst earnings forecasts extrapolate past trends in stock prices or in the book-to-market ratio. See Klein (1990) and Doukas *et al.* (2002).

(1996), Dechow and Sloan (1997), and Ciccone (2003). Based on US data, Dechow and Sloan cannot substantiate the view that the forecasts embedded in share prices are consistent with the simple extrapolation of past earnings and revenue growth (as suggested by Lakonishok *et al.* [1994]). On the other hand, they do find that share prices give too much weight to exceedingly optimistic analyst forecasts of long-term earnings growth.

Is the evidence for price reversals and momentum robust? De Bondt (2000) offers a survey with tests for fourteen countries. Among many other studies (including Fama and French [1998]), Schiereck *et al.* (1999) and Rouwenhorst (1998) examine whether the results for the United States may be due to chance (or, what is the same, collective data snooping). Schiereck *et al.* document the profitability of contrarian and momentum strategies in Germany between 1961 and 1991. Rouwenhorst documents price momentum in each of twelve European countries during the period 1980–95. Six-month past winners out-perform past losers by approximately 1 percent per month. The evidence is stronger for small firms. Jegadeesh and Titman (2001) confirm the robustness of their earlier findings in a separate way. They extend the sample period for the US by eight years (1990–8). In addition, they show that the performance of the strategy is negative between month 13 and month 60 after the time of portfolio formation. This effect ties in with the point of view that share prices are influenced by delayed overreactions to news that are eventually reversed.

Recently, some researchers have begun to develop theoretical models that aim to explain price momentum and price reversals within the same analytical framework. One perspective, already discussed, is that the speculative dynamics of stock prices are driven by false expectations of future profitability, i.e., overreaction followed by underreaction (De Bondt and Thaler [1985, 1987]; Barberis *et al.* [1998]). A different view, emphasized by Hong and Stein (1999), is that firm-specific information diffuses little by little among investors, and that traders cannot easily extract information from prices. Hong *et al.* (2000) offer evidence that supports the theory. Price momentum strategies appear to be most rewarding for stocks with low market capitalization and low analyst coverage. The effect of low coverage is especially significant for firms that are in financial distress. (With low coverage, it is easier for management to hide what happened.) Thus, "bad news travels slowly."[47]

---

[47] A third behavioral theory is the overconfidence model formulated by Daniel *et al.* (1998). A fourth model is Barberis and Huang (2001). These authors model the equilibrium behavior of firm-level stock returns (1) when the representative investor is loss averse over the price fluctuations of individual stocks, or (2) when he is loss averse over the value of his equity portfolio. (The extent of narrow framing is a matter of mental accounting.) With individual stock accounting, the discount rate can change as a function of its past return performance. A stock that performed well will be seen by investors as less risky; a stock that performed poorly, more risky. The model accounts for a wide range of empirical facts. For instance, firm-level returns are excessively volatile and are predictable from lagged variables. Individual stock accounting also reproduces a value premium in the cross-section of firms.

Finally, other researchers have produced interesting new and related facts. First, Lee and Swaminathan (2000) believe that past trading volume provides a link between momentum and reversal strategies. For instance, firms with high past turnover exhibit glamour characteristics, i.e., they undergo negative earnings surprises and perform poorly. (Teh and De Bondt [1997] and Scott *et al.* [2003] report parallel findings but offer different interpretations.) Also, past trading volume predicts the magnitude and the persistence of price trends: for example, high volume winners experience faster momentum reversals. The market, it seems, is surprised by the disappointing earnings of high volume firms. Lee and Swaminathan link their conclusions, described as the "momentum life cycle hypothesis," to the work of Bernstein (1993). It may be that stocks move through periods of glamour and neglect, and that trading volume helps to identify where a stock is in the cycle. Share prices initially underreact but ultimately overreact to news.

Second, Asness (1997) and Piotroski (2000) present refinements of the winner–loser contrarian strategy. Asness' empirical analysis shows that, if the past is any indicator, it would be best for speculators to go long in cheap stocks that have started to turn upward and to go short in expensive stocks that have suffered a setback. This approach combines the insights of the contrarian and momentum strategies. Piotroski tries to improve the contrarian strategy by eliminating stocks from the portfolio that are likely to suffer financial distress. The Fama–French interpretation of value investing suggests that this may be costly, since the most risky firms should earn the highest returns. In fact, the opposite is true.

4.8 Actual and predicted earnings per share

I now return to the overreaction hypothesis, and I discuss additional evidence that is based on studies of actual and predicted earnings per share. One way to evaluate the hypothesis is to compare the stochastic process of annual earnings with the market expectation of that process implicit in stock prices. Quite a few studies find that annual accounting earnings follow a random walk with drift (e.g., Ball and Watts [1972]; Watts and Leftwich [1977]).[48] However, the analysis of Brooks and Buckmaster (1976) indicates that in some cases the random walk hypothesis must be amended. They study all US firms on Compustat with annual earnings data for nine or more years between 1954 and 1973. When the sample is stratified according to distance of a given observation from normal income, the earnings series in the outer strata revert to the preceding income levels.[49]

---

[48] Two other pioneering studies (with analysis of data from the United Kingdom) are Little (1962) and Whittington (1971).

[49] More recently, Fama and French (2000) use different methods but reach similar conclusions. Clearly, the fact that many time-series studies fail to reject the random walk hypothesis does

That the forecasts of earnings embedded in security prices are too extreme is indicated by the wide cross-sectional dispersion of PE multiples. This wide range appears illogical. It is difficult to reconcile with rational expectations and the Gordon growth model. Suppose that investors have no information other than the historical time series of earnings and that, for any individual firm, the discount rate can be expected to remain constant over time. Assume further that earnings growth rates do not deviate much between firms in the long run (say, over ten years) even if they vary significantly in the short run. In this case, unanticipated movements in earnings should leave PE ratios largely unchanged. The cross-sectional range in PE ratios should also be relatively steady. In addition, the range should be narrow since, by and large, it reflects the distribution of investor-required rates of return.

Of course, all these conjectures are false if PE multiples predict future corporate earnings with more precision than is possible on the basis of past income data alone. However, PE ratios are weak indicators of actual earnings growth. Beaver *et al.* (1980) construct a PE-based forecast model. When the model's accuracy is compared with that of a naive random walk (with drift), the PE model is marginally superior. Security prices behave "as if earnings are perceived to be dramatically different from a simple random walk process" (p. 3). Cragg and Malkiel (1968, 1982) show that PEs and financial analyst forecasts usually move together, but that neither variable is strongly correlated with realized earnings growth. Similar results also appear in Murphy and Stevenson (1967) who decide that "if the market judges future growth through the PE ratio, it is not a good judge" (p. 114).[50]

In many instances, the market forecast of earnings overreacts because it is a simple extrapolation of current trends – in the same way that security analyst and management forecasts are extensions of current trends (McEnally [1971]; Cragg and Malkiel [1968]; Fried and Givoly [1982]).[51] The empirical research on the relative precision of analyst, management, and time-series forecasts has generated much conflicting evidence. The safest conclusion is that they are about equally accurate and that disparities, if they exist, do not endure.[52] What looks certain is that analyst forecast errors are large (Dreman and Berry [1994]). The forecasts suffer from persistent optimism and overreaction bias,

---

not imply that changes in EPS cannot be predicted. It only means that such movements cannot be forecast on the basis of current and past EPS data. Among others, Chant (1980) and Freeman *et al.* (1982) present models that improve upon time-series forecasts by including variables such as industry stock price indices, the money supply and the book rate-of-return.

[50] Likewise, Malkiel and Cragg (1970) conclude "that if one wants to explain [stock] returns over a one-year horizon it is far more important to know what the market will think the growth rate of earnings will be next year rather than to know the realized long-term growth rate" (p. 616).

[51] For that reason, many studies (e.g., Ball and Brown [1968] and Watts [1978]) let a naive time-series model proxy for the market expectation of earnings.

[52] Compare, for example, Cragg and Malkiel (1968), Elton and Gruber (1972), Basi *et al.* (1976), and Imhoff and Pare (1982). Brown and Rozeff (1978) is one of few studies concluding that analyst forecasts are superior.

i.e., actual changes in EPS, up or down, are less than predicted changes (see, e.g., McDonald [1973]; Crichfield *et al.* [1978]; Malkiel and Cragg [1970]; Fried and Givoly [1982]; Elton *et al.* [1984]; De Bondt and Thaler [1990]; Easterwood and Nutt [1999]). Finally, a series of studies find serial dependence in consecutive analyst forecast errors and forecast revisions (e.g., Givoly and Lakonishok [1979]; Amir and Ganzach [1998]; Nutt *et al.* [1999]). Particularly influential in this regard is the work of Bernard and Thomas (1990) and Abarbanell and Bernard (1992).

When forecasting future EPS, analysts have a tendency to underestimate the permanence of past earnings shocks. This error is seen as an underreaction.[53] Easterwood and Nutt (1999) also conclude that analysts are too optimistic. Analysts overreact to positive earnings news but underreact to negative news. Givoly and Lakonishok (1984) and Brown (1996, 1997b) offer useful surveys of what has become a vast literature.

Analyst and management forecasts are significant to research in behavioral finance because they are produced by experts who have professional experience, time, resources, and incentives to be more accurate than other market participants.[54] Also, their individual projections are sold, directly or indirectly, to unsophisticated investors. Therefore, the mean of the estimates, i.e., the consensus forecast, seems bound to influence market prices. It is our closest proxy for the unobservable market expectation. Consonant with this conjecture, earnings surprises (Niederhofer and Regan [1972]; Fried and Givoly [1982]; Rendleman *et al.* [1982]) and changes in consensus forecasts (Peterson and Peterson [1982]) are key determinants of stock price movements. Zacks (1979) and Elton *et al.* (1981) show that the payoff from being able to assess the errors and revisions in the consensus estimate of EPS is larger than the payoff from a precise forecast of EPS itself.

Analysts are usually thought of as "smart money." The efficient markets hypothesis becomes less plausible, however, if experts too are subject to bias. Based on data for the UK, De Bondt and Forbes (1999) suggest that analysts herd in the sense that there is too little disagreement between them. In a clinical

---

[53] Elgers and Lo (1994) find that prior stock returns and earnings changes can be used to modify analyst predictions in a way that meaningfully improves their precision. For instance, for firms with poor earnings performance, analysts forecast greater reversals than are demonstrated by actual earnings. Markov and Tamayo (2006) offer a rational explanation for the predictability in analysts' forecast errors. The serial correlation pattern in analysts' quarterly earnings forecast errors is consistent, they say, with an environment in which analysts face parameter uncertainty and learn rationally about the parameters over time.

[54] As the various financial scandals of the last decade demonstrate (Partnoy [2003]; Berenson [2004]; Bogle [2005]), conflicts of interest permeate Wall Street and experts may have powerful incentives to mislead. For instance, analysts, investment bankers, journalists, and others may be keen to maintain good relations with corporate management. If they issue negative reports, they lose business. (For some telling anecdotes in this regard, see Gallant [1990] and Browning [1995].) Hong and Kubik (2003) find an empirical link between analyst optimism and career success. A long-standing Wall Street adage says that "you start as an analyst, but you end as an ambassador."

study, Cornell (2001) discusses the case of Intel. In the summer of 2000, nearly all analysts were very enthusiastic about Intel. In September 2000, however, Ashok Kumar (a superstar analyst) stated his belief that the demand for personal computers would grow at about 6 percent (rather than the 12 percent that was forecast). Also, on September 21, Intel management issued a press release warning that revenue growth for the third quarter would be positive but less than forecast. In response, the stock price dropped 30 percent and $120 billion of shareholder value was lost: a number so large that no reasonable discounted cash flow analysis can justify it. Yet, fewer analysts recommended Intel after the price drop than before.

In sum, security analysts' earnings forecasts are persistently very wide of the mark. Yet, analysts keep offering extreme predictions. Simultaneously, the data show excessive optimism, an unwillingness to deviate from the consensus, and a reluctance to accept news that runs against current beliefs. If this behavior also characterizes many investors and, ultimately, the market, we should not be surprised that stocks are systematically mispriced.

4.9 Conclusion

This chapter summarizes key elements of a new psychological theory of stock prices with special emphasis on the formation of investor beliefs and the quality of judgment. Important anomalies in the behavior of equity markets can be understood in the context of new experimental, empirical, and theoretical research. The shortcomings of human intuition play a decisive role in stock market bubbles. Related biases explain predictable momentum and reversals in prices.

While some economists choose to ignore behavioral finance, most professional or amateur investors agree that investor sentiment matters. People are human. Their preferences, beliefs, and actions show patterns that are not easily reconciled with the axioms of rationality. In many ways, shifting fashions are the lifeblood of the stock market (and the brokerage industry). Examples of investors becoming obsessed with a specific sector, industry, or firm abound. Traders may fall into the trap of buying at market highpoints and selling at market lowpoints. On the other hand, investment performance may improve with precise forecasts of novel cognitive frames that are about to catch on. In inefficient markets, the skill with which assets are acquired, managed, and disposed of is responsible for a large part of total return. Therefore, the quality of judgment and decision-making is critical.

Behavioral finance has already proven itself to be a productive framework for research. It has produced many new ideas and many new facts. It has started to rebuild asset pricing theory. With its emphasis on the realism of modeling assumptions (e.g., the replication of laboratory findings), it introduces discipline. With its guidelines for wise decision-making, it is pragmatic.

Although not emphasized here, shortcomings in intuitive judgment also have policy implications. Many investors are vulnerable: "Good people get hurt." Government may be able to limit the damage through education, regulation (e.g., financial reporting rules and capital market regulations), and other paternalistic methods (e.g., a social security system that guarantees retirement income). As explained by Stout (2002) and Levitt (1998), such policies strengthen financial markets which only exist and thrive "through the grace of investors."

4.10 References

Abarbanell, J. and V. L. Bernard, "Tests of analysts' overreaction/underreaction to earnings information as an explanation for anomalous stock price behavior," *Journal of Finance*, July 1992.

Abreu, D. and M. K. Brunnermeier, "Synchonization risk and delayed arbitrage," *Journal of Financial Economics*, 64, 341–60, 2002.

"Bubbles and crashes," *Econometrica*, 71, 173–204, 2003.

Ahlers, D. and J. Lakonishok, "A study of economists' consensus forecasts," *Management Science*, 29, 1113–25, 1983.

Allen, F. L., *Only Yesterday: An Informal History of the 1920s*, Perennial Library, 1931.

Amir, E. and Y. Ganzach, "Overreaction and underreaction in analysts' forecasts," *Journal of Economic Behavior and Organization*, 37, 3, 333–47, November 1998.

Andreassen, P. B., "On the social psychology of the stock market: Aggregate attributional effects and the regressiveness of prediction," *Journal of Personality and Social Psychology*, 53, 3, 490–6, 1987.

Arbel, A. and P. Strebel, "Pay attention to neglected firms! Even when they're large," *Journal of Portfolio Management*, Winter 1983.

Asch, S., "Opinions and social pressure," *Scientific American*, 193, 31–5, 1955.

Asness, C., "The interaction of value and momentum strategies," *Financial Analysts Journal*, 29, March–April 1997.

Azariadis, C., "Self-fulfilling prophecies," *Journal of Economic Theory*, 25, 380–96, 1981.

Ball, R., "Anomalies in relationships between securities' yields and yield-surrogates," *Journal of Financial Economics*, June–September 1978.

Ball, R. and P. Brown, "An empirical evaluation of accounting income numbers," *Journal of Accounting Research*, 6, 159–78, Autumn 1968.

Ball, R. and R. Watts, "Some time series properties of accounting earnings numbers," *Journal of Finance*, 27, 663–81, June 1972.

Bange, M. M., "Do the portfolios of small investors reflect positive feedback trading?" *Journal of Financial and Quantitative Analysis*, 35, 2, 239–55, June 2000.

Banz, R., "The relationship between return and market value of common stocks," *Journal of Financial Economics*, 9, 3–18, 1981.

Barberis, N. and M. Huang, "Mental accounting, loss aversion, and individual stock returns," *Journal of Finance*, 56, 4, 1247–92, August 2001.

Barberis, N., A. Shleifer, and R. Vishny, "A model of investor sentiment," *Journal of Financial Economics*, 49, 307–43, 1998.

Baron, J., *Thinking and Deciding*, Cambridge University Press, 1988.

Barro, R. and S. Fischer, "Recent developments in monetary theory," *Journal of Monetary Economics*, 2, 133–76, 1976.

Barth, M. E., J. A. Elliot, and M. W. Finn, "Market rewards associated with patterns of increasing earnings," *Journal of Accounting Research*, 37, 387–413, 1999.

Basi, B., K. Carey, and R. Twark, "A comparison of the accuracy of corporate and security analysts' forecasts of earnings," *Accounting Review*, 51, 244–54, April 1976.

Basu, S., "The information content of price–earnings ratios," *Financial Management*, 53–64, Summer 1975.

"Investment performance of common stocks in relation to their price–earnings ratios: A test of the efficient market hypothesis," *Journal of Finance*, 33, 3, 663–82, June 1977.

"The effect of earnings' yield on assessments of the association between annual accounting income numbers and security prices," *Accounting Review*, 53, 3, 599–625, July 1978.

"The relationship between earnings' yield, market value and return for NYSE common stocks: Further evidence," *Journal of Financial Economics*, 12, 129–56, June 1983.

Bauman, W. S. and R. Dowen, "Growth projections and common stock returns," *Financial Analysts Journal*, 79–80, July–August 1988.

Beaver, W., "Market efficiency," *Accounting Review*, 23–37, January 1981.

Beaver, W., R. Lambert, and D. Morse, "The information content of security prices," *Journal of Accounting and Economics*, 2, 3–28, 1980.

Beaver, W. and D. Morse, "What determines price–earnings ratios?" *Financial Analysts Journal*, 65–76, July–August 1978.

Becker, G., *The Economic Approach to Human Behavior*, University of Chicago Press, 1976.

Bell, F. W., "The relation of the structure of common stock prices to historical, expectational and industrial variables," *Journal of Finance*, 29, 187–97, March 1974.

Benishay, H., "Variability in earnings price ratios of corporate equities," *American Economic Review*, 51, 81–94, March 1961.

Berenson, A., *The Number: How the Drive for Quarterly Earnings Corrupted Wall Street and Corporate America*, Random House, 2004.

Bernard, V. L., "Stock price reactions to earnings announcements: A summary of recent anomalous evidence and possible explanations," in R. Thaler, *Advances in Behavioral Finance*, Russell Sage Foundation, 1993.

Bernard, V. L. and J. K. Thomas, "Evidence that stock prices do not fully reflect the implications of current earnings for future earnings," *Journal of Accounting and Economics*, 13, 305–40, 1990.

Bernstein, R., "The earnings expectations life cycle," *Financial Analysts Journal*, 49, 90–3, March–April 1993.

Bloomfield, R. and J. Hales, "Predicting the next step of a random walk: Experimental evidence of regime-shifting beliefs," *Journal of Financial Economics*, 65, 397–414, 2002.

Blume, L. E., M. M. Bray, and D. Easley, "Introduction to the stability of rational expectations equilibrium," *Journal of Economic Theory*, 26, 313–17, 1982.

Blume, L. E. and D. Easley, "Evolution and market behavior," *Journal of Economic Theory*, 58, 9–40, 1992.

Bogle, J. C., *The Battle for the Soul of Capitalism*, Yale University Press, 2005.

Brav, A. and J. B. Heaton, "Competing theories of financial anomalies," *Review of Financial Studies*, 15, 2, 575–606, 2002.

Bray, M. M., "Learning, estimation and the stability of rational expectations," *Journal of Economic Theory*, 26, 318–39, 1982.

Breeden, D., "An intertemporal asset pricing model with stochastic consumption and investment opportunities," *Journal of Financial Economics*, 7, 265–96, 1979.

Brooks, L. D. and D. A. Buckmaster, "Further evidence on the time series properties of accounting income," *Journal of Finance*, 31, 1359–73, December 1976.

Brown, B. W. and S. Maital, "What do economists know? An empirical study of experts' expectations," *Econometrica*, 49, 491–504, 1980.

Brown, L. D., "Analyst forecasting errors and their implications for security analysis: An alternative perspective," *Financial Analysts Journal*, January–February 1996.

"Analyst forecasting errors: Additional evidence," *Financial Analysts Journal*, November–December 1997(a).

"Earnings surprise research: Synthesis and perspectives." *Financial Analysts Journal*, March–April 1997(b).

Brown, L. D. and M. S. Rozeff, "The superiority of analysts' forecasts as measures of expectations: Evidence from earnings," *Journal of Finance*, 33, 1–16, March 1978.

Browning, E. S., "Please don't talk to the bearish analyst," *Wall Street Journal*, May 2, 1995.

Brunnermeier, M. K. and S. Nagel, "Hedge funds and the technology bubble," *Journal of Finance*, 59, 2013–40, 2003.

Canetti, E., *Crowds and Power*, Viking Press, 1962.

Cass, D. and K. Shell, "Do sunspots matter?" *Journal of Political Economy*, 91, 193–227, 1983.

Chan, L., J. Karceski, and J. Lakonishok, "The level and persistence of growth rates," *Journal of Finance*, 58, 643–84, 2003.

Chant, P. D., "On the predictability of corporate earnings per share behavior," *Journal of Finance*, 35, 13–21, March 1980.

Charest, G., "Dividend information, stock returns and market efficiency," *Journal of Financial Economics*, 6, 297–330, 1978.

Chen, H.-L. and W. F. M. De Bondt, "Style momentum within the S&P-500 Index," *Journal of Empirical Finance*, 11, 483–507, 2004.

Chen, J., H. Hong, and J. C. Stein, "Breadth of ownership and stock returns," *Journal of Financial Economics*, 66, 171–205, 2002.

Chopra, N., J. Lakonishok, and J. R. Ritter, "Measuring abnormal performance: Do stocks overreact?" *Journal of Financial Economics*, 31, 235–68, 1992.

Chordia, T. and L. Shivakumar, "Earnings and price momentum," *Journal of Financial Economics*, 80, 627–56, 2006.

Ciccone, S., "Does analyst optimism about future earnings distort stock prices?" *Journal of Behavioral Finance*, 4, 2, 59–64, 2003.

Cochrane, J. H., *Asset Pricing*, Princeton University Press, 2000.

Conlisk, J., "Why bounded rationality?" *Journal of Economic Literature*, 34, 669–700, 1996.

Cook, T. J. and M. S. Rozeff, "Size and price–earnings anomalies: One effect or two?" *Journal of Financial and Quantitative Analysis*, 19, 4, 449–66, December 1984.

Cooper, M., O. Dimitrov, and P. R. Rau, "A rose.com by any other name," *Journal of Finance*, 56, 6, 2371–88, December 2001.

Copeland, T. E. and D. Mayers, "The Value-Line enigma (1965–1978): A case study of performance evaluation issues," *Journal of Financial Economics*, 10, 289–321, 1982.

Cornell, B., "Is the response of analysts to information consistent with fundamental valuation? The case of Intel," *Financial Management*, 30, 1, 113–36, Spring 2001.

"Comovement as an investment tool," *Journal of Portfolio Management*, Spring 2004.

Cragg, J. G. and B. G. Malkiel, "The consensus and accuracy of some predictions of the growth of corporate earnings," *Journal of Finance*, 23, 1, 67–84, March 1968.

Expectations and the Structure of Share Prices, University of Chicago Press, 1982.

Crichfield, T., T. Dyckman, and J. Lakonishok, "An evaluation of security analysts' forecasts," *Accounting Review*, 53, 651–68, July 1978.

Cyert, R. M. and M. H. DeGroot, "Rational expectations and Bayesian analysis," *Journal of Political Economy*, 82, 521–36, 1974.

Daly, G. G. and T. H. Mayor, "Reason and rationality during energy crises," *Journal of Political Economy*, 91, 168–81, 1983.

Damasio, A., *Descartes' Error: Emotion, Reason, and the Human Brain*, G. P. Putnam's Sons, 1994.

Daniel, K., D. Hirshleifer, and A. Subrahmanyam, "Investor psychology and security market under- and overreactions," *Journal of Finance*, 53, 1839–85, December 1998.

Daniel, K., D. Hirshleifer, and S. H. Teoh, "Investor psychology in capital markets: Evidence and policy implications," *Journal of Monetary Economics*, 49, 139–209, 2002.

De Bondt, W. F. M., "A behavioral theory of the price/earnings ratio anomaly," Working Paper, Cornell University, March 1983.

"Stock price reversals and overreaction to news events: A survey of theory and evidence," in R. M. C. Guimaraes, B. G. Kingsman, and S. J. Taylor (eds.), *A Reappraisal of the Efficiency of Financial Markets*, Springer, 1989.

"What do economists know about the stock market?" *Journal of Portfolio Management*, 84–91, 1991.

Earnings Forecasts and Share Price Reversals, AIMR monograph, 1992.

"Betting on trends: Intuitive forecasts of financial risk and return," *International Journal of Forecasting*, 9, 3, 355–71, 1993.

"A portrait of the individual investor," *European Economic Review*, 42, 831–44, 1998.

"The psychology of underreaction and overreaction in world equity markets," in D. B. Keim and W. Ziemba (eds.), *Security Market Imperfections in Worldwide Equity Markets*, pp. 65–89, Cambridge University Press, 2000.

"Bubble psychology," in W. Hunter and G. Kaufman (eds.), *Asset Price Bubbles: Implications for Monetary, Regulatory, and International Policies*, pp. 205–16, MIT Press, 2002(a).

"Discussion of 'Competing theories of financial anomalies'," *Review of Financial Studies*, 15, 607–13, 2002(b).

"The values and beliefs of European investors," in K. Knorr Cetina and A. Preda (eds.), *The Sociology of Financial Markets*, pp. 163–86, Oxford University Press, 2005(a).

De Bondt, W. F. M. (ed.), *The Psychology of World Equity Markets*, Edward Elgar, 2005(b).

De Bondt, W. F. M. and W. Forbes, "Herding in analyst earnings forecasts: Evidence from the United Kingdom," *European Financial Management*, 5, 143–63, 1999.

De Bondt, W. F. M. and R. H. Thaler, "Does the stock market overreact?" *Journal of Finance*, 40, 3, 793–805, July 1985.

"Further evidence on investor overreaction and stock market seasonality," *Journal of Finance*, 42, 557–81, July 1987.

"A mean-reverting walk down Wall Street," *Journal of Economic Perspectives*, 3, 189–202, 1989.

"Do security analysts overreact?" *American Economic Review*, 80, 2, 52–7, May 1990.

"Financial decision making in markets and firms: A behavioral perspective," in R. A. Jarrow *et al.* (eds.), *Handbook of Finance*, pp. 385–410, Elsevier–North-Holland, 1995.

DeCanio, S. J., "Rational expectation and learning from experience," *Quarterly Journal of Economics*, 92, 47–57, 1979.

Dechow, P. M. and R. G. Sloan, "Return to contrarian investment strategies: Tests of naïve expectations hypotheses," *Journal of Financial Economics*, 43, 3–27, 1997.

De Franco, G., H. Lu, and F. P. Vasvar, "Wealth transfer effects of analysts' misleading behavior," *Journal of Accounting Research*, 45, 1, 71–110, March 2007.

Devenow, A. and I. Welch, "Rational herding in financial economics," *European Economic Review*, 40, 603–15, 1996.

Diether, K., C. J. Malloy, and A. Scherbina, "Differences of opinion and the cross-section of stock returns," *Journal of Finance*, 57, 5, 2113–41, October 2002.

Doukas, J. A., C. Kim, and C. Pantzalis, "A test of the errors-in-expectations explanation of the value/glamour stock returns performance: Evidence from analysts' forecasts," *Journal of Finance*, 57, 5, 2143–65, October 2002.

Dreman, D. N., *Psychology and the Stock Market*, Amacom, 1977.

The New Contrarian Investment Strategy, Random House, 1982.

Contrarian Investment Strategies: The Next Generation, Simon & Schuster, 1998.

Dreman, D. N. and M. Berry, "Analyst forecast errors and their implications for security analysis," *Financial Analysts Journal*, 30–41, May–June 1994.

"Overreaction, underreaction, and the low-P/E effect," *Financial Analysts Journal*, 21–30, July–August 1995.

Easley, D. and R. Jarrow, "The meaning and testing of market efficiency: A synthesis," Working Paper, Cornell University, October 1982.

"Consensus belief equilibrium and market efficiency," *Journal of Finance*, 38, 903–11, 1983.

Easterwood, J. C. and S. R. Nutt, "Inefficiency in analysts' earnings forecasts: Systematic misreaction or systematic optimism?" *Journal of Finance*, 54, 5, 1777–97, October 1999.

Eggleton, I., "Patterns, Prototypes, and Predictions: An Exploratory Study," *Studies on Information Processing in Accounting*, Supplement to *Journal of Accounting Research*, 14, 132–44, 1976.

"Intuitive time-series extrapolation," *Journal of Accounting Research*, 20, 68–102, Spring 1982.

Einhorn, H., "Learning from experience and suboptimal rules in decision making," in T. Wallsten (ed.), *Cognitive Processes in Choice and Decision Behavior*, Lawrence Erlbaum, 1980.

Einhorn, H. and R. Hogarth, "Confidence in judgment: Persistence of the illusion of validity," *Psychological Review*, 85, 395–476, 1978.

Eisner, R. and R. H. Strotz, "Flight insurance and the theory of choice," *Journal of Political Economy*, 69, 355–68, August 1961.

Elgers, P. T. and M. H. Lo, "Reductions in analysts' annual earnings forecast errors using information in prior earnings and security returns," *Journal of Accounting Research*, 32, 2, 290–303, Autumn 1994.

Elster, J., *Ulysses and the Sirens: Studies in Rationality and Irrationality*, Cambridge University Press, 1979.

Elton, E. J. and M. J. Gruber, "Earnings estimates and the accuracy of expectations data," *Management Science*, 18, 409–24, 1972.

Elton, E. J., M. J. Gruber, and M. N. Gultekin, "Expectations and share prices," *Management Science*, 27, 975–87, 1981.

"Professional expectations: Accuracy and diagnosis of errors," *Journal of Financial and Quantitative Analysis*, 19, 351–63, December 1984.

Fama, E. F., "The behavior of stock market prices," *Journal of Business*, 34, 105, January 1965(a).

"Random walks in stock market prices," *Financial Analysts Journal*, 55–9, September–October 1965(b).

"Efficient capital markets: A review of theory and empirical work," *Journal of Finance*, 25, 383–417, May 1970.

Foundations of Finance, Basic Books, 1976.

"Market efficiency, long-term returns, and behavioral finance," *Journal of Financial Economics*, 49, 283–306, 1998.

Fama, E. F. and K. R. French, "The cross-section of expected stock returns," *Journal of Finance*, 47, 2, 427–65, June 1992.

"Multifactor explanations of asset pricing anomalies," *Journal of Finance*, 51, 1, 55–84, March 1996.

"Value versus growth: The international evidence," *Journal of Finance*, 53, 1975–99, December 1998.

"Forecasting profitability and earnings," *Journal of Business*, 73, 161–75, 2000.

Figlewski, S., "Market efficiency in a market with heterogeneous information," *Journal of Political Economy*, 86, 581–97, August 1978.

"The informational effects of restrictions on short sales: Some empirical evidence," *Journal of Financial and Quantitative Analysis*, 16, 463–76, November 1981.

"Information diversity and market behavior," *Journal of Finance*, 37, 87–102, March 1982.

Fischhoff, B., "Hindsight does not equal foresight: The effect of outcome knowledge on judgment under uncertainty," *Journal of Experimental Psychology, Human Perception and Performance*, 1, 288–99, 1975.

Freeman, R. N., J. A. Ohlson, and S. H. Penman, "Book rate-of-return and prediction of earnings changes: An empirical investigation," *Journal of Accounting Research*, 20, 639–53, Autumn 1982.

French, K. R., "Stock returns and the weekend effect," *Journal of Financial Economics*, 8, 1, 55–69, March 1983.

Fried, D. and D. Givoly, "Financial analysts' forecasts of earnings," *Journal of Accounting and Economics*, 4, 85–107, 1982.

Friedman, B., "Optimal expectation and the extreme informational assumptions of rational expectations macromodels," *Journal of Monetary Economics*, 5, 24–41, 1979.

"Survey evidence on the 'rationality' of interest rate expectations," *Journal of Monetary Economics*, 6, 453–65, 1980.

Froot, K. and M. Obstfeld, "Intrinsic bubbles: The case of stock prices," *American Economic Review*, 81, 1189–1217, 1991.

Frydman, R., "Towards an understanding of market processes: Individual expectations, learning, and convergence to rational expectations equilibrium," *American Economic Review*, 72, 652–68, September 1982.

Fuller, R. J., L. C. Huberts, and M. J. Levinson, "Returns to E/P strategies, higgledy-piggledy growth, analysts' forecast errors, and omitted risk factors," *Journal of Portfolio Management*, 13–24, Winter 1993.

Gallant, D., "The hazards of negative research reports," *Institutional Investor*, July 1990.

Gibbons, M. R. and P. Hess, "Day of the week effects and asset returns," *Journal of Business*, 54, 579–96, October 1981.

Gilovich, T., *How We Know What Isn't So: The Fallibility of Human Reason in Everyday Life*, Free Press, 1991.

Gilovich, T., D. Griffin, and D. Kahneman, *Heuristics and Biases: The Psychology of Intuitive Judgment*, Cambridge University Press, 2002.

Gilson, S. C., "Investing in distressed situations: A market survey," *Financial Analysts Journal*, 8–27, November–December 1995.

Givoly, D. and J. Lakonishok, "The information content of financial analysts' forecasts of earnings," *Journal of Accounting and Economics*, 1, 165–85, 1979.

"Financial analysts' forecasts of earnings," *Journal of Banking and Finance*, 4, 221–33, 1980.

"The quality of analysts' forecasts of earnings," *Financial Analysts Journal*, 40–7, September–October 1984.

Givoly, D. and A. Ovadia, "Year-end tax-induced sales and stock market seasonality," *Journal of Finance*, 38, 1, 171–85, March 1983.

Gordon, M., *Finance, Investment and Macroeconomics*, Edward Elgar, 1994.

Graham, B., *The Intelligent Investor: A Book of Practical Counsel*, Harper, 1949.

Graham, B. and D. L. Dodd, *Security Analysis*, 1st edn, McGraw-Hill, 1934.

Greene, M. T. and B. D. Fielitz, "Long-term dependence in common stock returns," *Journal of Financial Economics*, 4, 339–49, 1977.

Grether, D. M., "Bayes rule as a descriptive model: The representativeness heuristic," *Quarterly Journal of Economics*, 95, 3, 537–57, November 1980.

Grether, D. M. and C. Plott, "Economic theory of choice and the preference reversal phenomenon," *American Economic Review*, 72, 569–74, September 1979.

Griffin, J. M. and M. L. Lemmon, "Book-to-market equity, distress risk, and stock returns," *Journal of Finance*, 57, 2317–36, October 2002.

Grossman, S. J., *The Informational Role of Prices*, MIT Press, 1989.

Grossman, S. J. and R. J. Shiller, "The determinants of the variability of stock market prices," *American Economic Review*, 71, 222–7, May 1981.

Grossman, S. J. and J. Stiglitz, "On the impossibility of informationally efficient markets," *American Economic Review*, 70, 393–408, June 1980.

Harrison, J. M. and D. M. Kreps, "Speculative investor behavior in a stock market with heterogeneous expectations," *Quarterly Journal of Economics*, 92, 323–36, May 1978.

Hastie, R. and R. Dawes, *Rational Choice in an Uncertain World: The Psychology of Judgment and Decision-Making*, Sage Publications, 2001.

Haugen, R. and N. Baker, "Commonality in the determinants of expected stock returns," *Journal of Financial Economics*, 41, 401–39, 1996.

Hayek, F. H., *Individualism and Economic Order*, University of Chicago Press, 1948.

Hellwig, M. F., "On the aggregation of information in competitive markets," *Journal of Economic Theory*, 22, 477–98, 1980.

"Rational expectations equilibrium with conditioning on past prices: A mean-variance example," *Journal of Economic Theory*, 26, 279–312, 1982.

Hickman, W. B., *Corporate Bond Quality and Investor Experience*, Princeton University Press, 1958.

Hirshleifer, D., "Security analysis and trading patterns when some investors receive information before others," *Journal of Finance*, 49, 5, 1665–98, December 1994.

"Investor psychology and asset pricing," *Journal of Finance*, 56, 1533–97, August 2001.

Hogarth, R. M., "Cognitive processes and the assessment of subjective probability distributions," *Journal of the American Statistical Association*, 70, 294, June 1975.

Judgment and Choice. The Psychology of Decision, Wiley, 1980.

Hogarth, R. M. and S. Makridakis, "Forecasting and planning: An evaluation," *Management Science*, 27, 115–38, February 1981.

Hong, H. and J. D. Kubik, "Analyzing the analysts: Career concerns and biased earnings forecasts," *Journal of Finance*, 58, 1, 313–51, February 2003.

Hong, H., T. Lim, and J. C. Stein, "Bad news travels slowly: Size, analyst coverage, and the profitability of momentum strategies," *Journal of Finance*, 55, 1, 265–95, February 2000.

Hong, H. and J. C. Stein, "A unified theory of underreaction, momentum trading, and overreaction in asset markets," *Journal of Finance*, 54, 2143–84, 1999.

Huberman, G., "Familiarity breeds investment," *Review of Financial Studies*, 14, 3, 659–80, Fall 2001.

Huberman, G. and T. Regev, "Contagious speculation and a cure for cancer: A non-event that made stock prices soar," *Journal of Finance*, 56, 1, 387–96, February 2001.

Imhoff, E. A. and P. V. Pare, "Analysis and comparison of earnings forecast agents," *Journal of Accounting Research*, 20, 429–39, Autumn 1982.

Jaffe, J., D. B. Keim, and R. Westerfield, "Earnings yields, market values, and stock returns," *Journal of Finance*, 44, 1, 135–48, 1989.

Janis, I. L., *Victims of Groupthink*, Houghton Mifflin, 1972.

Jarrow, R., "Heterogeneous expectations, restrictions on short sales, and equilibrium asset prices," *Journal of Finance*, 35, 1105–13, December 1980.

Jegadeesh, N. and S. Titman, "Returns to buying winners and selling losers: Implications for stock market efficiency," *Journal of Finance*, 48, 65–91, 1993.

"Profitability of momentum strategies: An evaluation of alternative explanations," *Journal of Finance*, 56, 2, 699–720, April 2001.

Jensen, M. C., "Some anomalous evidence regarding market efficiency," *Journal of Financial Economics*, 6, 95–101, 1978.

Jensen, M. C. and G. A. Benington, "Random walks and technical theories: Some additional evidence," *Journal of Finance*, 25, 469–82, May 1970.

Jones, C. J., D. Tweedie, and G. Whittington, "The regression portfolio: A statistical investigation of a relative decline model," *Journal of Business Finance and Accounting*, 3, 71–92, 1976.

Kahneman, D. and M. Riepe, "Aspects of investor psychology," *Journal of Portfolio Management*, 24, 4, 52–65, Summer 1998.

Kahneman, D., P. Slovic, and A. Tversky, *Judgment Under Uncertainty: Heuristics and Biases*, Cambridge University Press, 1982.

Kahneman, D. and A. Tversky, "Prospect theory: An analysis of decision under risk," *Econometrica*, 47, 263–91, March 1979.

"Choices, values, and frames," *American Psychologist*, 39, 4, 341–50, 1984.

Keim, D. B. and W. Ziemba (eds.), *Security Market Imperfections in Worldwide Equity Markets*, Cambridge University Press, 2000.

Keynes, J. M., *The General Theory of Employment, Interest and Money*, Harcourt Brace Jovanovich, 1936.

Kindleberger, C., *Manias, Panics, and Crashes: A History of Financial Crisis*, Basic Books, 1978.

Klein, A., "A direct test of the cognitive bias theory of share price reversals," *Journal of Accounting and Economics*, 13, 2, 155–66, 1990.

Klein, M., "The stock market crash of 1929: A review article," *Business History Review*, 75, 2, 325–51, Summer 2001.

Kunreuther, H., R. Ginsberg, L. Miller *et al.*, *Disaster Insurance Protection: Public Policy Lessons*, Wiley, 1978.

Lakonishok, J., "Stock market return expectations: Some general properties," *Journal of Finance*, 35, 921–30, September 1980.

Lakonishok, J., A. Shleifer, and R. W. Vishny, "Contrarian investment, extrapolation, and risk," *Journal of Finance*, 49, 1541–78, December 1994.

Langer, E., "The illusion of control," *Journal of Personality and Social Psychology*, 32, 311–28, 1975.

LaPorta, R., "Expectations and the cross-section of stock returns," *Journal of Finance*, 51, 5, 1715–42, December 1996.

LaPorta, R., J. Lakonishok, A. Shleifer, and R. Vishny, "Good news for value stocks: Further evidence on market efficiency," *Journal of Finance*, 52, 2, 859–74, June 1997.

Latane, H. A. and C. P. Jones, "Standardized unexpected earnings – a progress report," *Journal of Finance*, 32, 5, 1457–65, December 1977.

Laughhunn, D. J., J. W. Payne, and R. Crum, "Managerial risk preferences for below-target returns," *Management Science*, December 1980.

LeBon, G., *The Crowd. A Study of the Popular Mind*, Penguin Books, 1977 (originally published in 1895).

LeDoux, J., *The Emotional Brain*, Simon & Schuster, 1996.

Lee, C. M. C. and B. Swaminathan, "Price momentum and trading volume," *Journal of Finance*, 55, 5, 2017–69, October 2000.

LeRoy, S. F., "Expectations models of asset prices: A survey of theory," *Journal of Finance*, 37, 185–217, March 1982.

LeRoy, S. F. and R. Porter, "The present value relation: Tests based on implied variance bounds," *Econometrica*, 49, 555–74, May 1981.

Levitt, A., "The numbers game," Remarks by the Chairman of the Securities and Exchange Commission, New York University Center for Law and Business, September 28, 1998.

Levy, H., "Equilibrium in an imperfect market: A constraint on the number of securities in the portfolio," *American Economic Review*, 68, 643–58, September 1978.

Levy, R., "Random walks: Reality or myth?" *Financial Analysts Journal*, November–December 1967.

Lewellen, J. and J. Shanken, "Learning, asset pricing tests, and market efficiency," *Journal of Finance*, 57, 1113–45, 2002.

Libby, R. and P. C. Fishburn, "Behavioral models of risk taking in business decisions: A survey and evaluation," *Journal of Accounting Research*, 15, 272–92, Autumn 1977.

Little, I. M. D., "Higgledy piggledy growth," *Bulletin of the Oxford University Institute of Economics and Statistics*, 4, 387–412, November 1962.

Liu, J., D. Nissim, and J. Thomas, "Equity valuation using multiples," *Journal of Accounting Research*, 40, 1, 135–72, March 2002.

Lloyd-Davies, P. and M. Canes, "Stock prices and the publication of second-hand information," *Journal of Business*, 51, 1, 43–56, 1978.

Loewenstein, G. F., E. U. Weber, C. K. Hsee, and N. Welch, "Risk as feelings," *Psychological Bulletin*, 127, 2, 267–86, 2001.

Long, J. B., Jr., "Discussion," *Journal of Finance*, 36, 304–7, May 1981.

Loomes, G. and R. Sugden, "Regret theory: An alternative theory of rational choice under uncertainty," *Economic Journal*, 92, 368, 805–24, December 1982.

Lorie, J. and M. Hamilton, *The Stock Market: Theories and Evidence*, Irwin, 1973.

Lovell, M. C., "Tests of the rational expectations hypothesis," *American Economic Review*, 76, 110–24, 1986.

Lucas, R. E., "An equilibrium model of the business cycle," *Journal of Political Economy*, 6, 1113–44, December 1975.

Macauley, F. R., *Some Theoretical Problems Suggested by the Movement of Interest Rates, Bond Yields and Stock Prices in the United States Since 1856*, NBER, 1938.

MacCrimmon, K. R. and D. A. Wehrung, *Taking Risks: The Management of Uncertainty*, Free Press, 1986.

Maines, L. A. and J. R. M. Hand, "Individuals' perceptions and misperceptions of time series properties of quarterly earnings," *Accounting Review*, 71, 317–36, 1996.

Malkiel, B. G. and J. G. Cragg, "Expectations and the structure of share prices," *American Economic Review*, 601–17, September 1970.

Mandelbrot, B. and R. L. Hudson, *The (Mis)behavior of Markets*, Basic Books, 2004.

March, J. G. and Z. Shapira, "Managerial perspectives on risk and risk taking," *Management Science*, 33, 11, 1404–18, November 1987.

Markov, S. and A. Tamayo, "Predictability in financial analyst forecast errors: Learning or irrationality?" *Journal of Accounting Research*, 44, 4, September 2006.

Mayshar, J., "On divergence of opinion and imperfections in capital markets," *American Economic Review*, 73, 114–28, March 1983.

McCallum, B. T., "On non-uniqueness in rational expectations models," *Journal of Monetary Economics*, 11, 139–68, 1983.

McDonald, C., "An empirical evaluation of the reliability of published predictions of future earnings," *Accounting Review*, 48, 502–10, July 1973.

McEnally, R. W., "An investigation of the extrapolative determinants of short-run earnings expectations," *Journal of Financial and Quantitative Analysis*, 6, 2, 687–706, March 1971.

McWilliams, J., "Prices, earnings, and PE ratios," *Financial Analysts Journal*, 137–42, May–June 1966.

Merton, R. C., "An intertemporal capital asset pricing model," *Econometrica*, 41, 867–87, September 1973.

Michaely, R., R. H. Thaler, and K. L. Womack, "Price reactions to dividend initiations and omissions: Overreaction or drift?" *Journal of Finance*, 50, 573–608, June 1995.

Miller, E., "Risk, uncertainty and divergence of opinion," *Journal of Finance*, 32, 4, 1151–68, September 1977.

Miller, M. H. and F. Modigliani, "Dividend policy, growth and the valuation of shares," *Journal of Business*, 34, 411–33, October 1961.

Mishkin, F. S., "Are market forecasts rational?" *American Economic Review*, 71, 295–306, June 1981.

Moskowitz, T. J. and M. Grinblatt, "Do industries explain momentum?" *Journal of Finance*, 54, 4, August 1999.

Murphy, J. E., Jr. and H. W. Stevenson, "Price/earnings ratios and future growth of earnings and dividends," *Financial Analysts Journal*, 23, 111–14, November–December 1967.

Muth, J. F., "Rational expectations and the theory of price movements," *Econometrica*, 29, 315–35, July 1961.

Mutz, D. C., *Impersonal Influence: How Perceptions of Mass Collectives Affect Political Attitudes*, Cambridge University Press, 1998.

Neill, H. B., *The Art of Contrary Thinking*, Caxton Printers, 1954.

Nicholson, F., "Price ratios in relation to investment results," *Financial Analysts Journal*, 105–9, January–February 1968.

Niederhofer, V. and P. Regan, "Earnings changes and stock prices," *Financial Analysts Journal*, May–June 1972.

Nisbett, R. and L. Ross, *Human Inference: Strategies and Shortcomings of Social Judgment*, Prentice-Hall, 1980.

Nozick, R., *The Nature of Rationality*, Princeton University Press, 1993.

Nutt, S. R., J. C. Easterwood, and C. M. Easterwood, "New evidence on serial correlation in analyst forecast errors," *Financial Management*, 28, 106–17, Winter 1999.

Ofek, E. and M. Richardson, "DotCom mania: The rise and fall of internet stock prices," *Journal of Finance*, 58, 3, 1113–37, June 2003.

Oppenheimer, H. R. and G. G. Schlarbaum, "Investing with Ben Graham: An ex ante test of the efficient markets hypothesis," *Journal of Financial and Quantitative Analysis*, 16, 341–60, September 1981.

Partnoy, F., *Infectious Greed: How Deceit and Risk Corrupted the Financial Markets*, Henry Holt, 2003.

Payne, J. W., "Task complexity and contingent processing in decision making: An information search and protocol analysis," *Organizational Behavior and Human Performance*, 16, 366–87, 1976.

Peavy, J. W. and D. A. Goodman, "The significance of P/Es for portfolio returns," *Journal of Portfolio Management*, 10, 43–7, Spring 1983.

Perkins, A. B. and M. C. Perkins, *The Internet Bubble*, HarperBusiness, 1999.

Peterson, D. and P. Peterson, "The effect of changing expectations upon stock returns," *Journal of Financial and Quantitative Analysis*, 17, 799–813, December 1982.

Piotroski, J. D., "Value investing: The use of historical financial statement information to separate winners from losers," *Journal of Accounting Research*, 38, 1–41, 2000.

Plous, S., *The Psychology of Judgment and Decision-Making*, McGraw-Hill, 1993.

Rabin, M., "Psychology and economics," *Journal of Economic Literature*, 36, 11–46, 1998.

Reinganum, M. R., "Misspecification of capital asset pricing: Empirical anomalies based on earnings' yields and market values," *Journal of Financial Economics*, 9, 19–46, 1981.

Rendleman, R. J., C. P. Jones, and H. A. Latane, "Empirical anomalies based on unexpected earnings and the importance of risk adjustments," *Journal of Financial Economics*, 10, 269–87, 1982.

Roll, R., "A critique of the asset pricing theory's tests," *Journal of Financial Economics*, 4, 129–76, 1977.

   "Vas ist das? The turn-of-the-year effect and the return premia of small firms," *Journal of Portfolio Management*, 9, 18–28, Winter 1983.

Rose, A. M., "Rumor in the stock market," *Public Opinion Quarterly*, 15, 3, 461–86, Autumn 1951.

Rosenberg, H., *The Vulture Investors*, HarperBusiness, 1992.

Ross, S. A., "The arbitrage theory of capital asset pricing," *Journal of Economic Theory*, 13, 341–60, 1976.

Rouwenhorst, K. G., "International momentum strategies," *Journal of Finance*, 53, 1, 267–84, February 1998.

Royster, V., "An innocent abroad," *Wall Street Journal*, April 20, 1983.

Rozeff, M. S. and W. R. Kinney, "Capital market seasonality: The case of stock returns," *Journal of Financial Economics*, 3, 379–402, October 1976.

Rubinstein, M., "Securities market efficiency in an Arrow–Debreu economy," *American Economic Review*, 65, 812–24, 1975.

"Rational markets: Yes or no? The affirmative case," *Financial Analysts Journal*, 57, 3, 15–29, 2001.

Schiereck, D., W. De Bondt, and M. Weber, "Contrarian and momentum strategies in Germany," *Financial Analysts Journal*, 104–16, November–December 1999.

Schmalensee, R., "An experimental study of expectation formation," *Econometrica*, 44, 17–41, January 1976.

Schoemaker, P. J. H., "The expected utility model: Its variants, purposes, evidence and limitations," *Journal of Economic Literature*, 20, 529–63, June 1982.

"Determinants of risk-taking: Behavioral and economic views," *Journal of Risk and Uncertainty*, 6, 49–73, 1993.

Schwartz, H., *Rationality Gone Awry? Decision-Making Inconsistent with Economic and Financial Theory*, Praeger, 1998.

Scott, J., M. Stumpp, and P. Xu, "News, not trading volume, build momentum," *Financial Analysts Journal*, 45–54, March–April 2003.

Searle, J. R., *Rationality in Action*, MIT Press, 2001.

Shanken, J., "The arbitrage pricing theory: Is it testable?" *Journal of Finance*, 37, 1129–40, December 1982.

Shefrin, H., *Beyond Greed and Fear: Understanding Behavioral Finance and the Psychology of Investing*, Oxford University Press, 1999.

A Behavioral Approach to Asset Pricing, Elsevier Academic Press, 2005.

Shefrin, H. (ed.), *Behavioral Finance*, Edward Elgar, 2001 (3 vols.).

Shiller, R. J., "The volatility of long-term interest rates and expectation models of the term structure," *Journal of Political Economy*, 87, 1190–1219, December 1979.

"Do stock prices move too much to be justified by subsequent changes in dividends?" *American Economic Review*, 71, 421–36, June 1981.

"Stock prices and social dynamics," *Brookings Papers on Economic Activity*, 1984, 457–510, 1984.

Market Volatility, MIT Press, 1989.

Irrational Exuberance, Princeton University Press, 2000.

Shleifer, A., *Inefficient Markets*, Oxford University Press, 2000.

Shleifer, A. and R. W. Vishny, "The limits of arbitrage," *Journal of Finance*, 52, 35–55, March 1997.

Simon, H. A., *Administrative Behavior: A Study of Decision-Making Processes in Administrative Organization*, Free Press, 1945.

Models of Man: Social and Rational, Wiley, 1957.

Reason in Human Affairs, Stanford University Press, 1983.

Skinner, D. J. and R. G. Sloan, "Earnings surprises, growth expectations, and stock returns, or don't let an earnings torpedo sink your portfolio," *Review of Accounting Studies*, 7, 289–312, 2002.

Sloan, R.G, "Do stock prices fully reflect information in accruals and cash flows about future earnings?" *Accounting Review*, 71, 3, 289–315, July 1996.

Slovic, P., "Information processing, situation specificity, and the generality of risk-taking behavior," *Journal of Personality and Social Psychology*, 22, 128–34, 1972(a).

"Psychological study of human judgment: Implications for investment decision-making," *Journal of Finance*, 27, 4, 779–99, September 1972(b).

"Rational actors or rational fools: Implications of the affect heuristic for behavioral economics," in T. Gilovich *et al.* (eds.), *Heuristics and Biases: The Psychology of Intuitive Judgment*, Cambridge University Press, 2002.

Smelser, N. J., *Theory of Collective Behavior*, Free Press of Glencoe, 1963.

Smith, V., G. Suchanek, and A. Williams, "Bubbles, crashes, and endogenous expectations in experimental spot asset markets," *Econometrica*, 56, 5, 1119–51, September 1988.

Stiglitz, J., "Pareto-optimality and competition," *Journal of Finance*, 36, 235–51, May 1981.

Stout, L. A., "The investor confidence game," 9th Annual Abraham L. Pomerantz Lecture, Brooklyn Law School, 2002.

Taussig, F. W., "Is market price determinate?" *Quarterly Journal of Economics*, 35, 394–411, May 1921.

Teh, L. and W. F. M. De Bondt, "Herding behavior and stock returns: An exploratory investigation," *Swiss Journal of Economics and Statistics*, 133, 293–324, 1997.

Temin, P. and H.-J. Voth, "Riding the South Sea Bubble," *American Economic Review*, 94, 5, 1654–68, December 2004.

Timmerman, A., "How learning in financial markets generates excess volatility and predictability in stock prices," *Quarterly Journal of Economics*, 108, 1135–45, 1993.

Tirole, J., "On the possibility of speculation under rational expectations," *Econometrica*, 50, 1163–81, September 1982.

Townsend, R., "Market anticipations, rational expectations, and Bayesian analysis," *International Economic Review*, 19, 481–94, June 1978.

Tversky, A., "Intransitivity of preferences," *Psychological Review*, 76, 31–48, 1969.

Tversky, A. and D. Kahneman, "Judgment under uncertainty: Heuristics and biases," *Science*, 185, 1124–31, 1974.

"Rational choice and the framing of decisions," *Journal of Business*, 59, 67–94, October 1986.

Umstead, D. A., "Forecasting stock market prices," *Journal of Finance*, 32, 427–41, May 1977.

Verrecchia, R. E., "On the theory of market efficiency," *Journal of Accounting and Economics*, 1, 77–90, 1979.

"Consensus beliefs, information acquisition, and market information efficiency," *American Economic Review*, 70, 874–84, December 1980.

"Information acquisition in a noisy rational expectations economy," *Econometrica*, 50, 1415–30, November 1982.

Vlek, C. and P. J. Stallen, "Rational and personal aspects of risk," *Acta Psychologica*, 45, 273–300, 1980.

Wärneryd, K.-E., *Stock-Market Psychology: How People Value and Trade Stocks*, Edward Elgar, 2001.

Watts, R., "Systematic abnormal returns after quarterly earnings announcements," *Journal of Financial Economics*, 6, 127–50, 1978.

Watts, R. and R. Leftwich, "The time series of annual accounting earnings," *Journal of Accounting Research*, 15, 253–71, Autumn 1977.

Weber, E. U. and R. A. Milliman, "Perceived risk attitudes: Relating risk perception to risky choice," *Management Science*, 43, 2, 123–44, February 1997.

Whittington, G., *The Prediction of Profitability and Other Studies of Company Behaviour*, Cambridge University Press, 1971.

Williams, J. B., *The Theory of Investment Value*, North-Holland, 1956 (reprint of the 1938 edition).

Working, H., "The investigation of economic expectations," *American Economic Review*, 39, 150–66, May 1949.

"A theory of anticipatory prices," *American Economic Review*, 48, 188–99, May 1958.

Zacks, L., "EPS forecasts – accuracy is not enough," *Financial Analysts Journal*, 35, 53–5, March/April 1979.

Zarnowitz, V., "The accuracy of individual and group forecasts from business outlook surveys," *Journal of Forecasting*, 3, 11–26, 1984.

Zarowin, P., "Does the stock market overreact to corporate earnings information?" *Journal of Finance*, 44, 5, 1385–99, December 1989.

5 Inter-temporal choice and self-control: saving and borrowing

PAUL WEBLEY AND ELLEN K. NYHUS

Many of the decisions we make on a day-to-day basis involve inter-temporal choice. We have to decide what to eat, whether to exercise and when to go to bed. These decisions involve a trade-off between immediate gratification and long-term consequences: the toffee pudding will be delicious but will contribute to a thickening waistline; going for a jog might be painful, but one will be healthier for it; reading documents in the evening means there is no time to watch the football, but the meeting next day will be much more successful as a result. All decisions that implicate consequences at different points in time are inter-temporal choices.

The term inter-temporal choice is used to denote choices between outcomes occurring at different points in time. For example, when we choose between receiving something today at one price and receiving the same thing in a year at a lower price, we have to make trade-offs between the differences in costs and the time we have to wait for the benefits. Many economic decisions involve such trade-offs, but probably the best example is when we choose between spending money today and spending at some time in the future. We do this when we save (spend less now so that we can spend in the future) and borrow (spend more now and less in the future).

In this chapter we will look first at the standard economic model of inter-temporal choice, consider some of the relevant evidence on the assumptions that underpin this model, and then explore the relevance of self-control. In the second part we consider behavioural saving models and some of the issues highlighted in recent savings research that cast light on models of inter-temporal choice. This review reveals that tests of behavioural models are based on different types of methods depending on the behaviour under investigation. So studies of inter-temporal decision making and the various factors that may influence a particular choice are predominantly based on experimental research whereas studies of saving and borrowing are mainly based on analyses of data collected through self-report surveys or data provided by financial institutions or national databases. We have not produced an overall model of the determinants of saving and borrowing behaviour (that is beyond us) but we hope that the chapter will encourage the integration of the more social psychological approaches to saving and borrowing considered in the second part (for example, on savings motives) with the more individualistic approaches considered in the first.

5.1 The economic model of inter-temporal choice

The standard economic model for the analysis of inter-temporal choices is the discounted utility model (DU model) put forward by Samuelson in 1937, and further elaborated by Fishburn and Rubinstein (1982). In this model it is assumed that the decision maker aims to maximize the sum of utilities derived from consumption across all future time periods. Because individuals are impatient, and prefer to consume things now, future utility is 'discounted' by the decision maker's subjective discount rate, or rate of time preference. Thus something which gave the decision maker 100 units of utility now would give 95 units in period 2, if the subjective discount rate was 5 per cent. If time preference (the subjective discount rate) is high, this means that additional consumption in the present is valued relatively higher than additional consumption in the future, while if it is low, additional future consumption is given a relatively high weight compared to additional present consumption.

In most analyses and models of inter-temporal choice, it is assumed that the time preference rate is positive. A positive discount rate causes future consumption to be devalued when compared to present consumption, so this assumption implies that a decision maker will maximize utility by choosing a consumption stream that involves consuming *all* available resources in the present. However, it is usually also assumed that we have diminishing marginal utility from consumption. This means that we get less utility from the second unit of consumption than from the first, and even less utility from the third unit than the second, and so on. Hence, due to diminishing marginal utility, the decision maker is assumed to prefer spreading consumption evenly over all future time periods in order to maximize total utility. If we have only two units to consume, we will derive more utility from consuming one today and one tomorrow instead of both today. These two assumptions imply a preference for spreading consumption over all future periods, with a tendency to prefer a somewhat higher consumption in the present.

The DU model is further based on assumptions of complete and continuous preferences. It also assumes that the decision maker's preferences are transitive, which means that if we prefer X to Y and Y to Z, we will prefer X to Z. Frederick, Loewenstein and O'Donoghue (2002) clarify other important assumptions: (1) that decision makers are assumed to update their inter-temporal choices when they get new opportunities; (2) that utility derived from consumption in one period is independent of what has been consumed in other periods – this means that we should not let the choice of dinner today be affected by what we had for dinner yesterday or what we expect to have for dinner tomorrow; (3) that utility in one period is independent of utility in other periods, meaning that the decision maker is indifferent as to whether there is a smooth consumption profile or a fluctuating one, as long as the sum of the utility from each period is the same; (4) that we apply the same rate of time preference for all types of consumption – this means that the time preference rate we use when making choices concerning food is the same as the rate we use when making choices about furniture; (5) that utility derived from a specific outcome is unaffected by when the outcome takes place – this means that we should enjoy an ice cream just as much on a cold winter day as on a hot day in the summer. As Frederick *et al.* (2002) note, despite the fact that the creators of the DU model warned against using the model as a descriptive model of inter-temporal choice and that economists agree that many of these assumptions are unrealistic, the DU model has been the most widely used model of inter-temporal choice.

5.2   The variability of subjective discount rates

Several experiments have shown that most of the assumptions underlying the DU model are not supported by the evidence. In particular, numerous studies show that one of the most important assumptions, a constant discount rate, seems to be unrealistic. Decision-specific factors like the timing of receipts and payments and the size of the outcomes involved in the decisions have been found to influence the discount rate used.

Several studies have found that higher discount rates are used for events closer in time than for events further away. Thaler (1981) demonstrated that the average discount rates varied inversely with the length of the period the individuals had to wait for rewards. These results were later replicated by Benzion, Rapoport and Yagil (1989) and Shelley (1993) using larger samples. They found that the average rate of time preference decreased with the length of period to be waited both for payments and for receipts. Frederick *et al.* (2002) reported that this has been found for studies using periods up to one year, while the impact of time on time preference disappears for periods beyond one year. Read (2001) proposed that 'sub-additive discounting' can explain the relationship found between time preference and time, since respondents may respond not only to the delay but also to the length of the intervals involved in the decisions. He found that the average discount rate inferred from decisions involving three successive periods of eight months (from month 0 to month 7, month 8 to month 15 and month 16 to month 23) is higher than the discount rate inferred from decisions concerning twenty-four months (month 0 to month 23). Read *et al.* (2004) found that the effect of the time interval on the discount rate disappears if dates rather than time intervals are used when asking people about how much compensation they want for waiting.

The size of the rewards and payments involved in inter-temporal decisions has also been found to have a negative relationship with the discount rates used (this is called the magnitude effect). The average inferred discount rates used for small amounts have been surprisingly high, while those used for larger amounts are more reasonable. This has been found in the hypothetical choice situations used by Benzion *et al.* (1989), Horowitz (1991), Shelley (1993) and Thaler (1981). Two different explanations for this phenomenon have been proposed (Loewenstein and Thaler, 1989). The first explanation focuses on how outcomes are actually perceived. The findings suggest that people react not only to relative changes but also to absolute differences in amounts. For example, the perceptual difference between €100,000 now and €110,000 in a year appears greater than the difference between €1,000 now and €1,100 in a year, and people might therefore be less willing to wait for the €100 than for the €10,000. This explanation has been denoted 'the absolute magnitude effect' (Loewenstein and Prelec, 1992; Loewenstein and Thaler, 1989). The second explanation relies on the notion of mental accounting (Shefrin and Thaler, 1988). It is argued that small windfalls, like €1,000, are entered into a mental current account, while large windfalls, like €100,000, are entered into a mental savings account. The propensity to consume from these two accounts is assumed to be different, which might affect the way the cost of delaying is perceived. Waiting for a small windfall might be perceived as foregone consumption whereas waiting for a larger windfall is more likely to be perceived in terms of foregone interest.

Moreover, results from experiments show that the framing of the decision situation has an effect on the discount rate. People typically discount receipts more than payments (Benzion *et al.*, 1989; Thaler, 1981). Receipts refer to money the decision maker is to receive – for example, a lottery premium or a bonus – while payments refer to money the decision maker is to pay – for example, a bill. Thaler (1981) suggested that the effects of framing might stem from a tendency to undervalue opportunity costs relative to 'out-of-pocket-costs'. Studies by Benzion *et al.* (1989), Loewenstein (1988) and Shelley (1993) showed that people use higher discount rates when they make decisions which involve delay of receipts than when the decisions involve a speeding-up of the receipts. For example, Loewenstein (1988) found that the amount required to compensate for delaying receiving a VCR by a given interval was between two and four times greater than the amount subjects were willing to sacrifice to speed up the receipt of the VCR by the same interval. However, when the decision involves payments the results are reversed: respondents use higher discount rates for expeditions than for delays of payments.

Loewenstein (1988) and Shelley (1993) reinterpreted the findings outlined above and argued that the effects of outcome sign (receipt vs. payment) and question framing (delays vs. speeding-up) should be combined instead of being interpreted independently. They define delay of rewards and speed-ups of payments as 'immediate losses' while speed-ups of rewards and delays of payments are defined as 'immediate gains'. This definition of gains and losses rests on the assumptions that people generally are concerned with changes in the present or the immediate future and that outcomes are defined as gains or losses depending on whether they imply an increase or decrease in immediate utility relative to the original plan. This interpretation of the effects of near-term outcomes has been used to elaborate a model that explains the effects of framing in terms of reference point shifts (Loewenstein, 1988; Loewenstein and Prelec, 1992; Shelley, 1993). When, for example, an individual is asked how much he is willing to pay in order to speed up a delivery of a good that he was supposed to receive at some point in the future, his reference point is neutral. He has not yet psychologically adapted to possessing the good and speeding up the delivery is perceived as an immediate gain. However, if the delivery of the good was supposed to be in the present, and he is asked how much he wants in compensation in order to agree to postpone the receipt, his reference point is higher than in the speed-up situation since he has adapted to the thought of having the good. In this delay situation, 'not having the good' will be perceived as an immediate loss, causing the individual to feel deprived. The compensation wanted for this delay has been found to be higher than what the individual is willing to pay for speeding up delivery of something he was not supposed to have in the present. This means that people implicitly use higher subjective discount rates in immediate loss situations than in immediate gain situations.

The results discussed above show that the discount rate is not a constant, as assumed in the DU model, but situation-specific. This makes the measurement of time preference rates difficult, since the results often depend on the characteristics of the questions used or the situations observed to infer discount rates. It is also difficult to decide if a certain result of an experiment which is inconsistent with the DU model is evidence of the assumptions of the model being unrealistic or an artefact of the method used.

5.3   Inter-temporal inconsistency

Exponential discounting means that future alternatives are discounted at a constant rate, that is, the same discount rate is used when calculating the net value of outcomes occurring one month hence, one year hence or ten years hence. Some of the experimental evidence reported above suggests, however, that people use a higher discount rate for events closer in time than for events further away. An implication of this is that the discount function has a hyperbolic form rather than an exponential one. A consequence of hyperbolic discounting is what Strotz (1955–6) called 'dynamic inconsistency', which means that we will not follow our own plans. Typical decisions that are dynamically inconsistent are those that imply a conflict of short-time and long-term goals: for example, eating vs. weight control, smoking vs. being healthy, impulse buying vs. saving for retirement, staying out with friends vs. doing homework.

Hyperbolic discounting and inter-temporal inconsistency have been illustrated by Ainslie (1992) with the following figures. The graphs illustrate the

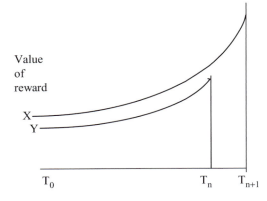

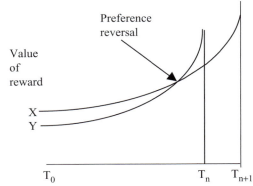

Figure 5.1 Preferences under constant discount rates: stable preferences. Adapted from Ainslie, G. *Picoeconomics: The Strategic Interaction of Successive Motivational States within the Person*, Copyright 1992, with permission from Cambridge University Press

Figure 5.2 Preferences when discount rate changes as a function of time: preference reversal. Adapted from Ainslie, G. *Picoeconomics: The Strategic Interaction of Successive Motivational States within the Person*, Copyright 1992, with permission from Cambridge University Press

present value assigned to two alternatives after discounting them to comparable present values.

Figure 5.1 illustrates an individual's preferences and behaviour when a constant discount rate is used. At time T_0 the individual prefers alternative X, which is larger but is available at a later point in time than alternative Y. As time T_n approaches, the decision maker still considers alternative X better than alternative Y because the decision maker uses the same discount rate when evaluating the alternatives. The constant rate of discounting produces preference curves that are exponential and proportional to each other so they never cross. The decision maker waits for alternative X, which is available at time T_{n+1}. Figure 5.2 shows preferences and behaviour when the discount rates are higher for events close in time than events further into the future. At time T_0, the individual prefers alternative X to Y as in the first example. However, as the time when alternative Y is available approaches, the discount rate used for discounting the value of the two alternatives increases, so that alternative X at a certain point is perceived as having a lower present value than alternative Y. This causes a shift of preferences. The alternative closest in time is discounted with a much higher rate, so after a certain point it has the highest present value. The change in discount rates produces the hyperbolic preference curves which result in the curves crossing. The result is that alternative Y is chosen, in spite of the initial preference for alternative X. Ainslie (1975) reviewed numerous studies on this kind of inconsistent behaviour, which has been found among birds, animals, children and adults. Preferences for two goods available at two different points in time are better described by hyperbolic curves than by exponential ones.

Loewenstein (1996) considered why inconsistent behaviour is induced in some situations but not others. He attributed 'inconsistent behaviour' to the role of visceral factors (e.g. hunger, thirst, mood, emotion, physical pain) rather than to a change in preferences. Loewenstein identified three important differences between preferences and visceral factors. First, visceral factors change more quickly than preferences since they are associated with external circumstances such as stimulation and deprivation. As a result, it is more difficult to foresee them and defend oneself against them. Second, visceral factors draw on different neuropsychological mechanisms than preferences. Neurological research has found that the core of the brain (the limbic system) uses chemical regulation to control body functions, and different configurations of these chemicals are experienced as hunger, thirst, sleepiness, elation, depression, etc. Preferences, on the other hand, consist of information stored in memory concerning the relative desirability of different goods and activities. Finally, visceral factors are difficult to store in memory. We have a limited ability to store information about visceral sensations since it is difficult to imagine hunger, pain, anger or other passions when we are not experiencing them. Consequently, it will be difficult to consider visceral sensations when planning future behaviour even though we have experienced the sensations in the past. Loewenstein suggested that the role of visceral factors should be included in models of inter-temporal choice, so that impulsive behaviour is not regarded as an irrational shift in preferences. Preferences remain stable but other factors that interact with them in determining behaviour, such as being offered an unhealthy snack when hungry, must be taken into account when predicting behaviour.

5.4   Self-control in inter-temporal choice

Experiments have shown that individuals and animals in some situations choose a small reward available immediately instead of a larger one available later. However, if people always showed this type of behaviour, everybody would be without education, in debt and unable to hold down a regular job. As Loewenstein (1996) pointed out, it seems as if some types of behaviour are more likely to be dynamically inconsistent than others. But even for these types of behaviour, people seem to be able to stick to their long-term plans; in most situations people are able to delay gratification in order to achieve their long-term goals. Hence, time preference cannot be the only factor that influences inter-temporal choices.

The concept of self-control has been linked to economic behaviour at least since Adam Smith discussed self-command in the *Theory of Moral Sentiments*.[1] Theories including self-control recognize that delaying pleasure to a

---

[1] See Loewenstein, 1992; Wärneryd, 1989; 1999.

later time can be challenging. Schelling (1984) defined self-control as those efforts made to avoid or resist behaving inconsistently. The story about Ulysses and the sirens has often been used to illustrate such efforts (e.g. Strotz, 1955–6; Elster, 1979; Ainslie, 1992; 1993). In order to resist the tempting song of the sirens, Ulysses used two main techniques. He used *prior commitment*, by being tied to the ship's mast so that it was impossible for him to follow his urge to steer the ship off-course, and *exposure avoidance*, by putting wax in the ears of his crew so that they were deaf to the sirens and therefore not tempted. An example of prior commitment in the economic domain would be buying illiquid assets in order to prevent oneself from overspending, and an example of exposure avoidance would be avoiding shopping malls. A third self-control technique is consistent planning (Ainslie, 1992; 1993; Strotz, 1955–6). Using strategies of consistent planning means choosing the best of the plans that one believes it is possible to follow. Ainslie explained this technique by arguing that the process underlying impulse control can be modelled as a repetitive, inter-temporal prisoner's dilemma, and that one choice will set precedents for later ones. Since a person wants to act rationally in his future choices, he may choose to act rationally in the present due to a belief that it will serve as an example of future behaviour. Hence, according to Ainslie, self-control is most likely to be observed for choices that will be repeated.

5.5   How does the ability to wait develop?

Strotz (1955–6) assumed that most of us are born with hyperbolic discount functions, but that these are modified through parental and social teaching. He divided consumers into three groups. The 'thrifty' were trained so effectively that the original discount function had been substituted with an exponential one. Self-control is not necessary for them, as inconsistency problems do not occur. The 'Pre-committers' have been taught to plan and behave consistently, but without having their tastes altered. They will need to use pre-commitment in order to stick to their original plans. The 'spendthrifts' are people who, because of a lack of training or insight, have never learned to behave consistently and for whom the inter-temporal tussle remains unsolved. Strotz argued that we find these among the lower-income classes.

Psychologists have for decades studied how self-regulation and the ability to wait for larger rewards develop and how the ability of self-regulation differs between individuals. Typically, such experiments have required children of different age groups, genders and social class to wait for a larger reward in the presence of a small immediate reward (Mischel, Shoda and Rodriguez, 1989). This research has revealed that the delayed reward has to be of a certain size before children are motivated to wait, consistent with the findings reported above of adults using higher discount rates for small amounts than for large amounts. Moreover, children's willingness to wait is associated with the perception of risk associated with waiting. Furthermore, a stronger focus on the delayed reward increased the ability to wait. This research has also revealed the strategies used by children in order to be able to wait. These typically involve attempts to control attention so that thinking about the immediate reward is avoided. In the laboratory such strategies included singing, trying to sleep or thinking fun thoughts. These experiments reveal individual differences in the ability to wait, and a few studies have shown how this is related to behaviour later in life. Children found able to wait for a reward at age four were described as more successful by their parents at age fourteen and had higher SAT scores (Mischel, Shoda and Peake, 1988; Shoda, Mischel and Peake, 1990). Ayduk *et al.* (2000) found that the ability to wait in young age is related to positive behaviours in adulthood, such as obtaining a higher education level.

Metcalfe and Mischel (1999) proposed a model describing how two systems in the brain (the hot and impulsive 'go system' and the cool and cognitive 'know system') interact and determine a person's ability to wait. The model has two interactive systems. The emotional 'hot' system is specialized for quick emotional processing. It is simple and fast and consists of relatively few representations or 'hot spots' that trigger reflexive actions. The hot system is assumed to develop early in life and is dominant in young infants. The cognitive 'cool' system is an emotionally neutral 'know' system: cognitive, complex, deliberate and contemplative. It consists of a network of informational cool nodes that are connected to each other and which generates rational and planned behaviour. The hot and the cool systems are assumed to interact when activated by external referents. The hot spots and cool nodes that share the same external referent are therefore linked to one another. Hot spots can be evoked by activation of the corresponding cool nodes and vice versa. Self-control problems typically arise when hot spots cannot access the corresponding cool node, so that the cool system's regulation of the behaviour is non-existent. The child's increased ability to delay gratification as it grows older is explained by the developmental lag between the two systems. The hot system is present at birth whereas the cool system develops with age. Both the hot and cool systems are heavily influenced by biological dispositions, learning and maturation, which may explain the observed individual differences in ability to delay gratification. Metcalfe and Mischel report that high stress levels seem to reduce access to the cool system, so that stressful situations make the individual unable to redirect activity away from the hot system. Low to moderate stress levels, on the other hand, may strengthen the impact of the cool system.

Developments in neuroeconomics (see the chapter in the present collection by Lohrenz and Montague) support a model of two interrelated systems in the brain (Camerer, Loewenstein and Prelec, 2005). Neuroscience uses brain activity imaging and other techniques to infer details about how the brain works: for example, to map the interplay between controlled and automatic processes and the brain's cognitive and affective systems. In neuroeconomics this is used to learn more about which parts of the brain are active when making economic decisions. For example, McClure *et al.* (2004) have found that different parts of the brain are active when making inter-temporal choices where one of the alternatives involves immediate gratification compared to choices where both alternatives concern future gratification. They scanned people using functional magnetic resonance imaging (fMRI) while they made preference judgements between monetary rewards. They found that parts of the limbic (the affective) system associated with the midbrain dopamine system were activated when making judgements about alternatives where one involved immediately available rewards. When the subjects chose between alternatives where all rewards would be available in the future, the regions of the lateral prefrontal cortex and posterior parietal cortex were active. McClure *et al.* also found that the relative activity of the two systems predicted the judgements that subjects made. A greater relative activity in the affective systems was associated with more frequent choices of earlier rewards. This supports the notion of a hot and cool system, where immediate gratification typically activates the hot system.

Murayen and Baumeister (2000) proposed that self-control may be regarded as a resource that can be depleted. We have to apply self-control in many ways in our everyday life so that various tasks and duties are fulfilled. Experiments in which respondents are asked to do two self-control tasks in succession show that respondents who have had to exercise more self-control in the first task or use their brain in other ways are less able to exercise self-control in the second. For example, Shiv and Fedorikhin (1999) instructed participants to memorize numbers. One group were asked to memorize a two-digit number, while the other group were asked to memorize a seven-digit number. They were then asked to go to a different room in the building. On the way to the other room, they were presented with a choice between a slice of cake or a bowl of fruit salad. Of those asked to remember the seven-digit number, 59 per cent chose the cake, while only 37 per cent of those asked to remember the two-digit number chose the cake. These findings suggest that brain effort may reduce our ability to exercise self-control. It is as though the influence of the cognitive system decreases with demand for performance of cognitive tasks. Hence, stress or previous situations which have required self-control may reduce an individual's ability to exercise self-control again. Vohs and Faber (2007) showed that this also applies to spending behaviour. Respondents who first had to do attention-control tasks requiring self-controlling behaviour gave more impulsive purchasing responses than respondents who had not been asked to do attention-control tasks. The respondents who had used self-control in the first task and therefore had a depleted resource expressed higher willingness to pay for a variety of items and spent more money and bought more items in an unanticipated buying situation than the other respondents.

5.6 Inter-temporal choice, saving and borrowing

On the face of it, saving and borrowing are perfect exemplars of inter-temporal choice. What is saving, after all, but a decision to spend in the future (on holidays, on living in retirement) instead of spending in the present? Conversely, when we borrow money, we spend in the present rather than in the future (when we must pay back the borrowed funds). So we might expect the models of inter-temporal choice discussed above to shed a great deal of light on saving and borrowing. In reality, whilst they provide some illumination, there are a number of factors which limit a straightforward application of these models to saving and borrowing. We will consider these below, but before we do so, we need to tackle some definitional issues.

We probably all think we know what saving and borrowing are. Saving is putting money aside on a regular basis so that we can buy a car, whereas borrowing is taking out a loan in order to buy the car now. But is the meaning of saving quite as self-evident as it might appear?

At a formal level saving is quite easy to define. Since income can either be spent or saved, saving is simply income that has not been spent (whether by an individual, a family or a nation). But to make sense of this, it is necessary to specify an accounting period. If a child is given £5 a week pocket money, saves it for four weeks and then spends £20 on a computer game, she has saved a lot considered on a weekly basis, but has saved nothing over the month. She is clearly making an inter-temporal choice, trading off the joys of spending £5 on her normal weekly fare against the pleasure of playing the game in a month's time, but (using a monthly accounting period) has saved nothing. This might seem like nit-picking, but when we consider empirical studies of saving, the accounting period used matters a great deal, as it has a considerable impact on who is considered as having saved, as well as the amounts that have been saved. In this case, we would have no difficulty, conceptually at least, in recognizing that the child had saved, even if we were unable to detect it with our usual methods of measurement. But what if she had not spent her £5 on the Saturday she received it, but on the following Friday. Again, using a weekly accounting period she would have saved nothing, but equally she has made another inter-temporal choice. Neither she nor her parents would probably describe her behaviour as saving, but saved she has (using a daily accounting period). There are two points to take away from this: first that the accounting period matters, and we will often be unable to detect empirically that saving has occurred, and second that everyday understandings may (sometimes) get in the way of our understanding of a phenomenon.

In a chapter this size it is not possible to do justice to the extensive literature on saving and borrowing. Rather than attempt the impossible, our aim here is first to consider behavioural saving models and then to review a number of issues that emerge in recent savings research that link directly to models of inter-temporal choice.

5.7 Behavioural saving models

A number of 'behavioural' saving theories have been developed which are closely linked with models of inter-temporal choice. Three models will be briefly considered.

5.7.1 The behavioral life-cycle model

Whilst the model of inter-temporal choice can in principle apply to any time periods, most theoretical effort in economics has focused on how individuals deal with income across their lifespan. The seminal theory is Modigliani and Brumberg's (1954) life-cycle hypothesis. This says that saving at any stage of a person's life-cycle can be predicted from his current income and wealth, expectation of future income and life expectancy, by finding the stream of consumption that will maximize the total utility for all future periods. The theory predicts that young people will borrow to pay for consumption, the middle-aged save for retirement and the old will 'dis-save' – that is, spend those savings. A similar approach was taken by Friedman (1957) with his permanent income hypothesis. The important difference between this and the life-cycle hypothesis is that the permanent income is not the same as expected lifetime earnings. Friedman was also clear that people do not necessarily have a lifetime plan and may use a much shorter time horizon.

In both of these models, a consumer is assumed to be able to distribute income over the lifespan – in other words, the assumption is that people are completely rational and that self-control is unproblematic. Shefrin and Thaler (1988) developed an alternative approach, the 'behavioral life-cycle model'. This treats saving decisions as the consequence of a conflict between two inconsistent personae. The 'planner' cares about the long term whereas the 'doer' only cares about the present and the short term. The 'planner' attempts to control the 'doer's' spending by using mental accounts and rules of thumb. Three mental accounts are assumed to operate: current income, current assets and future income. The propensity to spend is assumed to be greatest for the current income mental account and least for the future income mental account.

There is some evidence that supports the predictions of the behavioural life-cycle model. For example, Shefrin and Thaler (1988) report that the self-reported propensity to spend from regular payments was greater than that for equivalently valued lump sum payments, which provides support both for the existence of mental accounts and for different propensities to consume from them. If we relate this to the model of how the affective and cognitive systems in the brain work, it may be that the thought of using present income, which is available immediately, is more likely to activate the affective system than the thought of using savings (current assets) or future income, which may require some efforts to get hold of and therefore are less likely to activate emotions.

5.7.2 The buffer-stock model

Another approach is the so-called 'buffer-stock' model of saving (Carroll, 1997). This model takes into account the high rates of time preference found in empirical studies and assumes that people are impatient and so want to consume in the present. However, a further assumption is that people are anxious that they may not have sufficient money in the future, which motivates saving. People are therefore assumed to have a target for their saving (the buffer) based on the ratio between their wealth and their income. If wealth is below target, people are prudent, whereas if it is above target, people spend. The more uncertain future income is, the higher the buffer-stock saving target will be. There is quite a lot of evidence for this model. Samwick (1998), Gourinchas and Parker (1999) and Zhou (2003) all found that young people engage in buffer-stock saving, while older people tend to save for retirement.

5.7.3 The golden-eggs model

In two papers Laibson (1997; 1998) explores the impact of illiquid assets ('golden eggs') on saving behaviour. Laibson views illiquid assets (a house is a good exemplar) as a pre-commitment device that limits over-consumption. Wealth that is illiquid cannot be used to smooth consumption when income is low. This explains why we observe that household consumption tracks household income more closely than an adherence to the life-cycle hypothesis would lead us to expect. The model also predicts that financial innovations that increase liquidity would lead to a decline in saving, which is what has been seen in many western countries (Maital and Maital, 1994).

Hyperbolic discounting can also explain why people borrow whilst also having savings (Harris and Laibson, 2001; Laibson *et al.*, 2003). The key idea is that a person's willingness to save for retirement is greater in the present than the willingness she expects to have at a later period in her life. An individual will therefore acquire illiquid assets for retirement quite deliberately as a pre-commitment strategy so as to impose restrictions on the spending of future selves.

5.8 Expectations, uncertainty and time horizons

Future expectations are obviously highly relevant to decisions about whether to spend now or save for the future. If one anticipates a future increase in income, current spending decisions are likely to be very different to a situation where a reduction in income is anticipated or large increases in expenditure are on the horizon. Similarly, if a person's expectations about future income are very uncertain, saving is much more likely.

Katona (1975) carried out a large number of studies on the relationship between saving and people's expectations of future economic conditions (optimism or pessimism). He believed that saving is a result of both ability to save (linked to disposable income) and willingness to save (linked to how optimistic or pessimistic a person feels about both their personal situation and the economy). Such optimism was measured using the 'Index of Consumer Sentiment' (ICS). This consists of five questions, two on expectations about the personal financial situation, two on expectations about the national economy as a whole, and one on expectations about the market situation.

Van Raaij and Gianotten (1990) found that the expectation-oriented questions about the household financial situation were better predictors of saving than the questions concerning the development of the general economic situation. Expectations about the household financial situation were positively correlated with savings. Brown *et al.* (2005) provide similar evidence concerning the link between expectations and borrowing. They used samples derived from the 1995 and 2000 waves of the British Household Panel Survey. The measure of borrowing was fairly straightforward (a question about unsecured borrowing which just asked *how much in total do you owe?*) as was the measure of expectations (where participants had to judge how well off they would be financially in a year's time). These were clearly linked – those with more optimistic expectations about the future tended to have borrowed more.

Another issue of interest is the effect of uncertainty about income changes. Carroll (1994) found that income uncertainty had a depressing effect on consumption. Similar results have been found in studies by Banks, Blundell and Brugiavini (1995), Guiso, Jappelli and Terlizzese (1992) and Lusardi (1993). This means that uncertainty will mediate the effects of expectation on saving. Optimistic expectations concerning future income might not lead to more spending if the uncertainty of its realization is high. Both expectations and uncertainty must therefore be taken into account.

Time horizons have been measured by asking people about whether they make plans or not with respect to economic decisions and about the length of their planning horizon. Responses to these questions suggest that time horizons show considerable variation between individuals and between purchasing situations. The conclusion from many studies is that people with a longer planning horizon save more. For example, Wärneryd (2000) found that a future time perspective was positively related to financial situation, saving habits and savings.

It is clear that whether individuals are pessimistic or optimistic, such expectations will affect the financial decisions that they make. So individuals who believe (rightly or wrongly) that their income will be higher in the future will be more likely to borrow to spend now on the ground that they will be easily able to pay the money back later. Those who face greater income uncertainty will consume less and save more. These adjustments of consumption and savings are in line with the predictions of the DU model and the life-cycle model. If we expect a higher income in the future, the marginal utility of consumption in the future is likely to be lower than the marginal utility of consumption in the present (assuming a diminishing marginal utility for consumption). Hence, in times of optimism with regard to one's future economic situation, increasing present consumption may be the rational thing to do. Likewise, when one's future income is uncertain, it is rational to reduce consumption in the present. Short time horizons, however, cannot be seen as rational unless one has a terminal disease or other reasons for believing that periods beyond, for example, three years, should not be considered when making saving and spending decisions. Use of short time horizons seems to increase impatience, which is logical since outcomes further into the future are completely ignored. Short time horizons seem to be one reason why some people use very high discount rates when deciding how much to spend in the present.

5.9 Saving motives

Why do people save, and how does this relate to economic models of inter-temporal choice? Keynes (1936) identified eight motives for saving, a list that has stood the test of time. According to Browning and Lusardi (1996), only one motive – to create a lump sum of money for making down-payments for expensive and durable goods – needs to be added, though in our view this is just a variant of motive 6. This is Keynes' list:

(1)   to build up a reserve against unforeseen contingencies (the precautionary motive)
(2)   to provide for the anticipated future relationship between income and needs (the life-cycle motive)
(3)   to enjoy interest (the inter-temporal substitution motive)
(4)   to enjoy a gradually improving expenditure (the improvement motive)
(5)   to enjoy a sense of independence and power to do things (the independence motive)
(6)   to secure a masse de manoeuvre to carry out speculative or business projects (the enterprise motive)
(7)   to bequeath a fortune (the bequest motive)
(8)   to satisfy pure miserliness (the avarice motive)

Most economic theories of saving concentrate on motive 2 (the most obvious reason for saving today is to spend tomorrow), though recent theories, for example Carroll's buffer-stock model, also focus on motive 1 (the need to have a reserve for emergencies).

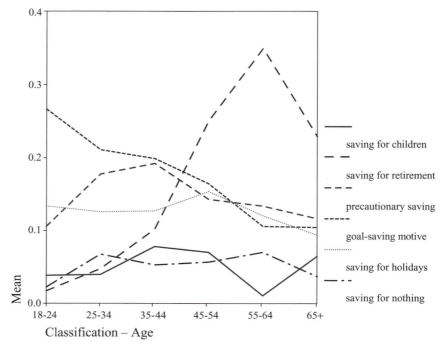

Figure 5.3 Savings motives in the UK. Adapted from Webley and Burgoyne, 2003

There is now a large body of literature that has investigated the importance of different motivations to save. The earliest example is the work of Katona (1975), who showed that the most important motive for saving was 'emergencies', followed by the desire to have funds in reserve for necessities, with saving for interest and the bequest motive both being unimportant. The importance of the precautionary motive across a wide range of countries (e.g. Alessie, Lusardi and Aldershof, 1997; Horioka and Watanabe, 1997) has been confirmed, as has lack of importance of the bequest motive. The pattern of the importance varies across countries and different groups (for example, Japanese families save mainly for retirement and for precautionary reasons, whereas immigrant Canadians of SE Asian origins save mainly for emergencies and for their children's education) but in no country is the precautionary motive unimportant and the pattern of importance of savings motives across the lifespan is consistent. A recent example involves the studies carried out by Webley and Burgoyne (2003) using Lloyds TSB's savings monitor. Their results show that being prepared for emergencies (having a 'buffer') is indeed an important motive in the UK for saving at all ages, but is never the most important motive (which for young adults is saving for particular goals – cars, houses, etc., and for older adults is saving for retirement) (see figure 5.3). These results also confirm that saving for a buffer is more important to younger people while older people tend to save for retirement.

Problems with this and the similar studies of savings motives described above are threefold. First, they rely on respondents indicating how important a set of stated motives are for saving. But the list provided may not be complete and prompting individuals in this way may result in them endorsing motives that were not actually in their mind. Second, it is not at all clear how the strength of different savings motives actually relates to saving behaviour. Third, some saving may satisfy many motives at the same time. For example, saving by investing in a house may satisfy the goal-saving motive (saving for the house itself), the precautionary-saving motive, the retirement-saving motive as well as the bequest motive. The equity may be used to satisfy different needs, although it is not certain which one it eventually will be used for at the time the decision to invest in a house is made. The questions used in surveys have not allowed respondents to clarify if and how the same money may be used for different purposes depending on future circumstances.

One study that overcomes the first problem (but not the second and third) is that of Canova, Manganelli Rattazzi and Webley (2005). A total of 141 British adults answered a mail-questionnaire and 97 participants stated that they intended to save during the next twelve months. Those intending to save had to provide four reasons why they wanted to save, then explain why these reasons were important, and they were then asked to give further justifications. The savers were more positive about the economic situation of the UK and were more optimistic. The analysis of the reasons for saving revealed three general orientations: (1) the need to avoid debt and achieve a certain security in life (essentially a precautionary motive), (2) the desire for self-gratification (holidays, etc.) (the reason that emerged overall as the most significant, and that relates very directly to the life-cycle motive) and (3) a focus on old age (which links to both the precautionary and the life-cycle motive). What was distinctive here was that saving for retirement was important to guarantee gratification rather than security.

This work confirms that economists were right to concentrate on life-cycle saving and buffer saving, the motives that have linked most closely to inter-temporal choice models. The pattern of change of importance over the lifespan found in surveys is similar to that proposed by Fisher (1930), who discussed factors that would influence the rate of time preference. He described the following typical life-cycle profile. A child will be impatient because children in general lack foresight and self-control. A young man will still have a high degree of impatience, because he expects large increases in income. When he has settled down and has a family, the impatience will decrease, because he will be forced to think more about meeting future needs. In the 'empty-nest' stage, the impatience will increase due to a shorter expected remaining lifetime. In addition, Fisher noted that uncertainty about future income streams would decrease impatience to spend. There is still little research linking saving motives to the rate of time preference, but the evidence found so far suggests that Fisher's views about the association between motives to save and the variation in time preference over the lifespan are plausible.

5.10   The social dimension

One major problem with models of inter-temporal choice and models of saving is that, like many theories in economics, they are highly individualistic. The models say nothing about how household saving decisions may play out in practice (one can imagine that the intra-psychic approach of Shefrin and Thaler might equally well work in a family, with one spouse being a 'planner' and the other a 'doer'). They also assume that individuals act in a self-contained way and that the saving or inter-temporal behaviour of others has no relevance to individual choices.

As in other areas (see the chapter by Burgoyne and Kirchler in this volume), it is important to understand both individual and household saving. Daniel and Webley (1998) studied households in the south-west of England and found that there was a positive correlation between the scores of spouses on most psychological variables (such as measures of impulsiveness and future orientation). Similar findings are reported by Webley and Nyhus (2006). Daniel and Webley report that these correlations were higher for those couples who had been married longer (which suggests that a convergence of dispositions happens over time) whilst Webley and Nyhus report that spouses have similar experiences of economic socialization. Using psychological information from each couple member significantly improved predictions for total savings and regular saving in both studies.

The DU model assumes that that behaviour is independent of other people's preferences and choices. Social scientists such as anthropologists (e.g. Douglas and Isherwood, 1996), marketers (e.g. Coleman, 1983) and social psychologists (e.g. Baxter, 1988; Crosby, 1976) have, on the other hand, long recognized that consumer behaviour cannot be fully understood unless consideration is given to the effects of interpersonal influence. Unfavourable comparisons with peers have also been proposed as a factor that may increase temptation (Hoch and Loewenstein, 1991). The first attempts to define saving models that included notions of social comparison were those of Brady and Friedman (1947), Duesenberry (1949) and Modigliani (1949). Duesenberry (1949), for instance, proposed a saving model that focused on relative income and past income. He argued that consumption expenditures are strongly influenced by comparisons with other persons' consumption. His theory was built on the belief that people compare themselves to people they meet on a regular basis. Hence an individual's saving decisions may depend on 'the frequency with which he has to make an unfavourable comparison between the quality of the goods he uses with those used by others' (Duesenberry, 1949, p. 31). Consumption patterns would therefore spread through groups in society that share commonalities (e.g. neighbours or work colleagues). More recently, Schor (1998) has proposed that people tend to compare themselves to the lifestyles and consumption patterns they are exposed to through the mass media rather than to their neighbours.

Duesenberry's theory has been rather downplayed in the economic literature. A couple of studies, however, show that models of saving and borrowing behaviour may be improved by allowing for interdependent preferences. Kapteyn (2000) found that the incomes in one's reference group have an unambiguously negative effect on savings. Respondents were asked about the average total net income per year of the 'households of their acquaintances', which Kapteyn (2000) assumed represented the reference group of the respondents. He found that reported reference group incomes tended to be lower than the respondents' own household incomes. Although the measures of saving used in this study were rather rough, the results were convincing: household income and reference group income were significant predictors of household saving. Schor (1998) estimated a savings function which included variables intended to capture the impact of interpersonal comparisons on savings behaviour and compared it to a model that did not contain such variables. One model contained socio-economic variables such as income, age, sex, occupation and education level, while the other model also included a comparative variable capturing the respondents' perception of how well off they are compared to their reference group. Using a sample of middle- and upper-middle-class people from the United States, she found that the comparison variable improved the performance of the model and that it had great impact on the expected saving. Those who believed that they had a worse financial situation compared to their reference group reported lower expected savings. Interestingly, she also found a negative relationship between expected saving and daily hours spent watching television. So it may be the case, as suggested by Hoch and Loewenstein (1991), that unfavourable comparisons between one's own situation and the consumption level of 'others' may produce spending temptations. Moreover, if it is the case that repeated temptations deplete cognitive resources, people who are constantly exposed to people who they perceive as better off are more likely to give in to spending temptations in the end.

5.11 The development of saving by children and adolescents and its relationship with inter-temporal choice behaviour

Consistent with the findings that ability to wait increases with age, saving increases with age (Ward, Wackman and Wartella, 1977; Furnham and Thomas, 1984), and this is not simply a result of the fact that income also increases with age. The savings motives of children are rather different to those of adults (not surprisingly as their parents protect them in case of emergencies).

Thus, according to Furnham and Thomas, older children save because they anticipate needing money in the future whereas younger children save for concrete targets (such as a computer game). Older children are much more likely to save using saving accounts in financial institutions, which is partly the result of an increased ability to use pre-commitment strategies.

We earlier described how children learn to wait. In delay experiments the price the child has to pay to get the bigger reward is the time she has to sit and wait. In saving, a child does not have to wait in the same way and has to make a whole series of decisions (to add to savings, to withdraw) over time. But some of the things children are learning, such as the control of their attention and how to implement personal rules, will be helpful in learning how to save.

A broader picture of the processes underlying saving by children can be found in the series of studies of saving carried out by Webley and his colleagues (Webley, Levine and Lewis, 1993; Sonuga-Barke and Webley, 1993; Otto, Schots, Westerman and Webley, 2006). Sonuga-Barke and Webley carried out a number of studies using a savings board game. Children earned tokens on an operant task and then played a board game which was designed to present them with problems similar to those that they might experience in the real world. In one study, for instance, children were faced with temptation in the form of a sweet shop. Solutions to these problems were available in the game and these included a bank, where money could be deposited to keep it safe. The exact problems and solutions represented on the board game varied from one study to the next, but in each case there was a toyshop, where the child chose the target toy to save for, and a bank.

Otto *et al*. (2006) used a board game of a different design which also included tempting shops, and had banks as one of the possible solutions. During the game the board 'unfolded', which meant that the children were dealing with an unknown future: they did not know how long the game would last nor what opportunities (or problems) would be encountered as the game proceeded. It was also possible to manipulate income uncertainty in this game.

Webley, Levine and Lewis (1993) took a rather different approach and operationalized the problem of saving temporally rather than spatially. They used a play economy set up in a suite of rooms, where a range of activities were available. Some activities (e.g. a library of children's books) were free, but others, such as playing a computer game, cost a fixed amount. For other activities, buying sweets from a shop and drinks from a café, the costs varied. The experiment lasted a 'speeded-up' week, where each day lasted ten minutes. During each 'day' each child would be given ten tokens and spent ten minutes in a room where a free, a fixed-cost and a variable-cost activity were available. In order to obtain their target toy, chosen at the beginning of the study, children had to save seventy tokens out of the ninety they were given in the course of the game. Sixty tokens were given out as pocket money and there was an initial endowment of thirty tokens in a bank account.

All these studies investigated saving in different ways but the results provide a consistent picture. By the time they are six years old, children have learnt that saving is an activity that has a social value. To be patient, to be thrifty, to exercise self-control, to think about the future are all seen (by the adult world) to be virtuous. The children do not like saving much (immediate consumption is much more fun) and they are not very good at it. In one of the board games, for example, children could deposit their tokens in a bank before they went past the sweet shop and then take them out again when they had passed the danger. The four-year-olds used the bank randomly. Six-year-olds used the bank but not consistently, whereas nine- and twelve-year-olds both used and understood the function of the bank. Mary, aged nine years, said 'I won't take it out of the bank as I don't want to be tempted.' In the play economy six-year-olds also showed a limited ability to save, and half of them did not manage to save at all. Many children at this age saw money saved as money lost. By the time children are in the nine-to-twelve age range they will seem to understand the problem that saving helps to solve. But they have developed a range of other strategies for getting hold of money when they need it (saving is only one possible way of achieving this end). These are nearly always techniques for obtaining money from their parents and other relatives. Negotiating, arguing with, and emotional blackmailing of parents are all possible options – in other words, their economic behaviour is also social behaviour and to do it justice we need to understand it within a social context.

One important context is the family. Webley and Nyhus (2006) used Dutch panel data to compare the future orientation, conscientiousness and saving of young people aged sixteen to twenty-one with those of their parents in order to explore the notion that an approach to economic problems and decisions is transferred from one generation to the next. Their results showed that parental behaviour (such as discussing financial matters with children) and parental orientations (conscientiousness, future orientation) had a weak but clear impact on children's economic behaviour. Conscientious parents tended to have conscientious children. In a follow-up study which looked at grandparents as well as parents in both Norway and England, Nyhus and Webley (2005) confirmed these findings, although the relationships were relatively weak and mothers had a greater impact than fathers.

How does this developmental work relate to the discounted utility model? The reader will recall that Strotz (1955–6) believed that we are born with hyperbolic discount functions, but that we learn to deal with them through parental and social teaching. It is clear that what children are learning is self-control and planning strategies, and general approaches to economic life. Adults have learned to live in a world where they must plan for a lifetime much longer than that in which their preferences and predispositions evolved (see the chapter by Lea in this volume). They have a wide range of institutional commitment devices (illiquid assets of one kind or another, contracts for regular saving, etc.)

to save themselves from themselves. But their basic preference for the here and now remains.

5.12 Conclusions

The psychology of inter-temporal choice is intriguing and is relevant to many of our daily decisions. Research over the past decades has given us much more insight into factors that influence such choices and – now – how the brain functions when making these decisions. This has increased our understanding of behaviours related to spending, saving and borrowing, and helped explain why observed behaviour deviates from the predictions of the rational model. The psychology of inter-temporal choice is, however, also very complex and difficult to study. Experiments have revealed many different factors that seem to influence the preference for present consumption over delayed consumption. In particular, the observation that consumers are affected by framing effects makes it difficult to predict behaviour outside the laboratory. The choice between consumption today and consumption tomorrow may depend on how the consumer interprets the choice situation, which puts a premium on research to find out how framing works in everyday life settings. This may interact with dispositions such as optimism and future orientation or situational factors such as a relatively low income level which may make the consumer feel chronically deprived.

The study of the psychology of saving and borrowing behaviour is, if anything, even more challenging. There are several reasons for this. First, saving during a certain period is a consequence of a series of inter-temporal decisions. So far, we know little about consistency in inter-temporal choices, although some findings suggest that it is reasonable to expect that a person who delays gratification in one situation is likely to do so in another. Some research even suggests that this tendency to delay gratification is shaped in childhood and adolescence and that delay of gratification behaviour in childhood predicts behaviour in adulthood. But there are still too many consumers showing inconsistency in their delay of gratification behaviour to conclude that ability to delay gratification is a consistent disposition. For example, a person who has been able to save and become rich may still be overweight and smoke. Second, there are challenges associated with defining who is a saver and who is a borrower since this may vary depending on the accounting period used when making the classification. This may in certain cases lead to wrong conclusions about what factors typically characterize a saver and what factors typically characterize a borrower. It may be necessary to focus on accounting periods of different lengths as well as to look at behaviour over long periods in order to be able to classify consumers appropriately. Third, many consumers share accommodation with their family and are likely to make a large number of consumption and borrowing decisions in collaboration with them. Hence, in order to predict their saving and borrowing it may well be necessary to know the inter-temporal consumption preferences of all household members as well as their relative influence in family decision making. This is still an area that needs more research efforts before we know how to weigh diverging preference patterns among family members when predicting their behaviour. Fourth, it is still not clear how the two research streams on saving behaviour should be combined. On the one hand, we have experimental evidence that shows individual and situational factors that may influence inter-temporal consumption decisions. On the other hand, we have survey evidence that shows that saving behaviour is related to variables such as time horizon, future orientation, saving motives and saving attitudes. It is still premature to combine these findings in order to build a psychological model of saving behaviour.

The saving literature is a good example of how psychology can contribute towards explaining and predicting economic behaviour. The traditional economic models which do not consider the psychological mechanisms underlying saving and borrowing behaviour have shown limited predictive power and contribute little to explaining observed behaviour. They also fail to provide the basis for sound advice about how saving can be stimulated so that individual or national saving targets are reached. The research presented in this chapter shows that use of psychological insights is a fruitful way to improve the traditional models. It should therefore encourage further research on the psychological mechanisms underlying saving behaviour with the aim of constructing saving and consumption models which incorporate both the effect of socio-economic and psychological variables and any interaction between them.

5.13 References

Ainslie, G. (1975). Specious reward: A behavioral theory of impulsiveness and impulse control. *Psychological Bulletin*, 82, 463–96.

(1992). *Picoeconomics: The Strategic Interaction of Successive Motivational States within the Person*. New York: Cambridge University Press.

(1993). Picoeconomics. A bargaining model of the will and its lapses. Paper presented at the Marcus Wallenberg Symposium, Will and Economic Behavior, Stockholm School of Economics, Stockholm.

Alessie, R., Lusardi, A., and Aldershof, T. (1997). Income and wealth over the life-cycle: Evidence from panel data. *Review of Income and Wealth*, 43, 1–31.

Ayduk, O., Mendoza-Denton, R., Mischel, W., Downey, G., Peake, P. K., and Rodriguez, M. (2000). Regulating the inter-personal self: Strategic self-regulation for coping with rejection sensitivity. *Journal of Personality and Social Psychology*, 79 (5), 776–92.

Banks, J., Blundell, R., and Brugiavini, A. (1995). Income uncertainty and consumption growth. IFS working paper (ifsewp: 95–13). London: Institute for Fiscal Studies.

Baxter, J. L. (1988). *Social and Psychological Foundation of Economic Analysis*. New York: Harvester Wheatsheaf.

Benzion, U., Rapoport, A., and Yagil, J. (1989). Discount rates inferred from decisions: An experimental study. *Management Science*, 35, 270–84.

Brady, D. S., and Friedman, R. D. (1947). Savings and the income distribution. *Studies in Income and Wealth*, 10, 247–65.

Brown, S., Garino, G., Taylor, K., and Price, S. W. (2005). Debt and financial expectations: an individual- and household-level analysis. *Economic Inquiry*, 43, 100–20.

Browning, M., and Lusardi, A. (1996). Household savings: Micro theories and micro facts. *Journal of Economic Literature*, 34, 1797–1855.

Camerer, C. F., Loewenstein, G. F., and Prelec, D. (2005). Neuroeconomics: How neuroscience can inform economics. *Journal of Economic Literature*, 43, 9–64.

Canova, L., Manganelli Rattazzi, M., and Webley, P. (2005). The hierarchical structure of saving motives. *Journal of Economic Psychology*, 26, 21–34.

Carroll, C. D. (1994). How does future income affect current consumption? *Quarterly Journal of Economics*, 109, 111–47.

(1997). Buffer-stock saving and the life cycle/permanent income hypothesis. *Quarterly Journal of Economics*, 112, 1–56.

Coleman, R. P. (1983). The continuing significance of social class to marketing. *Journal of Consumer Research*, 10, 265–80.

Crosby, F. (1976). A model of egoistic relative deprivation. *Psychological Review*, 83, 85–113.

Daniel, T., and Webley, P. (1998). Individual differences and research into saving. In workshop on individual differences in economic behaviour. International Centre for Economic Research, Turin, March 1998.

Douglas, M., and Isherwood, B. (1996). *The World of Goods. Towards an Anthropology of Consumption*. London: Routledge.

Duesenberry, J. S. (1949). *Income, Saving and the Theory of Consumer Behavior*. Cambridge, MA: Harvard University Press.

Elster, J. (1979). *Ulysses and the Sirens. Studies in Rationality and Irrationality*. New York: Cambridge University Press.

Fishburn, P. C., and Rubinstein, A. (1982). Time preference. *International Economic Review*, 23, 677–94.

Fisher, I. (1930). *The Theory of Interest as Determined by Impatience to Spend Income and Opportunity to Invest It*. New York: Macmillan.

Frederick, S., Loewenstein, G., and O'Donoghue, T. (2002). Time discounting and time preference: A critical review. *Journal of Economic Literature*, 40, 351–401.

Friedman, M. (1957). *A Theory of the Consumption Function*. Princeton, NJ: Princeton University Press.

Furnham, A., and Thomas, P. (1984). Adults' perception of economic socialization of children. *Journal of Adolescence*, 7, 217–31.

Gourinchas, P.-O., and Parker, J. (1999). *Consumption Over the Lifecycle* (NBER Working Paper No. 7271). Cambridge, MA: National Bureau of Economic Research.

Guiso, L., Jappelli, T., and Terlizzese, D. (1992). Earnings uncertainty and precautionary saving. *Journal of Monetary Economics*, 30, 307–37.

Harris, C. J., and Laibson, D. (2001). Dynamic choices of hyperbolic consumers. *Econometrica*, 69, 935–57.

Hoch, S. J., and Loewenstein, G. F. (1991). Time-inconsistent preferences and consumer self-control. *Journal of Consumer Research*, 17, 492–507.

Horioka, C. Y., and Watanabe, W. (1997). Why do people save? A micro-analysis of motives for household saving in Japan. *Economic Journal*, 107, 537–52.

Horowitz, J. K. (1991). Discounting money payoffs: An experimental analysis. In S. Kaish and B. Gilad (eds.), *Handbook of Behavioral Economics*, vol. 2B, pp. 309–24. Greenwich: JAI Press.

Kapteyn, A. (2000). Saving and reference groups. Mimeo. Tilburg University.

Katona, G. (1975). *Psychological Economics*. New York: Elsevier.

Keynes, J. M. (1936). *The General Theory of Employment Interest and Money*. London: Macmillan.

Laibson, D. (1997). Golden eggs and hyperbolic discounting. *Quarterly Journal of Economics*, 112, 443–77.

(1998). Life-cycle consumption and hyperbolic discount functions. *European Economic Review*, 42, 861–71.

Laibson, D., Repetto, A., and Tobacman, J. (2003). A debt puzzle. In P. Aghion, R. Frydman, J. Stiglitz, and M. Woodford (eds.), *Knowledge, Information, and Expectations in Modern Macroeconomics: In Honor of Edmund S. Phelps*, pp. 228–66. Princeton, NJ: Princeton University Press.

Loewenstein, G. F. (1988). Frames of mind in intertemporal choice. *Management Science*, 34, 200–14.

(1992). The fall and rise of psychological explanations in the economics of intertemporal choice. In G. F. Loewenstein and J. Elster (eds.), *Choice Over Time*, pp. 3–34. New York: Russell Sage Foundation.

(1996). Out of control: Visceral influences on behavior. *Organizational Behavior and Human Decision Processes*, 65, 272–92.

Loewenstein, G. F., and Prelec, D. (1992). Anomalies in intertemporal choice: Evidence and an interpretation. *Quarterly Journal of Economics*, 107, 73–97.

Loewenstein, G. F., and Thaler, R. H. (1989). Anomalies: Intertemporal choice. *Journal of Economic Perspectives*, 3, 181–93.

Lusardi, A. (1993). *Precautionary Saving and Subjective Earnings Variance* (VSB-CentER savings project progress report No. 16). Tilburg, the Netherlands: Tilburg University, CentER for Economic Research.

McClure, S. M., Laibson, D. I., Loewenstein, G., and Cohen, J. D. (2004). Separate neural systems value immediate and delayed monetary rewards. *Science*, 306, 503–7.

Maital, S., and Maital, S. L. (1994). Is the future what it used to be? A behavioral theory of the decline of saving in the West. *Journal of Socio-Economics*, 23, 1–32.

Metcalfe, J., and Mischel, W. (1999). A hot/cool system analysis of delay of gratification: Dynamics of willpower. *Psychological Review*, 106 (1), 3–19.

Mischel, W., Shoda, Y., and Peake, P. K. (1988). The nature of adolescent competencies predicted by preschool delay of gratification. *Journal of Personality and Social Psychology*, 54, 687–96.

Mischel, W., Shoda, Y., and Rodriguez, M. L. (1989). Delay of gratification in children. *Science*, 244, 933–8.

Modigliani, F. (1949). Fluctuations in the saving–income ratio: A problem in economic forecasting. *Studies in Income and Wealth*, 11, 371–438.

Modigliani, F., and Brumberg, R. (1954). Utility analysis and the consumption function: An interpretation of cross-section data. In K. K. Kurihara (ed.), *Post-Keynesian Economics*, pp. 388–438. New Brunswick, NJ: Rutgers University Press.

Murayen, M., and Baumeister, R. F. (2000). Self-regulation and depletion of limited resources: Does self-control resemble a muscle? *Psychological Bulletin*, 126, 247–59.

Nyhus, E. K., and Webley, P. (2005). The inter-generational transmission of future orientation and saving preferences. Paper presented at the Thirtieth Annual Conference of IAREP, Prague, September 2005.

Otto, A. M. C., Schots, P. A. M., Westerman, J. A. J., and Webley, P. (2006). Children's use of saving strategies: An experimental approach. *Journal of Economic Psychology*, 27, 57–72.

Read, D. (2001). Is time-discounting hyperbolic or subadditive? *Journal of Risk and Uncertainty*, 23, 5–32.

Read, D., Orsel, B., Rahman, J., and Frederick, S. (2004). Four score and seven years from now: The 'date/delay effect' in temporal discounting (Working Paper LSEOR 04.65). Department of Operational Research, London School of Economics and Political Science.

Samuelson, Paul A. (1937). A note on measurement of utility. *Review of Economic Studies*, 4, 155–61.

Samwick, A. A. (1998). Discount rate heterogeneity and social security reform. *Journal of Development Economics*, 57, 117–47.

Schelling, T. C. (1984). Self-command in practice, in policy and in a theory of rational choice. *American Economic Review, Papers and Proceedings*, 74, 1–11.

Schor, J. B. (1998). *The Overspent American*. New York: Basic Books.

Shefrin, H. M., and Thaler, R. H. (1988). The behavioral life-cycle hypotheses. *Economic Inquiry*, 26, 609–43.

Shelley, M. K. (1993). Outcome signs, question frames, and discount rates. *Management Science*, 39, 806–15.

Shiv, B., and Fedorikhin, A. (1999). Heart and mind in conflict: Interplay of affect and cognition in consumer decision making. *Journal of Consumer Research*, 26, 278–82.

Shoda, Y., Mischel, W., and Peake, P. K. (1990). Predicting adolescent cognitive and social competence from preschool delay of gratification: Identifying diagnostic conditions. *Developmental Psychology*, 26, 978–86.

Sonuga-Barke, E. J. S., and Webley, P. (1993). *Children's Saving*. Hove: Erlbaum.

Strotz, R. H. (1955–6). Myopia and inconsistency in dynamic utility maximization. *Review of Economic Studies*, 23, 163–80.

Thaler, R. H. (1981). Some empirical evidence on dynamic inconsistency. *Economic Letters*, 8, 201–7.

Van Raaij, W. F., and Gianotten, H. J. (1990). Consumer confidence, expenditure, saving and credit. *Journal of Economic Psychology*, 11, 269–90.

Vohs, K. D., and Faber, R. J. (2007). Spent resources: Self-regulatory resource availability affects impulse buying. *Journal of Consumer Research*, 33, 537–48.

Ward, S., Wackman, D. B., and Wartella, E. (1977). *How Children Learn to Buy.* London: Sage Publications.

Wärneryd, K.-E. (1989). On the psychology of saving: An essay on economic behaviour. *Journal of Economic Psychology*, 4, 297–317.

(1999). *The Psychology of Saving. A Study on Economic Psychology.* Cheltenham: Edward Elgar.

(2000). Personality: future-orientation, self-control and saving. Paper presented at the XXVII International Congress of Psychology, Stockholm

Webley, P., and Burgoyne, C. B. (2003). Saving behaviour in Britain. Paper presented at the IAREP workshop, Kristiansand, December 2003.

Webley, P., Levine, R. M., and Lewis, A. (1993). A study in economic psychology: Children's saving in a play economy. In S. Maital and S. Maital (eds.), *Economics and Psychology*, pp. 61–80. Cheltenham: Edward Elgar.

Webley, P., and Nyhus, E. K. (2006). Parents' influence on children's future orientation and saving. *Journal of Economic Psychology*, 27, 140–64.

Zhou, Y. (2003). Precautionary saving and earnings uncertainty in Japan: A household-level analysis. *Journal of Japanese and International Economies*, 17, 192–212.

6 Financial decisions in the household

CAROLE BURGOYNE AND ERICH KIRCHLER

6.1 Introduction

Why should we be interested in studying intra-household economic behaviour? There are many reasons. First, the household is a prime site for cooperation, negotiation of conflicts of interest and settlement of disagreements. Many issues will concern money and other resources. Whilst serious conflicts are relatively rare in enduring relationships (McGonagle, Kessler and Schilling, 1992; Straus and Sweet, 1992), partners may disagree about a whole host of issues almost daily (Gottman, 1994; Holmes, 1989; Surra and Longstreth, 1990). This makes the household a natural target for researchers in economic psychology. Secondly, those with statutory duties concerning families need accurate information on which to base the development of policies. It goes without saying that government policy can impact upon individuals within households (through changes, for example, in the tax and benefit laws). However, the decisions taken by individuals within households can also have significant effects upon the economy, given that private households dispose of a major part of a nation's financial resources. Another example of this is the dramatic increase in the number of lone parent families following the liberalization of divorce laws in most European countries in the 1970s and 1980s and the consequent rise in welfare expenditure. Thirdly, the convenient assumption, by both researchers and policy makers in the past, that a household is essentially an income-pooling entity with a common standard of living, has been shown to be misguided. It is now well documented that inequalities in the wider economy can be reflected in differential access to household money and other resources. Given the obvious links between money and power (see Pahl, 1995), this clearly has ramifications for the physical and psychological welfare of economically weaker household members (see Webley, Burgoyne, Lea and Young, 2001, pp. 82–3). For example, measures of welfare based on an assumption of income sharing in the household will seriously underestimate individual poverty. Finally, economic models that fail to take account of systematic variations in household financial practices will inevitably be less accurate in predicting the impact of policies aimed (for example) at enhancing the well-being of children, encouraging debt avoidance or saving for a pension.

However, getting a clear picture of economic behaviour within the household is far from easy. From the outset, we are dealing with an entity that is relatively private and difficult to define, with fuzzy boundaries which may change over time (Kirchler, Rodler, Hoelzl and Meier, 2001; Wilkes, 1995). It is subject to many different influences at both micro- and macro-economic levels, and there is a great deal of variability both within and between households. The composition and activities of a household may change quite abruptly with the arrival and departure of children or with movements in and out of the labour market. Not all households are composed of couples or 'traditional' families, and families as well as couples may extend across a number of different households (Gershuny, 2000). A further complication is that within the family, financial practices can be constructed in two opposing discourses – those of economic versus social exchange. Many household activities (such as cooking meals for the family or carrying out household repairs) contain elements of both, that is, they are clearly economic activities but can also be seen as expressions of care-giving or love (see Webley *et al.*, 2001), and accounts will differ depending on how one approaches the question. The 'rules' governing economic exchange tend to be at odds with those of social exchange, especially within intimate family relationships (Curtis, 1986). For example, it is generally accepted that one has the right to own and control one's earnings; at the same time, the belief that marriage should be a partnership with shared resources is widely endorsed. Couples may attempt to resolve this contradiction in many different ways. When it comes to the allocation of benefits and burdens, people may draw upon different rules of distributive justice, such as equity, equality and need (Deutsch, 1975). If money is allocated on the basis of equity, then the biggest contributor is entitled to a greater share of the 'cake'. In contrast, an equality rule would dictate that everyone has an equal share, regardless of contribution. Even if need is taken as a criterion, this still leaves unresolved who will determine when, and to what extent, a need exists. When we add to this powerful mix the notion that love and money are in many respects incommensurable (Foa, 1971), then it is not difficult to see why economic issues in this context may give rise to feelings of ambivalence and ambiguity. Conflicts of interest, inequalities and power struggles, both overt and covert, all contrive to make household economic behaviour a somewhat thorny topic of investigation (Webley *et al.*, 2001).

6.2 Heterogeneity of households and families

Current researchers have largely discarded the earlier practice of relying upon the reports of one partner, though much of the previous research has focused upon relatively traditional family households comprising a married couple and their dependent children (Burgoyne, 2004; Kirchler *et al.*, 2001). However, the stereotypical image of a family as comprising one man and one woman plus (2.4) children accounted for only 42 per cent of households in Europe in 1998 (Antonides and van Raaij, 1998) and traditional marriage throughout the Western world is declining rapidly as alternative family forms become more widespread (Seltzer, 2004; Cherlin, 2004; Kiernan, 2004). Marriage is now just one option: it has almost become a lifestyle choice, and its nature, meaning and practice are shifting in parallel with other social changes. For example: many women now spend time developing a career before considering marriage and childbirth (Ermisch and Francesconi, 2000; Social Trends, 2004; Wunderink, 1995), and a substantial number continue in paid employment thereafter. Remarriage has become more common following the liberalization of the divorce laws, and alternatives to marriage are now more acceptable than was the case for previous generations. One of the most notable changes in the last quarter of the twentieth century was the huge increase in the number of couples living together without marrying, many also having children outside wedlock. The increasing acceptability of same-sex unions has led to new legislation in some countries that can offer marriage or marriage-like rights and responsibilities to same-sex couples: at the time of writing, same-sex marriage is permitted in Belgium, the Netherlands, Spain, Canada, and the US state of Massachusetts. The UK enacted a form of Civil Partnerships legislation in December 2004 and the UK Law Commission is actively considering an extension of such legislation to include cohabiting couples. However (as we see later), policy based on the presumed marital model of financial interdependence may be out of step with what couples are actually doing.

In sum, more than at any other time in the last hundred years, couples in Western societies seem to have more freedom to determine the type of intimate relationship they have, and their respective roles within it. Barlow, Duncan, James and Park (2005, p. 92) put it succinctly: 'The social structures that gave marriage its power to attract people into, and hold them in, partnerships for life have been greatly weakened. Externally imposed religious and moral codes are a declining force, women's financial and emotional independence has increased, people see partnership more as a part of personal fulfilment than a social duty, sex and childbearing are now separated from marriage, and both divorce and cohabitation are accepted and pervasive.'

This is clearly a topic that could take us far beyond the scope of this chapter. Therefore we have confined our discussion to those areas most studied: money management and decision making in family households. For the purposes of this chapter we shall use the terms 'household' and 'family' fairly loosely to refer to households involving intimate relationships between two adults, who may or may not have resident children, and lone parent households with one or more dependent children. We begin by examining money management, persuasion and negotiation in traditional heterosexual couples.

6.3 'Traditional' households

6.3.1 Money management in heterosexual marriage

The stereotypical roles of male breadwinner and female carer have been described by Becker (1973) as a rational use of human capital for individual utility-maximizers, and it is the model that many heterosexual couples currently follow (see also Grossbard-Schechtman, 1993). They do so not just for the sake of tradition (though that is certainly a factor) but because it makes sense for each individual couple to adhere to this pattern when male earnings are (typically) higher than women's and the latter bear the children. Becker's (1973) thesis is that marriage offers gains in trade by means of specialized human capital, the sharing of public goods (e.g., the family home) and economies of scale. This model also assumes that women will invest primarily in domestic capital since women have a 'comparative advantage' in bearing and caring for children.

However, Becker has been criticized for ignoring a great many factors that constrain the choices of real couples, such as the typically lower wage rates for women, and normative expectations about who will provide child-care (Bergmann, 1986; 1995; see also Webley *et al.*, 2001, pp. 79–82). In addition, the traditional division of labour in heterosexual marriage exposes women to economic risk. This is a recurrent finding from a variety of research approaches (e.g., Pahl, 1989; 1995). Despite a public rhetoric depicting (Western) marriage as a partnership of equals (Reibstein and Richards, 1993), few seem to achieve this ideal in practice. Men are more likely to start off with greater earnings than their wives and are more likely to become the principal breadwinners when a couple has children. The resulting disparity between male and female incomes can result in a lower standard of living for wives than husbands within the same household, and less say in decision making. It can also make women financially vulnerable in societies with a high divorce rate.

This vulnerability may be offset or enhanced to the extent that 'market forces' are allowed to enter the household. One important factor here is the way that a couple chooses to treat income and other financial assets. Pahl (1989) identified a number of systems of money management and her typology has been widely used. It includes:

> *The Female Whole Wage system*: where the wife manages all household money apart from the husband's personal spending money;
>
> *The Male Whole Wage system*: in which the husband manages all finances; this can leave the wife with no access to any money;
>
> *The Housekeeping Allowance system*: where the main earner – typically a male breadwinner – gives their partner a sum to cover household expenses and retains control of the rest;

The Pooling system: where most or all of household income is combined – often in a joint account; and

The Independent Management system: where each partner keeps their income in a separate account – more typical for dual-earner couples.

Surveys in the UK during the 1990s (e.g., Laurie and Rose 1994) showed that around half of all couples were using a pooling system, about 36% used a whole wage system, 11% used a housekeeping allowance and around 2% had independent management. More recent studies have observed an increasing use of a hybrid system labelled Partial Pooling (Burgoyne, Clarke, Reibstein and Edmunds, 2006; Pahl, 2005) and we shall examine this system later on. Pahl (2005) also reports increasing individualization in finances in countries as diverse as Spain and Sweden.

An important distinction has been made by Pahl (1989) and others between overall control of money (or strategic power) and management (or executive power). These have different implications for access to personal spending money and the right to allocate money for different purposes. Thus, the female whole wage system may leave overall control in the hands of a male bread-winner who can set priorities for the use of the money that his wife manages on a day-to-day basis. It is also important to realize that pooling may be more apparent than real, with the potential for one partner to have more say on how the money is to be used (Vogler and Pahl, 1994). Male-dominated systems (such as the housekeeping allowance system and male-controlled pooling) are more likely to occur at higher income levels. Women typically have the more onerous task of making ends meet at lower income levels.

There are a number of possible explanations for the financial inequalities that seem to creep into many marriages. First, making a significant financial contribution, especially as the main breadwinner, is both more visible and accorded more privilege (such as greater access to money for personal use, more 'say' in decision making, etc.) than other types of input such as housework or childcare. The situation for mothers who reduce their earning power tends to deteriorate over time as their labour market human capital diminishes (James, 1996; Webley *et al.*, 2001). Secondly, even when partners have a joint account and try to treat money as a collective resource, the source of that income – i.e., who has earned or contributed it – is difficult to ignore (Burgoyne, 1990; Burgoyne and Lewis, 1994; Burgoyne, Clarke, Reibstein and Edmunds, 2006). Another factor is marital ideology, such as a traditional or 'modern' view of marriage and of marital roles (see Reibstein and Richards, 1993). Traditionally the man has the final say, or sets the financial agenda (Pahl, 1989). The degree of commitment is also important, with couples less likely to see money as collectively owned (whatever system they use) when there are doubts about the stability of the relationship (see Burgoyne and Morison's 1997 study of second marriages; Vogler, 2006).

Gender also sets the parameters for other types of behaviour in heterosexual couples. Men are more likely to allocate benefits on the basis of equity whereas women are more likely to opt for equality (Burgoyne and Lewis, 1994). Even in a country like Sweden which is renowned for its attention to equality, Nyman (1999) argues that 'real' equality will remain just an ideal when men are still able to set the overall agenda for money management and women are expected to put the interests of the family before their own. In Nyman's study, the couples had arranged to cover all household expenses jointly, leaving each partner with an equal amount of money for personal use. However, as the wives had day-to-day practical responsibility for meals and childcare, they tended to use their own personal spending money as a buffer to even out household expenses and this was not accounted for. The men seemed able to ignore their wives' pleas to change the way that these expenses were managed, and the women seemed reluctant to press the issue in case it led to conflict. Thus, systems of management that should have left these dual-income partners with equal access to personal spending money paradoxically led to the familiar inequalities associated with gender (see Elizabeth, 2001).

6.3.1.1   Beliefs about financial practices in 'traditional' marriage

We have discussed a number of possible explanations for inequalities in marriage. But do people really think that household money should be shared equally, even when partners are contributing different amounts? This issue was investigated in two studies by Burgoyne and Routh (2001) and Sonnenberg, Burgoyne and Routh (2005). The latter used a series of vignettes describing (a) a couple who were getting married, and (b) a couple about to have their first baby. In both types of vignette, the relative incomes of the partners were varied so that sometimes they earned equally and sometimes one partner was the breadwinner, or earned much more than their partner. Participants in Burgoyne and Routh's (2001) study were asked to choose the 'best' and 'fairest' of a list of possible systems of money management (based upon Pahl's typology), and to say whether or not one partner should have more personal spending money. Overall, regardless of relative income, the most frequently chosen 'best' option was pooling all money and making joint decisions about it. Respondents also tended to identify their choice as the 'fairest'. However, for a significant minority, the partner earning relatively more money was deemed to be entitled to more personal spending money. A similar pattern of results was obtained by Sonnenberg *et al.* (2005). However, one noteworthy new finding was that when the woman was depicted in the role of mother, her income was seen as being by default for the family, with less individual freedom to own and control it. In contrast, the man in the role of father seemed to be accorded a higher degree of financial autonomy. This echoes Nyman's (1999) findings, and those of Pahl (1995), who noted that women tend to be more 'family-focused' than men, typically contributing a larger proportion of their income to the family. Some recent work on bargaining experiments also supports gender differences: both sexes expect women to be more generous in their allocations and to be content with receiving less (Solnick, 2001).

6.3.1.2   Persuasion and negotiation

The freedom to determine the nature of one's relationship, one's role, as well as individual interests and joint goals, requires a complex process of negotiation and decision making. This process has to take account of both individual-level concerns (such as expectations about the relationship: its permanence, stability and individual commitment) and wider economic factors. Such concerns will influence the way that couples try to pursue their own and mutual goals, how they deal with money, and how they make decisions about saving and spending.

Investigations into traditional household spending decisions have identified a number of common patterns. Depending on the type of good, one member of the household may instigate a decision to buy and simply go ahead with the purchase. However, if the decision involves an expensive and infrequent purchase that is socially visible and used by both spouses or all family members (such as an apartment or a car), then there is likely to be a more extensive decision process, which could involve all members of the household (Kirchler,1989; Kirchler *et al.*, 2001).

Joint decision processes are also more likely to occur in the absence of an impulsive or habitual decision. One or both partners may gather information about possible alternatives, evaluate them against needs, and then make a choice. Partners may differ in their interests and the type of information they consider relevant, and so may disagree on which alternative is best. The partners may find their preferred option overruled and may have to change their mind or reach a compromise (Bohlmann and Qualls, 2001). They may also have to make a trade-off between satisfying their individual wants and needs, and maintaining a harmonious relationship.

If partners have divergent views and wish to avoid a heated conflict whilst achieving their individual goals, the decision may pass through a number of stages. They may move to and fro between the stage of wanting the good and gathering relevant information; they may try, by factual argument, manipulation, flattery or threats, to persuade the other to yield, or they may offer an exchange deal, such as performing a household service or offering another favour in return.

Kirchler *et al.* (2001) identified eighteen different tactics that spouses might use to persuade their partners (see table 6.1). Some of these tactics are designed to avoid conflicts (tactics 13, 14 and 15 in table 6.1): these usually derive from role segregation or social norms which assign roles and influence either to the woman or to the man, a process known as *role competence*. This allows one partner to take on particular tasks by default, including responsibility and control over that sphere of decision making. Once task areas have been assigned or assumed in this way, partners generally accept that one will act autonomously, but with the other's wishes in mind.

A second category of tactics is concerned with 'problem solving' (e.g., tactic 18 in table 6.1). These tactics include reasoned arguments and factual information which serve to clarify the situation, typically used when partners

Table 6.1 *Classification of tactics. From Kirchler, E. et al. 2001.* Conflict and decision making in close relationships. *Reprinted with permission from The Psychology Press, a member of the Taylor & Francis Group*

Tactic content	Tactic label	Examples
Emotion	1. Positive emotions	Manipulation, flattery, smiling, humour, seductive behaviour.
	2. Negative emotions	Threats, cynicism, ridicule, shouting.
Physical force	3. Helplessness	Crying, showing weaknesses, acting ill.
	4. Physical force	Forcing, injuring, violence, aggression.
Resources	5. Offering resources	Performing services, being attentive.
	6. Withdrawing resources	Withdrawing financial contributions, punishing.
Presence	7. Insisting	Nagging, constantly returning to the subject, conversations designed to wear down opposition.
	8. Withdrawal	Refusing to share responsibility, changing the subject, going away, leaving the scene.
Information	9. Open presentation of facts	Asking for cooperation, presenting one's own needs, talking openly about importance/interest to self.
	10. Presenting false facts	Suppressing relevant information, distorting information.
Persons	11. Indirect coalition	Referring to other people, emphasizing utility of purchase to children.
	12. Direct coalition	Discussing in the presence of others.
Fact	13. Fait accompli	Buying autonomously, deciding without consulting partner.
Role segmentation	14. Deciding according to roles	Deciding autonomously according to established role segmentation.
	15. Yielding according to roles	Autonomous decision by partner according to role.
Bargaining	16. Trade-offs	Offers of trade-offs, bookkeeping, reminders of past favours.
	17. Integrative bargaining	Search for the best solution to satisfy all concerned.
Reasoned argument	18. Reasoned argument	Presenting factual arguments; logical argument.

Note: Some studies of tactics take account of all eighteen tactics. Occasionally fifteen tactics are discussed. In these cases, tactics 13, 14 and 15 are omitted. A few other studies examine seventeen tactics. There, tactic 15 is omitted.

are in general agreement about their basic aims and are trying to realize them jointly. For example, if they agree that they need a new car, and they also agree on the essential characteristics (e.g., inexpensive, comfortable, safe), their task is relatively straightforward. They simply have to collect information, clarify areas of doubt, evaluate the various alternatives and select the car most likely to fulfil their requirements.

The 'persuasion' tactics (1 to 12 in table 6.1) are likely to be used if partners have conflicting values. Since neither is likely to be convinced by reasoned argument, such tactics may include the use of positive or negative emotions, (e.g., seductive behaviour, threats, cynicism), acting in a helpless way, coercion, etc. In probability and value conflicts, bargaining tactics may also come into play (e.g., tactics 16 and 17 in table 6.1). These may involve 'tit-for-tat' with (for example) offers of trade-offs, 'bookkeeping' and reminders of past favours. Alternatively, 'integrative bargaining' may lead to a search for additional alternatives and options in order to find a solution that satisfies everyone without the need for trade-off or compromise.

However, reaching an agreement does not necessarily signal the end of the decision process. The partner who has dominated the decision may incur an influence 'debt' which could mean having to yield more readily in the next decision. Similarly there may be benefit or 'utility' debts. In his model of purchasing decisions, Pollay (1968) assumes that the utility or benefit of a good is a function of the strength of a partner's need for that good, the frequency of use, and the anticipated degree of satisfaction. For example, if one partner wants to buy an expensive item of clothing and seeks the other's consent, the purchase may go ahead if it coincides with the other's taste and the latter agrees to the purchase. Even when there is no disagreement, the partner who will actually wear the item has incurred 'benefit debts'. Depending on the way that the couple usually deals with the regulation of disparities in benefits, the other partner may expect more acquiescence next time they want to buy something. Thus, a decision is not complete until the partners have agreed explicitly or implicitly on whether there has been an asymmetrical distribution of benefits, and how this should be dealt with.

6.3.1.3   Gender differences in spending decisions

Consumer research interest in 'traditional' family decision making has typically centred on spending decisions and the relative influence of husband and wife. Does the male or female partner have the final say, or do they decide jointly? Are children given a voice in the decision, and if so, on what goods? However, research shows that simply asking people about the outcomes of decisions is unlikely to tell us much about the underlying processes, and may give us a misleading picture of relative influence for different types of decisions.

The Vienna Diary Study (Kirchler et al., 2001) provided a unique opportunity to explore in depth the underlying processes and outcomes of decision making over the period of a year. Participants included forty married and cohabiting couples who had at least one child of school age. The individual partners kept a daily diary of their discussion and decision making. Kirchler *et al.* found that everyday life typically left partners little time for shared activities, not even disagreements. Couples spent only about three to four hours a day in each other's company, including time spent on chores. On average (including weekends and holidays) they managed to talk for only about an hour a day. The most frequent topic of conversation was the children (discussed on 80% of days); leisure and friends came next, followed by work (especially paid employment) and spending.

Of course this was a special sample of individuals, since they had to keep a detailed diary of their topics of discussion and disagreement for a year. Nonetheless, conversations involving disagreement were recorded in only 2.5% of the cases. Although economic discussions took place less often than those relating to the children, friends and leisure, and work, they were more likely to involve conflict (3.6% of conversations, compared to 2.3% about work, 1.9% about children, 3.1% about the relationship, and 2% about leisure). Focusing just on the total number of conflicts reported, about 23% concerned economic matters, 21% were about work, 20% about leisure, 20% about children and 16% about the relationship. Thus, the most likely cause of conflict is disagreement over spending or some other economic issue. Overall, women reported having about 49% of the influence and men 51%. In around 55% of decisions involving conflict one or other partner had more influence. However, situations where one partner had *total* say were rare, reported in only 1% to 2% of cases. Women said they had no influence in 1.5% of the decisions reported, but decided autonomously in another 2.3%. The respective proportions for men were 1.5% and 1.2%. Where discussions were about economic matters, men tended to have more influence (54%) than the women (46% on average).

The results of a series of studies undertaken between 1956 and 1988 on the relative influence of men and women in economic decision making also suggest (at first glance) that both partners have roughly equal say (Kirchler, 1989). In the classical questionnaire studies of Davis and Rigaux (1974), participants were asked who made particular decisions. Davis and Rigaux distinguished four categories of control: decisions controlled by (a) the man; (b) the woman; (c) jointly; and (d) sometimes the man, sometimes the woman. They found typical role specialization, with the husband being responsible for insurance and car expenditures, the wife for kitchen and cooking items, and both partners for holiday decisions. Also, the proportion of joint decisions seemed to decline between the initiation and information-seeking stages, rising again around the point of purchase.

In a review of the literature, Kirchler (1989) showed that, on average just over half (53%) of decisions were reached jointly, with the remainder taken slightly more often by men alone (52%) than by women (48%). However, relative influence was found to vary with the topic at stake and, in purchase decisions, with the good under discussion, typically along traditional (stereotypical) gender lines: technical items were the man's responsibility, kitchen items the wife's. Purchases of cars, cameras, TV or stereo were dominated by the husband. Wives decided on household furnishings, the kitchen, providing and preparing meals, care of the home and items connected with health and body-care. Kirchler *et al.* (2001) also confirmed Davis and Rigaux's (1974) findings of a stereotypical gender role specialization in purchase decisions.

Thus despite an apparent overall balance in the distribution of influence, men and women dominated decisions in different areas, at least in these earlier studies: men being responsible for expensive, technical matters, women for aesthetic ones and for more everyday, mundane items (Kirchler, 1989). Even when it was the characteristics of the product that were under consideration (not just the type of product) the picture still reflected traditional expectations: it was more often the man who decided what price was acceptable and what method of payment to use, while the woman decided on the design.

However, Cunningham and Green (1974) detected a shift in partners' influence patterns between the 1950s and 1970s. In view of the social changes alluded to earlier and the way that societal representations of female and male roles have also changed since the 1970s (Diekman and Eagly, 2000; Eagly, 2001), one might expect much less sex-role segregation in decision making today. Indeed, Meier, Kirchler and Hubert (1999) report that female partners currently have more influence in financial investment decisions than in the past. However, the extent to which there has been an overall change in decision making is unclear. For example, Muehlbacher, Hofmann, Kirchler and Roland-Lévy (2007) found that sex-role specialization was only slightly less pronounced in their younger respondents than in the older ones. Thus, as we observed with money management, it appears that some aspects of male–female dominance within the household are especially resilient to change.

6.3.2 Money in second marriages

Given the high rate of remarriage, research on economic behaviour in such couples is somewhat scanty. One in four of all marriages in the USA in 1989 (Coleman and Ganong, 1989) and one in three of all weddings in 1993 in the UK (Office of Population Censuses and Surveys, 1993) involved a remarriage for one or both partners. These couples may have dependent children from one or more previous unions, as well as children of the remarriage. With a range of potential step-relationships (siblings, grandparents, etc.) the tensions that can arise over money and other issues can be enormous. These 'reconstituted' families also tend to be poorer than first families (Cockett and Tripp, 1996). This can add to the stresses and potential conflicts associated with trying to reconcile different financial habits (Coleman and Ganong, 1989). Couples may have to deal with maintenance payments or debts and this may entail continuing (sometimes acrimonious) relationships with former partners.

Studies in the USA suggest that money is treated in much the same way as in a first marriage (Coleman and Ganong, 1989; Lown and Dolan, 1994). However, couples were asked only general questions such as whether they had a 'one-pot' or 'two-pot' system. Given the normative pressures to present one's marriage in a positive light, such an approach is likely to overstate the extent to which money is pooled. To counter this, Burgoyne and Morison (1997) asked detailed questions about the handling of money on a day-to-day basis. They found a greater degree of separation in control and ownership of money and other assets than is typically the case for married couples in general. About half of their couples were using a form of independent management. In some cases, this separation was quite deliberate; those with children from previous relationships felt that they were holding resources 'in trust' for their own children and wanted to ensure that the latter would inherit what they saw as rightfully theirs. Some couples had avoided merging money because the potential threat of divorce or separation was now more salient, whilst others wanted to keep their current partner out of assessments for maintenance payments to former spouses. Some of the men felt that they had been 'ripped off' in divorce settlements with former wives and wanted to keep control of any assets they brought into the second marriage. For the women's part, although generally less wealthy than their new partners, many felt they had more independent access to resources than in their first marriages and were reluctant to give this up. Similar findings have been observed in New Zealand by Fleming and Atkinson (1999) and in the Netherlands by Buunk and Mutsaers (1999).

Thus far we have seen that equality in marriage is rarely achieved, though people generally endorse it and – in principle – would opt for a system of money management that gives both partners a relatively equal say in how the household income is used. As mentioned earlier, recent and proposed changes in UK partnership legislation are based on just such a presumption of sharing and mutual financial responsibility in marriage. However, it is unclear whether this 'marriage' model would be relevant for the various marital alternatives. Indeed, as we see below, such assumptions may be unwarranted even for couples who are currently choosing to marry.

6.3.3 Today's newly-weds

In view of the rapid social changes outlined earlier, today's young brides are likely to be older and more financially independent than their mothers and grandmothers. They may also expect to retain a greater degree of financial autonomy. Will the current cohort of newly-weds be more successful in achieving the egalitarian ideal? Burgoyne and colleagues were able to address these and related questions in a longitudinal qualitative study funded by the Lord Chancellor's Department (a former UK Government Department). The detailed findings have been reported in Burgoyne, Clarke, Reibstein and Edmunds (2006) and Burgoyne, Reibstein, Edmunds and Dolman (2007). Separate interviews were carried out with each partner in sixty-two couples just before their wedding and again with forty-two of the couples a year later. Although none had been married before and the majority had already been cohabiting at the time of the initial interviews, few were using joint pooling systems before the wedding (see table 6.2). A year later, there had been some merging of

Table 6.2 *Money management at the time of the wedding and about one year later.*
Reprinted from Journal of Economic Psychology, *28(2), Burgoyne, C. et al., 'Money*
management systems in early marriage: factors influencing change and stability',
pp. 214–28, Copyright 2007, with permission from Elsevier

System of management	*N* at T1	*N* at T2	Comments
Independent Management (IM)	17	IM: 6 PP: 7 P: 4	Those still using IM becoming more flexible, merging; others have started treating money in a more collective way, some now having mortgages and/or expecting their first child
Partial Pooling (PP)	17	PP: 12 P: 5	Further merging of finances, especially those who have started a family
Pooling (P)	5	P: 5	Unchanged
Whole Wage (WW)	3	WW: 1 IM: 1 P: 1	Some have moved towards a slightly more collective view of money

N = 42 couples

finances: the numbers using total pooling had tripled, and partial pooling had also increased, largely due to movement out of independent management. None of the couples at either time were using a housekeeping allowance system.

There were important differences between pooling and partial pooling. The couples using the latter system had their earnings paid direct into their individual accounts, and they transferred an agreed sum (or proportion) into a joint account for shared expenses. Many kept considerable sums of money and other assets separately. Partial pooling was motivated mainly by a desire to achieve independence, autonomy and some financial privacy as well as a sense of financial 'identity'. In contrast, those who used a total pooling system paid both incomes initially into a joint account, with some transferring small amounts purely for personal spending money into separate personal accounts.

Merging finances was often prompted by economic factors, such as taking on a mortgage or starting a family. However, couples were likely to go only as far as partial pooling unless there was also a commitment to shared ownership of household resources. The latter seemed to be the main determinant of starting with a joint account or moving towards pooling over time. A year after the wedding, couples with a more collective sense of ownership were significantly more likely to be pooling (more of) their incomes, and there was a significant change in this trend between the first and second interviews. (See tables 6.3a and 6.3b.)

Couples with pooling systems were more likely to be explicit about treating all resources collectively, and to say that all of the money was 'ours', than those using either independent management or partial pooling, more of whom saw a substantial proportion of the money as individually owned.

Table 6.3a *Ownership and financial systems at time 1*

System Ownership	Pooling	Part-Pooling	Independent Management	Whole Wage	Totals
Shared	4	3	2	1	10
Distinct	0	13	9	1	23
Transitional	1	1	6	1	9
Totals	5	17	17	3	42

Table 6.3b *Ownership and financial systems time 2*

System Ownership	Pooling	Part-Pooling	Independent Management	Whole Wage	Totals
Shared	14	3	1	0	18
Distinct	0	14	3	1	18
Transitional	1	2	3	0	6
Totals	15	19	7	1	42

This section has examined economic behaviour in married couples and how this may be changing in parallel with other social changes. Next, we consider some of the newer alternative forms of partnership.

6.4 Alternatives to marriage

6.4.1 Heterosexual cohabiting couples

It is only relatively recently that investigators have started treating this fast-growing population as worthy of separate investigation. Across the fifteen member states of the European Community in 1996, 11% of men and women aged 20–24 were cohabiting, 13% of those aged 25–29, and 10% of those aged 30–34 (Kiernan, 1999). In 2002, 25% of all unmarried adults in the UK aged between 16 and 59 years were cohabiting, and this seems set to increase further (National Statistics, 2004). A quarter of all births in the UK are now to cohabiting couples (Social Trends, 2004). The figure in the USA is even higher: one in three births takes place outside marriage and there is a similar ratio in Canada (Cherlin, 2004). Another form of partnership that is becoming more common is 'living apart together'; a recent study indicated that three in ten men and women aged 16 to 59 in the UK who are not currently married or cohabiting say they have a regular partner (Population Trends, 2005).

One key finding in the UK is that 56% of the general population and 59% of cohabitants believe (falsely) that there is still a legal entity called 'common-law marriage' and that couples who have cohabited for some specified period acquire the same rights as legally married couples (Barlow *et al.*, 2001; 2005).

This confusion may partly be due to the state of the current law in the UK which is somewhat confused and contradictory. Cohabiting couples are treated as if married for the purposes of tax and benefit law, but in other respects (e.g., wills and property rights) the law treats them as unrelated individuals. Perhaps more surprising is the finding that even when couples are aware that the law does not offer them the same protection as if they were married, very few take any legal steps such as making wills or formal agreements about housing (Barlow *et al.*, 2005). There are interesting research questions here for economic psychologists: is it due to over-optimism about the durability of the relationship, a refusal by one partner to cooperate, or a reluctance to allow 'cold' issues of cash, death, etc., into the relationship? Whatever the reason, extending the legal rights and benefits of marriage to these couples is somewhat complex since some are actively seeking to avoid marriage-like obligations whereas others would embrace them.

A study by Ashby and Burgoyne (2005) found both a prevalence of independent management and an emphasis on achieving a balanced and fair money management system. However, there was a surprising degree of complexity underlying the use of independent management, which suggests the need for further development of Pahl's (1995) typology. Each couple seemed to apply this system in an idiosyncratic way and with different underlying meanings for individual partners. Some findings were similar to those of Burgoyne *et al.*'s (2006) study with newly-weds. For example, keeping money separately did not necessarily mean that cohabiting partners were not prepared to support each other financially, and some did in fact support each other in much the same way as those who were pooling their money. Also, as Elizabeth (2001) has observed, partners only felt free to spend their money as they wished after joint expenses had been paid, so there were limitations placed upon their independence. Couples had to negotiate how much money each partner would contribute (and from which account), what was defined as a joint expense, and who would ensure that bills were paid. This was even more tricky when there was a large disparity in earnings. It was notable, however, that independent management did not provide much protection to the economically weaker partner – in some cases quite the reverse (see Elizabeth, 2001). Overall, Ashby and Burgoyne's findings showed that the reasoning behind financial arrangements was quite complex. However, when asked about potential legal changes, many of the couples said they would welcome more legal rights and responsibilities towards their partner, particularly with respect to inheritance.

One important issue that has often been overlooked in previous research is the great diversity in cohabitation, and the impact that this may have on the treatment of money. Money management depends on whether the relationship is seen as a long-term alternative to marriage, as a prelude to marriage or as a temporary arrangement – perceptions that may change over time (Ashby and Burgoyne, 2005). Another issue is that cohabitation is often seen in a negative light as a 'retreat' from marriage, with a fear that the institution of marriage is being undermined. Some couples do regard cohabitation as a valid alternative to marriage, and some feel that they are as good as married already (Barlow *et al.*, 2001). However, there is also evidence from studies in the USA that marriage can signify for some the achievement of an enhanced socio-economic status (Smock and Manning, 2004; Smock, Manning and Porter, 2005; Seltzer, 2004). Some low-income cohabiting couples valued marriage highly but felt they had to overcome certain obstacles before they would marry (Kiernan, 2004). Smock *et al.* (2005) found that the likelihood of getting wed was sensitive to men's ability to provide, with financial stress and conflict acting as an indirect barrier to marriage. Lower income cohabitees wanted to get out of debt, own their own homes, have a stable income and be able to afford a 'real' wedding before they would contemplate getting married.

Financial practices in some types of cohabiting couples may differ from those in marriage. Work by Vogler (2005) shows that marital status has an independent effect on money management (controlling for other variables), with separate systems more likely in cohabitation. Whereas 'nubile' (young without children) and post-marital cohabitors were more likely to use partial pooling and independent management systems, those with a biological child used housekeeping allowance systems more than their married counterparts, especially when the man was unemployed or in the working or intermediate classes. Childless cohabitors, especially when the woman was in a professional or managerial position and the man was under fifty-five, were more likely to adopt a relatively egalitarian co-provisioning approach to money.

In other respects, cohabiting couples appear all too similar to their married counterparts. Avellar and Smock (2004) found that gender inequalities in access to finances were just as likely in cohabiting unions and that, after dissolution, women's incomes were likely to drop by 33% (compared with 10% for men). Although women leaving cohabiting unions appeared not to suffer quite as large a drop in their finances as those getting divorced, the differences were relatively small when the women had custody of children.

6.4.2 Same-sex couples

To date, there is relatively little research on the economic behaviour of same-sex couples (but see Blumstein and Schwartz, 1983; Dunne, 1997). The first UK study to examine this in some depth revealed that very few lesbian and gay couples were pooling all their income, though a majority pooled some money to cover joint expenses (Burns, Burgoyne, Clarke and Ashby, 2005). As with the cohabiting couples discussed earlier, this lack of pooling did not necessarily imply disunity; it may partly be due to the risks of merging finances in the absence of legal regulation. It will be interesting to see whether the introduction of the Civil Partnerships legislation in the UK has any impact on this behaviour. Burns *et al.*'s participants were also keen to emphasize the importance of fairness and equality in the relationship. However, these are contested concepts and what they meant in practice varied a great deal from one couple to another. For example, contributions could be described as *both* equal *and* proportional; further analysis is required to tease out the way that these concepts are being applied. Being financially dependent on one's partner was to be avoided, though most said they were prepared to support each other financially if necessary. However, contrary to the assumptions of the new legislation, such support seemed in many cases to be time-limited, for example, until the supported partner could find another job, and many seemed to endorse an ethic of co-independence rather than mutual dependence. An analysis of large-scale survey data from the same study (Burgoyne, Clarke and Burns, forthcoming) will allow us to test the generality of these findings. We shall also explore the relationships between relative earning power and financial practices, as well as potential similarities and differences between female and male couples.

The studies we have outlined above highlight the diversity of economic decisions in the household. They encompass negotiations about who will provide for the couple or family, who will provide childcare, and how the household chores will get done. A couple also has to decide whether to aim for equality of contribution or of outcome, and how to achieve a fair balance of benefits and burdens. Moreover, the meaning of concepts such as *autonomy* or *financial contribution* may be gender-specific. One example is the common aphorism that an independent man is one who is not reliant on paid employment, whereas an independent woman is one who is not financially dependent on someone else. More research is needed on the economic arrangements of same-sex couples, but, as we have seen, gender is an important factor in the treatment of money in heterosexual cohabitation and marriage. Men and women also differ in their financial preferences, with wives tending to be more conscientious, more motivated to save and less willing to take on debt or financial risks than their husbands, with the latter tending to be more future-oriented (Nyhus, 2005). Today's new couples still assume that the woman will take principal responsibility for childcare, especially in the early years, and this usually means a reduction in women's incomes and earning power. However, even when both partners are employed full-time, men still do less than half of the household work (Crompton, Brockmann, and Wiggins, 2003; Brandstätter and Wagner, 1994). Thus, whilst some aspects of couple relationships have been changing rapidly, others appear to be much more resistant to change.

6.5 Conclusions

The changing nature of marriage and the increasing prevalence of alternative forms of partnership have raised concerns in some quarters about the 'deinstitutionalization' and 'individualization' of marriage, with an attendant erosion of concepts such as commitment and obligation (see Lewis, 2001; Cherlin, 2004). Others are more concerned by the apparent 'retreat' from marriage as indicated in increasing rates of cohabitation. However, as Amato (2004) argues, whether or not this is seen as a problem depends on whether one takes an institutional or an individual perspective. Fears about what has been termed an 'ethic of expressive individualism' (Cherlin, 2004) may to some extent be unfounded. People are still performing the functions of marriage even if the forms are more diverse (Barlow *et al.*, 2005). Earlier moral discourses in terms of rights and responsibilities still exist, albeit with different content. As Gerson (2002, pp. 12–14) so aptly puts it: 'As adult partnerships have become more fluid and voluntary, [couples] are grappling with how to form relationships that balance commitment with autonomy and self-sufficiency.'

Nonetheless, the increasing diversity of family life-cycles and family forms that has emerged in the last couple of decades has certainly weakened the predictive power of earlier models of behaviour based on demographic or socio-economic variables (Nyhus, 2005). The current proliferation of research on couple relationships other than heterosexual marriage should provide us with valuable information on the ways that economic behaviour within households may be adapting to new social and economic demands. However, there is one important issue that remains to be resolved: how to aggregate the information from two individuals within a household when they may not always agree about such basic 'facts' as level of household income, or how much they are able to save (Kirchler *et al.*, 2001). Although Nyhus (2005) found that couples using the joint pool were more likely to give similar accounts of their economic situation than those using other systems, there were still significant differences in their reports. This led her to conclude that household finances resemble more of a 'duel' than a 'duet'.

Does our exploration of economic behaviour in the household support this view? To a great extent, we think it does. First, and most importantly, we discern one common thread: money in intimate relationships (of all types) is 'relational' (Nyman, 2003). In other words, the treatment of economic resources and decision making can only be understood within the context of the relationship within which they are embedded. Moreover, the relationship may be constrained, shaped or facilitated by the way that such issues are handled. Nyman (2003) argues that, in order for one partner to have influence in the relationship, their financial contribution needs to remain visible. But of course this very visibility can make dependence all the more obvious if one partner is unable to maintain that contribution (Burgoyne, 2005). If the couple operates according to the principle of equity, then this can make it seem legitimate for the main contributor to have better access to personal spending money and a greater 'say' in decision making (cf. Elizabeth, 2001).

Paradoxically, pooling of income can allow the power of the main contributor to remain unchallenged and hidden, especially if the partner contributing less (or not at all) lacks that sense of entitlement that seems to go hand in hand with earning. Even when there is no obvious attempt to exercise such power, being supported financially can be a two-edged sword. It may be experienced as an expression of love but at the same time may create a diffuse feeling of obligation. Attempts to circumvent this by using a separate system of finances (such as independent management) in new marriages and perhaps both same-sex and heterosexual cohabitation also seem doomed to failure. As Elizabeth (2001) has noted, couples adopt independent management in order to resist the assumption (implicit in heterosexual marriage) of women's financial dependence, and to maintain equality between the partners. However, as Ashby and Burgoyne (2005) also found, when there is a significant disparity in incomes, the economically more powerful partner has the potential to influence the other's freedom either by insisting on equal contributions (which leaves them with less personal spending money) or by 'helping them out' (and thereby demonstrating their own power and the other's weakness). 'Used to oppose the constraints of financial dependence, independent money management is unable to produce unfettered independence' (Elizabeth, 2001). So again, paradoxically, independent management can also partially disguise and facilitate the power of the higher earner – in contradiction to the expectations of many who adopt this system.

Thus, despite the emphasis on independence and financial 'identity' in current forms of partnership, some of the old inequalities still seem to emerge somewhere – a bit like squeezing a balloon. As Elizabeth (2001) points out, if couples focus on equality of contribution, then equality of access, equal personal spending money and equal control become elusive. Is there a solution? It takes a great deal of commitment to treat household resources and decision making in a truly collective way and this may apply regardless of the legal status of the partnership. However, if a couple is really serious about achieving equality, then it should not be impossible. One possible way would be to pool all income, cover *all* joint expenses (see Nyman 2003) and split any remaining money between them. If a significant proportion of couples were to organize money in this way, then future research might reveal some interesting new patterns in household economic behaviour where gender-associated issues of financial power are less in evidence.

6.6   References

Amato, P. R. (2004). Tension between institutional and individual views of marriage. *Journal of Marriage and Family*, 66, 959–65.

Antonides, G., and van Raaij, F. (1998). *Consumer Behaviour: A European Perspective*. Chichester: Wiley.

Ashby, K. J., and Burgoyne, C. B. (2005). Independently together: an exploratory study of money management in cohabiting couples. *Proceedings: 30th Annual*

Congress: International Association for Research in Economic Psychology. Absurdity in the Economy, Prague, 21–24 September.

Avellar, S., and Smock, P. J. (2004). The economic consequences of the dissolution of cohabiting unions. *Journal of Marriage and Family*, 67, 315–27.

Barlow, A., Duncan, S., James, G., and Park, A. (2001). Just a piece of paper? Marriage and cohabitation. In A. Park, K. Curtice, K. Thomson, L. Jarvis and C. Bromley (eds.), *British Social Attitudes: The 18th Report – Public Policy and Social Ties*, pp. 29–57. London: Sage.

  (2005). *Cohabitation, Marriage and the Law*. Oxford: Hart.

Becker, G. S. (1973). A theory of marriage: part I. *Journal of Political Economy*, 81, 813–46.

Bergmann, B. (1986). *The Economic Emergence of Women*. New York: Basic Books.

  (1995). Becker's theory of the family: preposterous conclusions. *Feminist Economics*, 1, 141–50.

Blumstein, P., and Schwartz, P. (1983). *American Couples: Money, Work, Sex*. New York: William Morrow and Company Inc.

Bohlmann, J. D., and Qualls, W. J. (2001). Household preference revisions and decision making: the role of disconfirmation. *International Journal of Research in Marketing*, 18, 319–39.

Brandstätter, H., and Wagner, W. (1994). Erwerbsarbeit der Frau und Alltagsbefinden von Ehepartnern im Zeitverlauf. *Zeitschrift für Sozialpsychologie*, 25, 126–46.

Burgoyne, C. B. (1990). Money in marriage: how patterns of allocation both reflect and conceal power. *Sociological Review*, 38, 634–65.

  (2004). Heart-strings and purse-strings: money in heterosexual marriage. *Feminism and Psychology*, 14, 165–72.

  (2005). Evolving systems of money management in newly-weds. *Proceedings: 30th Annual Congress: International Association for Research in Economic Psychology. Absurdity in the Economy*, Prague, 21–24 September.

Burgoyne, C. B., Clarke, V., and Burns, M. L. (forthcoming). Money management and views about Civil Partnerships in same sex couples: results from a UK survey of non-heterosexuals.

Burgoyne, C. B., Clarke, V., Reibstein, J., and Edmunds, A. M. (2006). 'All my worldly goods I share with you'? Managing money at the transition to heterosexual marriage. *Sociological Review*, 54, 619–37.

Burgoyne, C. B., and Lewis, A. (1994). Distributive justice in marriage: equality or equity? *Journal of Community and Applied Social Psychology*, 4, 101–14.

Burgoyne, C. B., and Morison, V. (1997). Money in remarriage: keeping things simple – and separate. *Sociological Review*, 45, 363–95.

Burgoyne, C. B., Reibstein, J., Edmunds, A. M., and Dolman, V. A. (2007). Money management systems in early marriage: factors influencing change and stability. *Journal of Economic Psychology*, 28(2), 214–28.

Burgoyne, C. B., and Routh, D. A. (2001). Beliefs about financial organisation in marriage: the 'equality rules OK' norm? *Zeitschrift für Sozialpsychologie*, 32, 162–70.

Burns, M., Burgoyne, C. B., Clarke, V., and Ashby, K. J. (2005). Money talks? Same-sex partners discuss money management in their relationships. *Proceedings: 30th*

Annual Congress: International Association for Research in Economic Psychology. Absurdity in the Economy, Prague, 21–24 September.

Buunk, B. P., and Mutsaers, W. (1999). Equity perceptions and marital satisfaction in former and current marriage: a study among the remarried. *Journal of Social and Personal Relationships*, 16, 123–32.

Cherlin, A. J. (2004). The deinstitutionalisation of American marriage. *Journal of Marriage and Family*, 66, 848–61.

Cockett, M., and Tripp, J. (1996). *The Exeter Family Study*. Exeter: University of Exeter Press.

Coleman, M., and Ganong, L. H. (1989). Financial management in stepfamilies. *Lifestyles: Family and Economic Issues*, 10, 217–32.

Crompton, R., Brockmann, M., and Wiggins, R. D. (2003). A woman's place. In A. Park (ed.), *British Social Attitudes, 20th Report*. London: Sheldon Press.

Cunningham, I., and Green, R. (1974). Purchasing roles in the US family, 1955 and 1973. *Journal of Marketing*, 38, 61–96.

Curtis, R. F. (1986). Household and family in theory of inequality. *American Sociological Review*, 51, 168–83.

Davis, H. L., and Rigaux, B. P. (1974). Perception of marital roles in decision processes. *Journal of Consumer Research*, 1, 51–62.

Deutsch, M. (1975). Equity, equality, and need: what determines which value will be used as the basis of distributive justice? *Journal of Social Issues*, 31, 137–49.

Diekman, A. B., and Eagly, A. H. (2000). Stereotypes as dynamic constructs: women and men of the past, present, and future. *Personality and Social Psychology Bulletin*, 26, 1168–71.

Dunne, G. A. (1997). *Lesbian Lifestyles: Women's Work and the Politics of Sexuality*. London: Macmillan.

Eagly, A. H. (2001). Social role theory of sex differences and similarities. In J. Worell (ed.), *Encyclopedia of Women and Gender*, vol. II, pp. 1069–78. San Diego, CA: Academic Press.

Elizabeth, V. (2001). Managing money, managing coupledom: a critical examination of cohabitants' money management practices. *Sociological Review*, 49, 389–411.

Ermisch, J., and Francesconi, M. (2000). Patterns of household and family formation. In R. Berthoud and J. Gershuny (eds.), *Seven Years in the Lives of British Families: Evidence of the Dynamics of Social Change from the British Household Panel Survey*, pp. 21–44. Bristol: Policy Press.

Fleming, R., and Atkinson, T. (1999). *Families of a Different Kind*. Waikanae, New Zealand: Families of Remarriage Project.

Foa, U. G. (1971). Interpersonal and economic resources. *Science*, 171, 345–51.

Gershuny, J. (2000). *Changing Times*. Oxford: Oxford University Press.

Gerson, K. (2002). Moral dilemmas, moral strategies, and the transformation of gender. *Gender and Society*, 16, 8–28.

Gottman, J. M. (1994). *What Predicts Divorce? The Relationship Between Marital Processess and Marital Outcomes*. Hillsdale, NJ: Erlbaum.

Grossbard-Schechtman, S. (1993). *A Theory of Marriage, Labor and Divorce*. Boulder: Westview Press.

Holmes, J. G. (1989). Trust and the appraisal process in close relationships. In W. H. Jones and D. Perlman (eds.), *Advances in Personal Relationships*, vol. II, pp. 57–104. London: Jessica Kingsley.

James, S. (1996). Female household investment strategy in human and non-human capital with the risk of divorce. *Journal of Divorce and Remarriage*, 25, 151–67.

Kiernan, K. (1999). Cohabitation in Western Europe: investigating changes in patterns of forming relationships. *Population Trends*, 96, downloaded from National Statistics On-line.

(2004). Redrawing the boundaries of marriage. *Journal of Marriage and Family*, 66, 980–7.

Kirchler, E. (1989). *Kaufentscheidungen im privaten Haushalt. Eine sozialpsychologische Analyse des Familienalltages*. Göttingen: Hogrefe.

Kirchler, E., Rodler, C., Hoelzl, E., and Meier, K. (2001). *Conflict and Decision Making in Close Relationships*. Hove, East Sussex: Psychology Press.

Laurie, H., and Rose, D. R. (1994). Divisions and allocations within households. In N. Buck, J. Gershuny, D. Rose and J. Scott (eds.), *Changing Households: The British Household Panel Survey*, pp. 220–42. Colchester: University of Essex.

Lewis, J. (2001). *The End of Marriage? Individualism and Intimate Relationships*. Cheltenham: Edward Elgar.

Lown, J. M., and Dolan, E. M. (1994). Remarried families' economic behavior: Fishman's model revisited. *Journal of Divorce and Remarriage*, 22, 103–19.

McGonagle, K. A., Kessler, R. C., and Schilling, A. E. (1992). The frequency and determinants of marital disagreements in a community sample. *Journal of Social and Personal Relationships*, 9, 507–24.

Meier, K., Kirchler, E., and Hubert, A.-C. (1999). Savings and investment decisions within private households: spouses' dominance in decisions on various forms of investment. *Journal of Economic Psychology*, 20, 499–519.

Muehlbacher, S., Hofmann, E., Kirchler, E., and Roland-Lévy, C. (2007). Household decision making: changes of female and male partners' roles? *New Journal of Social Psychology*, in press.

National Statistics (2004). *Living in Britain: A Summary of Changes Over Time. Marriage and Cohabitation*, Retrieved from www.statistics.gov.uk/lib2002/.

Nyhus, E. K. (2005). Duet or duel in intra-household decision making? In A. M. Fulgseth and I. A. Kleppe (eds.), *Anthology for Kjell Gronhaug in Celebration of His 70th Birthday*, pp. 69–99. Bergen: Fagbokforlaget.

Nyman, C. (1999). Gender equality in the 'most equal country in the world'? Money and marriage in Sweden. *Sociological Review*, 47, 766–93.

(2003). The social nature of money: meanings of money in Swedish families. *Women's Studies International Forum*, 26, 79–94.

Office of Population Censuses and Surveys (OPCS) (1993). *Marriage and Divorce Statistics*. London: HMSO.

Pahl, J. (1989). *Money and Marriage*. London: Macmillan.

(1995). His money, her money: recent research on financial organisation in marriage. *Journal of Economic Psychology*, 16, 361–76.

(2005). Individualisation in couple finances: who pays for the children? *Social Policy and Society*, 4, 381–2.

Pollay, R. W. (1968). A model of family decision making. *British Journal of Marketing*, 2, 206–16.

Population Trends (2005). 122 (Winter). Retrieved 28 March 2006 from www.statistics.gov.uk/statbase/Product.asp?vlnk=6303.

Reibstein, J., and Richards, M. P. M. (1993). *Sexual Arrangements: Marriage and the Temptation of Infidelity*. New York: Scribners.

Seltzer, J. A. (2004). Cohabitation in the United States and Britain: demography, kinship, and the future. *Journal of Marriage and Family*, 66, 921–8.

Smock, P. J., and Manning, W. D. (2004). Living together unmarried in the United States: demographic perspectives and implications for family policy. *Law and Policy*, 26, 87–117.

Smock, P. J., Manning, W. D., and Porter, M. (2005). 'Everything's there except the money': how money shapes decisions to marry among cohabitors. *Journal of Marriage and Family*, 67, 680–96.

Social Trends (2004). 34. *National Statistics*. Retrieved 28 March 2006 from www.statistics.gov.uk/socialtrends.

Solnick, S. J. (2001). Gender differences in the ultimatum game. *Economic Inquiry*, 39, 198–200.

Sonnenberg, S., Burgoyne, C. B., and Routh, D. A. (2005). Income disparity and choice of financial organisation in the household: some experimental evidence. *Proceedings: 30th Annual Congress: International Association for Research in Economic Psychology. Absurdity in the Economy*, Prague, 21–24 September.

Straus, M., and Sweet, S. (1992). Verbal/symbolic aggression in couples: incidence rates and relationships to personal characteristics. *Journal of Marriage and the Family*, 54, 346–57.

Surra, C. A., and Longstreth, M. (1990). Similarity of outcomes, interdependence, and conflict in dating relationships. *Journal of Personality and Social Psychology*, 59, 501–16.

Vogler, C. (2005). Cohabiting couples: rethinking money in the household at the beginning of the twenty-first century. *Sociological Review*, 53, 1–29.

Vogler, C., Brockmann, M., and Wiggins, R. D. (2006). Intimate relationships and changing patterns of money management at the beginning of the twenty-first century. *British Journal of Sociology*, 57, 455–82.

Vogler, C., and Pahl, J. (1994). Money, power and inequality within marriage. *Sociological Review*, 42, 263–88.

Webley, P., Burgoyne, C. B., Lea, S. E. G., and Young, B. M. (2001). *The Economic Psychology of Everyday Life*. Hove, East Sussex: Psychology Press.

Wilkes, R. E. (1995). Household life-cycle stages, transitions, and product expenditures. *Journal of Consumer Research*, 22, 27–42.

Wunderink, S. (1995). Is family planning an economic decision? *Journal of Economic Psychology*, 16, 377–92.

7 Corporate social responsibility: the case of long-term and responsible investment

DANYELLE GUYATT

This chapter focuses on the role of institutional investors in the promotion of corporate social responsibility (CSR). Corporate scandals have become a common headline in the financial news across the world over recent years, including high-profile collapses such as Enron, Worldcom and Parmalat. Beyond the issue of corporate governance standards, societal expectations of what is acceptable corporate conduct have also shifted, with concern expressed about issues such as the impact of corporations on the environment, local communities, labour standards, human rights and business practices in developing countries. This shift in societal expectations has corresponded with heightened demands for improved corporate governance and calls for greater transparency and accountability to stakeholders.

Against that backdrop, the potential influence of large shareholders, such as institutional investors, has increasingly come into focus as a means of improving the allocative efficiency of the market. A more holistic understanding of investor behaviour is needed to consider the wider role of institutional investors: one that challenges the neoclassical definition of 'rational behaviour' and the notion of market efficiency within the Efficient Market Hypothesis (EMH).[1] Research into the attitude, beliefs and behaviour of economic actors that invest in ethical and socially responsible investment funds (Lewis, 2002) built on the idea that economic behaviour has both an economic and a moral dimension. Also of relevance is the growing body of evidence in the field of behavioural finance of non-Bayesian (irrational) behaviour amongst financial market investors that calls into question our understanding of investor behaviour, with evidence of short-termism and herding at the institutional level. Finally, to the extent that responsible investment practices are

---

[1] According to the EMH, market prices should 'instantaneously and fully reflect all relevant available information' (Blake *et al.*, 2000: 390), broadly meaning that market prices reflect the fundamental value of securities. Within the efficient market theory, three main variations of the EMH have emerged in the literature (Blake *et al.*, 2000: 392–3): (1) the weak form (where current security prices instantaneously and fully reflect all information contained in the past history of security prices); (2) the semi-strong form (where current security prices instantaneously and fully reflect all publicly available information about security markets); and (3) the strong form (where current security prices instantaneously and fully reflect all known information about securities markets, including privately available inside information). In general, reference to market efficiency across the financial sector refers to the semi-strong form.

unconventional amongst institutional investors, the notion of 'conventions' in economics, social psychology, sociology and anthropology also provides valuable insights for developing a deeper understanding of investor behaviour that may assist in any deliberations about promoting responsible investment and the advancement of CSR.

Drawing from these schools of thought, this chapter sets out an expanded definition of the notion of 'investor responsibility': focusing less on the shortcomings of corporate behaviour and more on the flaws with institutional investor behaviour and how these might be redressed to improve the allocative efficiency of the market. This will be referred to as long-term responsible investment (LTRI). The arguments for and against LTRI amongst institutional investors will be discussed, before moving on to present data and evidence that suggests LTRI still remains on the fringe of mainstream institutional investment practices. Finally, it will be argued that literature on behavioural inefficiencies and the role of conventions could make a valuable contribution to further understanding, and possibly improving the efficiency of, investor behaviour in terms of meeting institutional objectives and fulfilling beneficiaries' needs.

7.1 Definitions

As the notion of 'responsible investment' has evolved, different definitions and interpretations of what it means have emerged. As set out by Sparkes and Cowton (2004), different terms have been used in the academic literature, including: social, green, divergent, ethical and socially responsible investment. It is the latter two that are most commonly referred to, with ethical investment representing the 'older' term, originating from religious investors in the US, the UK and Australia (Sparkes and Cowton, 2004: 46). Socially responsible investment (SRI) has emerged as a more commonly used, widespread term across the academic community, since it is said to better capture the objectives of different investor groups that may be driven by a combination of value and profit-based objectives (Sparkes, 2001). There is also a raft of literature concerned primarily with corporate governance and shareholder activism responsibilities of institutional investors, where reference to the term 'SRI' is less common (Davis, 2002; Friedman and Miles, 2001; Gompers and Metrick, 2001; Graves and Waddock, 1994; Mallin, 1999, 2001; Useem, 1996; and Webb *et al.*, 2003).

There appears to be even more variation in the terminology used to describe responsible investment practices across the institutional investment community. For example, a content analysis carried out on twenty websites of international investment institutions[2] found that 'SRI' was only used by 35% of

---

[2] This analysis was carried out in December 2004 as part of the development of a research proposal for the Mistra research grant on sustainable investment. The institutions used for the analysis were all present at the Triple Bottom Line Investment Conference in Amsterdam, 11–12 November 2004.

those surveyed, where they describe their task as one in which they seek to encourage companies they hold shares in to adopt CSR policies. This was generally defined to mean that they assess environmental, social and corporate governance performance (ESG) alongside financial performance. The other dominant term used was the 'environment', where 15% of the websites analysed refer to responsibility in terms of the environment and the need to manage the risks associated with economic, environmental and geopolitical trends. Another 15% refer to 'corporate governance', where good corporate governance was described as being critical to creating sustainable, long-term value for all stakeholders. 'Long-term' was a phrase used by 15% of those analysed, with the aim to take a long-term view towards investing that integrates responsibility factors with fundamental financial research. Finally, 20% of investors referred to all of the categories listed above when defining their investment philosophy, with no unifying term or definition used. Whilst some institutions referred to their Code of Ethics, none of them used the term 'ethical' when describing their investment policy. Many of the institutions also emphasized the importance of performance and 'the bottom line' as drivers for adopting a responsible investment policy.

In an effort to bring together the terms used in the academic community with those used amongst practitioners, the notion of LTRI will be proposed. LTRI is the situation whereby institutional investors integrate financial, corporate governance, social and environmental criteria into the investment process in the pursuit of long-term portfolio returns. In doing so, institutions take into consideration beneficiaries' financial needs and their wider objectives regarding the way in which their savings are invested over the long term. Wider objectives might encompass, but are not restricted to, the promotion of positive ESG outcomes. LTRI is a more embracing concept than SRI, since the latter tends to place more emphasis on ESG criteria and on changing corporate behaviour, whereas LTRI is focused on investor behaviour, particularly the importance of the long-term investment horizon and responsiveness to beneficiary needs. The notion of LTRI acknowledges that investor behaviour is not always optimal as expounded by portfolio theory, with a raft of behavioural finance literature suggesting that investor biases and inefficiencies prevail. Consequently, it will be argued that adopting an LTRI approach to investing is, in some way, an attempt to redress some of the shortcomings with investor behaviour, whilst at the same time having a positive influence on corporate conduct.

7.2 The case for LTRI amongst institutional investors

The next thing to establish is why this discussion focuses on institutional investors as opposed to other investor groups.[3] There are three main reasons

---

[3] Institutional investors include wholesale institutions such as pension funds and insurance companies, as well as retail institutions such as mutual funds. There are also non-profit institutions such as charities, religious foundations and environmental groups.

for this. First, it is often argued that, owing to the agency problem that is inherent in the structure of the modern corporation, institutional investors have wider responsibilities to protect beneficiaries' interests. Second, there is growing evidence and support for the idea that as large and powerful owners of corporate equity, institutional investors can and do have significant influence over corporate conduct (and that this influence is not always a positive one). Finally, there is growing evidence to suggest that institutional investors could benefit from acting as long-term responsible investors given the long-term nature of their liabilities and the possibility for an improvement in corporate and, ultimately, portfolio performance.

7.2.1   The agency problem

The notion that there might be a problem with the structure of the modern corporation and the principal–agent problem that arises as a result of the separation of ownership and control dates back to as early as 1776 when Adam Smith in *The Wealth of Nations* (p. 700) opined that we cannot expect directors who manage other people's money (shareholders) to be as vigilant as if it was their own, concluding that: 'Negligence and profusion, therefore, must prevail, more or less, in the management of the affairs of such a company.' Berle and Means (1932) later considered the modern corporation and the weakening of control by shareholders following the separation of ownership and control in the formation of publicly listed companies. They noted that before publicly listed companies emerged, traditional property relationships gave shareholders a set of definite rights, and that investment involved owning a stake in a company for the long term and playing an active part in the direction of that company. The shift in decision-making responsibility from shareholders to company directors resulted in the new role of the stockholder being subverted to that of a passive supplier of capital. As Berle and Means argued, this created a risk that the bulk of industry could be operated by trustees for the sole benefit of inactive and irresponsible security owners.

Further insights into the agency problem were put forward by Jensen and Meckling (1976) who suggested that it created a need for monitoring activities to protect the interests of the owners (principals) against the self-interested utility-maximizing managers (agents), such as through auditing and formal control mechanisms. To reduce the cost of such monitoring activities associated with the agency problem, Jensen and Meckling argued that monitoring would 'become specialised to those institutions and individuals who possess comparative advantages in these activities' (1976: 354). In other words, through specialization and refinement of monitoring skills, the market system could provide the mechanism by which corporations could be more efficiently held to account.

Institutional investors may indeed have some degree of comparative advantage for such monitoring activities and therefore the ability to reduce the 'social cost' associated with the agency problem. It is on this basis that much literature has emerged in support of a more active involvement of institutional investors in the corporate governance function and the advancement of beneficiaries' wider long-term interests. Drawing from stakeholder theory,[4] Lydenberg and Paul (1997) and Cowton and Crisp (1998) suggested that investors carry responsibilities that require a certain degree of involvement in promoting responsible behaviour amongst the corporations in which they invest. They argued that the agency problem and the asymmetric nature of risk to stakeholders in the structure of the modern corporation might encourage anti-social behaviour, such as firms externalizing environment costs in their pursuit of profit maximization. Sparkes (2001) built on this idea to argue that since pension funds enjoy a privileged position in society,[5] they should repay such privileges by acting in a socially responsible manner and promoting responsible business conduct through their investment activities. Monks (2001) also voiced support for the idea that institutional investors can and should ensure accountability for the modern firm.

7.2.2 Size, power and influence

The importance of institutional investors as owners of listed corporate equity has grown considerably, to the point where they have become the dominant shareholders in many markets. According to the OECD (2004), in 1999 the value of assets owned by insurance companies, pension funds and collective investment schemes or mutual funds amounted to the equivalent of 144% of the GDP of OECD countries, compared with only 38% in 1980. A breakdown of equity holdings by G7 countries is illustrated in table 7.1. The data shows that, at the end of 2000, around 40% of equity in the US and the UK was owned by domestic institutional investors, 20% in Germany, Japan and Canada, and 10% in France and Italy.

The size of institutional investors gives them a potentially strong level of influence over corporations, both in formal arenas such as at annual general meetings (AGMs), and also through informal discussions and gaining access to corporate managers through various engagement activities. Indeed, some argue that without the active support of institutional investors it would be difficult for UK shareholders to raise matters of concern at AGMs or to influence corporate decisions through proxy votes and other such means (Taylor, 2000; Friedman and Miles, 2001). Added to that is the expert knowledge that

---

[4] The agency problem and the apparent 'social costs' as a result of the shortcomings with the modern corporation gave rise to the birth of stakeholder theory, where Freeman (1984) expounded the wider responsibilities of corporate managers to their stakeholders. He wrote of the need for managers to enhance shareholder value through engaging with stakeholders for long-term value creation.

[5] For illustrative purposes, they might enjoy benefits such as tax relief on contributions, immunity from capital gains tax and employers' contributions not being treated as taxable income.

Table 7.1 *Corporate equity holders by sector, end of 2000 (percentage of total). Reprinted from Davis, E. P.* Institutional investors, corporate governance and the performance of the corporate sector, *working paper: The Pensions Institute, Birkbeck College, London, Copyright 2002, with permission*

	UK	US	Germany	Japan	Canada	France	Italy
Households	20	35	17	18	41	21	35
Companies	4	14	31	24	25	35	28
Public sector	0	1	3	2	3	3	6
Foreign	37	9	16	18	6	20	14
Financial	39	41	33	38	25	21	17
Banks	2	2	12	12	3	12	8
Life/Pension	27	23	8	17	12	4	4
Mutual funds	9	16	13	3	8	5	6
Institutional investors	36	39	21	20	20	9	10

Adapted from national balance sheet data. Share of banks, life/pension and mutual funds may not add up to financial sector total given holdings by other financial institutions.

investment professionals have (over, say, non-expert private investors) which puts them in a better position to be able to scrutinize business practices and identify investment risks. Indeed, as Robert Reich (former US Labor Secretary) (1994) stated with regard to the experience in the US: 'Pension funds are becoming perhaps the most vigilant and influential custodians of long-term corporate strategy . . . as any CEO will tell you, nothing concentrates the mind so much as an inquiry from a major institutional investor about his or her company's practices.'

7.2.3   Acting as a long-term responsible investor may bolster returns

7.2.3.1   Extend horizon to better match liabilities

It is well known that institutional investors have long-term liabilities and future obligations to beneficiaries that span some twenty years or more. A long-term investment horizon therefore better fits with an institution's long-term funding obligations to its beneficiaries. On this basis, it has been argued that institutional investors are the ideal candidates to benefit from extending the investment horizon and taking an interest in the long-term performance of the companies/securities in which they invest (Sparkes, 2002; Monks, 2001).

7.2.3.2   Resist short-term fads, bubbles and herding

There is mounting evidence to suggest that institutional investors are at risk of getting caught up in short-term fads, speculative bubbles and herding (Shiller, 2000; Shleifer, 2000; and Sias, 2004). Such phenomena are not only a threat for non-professional individual investors, or so-called 'irrational' noise traders

(Shleifer and Summers, 1990), but can also infiltrate the behaviour and investment decisions of well-informed, professional investors that manage funds on behalf of long-term investment institutions. On this basis, lengthening the investment horizon and focusing more on the long-term needs of a fund's beneficiaries could reduce the risk of getting caught up in such short-term activities. This, in turn, could increase the likelihood that investment decisions are based more on long-term fundamental valuations and less on the short-term vagaries of the market.

7.2.3.3 Reduce transaction costs

By taking a longer-term view and minimizing short-term trading activity, institutional investors have the potential to reduce the trading costs associated with investment management. Studies in the US have found that mutual funds and pension funds tend to underperform their benchmarks over the long term[6] and that one of the factors contributing to this underperformance could be the high level of transaction costs incurred as a result of their trading activities. Supporting this is a study by Gompers and Metrick (2001) which found that institutional investors tended not to earn supernormal profits and that this could be because of fees and high transaction costs (2001: 247). Transaction costs could also be exacerbated by the fact that institutional investors are typically large, real money investors, meaning that it could be more difficult for them to shift portfolio holdings without incurring a financial penalty either through slower than optimal implementation (small, incremental changes in portfolio holdings to remain anonymous in the market), or simply because large trades might incur higher costs through wider bid/offer spreads (particularly in periods of low levels of market liquidity and/or for smaller, less liquid security holdings).

7.2.3.4 Improve corporate performance

The fourth reason as to why LTRI may be beneficial for institutional investors draws from evidence that suggests there could be an improvement in the performance of corporations in which they are invested as a result of taking a longer-term perspective that focuses on good corporate governance (CG) and corporate responsibility (CR) practices. For example, the Business in the Community (BiTC) report (1998) outlined the links between good CG, CR and an improvement in corporate performance to evolve around three themes of building business, building people and building trust.

The influence of shareholder activism on a firm's performance has been examined and produced somewhat mixed results. For example, Smith (1996) looked at shareholder activism to find out whether there are benefits and,

---

[6] Jensen (1968) studied US mutual funds in the period 1945–64 and found evidence of persistent pension fund underperformance over the long term. A more recent paper by Lakonishok *et al.* (1992), also on the mutual fund industry in the US, found these investors underperformed their benchmarks over time.

through a case study of CalPERS' actions, found that when activism is successful in changing a company's governance structure, then it can result in a statistically significant increase in shareholder wealth. Officials at CalPERS estimated total annual costs of activism to be $500,000 and this figure was used by Smith (1996: 251) to compute the net benefit: 'On net, activism appears to be beneficial to CalPERS, as the value increase of its holdings from activism is almost $19 million over the 1987–93 period (for the 34 firms with sufficient data), while its estimated costs of activism over the same period were approximately $3.5 million ($500,000 per year).' Admati *et al.* (1994) modelled large shareholders with diversified portfolios and found that there was an incentive to expend resources in monitoring management and that activism arises as an equilibrium condition when the expected gains exceed the likely costs. Building on this notion, Ayres and Cramton (1993) argued that institutional investors who commit to holding a firm's equity have increased credibility and influence in monitoring management and, by increasing the chance of success, they increase the expected benefits of activism. A study by Nesbitt (1994) also used a sample of firms targeted by CalPERS and found a significant long-run positive abnormal long-term stock price performance of firms following targeting activities. In contradiction to these findings, Wahal (1996) found that there was no evidence of an improvement in the long-term stock price performance of targeted firms. Karpoff *et al.* (1996) also found that shareholder initiatives had little effect on operating returns, company share values and management turnover.

Other efforts to quantify the effect of engagement activities on corporate conduct include a study by Davis (2002) which explored the effect of institutional corporate governance on corporate performance. He examined the empirical relationship between institutional shareholding and corporate-sector performance at the economy-wide level and found evidence that suggested: firstly, institutional pressure could be effective in raising the long-run level of real dividends; secondly, institutional investors exert a negative influence on 'wasteful' investment; and finally, total factor productivity growth may be stimulated by domestic institutions' activity and corporate governance pressure. He concluded that by improving CG, institutions were found to have the capacity to boost elements of corporate-sector performance at the macroeconomic level.

Gompers *et al.* (2003) looked at shareholder rights and constructed a 'Governance Index' to proxy for the level of shareholder rights of 1,500 large firms during the 1990s. The study found, amongst other things, that firms with a stronger exercise of shareholder rights had higher firm value, higher profits, higher sales growth, lower capital expenditures, and made fewer corporate acquisitions. This suggests that investors who utilize their capability to influence managers through corporate governance mechanisms will likely benefit from their activities as the exercise of such rights are correlated with better firm performance.

On the wider issue of ESG criteria, there is growing evidence to suggest that 'responsible' behaviour would not only potentially contribute to sustainable development and benefit society at large, but could also improve the long-term performance of corporations. Some studies have framed their inquiry in terms of comparing screened portfolio performance (which incorporates elements of ESG criteria) with an unscreened portfolio of similar risk and have found no statistically significant difference in returns (Grossman and Sharpe, 1986; Guerard, 1997; and Teoh *et al.*, 1999). However, other studies have found that there is some positive relationship between good governance and responsibility and corporate performance, suggesting that there may be some improvement in portfolio performance for investors that promote responsible behaviour. The main link to quantifying the intangibles is to view irresponsible behaviour as a risk to corporate reputation, where studies such as Waddock and Graves (1997) found a strong relationship between corporate reputation and ratings of corporate responsibility. Statman (2000) compared the returns of socially conscious and conventional funds and found that socially responsible mutual funds performed better than the conventional funds of equal asset size, although the difference was not statistically significant. Another study by Verschoor (1998) found that the financial performance of those companies with a commitment to ethics ranks higher than that of those which do not have such a commitment.

On balance, the evidence suggests that there at least does not appear to be a performance *penalty* for investing in a long-term responsible manner and there is some evidence to suggest that it could actually *improve* corporate performance over the long term. It is also worth noting that shareholder activism and the promotion of governance and ESG criteria is still relatively new and it may be too early to judge the merit of this approach based on performance data since the benefits will likely become more apparent over the longer term.

7.3 The case against institutional investor involvement

7.3.1 The free-rider problem

Webb *et al.* (2003) proposed some counter-arguments to institutional investor involvement in wider issues of import to beneficiaries. Indeed, they argued that institutional investor involvement in, for example, ESG issues could create anomalies in the efficient functioning of the capital market, increase transaction costs and create free-rider problems. Their concern focused on the recommendations made by the Hampel Report (1999) on 'the role of shareholders'. The concern of Webb *et al.* was that the transaction costs in monitoring such activities would be high, and ill-informed investors could free-ride off the better-informed investors on such matters. They also argued that there is a risk for institutional investors with taking a long-term view given that the financial markets operate with a short-term horizon. The authors concluded that there was a lack of incentive for institutional investors to become more active and long term in their investment approach.

The market efficiency arguments put forward by Webb *et al.* do not recognize that inefficiencies have already been found to prevail and, as argued earlier, some of these may in fact be a result of the short-termist approach of the investment community. As to the free-rider problem, this is not necessarily a problem for wholesale investment institutions over the long term since their ultimate objective is not to compete with each other but to invest in a way that provides their beneficiaries with a secure financial future whilst satisfying their wider objectives. Moreover, if LTRI became more widely accepted, then the transaction and research costs would likely decline over time as it becomes built into convention.

7.3.2   The fiduciary duty and LTRI

7.3.2.1   Fiduciary duty

Trustees of institutional investment organizations have a fiduciary duty, or legal responsibility, to act in the best interests of their beneficiaries. 'Acting in the best interest' means ensuring that beneficiary interests are not damaged by gross incompetence or mismanagement by the trust or the investment committee responsible for making the investment decisions. If the beneficiaries believe that their best interests have not been protected or advanced, trustees and investment managers can be held liable and sued for a breach of fiduciary duty. Most trustees in pension funds and charities do not have specialist investment knowledge and there is generally no legal requirement for them to have such knowledge in most countries. For example, in the UK there is the requirement only that they 'obtain proper advice' about it (Myners Review, 2001: 5). As a result, they rely heavily on external advice from investment consultants who grade and scrutinize the fund managers in the marketplace.

7.3.2.2   Prudent person rule

As a means of managing the risks associated with fiduciary duty responsibilities, trustees rely on the prudent person rule that requires fund managers to act in a prudent manner when carrying out their investment management responsibilities. Without listing the details of all the laws that apply within each country,[7] for the purposes of this discussion we need be concerned only with the goal of the regulations: to ensure that institutional assets are managed prudently and in a manner that is in the best interest of beneficiaries. The prudent person rule suggests that the investment process must be coherent and justifiable and that the institution has investment principles that are transparent, robust and testable. Del Guercio (1996) found evidence to suggest

---

[7] To varying degrees the prudent person rule or fiduciary duty to act in the best interests of beneficiaries applies to OECD countries, including Australia, Canada, Finland, Germany, Italy, Japan, the Netherlands, Sweden, the UK and the US.

that prudence distorts investment decisions and results in some institutional investors tilting their portfolios towards equities that they consider to be more prudent, such as large cap stocks or higher-grade bonds. Investment managers are therefore encouraged to err on the side of caution to ensure that their decisions are justifiable in the event of a lawsuit that might be filed against them by the board of trustees whose funds they manage. The £100m lawsuit filed by the trustees of Unilever against the pension fund manager Mercury Asset Management in October 2000 for negligence was a clear illustration of how trustees can, and do, hold fund managers to account.

7.3.2.3 Fiduciary duty is compatible with LTRI

The 'best interest' of beneficiaries has generally been interpreted to mean that it is in their best *financial* interest, which translates to a goal of maximization of portfolio return for a given level of risk as expounded in modern portfolio theory. Many mainstream investment managers are sceptical as to whether portfolio diversification and financial return are compatible with other considerations that might be less tangible and immediate in terms of their short-term impact on the share price – such as shareholder activism, governance and wider investment criteria. There is no definitive answer as to what constitutes the 'best interest' of beneficiaries, but prevailing legal opinions suggest that as long as activism, governance and wider investment criteria will not adversely impact on financial return (and there is evidence to suggest that it actually enhances return, as presented earlier) then it is within the legal boundaries to take these factors into consideration. Indeed, a recent UN-sponsored study carried out by Freshfields (2005) suggested that the notions of prudence and fiduciary obligations have been interpreted too narrowly by investment agents, and that such requirements do not preclude an institution from extending its investment horizon and taking wider issues into account in the investment management process.

7.4 What are institutional investors doing?

7.4.1 LTRI is still not mainstream

There has been significant growth in the proportion of institutional assets that take ESG criteria into account across the major investment markets. Table 7.2, reproduced from Sparkes (2001), shows the rapid growth in this sector in the UK, defined as 'the SRI investment universe', which translates to those investors who apply (to varying degrees) wider governance and ESG criteria across their equity investments.

More recently, the launch of the Principles for Responsible Investment in April 2006 has gained significant support from the investment community, with $10 trillion assets under management represented as signatories for the principles as of October 2007. According to Eurosif (2007) the SRI market now

Table 7.2 *Size of the SRI investment market. Reprinted from Sparkes, R. 'Ethical investment: whose ethics, which investment?'* Business Ethics: A European Review, *10(3), pp. 194–205, Copyright 2001, with permission from Blackwell Publishing*

Growth in UK SRI investment universe (GBP, billion)			
	1997	1999	2001
Church investors	12.5	14.0	13.0
SRI unit trusts	2.2	3.1	3.5
Charities	8.0	10.0	25.0
Pension funds	0.0	25.0	80.0
Insurance companies	0.0	0.0	103.0
Total	22.7	52.2	224.5

represents 10% of worldwide equity investing, with the global SRI market estimated to be $3.6 trillion assets under management. Of this, Eurosif estimates that 64% of investors are North American based, with 35% in Europe and 1% in Australasia. These estimates are based on an expanded definition of SRI that includes negative and positive screening, best in class strategies, engagement and integration. In the US, according to a Social Investment Forum report (2005), there has been a strong level of growth, with assets involved in social investing rising 4 per cent faster than all professionally managed investment US assets. In cumulative terms, the report (p. 1) states that the 'SRI universe has increased more than 258 percent from 1995 to 2005, while the broader universe of assets under professional management in the US has grown less than 249 percent from $7 trillion in 1995 to $24.4 trillion in 2005.' Despite the encouraging level of growth in SRI-related funds under management, it would be premature to conclude that responsible investment has moved into the mainstream amongst global institutional investors. The data fails to consider the rate of growth relative to the size of the total investment market. Recent estimates of the SRI assets under management as a proportion of the total investment market in the UK put it as less than 1%,[8] suggesting that this type of investing is still a long way from being 'mainstream'. Haigh and Hazelton (2004) also estimated that SRI funds under management (retail and wholesale) accounted for no more than 0.4% of total funds under management in Europe between December 1999 and 2001, 0.2% in the US for the period September 2000 to 2002 and 0.3% in Australia over the same period. The apparent low level of adoption and integration into total funds under management is consistent with the findings of two reports by Just Pensions (Coles and Green, 2002; Gribber and Faruk, 2004) which found evidence to suggest that

---

[8] Christian Aid (2004) computed from the International Financial Services London, Fund Management Report 2003 that the total value of the UK investment market (including all assets) was £2.6 trillion and from the UK Social Investment Forum that SRI funds were worth £225 billion.

whilst lip service is being paid to responsible investing through the inclusion of a statement within the Statement of Investment Principle policy document, there is little evidence to suggest that mainstream investors have integrated these goals into the investment process.

On the question of shareholder activism and engagement strategies, Sparkes and Cowton (2004) rightly suggested that the increasing use of engagement activities is a positive development in terms of the potential influence it could yield over corporate conduct. However, the fact that there is *potential* for fund managers to engage on these broader issues does not mean that it is actually happening. Mainstream fund managers have always spoken to company directors about issues that are considered to be important to the maximization of shareholder value, so claims of shareholder 'engagement' do not, in themselves, provide us with any information on what issues are being raised through the engagement process. Indeed, a recent survey conducted by the World Economic Forum (2004) reported that mainstream investors express little interest in corporate governance and responsibility, based on the opinion of CEOs in twenty-six global companies. According to the report, two-thirds of mainstream investors only ask questions about these issues *occasionally* and more were reported never to ask such questions (15%) than to do so often (12%). The evidence and data suggest that LTRI is still a long way off being integrated into the institutional investment management and engagement process of global institutional investors.

7.4.2 Short-termist tendencies

Case studies carried out on three UK investment institutions found evidence to suggest that fund managers grapple with being pulled towards a short-term investment horizon, despite their respective institutions all having adopted a policy to invest in a long-term responsible manner (Guyatt 2005: 141).[9] Many fund managers interviewed as part of this study argued that because the rest of the market invested with a short-term horizon, they felt they also had to do so, as illustrated by the following statement:

> If the whole market became more long term and was trading on a 10 year outlook then it would be fine [to be longer term], but they're not so you just have to trade on what they're trading on . . . it's just what you've got to do really . . . if I were to take a 10 year forecast it would be hopeless . . .

The discourse used, such as 'trading' rather than referring to the task at hand as 'investing', was how many interviewees described their job and further

---

[9] These case studies were carried out as part of a PhD thesis. Whilst these case studies were based on UK institutions, the participants were all global investors, and the nature of the interconnected global investment market increases the likelihood that behavioural biases at the market level in one country might be mirrored across the wider global market. The findings were also tested against a wider investor audience for feedback at conferences and meetings during the course of the research, including investors based in the US, Europe, Canada and Australia. Based on the feedback received, there was strong agreement with the overall findings and conclusions of the case study research.

illustrated the disparity between investors' own objectives and that at the institutional level. From the fund manager's perspective, taking a longer-term view was seen as riskier as they feared that if they got it wrong for a period of time then they would be penalized (through a lower annual bonus payment or even losing their job).

The implications of being pulled towards the short term are that, firstly, it increases the risk of excessive trading and higher transaction costs that erode portfolio returns (Odean, 1999). Secondly, short-termism also increases the risk that fund managers' decisions might get caught up in short-term market volatility and excessive bubbles or crashes that affect the market over time, whilst at the same time precluding the integration of longer-term drivers of shareholder value (such as good corporate governance and responsibility). Finally, short-termism makes it more difficult for fund managers to incorporate issues related to corporate responsibility into investment decisions as these are considered by the investment community to have more impact over the long term rather than being reliable near-term drivers of the stock price, as illustrated by the following quote from one interviewee:

> The big difficulty is that a lot of the reputational issues and environmental issues play out over a very long period of time and it's only one factor in the process and if the market isn't looking at it you can sit there for a very long time on your high horse saying 'this company is a disaster, it shouldn't be trusted' and you can lose your investors an awful lot of money.

7.4.3 Herding/gravitation to the 'defensible'

Another challenge associated with LTRI that emerged from analysis of the case study data was the gravitation towards decisions that are considered by fund managers to be easier to defend (Guyatt, 2005: 143). Tried and trusted conventions that are accepted in the market appear to make it easier for investors to justify their decision to others, hence minimizing the risk of getting 'talked out of it quickly'. Since responsible investment is still a relatively new development and is unconventional, investment decisions that are more heavily weighted to these issues might be harder to substantiate, as they are less widely (trusted) and applied across the market. Indeed, in the words of one fund manager, investors need to believe that they can trust people to support the basis of their investment decisions; the less trust that is in place the more they will be tempted to make decisions that are underpinned by more conventional and 'popular' criteria that will be easier to defend in the event that it proves to be wrong:

> if the trust is not in place, you are far more likely to get a fund manager making decisions looking over his shoulder. He tends to gravitate towards those decisions which can be most easily defended after the fact in case he gets them wrong. And that's a natural human instinct. And we don't want that.

Due to the fact that LTRI is unconventional, it is perceived to be riskier than a more conventional approach to investing. This 'safety in numbers' principle applies to any investment professional but arguably presents an even greater challenge for so-called responsible investors because the criteria they set out to incorporate are different to those of the wider market.

7.4.4 LTRI not integrated into valuation framework

Another recurring theme that emerged during analysis of the case study data related to the difficulties associated with integrating and valuing the intangibles associated with LTRI (Guyatt, 2005: 144–5). Whilst most investors generally believed there was theoretical merit in taking these issues into account, in reality they explained that they are difficult to incorporate into the prevailing and well-accepted (market-wide) conventions, whereby valuations and investment decisions are largely underpinned by identifying short-term mis-pricings based on well-accepted financial criteria,[10] as indicated by the following statement made by a fund manager:

> You know, it is all about customer relationships, supplier relationships, you know reputational risk, brand reputation, you know it's in there . . . so you've got to look at it. If you can somehow get it into a financial ratio somewhere it should be done.

The discourse suggests that incorporating these 'extra-financial' variables into financial ratios and investment decisions is by no means a straightforward task, as illustrated by the use of words such as 'somehow' and 'somewhere'. Reflecting the apparently different skills required for investing in a long-term responsible manner, the participating case study institutions had all hired an external or created an internal specialist team of 'responsible investment' researchers. This 'two-team' approach appears to have taken some of the pressure off core investors to incorporate these issues into their investment decisions, allowing them to continue investing on the basis of more conventional financial criteria, as indicated by the following comment made by a fund manager:

> Tangible financial criteria are the most important thing . . . if we were going to bring in socially responsible factors then I'd only be interested in those if I thought they were going to have an impact on the tangible financials.

Thus tangible financials appear to be given a higher priority than other less tangible inputs that might also contribute to long-term shareholder value; moreover, these issues are considered distinct from each other. Lack of integration of LTRI principles into the core valuation and investment decision-making process is problematic for a number of reasons. First, it could send a mixed message to companies and may therefore undermine an institution's ability to

---

[10] The financial criteria most commonly referred to by interviewees as conventional in the marketplace include the net present value of the stock's expected income stream such that cash flow return on investment can be estimated. Close attention is paid to financial ratios such as return on equity, return on capital employed, sales growth, price/earnings ratios and technical/momentum indicators (see Hellman (2000) for a comprehensive evidence-based study of information used by institutional investors).

influence corporate behaviour. Secondly, it runs the risk of becoming a policy that represents 'window dressing' more than a true reflection of the way in which an institution's assets are actually being managed. Finally, it could reduce the overall credibility of LTRI within the investment community and hence undermine the potential for its wider adoption by other institutional investors.

7.5   Behavioural insights for the study of LTRI

7.5.1   Shortcomings with the Efficient Market Hypothesis

The vast body of literature on investor responsibility has tended to focus on building the normative case for its adoption. Whilst making an important contribution to thinking in this field, there is a need to move beyond these arguments to consider *why* such practices remain on the periphery in terms of how institutional assets are managed. Drawing from the case study evidence summarized above, the practices of short-termism, herding and narrow application of investment criteria at the fund manager level are contrary to fulfilling an institution's objective to invest in a long-term responsible manner. Moreover, these behavioural shortcomings are reflective of the investor biases/inefficiencies that have been identified in the behavioural finance literature at the market level, evidence of which casts some doubt as to the validity of the EMH. For example, evidence has been found to show that overconfidence of investors exists, whereby investors overestimate the precision of their information signal (Camerer and Lovallo, 1999; Cosmides and Tooby, 1996; Daniel *et al.*, 1998; Shefrin and Statman, 1994; Stephan, 1999; Stephan and Kiell, 2000; and Tversky and Kahneman, 1974). This is related to the studies on over- and under-reaction (De Bondt and Thaler, 1985; Dreman and Berry, 1995) where it has been shown that investors tend to overvalue the best stocks and undervalue the worst, which, in turn, is usually driven by an extrapolation of recent performance (Andreassen, 1988; De Bondt, 1993; and Shleifer and Vishny, 1990). Furthermore, evidence of herding has been found in mutual funds (Grinblatt *et al.*, 1995; Wermers, 1999) and in pension funds (Lakonishok *et al.*, 1992; Nosfinger and Sias, 1999; Scharfstein and Stein, 1990; and Sias, 2004). There is also a body of research that focuses on the relationship between investor behaviour and the short-term investment horizon (see, for example, Froot *et al.*, 1992; Stein, 1989), with growing evidence to suggest that myopic behaviour prevails in the financial market (for example, Black and Fraser, 2000; Cuthbertson *et al.*, 1997; Frederick *et al.*, 2002; Miles, 1993; and Nickell and Wadhwani, 1987). Finally, Shiller (2000) discussed the prevalence and drivers of fads and fashions and excess volatility that have been found to pervade the market over time, further adding to the weight of evidence of non-Bayesian (irrational) investor behaviour.

Despite the mounting evidence of investor inefficiencies and biases, proponents of the EMH contend that as long as fund managers fail systematically to 'beat the market' over the long term, the notion of market efficiency cannot be rejected (Fama, 1998). However, portfolio managers' inability to beat the market might be better explained by investor inefficiencies owing to a combination of psychological and institutional influences, rather than a validation of the EMH. The many psychological influences on investor behaviour that might contribute to these inefficiencies can be narrowed down to outgrowths of heuristic simplification, self-deception and emotion-based judgements (Hirshleifer, 2001). Daniel et al. (2002) highlighted how heuristic simplification might help to explain many biases such as availability effects (heavy focus on information that stands out), framing effects (where the description of a situation affects judgement), money illusion (where nominal prices affect perceptions) and mental accounting (tracking gains/losses relative to arbitrary reference points). In addition, self-deception can explain overconfidence, biased self-attribution, confirmatory bias (interpreting information in a way that is consistent with one's pre-existing beliefs) and hindsight bias. Finally, feeling- or emotion-based judgements can explain mood effects (optimism/pessimism), attribution errors related to mood and problems of self-control (such as fear of risky choices). The institutional impediments that may contribute to investor inefficiencies include factors such as the high costs associated with short selling (Shiller, 2000) and the prudent person rule that applies to institutional investors, which has been found to distort investment decisions (Del Guercio, 1996).

7.5.2   Influence of dominant conventions on behaviour

It has been argued in this chapter that it is still not 'conventional' amongst global institutional investors to adopt or implement an active long-term, responsible investment policy. By implication, institutions that adopt such a policy are challenging prevailing conventions and taking on board the perceived risk of being different to the rest of the market. 'Convention', as defined in the Oxford English Dictionary, refers to 'a usual or accepted way of behaving, especially in social situations, often following an old way of thinking or a custom in one particular society'. In the context of institutional investors, conventions therefore refer to the way in which assets are usually managed and what is deemed to be 'acceptable' behaviour within the financial market setting.

Whilst herding tendencies as identified in the behavioural finance literature are an important element of the mechanisms by which conventions are adhered to, by defining such behaviour as transitory in terms of the forever-changing 'consensus opinion', such conceptualizations run the risk of underestimating the deep, structural role that conventions play in influencing investor behaviour (Bibow et al., 2005). Conventions encompass behaviour amongst investors that goes far beyond merely following the transitory fads and fashions that periodically pervade the financial market. Rather, conventions represent a schema of the workings of the market that are shared by investors and formed on the basis of their beliefs, experiences and knowledge. Indeed, as the case study evidence suggested, conventions are the structural underpinnings that guide investor behaviour based on their shared understanding of how the financial market works. Sugden (1986) rightly argued that solutions to market failure need not always be best dealt with through government regulation but may be more effectively managed by the relevant market agents themselves. The implications of this statement in terms of institutional investor behaviour and the observed shortcomings with the workings of the financial market are profound; most significantly, it suggests that the potential impact of coordination between institutional investors in solving the market's shortcomings and investing in a long-term responsible manner should not be underestimated.

7.5.3   Allocative efficiency of the market

From a welfare and allocative efficiency perspective, the 'beat the market' definition of market efficiency is too narrowly defined and fails to recognize that the 'ultimate function of the financial market is not to allow agents to speculate over future movements in prices, but rather (over time) to allocate consumption in the lifetime in an optimal manner and (at a certain point in time) to allocate funds to the most productive investment opportunities' (Stracca, 2004: 395). Allocative efficiency is therefore about how well market prices allocate resources and will be influenced by factors such as the skills of market participants, the factors driving their decision-making process, the way market agents interact and the criteria used to estimate long-term shareholder value. In that sense the *determination* of the price-setting process is more important in terms of the resource allocation implications than is the actual price set in the market. As pointed out by Stracca (2004: 400), the allocative implications of investor inefficiencies are deserving of further attention to assess 'whether the fact that behavioural biases distort asset prices in large and competitive markets has a significant implication on the quality of the allocation of capital and ultimately on long-term economic growth and welfare, namely on the economic efficiency of financial market prices'. Whilst there has been some research on the potential impact of behavioural biases and inefficiencies on the determination of asset prices, more research is needed to assess the implications on resource allocation and the market's ability to function in an efficient manner. Daniel *et al.* (2002) provide a thorough overview of the prevailing literature on this subject, arguing first and foremost that the bubble in US internet shares could be interpreted as evidence in itself that 'market inefficiency causes real misallocation of resources' (Daniel *et al.*, 2002: 174).

In addition to these effects, Daniel *et al.* (2002) point to a study by Chirinko and Schaller (2001) which found evidence that the 1980s stock market boom and mis-valuation in asset prices in Japan was associated with an increase in business fixed investment by at least 6–9 per cent during 1987–9 (around 1–2 per cent of GDP). Furthermore, Wurgler (2000) found evidence to suggest that capital allocations are better in countries with more firm-specific information in domestic stock prices. Daniel *et al.* (2002: 174) argued that this points to a strong link between market efficiency and economic performance: 'If less-informative stock prices are also more subject to psychological bias, then this finding suggests that there is a link between market efficiency and resource allocation.' Finally, Daniel *et al.* argue that there is some evidence that points to investor bias contributing to an exaggeration in the peaks and troughs in a business cycle, since investors have been found to be overly pessimistic (optimistic) about equity risk at the time of business cycle troughs (peaks). By way of evidence, Cochrane (1991) found that production at the firm level responds to movements in the business cycle and variability in returns. To the extent that firms respond to movements in equity prices by varying their investment and production levels, investor inefficiencies could be contributing to a misallocation of resources.

On the basis of the arguments and evidence presented above, there appears to be a link between the behaviour of investors and the efficient functioning of the market through the investment mechanism. Inefficient investor behaviour can have unfavourable resource allocation implications either directly by adversely influencing the behaviour of corporations, or indirectly by exacerbating the peaks and troughs of the business cycle. Further research that unites the complementary theories of investor responsibility, behavioural finance and portfolio theory with the study of investor behaviour is needed to expand our knowledge of the social, economic and psychological influences on investor behaviour. This knowledge, in turn, may not only assist in bolstering the wider credibility of responsible investment practices beyond the normative, often ethically based, arguments that underpin much of the responsible investment literature, but could also contribute to developing a more holistic theoretical framework to study investor behaviour and market efficiency.

7.6 Conclusion

Whilst there are signs of change, the data and arguments presented in this discussion suggest that the majority of global institutional investors do not invest in a long-term responsible manner. The gap between theoretical principles and practice is at odds with the benefits of LTRI, including the potential improvement in portfolio performance through better matching the asset management horizon with an institution's long-term liability obligations; reducing the risk of getting caught up in short-term fads, speculative bubbles and herding tendencies; reducing transaction costs; and improving long-term corporate performance. In addition, it has been argued that LTRI might be more consistent with an institution satisfying the wider concerns of its beneficiaries, as well as representing a more effective use of its market size and power. The challenge for researchers and policy makers alike is to develop a broader, multi-disciplinary understanding of investor behaviour that questions the notion of rationality and market efficiency. This, in turn, would help to shift the focus of research on responsible investment away from normative-based arguments, and more towards those based on evidence of investor behaviour and market realities.

By way of illustration, whilst herding is a well-documented and researched pattern of behaviour that has been found to prevail amongst institutional investors, the literature on this subject has primarily focused on measuring and testing for herding, with some consideration also given to the psychological factors that might drive such behaviour (such as information cascades, reputational and investigative herding). Little consideration has been given to what factors investors might be herding on, and the implications of herding in terms of long-term portfolio returns and the efficient functioning of the market. In the absence of this knowledge, it is difficult to assess whether herding represents an opportunity to exploit or a risk for institutional investors to manage. It is in this regard that the notion of conventions could potentially play an important role in extending existing research on herding and unravelling its machinations: namely to consider the deeper, structural underpinnings of investor behaviour, including their investment beliefs and the way in which investors justify their behaviour to others. A clearer delineation of these components would assist researchers and institutional investors alike to assess the implications of herding both at the micro-level in terms of an institution fulfilling its long-term objective to invest in a long-term responsible manner, and at the macro-level when considering its effect on the allocative efficiency of the market.

7.7 References

Admati, A., Pfleiderer, P., and Zechner, J. (1994), 'Large shareholder activism, risk sharing, and financial market equilibrium', *Journal of Political Economy*, 102(6): 1097–1130.

Andreassen, P. B. (1988), 'Explaining the price–volume relationship: The difference between price changes and changing prices', *Organisational Behaviour and Human Decision Processes*, 41(3): 371–89.

Ayres, I., and Cramton, P. (1993), 'An agency perspective on relational investing', Working Paper, Stanford University, Stanford, CA.

Berle, A. A., and Means, G. C. (1932), *The Modern Corporation and Private Property*, New York: Macmillan.

Bibow, J., Lewis, P., and Runde, J. (2005), 'Uncertainty, conventional behaviour, and economic sociology', *American Journal of Economics and Sociology*, 64(2): 507–32.

Black, A., and Fraser, P. (2000), 'Stock market short-termism – An international perspective', *Journal of Multinational Financial Management*, 12: 135–58.

Blake, D., Lehmann, B., and Timmermann, A. (2000), 'Performance clustering and incentives in the UK pension fund industry', Pensions Institute, June, www.pensions-institute.org.

Camerer, C., and Lovallo, D. (1999), 'Overconfidence and excess entry: An experimental approach', *American Economic Review*, 89(1): 306–18.

Chirinko, R. S., and Schaller, H. (2001), 'Business fixed investment and bubbles: The Japanese case', *American Economic Review*, 91: 663–80.

Christian Aid (2004), 'Behind the mask: The real face of corporate social responsibility', January, www.christianaid.org.uk.

Cochrane, J. H. (1991), 'Production based asset pricing and the link between stock returns and macroeconomic fluctuations', *Journal of Finance*, 46: 209–38.

Coles, D., and Green, D. (2002), 'Do UK pension funds invest responsibly? A survey of current practice on socially responsible investment', sponsored by Just Pensions, www.justpensions.org.

Cosmides, L., and Tooby, J. (1996), 'Are humans good intuitive statisticians after all? Rethinking some conclusions from the literature on judgement under uncertainty', *Cognition*, 58(1): 1–73.

Cowton, C., and Crisp, R. (1998), *Business Ethics: Perspectives on the Practice of Theory*, Oxford: Oxford University Press.

Cuthbertson, K., Hayes, S., and Nitzsche, D. (1997), 'UK stock prices and returns', *Economic Journal*, 107: 986–1008.

Daniel, K., Hirshleifer, D., and Subramanyam, A. (1998), 'Investor psychology and security market under- and overreactions', *Journal of Finance*, 53: 1839–85.

Daniel, K., Hirshleifer, D., and Teoh, S. H. (2002), 'Investor psychology in capital markets: Evidence and policy implications', *Journal of Monetary Economics*, 49: 139–209.

Davis, E. P. (2002), 'Institutional investors, corporate governance, and the performance of the corporate sector', Working Paper, Pensions Institute, Birkbeck College, London.

De Bondt, W. F. M. (1993), 'Betting on trends: Intuitive forecasts of financial risk and return', *International Journal of Forecasting*, 9(3): 355–71.

De Bondt, W. F. M., and Thaler, R. H. (1985), 'Does the stock market overreact?' *Journal of Finance*, 40: 793–805.

Del Guercio, D. (1996), 'The distorting effect of the prudent-man laws on institutional equity investments', *Journal of Financial Economics*, 40: 31–62.

Dreman, D. N., and Berry, M. A. (1995), 'Overreaction, underreaction, and the low-P/E effect', *Financial Analysts Journal*, July/August: 21–30.

Eurosif (2003), 'Report on socially responsible investment among European institutional investors', European Sustainable and Responsible Investment Forum, www.eurosif.org.

   (2007) 'What do investors want?' A presentation delivered by Matt Christensen to the PFS Program and Bucharest Stock Exchange, June 2007, www. pfsprogram.org.

Fama, E. F. (1998), 'Market efficiency, long-term returns and behavioural finance', *Journal of Financial Economics*, 49: 283–306.

Frederick, S., Loewenstein, G., and O'Donoghue, J. (2002), 'Time discounting and time preference: A critical review', *Journal of Economic Literature*, 40(2): 351–401.

Freeman, R. E. (1984), *Strategic Management: A Stakeholder Approach*, Boston, MA: Pitman.

Freshfields, Bruckhaus & Deringer (2005), 'A legal framework for the integration of environmental, social and governance issues into institutional investment', produced for the Asset Management Working Group of the UNEP Finance Initiative, October.

Friedman, A. L., and Miles, S. (2001), 'Socially responsible investment and corporate social and environmental reporting in the UK: An exploratory study', *British Accounting Review*, 33: 523–48.

Froot, K. A., Scharfstein, D. S., and Stein, J. C. (1992), 'Herd on the street: Informational inefficiencies in a market with short-term speculation', *Journal of Finance*, 47(4): 1461–84.

Gompers, P., Ishii, J., and Metrick, A. (2003), 'Corporate governance and equity prices', *Quarterly Journal of Economics*, February: 107–55.

Gompers, P., and Metrick, A. (2001), 'Institutional investors and equity prices', *Quarterly Journal of Economics*, February: 229–59.

Graves, S. B., and Waddock, S. A. (1994), 'Institutional owners and corporate social performance', *Academy of Management Journal*, 37(4): 1034–46.

Gribber, C., and Faruk, A. (2004), 'Will UK pension funds become more responsible? A survey of trustees', Ashbridge Centre for Business and Society, sponsored by Just Pensions, www.justpensions.org.

Grinblatt, M., Titman, S., and Wermers, R. (1995), 'Momentum investment strategies, portfolio performance, and herding: A study of mutual fund behaviour', *American Economic Review*, 85: 1088–1105.

Grossman, B., and Sharpe, W. (1986), 'Financial implications of South Africa divestment', Stanford Graduate School of Business Research, Paper No. 872.

Guerard, J. B. (1997), 'Is there a cost to being socially responsible in investing? It costs nothing to be good', *Journal of Forecasting*, 16: 475–89.

Guyatt, D. (2005), 'Meeting objectives and resisting conventions: A focus on institutional investors and long-term responsible investing', *Journal of Corporate Governance*, 5(3): 139–50.

Haigh, M., and Hazelton, J. (2004), 'Financial markets: A tool for social responsibility?' *Journal of Business Ethics*, June, 52(1): 59–71.

Hampel, Sir Ronnie (1999), Committee on Corporate Governance Final Report, London: Gee Publishing.

Hellman, N. (2000), 'Investor behaviour: An empirical study of how large Swedish institutional investors make equity investment decisions', unpublished PhD dissertation, Stockholm School of Economics.

Hirshleifer, D. (2001), 'Investor psychology and asset pricing', *Journal of Finance*, 56: 1533–97.

Jensen, M. C. (1968), 'The performance of mutual funds in the period 1945–1964', *Journal of Finance*, 23(2): 389–416.

Jensen, M. C., and Meckling, W. H. (1976), 'Theory of the firm: managerial behaviour, agency costs and ownership structure', *Journal of Financial Economics*, 3(4): 305–60.

Karpoff, J., Malatesta, P., and Walkling, R. (1996), 'Corporate governance and share-holder initiatives: Empirical evidence', *Journal of Financial Economics*, 42: 365–95.

Lakonishok, J., Shleifer, A., and Vishny, R. W. (1992), 'The impact of institutional trading on stock prices', *Journal of Financial Economics*, 32: 23–43.

Lewis, A. (2002), *Morals, Markets and Money: Ethical, Green and Socially Responsible Investment*, London: Pearson Education.

Lydenberg, S., and Paul, K. (1997), 'Stakeholder theory and socially responsible investing: Toward a convergence of theory and practice', IABS Meeting, Sandestin, FL, 9 March.

Mallin, C. (1999), 'Financial institutions and their relations with corporate boards', *Corporate Governance*, 7(3): 248–55.

  (2001), 'Institutional investors and voting practices: An international comparison', *Corporate Governance*, 9(2): 118–26.

Miles, D. (1993), 'Testing for short-termism in the UK stock market', *Economic Journal*, 103: 1379–96.

Monks, R. A. G. (2001), *The New Global Investors*, New York: Capstone.

Myners Review (2001), 'Institutional investment in the UK: A review', a study commissioned by the UK Government, March, www.hm-treasury.gov.uk.

Nesbitt, S. L. (1994), 'Long-term rewards from shareholder activism: A study of the CalPERS effect', *Journal of Applied Corporate Finance*, 6: 75–80.

Nickell, S., and Wadhwani, S. (1987), 'Myopia, the dividend puzzle, and share prices', Centre for Labour Economics, London: London School of Economics.

Nosfinger, J. R., and Sias, R. W. (1999), 'Herding and feedback trading by institutional and individual investors', *Journal of Finance*, December, 54(6): 2263–95.

Odean, T. (1999), 'Do investors trade too much?' *American Economic Review*, December, 89(5): 1279–99.

OECD (2004), 'Principles of corporate governance', www.oecd.org/dataoecd/41/32/33647763.pdf.

Reich, R. (1994), 'Pension funds on watchdog role', *Sunday Telegraph*, 10 July 1994.

Scharfstein, D. S., and Stein, J. C. (1990), 'Herd behaviour and investment', *American Economic Review*, 80(3): 465–79.

Shefrin, H., and Statman, M. (1994), 'Behavioural capital asset pricing theory', *Journal of Financial and Quantitative Analysis*, 29(3): 323–49.

Shiller, R. J. (2000), *Irrational Exuberance*, Princeton: Princeton University Press.

Shleifer, A. (2000), *Inefficient Markets: An Introduction to Behavioral Finance*, Oxford: Oxford University Press.

Shleifer, A., and Summers, L. (1990), 'The noise trader approach to finance', *Journal of Economic Perspectives*, 4: 19–33.

Shleifer, A., and Vishny, R. (1990), 'Equilibrium short horizons of investors and firms', *American Economic Review Papers and Proceedings*, 80(2): 148–53.

Sias, R. W. (2004), 'Institutional herding', *Journal of Behavioral Finance*, 5(3): 181–95.

Smith, A. (1776) *The Wealth of Nations*, 1st edn.

Smith, M. P. (1996), 'Shareholder activism by institutional investors: Evidence from CalPERS', *Journal of Finance*, 51(1): 227–52.

Sparkes, R. (2001), 'Ethical investment: Whose ethics, which investment?' *Business Ethics: A European Review*, 10(3): 194–205.

—— (2002), *Socially Responsible Investment: A Global Revolution*, Chichester: Wiley.

Sparkes, R., and Cowton, C. J. (2004), 'The maturing of socially responsible investment: A review of the developing link with corporate social responsibility', *Journal of Business Ethics*, 52(1): 45–58.

Statman, M. (2000), 'Socially responsible mutual funds', *Financial Analysts Journal*, 56(3): 30–9.

Stein, J. (1989), 'Efficient capital markets, inefficient firms: A model of myopic corporate behaviour', *Quarterly Journal of Economics*, 104: 655–9.

Stephan, E. (1999), 'The role of judgmental heuristics in financial decisions', *Finanzpsychologie*, Munich: Oldenbourg Verlag.

Stephan, S., and Kiell, G. (2000), 'Decision processes in professional investors: Does expertise moderate judgemental biases?' IAREP/SABE Conference Proceedings: Fairness and Competition: 416–20.

Stracca, L. (2004), 'Behavioral finance and asset prices: Where do we stand?' *Journal of Economic Psychology*, 25: 373–405.

Sugden, R. (1986), *The Economics of Rights, Co-operation and Welfare*, Oxford: Basil Blackwell.

Taylor, R. (2000), 'How new is socially responsible investment?' *Business Ethics: A European Review*, 9(3): 174–9.

Teoh, S. H., Welch, I., and Wazzan, C. P. (1999), 'The effect of socially activist investment policies on the financial markets: Evidence from the South African boycott', *Journal of Business*, 72(1): 35–55.

Tversky, A., and Kahneman, D. (1974), 'Judgement under uncertainty: Heuristics and biases', *Science*, 185: 1124–31.

US Social Investment Forum (2005), 'Report on socially responsible investing trends in the United States', Social Investment Forum, Industry Research Program, 10-Year Review, www.socialinvest.org.

Useem, M. (1996), *Investor Capitalism: How Money Managers Are Changing the Face of Corporate America*, New York: Basic Books.

Verschoor, C. C. (1998), 'A study of the link between a corporation's financial performance and its commitment to ethics', *Journal of Business Ethics*, 17: 1509–16.

Waddock, S. A., and Graves, S. B. (1997), 'The corporate social performance–financial performance link', *Strategic Management Journal*, 18(4): 303–19.

Wahal, S. (1996), 'Public fund activism and firm performance', *Journal of Financial and Quantitative Analysis*, 31(3): 1–23.

Webb, B., Beck, M., and McKinnon, R. (2003), 'Problems and limitations of institutional investor participation in corporate governance', *Corporate Governance* 11(1): 65–73.

Wermers, R. (1999), 'Mutual fund herding and the impact on stock prices', *Journal of Finance*, 54: 581–622.

World Economic Forum (2004), 'Values and value: Why global corporate citizenship matters', a survey of CEOs and CFOs of twenty-six leading international companies, www.weforum.org.

Wurgler, J. (2000), 'Financial markets and the allocation of capital', *Journal of Financial Economics*, 58: 187–214.

PART III

Consumer behaviour in the private sector

8 Consumption and identity

RUSSELL BELK

8.1 You are what you consume

8.1.1 Who are you?

There are a number of ways in which we might respond to a question that asks us to identify ourselves. Although the salience and sequence of possible answers differs culturally and situationally, for many of us our name is likely to be the first response that comes to mind. This is an enduring marker that we may carry throughout a lifetime and in some cultures it may say much about our ancestry, home region, and caste. We may nevertheless change our family name upon marriage or divorce, use nicknames or more familiar variants of our given names, or attach a title that says something about our sex, age, or our marital, professional, religious, or hereditary status. When we have a choice of names, the name we choose may reveal much about us, including our cultural identity (Mathews 1996). Our name is perhaps our most central possession and is both a signifier of self and the signified to which other consumption signifiers attach (Kaplan and Bernays 1997). We have only to add an "'s" to our name in order to claim other things as ours. In so doing we may either borrow from or extend to these things a part of our identity. It is for this reason that consumption and identity are to varying degrees co-constituent of each other. That is, at least in part, we are what we consume and what we consume is us.

Another common response to the query "Who are you?" is to state our vocational role or qualifications by indicating our occupation, rank, job title, or educational degrees. Other responses that might come to mind, especially if we are away from home, are those that identify us by our nationalities, ethnicities, places of residence, employers, religions, or other loyalties. Whereas this might have once meant claiming to be a subject, soldier, or representative of King So-and-So, today it might also mean claiming to be a fan of a particular football club, musical group, or other devotional cult.

As some of these examples suggest, we may identify our selves through what we consume and have rather than through what we produce, know, or do. Historically and with growing affluence this identification with consumption has become increasingly common, especially in our non-verbal statements of our identities. Non-verbal statements of identity are largely visual, although they could be olfactory as with some of the things we might eat, smoke, or dab on our bodies. Just as the non-verbal claims of advertisements may be stronger in impact because they are less likely than verbal claims to be challenged or counter-argued, non-verbal signs of self may have a strong impact on others because they allow us to "say" things we would not dare say verbally and nevertheless to remain confident that we will not be questioned about or asked to justify our implicit claims. We would hardly come up to a stranger and verbally say "I'm rich," "I'm sexy," "I'm a bicyclist," "I'm a Muslim," "I'm conventional," or "I'm a little wild." But we can easily convey such claims through the clothes we wear, the vehicles we drive, the fragrances we use, the electronic devices to which we attach ourselves, the clubs and shops we frequent, and the places where we live.

Of course we might instead try to define ourselves through internal characteristics such as our beliefs, skills, ideas, or knowledge. But even our beliefs have come to be regarded as possessions (Abelson 1986, 1989). More superficially we might identify our face and body as constituting our identity. But even body parts may be viewed as possessions and they can be augmented through the purchase of various other products or services (Belk 1987). Alternatively, we might send someone who inquires about our identity a résumé that, for an academic, will include a list of our publications. Publications, along with inventions, artworks, and other of our creations are possessions that we guard jealously and that are protected by intellectual property laws. But other intangible possessions that refer to our identity may be readily shared with others. Besides our résumé we might freely circulate flattering digital photographs, compositions, papers, and other announcements for self on our websites and blogs (e.g., Schau and Gilly 2003).

We may also adopt or create a template of interrelated consumption choices that exemplify a lifestyle. Such product constellations (Solomon and Assael 1987) can also define group identity in a neo-tribal manner (Maffesoli 1996). The role of consumption in contributing to group identity is best seen in "marker goods" (Douglas and Isherwood 1979) that act as symbolic badges of inclusion and exclusion. In the US, gang members normally signal their affiliation through their clothing, colors, styles, and other fashion choices. When a single brand becomes the focus of group identification the group may be called a brand cult (Belk and Tumbat 2005), consumption community (Boorstin 1973), idioculture (Fine 1979), brand community (Muñiz and O'Guinn 2001), or consumption subculture (Schouten and McAlexander 1995). Such affiliations often go beyond consumption-based lifestyles and also involve myths, rituals, dogma and other quasi-religious elements. The consumption object can take on sacred characteristics in such cases (Belk, Wallendorf, and Sherry 1989). Such spiritual deepening of the meanings of our possessions not only increases the passion of our attachments to these objects, it also ennobles the lifestyle or group with which these possessions are affiliated.

The contributions of consumption to defining or expressing identity that have been discussed thus far tend to assume that we carry with us a relatively stable and enduring sense of self. They implicitly invoke a type theory of personality. But it is also possible to see products, services, and brands as instead representing facets or traits of the individual. Various authors (e.g., Cushman 1990; Elliott and Wattanasuwan 1998; Firat and Venkatesh 1995) have suggested that postmodern self is fractionated, unstable, and lacks a center or core. For such a self, selected consumption choices are more akin to trait theories of personality and allow playing with identity, mixing and matching, and trying on new aspects of self. Our appearance, for example, may be regarded as a costume that allows us to play with alternative identities (e.g., children playing in grown-up clothing, adults at a masquerade party, cosmetic "makeovers"). Others suggest that identity is more situational (e.g., Schenk and Holman 1980; Stayman and Deshpande 1989). Thus, we might be a mild-mannered person at work, but an aggressive and flamboyant skier. Even though wearing a uniform often signals a stable authority position (e.g., a police officer, train conductor, plane pilot), it may also signal a temporary liminal status that we take on during a role transition (e.g., a graduation robe, wedding dress, hospital gown).

8.1.2 Our possessions and our selves

Regardless of whether they are temporary or enduring, identify an individual or a group, are internal or external, playful or serious, our possessions are regarded as part of our extended self (Belk 1988). One of the premises of the concept of extended self is that the self may exist at several levels, such as those of the individual, the family, the community, and the nation. However, rather than being layers of self-identity, Tian and Belk (2005) found that the home and work selves contend with one another for primacy and that this is seen in the self-extending possessions found in homes and offices. On the one hand, the workplace and work tasks now intrude into the home through mobile phones, e-mail, and other electronic devices facilitating and symbolizing work outside of the office. On the other hand, photos, phone calls, and mementoes of the family displayed in the workplace act as cues to the home self while at work. These patterns also support the existence of multiple selves rather than self as an integrated whole.

Although there were earlier studies of possessions as extensions of self (e.g., Belk 1978; Cooper 1972, 1974; Duncan and Duncan 1976; Grubb and Hupp 1968; Luft 1957; Proshansky 1978; Volkan 1974) and the concept can be traced back as far as William James (1890), perhaps the most comprehensive research on extended self is that of Csikszentmihalyi and Rochberg-Halton (1981). Based on a three-generation study of Chicago area families, they found that the forty- to fifty-year-old generation was the most likely to cite status and power as the gratifications derived from their favorite possessions. Younger generations in the same family were more likely to value their possessions for what they could help them do (e.g., play music, perform athletically). And the oldest generation was more likely to treasure possessions that represented others (e.g., photos, gifts). It is notable that all three generations vested an important part of their identities in possessions, but they did so for different reasons. The youngest generation relished things that helped them perform. The middle generation cited possessions that showed what they had achieved. And the oldest generation thought themselves best represented by possessions that showed their links to other people.

Other researchers have also found that the role of possessions in identity changes systematically over the life course (Dittmar 1992; Gentry, Baker, and Kraft 1995; Kamptner 1990; Livingstone and Lunt 1991; Lunt and Livingstone 1992). At the extremes of the life cycle, possessions play an important role in identity during infancy as well as later in life as death comes closer. During infancy the child first learns to distinguish self from environment and mother via the kinesthetic feedback and the contingency of being able to act upon objects in the environment (Seligman 1975). When the child and its mother are separated, often the "security blanket" of a transitional object associated with the mother can provide feelings of comfort (Winicott 1953; Furby and Wilke 1982). By providing greater feelings of independence from mother, transitional objects may aid in identity formation (Bowlby 1969). Some have suggested that this use of security objects continues into adulthood through objects such as collections (Gulerce 1991; Muensterberger 1994).

During old age, when death normally approaches, people may use their possessions as representations of themselves in an attempt to assure that this part of them will live on and that they will be remembered (Unruh 1983; Belk 1988). They may be quite strategic about this, striving to complete the life-long process of identity construction and reconstruction by transferring treasured possessions to family members (Price, Arnould, and Curasi 2000; Curasi, Hogg, and Maclaren 2004). In Asante Ghana, Bonsu and Belk (2003) found that this identity reconstruction process can continue after death as the survivors seek to change the way the dead will be remembered, using the lavishness of funeral rituals to achieve this.

8.1.3 Loss of possessions and loss of self

If death threatens a loss of identity and passing on heirloom possessions can help to ameliorate this threat, what of the traumatic loss of self-signifying possessions before death? Those who have lost self-signifying possessions to theft often report feelings of violation and pollution akin to being raped (Maguire 1980; Papp 1981; Van den Bogaard and Wiegman 1991). Sayre (1994) found that for victims who lost their homes to a wildfire in California there were feelings of loss of self and mourning. Likewise Ikeuchi, Fujihara, and Dohi (1999) found that victims of earthquakes in both Japan and California experienced a loss of extended self, especially for those in Japan. The authors attribute the cultural differences in their findings to the notion of identity being more internal in the United States and more external in Japan. This explanation is consistent with Pavia (1993, p. 426), who found that dying AIDS patients in the US felt a greater sense of loss from immaterial, inner things:

> These informants associated the greatest loss of self with the loss of jobs, energy, and motivation rather than with the loss of material goods . . . Someone who identifies closely with an art collection does not say "I am an art collection," instead he or she says, "I am an art collector," which implies that "I have the means to acquire art" (e.g., money, appropriate knowledge, the right connections, etc.). This person may lose the art collection, and suffer a loss of self, but still retain the means to collect (e.g., a theft of the collection); or the person may lose the collection as well as the means to collect, and suffer an extraordinary deep loss of self. This deep loss of self is the type of loss experienced by the informants and may describe why the loss of their material goods was described as relatively less important than other losses.

For those who lose possessions but do not face a debilitating terminal illness like AIDS, there is often a chance to reconstitute the material aspects of their identity. This is predicted by the compensatory symbolic self-completion process hypothesized by Wicklund and Gollwitzer (1992). Thus, Sayre and Horne (1996) found that insured firestorm victims in California very purposefully reconstructed and upgraded their identities through reacquisition of newer and better replacement possessions.

The process of self-completion and intentionally fashioning the self can also be seen in other contexts. Schouten (1991a, 1991b) found that those contemplating cosmetic surgery go through a liminal state of playfully imagining transformed selves. These possible selves (Markus and Nurius 1986) are very likely facilitated or conjured by advertising for other supposedly self-tranformative products like fragrances, clothing, automobiles, tourism, cosmetics, and any number of other products and services (Belk 1991). It is not without reason that advertising has been called a magic system (Williams 1980). What consumers may seek is nothing less than a Cinderella-like transformation, in which a purchase magically transforms them into a completely different self. This is what was found in one study of consumer desire (Belk, Ger, and Askegaard 2003). But the authors also found that upon acquiring the objects of their desires, consumers missed the former state of longing and the hope for a better self and soon transferred their longing to some new object that became vested with similar self-tranformative hopes.

8.1.4 The role of culture

As hinted at in the comparison of reactions to losses of possessions to earthquakes in the US and Japan (Ikeuchi, Fujihara, and Dohi 1999), both the notion of self-identity and the role of consumption in expressing, shaping, extending, and managing identity may vary culturally. Much work remains to be done in this area, but it is clear that there are cultural differences. Wallendorf and Arnould (1988) studied favorite possessions in the US and Niger. Not only were the objects chosen different in the two cultures (e.g., more religious objects and brightly colored bowls in Niger; more clothing and photos in the US), so were their meanings. In Niger, favorite objects were more often those that represented status, while in the US they were more likely to be objects that represented other people. Mehta and Belk (1991) compared favorite possessions of East Indians in India to those of Indian immigrants to the US. They found few possessions that represented India among the Indian resident group, but many such possessions in the immigrant group (e.g., replicas of the Taj Mahal, collections of Indian music, collections of Bollywood movies). They concluded that possessions were a key part of identity reconstruction among immigrants. Similar findings have been obtained by Joy and Dholakia (1991) with Indian immigrants in Canada and by Bih (1992) among Chinese students in the US. Jain and Joy (1997) found that female Indians in Canada used gifts of gold jewelry from family members to maintain ties between generations and between family on different continents. Belk (1992b) found that by moving treasured possessions we also attempt to transplant part of our identity from one place to another.

Dittmar (1992) suggested that one way that groups use possessions to define collective identity is to differentiate their consumption from that of outgroups. Likewise Englis and Solomon (1997) described avoidance products that are eschewed not because the consumer dislikes them, but rather because they are associated with a group from which we would like to disassociate ourselves. But Eckhardt and Houston (1998) found that among more collectivist Chinese consumers, this concern for how disliked others may perceive us is largely irrelevant. Wong (1997) found that those with a more collectivist orientation are less materialistic and less concerned with defining self via possessions. Nevertheless she also noted the paradoxical observation that luxury goods are highly important in Asian societies. This likely has more to do with trying to enhance collective self through "face work" (Wong and Ahuvia 1998; Zhou and Belk 2004).

8.2 Implications of identity-seeking through consumption

There are many implications of the phenomenon of deriving an important part of our identities through what we consume. They include considerations of the effect on gift-giving, vicarious consumption, care of possessions, product disposition, and the attempt to derive or construct meaning in life (Belk 1988). Two consumption phenomena that will be used to highlight the importance of identity issues are materialism and sharing. While materialism is a potentially negative consequence of finding identity in consumption, sharing is a potentially positive consequence.

8.2.1 Materialism and compulsive consumption

One outcome of attempting to construct our identities through what we consume is that possessions and expenditures may become all-important in our lives. Materialism has been defined as the importance a person attaches to possessions (Belk 1985). At its highest levels materialism manifests itself as the belief that possessions are the primary source of happiness or unhappiness in life. In this conception the subcomponents of materialism are possessiveness, non-generosity, and envy. Studies have consistently found that those who are more materialistic are less happy and have lower feelings of well-being (Belk 1985; Richins and Dawson 1992; Kasser and Ryan 1993; Kasser 2003). Although it is not clear whether people are unhappy because they are materialistic or if they instead turn to materialism because they are unhappy, it is clear that a materialistic orientation to life does not bring happiness. Ger and Belk (1999) found that informants in Turkey, the US, northern Europe, and Romania all claimed to believe that materialism is bad and does not bring happiness. Nevertheless, these same informants were nearly unanimous in desiring more money and more and better possessions, thus exhibiting the materialism they ostensibly condemned. These people found various ways to justify or excuse their materialistic desires, such as claiming that these desires were for the sake of their families, that they deserved such rewards, or that because they were not tempted to buy frivolous gadgets (which northern Europeans attributed to American consumers) they were not really materialistic. Such rationalizations may help materialistic consumers to feel better about their desire to enhance self through consumption, but they do not make such consumption any more fulfilling.

Another negative consequence for some consumers pursuing self-definition through consumption is compulsive buying. Faber defines compulsive buying as "chronic, repetitive purchasing that becomes a primary response to negative feelings and that provides immediate short-term gratification, but that ultimately causes harm to the individual and/or others" (Faber 2000, p. 29). Compulsive buying is also related to materialism. By comparing a sample of compulsive buyers to a sample of general consumers, O'Guinn and Faber (1989) found that compulsive buyers are significantly more materialistic and score higher on the subtraits of envy and non-generosity. The type of materialism involved here is not the positive instrumental materialism described by Csikszentmihalyi and Rochberg-Halton (1981); rather it is the type they term terminal materialism, with only negative consequences. For instance, Faber, O'Guinn, and Krych (1987) found that many compulsive purchasers never used the items they bought or even removed them from their original bags and boxes. Therefore it is not surprising that the possessiveness component of materialism was not found to differentiate compulsive consumers (O'Guinn and Faber 1989). Rather, this line of research has found that compulsive buyers feel temporarily self-enhanced by the attentions of store personnel and delivery people. Their desire for attention also shows in that many of the objects they compulsively buy are intended as gifts for others. Some, in fact, buy almost exclusively for others. This suggests that they too may justify their buying, as did Ger and Belk's (1999) materialists, by claiming "It's not for me."

The relationship of compulsive buying to attempts at self-enhancement is evident in the cues prompting compulsive buying (Faber and Christenson 1996). They include not just opportunities (e.g., sales, credit cards, bargains) but also negative self-images (e.g., feeling fat, bored, stressed, angry, hurt, or irritable). Dittmar (2000) also found that compulsive buying is most likely to occur when a negative self-image is salient and is most likely to result in purchases of body-care products, footwear, clothing, and jewelry. Notably, all of these product categories are related to self-image. While compulsive buyers are not exclusively female, these studies also reveal that far more women than men are diagnosed as compulsive buyers (e.g., Campbell 2000).

8.2.2 Sharing

If women are more likely to become compulsive buyers, they are also more likely to engage in a more positive aspect of the pursuit of identity through consumption: sharing. While owning something means that we can share it with others, feelings of possessiveness and attachment toward the things we possess discourage sharing (Ball and Tasaki 1992; Belk 1992a; Kleine and Baker 2004; Schultz, Kleine, and Kernan 1989; Sivadas and Venkatesh 1995; Wallendorf and Arnould 1988). Since non-generosity is a component of materialism (Belk 1985), it is to be expected that materialistic people are less willing to share what they have with others. The same is true with regard to at least some aspects of the extended self. If we regard a possession as a part of our extended self, we are more likely to retain it rather than share it (Belk 1988; Kleine, Kleine, and Allen 1995). Even with a bodily organ, the more we regard it as a part of our identity, the less willing we are to be an organ donor (Belk 1987, 1990). The process of incorporating an object into our identity is termed cathexis and objects that are so incorporated are beneficiaries of the endowment effect (Kahneman, Knetsch, and Thaler 1990).

But we also have a part of extended self that includes other people. We may make sacrifices not only of money, time, and possessions to groups of people ranging from our family to our nation, we may sometimes even sacrifice our life for these others. We have already seen that with family heirlooms there may even be an anxiousness to share these possessions with kin who may thereby remember us and grant us a certain immortality (e.g., Price, Arnould, and Curasi 2000). Not only with inheritances however, but with gift-giving generally, we are often quite happy to share a part of our resources with loved others. Ideally, the gift should be perfectly attuned to the self of the recipient rather than reflect the giver's tastes (Belk 1996). The gift-giving and gift-receiving ritual is itself an act of extending and partially merging the selves of the two actors into one. Even when this bond is already well formed, as between spouses and between parents and children, gift-giving ritually reinforces these bonds. Although Dittmar (1992) worried that giving a gift imposes an identity on the gift recipient, this appears to be an infrequent occurrence. Belk and Coon (1993) found a shift over time in dating relationships from instrumental economic exchange to social exchange, and finally to agapic love (from the Greek *agape*, meaning self-sacrificing, unconditional, or thoughtful love). As this ideal progression occurs, the gift-giver grows ever more attentive to pleasing the recipient.

There is also another type of possession that we may be happy to share with others. These are the intangible possessions that we can give to others without losing them for ourselves. With the Internet and e-mail for example, we can post messages to bulletin boards, participate in online chat rooms, and send photos, music, movies, and messages to both friends and strangers. This has prompted some to suggest that consumerism is being replaced by the high-tech gift economy (Pinchot 1995; Barbrook 2005; Coyne 2005). Examples include the many contributors to open-source software like Linux (Bergquist 2003; Bergquist and Ljungberg 2001), sharing music and video files via Napster and its successors (Giesler 2006), "freeware" (Raymond 2001), and a variety of virtual communities sharing expertise, enthusiasm, and information (Barbrook and Cameron 2001; Rheingold 2000).

Whether or not we are entering a new era in which the high-tech gift economy supplants consumerism, it is evident that the gift economy has by no means disappeared in contemporary society as Mauss (1990) forecast would happen. The persistence and growth of the gift economy in an age of possessive individualism, commodity fetishism, and crass materialism is a powerful demonstration that there is more to life than enhancing status and defining self through an endless parade of consumption choices. Perhaps those who call for opposing consumerism, materialism, and lifestyle complexity through downshifting (e.g., Schor 1998) dematerializing (e.g., Hammerslough 2001), or voluntary simplicity (e.g., Elgin 1998) need look no farther than the gift economy to find a more viable alternative to, and check on, competitive status seeking.

8.3   Brand identity and consuming counterfeits

Consumers are not the only ones who seek an identity through branded products and services; so do those who market these brands (e.g., Frank 1997; Quart 2003; Holt 2004). Although marketers do not seek to create identities for their brands in quite the same way that consumers seek identity through brand consumption, it has been proposed that brand identities be measured through personality inventories in a manner similar to measuring human personalities (Aaker 1997). Moreover, the two identities are interdependent – the image of the brand user draws on the image of the brand and the image of the brand draws on the image of the brand user (Belk 1978; Wong and Zaichkowsky 1999). The marketer has the additional tools of advertising, selective distribution, product design, packaging, and pricing to influence its brand image however.

In some instances the brand derives its personality from a fictitious person associated with it, as with Aunt Jemima, Betty Crocker, Tony the Tiger, or Uncle Ben (Lury 2004). In other cases, the brand derives its personality from the company owner or founder, as with Tommy Hilfiger, Martha Stewart, Ralph Lauren, Donna Karan (DKNY), or Coco Chanel (Twitchell 2004). Sometimes it is a celebrity endorser such as Michael Jordon or Tiger Woods who lends his or her personality to the brand (McCracken 1989). And in still other cases, it is celebrity brand users who help shape a brand image, as when Malcolm Forbes and Elizabeth Taylor rode their Harley Davidson motorcycles into the limelight.

The power of brand identity means that a well-known brand can command a premium price and achieve greater brand loyalty. In the case of luxury brands, this is so much the case that they can sell at a price that can be tenfold or more higher than the price charged by non-luxury brands (Frank 1999; Twitchell 2003). Common luxury goods categories are automobiles, travel, alcoholic beverages, clothing, accessories, and fragrances. It might be assumed that the primary market for luxury goods consists of affluent consumers in affluent countries, and there is indeed a large market in these countries (Dubois and Laurent 1993, 1995). But not all affluent countries have values supporting luxury goods. For example, despite comparable incomes, France is very receptive to luxury goods, while Australia is not (Tidwell and Dubois 1996). And among the largest markets for Western luxury goods are Asian locales including Japan, Korea, Singapore, Hong Kong, Taiwan, and mainland China (Dubois and Laurent 1994a; Wong and Ahuvia 1998; Wong and Zaichkowsky 1999). While it is partly the newly affluent in these rapidly growing economies who are attracted to luxury goods, it is also the less than affluent who are attracted to luxury brands in Asia and elsewhere. They enter these markets in several different ways. One is by virtue of occasional excursions into the luxury brand domains. These "excursionists" cannot afford to buy luxury brands consistently, but through occasional purchases they demonstrate that they prefer owning a few luxury brands to owning many more non-luxury brands (Dubois and Laurent 1994b, 1996). Another strategy is to sacrifice to be able to buy luxury brands. This sometimes results in what may appear to be illogical compromises such as sacrificing eating in order to afford a refrigerator into which the consumer cannot afford to put food (Belk 1999).

And yet another strategy for non-affluent consumers to afford luxury brands is to buy counterfeits. As Abbas (2002) points out, the counterfeit highlights problems that arise from widespread exposure to global brands and far less widespread ability to afford these marks of modernity and participation in global consumer culture. At the same time Abbas (2002, pp. 316–17) suggests that the counterfeit may not be the only fake: the "designer watch is already, in a sense, a fake . . . Part of the animus directed against the fake, especially on the part of the producers of taste, comes we might suspect from the fact that it threatens to expose such goods themselves to the charge of fakery." As Hopkins, Kontnik, and Turnage (2003) point out, as much as US $500 billion of counterfeit goods are sold each year, with a substantial amount of this being for the luxury goods that Abbas (2002) argues are themselves a type of fake. In an eight-country study of consumer ethics, one of the three scenarios posed by Belk, Devinney, and Eckhardt (2005) involved buying a counterfeit Louis Vuitton suitcase or wallet. Almost universally in both the more affluent world (the US, Sweden, Germany, Spain, Australia) and the less affluent world (China, India, Turkey) consumers said that they were not upset by such purchases and many justified such behavior by arguing that the prices of the originals are the real immorality. Still, there was one key difference between those in the more affluent and those in the less affluent world. The more affluent consumers said they might buy such goods because it was a fun thing to do that they could later joke about with friends (e.g., "You won't believe what I paid for this!"). Those in the less affluent world however would not tell their friends and would feel shame if their deception was discovered (Chuchinprakarn 2003). As Gentry, Putrevu, Shultz, and Commuri (2001) found, those in Asian countries who are attracted to counterfeit goods would buy the "real thing" if they could afford it. But since they cannot, they make do with the counterfeit in an effort to achieve what they regard as a level of decency and dignity in a brand-conscious world. In other words, they attempt to enhance their identity through deception. Chuchinprakarn (2003) also found that university students who are more materialistic and from less affluent families are more likely to buy counterfeit goods. This too suggests that buying counterfeit goods in Asia is an attempt to keep up, fit in, and cultivate face and dignity.

8.4   Conclusion

Just as advertising and packaging help to create an identity for a branded good, consumer use of branded goods can be seen as an advertisement for, and packaging of, the self in an effort to proclaim a self-identity (Pavitt 2000). The notion of self as brand is one that has been criticized (e.g., Quart 2003) because it involves a commodification of the self and because it defines the self based more on the extended self rather than through some inner sense of the person. If we judge and relate to other people because of what they have rather than who they are in some more intrinsic sense, we have given in to the superficial world encouraged by advertising. If we seek to win others' favor through bestowing them with material gifts, we have similarly given in to a commodity-based system of human relationships. And if we define ourselves through what we have, we become vulnerable to an existential question posed by Erich Fromm (1976, p. 76): "If I am what I have and if what I have is lost, who then am I?"

8.5 References

Jennifer L. Aaker, "Dimensions of brand personality," *Journal of Marketing Research* 34 (1997), 347–56.

Ackbar Abbas, "Theory of the fake," in *HK Lab*, Laurent Gutierrez, Ezio Manzini, and Valérie Portefaix (eds.) (Hong Kong: Map Book Publishers, 2002), 312–23.

Robert Abelson, "Beliefs are like possessions," *Journal for the Theory of Social Behavior* 15 (1986), 223–50.

"Beliefs as possessions – A functional perspective," in *Attitude Structure and Function*, Anthony R. Pratkanis and Deborah A. Prentice (eds.) (Hillside, NJ: Lawrence Erlbaum, 1989), 361–81.

A. Dwayne Ball and Lori H. Tasaki, "The role and measurement of attachment in consumer behavior," *Journal of Consumer Psychology* 1 (1992), 155–72.

Richard Barbrook, "The hi-tech gift economy," *First Monday*, www.firstmonday. org/issues/issue3_12/barbrook/index.html (2005).

Richard Barbrook and Andy Cameron, "Californian ideology," in *Crypto Anarchy, Cyberstates, and Pirate Utopias*, Peter Ludlow (ed.) (Cambridge, MA: MIT Press, 2001), 363–87.

Russell W. Belk, "Assessing the effects of visible consumption on impression formation," *Advances in Consumer Research* 5 (1978), 39–47.

"Materialism: Trait aspects of living in the material world," *Journal of Consumer Research* 12 (1985), 265–80.

"Identity and the relevance of market, personal, and community objects," in *Marketing and Semiotics: New Directions in the Study of Signs for Sale*, Jean Umiker-Sebeok (ed.) (Berlin: Mouton de Gruyter, 1987), 151–64.

"Possessions and the extended self," *Journal of Consumer Research* 15 (1988), 139–68.

"How perceptions of the body influence organ donation and transplantation: Me and thee versus mine and thine," in *Psychological Research on Organ Donation*, James Shanteau and Richard J. Harris (eds.) (Washington, DC: American Psychological Association, 1990), 139–49.

"The ineluctable mysteries of possessions," *Journal of Social Behavior and Personality* 6 (1991), 17–55.

"Attachment to possessions," in *Human Behavior and Environment: Advances in Theory and Research*, vol. XII, *Place Attachment*, Irwin Altman and Setha Low (eds.) (New York: Plenum Press, 1992a), 37–62.

"Moving possessions: An analysis based on personal documents from the 1847–1869 Mormon migration," *Journal of Consumer Research* 19 (1992b), 339–61.

"The perfect gift," in *Gift Giving: A Research Anthology*, Cele Otnes and Richard F. Beltramini (eds.) (Bowling Green, OH: Bowling Green University Popular Press, 1996), 59–84.

"Leaping luxuries and transitional consumers," in *Marketing Issues in Transitional Economies*, Rajiv Batra (ed.) (Norwell, MA: Kluwer, 1999), 38–54.

Russell W. Belk and Gregory Coon, "Gift-giving as agapic love: An alternative to the exchange paradigm based on dating experiences," *Journal of Consumer Research* 20 (1993), 393–417.

Russell W. Belk, Timothy Devinney, and Giana Eckhardt, "Consumer ethics across cultures," *Consumption, Markets and Culture* 8 (2005), 275–90 (with accompanying DVD).

Russell W. Belk, Güliz Ger, and Søren Askegaard, "The fire of desire: A multi-sited inquiry into consumer passion," *Journal of Consumer Research* 30 (2003), 326–51.

Russell W. Belk and Gülnur Tumbat, "The cult of Macintosh," *Consumption, Markets and Culture* 8 (2005), 205–18.

Russell W. Belk, Melanie Wallendorf, and John Sherry, "The sacred and the profane in consumer behavior: Theodicy on the odyssey," *Journal of Consumer Research* 15 (1989), 1–38.

Magnus Bergquist, "Open source software development as gift culture: Work and identity formation in an Internet community," in *New Technologies at Work: People, Screens, and Social Virtuality*, Christina Garsten and Helena Wulff (eds.) (Oxford: Berg, 2003), 223–341.

Magnus Bergquist and Jan Ljungberg, "The power of gifts: Organizing social relationships in open source communities," *Information Systems Journal* 11 (2001), 305–20.

Herng-Dar Bih, "The meaning of objects in environmental transitions: Experiences of Chinese students in the United States," *Journal of Environmental Psychology* 12 (1992), 135–47.

Samuel K. Bonsu and Russell W. Belk, "Do not go cheaply into that good night: Death ritual consumption in Asante, Ghana," *Journal of Consumer Research* 30 (2003), 41–55.

Daniel J. Boorstin, *The Americans: The Democratic Experience* (New York: Random House, 1973).

John Bowlby, *Attachment and Loss*, vol. I (London: Hogarth, 1969).

Colin Campbell, "Shopaholics, spendaholics, and the question of gender," in *I Shop, Therefore I Am: Compulsive Buying and the Search for Self*, April Lane Benson (ed.) (Northvale, NJ: Jason Aronson, 2000), 57–75.

Supanat Chuchinprakarn, "Consumption of counterfeit goods in Thailand: Who are the patrons?" *European Advances in Consumer Research* 6 (2003), 48–53.

Clare Cooper, "The house as symbol," *Design and Environment* 3 (1972), 3–37.

"The house as a symbol of the self," in *Designing for Human Behavior*, Jon Lang *et al.* (eds.) (Stroudsburg, PA: Dowden, Hutchinson and Ross, 1974), 130–46.

Richard Coyne, *Cornucopia Limited: Design and Dissent on the Internet* (Cambridge, MA: MIT Press, 2005).

Mihaly Csikszentmihalyi and Eugene Rochberg-Halton, *The Meaning of Things: Domestic Symbols and the Self* (Chicago: University of Chicago Press, 1981).

Carolyn Folkman Curasi, Margaret Hogg, and Pauline Maclaren, "Identity, consumption and loss: The impact of women's experience of grief and mourning on consumption in empty nest households," *Advances in Consumer Research* 31 (2004), 615–22.

Phillip Cushman, "Why the self is empty: Toward a historically situated psychology," *American Psychologist* 45 (1990), 599–611.

Helga Dittmar, *The Social Psychology of Material Possessions: To Have Is to Be* (New York: St. Martin's Press, 1992).

"The role of self-image in excessive buying," in *I Shop, Therefore I Am: Compulsive Buying and the Search for Self*, April Lane Benson (ed.) (Northvale, NJ: Jason Aronson, 2000), 105–32.

Mary Douglas and Baron Isherwood, *The World of Goods: Towards an Anthropology of Consumption* (New York: W. W. Norton, 1979).

Bernard Dubois and Gilles Laurent, "Is there a Euro consumer for luxury goods?" *European Advances in Consumer Research* 1 (1993), 58–69.

"Attitudes towards the concept of luxury: An exploratory analysis," *Asia Pacific Advances in Consumer Research* 1 (1994a), 273–8.

"The functions of luxury: A situational approach to excursionism," *Advances in Consumer Research* 23 (1994b), 470–7.

"Luxury possessions and practices: An empirical scale," *European Advances in Consumer Research* 2 (1995), 69–77.

James S. Duncan and Nancy G. Duncan, "House as presentation of self and the structure of social networks," in *Environmental Knowing: Theories, Research, and Methods*, Reginald G. Gollege (ed.) (Sroudsburg, PA: Dowden, Hutchinson and Ross, 1976), 247–53.

Giana M. Eckhardt and Michael J. Houston, "Consumption as self-presentation in a collectivist society," *Asia Pacific Advances in Consumer Research* 3 (1998), 52–8.

Duane Elgin, *Voluntary Simplicity, Revised Edition: Toward a Way of Life That Is Outwardly Simple, Inwardly Rich* (New York: Harper, 1998).

Richard Elliott and Kritsadarut Wattanasuwan, "Consumption and the symbolic project of the self," *European Advances in Consumer Research* 3 (1998), 17–20.

Basil G. Englis and Michael R. Solomon, "I am not, therefore I am: The role of avoidance products in shaping consumer behavior," *Advances in Consumer Research* 24 (1997), 61–3.

Ronald J. Faber, "A systematic investigation into compulsive buying," in *I Shop, Therefore I Am: Compulsive Buying and the Search for Self*, April Lane Benson (ed.) (Northvale, NJ: Jason Aronson, 2000), 27–53.

Ronald J. Faber and G. A. Christenson, "In the mood to buy: Differences in mood states experienced by compulsive buyers and other consumers," *Psychology and Marketing* 13 (1996), 803–20.

Ronald J. Faber, Thomas C. O'Guinn, and Raymond Krych, "Compulsive consumption," *Advances in Consumer Research* 14 (1987), 132–5.

Gary A. Fine, "Small groups and culture creation: The idioculture of a Little League Baseball team," *American Sociological Review* 44 (1979), 733–45.

A. Fuat Firat and Alladi Venkatesh, "Liberatory postmodernism and the reenchantment of consumption," *Journal of Consumer Research* 22 (1995), 239–67.

Robert Frank, *Luxury Fever: Why Money Fails to Satisfy in an Era of Excess* (New York: Free Press, 1999).

Thomas Frank, *The Conquest of Cool: Business Culture, Counterculture, and the Rise of Hip Consumerism* (Chicago: University of Chicago Press, 1997).

Erich Fromm, *To Have or to Be* (New York: Harper & Row, 1976).

Lita Furby and Mary Wilke, "Some characteristics of infants' preferred toys," *Journal of Genetic Psychology* 140 (1982), 207–19.

Jim Gentry, Stacey Menzel Baker, and Frederic B. Kraft, "The role of possessions in creating, maintaining, and preserving one's identity: Variation over the life course," *Advances in Consumer Research* 22 (1995), 413–18.

James W. Gentry, Sanjay Putrevu, Clifford Shultz II, and Suraj Commuri, "How now Ralph Lauren? The separation of brand and product in a counterfeit culture," *Advances in Consumer Research* 28 (2001), 258–65.

Güliz Ger and Russell W. Belk, "Accounting for materialism in four cultures," *Journal of Material Culture* 4 (1999), 183–204.

Markus Giesler, "Consumer gift systems," *Journal of Consumer Research* 33 (2006), 283–90.

Edward L. Grubb and Gregg Hupp, "Perception of self: Generalized stereotypes, and brand selection," *Journal of Marketing Research* 5 (1968), 58–63.

Aydan Gulerce, "Transitional objects: A reconsideration of the phenomena," *Journal of Social Behavior and Personality* 6 (1991), 187–208.

Jane Hammerslough, *Dematerializing: Taming the Power of Possessions* (Cambridge, MA: Perseus Publishing, 2001).

Douglas B. Holt, *How Brands Become Icons: The Principles of Cultural Branding* (Boston: Harvard Business School Press, 2004).

David M. Hopkins, Lewis T. Kontnik, and Mark T. Turnage, *Counterfeiting Exposed: Protecting Your Brand and Customers* (Hoboken, NJ: John Wiley & Sons, 2003).

Hironi Ikeuchi, Takehiro Fujihara, and Itsuko Dohi, "Involuntary loss of extended self of victims of great Hanshin earthquake and Northridge earthquake," *European Advances in Consumer Research* 4 (1999), 28–36.

Arvind K. Jain and Annamma Joy, "Money matters: An exploratory study of the socio-cultural context of consumption, saving, and investment patterns," *Journal of Economic Psychology* 18 (1997), 649–75.

William James, *The Principles of Psychology*, vol. I (New York: Henry Holt, 1890).

Annamma Joy and Ruby Roy Dholakia, "Remembrances of things past: The meaning of home and possessions of Indian professionals in Canada," *Journal of Social Behavior and Personality* 6 (1991), 385–402.

Daniel Kahneman, Jack L. Knetsch, and Richard Thaler, "Experimental tests of the endowment effect and the Coase theorem," *Journal of Political Economy* 99 (1990), 1325–48.

Laura Kamptner, "Personal possessions and their meanings: A life span perspective," *Journal of Social Behavior and Personality* 6 (1990), 209–28.

Justin Kaplan and Anne Bernays, *The Language of Names: What We Call Ourselves and Why It Matters* (New York: Simon and Schuster, 1997).

Tim Kasser, *The High Price of Materialism* (Cambridge, MA: MIT Press, 2003).

Tim Kasser and R. M. Ryan, "A dark side of the American Dream: Correlates of financial success as a central life aspiration," *Journal of Personality and Social Psychology* 64 (1993), 410–22.

Sonia Livingstone and Peter K. Lunt, "Generational and life cycle differences in experiences of ownership," *Journal of Social Behavior and Personality* 6 (1991), 229–42.

Joseph Luft, "Monetary value and the perception of persons," *Journal of Social Psychology* 46 (1957), 245–51.

Peter K. Lunt and Sonia M. Livingstone, *Mass Consumption and Personal Identity* (Buckingham, UK: Open University Press, 1992).

Celia Lury, *Brands: The Logos of the Global Economy* (London: Routledge, 2004).

Michel Maffesoli, *The Time of the Tribes: The Decline of Individualism in Mass Society*, Don Smith, trans. (Thousand Oaks, CA: Sage, 1996).

Mike Maguire, "The impact of burglary upon victims," *British Journal of Criminology* 20 (1980), 261–75.

Hazel Markus and Paula Nurius, "Possible selves," *American Psychologist* 41 (1986), 954–69.

Gordon Mathews, "Names and identities in the Hong Kong cultural supermarket," *Dialectical Anthropology* 21 (1996), 399–419.

Marcel Mauss, *The Gift: The Form and Functions of Exchange in Archaic Societies*, Ian Cunnison, trans. (New York: Norton, 1990).

Grant McCracken, "Who is the celebrity endorser?" *Journal of Consumer Research* 15 (1989), 310–21.

Raj Mehta and Russell W. Belk, "Artifacts, identity, and transition: Favorite possessions of Indians and Indian immigrants to the United States," *Journal of Consumer Research* 17 (1991), 398–411.

Werner Muensterberger, *Collecting, an Unruly Passion: Psychological Perspectives* (Princeton, NJ: Princeton University Press, 1994).

Albert M. Muñiz, Jr. and Thomas C. O'Guinn, "Brand community," *Journal of Consumer Research* 27 (2001), 412–33.

Thomas C. O'Guinn and Ronald J. Faber, "Compulsive buying: A phenomenological approach," *Journal of Consumer Research* 16 (1989), 147–57.

Warren R. Papp, "Being burglarized: An account of victimization," *Victimology: An International Journal* 6 (1981), 297–305.

Teresa Pavia, "Dispossession and perceptions of self in late stage HIV infection," *Advances in Consumer Research* 20 (1993), 425–8.

Jane Pavitt, "In goods we trust?" in *Brand-New*, Jane Pavitt (ed.) (London: V&A Publications, 2000), 19–51.

Gifford Pinchot, "The gift economy," *In Context: A Quarterly of Humane Sustainable Culture*, www.context.org/ICLIB/IC41/PinchotG.htm (1995).

Linda L. Price, Eric J. Arnould, and Carolyn Folkman Curasi, "Older consumers' disposition of special possessions," *Journal of Consumer Research* 27 (2000), 179–201.

Harold W. Proshansky, "The city and self-identity," *Environment and Behavior* 10 (1978), 147–69.

Alissa Quart, *Branded: The Buying and Selling of Teenagers* (New York: Basic Books, 2003).

Eric Steven Raymond, "The hacker milieu as gift culture," *Future Positive*, http://futurepositive.synearth.net/stories/storyReader$223 (2001).

Howard Rheingold, *The Virtual Community: Homesteading on the Electronic Frontier* (Cambridge, MA: MIT Press, 2000).

Martha L. Richins and Scott Dawson, "A consumer values orientation for materialism and its measurement," *Journal of Consumer Research* 19 (1992), 303–16.

Shay Sayre, "Possessions and identity in crisis: Meaning and change for victims of the Oakland firestorm," *Advances in Consumer Research* 21 (1994), 109–14.

Shay Sayre and David Horne, "I shop, therefore I am: The role of possessions for self definition," *Advances in Consumer Research* 23 (1996), 323–8.

Hope J. Schau and Mary C. Gilly, "We are what we post? Self-presentation in personal web space," *Journal of Consumer Research* 30 (2003), 385–414.

Carolyn Schenk and Rebecca Holman, "A sociological approach to brand choice: The concept of situational self image," *Advances in Consumer Research* 7 (1980), 610–14.

Juliet B. Schor, *The Overspent American: Upscaling, Downshifting, and the New Consumer* (New York: Basic Books, 1998).

John W. Schouten, "Personal rites of passage and the reconstruction of self," *Advances in Consumer Research* 18 (1991a), 49–51.

"Selves in transition: Symbolic consumption in personal rites of passage and identity reconstruction," *Journal of Consumer Research* 17 (1991b), 412–25.

John W. Schouten and James H. McAlexander, "Subcultures of consumption: An ethnography of the new biker," *Journal of Consumer Research* 22 (1995), 43–62.

Susan E. Schultz, Robert E. Kleine III, and Jerome B. Kernan, "'These are a few of my favorite things': Toward an explication of attachment as a consumer behavior construct," *Advances in Consumer Research* 16 (1989), 359–66.

Susan Schultz Kleine and Stacey Menzel Baker, "An integrative review of material possession attachment," *Academy of Marketing Science Review* 1 (2004), 1–39.

Susan Schultz Kleine, Robert E. Kleine III, and Chris T. Allen, "How is a possession 'me' or 'not me'? Characterizing types and an antecedent of material possession attachment," *Journal of Consumer Research* 22 (1995), 327–43.

Martin E. P. Seligman, *Helplessness* (San Francisco: Freeman, 1975).

Eugene Sivadas and Ravi Venkatesh, "An examination of individual and object-specific influences on the extended self and its relation to attachment and satisfaction," in *Advances in Consumer Research* 22 (1995), 406–12.

Michael R. Solomon and Henry Assael, "The forest or the trees? A gestalt approach to symbolic consumption," in *Marketing and Semiotics: New Directions in the Study of Signs for Sale*, Jean Umiker-Sebeok (ed.) (Berlin: Mouton de Gruyter, 1987), 189–218.

Douglas M. Stayman and Rohit Deshpande, "Situational ethnicity and consumer behavior," *Journal of Consumer Research* 16 (1989), 361–71.

Kelly Tian and Russell W. Belk, "Extended self and possessions in the workplace," *Journal of Consumer Research* 32 (2005), 297–310.

Paula Tidwell and Bernard Dubois, "A cross-cultural comparison of attitudes toward the luxury concept in Australia and France," *Asia Pacific Advances in Consumer Research* 2 (1996), 31–5.

James B. Twitchell, *Living It Up: America's Love Affair with Luxury* (New York: Simon and Schuster, 2003).

Branded Nation: The Marketing of Megachurch, College, Inc., and Museumworld (New York: Simon and Schuster, 2004).

David R. Unruh, "Death and personal history: Strategies of identity preservation," *Social Problems* 30 (1983), 340–51.

Joop Van den Bogaard and Oene Wiegman, "Property crime victimization: The effectiveness of police services for victims of residential burglary," *Journal of Social Behavior and Personality* 6 (1991), 329–62.

Vanik D. Volkan, "The linking objects of pathological mourners," in *Normal and Pathological Responses to Bereavement*, John Ellard *et al.* (eds.) (New York: MSS Information Corporation, 1974), 186–202.

Melanie Wallendorf and Eric J. Arnould, "'My favorite things': A cross-cultural inquiry into object attachment, possessiveness, and social linkage," *Journal of Consumer Research* 14 (1988), 531–47.

Robert Wicklund and Peter Gollwitzer, *Symbolic Self-Completion* (Hillsdale, NJ: Lawrence Erlbaum, 1992).

Raymond Williams, "Advertising: The magic system," in *Problems in Materialism and Culture: Selected Essays*, Raymond Williams (London: Verso, 1980), 170–95.

D. W. Winicott, "Transitional objects and transitional phenomena," *International Journal of Psychoanalysis* 34 (1953), 89–97.

Angela Chung Yan Wong and Judith Lynne Zaichkowsky, "Understanding luxury brands in Hong Kong," *European Advances in Consumer Research* 4 (1999), 310–16.

Nancy Y. C. Wong, "Suppose you own the world and no one knows? Conspicuous consumption, materialism and self," *Advances in Consumer Research* 24 (1997), 197–203.

Nancy Y. Wong and Aaron C. Ahuvia, "Personal taste and family face: Luxury consumption in Confucian and Western societies," *Psychology and Marketing* 15 (1998), 430–41.

Nan Zhou and Russell W. Belk, "Chinese consumer readings of global and local advertising appeals," *Journal of Advertising* 33 (2004), 63–76.

9 Wealth, consumption and happiness

AARON AHUVIA

The question of the relationship between wealth and happiness is an ancient one, addressed in the early writings of major religions and in Greek philosophy. Many religious and philosophical thinkers have argued that money does not buy happiness; whereas the general public have seen things quite differently. Recent empirical work has allowed us to bring data to bear on this question, with fascinating results.

Most of this research on happiness (i.e. subjective well-being) assumes that people can assess their own thoughts and feelings with reasonable accuracy. In this sense, it is no different from the overwhelming majority of psychological research, which relies on self-report measures. These self-report measures fall into several categories. Some assess global life satisfaction, for example by asking questions such as: looking at your life as a whole these days, how satisfied with your life would you say you are? Others assess satisfaction with various domains of life, such as financial situation, health, family life, etc. Judgements of life satisfaction are cognitive, that is to say, they are *thoughts* about how well one is doing. Other measures focus on affect, one's emotional life. Recently, researchers have started using the experience sampling methodology (Kahneman and Sugden 2005), in which respondents are contacted through a beeper at various points in the day, and write down what they are doing and how they feel at that moment. Although highly promising, the expense of the experience sampling approach has limited its popularity.

The website for the International Society for Quality of Life Studies contains a search engine for finding appropriate measures, and it is linked to a list of 894 different scales and measures for assessing quality-of-life-related issues. While measures of life satisfaction and emotional well-being are the most commonly used, other measures look at issues including meaning in life, self actualization, mental health and physiological measures of stress. All of these measures illuminate important aspects of well-being, and I am particularly sympathetic with the call for more studies on respondents' sense of leading a meaningful life (Ryff and Keyes 1995). But, for this review, I will focus primarily on studies where the dependent variable is one or more measure of positive affect, negative affect and/or life satisfaction. Blanchflower and Oswald (2004) found that the decision to use either affect or life satisfaction as a dependent variable made no substantial difference in their microeconomic analysis. Since this chapter presents a general overview of the findings in this area, I will use the term *happiness* very broadly, to refer to any of these measures or their combination. For a more detailed look at how each of these elements of happiness may be differentially affected by economic factors, see Ahuvia and Friedman (1998).

Can happiness measures be trusted? There are good reasons for thinking the answer is yes, at least as general indicators of people's subjective life experience. People's assessment of their own happiness tends to remain fairly stable over time, indicating that it is a global judgement about life rather than primarily a response to momentary conditions (Diener 1984). However, measured happiness does change in the expected direction with major positive and negative life events (Frijters 2004). People who see themselves as happy have positive daily mood ratings, recall more positive and less negative events in their lives, smile more, and are seen as happy by others who know them well (Myers and Diener 1995, Fernandez-Dols and Ruiz-Belda 1990). One common objection to these measures is that happiness is too subjective to be studied empirically; in this regard it is worth noting a growing body of research linking self-reported happiness to specific brain states (Sutton and Davidson 1997). Finally, the conclusions reported here are well replicated, summarizing hundreds of studies that have been conducted using a variety of measures, methods and respondent populations. (For other reviews see Ahuvia and Friedman 1998, Diener and Biswas-Diener 2002, Frey and Stutzer 2002a, 2002b, Layard 2005.)

After valid and reliable measures of happiness were established, there was a lot of initial research that simply observed whether wealthier people were happier than those on lower incomes. This research has been well reviewed previously (Ahuvia and Friedman 1998, and Diener and Biswas-Diener 2002), so the material covered in these previous reviews will only be summarized here. The current review will focus most heavily on work done since 1998, when the present author last summarized work on this topic.

9.1 Personal wealth and individual happiness

9.1.1 The relationship is present, but weak

When looked at in isolation from other variables, the relationship between income and happiness is consistently present, and consistently weak. Figure 9.1 presents a typical illustration of the relationship. Dollars have been converted into 1996 equivalents, and adjusted for household size. The happiness score is based on a simple three-point scale of 'not too happy' $= 1$, 'pretty happy' $= 2$, and 'very happy' $= 3$. As is regrettably common, the data on the very highest income category available in the survey (the top 10 per cent) are difficult to interpret, since they cover people with incomes starting at \$40,000 and go up to include the richest people on earth. Therefore, the graph includes only the first nine income deciles. Although it appears in this particular data set

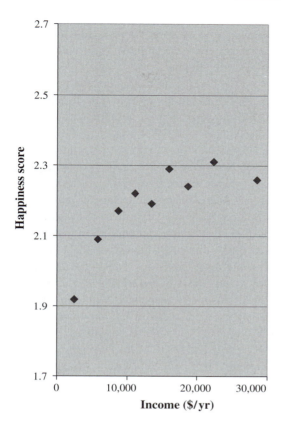

Figure 9.1 Income and happiness in the US, 1972–4. Reprinted from the National Opinion Research Center's General Social Survey, with permission

that happiness actually declines at around $30,000 per year, this is most likely a minor random fluctuation, since numerous studies show that the effect of income remains slightly positive even at higher income levels.

Most of this research on happiness (or subjective well-being (SWB)) assumes that people can assess their own thoughts and feelings with reasonable accuracy. Proponents of a connection between wealth and happiness emphasize that a statistically significant connection has been found in almost every study on the topic (for the few exceptions, see Arthaud-day and Near 2005, pp. 518–19). Conversely, authors who wish to argue that money is not closely related to SWB once basic needs have been met, focus on the weakness of this connection among the non-poor population.

Just how weak is the connection between money and happiness? Typical studies in developed economies indicate that income explains only about 2–4.5 per cent of the difference in happiness between individuals. A more sophisticated multilevel analysis by Schyns (2000) found that individual income explained only 2.5 per cent of the difference in happiness between people. Other studies have suggested ways of improving measures of income (Hsieh 2004, Saris 2001), but the results find that, at most, 5 per cent of the difference in happiness can be explained by income.

What is more, even the 5 per cent figure may overstate the case that money leads to happiness. Spurious correlations are possible because high-paying jobs also tend to have other rewards such as autonomy and relatively interesting work, which are associated with SWB (Argyle 1996). Unemployment is another likely cause of spurious correlations, since unemployment both brings a loss of income and has strong negative effects on happiness over and above the associated loss of wages (Clark, Georgellis and Sanfey 1999, Oswald 1997). Heavy consumer debt is another possible cause of spurious correlation because it significantly reduces happiness regardless of income level (Ahuvia and Friedman 1998), but it is more common among those with lower incomes (Lea, Webley and Walker 1995). The case of consumer debt is also interesting because at any given income level, increased debt indicates increased consumption. If wealth leads to happiness by increasing consumption, we might expect consumer debt to be positively associated with happiness. In fact, at any given income level, debt is associated with less happiness, and saving (i.e. reduced consumption) is associated with greater happiness (Ahuvia and Friedman 1998, Douthitt, MacDonald and Mullis 1992). Finally, Easterlin (2001b) reports that social class makes a large difference in how happy people are, but rising individual incomes over the life cycle do not increase happiness. One possible interpretation of this is that variables other than the level of one's consumption, like crime and single-parent families, may decrease the happiness of poorer people.

These arguments also arise when one looks at data comparing the average level of happiness in various nations. There is no question that, on average, the citizens of wealthy countries report more happiness than do people in poorer countries. But some researchers question if the observed correlation between GDP per capita and average level of happiness is driven by higher levels of consumption in the developed world. Helliwell (2003) looked at forty-nine countries, including some poor countries, and found that the correlation between national income and average level of happiness goes away after controlling for variables like quality of government, health and social connections. Similarly, Alesina, Di Tella and MacCulloch (2001) found that, after controlling for unemployment rate, income distribution and inflation, there was no correlation between real GDP per capita and happiness in the twelve European countries studied. It should, however, be noted that many of these variables, like health, are related to a country's wealth.

Finally, rather than wealth causing happiness, the causation could lie in the other direction. Aspects of a happy personality, such as optimism, have been shown to lead to higher incomes (Argyle 1996, Diener and Lucas 1999, Myers and Diener 1995). The influence of these personality variables can be so powerful, as noted in Cummins' (2000a) review study, that when income is included in models, along with psychological variables such as optimism, control and self-esteem, it does not show unique significance.

9.1.2 Money matters more to the poor

If money has little impact on happiness, does this mean we shouldn't worry about poverty? Most researchers reject this harsh conclusion by assuming a diminishing marginal utility for income, yielding a curvilinear relationship between income and happiness, so that a dollar provides more happiness to a poor person than it does to a rich person (Veenhoven 1991). The correlations between income and happiness mentioned above average together the strong effects of increased income on the poor with the much weaker effects of increased income on the non-poor. So, most of the variance explained in these correlations comes from alleviating the unhappiness of the very poor, rather than improving the living standard of the non-poor (Argyle 1999, Burchardt 2005, Firebaugh and Tach 2005, Hsieh 2004, Schyns 2003).

If the relationship between income and happiness is curvilinear, we would expect to see higher income-to-happiness correlations among the poor, who are at the more vertical part of the curve. Consistent with this, a review by Cummins (2000a) found that, among the non-poor, the correlation between income and happiness averaged only .14, but it increased to .26 among the poor. Furthermore, if the benefits of added income accrue mostly at the very low end of the distribution, we would expect the correlation between income and happiness to be higher in poor countries that don't have adequate social safety nets, and indeed, this is the case (Schyns 2003). For example, Biswas-Diener and Diener (2001) found a correlation of .45 between income and life satisfaction in the slums of Calcutta, even after controlling for other variables. And Saris (2001) found a significant improvement in the fit by moving from a linear to a curvilinear model for Russian data, where income explained a remarkably high 9 per cent of the variance in happiness.

Some authors have found evidence of a rather abrupt inflection point at around the income level where basic needs are met, and after that point the influence of income on happiness drops off sharply (Ahuvia and Friedman 1998, Argyle 1999, Cummins 2000a, Fuentes and Rojas 2001, Lever 2004). The approximate location of this inflection point varies across studies. Ahuvia and Friedman (1998) place it at around $20,000 per year in the US, Frey and Stutzer (2002a) place it at around $10,000 per year per capita when looking at national GDP data, and Fuentes and Rojas (2001) find that in Mexico it is as low as at $320 (US dollars, after conversion from Mexican pesos). For people with incomes above that inflection point, most studies find an extremely small but still measurable correlation between income and happiness (Schyns 2003), although, in other studies, the correlation between income and happiness among the non-poor becomes non-significant (Lever 2004).

Despite its intuitive appeal and the almost universal acceptance of the curvilinear relationship between income and happiness, not all evidence supports its veracity. When the average level of happiness for various nations is compared, rich countries are dependably happier than poor countries. Many studies have looked for a curvilinear relationship in this international data, but found a linear relationship instead (Diener, Sandvik, Seidlitz and Diener 1993, Diener, Diener and Diener 1995, Schyns 1998). However, this may be due largely to the fact that the data contain two distinct clusters of nations, the rich and happy versus the poor and less happy; and this type of clustering of data points makes any curvilinear relationship difficult to detect (Schyns 2003, p. 76). Easterlin (2005a) also raises concerns about the assumption of diminishing marginal returns on income. He recognizes that data from a single point in time show a curvilinear relationship between income and happiness, but argues that the expected patterns don't show up when looking at changes in individual or national income over time. Easterlin's arguments on these issues will be addressed in more detail when we look at the hedonic treadmill and economic growth.

Despite these legitimate concerns, the preponderance of the data still suggests a curvilinear relationship between wealth and happiness. In sum, the currently available data suggest that among the truly poor, the relationship between income and happiness is moderately strong. Once one's basic needs have been met, the relationship between income and happiness continues to be measurable but becomes extremely small, and of negligible practical significance.

9.1.3 Why is the relationship so weak?

Money is the ultimate resource which can be converted into almost anything one might desire. Why, then, is the relationship between wealth and happiness so small, especially among the non-poor? The answer seems to lie in a variety of complementary causes.

9.1.3.1 Among the non-poor, satisfaction with income matters more than income per se

First, while one's actual income has little relationship to one's happiness, *satisfaction* with one's finances does have a moderately strong relationship to life satisfaction as a whole, with correlations around .40–.50 (Ahuvia and Friedman 1998). This suggests that when people introspect about the impact of their own financial situation on their life as a whole, they compare their subjective sense of overall well-being to their subjective sense of their financial situation, and indeed the two are highly correlated. This may lead them to believe that their income is a major determinant of their happiness. But it seems that people often miss the fact that their objective financial situation has only a moderate connection to their subjective feelings about their situation (Diener and Oishi 2000, Fuentes and Rojas 2001).

Part of this is due to materialism, which is a dispositional tendency to, among other things, see one's standard of living as inadequate regardless of how much one actually earns (Burchardt 2005, Kasser 2002, Richins and Rudmin 1994, Ryan and Dziurawiec 2001, Sirgy, Lee, Larsen and Wright 1998). For example, in a recent survey of the very wealthy, 33 per cent of respondents with more than $10 million in investable assets reported that having enough money is a constant worry in their life (PNC Advisors 2005). Perhaps not surprisingly then, materialism or other forms of high-income aspirations are associated with unhappiness (Kasser 2002, Sirgy 1997, Stutzer 2004, Stutzer and Frey 2004). From this we can see that one's sense of financial satisfaction is largely a result of one's psychological disposition, rather than simply being a reaction to one's actual situation.

The relationship between satisfaction with specific life domains (e.g. standard of living, friends, work, neighbourhood, etc.) and overall life satisfaction is addressed in research on the 'bottom-up' versus the 'top-down' theories of happiness. The common-sense view is called the 'bottom-up' theory of happiness, where overall life satisfaction is a combination of people's satisfaction with various life domains such as family, work, income, etc. In contrast, the 'top-down' perspective holds that overall life satisfaction is largely due to genetics and/or stable personality factors; for example, some people are genetically predisposed towards anxiety and this lowers their happiness (Cummins 2000b, Diener and Lucas 1999, Lykken and Tellegen 1996). Research on the top-down model has shown that this dispositional sense of overall life satisfaction often spills over into specific life domains (e.g. people reason that if their life as a whole is good, their income must also be good), thus causing most of the correlation between domain satisfaction and overall life satisfaction (Mallard, Lance and Michalos 1997, Veenhoven 1996). These top-down effects are particularly strong in material domains such as satisfaction with one's income and home (Lance, Mallard and Michalos 1995). As Diener and Oishi (2000, p. 14) noted, 'people's global feelings about their lives are more important predictors of whether they'll be satisfied with their income than is their objective income!'

In sum, actual income is only loosely linked to income satisfaction, since income satisfaction reflects a large dispositional tendency for some individuals to be more satisfied with their financial situation than others (Ahuvia and Wong 2002). Income satisfaction, in turn, is only one of many life domains that influence overall life satisfaction. And while the connection between income satisfaction and life satisfaction is moderately strong, much of the correlation reflects the effects of overall life satisfaction on income satisfaction, rather than the other way around. Since the causal influences of income on income satisfaction, and income satisfaction on overall life satisfaction, are both fairly weak, it is not surprising that the causal influence of income on overall life satisfaction is very limited. This being the case, why is the relationship between income and happiness moderately strong among the poor?

9.1.3.2 Among the poor, income satisfaction per se may be largely beside the point

Veenhoven (1991) argues for livability theory, in which income increases happiness for the very poor by meeting basic needs, not by increasing income satisfaction per se. Consistent with livability theory, Groot and Van Den Brink (2000) found that in the Netherlands, when the wealthiest people in their sample received an increase in income, they quickly raised their income expectations to even higher levels and hence felt little happiness as a result (we will look at this 'preference drift' in more detail below), but this effect was not found among low-income respondents. This is interpreted as indicating that among lower income groups, money is used to meet basic needs, so preference drift doesn't occur. Biswas-Diener and Diener (2001) also presented evidence consistent with livability theory. As noted above, the connection between income satisfaction and actual income is generally weak but measurable; but Biswas-Diener and Diener (2001) found that within extremely impoverished populations in Calcutta, the correlation was so weak it did not reach statistical significance. Perhaps this was because even the relatively better off respondents in their sample had lifestyles so far below those they saw in the media (Ger and Belk 1996) that the income differences between the very poor respondents and the very *very* poor respondents had no measurable effect on income satisfaction. Nonetheless, even though income satisfaction had no influence on overall happiness, objective income had a very large and robust effect on overall happiness. In sum, this suggests that among the very poor, income may increase happiness not primarily by increasing income satisfaction, but by providing tangible benefits (nutrition, medicine, etc.) that have more direct effects on subjective well-being.

9.1.3.3 The hedonic treadmill and the durability bias

Disillusioned proponents of the idea that money leads to happiness can take some solace from the fact that it's not just money that disappoints; almost nothing that people expect will bring happiness has its anticipated effect. Part of this is because happiness is determined much more by how one thinks about the world, than by the way the world actually is (Lyubomirsky 2001), so changes to the external world have relatively little impact on subjective well-being. In what is called the 'durability bias', people tend to overestimate how much changes in their circumstances will affect their level of happiness, and, in particular, they greatly overestimate how long the changes in happiness will last (Gilbert, Pinel, Wilson, Blumberg and Wheatley 1998). This is true for negative events, such as having your political party lose an election, not getting tenure, or the dissolution of a romantic relationship (Gilbert *et al.* 1998), where people underestimate how quickly and thoroughly they will recover emotionally. And it is true for positive events, such as winning a lottery (Brickman, Coates, and Janoff-Bulman 1978) or the more mundane case of getting a higher income (Fuentes and Rojas 2001). The durability bias reflects a psychological process called 'adaptation', where people get used to a new situation and its emotional impact goes away (Kahneman and Sugden 2005). One big exception to this rule of adaptation seems to be the quality of interpersonal relationships, where evidence suggests they have a profound and lasting impact on happiness (Myers and Diener 1997), and people tend to underestimate their importance when making decisions (Dunn, Wilson and Gilbert 2003).

The durability bias is a more general term for what, in the case of income, has been called the 'hedonic treadmill'. For example, getting a better car provides a short-term boost in mood, but this quickly fades and your happiness goes back to normal. Now, you would need an even better car to elevate mood again, and the cycle could go on indefinitely (Layard 2005). So, like a person on a treadmill, we run and run, yet always stay in the same place. Stutzer and Frey (2004) provide evidence that increasing income aspirations undermine the effect of increases in income on happiness, by showing that the relationship between income and life satisfaction increases dramatically after income aspirations are controlled for.

If the hedonic treadmill exists, we would expect to see strong effects on happiness from recent changes in income, but little or no lasting effects. Some support for this has been found. Using retrospective measures, several studies have found that recent perceived improvements in living standards are related to happiness (e.g. Graham and Pettinato 2002). Using longitudinal panel data measuring income, Clark (1999) found that job satisfaction was tied to changes in wages, independent of absolute wage level. Also using panel data, several studies have found effects from changes in actual income on happiness or income satisfaction, even after controlling for the absolute income level (Chan, Ofstedal and Hermalin 2002, Ravallion and Lokshin 2001, Schyns 2003).

But not all data is supportive of the hedonic treadmill hypothesis (Diener, Sandvik, Seidlitz and Diener 1993). In studies that found the expected effects from changes in income, these effects were not generally strong enough to explain the positive correlation between income and happiness completely. Findings from Burchardt (2005) are even more problematic. In this carefully done longitudinal study, Burchardt finds the expected pattern for people who have experienced a loss in income; i.e. for any given income level, people who have experienced a drop in income are less satisfied with their incomes than are people who have had steady incomes. The negative effects of a drop in income remain even when data is examined over a ten-year period, indicating that adaptation to reduced incomes occurs slowly. Counter-intuitively though, people who have had an increase in income are also *less* satisfied than are people whose income remains constant. Some clues to this mystery can be found by breaking the respondents down into income quintiles, and these clues show that it might not be incompatible with adaptation theory after all. For the three middle quintiles, there was no difference in income satisfaction between people whose income recently increased to a given level, and people whose income had been holding constant at that level. For the highest income quintile, Burchardt finds the expected pattern where people who have had a recent increase in income are more satisfied with their income than those whose incomes have remained steady (see also Groot and Van Den Brink 2000). But, looking at the lowest income quintile, we get strong findings in the other direction; i.e. people with increasing income are less satisfied with their income than are people with low but stable income. It may be that for the lowest income quintile, increases in income make further increases seem possible, thus whetting respondents' appetite for more, and making them dissatisfied with their actual income.[1]

If this explanation for Burchardt's (2005) findings is correct, we see not only adaptation, but *hyper-adaptation*. In some cases, adaptation to an increase in income can 'overshoot' current income and lead to even greater dissatisfaction. This notion of hyper-adaptation is consistent with findings from Graham and Pettinato (2002), who looked at the effects of economic growth in Russia and Peru. They found that, in general, growth can promote happiness through upward mobility and optimism about the future. But they also uncovered a group of people they called 'frustrated achievers' who were disappointed at the slow rate of improvement and, despite objective improvements in their living standards, felt they were not doing well, thus depressing overall happiness scores.

9.1.3.4 Adaptation and material norms

Adaptation tells us that an increase in income is promptly followed by an increase in how much income one desires, so that however much one makes, it never seems to be enough. Saris (2001) provides interesting evidence for this by using a model that statistically removes the influence of past income on the current relationship between income and life satisfaction. Saris finds that, in Russia, this boosts the relationship from .18 to .56,[2] from which he concludes that 'the best interpretation of the income effect is that it is an effect of the change in income and not so much of income itself' (pp. 132–3). In a stunning example of adaptation to income, PNC Advisors (2005, p. 2, emphasis in original) report that

> When asked how much they needed to feel financially secure in the future, respondents consistently cited a need to approximately *double* their current level of assets. Those with $10 million or more felt they needed a median of $18.1 million; those with $5 million or more need $10.4 million, and those with half a million to $1 million said they needed $2.4 million.

---

[1] This is similar to the historian's adage that revolutions don't occur just because people have been oppressed for a long time. Rather, they occur when downtrodden populations start to see improvements in their lives, thus suggesting that further improvements are possible.

[2] The same analysis was conducted in Germany with similar, although far less dramatic, results.

This raises the question of where our norms for a desirable standard of living come from. Adaptation can be seen as the result of two different but related processes (Stutzer and Frey 2004). The first process, called habituation or adjustment, refers to decreasing responsiveness to repeated stimuli (Frederick and Loewenstein 1999). This process is not social; for example, getting used to eating spicy foods after a while would occur even if a person lived in complete isolation. The other aspect of adaptation has to do with social influences, like comparisons to other people or media images (Stutzer 2004). Experimental studies have shown that people make relative income judgements and this influences their happiness (Smith, Diener and Wedell 1989).

Michalos' (1985) Multiple Discrepancy Theory (MDT) sees unhappiness as stemming from large 'Have–Want' discrepancies. MDT is consistent with data which shows the Have–Want discrepancy for income to be significantly correlated with overall life satisfaction (Lance, Mallard and Michalos 1995) and pay satisfaction (Rice, Phillips and McFarlin 1990). The 'want' part of the Have–Want discrepancy is sometimes called the 'material norm'. MDT sees this material norm as a function of many variables, including 'what relevant others have, the best one has had in the past, what one expected to have in the past, what one expects to have in the future, what one deserves, and what one needs' (Lance, Mallard and Michalos 1995, p. 69). Festinger's (1954) seminal work on this topic claims that norms, like the material norm, are based on our observation of similar and proximate others. But attempts to test hypotheses derived from this theory have met with mixed results outside of the laboratory. For instance, people with a given income level are not happier when surrounded by people poorer than themselves and are not less happy when they are poorer than their neighbours (Diener, Sandvik, Seidlitz and Diener 1993). People seem to compute these norms in a more sophisticated way than simply looking at their neighbours. Work by Clark and Oswald (1996) and Drakopoulos and Theodossiou (1997) suggests that people may intuitively calculate an estimate of what someone with their education and demographic background normally earns, and use this as the partial basis for their material norm. Other studies have found support that people's perceptions of their parents' earning (McBride 2001) and that of American families in general (Mookherjee 1992, 1998) act as psychological anchors for establishing a person's material norm. Age may also affect the material norm. Campbell, Converse and Rodgers (1976) found evidence that retired people lower their income (and other) expectations, and thus in retirement average happiness increases while objective standard of living decreases.

Van Praag and Frijters (1999), using what they call the Leyden Approach, present evidence that people's idea of what constitutes a 'good income' depends in part on pragmatic issues like family size, but also depends on their current, past and anticipated future income, in that order of importance (van Praag and Frijters 1999). Because standards for a 'good income' depend a lot on one's current income, van Praag and Frijters recognize that the hedonic treadmill (which they call 'preference drift') will occur. Van Praag (1993) estimates that about 60% of the psychological benefits from any increase in income will be nullified by preference drift, but that still leaves 40%. Stutzer and Frey (2004) find that preference drift eats about 33% of the possible increases in happiness from an increase in income, but note that this figure underestimates the total loss in happiness since it excludes some important factors. Looking at Canadian data, Michalos (1989) found that 'although estimated needs increased 140% in the twelve-year period, these estimates still lagged behind the 199% increase in actual incomes', thus indicating a preference drift of about 70%. These studies suggest that preference drift is a matter of degree, and there is some lasting increase in happiness from an increase in wages, albeit a significantly smaller increase than one might otherwise expect.

While the idea that 60–70% of any increase in one's standard of living will be nullified by preference drift may strike some as a radical critique of conventional economic assumptions, it is actually more moderate than the competing claim that the hedonic treadmill eventually eliminates 100% of the psychic gains that might have accompanied increased income. Van Praag and Frijters (1999, p. 422) believe a consumer who gets *no* lasting psychic benefit from a raise in pay is 'a pathological case that has not been found in reality'. But Easterlin (1974, 1995, 2001a, 2001b) believes that it describes us all. In Easterlin's view, among the non-poor (and perhaps even among the poor (Easterlin 2005a)), adaptation to the tangible benefits of one's income eventually becomes complete. Easterlin emphasizes that within any given country, the rich are happier than the poor, but sees this as based entirely on social comparison of relative incomes, rather than any lasting benefits of tangible increases in living standards. Easterlin (2001a, 2005a) finds evidence for this position in data on happiness over the life cycle. As people get older, their incomes tend to increase towards middle age but then decrease as they enter retirement. One might expect their level of happiness to track their income, but instead, happiness is basically flat over the life cycle, even rising slightly in older age (Argyle 1999).

If it is true that adaptation eventually destroys most or all of the psychological benefits produced by an increasing income, what does this say about the desirability of economic growth?

9.2 National income and happy societies

The data comparing average levels of happiness in different countries present a puzzle that has become known as Easterlin's paradox (1974). The paradox refers to a conflict between the findings of cross-sectional data and those of time-series data. Cross-sectional data clearly show a weak but consistent correlation between income and happiness, yet time-series data do not replicate this effect. The same basic pattern is found on the macro-level, when we analyse the average levels of happiness in various countries, and compare these over time to changes in GDP per capita. At any point in time, rich countries tend to report significantly higher average levels of happiness than do poor countries (Cummins 1998, Diener and Oishi 2000). But tracking any given country over time, rising GNP per capita does not seem to translate into rising average levels of happiness (although this statement is under dispute, as we will see).

The most parsimonious way to explain this is through a strong form of the relative income hypothesis. In this view, the only benefit of income is status derived from social comparison, i.e. having more than someone else. Within a country, income correlates with happiness because, as people compare themselves to others, the people at the top feel good and the people at the bottom feel bad. Similarly, comparing average levels of happiness between countries, poor countries are on average less happy because their citizens compare themselves to what they see as first-world living standards, and feel unhappy as a result. In today's global economy consumers may judge their lifestyle against a 'world standard package of goods' that is influenced by international media and advertising (Ger and Belk 1996, O'Guinn and Shrum 1997). It is worth noting that Ger and Belk (1996) found that people in poorer countries tended to have the highest expectations for what goods they saw as necessities. This suggests that, rather than comparing themselves to their immediate neighbours, people in less developed countries may be comparing themselves to the lifestyles they see on American television, making their upward social comparison even more painful.

If money brings happiness exclusively through social comparison, individuals can increase their happiness by moving up in the relative income distribution. But since relative position is a zero-sum game, economic growth cannot make a society as a whole become happier – a rising tide lifts no boats.

Another possible explanation of the Easterlin paradox focuses on adaptation rather than social comparison. People simply increase their material norm at the same pace as their income, and hence happiness never improves. If this is true, though, why do we see a correlation between income and happiness at any given point in time? Wouldn't the rich and the poor alike have adapted to their lot in life, and have on average the same levels of happiness? A possible answer to this could be found in the discussion above about possible sources for a spurious correlation between income and happiness. For example, at the individual level marriage has a profound positive effect on happiness (Di Tella and MacCulloch 2005); since the marriage rate is positively correlated with income, this could create a spurious correlation between income and happiness. At a national level, I also discussed above a series of studies showing that if factors like individualism or good government were controlled for, the correlation between GDP per capita and national average levels of happiness goes away.

The social comparison explanation and the adaptation explanation can, of course, be combined so that each explains part of the phenomenon. Whatever the explanation, if it is true that economic growth does not increase average levels of happiness, this goes beyond a critique of GDP as a measure, and calls into question basic modernist ideas about progress (Eckersley 2000). Not surprisingly, the claim that economic growth does not lead to greater happiness has provoked a major debate that is still far from being resolved. This debate revolves around two key issues. First, is it true that countries are, in general, not getting happier over time? Second, is it possible that increases in GDP per capita do make countries happier, but this improving happiness is offset by other negative social trends?

9.2.1   Are countries getting happier?

Is it really true that countries have not been getting happier? The evidence is overwhelming that improvements in happiness have not kept pace with increases in wealth. But there is less certainty about whether levels of national happiness have remained totally flat, or have been slowly creeping upward, at least in some countries.

Easterlin (2005b) reviews a large body of evidence suggesting that, in general, longitudinal data show the level of happiness in most countries to be essentially flat over time. He concludes that 'countries with quite similar rates of economic growth have quite disparate trends in happiness, and that significant positive cases tend to be the exception, not the rule in countries with similar economic growth' (p. 440). In a commonly cited example, Easterlin (1995) presents data that show that the average level of happiness in Japan remained unchanged between 1958 and 1986, despite the fact that Japan's economic rise over that period was enormous. Japan is a problematic example to use, because on the one hand it did have enormous growth, but on the other hand it is a glaring exception to the normal correlations between GDP per capita and happiness. However, other studies also support Easterlin's general view. Stutzer and Frey (2004) find that after a rise in income, the related processes of habituation and social comparison fully nullify any lasting effect on happiness. Blanchflower and Oswald (2004) report that happiness in the US has actually been declining, and happiness in Britain has been flat, even as their economies have grown. Myers (1992) reports that between 1957 and 1990 the percentage of Americans who considered themselves 'very happy' remained unchanged despite a doubling of per capita income in constant dollars (see also Campbell 1981, Diener 1984).

On the other side of this debate, Veenhoven and Hagerty (2006) uncovered additional sources of time-series data that allowed them to look at trends over longer periods of time and in more countries. They found a very slight upward trend in happiness in both the US and Europe. This is consistent with Oswald's (1997) and Andrews' (1991) findings for the US, and Diener and Oishi's (2000) findings for Germany, Denmark and Italy. Veenhoven and Hagerty also found upward trends for happiness in the less developed countries where data was available, and the amount of improvement in happiness was much greater in these countries than it was in the US or Europe. This pattern is consistent with the idea that economic growth in poor countries can help people meet their basic needs, which impacts happiness directly, whereas the impact of economic growth on happiness in already developed nations is much less pronounced. Frijters (2004) found that after unification, 'East Germans experienced a continued improvement in life satisfaction to which increased household incomes contributed around 12 percent' (p. 649). In sum, because of limitations in the quality, duration and consistency of available data, no conclusive judgement can currently be reached as to whether happiness has been virtually flat or has been improving slightly.

9.2.2 Are other factors suppressing the relationship between national GDP changes and happiness?

Research on preference drift has found that rising expectations destroy most, but not all, of the psychic benefits from an increase in income. This would suggest that economic growth should lead to slight improvements in average levels of happiness. Under this scenario, the benefits of economic growth would be weak and easily overcome if other trends, such as increased pollution or longer work hours, were pushing happiness downward. Hagerty (2000) finds some support for this notion. His analysis shows that as communities get richer, higher absolute income levels create higher levels of happiness. But economic growth is often accompanied by increased inequality. Increased inequality raises the happiness of those at the top, but lowers it for those at the bottom. Since there are a lot more people at the bottom than the top, the net effect of increasing inequality is to decrease overall happiness (see also Alesina, Di Tella and MacCulloch 2001). Hagerty suggests that this is why economic growth in the US is not leading to much increased happiness, while economic growth in some more egalitarian European countries has led to increased levels of happiness. However, Schyns (2003) looked at forty countries in the World Values Survey using a multi-level model that simultaneously estimated individual and national level effects, and did not find similar negative effects for inequality.

Di Tella and MacCulloch (2005) also investigated this issue. Using large-scale time-series surveys in Europe and the US, they looked at the effects of economic growth on happiness, while statistically factoring out changes in life expectancy, environmental pollution, unemployment, inflation, unemployment benefits available, crime rate, divorce rate, working hours, economic openness to imports, government consumption, inequality, divorce rate, family size, and other factors. While some of these factors had moved in a negative direction, decreasing overall happiness, others had moved in a positive direction. On balance, the overall effect of these other variables was to *increase* happiness. So, rather than offering a solution to Easterlin's paradox by demonstrating negative social trends that offset the happiness caused by economic growth, they just make the paradox all the more vexing. If there is some social trend going on worldwide that is counteracting the positive effects of economic growth, it has yet to be discovered.

9.2.3 Does economic growth improve SWB in the very long term by changing culture?

Ahuvia (2002) argues that economic development is linked to happiness, but only in the *very* long run. Economic growth is important for meeting basic human needs. But beyond that, it also creates the preconditions for cultural and political change, and it is these social changes that ultimately have the greatest influence on happiness. Historically, this has been a multigenerational process occurring over hundreds of years. So, the rate of change in US happiness reported by Veenhoven and Hagerty (2006), where it would take 167 years to move the average happiness level up one point on a ten-point scale, is in line with this type of slow historical transformation. In particular, Ahuvia argues that 'cultures of happiness' allow people to make major life decisions like whom they will marry, or what their career will be, based on what they will find most personally fulfilling, allowing people to achieve higher levels of happiness.

It is clear that culture and related national or regional level variables have a strong influence on happiness. Helliwell (2003) found that the strong correlation between GDP per capita and average national levels of happiness is almost completely eliminated by controlling for region-specific determinants of happiness, such as culture. Schyns (2003) used a multi-level approach to look simultaneously at individual income and the effects of living in a rich country. She found that living in a rich country has an independent effect which is much stronger than individual level variables such as personal income. So we know that culture has a profound influence on happiness, and it is also known that the cultures that are most associated with happy societies allow people the freedom to make important life choices and express their thoughts and values (Diener, Diener and Diener 1995). Looking at a particular contemporary instance of this cultural change process, Kedem-Friedrich and Al-Atawneh (2004) found that Bedouin women in Israel were happier when they led more modern lives, provided that they saw their husbands as being fairly supportive of their more modern lifestyle. However, if the woman's modern lifestyle caused marital conflict, a more modern lifestyle was associated with lower happiness.

Richer countries tend to be more individualistic, and individualism is very strongly correlated with happiness at a national level (Cummins 1998, Myers and Diener 1995). As Schyns (2003) cautions, individualism, democracy and economic prosperity are bound together in a cycle of modernization that is very difficult to disentangle (with correlations as high as .85). However, when attempts have been made to pull these factors apart, the results provide only mixed support for Ahuvia's cultures of happiness thesis. Consistent with Ahuvia's thesis, Diener, Diener and Diener (1995) found that when individualism is controlled for, the correlation between GNP per capita and happiness goes away, but when GNP per capita is controlled for, the correlation between individualism and SWB is reduced but remains significant. However, Schyns (2003) conducted a similar analysis on a different data set, and found just the opposite results.

9.3 If money doesn't buy happiness, why do we act like it does?

Economists have long assumed that situations where people behave in ways that run counter to their own happiness are rare exceptions, not deserving of serious consideration. We are seeing here, though, that people make choices that don't maximize their happiness with great regularity and consequence. There are two main reasons why people might behave in ways at odds with their own happiness: biased processing and multiple goals. The biased processing approach maintains that consumers are trying to maximize happiness, but are bad at it due to various biases and heuristics (Layard 2005). And indeed, people seem to be astonishingly bad at predicting how happy some turn of events will make them, and also seem unable to learn from their mistakes. For example, van Praag and Frijters (1999) and Easterlin (2001b) argue along the same lines in explaining why people think more money will make them happy, when in fact it does not. Essentially, people have a psychological bias that prevents them anticipating the way their aspirations will adjust to their improved circumstances. So, when they contemplate getting a rise in pay, they imagine how happy they would be with that income, if their material norm remained unchanged. Yet, time and time again, their material norm does change after receiving a rise, and they seem to have great difficulty in taking this into account when making decisions.

Frey and Stutzer (2004) further refine this view. They argue that several biases combine to cause people to overvalue extrinsic benefits (e.g. wealth and prestige) and undervalue intrinsic benefits (e.g. family time) when making decisions. (For a fuller discussion of the extrinsic/intrinsic dichotomy see Kasser (2002).) To illustrate this point, they use the example of making a choice to take a job that offers a higher salary, but requires a longer commute. The commute cuts into time needed to pursue intrinsically rewarding activities like building social relationships, but provides income which can easily be translated into extrinsic rewards like status. They suggest that decision-making biases cause people to overvalue the income and undervalue the costs of the commute, thus leading them to accept the job when they should not. As empirical support for this hypothesis, they find that after controlling for a host of demographic variables, longer commuting times are closely associated with lower life satisfaction among respondents to the German Socio-Economic Panel Study (GSEPS). This runs counter to rational decision-making models, which suggest that commuting times and life satisfaction should be uncorrelated, since people would only choose to take a job with a long commute if it offered other advantages that compensated for this lost time. As further evidence for the psychological mechanism that they propose to explain this phenomenon, Frey and Stutzer hypothesize that people with a more extrinsic values orientation are particularly prone to making the mistake of overvaluing income relative to the loss of free time. To demonstrate this, they divide GSEPS respondents into those who primarily value intrinsic rewards (family, friends and religion) versus those who primarily value extrinsic rewards (income, influence on political decisions and career success). They then show that the negative correlation between commuting time and life satisfaction only exists in the extrinsically oriented group.

Advocates of the multiple goals perspective generally acknowledge that these cognitive biases exist, but question whether these biases represent the complete explanation for behaviors that work against happiness. The multiple goals perspective holds that while happiness is extremely important to people, it is just one of several goals underlying human action (Ahuvia 2002, 2006). Examples of these other goals include gaining honour or prestige, complying with social expectations, being sexually attractive, etc. In contrast to arguments that people only want these things because they hope to become happier, the multiple goals perspective holds that people sometimes value these things as ends in themselves, on a par with happiness. As Ahuvia (2002, p. 31) writes, for some people it is just as possible that they 'seek social recognition with the ultimate goal of personal happiness' as it is that they 'seek happiness with the ultimate goal of getting others to think well of them for having such a pleasant affect'. Frijters (2000) looked empirically at this question, and consistent with the multiple goals perspective, found only weak and limited evidence that people try to maximize general satisfaction.

In the multiple goals perspective, then, part of the reason people don't always achieve happiness is that they are implicitly trying to achieve goals that may conflict with happiness. If this is the case, people have multiple motivational systems that at times conflict with each other, rather than just one unified motivational system that maximizes a single goal such as utility. These motivational systems may have evolved at different times in our history and may operate through different neurological mechanisms. Which of these motivational systems eventually wins out and controls our behavior may be the result of factors like what mood we are in, if we feel threatened, whether social expectations are momentarily salient to us, or how much alcohol we have consumed; rather than a utility maximizing master algorithm.

9.4 Happiness and utility

Views in economics on the measurability of utility can be divided into four historical stages (Bruni 2004). The early classical economists spoke directly about happiness, which they saw in the Aristotelian sense of eudaemonia (i.e. human flourishing), which is dependent on virtuous actions. In the second stage, economic language shifted from 'happiness' to 'utility', which is a less morally charged concept, defined as the subjective balance of pleasures and pains (Bentham 1789/1948). This experienced utility was believed to be measurable (Frey and Stutzer 2002b, Layard 2005); for example, Edgeworth proposed the idea of a 'hedonometer', a machine to measure happiness (Dixon 1997). In the third stage, Robbins (1935) led a revolution in the field by arguing that subjective utility could not be measured and was therefore not a scientific concept. Samuelson (1938) proposed what is in essence 'decision utility' (Frey and Stutzer 2002b, Kahneman and Sugden 2005); i.e. rather than being a psychological experience that occurs during or after consumption, utility is that which people try to maximize when choosing between alternatives. Therefore, people's choices reveal their preferences, which in turn reveal their utility function; hence, revealed preferences define utility. After the Second World War, this school of thought became known as the New Welfare Economics.

Robbins (1935) mirrored the ideas of psychological behaviourism (Watson 1913), which was in full swing in the 1930s. Behaviourism held that, to be truly scientific, psychological theories should be based only on directly observable behaviour without reference to mental constructs like ideas, feelings, motives, etc. Behaviourism eventually lost favour in psychology for two main reasons. First, evidence mounted that human behaviour could not be adequately explained without reference to mental constructs. And second, philosophy of science also came to accept that theories are often about constructs that are not directly observable, whether they be gravity or grief. We infer the action of these non-observable constructs through observing what we can; in the case of gravity, we observe the behaviour of physical objects; in the case of grief, we observe human behaviour either in situ or in the form of responses to a questionnaire. So the exclusion of non-observable constructs is an unscientific requirement.

We are, I would argue, at the beginning of a fourth stage in economic thinking on these issues – what Frey and Stutzer (2002a) call 'another revolution in viewing utility' (p. 43). In contrast to the analytic focus of the New Welfare Economics, I would call this fourth stage a period of *Economic Psychological Realism*, in which economists try to bring their models of decision making and utility more in line with empirical research in the social sciences. One day, the award of the 2002 Nobel Prize in Economics to Daniel Kahneman may come to be seen as the historical turning point towards economic psychological realism.

Not surprisingly, this move towards economic psychological realism has encountered resistance. The data on income and subjective well-being are remarkably inconsistent with widely held views about the benefits of material wealth. And it is this radical disjunction between the data and established theory that has, in an ironic way, limited the data's discussion in economics. Free market advocate Arnold Kling (2003) was refreshingly candid in arguing that since the data seems to contradict established theory, *there must be something wrong with the data*. Coming from the other side of the controversy, van Praag puts the opposite spin on the same phenomenon, writing that 'it is rather remarkable that mainstream economics for half a century . . . has followed a way which is so different from what is going on in the development of most sciences. Mostly science is *following* reality, instead of *ignoring* it' (1994, p. 88, emphasis in original). Nonetheless, attitudes do seem to be slowly changing in economics. Although many economists still view happiness as 'too subjective' to be studied scientifically, a growing body of research is now linking self-reported happiness to specific brain states (Sutton and Davidson 1997), which is encouraging some otherwise sceptical observers to take research on happiness more seriously.

Of course this change in economics is not inevitable – there is another option. Economists can simply define the problem out of existence. Recognizing that decision utility (the implicit weights given to various alternatives before a decision is made) and experience utility (the experienced psychological consequences of those decisions) are frequently not in sync, economists could opt to define decision utility as the only utility of disciplinary concern. For many descriptive or predictive tasks, this would be appropriate and sufficient. But if decision utility is the only utility studied in economics, then economics makes an implicit claim that a decision is a good decision simply because someone freely made it, regardless of the consequences. This would be a brave philosophic stand, but also one that would place economics outside of the mainstream of normative discourse, where things like happiness matter.

9.5 Future directions

The previous discussion has revealed several large questions that remain top priorities for research. Questions about economic growth are high on the list. We know that economic growth does not provide large long-term returns in happiness, but the question is still open as to whether it can at least provide smaller lasting returns that might build up to practical significance over the long run. This relates directly to the issue of poverty. We have good evidence that improving the living standards of the very poor produces strong and direct gains in happiness, but it's too early to declare the case closed. Further evidence on this issue is badly needed due to its clear policy implications. We should also consider the potential positive effects of economic growth on culture. Specifically, at least moderate levels of economic growth might pay off psychologically by increasing optimism. Along these same lines, a zero overall growth level means that for someone to increase their income, someone else must lose income. Given that people will still want to get ahead economically, what would the effect of a zero-growth economy be on social trust and harmony? While these questions mean that advocating zero economic growth per capita is at best premature, the data is quite compelling that a culture less obsessed with economic growth would be both psychologically and ecologically healthier (Brown and Kasser 2005).

Much of the previous discussion revolves around people's material aspirations and their link to both income and happiness. In this way, the literature on income is closely linked with materialism. But current work has often relied on very approximate proxy measures for these aspirations. The inclusion of good measures for material aspirations in large-scale longitudinal studies would help fill in one of the most problematic lacunae in this area. How material aspirations are set has implications for, among other things, tax policy. If one person's gain in consumption raises the material aspirations of those around him or her, then status consumption has negative externalities (Frank 1999). Like any good with negative externalities, it will be overconsumed. Thus, Frank (1999) advocates a consumption tax to shift resource allocation away from status consumption and towards leisure, health, education and other less status-focused pursuits. It's a simple argument, but it has yet to make real headway as a policy.

In future research, it would behove us to develop effective personal and social strategies for living a happy life in a consumer society (Seligman 2002). For example, Scitovsky (1992) suggests a strategy for enjoyable spending, where people focus their budget on things for which adaptation is slow. And Tatzel (2003) recommends developing low financial aspirations and moderate spending patterns. But work in this area is still in its infancy.

Finally, quality of life is often looked at using a combination of objective and subjective indicators. However, some proponents of subjective measures argue that, ultimately, happiness is the only thing that matters. For example, Ng (1997, p. 1849) writes that 'We want money (or anything else) only as a means to increase our happiness', and Stutzer and Frey (2004, p. 1) write that 'Economic activity is certainly not an end in itself, but only has value in so far as it contributes to human happiness.' This position is an intellectual descendant of Aristotle's (trans. 1962) view that eudaemonia (roughly translated as happiness) is the proper ultimate goal for all human action (Ahuvia 2006). Aristotle reasoned that every other goal, such as wealth or power, was only desired because it was hoped that it would lead to happiness; whereas happiness was desired as an end in itself and not a means to another end. Therefore, other goals were only valuable in so far as they produced happiness.

But is this the position we really want to take? As Veenhoven and Hagerty (2006) point out, at the very least we should be looking at longevity as well as happiness. And Cummins (2000b) argues that both objective and subjective measures of quality of life are important to get a full picture of a good life. Diener and Diener (1995) start with the assumption that happiness is just one value among many, and therefore look at numerous measures, such as scientific achievement, that reflect achievement in different societies on a wide range of human values. In this chapter I have been quite critical of economists' reluctance to look at happiness, but that's not the same as saying all we should look at is happiness.

9.6 Conclusion

A somewhat stark conclusion to this chapter must be that people's economic decisions don't match up well with their self-reports about their happiness, leaving researchers and theorists with a real dilemma. Either one argues that people are smart and rational enough to make decisions that maximize their utility, but incompetent at assessing their own utility; or, one is left with the symmetrical problem that people are competent enough to assess their own well-being, but not competent enough to use that information effectively in decision making. While neither alternative is very appealing, it seems that the second is the more likely of the two. After all, assessing one's own *subjective* well-being seems a fairly straightforward task, at least when compared to making decisions about the probable outcome of future events. So, if either of these processes is prone to go askew, it is more likely to be decision making. The model of rational economic man is elegantly simple, but it is no longer capable of explaining the extant data. As Einstein once said, theories should be made as simple as possible, but not simpler.

9.7 References

Ahuvia, Aaron C. 2002. 'Individualism/Collectivism and Cultures of Happiness: A Theoretical Conjecture on the Relationship Between Consumption, Culture and Subjective Wellbeing at the National Level', *Journal of Happiness Studies* 3: 23–36.

2006. 'Aristotle's Error and Revealed Preferences: If Money Doesn't Buy Happiness, Why Do We Act Like It Does?' working paper.

Ahuvia, Aaron C. and Friedman, Douglas 1998. 'Income, Consumption, and Subjective Well-being: Toward a Composite Macromarketing Model', *Journal of Macromarketing* 18: 153–68.

Ahuvia, Aaron C. and Wong, Nancy 2002. 'Personality and Values Based Materialism: Their Relationship and Origins', *Journal of Consumer Psychology* 12(4): 389–402.

Alesina, Alberto, Di Tella, Ravael and MacCulloch, Robert 2001. 'Inequality and Happiness: Are Europeans and Americans Different?' National Bureau of Economic Research (NBER): working paper 8198.

Andrews, Frank M. 1991. 'Stability and Change in Levels and Structure of Subjective Well-being: USA 1972 and 1988', *Social Indicators Research* 25: 1–30.

Argyle, Michael 1996. 'Subjective Well-being', in Avner Offer (ed.) *In Pursuit of the Quality of Life* (New York: Oxford University Press), pp. 18–45.

1999. 'Causes and Correlates of Happiness', in D. Kahneman, E. Diener and N. Schwarz (eds.) *Well-being: The Foundations of Hedonic Psychology* (New York: Russell Sage Foundation), pp. 353–73.

Arthaud-day, Marne L. and Near, Janet P. 2005. 'The Wealth of Nations and the Happiness of Nations: Why "Accounting" Matters', *Social Indicators Research* 74(3): 511–48.

Arthaud-day, Marne L., Rode, Joseph C., Mooney, Christine H. and Near, Janet P. 2005. 'The Subjective Well-being Construct: A Test of Its Convergent, Discriminant, and Factorial Validity', *Social Indicators Research* 74(3): 445–76.

Bentham, Jeremy 1789, reprinted 1948. *An Introduction to the Principles of Morals and Legislation*. Oxford: Blackwell.

Biswas-Diener, Robert and Diener, Ed 2001. 'Making the Best of a Bad Situation: Satisfaction in the Slums of Calcutta', *Social Indicators Research* 55: 329–52.

Blanchflower, David G. and Oswald, Andrew J. 2004. 'Well-being Over Time in Britain and the USA', *Journal of Public Economics* 88(7–8): 1359–86.

Brickman, Philip, Coates, Dan and Janoff-Bulman, Ronnie 1978. 'Lottery Winners and Accident Victims: Is Happiness Relative?' *Journal of Personality and Social Psychology* 36(8): 917–27.

Brown, Kirk Warren and Kasser, Tim 2005. 'Are Psychological and Ecological Well-being Compatible? The Role of Values, Mindfulness, and Lifestyle', *Social Indicators Research* 74(2): 349–68.

Bruni, Luigino 2004. 'The "Technology of Happiness" and the Tradition of Economic Science', *Journal of History of Economic Thought* 26(1): 19–43.

Burchardt, Tania 2005. 'Are One Man's Rags Another Man's Riches? Identifying Adaptive Expectations Using Panel Data', *Social Indicators Research* 74(1): 57.

Campbell, Angus 1981. *The Sense of Well-being in America: Recent Patterns and Trends*. New York: McGraw-Hill.

Campbell, Angus, Converse, Philip E. and Rodgers, Willard L. 1976. *The Quality of American Life*. New York: Russell Sage.

Chan, A., Ofstedal, M. and Hermalin, A. 2002. 'Changes in Subjective and Objective Measures of Economic Well-being and Their Interrelationship Among the Elderly in Singapore and Taiwan', *Social Indicators Research* 57: 263–300.

Clark, Andrew 1999. 'Are Wages Habit-Forming? Evidence from Micro-Data', *Journal of Economic Behavior and Organization* 39: 179–200.

Clark, Andrew, Georgellis, Yannis and Sanfey, Peter 1999. *Scarring: The Psychological Impact of Past Unemployment*. Laboratoire d'Economie d'Orléans: Orléans, France.

Clark, Andrew E. and Oswald, Andrew J. 1996. 'Satisfaction and Comparison Income', *Journal of Public Economics* 61: 359–81.

Cummins, Robert A. 1998. 'The Second Approximation to an International Standard for Life Satisfaction', *Social Indicators Research* 43: 307–34.

2000a. 'Personal Income and Subjective Well-being: A Review', *Journal of Happiness Studies* 1(2): 133–58.

2000b. 'Objective and Subjective Quality of Life: An Interactive Model', *Social Indicators Research* 52: 55–70.

Diener, Ed 1984. 'Subjective Well-being', *Psychological Bulletin* 95 (May): 542–75.

Diener, Ed and Biswas-Diener, Robert 2002. 'Will Money Increase Subjective Well-being? A Literature Review and Guide to Needed Research', *Social Indicators Research* 57: 119–69.

Diener, Ed and Diener, Carol 1995. 'The Wealth of Nations Revisited, Income and the Quality of Life', *Social Indicators Research* 36: 275–86.

Diener, Ed, Diener, Marissa and Diener, Carol 1995. 'Factors Predicting the Subjective Well-being of Nations', *Journal of Personality and Social Psychology* 69 (November): 851–64.

Diener, Ed and Lucas, Richard E. 1999. 'Personality and Subjective Well-being', in D. Kahneman, E. Diener and N. Schwarz (eds.) *Well-being: The Foundations of Hedonic Psychology* (New York: Russell Sage Foundation), pp. 213–29.

Diener, Ed and Oishi, Shigehiro 2000. 'Money and Happiness: Income and Subjective Well-being Across Nations', in E. Diener and E. Suh (eds.) *Culture and Subjective Well-being* (Cambridge, MA: MIT Press), pp. 185–218.

Diener, Ed, Sandvik, Ed, Seidlitz, Larry and Diener, Marissa 1993. 'The Relationship Between Income and Subjective Well-being: Relative or Absolute?' *Social Indicators Research* 28 (March): 195–223.

Di Tella, Rafael and MacCulloch, Robert 2005. 'Gross National Happiness as an Answer to the Easterlin Paradox?' working paper.

Dixon, Huw D. 1997. 'Controversy, Economics and Happiness, Editorial Note', *Economic Journal* 107: 1812–14.

Douthitt, Robin A., MacDonald, Maurice and Mullis, Randolph 1992. 'The Relationship Between Measures of Subjective and Economic Well-being: A New Look', *Social Indicators Research* 26 (June): 407–22.

Drakopoulos, S. A. and Theodossiou, I. 1997. 'Job Satisfaction and Target Earnings', *Journal of Economic Psychology* 18: 692–704.

Duesenberry, James S. 1949. *Income, Savings and the Theory of Consumer Behavior.* Cambridge, MA: Harvard University Press.

Dunn, Elizabeth W., Wilson, Timothy D. and Gilbert, Daniel T. 2003. 'Location, Location, Location: The Misprediction of Satisfaction in Housing Lotteries', *Personality and Social Psychology Bulletin* 29(11): 1421.

Easterlin, Richard A. 1974. 'Does Economic Growth Improve the Human Lot? Some Empirical Evidence', in P. A. David and M. W. Reder (eds.) *Nations and Households in Economic Growth* (New York: Academic Press), pp. 89–125.

1995. 'Will Raising the Incomes of All Increase the Happiness of All?' *Journal of Economic Behavior and Organization* 27: 35–47.

2001a. 'Life Cycle Welfare: Evidence and Conjecture', *Journal of Socio-Economics* 30(1): 31–61.

2001b. 'Income and Happiness: Towards a Unified Theory', *Economic Journal* 111(473): 465–84.

2005a. 'Diminishing Marginal Utility of Income? Caveat Emptor', *Social Indicators Research* 70(3): 243–55.

2005b. 'Feeding the Illusion of Growth and Happiness: A Reply to Hagerty and Veenhoven', *Social Indicators Research* 74(3): 429–43.

Eckersley, Richard 2000. 'The Mixed Blessings of Material Progress: Diminishing Returns in the Pursuit of Happiness', *Journal of Happiness Studies* 1(3): 267–92.

Fernandez-Dols, Jose-Miguel and Ruiz-Belda, Maria-Angeles 1990. 'Are Smiles a Sign of Happiness? God Medal Winners at the Olympic Games', *Journal of Personality and Social Psychology* 69(6): 1113–19.

Festinger, Leon 1954. 'A Theory of Social Comparison', *Human Relations* 7(2): 117–40.

Firebaugh, Glenn and Tach, Laura 2005. 'Relative Income and Happiness: Are Americans on a Hedonic Treadmill?' working paper.

Frank, Robert 1999. *Luxury Fever*. New York: Free Press.

Frederick, Shane and Loewenstein, George 1999. 'Hedonic Adaptation', in D. Kahneman, E. Diener and N. Schwarz (eds.) *Scientific Perspectives on Enjoyment, Suffering, and Well-being* (New York: Russell Sage Foundation), pp. 302–29.

Frey, Bruno S. and Stutzer, Alois 2002a. *Happiness and Economics: How the Economy and Institutions Affect Human Well-being*. Princeton, NJ: Princeton University Press.

2002b. 'What Can Economists Learn from Happiness Research?' *Journal of Economic Literature* 40 (June): 402–35.

2004. 'Economic Consequences of Mispredicting Utility', Working Paper no. 218, Institute for Empirical Research in Economics, University of Zurich.

Frijters, Paul 2000. 'Do Individuals Try to Maximize General Satisfaction?' *Journal of Economic Psychology* 21(3): 281–304.

2004. 'Investigating the Patterns and Determinants of Life Satisfaction in Germany Following Reunification', *Journal of Human Resources* 39(3): 649–74.

Fuentes, Nicole and Rojas, Mariano 2001. 'Economic Theory and Subjective Well-being: Mexico', *Social Indicators Research* 53(3): 289–314.

Ger, Guliz and Belk, Russell W. 1996. 'Cross-cultural Differences in Materialism', *Journal of Economic Psychology* 17 (February): 55–77.

Gilbert, Daniel T., Pinel, Elizabeth C., Wilson, Timothy D., Blumberg, Stephen J. and Wheatley, Thalia P. 1998. 'Immune Neglect: A Source of Durability Bias in Affective Forecasting', *Journal of Personality and Social Psychology* 75(3): 617–38.

Graham, C. and Pettinato, S. 2002. 'Frustrated Achievers: Winners, Losers and Subjective Well-being in New Market Economies', *Journal of Development Studies* 38(4): 100–40.

Groot, Wim and Van Den Brink, Henriette Maassen 2000. 'Life-satisfaction and Preference Drift', *Social Indicators Research* 50(3): 315–28.

Hagerty, Michael R. 2000. 'Social Comparisons of Income in One's Community: Evidence from National Surveys of Income and Happiness', *Journal of Personality and Social Psychology* 78(4): 764–71.

Helliwell, John F. 2003. 'How's Life? Combining Individual and National Variables to Explain Subjective Well-being', *Economic Modeling* 20: 331–60.

Hsieh, Chang-Ming 2004. 'Income and Financial Satisfaction Among Adults in the United States', *Social Indicators Research* 66(3): 249–66.

Kahneman, Daniel and Sugden, Robert 2005. 'Experienced Utility as a Standard of Policy Evaluation', *Environmental and Resource Economics* 32: 161–81.

Kasser, Tim 2002. *The High Price of Materialism*. Boston, MA: MIT Press.

Kedem-Friedrich, Peri and Al-Atawneh, Maged 2004. 'Does Modernity Lead to Greater Well-being? Bedouin Women Undergoing a Socio-cultural Transition', *Social Indicators Research* 67(3): 333–51.

Kling, Arnold 2003. 'Survey Says!?' www.techcentralstation.com/051403D.html, May 14.

Lance, Charles E., Mallard, Alison G. and Michalos, Alex C. 1995. 'Tests of the Causal Directions of Global-Life Facet Satisfaction Relationships', *Social Indicators Research* 34: 69–92.

Layard, Richard 2005. *Happiness: Lessons from a New Science*. New York: Penguin Press.

Lea, Stephen E. G., Webley, Paul and Walker, Catherine M. 1995. 'Psychological Factors in Consumer Debt: Money Management, Economic Socialization, and Credit Use', *Journal of Economic Psychology* 13 (December): 111–34.

Lever, Joaquina Palomar 2004. 'Poverty and Subjective Well-being in Mexico', *Social Indicators Research* 68(1): 1–33.

Lykken, David and Tellegen, Auke 1996. 'Happiness is a Stochastic Phenomenon', *Psychological Science* 7(3): 186–9.

Lyubomirsky, Sonja 2001. 'Why Are Some People Happier than Others? The Role of Cognitive and Motivational Processes in Well-being', *American Psychologist* 56(3): 239–49.

Mallard, Alison G. C., Lance, Charles E. and Michalos, Alex C. 1997. 'Culture as a Moderator of Overall Life Satisfaction – Life Facet Satisfaction Relationships', *Social Indicators Research* 40: 259–84.

McBride, M. 2001. 'Relative-Income Effects on Subjective Well-being in the Cross-section', *Journal of Economic Behavior and Organization* 45: 251–78.

Michalos, Alex C. 1985. 'Multiple Discrepancies Theory (MDT)', *Social Indicators Research* 16: 347–413.

   1989. 'Discrepancies Between Perceived Income Needs and Actual Incomes', *Social Indicators Research* 21: 293–6.

Mookherjee, Harsha N. 1992. 'Perceptions of Well-being by Metropolitan and Non-metropolitan Populations in the United States', *Journal of Social Psychology* 132(4): 513–24.

   1998. 'Perceptions of Well-being Among the Older Metropolitan and Non-metropolitan Populations in the United States', *Journal of Social Psychology* 138: 72–82.

Myers, David G. 1992. *The Pursuit of Happiness: Who Is Happy – and Why*. New York: William Morrow & Co.

Myers, David G. and Diener, Ed 1995. 'Who Is Happy', *Psychological Science* 6: 10–19.

   1997. 'The Pursuit of Happiness', *Scientific American*: 40–4.

Ng, Yew-Kwang 1997. 'A Case for Happiness, Cardinalism, and Interpersonal Comparability', *Economic Journal* 107: 1848–58.

O'Guinn, Thomas C. and Shrum, L. J. 1997. 'The Role of Television in the Construction of Consumer Reality', *Journal of Consumer Research* 23(4): 278–94.

Oswald, Andrew J. 1997. 'Happiness and Economic Performance', *Economic Journal* 107 (November): 1815–31.

PNC Advisors, Press Release, January 10, 2005. 'Many Wealthy Americans Have Done Nothing to Protect Assets and Are Worried about Financial Security, Family Values, According to Largest Study of Its Kind Released Today', Pittsburgh, PA: PNC Financial Services Group.

Ravallion, Martin and Lokshin, Michael 2001. 'Identifying Welfare Effects from Subjective Questions', *Economica* 68: 335–57.

Rice, Robert W., Phillips, Suzanne M. and McFarlin, Dean B. 1990. 'Multiple Discrepancies and Pay Satisfaction', *Journal of Applied Psychology* 75(4): 386–93.

Richins, Marsha L. and Rudmin, Floyd W. 1994. 'Materialism and Economic Psychology', *Journal of Economic Psychology* 15: 217–31.

Robbins, Lionel C. 1935. *An Essay on the Nature and Significance of Economic Science*, 2nd edn. London: Macmillan.

Ryan, Lisa and Dziurawiec, Suzanne 2001. 'Materialism and Its Relationship to Life Satisfaction', *Social Indicators Research* 55: 185–97.

Ryff, Carol D. and Keyes, Corey Lee M. 1995. 'The Structure of Psychological Well-being Revisited', *Journal of Personality and Social Psychology* 69(4): 719–27.

Samuelson, Paul A. 1938. 'A Note on the Pure Theory of Consumer's Behaviour', *Economica* 5(17): 61–71.

Saris, Willem E. 2001. 'The Relationship Between Income and Satisfaction: The Effect of Measurement Error and Suppressor Variables', *Social Indicators Research* 53(2): 117–36.

Schyns, Peggy 1998. 'Crossnational Differences in Happiness: Economic and Cultural Factors Explored', *Social Indicators Research* 43: 3–26.

   2000. 'The Relationship Between Income, Changes in Income and Life-satisfaction in West Germany and the Russian Federation: Relative, Absolute, or a Combination of Both?' in E. Diener and D. Rahtz (eds.) *Advances in Quality of Life Theory and Research* (London: Kluwer Academic Publishers), pp. 83–109.

   2003. *Income and Life Satisfaction: A Cross-national and Longitudinal Study*. Delft: Uitgeverij Eburon.

Scitovsky, Tibor 1992. *The Joyless Economy: The Psychology of Human Satisfaction*, rev. edn. New York: Oxford University Press.

Seligman, Martin E. P. 2002. *Authentic Happiness: Using the New Positive Psychology to Realize Your Potential for Lasting Fulfillment*. New York: Free Press.

Sirgy, Joseph M. 1997. 'Materialism and Quality of Life', *Social Indicators Research* 6: 1–34.

Sirgy, Joseph M., Lee, Dong-Jin, Larsen, Val and Wright, Newell 1998. 'Satisfaction with Material Possessions and General Well-being: The Role of Materialism', *Journal of Consumer Satisfaction/Dissatisfaction and Complaining Behavior* 11: 103–18.

Smith, Richard H., Diener, Ed and Wedell, Douglas H. 1989. 'Intrapersonal and Social Comparison Determinants of Happiness: A Range-Frequency Analysis', *Journal of Personality and Social Psychology* 56(3): 317–25.

Stutzer, Alois 2004. 'The Role of Income Aspirations in Individual Happiness', *Journal of Economic Behavior and Organization* 54(1): 89–109.

Stutzer, Alois and Frey, Bruno S. 2004. 'Reported Subjective Well-being: A Challenge for Economic Theory and Economic Policy', *Schmoller Jahrbuch* 124(2): 1–41.

Sutton, Steven K. and Davidson, Richard J. 1997. 'Prefrontal Brain Asymmetry: A Biological Substrate of the Behavioral Approach and Inhibition Systems', *Psychological Science* 8(3): 204–11.

Tatzel, Miriam 2003. 'The Art of Buying: Coming to Terms with Money and Materialism', *Journal of Happiness Studies* 4(4): 405–35.

van Praag, Bernard M. S. 1993. 'The Relativity of the Welfare Concept', in M. C. Nussbaum and A. Sen (eds.) *The Quality of Life* (Oxford: Clarendon), pp. 362–85.

    1994. 'Ordinal and Cardinal Utility: An Integration of the Two Dimensions of the Welfare Concept', in R. Blundell, I. Preston and I. Walker (eds.) *The Measurement of Household Welfare* (Cambridge: Cambridge University Press), pp. 86–110.

van Praag, Bernard M. S. and Frijters, Paul 1999. 'The Measurement of Welfare and Well-being: The Leyden Approach', in D. Kahneman, E. Diener and N. Schwarz (eds.) *Well-being: The Foundations of Hedonic Psychology* (New York: Russell Sage Foundation), pp. 413–33.

Veenhoven, Ruut 1991. 'Is Happiness Relative?' *Social Indicators Research* 24: 1–34.

    1996. 'Developments in Satisfaction Research', *Social Indicators Research* 37: 1–46.

Veenhoven, Ruut and Hagerty, Michael 2006. 'Rising Happiness in Nations 1946–2004: A Reply to Easterlin', *Social Indicators Research* 79(3): 421–36.

Watson, John B. 1913. 'Psychology as the Behaviorist Views It', *Psychological Review* 20: 158–77.

10 Comparing models of consumer behaviour

GERRIT ANTONIDES

10.1 Introduction

One of the earliest experiments on consumer behaviour was conducted by Edward Chamberlin (1948), who studied market equilibria for buyers and sellers of hypothetical goods.[1] In one version of such an experiment each of the buyers is given a different maximum buy price and each of the sellers is given a different minimum sell price. They then start negotiating with each other to buy or sell their hypothetical good. After each successful negotiation, the agreed price is called. At the end of the experiment, the participants are paid the difference (to their advantage) between the negotiated price and their given price. After a few negotiations, a market equilibrium arises, which equals the intersection of buyers' and sellers' cumulative (given) price distributions. Under these circumstances, economic theory apparently predicts the empirical results quite well.

Although economics was the first discipline dealing with consumer behaviour, other disciplines, including psychology, sociology and anthropology, have studied the issue later on from different perspectives. Currently, there are many theories of consumer behaviour, which frequently leads to confusion, as is evident from students asking: 'Which is the right theory of consumer behaviour?' Obviously, there is no right or wrong theory, although some theories are more adequate than others in answering questions in particular situations. Also, since consumer behaviour can be highly complex, theories about different aspects of behaviour are necessary in order to increase explanatory power concerning this behaviour. One way of dealing with complex consumer behaviour is to integrate existing theories into one overarching model (e.g., Nicosia, 1966; Howard and Sheth, 1969; Engel *et al.*, 1968). Although such models have some heuristic value, the amount of data required renders them impractical. Rather, we will focus on models answering particular problems. Here, different models of consumer behaviour will be described and their adequacy in answering questions and providing explanations will be assessed. Furthermore, a trend in the development of theories will be described.

---

[1] Modern versions of Chamberlin's experiments are reported in Smith (1962), Holt (1996) and Fels (1993).

The first consumer behaviour theories were largely based on assumptions of rational consumers, i.e., consumers who strive to obtain the best possible outcomes, given their preferences and available information. These models worked quite well at the beginning of the twentieth century, when goods were scarce and income was low. Later on, due to developments in manufacturing, consumers obtained more income and goods became widely available. Under these circumstances, consumer behaviour became less predictable from simple models. Hence, the models gradually became more complex, including such factors as perceptions, social effects, emotions and situational circumstances. Nowadays, marketing researchers face questions like: 'What are consumers doing right in front of the shelf?' Such questions indicate the great instability of consumer preferences and they demand even more detailed consumer models.

Without pretending to provide an exhaustive summary of consumer models in the literature, we will categorize the main approaches to explaining consumer behaviour by using a couple of simple distinctions.[2] Stanovich and West (2000) and Kahneman (2003) distinguished between System I and System II types of decision making, which will be employed here. System I is characterized by intuitive, largely unconscious, associative, automatic, heuristic and emotional decision processes, whereas System II is controlled, rule-based, systematic and analytic in nature. Many consumer models can be classified as based on either of these systems, and some models even include both system types. The second distinction is by discipline, i.e., economics and other disciplines. Since they are considered the most traditional types of theory, we start by considering System II types of models, then continue with the System I and mixed-type models. An overview of consumer models and their applications is provided in table 10.1. We conclude with a general discussion.

10.2 System II types of models

Both in economics and in the other social sciences, consumer behaviour models were developed using System II assumptions of decision processing. We will first deal with the economic models.

10.2.1 Economic models

Most neoclassical economic models can be categorized as System II types of models since consumer decision making is assumed to be rule-based, in agreement with certain axioms, and analytic, using all available information for optimal choice. Two models are especially relevant to the study of consumer behaviour: the theory of demand and the life-cycle model of consumption.

---

[2] One important aspect of consumer decision making is bargaining within households. Although both economic (e.g., Lundberg and Pollak, 1993) and psychological bargaining theories (e.g., Raiffa *et al.*, 2003; Bazerman *et al.*, 2000) exist, we leave out this aspect for reasons of space limitation.

Table 10.1 *Overview of consumer models and their applications*

	Concepts	Applications
System II models		
Demand theory	Engel curves	Consumption quota for housing, food, etc.
	Income elasticity	Defining necessary and luxury goods
	Price elasticity	Price setting, taxation
	Characteristics approach	Hedonic price functions
Life-cycle model	Consumption and saving	Wealth management
Theory of planned behaviour	Attitudes, social norms, perceived behavioural control	Prediction of intentions, assessments of consumer opinions regarding products, social environment and personal control
Consumer expectations	Consumer confidence	Saving, discretionary spending
	Product expectations	Customer satisfaction
System I models		
Heuristics	Simplified judgements	Assessing importance order of product attributes
	Contrast and compromise effects	Product presentation, category management, brand portfolio management
	Focusing on easy-to-evaluate attributes	Product comparisons
	Mental accounting	Categorization of income, expenditures and investments
	Judging series of events	Design of consumer experiences, consumer satisfaction
Loss aversion	Asymmetric risk preferences	Investor behaviour
	Endowment effect	Environmental evaluation, product trials, trade-ins
	Status quo bias	Brand switching
	Mental accounting	Hedonic editing of multiple gains and losses
	Sunk cost effect	Entrapment in decision making
Subjective discounting	Hyperbolic discount rates	Investment goods, life-cycle model, saving, borrowing
Psychophysics	Psychophysical laws	Utility of consumption
	Probability weighting	Decision making under uncertainty
Learning by conditioning	Classical and operant conditioning	Advertising, development of preference
Other processes	Motivations, values, lifestyles	Market segmentation, product development
	Perceptions	Advertising
	Other types of learning	New product development
Mixed-type processes	Conditions for information processing	Information needs for functional products and high-involvement products

10.2.1.1 Theory of demand

The neoclassical economic model is based on the maximization of utility, subject to budget and time constraints. Consumers derive utility, or pleasure, from the consumption of goods, and utility maximization results in preferences for the goods yielding the highest utility. On the basis of assumptions concerning consumer preferences, consumer demand has been explained primarily by income and prices of goods and services (Deaton and Muellbauer, 1980; Varian, 2002). Important theoretical notions include decreasing marginal utility of consumption (each additional consumption results in less pleasure than the previous one) and equal marginal utility of expenditures for all goods consumed (the last euro spent on your car and the last euro spent on a French dinner should result in equal addition of pleasure). These theoretical notions are employed to make predictions concerning optimal consumer choice.

From the theory of demand, several useful predictions can be made. Engel curves show the quantified relationships between budget shares spent on particular goods and income. They show how expenditures, for example on food, are related to the level of income: for example, proportionally less is spent on food with increasing income. In the early twentieth century, Engel curves were used in forecasting demand for food. Nowadays, demand has become much more complex and many other factors may appear in demand equations. However, for policy reasons, Engel curves are still used to monitor expenditures as a proportion of household budgets.

A related set of predictions concerns income elasticities, defined as the percentage change in demand due to a percentage change in income. If the income elasticity is between zero and one, the good is called a primary or necessary good. If the income elasticity is greater than one, the good is called a luxury good. Expenditures on necessary goods tend to increase less than proportionally with rising income; expenditures on luxury goods increase more than proportionally with rising income.[3] Defining goods as necessary or luxury goods may have implications for governmental policy concerning poverty. Some poverty definitions are based on the ability to consume necessary goods from the available budget. The distinction between necessary and luxury goods may influence the way value added tax or income tax is levied. Income elasticities may differ across countries and across time periods. For example, cars were previously classed as luxury goods but are now classed as necessary goods in the Netherlands.

Consumer demand is also influenced by price changes. In this respect, price elasticity is defined as the percentage change in demand due to a percentage change in price. Thus, price elasticity predicts how demand will change after a price change. If the price elasticity is in the -1 to 0 range, demand is relatively inelastic: for example, in the case of petroleum. If the price elasticity is smaller

---

[3] Special cases are income elasticities equal to zero (indifferent good), smaller than zero (inferior good) and equal to one (origin good).

than -1, demand is said to be elastic: for example, for cars. Price elasticities may be used by the government for setting excise tax and value added tax rates, and for setting prices of public goods. Such policies may be relevant in reaching certain objectives, such as increasing public health or improving the environment. Companies may use price elasticities to calculate expected turnover and profits at different prices of consumer goods.[4]

So far, demand theory has been applied to consumer goods where all brand varieties are treated as different goods. For many purposes, this approach is impractical since it tells us nothing about the nature of different goods. For this reason, the characteristics approach (Lancaster, 1971; Ratchford, 1979) assumes that consumer demand is based on the attributes, or characteristics, of consumer goods. In the characteristics approach, hedonic price functions are estimated, resulting in implicit marginal prices of product characteristics. For example, the price difference between a regular and a four-wheel-drive car can be estimated, given the marginal prices of the other characteristics. Then, the implicit marginal prices can be related to production factors and to consumer characteristics, such as income, family size and education (Agarwal and Ratchford, 1980). Characteristics models may be used by consumer goods producers to find the optimal amount of characteristics to be included in product design, in the price setting of goods with new attribute levels and in defining target consumer segments. The characteristics approach is very similar to choice modelling (McFadden, 2001; McFadden and Train, 1996) in which consumer choices are explained by product characteristics.

10.2.1.2 Economic life-cycle model

In economics, saving behaviour has been described by means of the life-cycle model (Modigliani, 1988). The simple form of this model assumes a striving for a permanent level of spending, equal to the average income over the entire life-cycle of a household. Since the highest income level is not achieved immediately, income at a younger age will be lower than the life-cycle average. At this stage borrowing prevails, for instance to buy education or a house. At a later age, income is usually higher than the life-cycle average. At this stage, a buffer is created which is spent during the spell thereafter (retirement). If in the meantime an unforeseen income shock occurs, the average level of spending will be adapted. The life-cycle model concerns saving as a precaution for old age but also as wealth management, namely if substantial savings for old age are privately invested. The latter motive aims at wealth increase whereas the former is primarily meant for delayed consumption (Wärneryd, 1989). These motives are particularly relevant for people without (sufficient)

---

[4] Furthermore, cross-price elasticities define changes in demand for a good due to changes in the price of a different good: for example, changes in the price of a Volkswagen car may influence demand for a Peugeot car. Cross-price elasticities may also be used to assess the strength of competition in a market.

pension arrangements, such as self-employed entrepreneurs. The economic life-cycle model enables predictions concerning saving, borrowing and wealth management at different consumer life-cycle stages.

Several shortcomings of the life-cycle model have been noted, including under-consumption at lower ages, under-saving at middle ages and under-consumption again at higher ages (Thaler, 1990). It appears that the level of spending tracks the level of income earned, rather than being stable. This may partly be due to myopic behaviour of consumers, leading to overweighting of immediate, relative to long-term, consequences of behaviour. When myopic consumer preferences are taken into account (Angeletos et al., 2001), the life-cycle model no longer predicts constant levels of spending, in agreement with actual consumer behaviour.

10.2.2 Psychological models

A few psychological models of consumer behaviour, including the theory of planned behaviour and expectations theory, explicitly capture mental processing of information in an optimal way.

10.2.2.1 Theory of planned behaviour

Attitude models in psychology have developed along similar lines to the utility concept in economics (Antonides, 1989). At first, attitude was considered as an undifferentiated evaluation or emotional reaction, which is similar to considering utility as an immediate sensation of preference. Later on, attitudes were defined as differentiated valuations based on beliefs and evaluations of particular aspects of situations (Rosenberg, 1956; Tolman, 1959). This conception of attitudes is similar to utility defined on weighted characteristics of goods and services.

Differentiated attitudes were further developed in the *theory of reasoned action* (Fishbein, 1966; Fishbein and Ajzen, 1975). In this theory, behaviour (*B*) is explained by intentions to perform an act (*BI*); behavioural intentions further depend on attitudes (*A*) and social norms (*SN*). Social norms can be considered as pressure from the social environment to behave in a particular way. The relationships can be specified as follows:

$$B \approx BI = w_1 \times A + w_2 \times SN = w_1(\Sigma_i\, b_i \times e_i) + w_2(\Sigma_j\, nb_j \times mc_j)$$
$$i = 1, \ldots, I;\, j = 1, \ldots, J \tag{1}$$

where w_1 and w_2 can be considered as regression weights correcting both for the different scales of attitudes and social norms and for their differential influence on behavioural intentions. Attitudes are further specified as the summated beliefs (*b*) about the *I* relevant attributes of an object, weighted by the evaluations (*e*) of these attributes. For example, a belief that the European Union encourages competition among firms can be weighted by the evaluation of competition as being a good or bad aspect of the EU. Different degrees of beliefs and evaluations can be measured by using Likert scales or semantic differential scales.

Social norms are considered as differentiated with respect to a number (J) of relevant social parties in the environment of the consumer: for example, family members, acquaintances, colleagues, etc. Consumers hold normative beliefs (nb) concerning these parties' convictions that the consumer should behave in a particular way, which are weighted by the motivation to comply (mc) with the respective social parties. For example, the consumer may have a normative belief that family members think that he/she should vote for the EU constitution. Furthermore, the consumer may or may not comply with the normative beliefs concerning the social parties. The weighted average of such beliefs constitutes the overall social norm component of the theory of reasoned action.

The performance of the theory of reasoned action has been assessed in a meta-study by Sheppard *et al.* (1988). They found an overall correlation of .53 between behaviour and behavioural intentions, and an overall correlation of .66 between behavioural intentions on the one hand and attitudes and social norms on the other hand, showing the relative success of the model. Apart from the statistical performance, the model yields rich information about consumer perceptions and evaluations of multiple attributes of goods and services, which is useful in product design and marketing.

A further development of the model comprises perceived behavioural control, i.e., a person's perceived ease or difficulty of performing a particular behaviour (Ajzen, 1991). An example is the belief that one has a high level of control in choosing between a number of different investment options. Perceived behavioural control may also be measured as the summated beliefs regarding aspects associated with personal control, weighted by the perceived impact of the control aspect in performing a particular behaviour. For example, the belief that one has ample time available for choosing a particular investment option could be weighted by one's opinion that available time makes it easy to choose an investment option. The extended model of reasoned action is called the *theory of planned behaviour*. Ajzen (1991) reports an average correlation of .71 between behavioural intentions on the one hand, and attitudes, social norms and perceived control on the other hand. Furthermore, by including perceived control, the effect of social norms tends to become less significant.

The theory of planned behaviour turns out to predict behavioural intentions quite well, partly due to the high degree of similarity in the measures of intention, attitudes, social norms and perceived control. By measuring these concepts in a very detailed way, it is possible to estimate the influence of each aspect separately. An application of such estimates is marketing communication directed at the most important aspects of attitudes, social norms and behavioural control in order to promote desired behaviour effectively. Other applications include marketing communication of strong brand characteristics, improving weak characteristics and developing desired but missing attributes.

10.2.2.2   Consumer expectations

Expectations are cognitive constructs concerning future circumstances, including income and consumption. Expectations play a part in the economic life-cycle model and in investment decision making (Muth, 1961). However, in economic models, no direct information on consumer expectations is used. In economic psychology, both the income and expectations concerning future income are used in explaining consumer spending and saving. In consumer behaviour theory, expectations concerning product performance are used in assessing consumer satisfaction.

Katona (1975) has developed both a theory and a measurement device concerning consumer expectations about the general economy and their own financial situation. In addition to income and prices, which determine the ability to spend, discretionary spending[5] may be influenced by consumers' willingness to spend, indicated by their economic expectations. When consumers have optimistic expectations they tend to spend more on discretionary items, and they borrow more and save less than when they have pessimistic expectations. In order to forecast consumer spending, consumer expectations are measured by statistical bureaux in many countries.

In consumer behaviour theory, consumer satisfaction is assumed to depend on both consumer expectations concerning product performance and the actual (perceived) product performance (Oliver, 1996). When product performance exceeds or meets expectations, consumer satisfaction results, otherwise consumers will be dissatisfied. Consumer satisfaction based on expectations has been measured by means of customer satisfaction barometers in several countries and in different industries (Fornell, 1992; Johnson *et al.*, 2002). Customer satisfaction measures provide feedback on changes occurring in the marketplace and may guide marketing effort and the consumer policy of the government. Furthermore, customer satisfaction may induce repeat buying and prevent brand switching (Rust *et al.*, 2004).

10.3   System I types of models

Frequently, consumers do not behave like rationalizing agents in a narrow sense. They have limited information capacities, they use both cognitive and affective choice processes, and they show great impatience. Insights developed around these decision aspects deviate from standard economic theory and the theory of planned behaviour. Since System I types of models are excluded

---

[5] Discretionary spending can be advanced or delayed at the consumer's free will or discretion, i.e., consumption of durable goods.

in standard economic theory, the distinction between economics and other disciplines is dropped here.

10.3.1 Heuristics

Given the abundant supply of goods and services, and consumers' limited information capacities, consumers frequently show satisficing behaviour, i.e., simplified information processing (Kahneman *et al.*, 1982; Simon, 1986), or delay their decisions (Iyengar and Lepper, 2000). A long list of simplified information processes exists, including simplified judgements about goods and services, contrast and compromise effects, focusing on easy-to-evaluate attributes, mental accounting, and judging a series of events by focusing on the peak and the end. These heuristics may become more and more important with the increasing freedom of choice in modern consumption markets (Schwartz, 2000, 2004).

10.3.1.1 Simplified judgements of goods and services

Especially in the case of time constraints and information overload (Jacoby, 1984), consumers may deviate from the theory of planned behaviour using simplified judgements and comparisons of attributes across different goods and services. Simplified judgements include:

– affect referral, i.e., acting on first impression or familiarity with the product, without further elaboration;
– conjunctive decision rule, i.e., using minimally required values of product characteristics to select the first product meeting the consumer's minimal requirements;
– disjunctive decision rule, i.e., using one or more outstanding product characteristics as the basis for choice;
– lexicographic decision rule, i.e., judging product characteristics in order of their importance, resulting in choice of a product with the highest values of the most important characteristics;
– sequential elimination rule, i.e., eliminating products not meeting one's minimal requirements to narrow the choice set;
– additive differences, i.e., conducting pairwise product comparisons based on the differences between product attributes.

Several simplified judgements may be used consecutively. For example, disjunctive and elimination rules may be applied to narrow the choice set, followed by disjunctive, lexicographic and additive difference rules (see Antonides and Van Raaij, 1998). Hence, for marketing researchers it is important to know the minimally required product attributes and the importance order of the attributes.

10.3.1.2   Contrast and compromise effect

In the first instance, product comparisons may help in selecting the best product alternative. However, there is a downside to this (Simonson, 1999; Simonson and Tversky, 1992). Consumers tend to prefer products more if they are contrasted with an inferior choice alternative. The contrast effect makes the product appear a good buy, whereas in isolation it is considered less attractive.

In a similar vein, adding a third choice alternative to a set of two products makes the middle option relatively attractive. It appears that consumers tend to compromise in that they dislike choosing an extreme option. An illustration of this is the observation that most people choose neither the cheapest nor the most expensive item from a restaurant's wine list.

Obviously, contrast and compromise effects are important in designing the array of a consumer's choices, for example in category management or in brand portfolio management.

10.3.1.3   Focusing on easy-to-evaluate attributes

Especially when products are evaluated in isolation, consumers tend to focus on easy-to-evaluate product characteristics (Hsee, 1996, 1998). For example, in judging the attractiveness of an ice cream, consumers pay attention to whether or not the ice cream cup looks overfilled or underfilled, rather than to the exact weight of the ice cream. Since normally we don't know how much an ice cream should weigh, the exact weight is a difficult-to-evaluate characteristic whereas the filling is easy to evaluate.

However, if consumers can compare the weight of two different ice creams, they will pay little attention to the filling of the cup. Other easy-to-evaluate characteristics in isolated judgement are the perfect or imperfect state of a product, and product design. Difficult-to-evaluate characteristics are, for example, sound quality of audio equipment or number of entries in a dictionary. In isolated product judgement, simplified information processing may include judgement by easy-to-evaluate characteristics.

Consumer preferences seem to be influenced by the presentation of products, either in isolation or in comparison with other products. To the benefit of consumers, comparisons of difficult-to-evaluate attributes should be made available easily, for example on the internet, or should be simplified by using a rating system such as stars. This is all the more relevant in societies which leave the production of public goods such as health care, telecommunications and utilities to the market.

10.3.1.4   Mental accounting

When consumers have difficulty judging their expenses or other financial transactions in relation to one another, they make up so-called mental accounts. A mental account is a category of transactions which are psychologically separated from other transactions. For example, people tend to make mental accounts for weekly food, entertainment and monthly clothing (Heath and Soll, 1996). When a particular budget becomes exhausted at the end of a period, they tend to spend less within that particular category.

Another instance of mental accounting is earmarking income for particular expenses. Kooreman (2000) found that spending on children's clothing is more sensitive to changes in child allowances than to other income sources. Shefrin and Thaler (1988) found that the marginal propensity to consume from the current income account is much higher than from the future wealth account, providing further evidence of mental accounting.

In the field of investment decision making, investors tend to make mental accounts of particular stocks they bought (Thaler, 1999). In contrast to financial economic advice, they are reluctant to close losing accounts even if they have made huge profits in other accounts. In other words, they try to close each account with a positive balance.

Mental accounting is important in designing ways of consumer spending and income payments. For example, in attempts to stimulate consumer spending, the government should prefer a repeated increase of the current income account to an occasional increase by a lump-sum amount (Thaler, 1990).

10.3.1.5 Judging a series of events

How do consumers consider a series of events, for example, watching a movie, taking a holiday, or evaluating their marriage? The optimal way of evaluating such event series would be to evaluate each event separately, then take the average of all evaluations. However, this seems way too complicated for the average consumer. A very simple heuristic that people seem to apply is to judge both the most extreme (peak) and the final outcome (end), and then average their judgements (Kahneman, 1994, 1999).

The peak–end rule effectively summarizes consumers' judgements of series of events resulting in satisfaction or dissatisfaction. Ross and Simonson (1991) found a preference for happy endings in consumers' evaluations of computer games on a diskette. Although they found a reverse end effect, Verhoef *et al.* (2004) found evidence for peak effects in telephone conversations between call-centre agents and their clients. The peak–end rule may be used in the design of consumer experiences consisting of a series of events, for example, in entertainment.

10.3.2 Loss aversion

Several System I processes are based on the phenomenon of loss aversion. Loss aversion occurs because of the experience of negative emotion when consumers evaluate choice alternatives that deviate negatively from a reference point. For example, when facing a loss with respect to their current level of wealth, consumers react negatively and try to avoid the loss. The aversion to a loss is roughly twice as strong as the attractiveness of a commensurate gain (Tversky and Kahneman, 1992). Furthermore, risk preferences differ between gains and losses. These observations have led to the development of a value function which has a concave shape for gains and a convex and relatively steep shape for losses. The value function describes pleasure and pain, like the economic utility function captures pleasure. However, the value function is defined by deviations from a reference point, whereas the utility function is defined by total assets.

10.3.2.1   Asymmetric risk preferences

The shape of the value function has several consequences for consumer behaviour. Since the function is concave in the gain area, consumers are risk averse for positive outcomes, such as consumption benefits and income gains. However, they are risk seeking for negative outcomes, such as lost money in gambling, and loss of time. Asymmetric risk preferences even influence behaviour on stock markets. It has been found that investors are risk averse for positive outcomes (selling their winning stocks relatively early) and risk seeking for negative outcomes (selling their losing stocks relatively late). See Shefrin and Statman (1985) and Odean (1998).

10.3.2.2   Endowment effect

Another consequence of the shape of the value function is the endowment effect (Kahneman *et al.*, 1990), resulting in a higher preference for goods that people own than for goods that they do not own.[6] This phenomenon dramatically influences valuations of non-market goods, including natural resources, depending on whether such resources are acquired or given up (Knetsch, 2000). A possible application of the endowment effect concerning market goods is that of free trials, suggesting a feeling of ownership, resulting in increased preference for the good (De Groot, 2003). Another application is the trade-in of a used car, by which the owner of the car prefers to receive a higher price for the used car than to pay a lower price for the new car (Purohit, 1995).

10.3.2.3   Status quo bias

A related phenomenon is the status quo bias, resulting in a general preference for status quo options as compared with alternative options (Samuelson and Zeckhauser, 1988). A striking example is the choice of car insurance in two different states in the US (Johnson *et al.*, 1993). In one state, insurance which included the right to sue was the standard option (buyers being entitled to pay a lower premium if they wished to exclude the right to sue), which was preferred by 75 per cent of the consumers. In another state, exactly the same insurance without the right to sue was the standard option (buyers being entitled to upgrade the insurance by including the right to sue at a higher premium), which was preferred by 80 per cent of the consumers. Although the standard

---

[6] Standard economic theory assumes that preference is independent of ownership of a good.

options differed between the states, they were overwhelmingly popular among consumers in both states. See Hartman *et al.* (1991) for an example concerning the electricity market. In marketing, the status quo bias may be used in presenting a brand as the status quo alternative that consumers obviously should buy. Status quo bias would also prevent consumers from switching from one supplier to another supplier of a good or service.

10.3.2.4   Mental accounting

Loss aversion also has implications for mental accounting in a different sense from budgeting or earmarking, mentioned before. The hedonic editing hypothesis (Thaler, 1985) predicts that people evaluate choice options in line with the asymmetric shape of the value function. According to this hypothesis, people would prefer to segregate gains and integrate losses. Furthermore, they would prefer to integrate smaller losses with larger gains, and to segregate smaller gains from larger losses (silver lining). Such processes may be used in presenting products and services in marketing: for example, for credit cards (integrating losses, segregating gains) and rebates (silver lining). However, further research into this matter has revealed that people may become sensitive to cumulative losses, contrary to the hedonic editing hypothesis (Thaler and Johnson, 1990). Hence, they would prefer to spread losses over time rather than experience multiple losses at the same time. In other words, when the accumulation of losses over time becomes evident, their marginal effect increases, in contrast to the shape of the value function. This effect even adds to the psychological motivation to avoid losses in general (Thaler, 1999). These findings may be used in multiple-product offerings (product bundling) and in payment and bonus schemes.

10.3.2.5   Sunk cost effect

The sunk cost effect is another example of loss aversion. Because losses are painful and hard to accept, people try to compensate prior losses, even when such actions do not maximize their expected utility. One example is investment decision making, in which unsuccessful prior investments are taken into account in further investment decisions, in an attempt finally to avoid the loss (Arkes and Blumer, 1985). Such behaviour goes against economic advice to take only future outcomes into account. Throwing good money after bad money may lead to a situation of entrapment, i.e., a downward spiral of attempts to overcome prior losses (Antonides, 1995). A good example of entrapment is the case of Nick Leeson, a financial manager at Barings Bank (1993–5) who speculated on the futures market, causing a $1.3 billion loss to the bank, which was eventually taken over by ING Bank for £1. In consumer behaviour, sunk cost may play a part in consuming (too much of) pre-paid items, such as a series of concerts, all-you-can-eat pizzas, tennis clubs, etc. (Thaler, 1980). Time investments may lead to similar effects (Soman, 2001).

Loss aversion appears as a powerful motive in consumer behaviour, which is expressed in various ways. The government and several utility companies already apply the system of advance payment of taxes and service charges, which are perceived as income reductions (forgone gains), in order to avoid payments in arrears, which are perceived as losses.

10.3.3 Subjective discounting

Consumers generally are impatient, i.e., they prefer present consumption to future consumption at a rate which is higher than market interest rates. For example, in buying too little energy-efficient electrical equipment, on average consumers show subjective discount rates exceeding 20 per cent (Antonides and Wunderink, 2001; Gately, 1980; Hausman, 1979). Subjective discount rates capture the personal rates of discounting future outcomes, which vary widely across consumers and situations. Low-income and optimistic consumers show relatively high subjective discount rates in the decision to replace a durable good (Antonides, 1990). Both young and old people have higher subjective discount rates than middle-aged people (Read and Read, 2004). Subjective discount rates are relatively high for decisions involving small amounts of money, short time intervals and positive outcomes (Thaler, 1981). Subjective discount rates are also high for compensation required to delay present outcomes as opposed to payment to advance future outcomes (Loewenstein, 1988) and for hedonic types of goods rather than functional types of goods (Gattig, 2002). Finally, subjective discount rates vary across life domains. For example, willingness to invest in consumption items may be uncorrelated with investments in one's health or precautionary behaviour (Fuchs, 1982).

Hyperbolic functions have become popular in modelling consumer impatience (Ahlbrecht and Weber, 1995; Laibson, 1997) and can be implemented quite easily in economic models. One example of such implementation is the economic life-cycle model mentioned earlier (Angeletos *et al.*, 2001). Hyperbolic discounting models help explain why consumers hold relatively few liquid assets, overuse their credit cards and reduce their consumption around retirement. Another example is the introduction of a new kind of employee saving scheme, based on future income changes (Benartzi and Thaler, 2004). Basically, employees were offered a pension saving scheme in which they agreed to save part of their future income increases. Note that the offer focused on future income from which the employees were less impatient to consume. Also, the offer focused on income increases, the saving of which did not feel as a loss but as a forgone gain. Both factors were very effective in increasing employee pension saving dramatically. Applications in marketing may include 'consume now, pay later' type of offers which are especially attractive to suppliers in situations of low market interest rates, and to consumers with low incomes or low income expectations.

10.3.4 Psychophysics

Psychophysical theory studies quantified relationships between objective and subjective stimuli: for example, between the magnitude of product attributes and subjective experience value. Although subjective experiences may be influenced by other System I processes in many ways, the basic psychophysical theory deals with the nature of relationships between objective stimulus inputs and subjective experiences (outputs) without paying attention to mental processing of incoming stimuli.

The well-known psychophysical laws of Weber, Fechner and Stevens deal with perceptual discrimination of (differences between) stimuli. Fechner and Stevens developed respectively logarithmic and double-logarithmic relationships between psychological sensations and objective stimuli (see, for example, Antonides, 1996). Such relationships may be used in modelling utility of consumption of products and product characteristics (Antonides, 1989).

It appeared that Stevens' power law could successfully be applied to the liking and disliking of wage rates, to the reported degree of poverty associated with levels of income (Rainwater, 1974) and to the perception of inflation (Batchelor, 1986). Also, psychophysical relations have been reported between perceived status and amount of income, status and years of schooling and status and years of acculturation (Hamblin, 1973). Furthermore, the psychophysical method has been used to find the money equivalence of non-monetary events (Galanter, 1990). A number of different shapes of the psychophysical relationship between income evaluation and income level have been investigated (Van Herwaarden and Kapteyn, 1979). The results favoured the logarithmic and lognormal functions against a number of alternatives, including the power law.

A related perceptual process is the perception of probabilities, relevant in consumer decision making under uncertainty. In prospect theory objective probabilities are subjectively weighted such that small probabilities are overweighted whereas intermediate probabilities are underweighted generally (Kahneman and Tversky, 1979). Prelec (2000) has studied several probability weighting functions capturing these perceptual phenomena.

It appears that psychophysical functions capture largely unconscious processes of stimulus evaluation, which can successfully be applied in understanding consumer perceptions and preferences.

10.3.5 Learning by conditioning

Learning theories may explain consumer preference formation and habitual consumption behaviour (e.g., routine purchase behaviour). Learning may be accomplished in different ways, including learning by insight or problem solving, social learning and learning by conditioning. Since learning by conditioning is a rather unconscious process, also taking place in animal learning, it seems to be based on System I processes to a large extent.

The Russian physiologist Pavlov studied automatic reflexes occurring during the intake of food. When food is placed in the mouth of a dog, salivation is the automatic reaction to this stimulus. This reflex is described as an *unconditioned response* (UR) to an *unconditioned stimulus* (US). Furthermore, it appeared that after repeated presentation of a light signal followed by the presentation of food, the dog started salivating in response to the light signal alone. Technically speaking, if a *conditioned stimulus* (CS) is repeatedly followed by an unconditioned stimulus (US), the preliminary unconditioned response (UR) becomes conditioned to the CS. Salivation upon presentation of the light signal is then called a *conditioned response* (CR). This learning process is described as *classical conditioning*.

It seems as if conditioning is taking place unconsciously, as a function of CS–US pairings only. However, subjects appear to take the information value of the CS into account, i.e., the extent to which the CS predicts or signals the occurrence of the US. If the US also appears in the absence of the CS, the information value of the CS is reduced and the likelihood of the CR is diminished. For example, if a jingle (US) paired with a brand name (CS) in a commercial is frequently heard elsewhere, the information value of the brand name disappears. In other words, the covariation of CS and US (or their contingency) is crucial in establishing the conditioning (Rescorla, 1988). Classical conditioning theory has important implications for the psychology of advertising.

Although classical conditioning is powerful in learning behaviour in controlled conditions, it does not explain why people learn in natural environments. Edward Thorndike studied animal behaviour, for example, in opening a cage (see Murray, 1983). He found that behaviour leading to desired results (contributing to opening the cage) was strengthened, which was called the Law of Effect. Thorndike's research was a forerunner of operant conditioning, in which reinforcements or punishments were given after a particular behaviour had been shown (Skinner, 1954). Whereas in classical conditioning, the conditioned stimulus is presented before or simultaneously with the unconditioned stimulus, in *operant conditioning* or instrumental learning, the reinforcement is contingent on the occurrence of the behaviour to be learned. Conditioning theory has powerful applications in behavioural therapy, advertising, biofeedback, education and instruction. Also, the outcomes of consumption, for example, satisfaction or dissatisfaction, serve as feedback on previous consumption decisions. This process is helpful in developing consumer preferences.

10.3.6 Other processes

Several other psychological processes, relevant to the study of consumer behaviour, may be classified as System I processes, although they will not be described in detail here (see, for example, Antonides and Van Raaij, 1998).

A number of motivations, driving consumer behaviour, have been distinguished in psychology, including instinct, homeostasis, emotions, social pressures (need for affiliation and power motives), cognitive motivations such as cognitive balance and attributions, and personality characteristics such as need for control, need for achievement, self-realization, time preference, need for cognition and self-monitoring.

Indirectly, values and lifestyles add to System I decision-making processes. Values and lifestyles may influence subjective weights attached to product characteristics, which is important in market segmentation. For example, social class and status may be important determinants of consumer choices.

Other factors than psychophysical phenomena may play a part in perceptual processes, such as visual illusions, Gestalt principles and framing effects, which are important in product advertising. Psychometric scaling of perceptions of risk (Slovic, 2000) and economic activities (Veldscholte *et al.*, 1998) is another example of perceptual System I type of processing.

Other factors than conditioning processes may have a role in consumer learning, including biological processes of maturation, social learning (e.g., in upbringing and education), and learning by insight or creativity. Such processes may have a role in the adoption of new products and services.

10.4 Mixed-type theories

Several theories can be classified as combining System I and System II processes. They can be characterized as dual-process models, and include the Elaboration Likelihood model (Petty and Cacioppo, 1986), the Heuristic–Systematic model (Chen and Chaiken, 1999), the Cognitive–Experiential model (Epstein, 1994), the Associative versus Rule-based system (Sloman, 1996), and the Affective–Analytic choice model (Mittal, 1988).

Several theorists, going back to Aristotle and Freud, have made distinctions with respect to the type of processing of information. Zajonc (1980) assumed that affect for an object or brand may be developed by holistic processes, excluding cognitive algebra. Cognitive theorists, for example Lazarus (1984), stated that objects are always perceived before evaluation and that at least unconscious information processing precedes affect. Rather than assuming that one of these processes is exclusive, most theorists assume that such processes may complement each other under some circumstances.

Several distinctions regarding dual processes have been made. Sloman (1996) distinguished between associative systems, operating on the basis of similarity and temporal contiguity, and rule-based systems, operating on symbolic structures. The rule-based system may suppress the associative system to some extent. Epstein (1994) distinguished between cognitive and experiential processes which are assumed to operate in parallel and to interact with each other. Chen and Chaiken (1999) distinguished between heuristic and systematic processes. They stated that the use of judgement-relevant heuristic rules depends on their availability, accessibility and applicability, and on one's motivational concerns. Systematic processes may operate conditional on the availability of cognitive resources. The latter assumption was investigated by Shiv and Fedorikhin (1999), who found that restricting a consumer's cognitive resources induced decisions based on affect associated with the choice alternatives. Hence, people who had to rehearse a seven-digit number preferred chocolate cake to fruit salad relatively more often than people who rehearsed a two-digit number.

In Mittal's model (1988), one mode of choice is through *information processing* where product attributes are evaluated and then combined into an overall choice by means of some cognitive algebra. The other choice mode is *affective processing* whereby a property of the product as a whole, such as its hedonic impact or social image, determines choice. It is proposed that products can be purely functional or have both utilitarian and expressive properties to varying degrees. The expressiveness of a product refers to its ability to fulfil various psycho-social goals such as to be pleasing to the senses and to bolster the ego. The more expressive a product is, the more affective processing there is. In addition, products can be more or less involving: in other words, there can be a greater or lesser motivation for the consumer to make the right choice. The more involving the product is, the more information processing will take place. Further, the reasons for choices made by affective processing are much harder to express than those for choices made by information-processing mode.

The latter assumption was supported by a study by Wilson *et al.* (1993), who asked participants to choose a product (an art poster) either with the knowledge that they would have to give reasons for their choices or under no such expectation. Those who knew they would have to justify their choices chose different kinds of posters than those who chose without knowing they would be asked their reasons for choice. Most significantly, the former group was subsequently less satisfied with their selected posters than the latter. Wilson and Schooler (1991) obtained similar results for choices of jams and college courses.

Both the effect of involvement and the effect of availability of cognitive resources on information processing are consistent with the elaboration likelihood model (Petty and Cacioppo, 1986). This model considers the factors that influence the likelihood of elaborated processing of information. It states that in the absence of a motivation and the ability to process information, attitude is likely to be based on peripheral cues, such as positive or negative affect, attractiveness or expertise of the information source, number of arguments, etc.

As a conclusion, it appears that consumers may use different choice processes, depending on conditions associated with the personality and skills of the consumer, the choice alternatives and the environment. The choice processes may either complement or substitute one another. One possible application is advertising that is matched with the type of consumer decision making (Dubé *et al.*, 1996).

10.5 Discussion

We have discussed several types of consumer behaviour theories which may be used to deal with different consumption problems. System II types of models assume controlled, rule-based, systematic and analytic types of decision making. The economic System II models capture broad systematic relationships between income, prices, expenditures and savings, assuming rule-based analytic decision making. Such models are especially useful in economic policy making, although some models may also be applied in price setting by firms. New developments in economic models frequently include insights from behavioural economics into standard economic theory, for example, concerning consumer time preferences.

The psychological System II models deal with planned behaviour and expectations. Planned behaviour models provide much insight into the relative effect of consumer opinions on purchase intentions. Such insight may be used in the marketing efforts of private companies and in social marketing. Relatively new theoretical developments include the consumer's personal control, and finding new areas of application, such as Aids prevention and food safety. Consumer expectations can be broken down into expectations concerning the financial situation and expectations concerning product performance. Expectations concerning the financial situation may be used in predicting aggregate consumer demand and consumer saving. Expectations concerning product performance may be used both at the brand level and at industry level. The latest theoretical development in this area is lifetime customer value, including a long-term perspective on consumer loyalty and repeat buying.

System I types of models assume heuristics, emotional and motivational decision processes, and unconscious, associative and automatic processes. Models of heuristics and biases have become popular both in psychology and in behavioural economics, and have many applications in consumer behaviour theory. They are based on the consumer's limited information capacity, which is hardly recognized in System II models. The relatively large number of documented heuristics gives the impression of a fragmented theory, which is probably in agreement with the current volatility of consumer behaviour noted in the introduction section. It is likely that new heuristics will be discovered without the prospect of a coherent, overarching theory developing soon.

Loss aversion and hyperbolic discounting theories are based on emotional and motivational processes. Loss aversion theories are structured around a common idea of asymmetric valuation of gains and losses with respect to a reference point. Subjective discounting captures the phenomenon of relatively large consumer impatience for positive consumption outcomes. Both theories are likely to be applied to more and more consumption problems in future research.

Both psychophysics and learning-by-conditioning theory can be considered as black-box approaches to consumer behaviour excluding mental processing. Both theories represent relatively early psychological research. The latest development is the subjective weighting of probabilities, which is relevant to consumer decision making under uncertainty.

Mixed-type models combine both System I and System II types of processes. These models have yielded conditions for using information processing, which may be applied in the marketing of consumer goods. Unresolved questions are whether System I and System II processes always operate in parallel, inhibit one another or operate in isolation. A related question is whether these processes are part of the same continuum – for example, information processing vs. affective choice – or exist in their own right. Possibly, neuropsychology may throw more light on this question in the future.

Although we have not provided a chronological account of the development of consumer behaviour theories, it seems clear that consumer behaviour has become less predictable over time. Also, changes in focus of psychological theory – that is, from intuitions to cognitions, then from cognitions to emotions – have stimulated the development of richer models of behaviour. Similarly the rise of behavioural and experimental economics has shown the shortcomings of the standard economic model. Hence, effort has been put into finding additional variables which help explain behaviour, including attitudes, social and personality variables, emotions and context variables. Diminished predictability and the awareness of it in research may have at least two causes:

(1) Consumption decisions are becoming more complex over time. This assumption is reasonable, given the growth in product variety and increased consumption budgets (see Schwartz, 2004).
(2) In measuring additional variables and decision processes in greater detail, it turns out that consumer preferences are unstable and frequently depend on the way they are measured, suggesting that they are also highly dependent on the context of choice (see Lichtenstein and Slovic, 2006).

Rather than favouring System I over System II (or the reverse), it seems that a combination of the two permits us to offer better explanations and make better predictions of consumer behaviour. Several possibilities for integrating the two systems seem to exist:

(1) High consumer impatience can be captured relatively easily in economic models, since it only requires replacing the interest rate with the consumer's subjective discount rate. This has already been accomplished in the work of Laibson (1997) and Angeletos et al. (2001).
(2) Psychophysics may be integrated in utility functions in economic models of consumer demand (see Antonides, 1989), multi-attribute utility and

attitude models (see Keeney and Raiffa, 1976; Fishbein and Ajzen, 1975), hedonic price functions (Agarwal and Ratchford, 1980) and economic welfare functions (see Van Praag and Frijters, 1999).

(3) Heuristics and biases may be integrated in the decision rules used in economic or psychological models of choice. For example, non-compensatory choices may replace compensatory choices in multi-attribute choice models (e.g., Hogarth and Karelaia, 2005). Another example is Carbone and Hey (1994), who modelled expected utility, subjective expected utility, rank-dependent expected utility, disappointment aversion, prospective reference and weighted utility theory in explaining their subjects' preference order of forty-four risky choices (see also Hey and Orme, 1994). An example from a different area is noise trader models in finance (De Long *et al.*, 1990). Here, rational traders, who base their decisions on fundamentals, are distinguished from noise traders, who base their decisions partly on irrational factors, for example optimism or pessimism. Noise traders give rise to a different source of risk which should be taken into account by the rational traders.

The development of such integrated models will bring economics and psychology closer together. Since the models will become increasingly complex, this development will be at the expense of theoretical elegance. However, because of their flexibility in dealing with different types of choice processes, they will be more realistic and explain behaviour better than before.

10.6 References

Agarwal, M. K. and B. T. Ratchford, 1980. Estimating demand functions for product characteristics: The case of automobiles. *Journal of Consumer Research* 7, 249–487.

Ahlbrecht, M. and M. Weber, 1995. Hyperbolic discounting models in prescriptive theory of intertemporal choice. *Zeitschrift für Wirtschafts- und Socialwissenschaften* 115, 535–68.

Ajzen, I., 1991. The theory of planned behaviour. *Organizational Behaviour and Human Decision Processes* 50, 179–211.

Angeletos, G.-M., D. Laibson, A. Repetto, J. Tobacman and S. Weinberg, 2001. The hyperbolic consumption model: Calibration, simulation, and empirical evaluation. *Journal of Economic Perspectives* 15(3), 47–68.

Antonides, G., 1989. An attempt at integration of economic and psychological theories of consumption. *Journal of Economic Psychology* 10, 77–99.

1990. *The Lifetime of a Durable Good*. Dordrecht: Kluwer Academic Publishers.

1995. Entrapment in risky investments. *Journal of Socio-Economics* 24(3), 447–61.

1996. *Psychology in Economics and Business*. Dordrecht: Kluwer Academic Publishers.

Antonides, G. and W. F. Van Raaij, 1998. *Consumer Behaviour: A European Perspective*. Chichester: John Wiley.

Antonides, G. and S. R. Wunderink, 2001. Subjective time preference and willingness to pay for an energy-saving durable good. *Zeitschrift für Sozialpsychologie* 32(3), 133–41.

Arkes, H. R. and C. Blumer, 1985. The psychology of sunk costs. *Organizational Behavior and Human Performance* 35, 124–40.

Batchelor, R. A., 1986. The psychophysics of inflation. *Journal of Economic Psychology* 7, 269–90.

Bazerman, M. H., J. R. Curhan, D. A. Moore and K. L. Valley, 2000. Negotiation. *Annual Review of Psychology* 51, 279–314.

Benartzi, S. and R. Thaler, 2004. Save more tomorrow: Using behavioural economics to increase employee savings. *Journal of Political Economy* 112(1), 164–87.

Carbone, E. and J. D. Hey, 1994. Discriminating between preference functionals: A preliminary Monte Carlo study. *Journal of Risk and Uncertainty* 8, 223–42.

Chamberlin, E. H., 1948. An experimental imperfect market. *Journal of Political Economy* 56 (2), 95–108.

Chen, S. and S. Chaiken, 1999. The heuristic–systematic model in its broader context. In: S. Chaiken and Y. Trope (eds.) *Dual-process Theories in Social Psychology*, pp. 73–96. New York: Guilford Press.

Deaton, A. and J. Muellbauer, 1980. *Economics and Consumer Behaviour*. Cambridge: Cambridge University Press.

De Groot, I. M., 2003. Product trials: The effects of direct experience on product evaluation. Unpublished doctoral thesis, Tilburg University, the Netherlands.

De Long, J. B., A. Shleifer, L. H. Summers and R. J. Waldmann, 1990. Noise trader risk in financial markets. *Journal of Political Economy* 98(4), 703–38.

Dubé, L., A. Chattopadhyay and A. Letarte, 1996. Should advertising appeals match the base of consumers' attitudes? *Journal of Advertising Research* 36(6), 82–9.

Engel, J. F., D. T. Kollat and R. D. Blackwell, 1968. *Consumer Behavior*. New York: Holt, Rinehart and Winston.

Epstein, S., 1994. Integration of the cognitive and the psychodynamic unconscious. *American Psychologist* 49(8), 709–24.

Fels, R., 1993. This is what I do, and I like it. *Journal of Economic Education* 24, 365–70.

Fishbein, M., 1966. The relationship between beliefs, attitude and behaviour. In: S. Feldman (ed.) *Cognitive Consistency*, pp. 199–223. New York: Academic Press.

Fishbein, M. and I. Ajzen, 1975. *Belief, Attitude, Intention and Behaviour*. Reading, MA: Addison-Wesley.

Fornell, C., 1992. A national customer satisfaction barometer: The Swedish experience. *Journal of Marketing* 56 (January), 6–21.

Fuchs, V. R., 1982. Time preferences and health: An exploratory study. In: V. R. Fuchs (ed.) *Economic Aspects of Health*, pp. 93–120. Chicago: University of Chicago Press.

Galanter, E., 1990. Utility functions for nonmonetary events. *American Journal of Psychology* 103, 449–70.

Gately, D., 1980. Individual discount rates and the purchase and utilization of energy-using durables: Comment. *Bell Journal of Economics* 11(1), 373–4.

Gattig, A., 2002. *Intertemporal Decision Making*. Groningen: Interuniversity Center for Social Science Theory and Methodology.

Hamblin, R. L. 1973. Social attitudes: Magnitude measurement and theory. In: H. M. Blalock Jr (ed.) *Measurement in the Social Sciences*, pp. 61–121. London: Macmillan.

Hartman, R. S., M. J. Doane and C.-K. Woo, 1991. Consumer rationality and the status quo. *Quarterly Journal of Economics* 106, 141–62.

Hausman, J. A., 1979. Individual discount rates and the purchase and utilization of energy-using durables. *Bell Journal of Economics* 10(1), 33–54.

Heath, C. and J. B. Soll, 1996. Mental accounting and consumer decisions. *Journal of Consumer Research* 23, 40–52.

Hey, J. D. and C. Orme, 1994. Investigating generalizations of expected utility theory using experimental data. *Econometrica* 62(6), 1291–1326.

Hogarth, R. M. and N. Karelaia, 2005. Simple models for multi-attribute choice with many alternatives: When it does and does not pay to face trade-offs with binary attributes. *Management Science* 51(12) 1860–72.

Holt, C. A., 1996. Trading in a pit market. *Journal of Economic Perspectives* 10, 193–203.

Howard, J. A. and J. N. Sheth, 1969. *The Theory of Buyer Behaviour*. New York: Wiley.

Hsee, C. K., 1996. The evaluability hypothesis: An explanation for preference reversals between joint and separate evaluations of alternatives. *Organizational Behaviour and Human Decision Processes* 67(3), 247–57.

    1998. Less is better: When low-value options are valued more highly than high-value options. *Journal of Behavioural Decision Making* 11(2), 107–21.

Iyengar, S. S. and M. R. Lepper, 2000. When choice is demotivating: Can one desire too much of a good thing? *Journal of Personality and Social Psychology* 79(6), 995–1006.

Jacoby, J., 1984. Perspectives on information overload. *Journal of Consumer Research* 19(4), 432–5.

Johnson, E. J., J. Hershey, J. Meszaros and H. Kunreuther, 1993. Framing, probability distortions, and insurance decisions. *Journal of Risk and Uncertainty* 7, 35–51.

Johnson, M. D., A. Herrmann and A. Gustafsson, 2002. Comparing customer satisfaction across industries and countries. *Journal of Economic Psychology* 23, 749–69.

Kahneman, D., 1994. New challenges to the rationality assumption. *Journal of Institutional and Theoretical Economics* 150, 18–36.

    1999. Objective happiness. In: D. Kahneman, E. Diener and N. Schwarz (eds.) *Well-being: The Foundations of Hedonic Psychology*, pp. 3–25. New York: Russell Sage.

    2003. A psychological perspective on economics. *American Economic Review* 93, 162–8.

Kahneman, D., J. L. Knetsch and R. H. Thaler, 1990. Experimental tests of the endowment effect and the Coase theorem. *Journal of Political Economy* 98(6), 1325–47.

Kahneman, D., P. Slovic and A. Tversky, 1982. *Judgment Under Uncertainty: Heuristics and Biases*. Cambridge: Cambridge University Press.

Kahneman, D. and A. Tversky, 1979. Prospect theory: An analysis of decision under risk. *Econometrica*, 47, 263–91.

Katona, G., 1975. *Psychological Economics*. New York: Elsevier.

Keeney, R. L. and H. Raiffa, 1976. *Decisions with Multiple Objectives: Preferences and Value Tradeoffs*. New York: John Wiley.

Knetsch, J. L., 2000. Environmental valuations and standard theory: Behavioural findings, context dependence and implications. In: T. Tietenberg and H. Folmer (eds.) *The International Yearbook of Environmental and Resource Economics 2000/2001: A Survey of Current Issues*, pp. 267–99. Cheltenham: Edward Elgar.

Kooreman, P., 2000. The labeling effect of a child benefit system. *American Economic Review* 90, 571–83.

Laibson, D., 1997. Golden eggs and hyperbolic discounting. *Quarterly Journal of Economics* 112(2), 443–77.

Lancaster, K., 1971. *Consumer Demand: A New Approach*. New York: Columbia University Press.

Lazarus, R. S., 1984. On the primacy of cognition. *American Psychologist* 39, 124–9.

Lichtenstein, S. and P. Slovic, 2006. *The Construction of Preference*. New York: Cambridge University Press.

Loewenstein, G., 1988. Frames of mind in intertemporal choice. *Management Science* 34(2), 200–14.

Lundberg, S. and R. Pollak, 1993. Separate spheres bargaining and the marriage market. *Journal of Political Economy* 101(6), 988–1010.

McFadden, D., 2001. Economic choices. *American Economic Review* 91(3), 351–78.

McFadden, D. and K. E. Train, 1996. Consumers' evaluation of new products: Learning from self and others. *Journal of Political Economy* 104, 683–703.

Mittal, B., 1988. The role of affective choice mode in the consumer purchase of expressive products. *Journal of Economic Psychology* 9, 499–524.

Modigliani, F., 1988. The role of intergenerational transfers and life-cycle saving in the accumulation of wealth. *Journal of Economic Perspectives* 2, 15–40.

Murray, D. J., 1983. *A History of Western Psychology*. Englewood Cliffs, NJ: Prentice-Hall.

Muth, J. F., 1961. Rational expectations and the theory of price movements. *Econometrica* 29, 315–35.

Nicosia, F. M., 1966. *Consumer Decision Processes: Marketing and Advertising Implications*. Englewood Cliffs, NJ: Prentice-Hall.

Odean, T., 1998. Are investors reluctant to realize their losses? *Journal of Finance* 53, 1775–98.

Oliver, R., 1996. *Satisfaction: A Behavioural Perspective on the Consumer*. Boston: Irwin McGraw-Hill.

Petty, R. E. and J. T. Cacioppo, 1986. The elaboration likelihood model of persuasion. In: L. Berkowitz (ed.) *Advances in Experimental Social Psychology*, vol. XIX, pp. 123–205. New York: Academic Press.

Prelec, D., 2000. Compound invariant weighting functions in prospect theory. In: D. Kahneman and A. Tversky (eds.) *Choices, Values, and Frames*, pp. 67–92. Cambridge: Cambridge University Press.

Purohit, D., 1995. Playing the role of buyer and seller: The mental accounting of trade-ins. *Marketing Letters* 6, 101–10.

Raiffa, H., J. Richardson and D. Metcalfe, 2003. *Negotiation Analysis*. Cambridge, MA: Belknap.

Rainwater, L., 1974. *What Money Can Buy: The Social Meaning of Poverty*. New York: Basic Books.

Ratchford, B. T., 1979. Operationalizing economic models of demand for product characteristics. *Journal of Consumer Research* 6, 76–85.

Read, D. and N. L. Read, 2004. Time discounting over the lifespan. *Organizational Behaviour and Human Decision Processes* 94, 22–32.

Rescorla, R. A., 1988. Pavlovian conditioning. It's not what you think it is. *American Psychologist* 43, 151–60.

Rosenberg, M. J., 1956. Cognitive structure and attitudinal affect. *Journal of Abnormal and Social Psychology* 53, 367–72.

Ross, W. T. and I. Simonson, 1991. Evaluations of pairs of experiences: A preference for happy endings. *Journal of Behavioural Decision Making* 4, 273–82.

Rust, R. T., K. N. Lemon and V. A. Zeithaml, 2004. Return on marketing: Using customer equity to focus marketing strategy. *Journal of Marketing* 68 (January), 109–27.

Samuelson, W. and R. Zeckhauser, 1988. Status quo bias in decision making. *Journal of Risk and Uncertainty* 1, 7–59.

Schwartz, B., 2000. The tyranny of freedom. *American Psychologist* 55(1), 79–88.
2004. *The Paradox of Choice*. New York: HarperCollins.

Shefrin, H. and M. Statman, 1985. The disposition to sell winners too early and ride losers too long. *Journal of Finance* 40, 777–92.

Shefrin, H. and R. H. Thaler, 1988. The behavioural life-cycle hypothesis. *Economic Inquiry* 26, 609–43.

Sheppard, B. H., J. Hartwick and P. R. Warshaw, 1988. The theory of reasoned action: A meta-analysis of past research with recommendations for modifications and future research. *Journal of Consumer Research* 15 (December), 325–43.

Shiv, B. and A. Fedorikhin, 1999. Heart and mind in conflict: The interplay of affect and cognition in consumer decision making. *Journal of Consumer Research* 26, 278–92.

Simon, H. A., 1986. Theories of bounded rationality. In: C. B. McGuire and R. Radner (eds.) *Decision and Organization*, pp. 161–76. Minneapolis: University of Minnesota Press.

Simonson, I., 1999. The effect of product assortment on buyer preferences. *Journal of Retailing*, 75(3), 347–70.

Simonson, I. and A. Tversky, 1992. Choice in context: Tradeoff contrast and extremeness aversion. *Journal of Marketing Research* 29, 281–95.

Skinner, B. F., 1954. The science of learning and the art of teaching. *Harvard Educational Review* 24, 86–97.

Sloman, S. A., 1996. The empirical case for two systems of reasoning. *Psychological Bulletin* 119, 3–22.

Slovic, P., 2000. *The Perception of Risk*. London: Earthscan Publications.

Smith, V. L., 1962. An experimental study of competitive market behaviour. *Journal of Political Economy* 70(2), 111–37.

Soman, D., 2001. The mental accounting of sunk time costs: Why time is not like money. *Journal of Behavioural Decision Making* 14(3), 169–85.

Stanovich, K. E. and R. F. West, 2000. Individual differences in reasoning: Implications for the rationality debate? *Behavioural and Brain Sciences* 23(5), 645–65.

Thaler, R. H., 1980. Toward a positive theory of consumer choice. *Journal of Economic Behaviour and Organization* 1, 39–60.

   1981. Some empirical evidence of dynamic inconsistency. *Economics Letters* 81, 201–7.

   1985. Mental accounting and consumer choice. *Marketing Science* 4, 199–214.

   1990. Saving, fungibility, and mental accounts. *Journal of Economic Perspectives* 4(1), 193–205.

   1999. Mental accounting matters. *Journal of Behavioural Decision Making* 12, 183–206.

Thaler, R. H. and E. J. Johnson, 1990. Gambling with the house money and trying to break even: The effects of prior outcomes on risky choice. *Management Science* 36(6), 643–60.

Tolman, E. C., 1959. Principles of purposive behaviour. In: S. Koch (ed.) *Psychology: A Study of a Science*, vol. II, pp. 92–157. New York: McGraw-Hill.

Tversky, A. and D. Kahneman, 1992. Advances in prospect theory: Cumulative representation of uncertainty. *Journal of Risk and Uncertainty* 5, 297–323.

Van Herwaarden, F. G. and A. Kapteyn, 1979. Empirical comparison of the shape of welfare functions. *Economics Letters* 3, 71–6.

Van Praag, B. M. S. and P. Frijters, 1999. The measurement of welfare and well-being: The Leyden Approach. In: D. Kahneman, E. Diener and N. Schwarz (eds.) *Well-being: The Foundations of Hedonic Psychology*, pp. 413–50. New York: Russell Sage.

Varian, H. R., 2002. *Intermediate Microeconomics: A Modern Approach*. London: W. W. Norton.

Veldscholte, C. M., P. M. Kroonenberg and G. Antonides, 1998. Three-mode analysis of perceptions of economic activities in eastern and western Europe. *Journal of Economic Psychology* 19, 321–51.

Verhoef, P. C., G. Antonides and A. N. de Hoog, 2004. Service encounters as a sequence of events: The importance of peak experiences. *Journal of Service Research* 7, 53–64.

Wärneryd, K.-E., 1989. On the psychology of saving. An essay on economic behaviour. *Journal of Economic Psychology* 10, 515–41.

Wilson, T. D., D. J. Lisle, J. W. Schooler, S. D. Hodges, K. J. Klaaren and S. J. LaFleur 1993. Introspecting about reasons can reduce post-choice satisfaction. *Personality and Social Psychology Bulletin* 19, 331–9.

Wilson, T. D. and J. W. Schooler, 1991. Thinking too much: Introspection can reduce the quality of preferences and decisions. *Journal of Personality and Social Psychology* 60, 181–92.

Zajonc, R. B. 1980. Feeling and thinking. *American Psychologist* 35, 151–75.

PART IV

Consumer behaviour in the public sector

11 Lay perceptions of government economic activity

SIMON KEMP

Many economic decisions are taken not by individuals, households or firms, but by governments. Often, particularly in democratic societies, these government decisions are made with the benefit of the citizens in mind.

There is a vast variety of such decisions. Some government decisions directly provide goods and services to people. Consider, for example, a decision to upgrade the standard of lighting on your street, a decision to buy new squadrons of aircraft for the air force, or a decision to increase spending on hospitals. Some decisions have to do with taxes and balancing the government's budget. Consider, for example, a local authority decision to raise the rate of tax on land, a decision to lower the rate of income tax for high earners, or a decision to run a substantial budget deficit this year. Other decisions regulate the way that markets, firms and individuals behave. For example, governments maintain and change health standards that restaurants must meet, a government might limit the number of cars that may be imported from another country, or it might reduce the number of licences to fish on a stretch of coastline.

We can ask important questions of these decisions. Do they really improve the lives of the people they affect? Do these decisions reflect people's preferences? Should the decisions reflect people's preferences? Answering such questions requires input from psychology.

11.1 Government and private decisions

To date, most research in the psychology of economic behaviour has focused on decisions made in the market sector. This may be partly because there are many more of these decisions than decisions made by governments. However, there are at least three reasons for thinking that psychology is really of special importance in government decision-making.

First, we need psychology to help measure how government activity affects us. How can we tell whether a particular policy provides value for us or improves our well-being? Obviously, this is at least in part a psychological issue. Moreover, one can argue that it is more important to use psychology to help determine the value or well-being that results from government activity than to determine the results of activity in the market economy. This is fundamentally because, while it is often possible to get a reasonable behavioural measure of how much value a market-supplied good or service produces for people, it is usually not possible to get such a behavioural measure for goods and services supplied by the government.

If behavioural measures of value are available, both psychologists and economists prefer to rely on them rather than on people's subjective reports. This is because they quite reasonably doubt whether people can and do report accurately about the value they receive from purchasing or using goods and services (e.g. Nisbett and Wilson, 1977). Behavioural measures of utility are certainly available and they are used in the private sector. So, for example, suppose I run a firm that makes and sells garden furniture. If people value the furniture and benefit from it, this can be very simply measured by sales. Generally, if they value it highly, they will buy it. My firm will respond by making and supplying more of such furniture. If the furniture is not much valued, sales will be low and my firm may go out of business or my shareholders may (eventually) decide to replace me with a more competent and responsive manager. Of course, sales are not a perfect measure – maybe the furniture will quickly fall to pieces after we have made our fortunes from it; maybe my manufacturing process causes such massive pollution problems that overall people's well-being is decreased by my firm – but they are at least a reasonably easily interpreted measure of utility.

By contrast, behavioural measures of the value of government decisions or activity are more difficult to come by. Of course, such measures are sometimes available and used. For example, continual traffic jams are a good indicator to a local government that some change should be made to the transport network. But what behaviour measures the value to citizens of a government decision to increase spending on the air force or primary schools? Often government activity itself intentionally channels behaviour and thus makes the behavioural measure useless. So, for example, a government may restrict the importation of foreign cars, but if the market share of cars made in one's home country then increases, this does not mean that a home-produced car now produces more well-being than a foreign one would have.

The relative lack of good behavioural measures to value government activity suggests that subjective ones be used instead, and later in this chapter we briefly consider some options.

Second, at least in democracies, the political process is expected to produce the government economic decisions that people value and want, and there has been considerable interest by public choice theorists in the relationship between the value people receive from governments and how they vote (e.g. Shughart and Razzolini, 2001). One common theory in this tradition, the median voter model, suggests that political parties should adopt the position taken by the median (or middle) voter on every position. So, for example, the level of health spending should optimally be that of the median voter on a continuum from the voter wanting most spending to the voter wanting least (Black, 1958/1987; Stigler, 1972; Tullock, 1976).

As we shall see below, a number of empirical studies indicate that the median voter model fails as an account of how government spending actually responds to people's preferences. However, its failure can also be anticipated on theoretical grounds. A very obvious problem is simply that governments make many more decisions than individuals have votes. Contrasting government decisions and those made in the market sector, Harris and Seldon (1979, p. 68) write: 'What sovereignty does the voter exercise through the ballot box? In place of the daily choice between myriad suppliers, the voter has a single option between two or three political parties every four or five years.' Research by political scientists indicates that elections are largely decided by voter perceptions of how the economy as a whole is doing and not very much by particular government spending or policy priorities (e.g. Alvarez *et al.*, 2000; Price and Sanders, 1995). In general, then, we could not expect how people vote in elections to be a sensitive measure of the way people value a particular government activity or policy, especially if it has not been an election issue. This expectation suggests we should look elsewhere for a suitable measure.

Third, a good deal of previous research has shown that people's thinking about economic issues contains a number of cognitive biases (see Kahneman and Tversky, 2000, or the earlier chapters of this book for recent reviews). For the most part, such cognitive biases have been studied in the context of people's decisions as consumers, but there are good reasons for thinking they might be even more pronounced in people's thinking about government than about private activities. As McCaffery and Baron (2004b, p. 434) point out:

> In private markets, arbitrage mechanisms, which allow some to profit from the biases of others, with overall prices showing little effect, can be expected to reduce the effects of bias . . . In the public sector, however, the absence of any simple, general arbitrage mechanism, such as the market itself . . . gives reason to believe that the adverse effects of cognitive biases can persist for long periods of time.

As we shall see below, there is evidence that people do not think about governmental activities in a strictly rational way. Of course, we should not forget here that cognitive biases might appear in the thinking of decision-makers as well as in the thinking of the general public.

11.2   How to value what governments do

In this section, we consider some of the methods that have been used to try to assess the worth of government activities. There have been a number of different approaches to the issue. As mentioned above, behavioural measures have sometimes been used (e.g. Clarke, 1998; Font, 2000), but, as argued above, many government activities do not lend themselves easily to

this means of assessment. Thus, most of the research has used different subjective measurement techniques which have obtained verbal or written statements from surveys of individual people affected by government decisions or
activity.

11.2.1 Subjective well-being

The most global measure used has probably been that of subjective well-being.
(For recent reviews, see, e.g., Diener *et al.*, 1999; Diener and Seligman, 2004;
Easterlin, 2002.) People are asked, for example, to rate how satisfied they are
with their life as a whole these days on a ten- or seven-point rating scale,
and the answers obtained from people in different circumstances or living
under different administrations are then compared. This method has an important advantage in that it attempts to measure directly the crucial concept of
well-being, and a number of important effects related to government decision-
making have been reported. For example, there is a substantial correlation
between average levels of well-being and average per capita income across
nations (Diener and Biswas-Diener, 2002). National instability may have a
very marked effect on well-being (e.g. Inglehart and Klingemann, 2000). It is
well established that becoming unemployed has a considerable and sometimes
very persistent adverse effect on people's well-being over and above what
one might expect from lowered income levels (e.g. Lucas *et al.*, 2004). An
intriguing finding from Frey and Stutzer's (2000) comparisons across the different cantons of Switzerland is that living under an administration with direct
democracy, where the citizens vote directly on a number of individual government decisions, appears to produce a small but measurable improvement in
personal well-being.

Of course, if one finds differences in well-being between two populations,
it is not always easy to pinpoint the cause of the differences. For example, the
populations of former West and East Germany have exhibited a substantial and
enduring difference in well-being that could be ascribed to a number of different
causes (Frijters *et al.*, 2003). There is a persistent finding that the increase in
income and material living standards in the USA after the Second World War
has been accompanied by no marked rise in average life satisfaction (Diener
and Suh, 1997), although Oswald (1997) argues that the slight effects obtained
may have some substantive significance. The absence of a marked effect is
often explained in terms of adjustment to the increased material wealth, but it
could also be attributed to an adjustment to an increase in pleasure or subjective
well-being itself, a 'satisfaction treadmill' as Kahneman (2000) terms it. Thus,
the results obtained from comparisons of subjective well-being measurement
often need to be interpreted with caution.

Another issue with the use of measures of subjective well-being is that they
are not particularly sensitive to changes in any objective variables, including

those that a government might control (Diener *et al.*, 1999). Most studies show that psychological variables (e.g. how extroverted people are or how good their coping strategies are) are more important determinants (e.g. Diener *et al.*, 1999). Thus, the measure may be better suited for evaluating major government decisions or major changes in government direction than minor ones. Some other measures are more focused on asking people to value particular government policies or programmes directly.

11.2.2 Contingent valuation

In the contingent valuation method, people are asked directly how much they would be willing to pay for a new government service or to have an old one continued (e.g. Hanley and Spash, 1993). There are a number of well-researched variants of the method. For example, the respondents might instead be asked how much they would be willing to accept to lose a service. As a general rule, there is no expectation that people are going to be actually asked to pay anything.

Contingent valuation has been very widely used to value individual public services, particularly environmental goods, and more details can be found in another chapter. A consequence of the widespread use, however, has been widespread scrutiny of the method itself, and this has led to the discovery of apparent biases and problems with it. For example, the measure is known to be rather insensitive to the quantity of the good, so that general public samples often appear willing to pay as much to retain one wilderness area as several (Baron and Greene, 1996). The apparent implication of this is that people value the provision of one wilderness area just as much as the provision of many of them, which seems hard to credit. The converse of people's insensitivity to quantities of the good which one would expect to affect their valuations is that their values are also affected by variables to which one would hope people were not sensitive. For example, contingent values can be strongly influenced by what respondents believe or are led to believe is currently spent on government activities (Baron and Maxwell, 1996; Kemp, 2003).

Respondents sometimes declare themselves reluctant to pay for public goods that they believe should be free. Baron (1997, p. 83) describes them as having 'protected values'. Such reluctance seems similar to the reluctance many people feel about giving money as a gift or donating a sum of money to your hosts rather than a bottle of wine when you go to a dinner party (e.g. Burgoyne and Routh, 1991), and is an indication that people do not regard money as a universally appropriate measure of value. This reluctance, together with empirical studies suggesting that more 'attitudinal' measures of value might underlie contingent values (Kahneman *et al.*, 1993; Kemp and Willetts, 1995a), also suggests asking people to value government activities directly.

11.2.3 Rating government activities

A number of measures are similar to contingent valuation in producing estimates of value but do not require respondents to nominate actual sums of
money. One method has simply been to ask people whether they would like to
see more, less or the same amount of money spent on a particular government
activity or range of government activities (e.g. Ferris, 1983, 1985). As we shall
see below, although this method provides only limited information, the results
obtained with it are often not trivial.

The psychophysical methods of magnitude estimation and category rating
have also been used to value government activities. In category rating, which is
the simpler and more widely used method, respondents simply value different
activities using a limited range of numbers (e.g. 0 to 10). One justification for
using it is that category rating has been widely used in psychology to study the
structure of people's attitudes and beliefs in a variety of situations. For example,
subjective well-being is often measured with category ratings (e.g. Diener
et al., 1999; Frey and Stutzer, 2000). Category rating has also been used to value
government activities directly, and it appears to yield useful insights into how
people think about government (e.g. Kemp and Willetts, 1995a, b). Like other
methods, category ratings are subject to a number of well-documented biases
(e.g. Poulton, 1989). For example, as Baron (1997) points out, the relative
insensitivity of people's valuations to quantity of the activity provided appears
when category ratings of value are used as well as in contingent valuation. (For
more detail, see Kemp, 2002.)

11.2.4 The ideal method

Ideally, we should like to have a method of measuring people's subjective
utility, well-being or perceptions of value that is not only reliable and valid,
but also delivers a cardinal or interval scale (cf. Stevens, 1946). We would like
a scale which was additive so that the utility delivered by government activity
A and that delivered by government activity B together equalled the sum of
the separate utilities. We should like a scale in which the utility derived or felt
by individual P from a government activity could be directly compared with
that derived by Q.

None of the existing methods of valuation comes close to achieving this
ideal. For example, of the methods reviewed above, only contingent valuation
could conceivably deliver additivity, and the empirical evidence indicates that
it does not. As we have just seen, two wilderness areas are not given twice the
value of one. Category ratings of the value of particular activities change with
the context provided by the questioner (e.g. whether presented alongside other,
highly valued activities or not) and the same may well be true for people's
estimates of their subjective well-being. Results obtained with the different
methods are certainly not always comparable.

However, although none of the methods is ideal, it would be a mistake to conclude that nothing of any real-world importance can ever be discovered by using them. Diener and Seligman (2004) have recently argued that regular national surveys of subjective well-being could be of enormous help in making policy decisions. Regular national surveys of the relative values perceived from different government activities would provide information of a somewhat different kind, but would also be valuable. Indeed, overall, it is surprising that at present relatively little effort is expended by governments on the regular gathering of *any* potentially useful information of this kind, and even less on its use. (Some research is undertaken, although not necessarily by governments. For example, the United States General Social Survey (e.g. Russell and Megaard, 1988) has often asked whether people would prefer to spend more, less or the same on different issues. The British Social Attitudes Survey includes questions about preferred spending. The Eurobarometer includes questions on people's happiness and satisfaction.)

11.3   Lay thinking about government activity

In this section, we consider attempts to value some of the present activities of government in the economy, and people's views on what the government should be doing.

11.3.1   What sorts of things should government do?

The last decades of the twentieth century saw the governments of many developed countries retreat from 'commanding heights of industry' that they had previously occupied. Industries as varied as telecommunications, railways, coal mines, post offices, pension plans and prisons were taken out of government hands and given or sold into private ones. These privatizations were, in part, motivated by economic considerations of likely efficiency, and often gave rise to opposition at the time which then quietened either to sullen resentment or to contentment. However, a number of questions have not been well answered: What kinds of things do people believe are appropriate for the government, and what kinds are appropriate for private owners? Does the thinking of the lay person mirror that of the economist?

Thompson and Elling (2000) reported on the results of a survey done in the state of Michigan, which asked respondents whether they would prefer supply by profit-making firms, non-profit-making organizations or the government for each of fourteen different services. Overall, there were clear majorities in favour of government supply for all but four services (garbage collection, clerical services, street cleaning and emergency medical services). Thus, even in the USA, whose citizens are generally thought to favour a small public sector, people felt that many services should be supplied by the government.

For example, government supply was clearly preferred for services which involved some kind of coercion (e.g. prisons, police, fire services).

Mahoney *et al.* (2005) questioned samples from New Zealand and the UK about the characteristics of services that made them appear more suitable for government or private supply. In Study 1 participants simply rated the importance of different characteristics for making the decision. In Study 2 the participants were presented with scenarios in which the characteristics of the services were systematically varied. In Study 3 they were presented with twenty-five services, ranging from national defence to swimming pools to bakeries, and asked who they would prefer to supply them and how the services rated on each of eight characteristics. Taken over the three studies, two variables seemed of particular importance in people's decisions in favour of government supply: that the service is necessary for people's health; and if the supplier of the service has a monopoly. People also favoured government supply when nearly everyone was likely to make use of the service, when the supply might involve pollution, and when the service was connected with education.

It is possible that people's preference for whether a service should be provided by government or by private enterprise is linked to the different methods of allocation frequently used by the two sectors. There has been some research into when people would prefer to distribute a scarce good using a market system (when presumably the price would rise) or using some form of rationing or regulation (e.g. Frey and Pommerehne, 1993). People are often happy to distribute scarce champagne using the market system, but goods necessary to people's health, the possibility of monopoly, and many people wanting the service lead respondents to prefer some form of regulation or rationing (Kemp, 1996). These three characteristics also emerged as important for people's preference for government suppliers.

Interestingly, the research suggests that the lay person's and the economist's (e.g. Stiglitz, 1988, ch. 3) reasons for preferring government provision of services are not quite the same. So, to take a single example, economists often use the term 'public good' to refer to a service, like defence or sewage treatment, that once provided is effectively provided to all. There is a well-developed economic theory suggesting that public goods are undersupplied by the market system, and thus a case for governments to provide such services (Samuelson, 1955). This case seems related to, but not quite the same as, the lay preference for government provision when the service is demanded by all. The economist's account does not normally single out health goods (as distinct from public health measures) as particularly suited for government involvement, but lay people often do. Nor does economics often put special stress on coercive services.

11.3.2 Spending priorities on existing services

Another chapter looks at the general question of how big government should be overall, and later in this one we examine briefly the issue of how much

Table 11.1 *Percentage of respondents favouring less, the same or more expenditure on six categories of US public spending. Reprinted from* Public Choice, *45(2), 1985, pp. 139–53, 'Interrelationships among public spending preferences: a micro analysis', Ferris, J. M., with kind permission from Springer Science and Business Media*

	Less	Same	More
Public education	7.9	33.0	59.1
Public welfare	49.4	25.3	25.3
Public housing	19.4	28.6	52.0
Public health	8.1	32.2	59.7
Highways	23.1	44.1	32.9
Defence	41.5	45.3	13.1

people actually know about both the costs of government services and how taxation pays for them. But, supposing people were agreed on how much money should be spent on government services generally or that some services should be provided by the government, how should the spending be allocated? What sorts of priorities do people have for spending money on, say, defence versus public hospitals?

If the median voter model applied to government spending on a service then we should find that the number of people advocating an increase in spending on a service would roughly match the number of people advocating decreased spending on the service. Indeed, the model should apply to all the services provided by government. A number of different studies on national spending in different countries, however, have found this prediction to fail, and frequently the respondents would particularly like to see increased spending on education and health (Ferris, 1983, 1985; Lewis and Jackson, 1985; Kristensen, 1982; Smith and Wearing, 1987; Zanardi, 1996). A sample of results, taken from Ferris's (1985) representative US study, is shown in table 11.1. Note that a clear majority of respondents (including, of course, the median respondent) favoured more spending in three of the six areas (public education, housing and health); the proportion wanting less spending on welfare nearly equals the total wanting the same or more spending; and for only one area (highways) was there an approximately equal number of respondents in the more and less categories.

Results from the General Social Survey indicate that at least some of these apparent mismatches have persisted over long periods of time in the USA. For example, the 2002 General Survey results also show a majority of respondents favouring more spending on health and education. But there can be changes over time too. The same survey (General Social Survey, 2002) showed more people believed there was too little current spending on defence than believed there was too much (although the median voter thought the spending on defence was 'about right'), a clear reversal of Ferris's (1985) finding.

Other studies using somewhat different subjective methods have found comparable patterns of mismatch, indicating that the results are not simply an artefact of using the 'more, the same, less' method. Thus, for example, respondents in 'budget games' do not evenly allocate a proposed budget cut or budget increase over different spending categories (De Groot and Pommer, 1987; Hockley and Harbour, 1983; Strauss and Hughes, 1976). Representative US respondents in 1999 wanted much larger increases in federal expenditure on medical research, the United Nations and education than on overseas aid or transportation, although reduction of the national debt recorded the largest desired increase (Center on Policy Attitudes, 2000). Kemp and Willetts (1995b) asked a representative sample of New Zealand respondents to category rate the value of existing government services. The results showed a very weak relationship between the rated value of the individual services and the amount spent on them. Education, the police and health services seemed to be particularly good value for money (i.e. they produced more value than would be expected from their cost); defence, unemployment benefits and a benefit for solo parents were seen as comparatively poor value for money. Note, incidentally, that despite the different countries, times and methodologies, these results were qualitatively quite similar to Ferris's (1985) US results.

Taken over a number of different studies, the conclusion is clear: governments (at least national governments; see Bondonio and Marchese, 1994, for an exceptional finding for the municipality of Milan) do not generally match their spending to the desires or values of the citizenry.

11.3.3 Health services

In recent years, the question of spending priorities has probably been most intensively investigated within the domain of health services. Both health systems that are largely state-funded (e.g. in the United Kingdom) and health systems that are largely funded through health insurance (e.g. in the United States) have found it impossible to meet the demand for the many operations, drugs and other health services that are now available. Writing of the US health system, Ubel (2000, p. xviii) reports: 'We cannot afford to give every health service to every person who could possibly benefit.' Some sort of rationing or prioritizing is necessary, and the systems proposed have generally tried to take into account possible benefits to the patients.

One much-researched system calculates Quality Adjusted Life Years (QALYs). (For detailed discussions, see, for example, Drummond *et al.*, 1997; Gold *et al.*, 1996; Kawachi *et al.*, 1990; Sloan, 1995; Staquet *et al.*, 1998.) In brief, the patient's expectancy of life with or without receiving a particular medical treatment is calculated. Each year of life is weighted by an estimate of the quality of life for that year (usually measured on a scale from 0, meaning dead, to 1). Thus, for example, I might have a life expectancy of three years with a quality of life of 0.5 in each year, giving a total of 1.5 QALYs, if I am left alone; and a life expectancy of five years with a quality of life of 0.7 for each year, giving a total of 3.5 QALYs, if I am treated with a procedure that costs $20,000. The value of the treatment is then 2.0 QALYs, and the treatment costs $10,000/QALY.

It is easy to see that this system enables us to make quantitative comparisons between different sorts of treatments carried out on different sorts of patients. Moreover, we can contrast procedures which save life with those that enhance it. It is not much more difficult to see that actually using this system or those like it (e.g. Gold *et al.*, 1996) is likely to give rise to all sorts of controversies, and, indeed, it has. So, for example, how should we actually measure the future quality of people's lives (e.g. Sloan, 1995)? Should we give extra weight to a procedure which saves life (raises the future quality from 0 to 0.5 say) rather than one which enhances it (raises the future quality from 0.5 to 1.0) (e.g. Ubel, 2000, ch. 10)? Should we treat 1 QALY next year the same as 1 QALY in ten years' time (Lipscomb *et al.*, 1996)? Is the system's implicit assumption that we should aim for the greatest good of the greatest number justified (Burrows and Brown, 1993)?

There are clearly parallels between the sorts of methodological and ethical decisions to be made here and those made in deciding the larger area of prioritizing within government budgets. Perhaps one of the bigger differences is that there has been more research within the narrower domain of health decisions, and the drawbacks and advantages of different decision-making methods are thus somewhat better understood within it.

11.3.4 Currency

So far we have considered what people think about services that a government or government-regulated agency provides or might provide. However, a large part of government activity involves regulation of economic activity rather than service provision. Some examples of this appear in other sections of this handbook: for example, the actions of government to preserve aspects of the environment or to protect the consumer (see also Bazerman *et al.*, 2001; Mayer, 1999). Here we briefly consider two other examples: the provision of a national currency and the restriction of imports.

I know of no research which has looked at the broad issue of what people expect from a currency, although there is a good deal of discussion of the issue in economics (e.g. Davies, 1996). However, there has been considerable study of people's expectation that the currency be stable and hence of the effects of currency inflation. Also, more recently some researchers have investigated psychological aspects of the recent replacement of a number of European national currencies by the euro.

In strict economic theory, it may not matter whether wages and prices stay stable over a year or if they both go up by 20 per cent: in either case the purchasing power of individuals stays the same. But perhaps the most basic finding about price and currency inflation is that people do not see it that way. Opinion polls during periods of inflation have regularly shown that people were concerned about it and found it damaging, and psychological research indicates that it might produce psychological stress and detract from people's economic well-being (e.g. Epstein and Bahad, 1982; Fisher, 1986).

We should not take this as an indication that people think irrationally about inflation. One far from irrational manifestation of the increased stress produced by inflation is the increased number of wage negotiations that are conducted at times of high inflation (Heyman and Leijonhufvud, 1995). When inflation is high, workers cannot wait for pay rises and employers cannot afford to make settlements in advance. Thus, they must negotiate more often and under greater pressure.

There is also good evidence that inflation acts so as to blur price information. In times of moderately high inflation, prices of different items do not all rise at exactly the same rate. However, people do not always perceive these different rates of price change and tend to recall all past prices as having risen in much the same way (Kemp, 1987). Shamir (1985) found that, when inflation in their country exceeded 100 per cent per year, many Israelis did not know the *current* prices of even everyday items.

It is also arguable that the control of inflation is one area where governments have listened to the public. Certainly, the industrialized world at the turn of the millennium witnessed considerably lower rates of inflation than were present in the 1970s and 1980s, and governments have often acted so as to strengthen the ability of central banks to control inflation.

Although many countries have changed their currency over the last hundred years or so, the recent replacement of many European national currencies by the euro was perhaps the biggest such change and certainly the most researched. The euro was phased in as the official currency of much of Europe over a three-year period from 1999 to 2002. Coins and notes were used from 1 January 2002, and national currencies phased out of everyday use during the following months.

Prior to the new currency's introduction, there was research into the expectations and attitudes people held about it. Certainly not everyone was wholeheartedly in favour of change, and personal resistance to the euro's introduction was, in many countries, found to be correlated with nationalism (e.g. Meier and Kirchler, 1998; Müller-Peters, 1998; Van Everdingen and Van Raaij, 1998). Although at one level this result is unsurprising, it serves as a demonstration that people do not always view economic events from a strictly economic perspective. A neat demonstration that thinking about prices is not always rational comes from the work of Ferrari and Lozza (2005). They found around the time of the currency change that Italians expected higher future price increases when they thought in lire (a currency which in the past had often been inflation-prone) than when they thought in euros.

The introduction of the euro led to a widespread belief that many stores and services had used the change as an opportunity to raise prices, even though official statistics indicated that actual price changes had been minimal (Muss-weiler and Strack, 2004). The research on inflation suggests that the introduc-tion of the new currency should make it more difficult to compare prices and this is what seems to have happened in the short term. However, the longer-term expectation must be that the euro will act to stabilize prices as well as to make price comparisons between the different countries that adopted the new currency easier (Mussweiler and Strack, 2004).

Finally, we might note that lay opinion was canvassed in many individual nations about whether to participate in the common currency. For example, France held a referendum to decide on participation in the European Monetary Union in 1992; Denmark (in 2000) and Sweden (in 2003) declined to use the euro after the proposal was rejected in referenda.

11.3.5   International trade

Although their views have never been formally compared, economists gener-ally seem to regard free international trade more highly than ordinary folk do (e.g. Roberts, 2001). One explanation for the lack of universal enthusiasm for free trade is that a change to trade (or any other) policy that is in the general public interest will still often harm the economic interests of some. For exam-ple, liberalizing European agricultural policies might be in the wider interests of Europeans (and many non-Europeans) but is likely to harm many European farmers. A good deal of research attention has thus focused on how small, interested groups can organize themselves so as to obtain a decision in their interests (e.g. Rowley, 2001).

It is also possible to think of psychological explanations why people might not favour free trade. For example, economic theories of trade tend to be framed in terms of the increased consumption possibilities that arise from freeing up trade. However, it may be that ordinary folk largely disregard the increased utility that may result from the new consumption possibilities, and focus instead on the utility obtained from employment. Many people fear the lowering of trade barriers because they or some of their compatriots might become unemployed. As a number of studies have shown that the psychological effects of unemployment extend well beyond what could be predicted from the loss of income and hence the loss of consumption possibilities (e.g. Lucas *et al.*, 2004), this is hardly an irrational fear, although whether freeing up trade does actually have a major effect on employment is a matter for both debate and ongoing empirical research (e.g. Irwin, 2002).

Some explanations do suggest economic irrationality on the part of ordinary folk. Economics, for example, stresses that both parties gain if reciprocal trade between them is made freer, but it is possible that people respond as though the gains were a 'fixed pie' and that gains to one country must be offset by losses to another (Bazerman *et al.*, 2001). Ricardo's (1817/1971) principle of comparative advantage, which is one of the traditional cornerstones of the economic argument for free trade, is not intuitively obvious, and is often poorly understood by lay folk. Moreover, people who misunderstand the principle are also likely to prefer the restriction of imported goods (Baron and Kemp, 2004).

At present very little research has been done on the psychology of trade, so we can only speculate on the most important reason or reasons why lay opinion differs (if it actually does) from that of economists. There may also be important differences between groups of people. For example, those in the developing world may think quite differently about the issues than those in the developed world. However, as lay thinking has at least some role in making trade decisions – both as electors of decision-makers and because the decision-makers are often themselves lay thinkers – it would appear important to know what this thinking is, and whether it should modify policy (e.g. by more careful consideration of employment issues) or whether it should be met by better education (e.g. in the principle of comparative advantage).

11.4   How well informed is lay thinking?

Governments do not always make exactly the economic decisions that lay people want. But should they? It is quite likely that there are situations in which government decision-makers are better informed and in a position to make better decisions on behalf of their citizens than the citizens are themselves. Particularly, one might expect this to be true where the issues are complex and where the average citizen has not had the time or motivation to think them through. In fact, people do not always appear to think rationally about government involvement in the economy, and quite often they appear to think about government activities in a way that oversimplifies the issues. In the preceding section, we noted that the principle of comparative advantage is not well understood by people, although whether this is an important reason for many people's lack of enthusiasm for free trade is not known. The US 2002 General Social Survey found that a majority of respondents believed the government gave too little assistance to the poor, but at the same time more respondents thought that welfare spending was too high than thought it was too low (General Social Survey, 2002.) Of course, this is not necessarily a contradiction: it may be that people would have liked to direct the spending in a different way (see, e.g., Kluegel and Smith, 1986; Williamson and Wearing, 1996). We consider below some research into three other areas, at least two of which seem to be imperfectly understood by lay people.

11.4.1   Taxation

The suspicion that people are not fully aware of how much tax they pay and that governments might try to take advantage of this lack of complete awareness is of long-standing (e.g. Mill, 1848/1909, pp. 864–6). More recently, a tendency to underestimate the tax one pays has sometimes been termed *fiscal illusion*, and it is often claimed that indirect sales or consumption taxes are more subject to this illusion than direct, and particularly income, tax (e.g. Heyndels and Smolders, 1995; Misiolek and Elder, 1988; Sorensen, 1992).

This claim finds some support in empirical research. For example, Cullis and Lewis (1985) found British taxpayers to be more knowledgeable about income tax than about indirect taxes. Certainly, belief in the possibility of this fiscal illusion is strong enough that, in most US states, the price actually charged for retail goods is often higher than the marked price, because sales tax is added on later. Visitors, who are often surprised by this practice, find that it is defended by their American hosts on the grounds that it makes the indirect sales tax visible.

Not all researchers have found evidence for fiscal illusion. For example, Misiolek and Elder (1988) recorded the per capita tax revenues and the complexity (and hence invisibility) of the tax system across the different US states. Fiscal illusion would lead one to expect that the tax take might be higher in states with the less transparent systems, but this result was not found. Sorensen (1992) found little evidence for fiscal illusion in Norway. Kemp (2005, Study 4) found New Zealand respondents actually overestimated the proportion of revenue obtained from a quite well-known and well-publicized consumption tax relative to that obtained from income tax. Gemmell *et al.* (2004) reported, to their own apparent surprise, that far from underestimating their tax, respondents to the British Social Attitudes Survey tended to overestimate both the income tax and the consumption (VAT) tax they were liable for. Perhaps unsurprisingly, individuals tended to be more biased against a particular tax if they (mis)perceived themselves as paying more of it.

McCaffery and Baron (2003, 2004a, b) have recently shown that people's thinking about taxation is subject to a number of other biases. For example, there is a metric effect: people prefer a more steeply progressive tax system when the tax system is described in percentage terms – e.g. you pay 30 per cent tax on earnings between $30,000 and $50,000 – than when it is described in dollar terms (McCaffery and Baron, 2003). People display a disaggregation bias in which they do not adjust progressivity in one tax to fully compensate for the lack of it in another (McCaffery and Baron, 2003). Overall, they suggest that

> [s]ubjects approach a given choice or decision problem with strong independent norms or ideals, such as, here, 'do no harm', 'avoid penalties', 'treat likes alike', 'help children', and 'expect the rich to pay more than the not-rich'. They then evaluate the choice-problem based on a norm made most salient by the formal presentation, ignoring the others. This leads to preference reversals and shifts in a complex area such as tax, where independently attractive ideas are often in conflict.   (McCaffery and Baron, 2004a, p. 679)

Overall, people often do not have a good idea either of how much tax they pay or of how improvements to the tax system should be brought about, although the patterns of misperception are themselves not completely understood. The lack of a complete understanding of people's misperceptions has not prevented a good deal of past speculation on the implications of misperceptions. Broadly speaking, writers have either drawn attention to the likelihood of governments expanding their power and influence because taxes are underestimated (e.g. West and Winer, 1980) or have suggested that governments are too reluctant to undertake really useful spending (e.g. Galbraith, 1969; Mill, 1848/1909; Smith and Wearing, 1987). This debate about the appropriate size of government is beyond the scope of this chapter (see chapter 12 of this volume), but it should be remarked that both possible misperceptions of tax and possible misperceptions of the costs of government services are highly relevant to it.

Finally, in this section we note one study indicating that people's views on taxation are quite malleable. Alvarez and McCaffery (2000) carried out a large-scale survey on the attitudes of US citizens to various budgetary and taxation issues. Unusually, this survey incorporated a manipulation: half of the respondents were presented with the (fair) statement that 'Many experts believe that the tax system, because of its marriage penalties and child-care relief, is biased against working mothers' (Alvarez and McCaffery, 2000, p. 6). A question regarding tax cuts followed, and those respondents (particularly if male) who were presented with the statement were significantly less attracted to an across-the-board tax rate cut. As the authors point out, the result suggests that 'attitudes towards particular forms of tax cuts, not well formed in any event, are easily unmoored' (p. 8).

11.4.2   Costs of providing government services

If people are to have a say in how revenue might be allocated to different government services, it would often be useful to them to know how much is currently spent on the services. (This is particularly true because people do not appear to distinguish the marginal and total utility of government services very well: e.g., Kemp, 1998.) The evidence, however, suggests that they have only a rather sketchy idea of costs. Sorensen's (1992) Norwegian respondents did not generally know what it cost to provide services like day nurseries or schools. Harris and Seldon (1979) found their British respondents produced cost estimates for specific services that were not only very variable but systematically biased: the costs of expensive services (e.g. education) were underestimated, those of relatively cheap items (e.g. unemployment benefits at the time) were overestimated. Kemp and Burt (2001) found a similar pattern in New Zealand. Some measure of the extent of the inaccuracy in this last study is given by the percentage of general public respondents who were able to nominate a cost figure (as dollars spent per capita per year) that was within a factor of two of the correct answer. At one extreme, *none* of the respondents was able to estimate the New Zealand per capita contribution to the World Health Organization within a factor of two (all overestimated); at the other, 37 per cent achieved within a factor of two accuracy for spending on schools.

Kemp (2003) provided either accurate or misleading information – respondents were presented with costs that were either higher or lower than the actual ones by a factor of three – on the current costs of providing government services, and found valuations of the services, as measured by category rating, were largely unaffected by the cost information, but preferred spending was markedly changed. To a good approximation, people's preferred spending on the services simply increased or decreased by a factor of three in line with the misleading information they were given. These results not only reinforce the earlier conclusion that people know little about the costs of providing government services, but also provide fresh evidence that the contingent valuation technique may not be the ideal way to value them.

11.4.3 Altruism

When people think about the provision of government services, trade, tax, currency or any other government-provided service, they might do so either by thinking of their own narrow self-interest or by taking into at least some account the interests of other people. It would probably be conceptually easier for policy-makers if they did the former, because then the different valuations, preferences and so on might simply be added up over the different individuals or different interest groups. However, there is strong evidence that people's views are actually an amalgam of self-interest and public interest.

For example, Hudson and Jones (1994) asked UK respondents to make a choice among different tax and spending levels considering their general preference, their self-interest or the public interest. The three types of choice were somewhat different and the results indicated that both self-interest and public interest were reflected in the general preference, with the latter predominating. A similar result has been reported for New Zealanders (Kemp and Burt, 2002).

The way people vote in elections and referenda also indicates that they think of others when they vote (e.g. Funk and Garcia-Monet, 1997). As an example, a referendum held in Roanoke, Virginia on supporting a scheme to prevent flooding provided a majority in favour of the scheme, even though the majority of the voters did not actually stand in risk of flooding (Shabman and Stephenson, 1994).

Yet another source of evidence that people often behave altruistically comes from public goods games. Such games, which have been frequently studied by experimental economists, give participants the choice of investing some part of their experimental wealth in a fund which benefits all the participants in the game. The actual choices made depend on a large number of variables, many of which have been experimentally studied, but a consistent finding is that people often do invest in the public good (Ledyard, 1995).

If people behave or think altruistically, to whom do they behave altruistically? Do they, for example, consider others in their family, their social class, their country, their continent (cf. the European Union or NAFTA), the world? Clearly, such questions are important for understanding how, for example, people think about social welfare, taxation or trade policy, but for the most part they have not yet been put, let alone answered, except in the context of 'layered prisoner's dilemma' games (Schwartz-Shea and Simmons, 1990).

In these games, participants may cooperate or defect. Cooperation tends to disadvantage the participant and an 'out-group' but benefits members of the 'in-group'; defection has the opposite effects. The cooperative strategy, which is frequently followed by participants, may be thought of as 'parochialism' (Schwartz-Shea and Simmons, 1991). Baron (2001) obtained results suggesting that parochialism might in part stem from a 'self-interest illusion' in which people see themselves as benefiting more from sacrifices they make for the in-group than they in fact do, and this illusion could be reduced when people were forced to calculate the actual outcomes. The idea of parochialism is also consistent with other findings indicating that people tend to support measures that benefit both themselves and people like themselves. So, as one of many similar examples, Brook *et al.* (1998, p. 96) found 'a clear tendency for individuals to be more sympathetic to spending on the sorts of benefits which they might receive themselves'. But whether this is because individuals are thinking of their own self-interest or thinking of others (who they may know personally) who are like themselves is not so clear.

Other findings from layered prisoner's dilemma games suggest further complexities. Schwartz-Shea and Simmons (1990) reported results indicating that the worthiness of the out-group was important in the decision, and that this apparent worthiness could be affected by discussion. Thus, results to date suggest that the degree to which people consider the interests of the different groups they belong to is both variable and manipulable, as one might expect from observation of political history.

11.4.4 The origins of lay attitudes and beliefs

We have seen that ordinary folk have beliefs, perceptions and attitudes about the government's role in the economy. But how do people acquire them? The answer is important because it would help tell us how much weight we should attach to these views. If, to take one improbable extreme, such views were entirely formed by social learning, this would suggest that government economic activity would be best to follow the dictates of economics, and the public should be educated to accept them. If, to take the other improbable extreme, such views had hard-wired or innate foundations, then these should be an important basis for deciding appropriate government economic activity.

The fact that government spending and roles in the economy differ from country to country suggests that social learning plays an important role in lay views. There are suggestive international differences in people's preferences for spending allocations. For example, people's views about how to allocate scarce goods differ between different countries and between those brought up in communist or capitalist societies, although the results are not simply explained by people invariably preferring what they grew up with (Kemp and Bolle, 1999).

On the other hand, at least some of the components of lay attitudes seem to be partly hard-wired. Many would concede that altruism is one such component (e.g. Ridley, 1997). A more controversial example is fairness. Fairness is a crucial component of people's perception of government economic activity. For example, is it fair that George and his six children receive more in unemployment relief than Alan does when working full-time in a job he rather dislikes? Is it fair that Carole will become unemployed if the free importation of cheap clothing is allowed?

A number of different aspects of fairness have been studied experimentally. One line of research has used ultimatum games. In this game (e.g. Güth *et al.*, 1982), two players are offered a resource if they agree on its distribution. Player A is first given the choice of how the resource should be divided, and player B can then only accept or reject the suggested division. If B accepts, the resource is divided according to A's suggestion; if B declines, neither A nor B gets anything. The game theoretic solution suggests rational unfairness: B should accept any positive offer, and thus A should offer as little as possible. In practice, research in an enormous range of human societies has shown that the game theoretic solution is rarely achieved by individuals, and that fairer (more equal) divisions than this are normal in all of these societies (Henrich *et al.*, 2005). The same research, however, also shows that there is variation between societies, and thus there must be a considerable social learning component in ultimatum game behaviour, and, accepting the game as a measure of fairness, differences in the way people in different societies think of fair behaviour.

Thus, the evidence to date suggests that the two extremes – all social learning or all hard-wired – are indeed improbable, but a number of important questions, particularly about the way in which complex perceptions are formed, remain unanswered.

11.5 Could governments do better?

Democratically elected representative governments probably do a reasonable but by no means perfect job of meeting the economic aspirations of their citizens. Before becoming too harsh in our condemnation of them, we might recall that the performance of non-elected governments seems worse. For example, no recent leader of a democratically elected government has spent a measurable proportion of his country's tax revenue in providing pensions for his mistresses (like Charles II of England), or building a splendid palace for himself and his courtiers (like Louis XIV of France), or launching an invasion of territory held by another and more powerful country (like President Galtieri of Argentina).

On the other hand, even given the patchy nature of the research to date, there are clearly instances where current government policies do not align with the view of the median citizen. Obviously governments could bring their policies into better alignment with these views, but should they? If citizens' views are not well thought out, and, as we have seen, some aspects of them appear not to be, governments might indeed sometimes know best, and the welfare of the citizens might be better served by a government that did not listen to them too closely.

This is, of course, a very old issue. It is raised, for example, in Plato's *Republic*, and it is perhaps most appropriately studied by political scientists. However, there has been some recent research of a psychological nature that bears on the issue. For example, Ölander *et al.* (1999; cited in Kemp, 2002, ch. 9) found that New Zealanders recognized they had little influence on government allocation decisions, would have liked more influence, but were aware that they did not have all the information they needed to make the right decisions.

A number of recent studies have examined economic (and other) decisions under direct democracy, in which people vote directly through referenda on different issues. A number of US states, of which California is probably the best known, and other administrations make use of referenda, including referenda on financial matters. Ingberman (1985) studied the use of referenda in US school budgets, finding that the outcomes are somewhat dependent on the type of voting procedures used. So, for example, does the defeat of a budget proposal result in the previous status quo or in no budget at all?

Some very interesting studies have also been carried out in Switzerland. These make use of two peculiarities of Swiss democracy: many Swiss decisions are made at the canton (state) rather than the federal level; and the cantons differ in the extent to which they use either direct democracy, in which measures are voted on directly by the citizens, or representative democracy, in which measures are voted on by elected representatives of the citizenry (e.g. Pommerehne, 1990). Hence comparisons between cantons with different democratic procedures can be made. The evidence suggests that in cantons with direct democracy there is a better match between the voters' preferences for different government-supplied services and what is actually supplied (Frey, 1994). Moreover, people who live in such cantons are actually slightly happier than those who live in cantons where representative democracy prevails (Frey and Stutzer, 2000).

It is not simply that people get more of what they want in direct democracy. There are also indications that people in direct democracies make more effort to inform themselves about the issues before voting. Participation rates in the voting and the level of discussion generated are often high (Feld and Kirchgässner, 2000). Benz and Stutzer (2004) found that the level of knowledge in answer to three questions testing political knowledge (e.g. 'Who was the President of the Federal Council in 1995?') was higher in cantons with more direct democracy, even though the questions asked referred to the federal system rather than the particular canton. As the authors point out, such results suggest that 'voter information should be treated as endogenously determined by political institutions' (Benz and Stutzer, 2004, p. 31).

It is at least possible that the next decades will see more economic decisions made in this way and that, partly because the decisions are made by the citizens directly and partly because people's thinking about such issues will in consequence become more sophisticated, the present gap between what people want and what they get will reduce.

11.6 References

Alvarez, R. M. and McCaffery, E. J. 2000. *Is there a gender gap in fiscal political preferences?* Los Angeles: USC Law School, Olin Research Paper No. 00–5.

Alvarez, R. M., Nagler, J. and Willette, J. R. 2000. 'Measuring the relative impact of issues and the economy in democratic elections', *Electoral Studies* 19: 237–54.

Baron, J. 1997. 'Biases in the quantitative measurement of values for public decisions', *Psychological Bulletin* 122: 72–88.

Baron, J. 2001. 'Confusion of group interest and self-interest in parochial cooperation on behalf of a group', *Journal of Conflict Resolution* 45: 283–96.

Baron, J. and Greene, J. 1996. 'Determinants of insensitivity to quantity in valuation of public goods: Contribution, warm glow, budget constraints, availability, and prominence', *Journal of Experimental Psychology: Applied* 2: 107–25.

Baron, J. and Kemp, S. 2004. 'Support for trade restrictions, attitudes, and understanding of comparative advantage', *Journal of Economic Psychology* 25: 565–80.

Baron, J. and Maxwell, N. P. 1996. 'Cost of public goods affects willingness to pay for them', *Journal of Behavioral Decision Making* 9: 173–83.

Bazerman, M. H., Baron, J. and Shonk, K. 2001. *'You Can't Enlarge the Pie': Six Barriers to Effective Government*. New York: Basic Books.

Benz, M. and Stutzer, A. 2004. 'Are voters better informed when they have a larger say in politics? Evidence for the European Union and Switzerland', *Public Choice* 119: 31–59.

Black, D. 1987. *The Theory of Committees and Elections*. Boston: Kluwer. (Originally published in 1958.)

Bondonio, P. and Marchese, C. 1994. 'Equilibrium in fiscal choices: Evidence from a budget game', *Public Choice* 78: 205–18.

Brook, L., Preston, I. and Hall, J. 1998. 'What drives support for higher public spending?' In P. Taylor-Gooby (ed.), *Choice and Public Policy: The Limits to Welfare Markets*, pp. 79–101. London: Macmillan.

Burgoyne, C. B. and Routh, D. A. 1991. 'Constraints on the use of money as a gift at Christmas: The role of status and intimacy', *Journal of Economic Psychology* 12: 47–69.

Burrows, C. and Brown, K. 1993. 'QALYs for resource allocation: Probably not and certainly not now', *Australian Journal of Public Health* 17, 278–86.

Center on Policy Attitudes. 2000. *Americans on the federal budget (Sept. 2000): Allocating the discretionary budget*. Downloaded from www.policyattitudes.org/ OnlineReports/Budget on 24 February 2006.

Clarke, P. M. 1998. 'Cost–benefit analysis and mammographic screening: A travel cost approach', *Journal of Health Economics* 17: 767–87.

Cullis, J. G. and Lewis, A. 1985. 'Some hypotheses and evidence on the tax knowledge and preferences', *Journal of Economic Psychology* 6: 271–87.

Davies, G. 1996. *A History of Money: From Ancient Times to the Present Day*. Cardiff: University of Wales.

De Groot, H. and Pommer, E. 1987. 'Budget-games and the private and social demand for mixed public goods', *Public Choice* 52: 257–72.

Diener, E. and Biswas-Diener, R. 2002. 'Will money increase subjective well-being?' *Social Indicators Research* 57: 119–69.

Diener, E. and Seligman, M. E. P. 2004. 'Beyond money: Toward an economy of well-being', *Psychological Science in the Public Interest* 5: 1–31.

Diener, E. and Suh, E. 1997. 'Measuring quality of life: Economic, social and subjective indicators', *Social Indicators Research* 40: 189–216.

Diener, E., Suh, E. M., Lucas, R. E. and Smith, H. L. 1999. 'Subjective well-being: Three decades of progress', *Psychological Bulletin* 125: 276–302.

Drummond, M. F., O'Brien, B. J., Stoddart, G. L. and Torrance, G. W. 1997. *Methods for the Economic Evaluation of Health Care Programmes*, 2nd edn. Oxford: Oxford University Press.

Easterlin, R. A. (ed.) 2002. *Happiness in Economics*. Cheltenham: Edward Elgar.

Epstein, Y. M. and Bahad, E. Y. 1982. 'Economic stress: Notes on the psychology of inflation', *Journal of Applied Social Psychology* 12: 85–99.

Feld, L. P. and Kirchgässner, G. 2000. 'Direct democracy, political culture, and the outcome of economic policy: A report on the Swiss experience', *European Journal of Political Economy* 16: 287–306.

Ferrari, L. and Lozza, E. 2005. 'Psychological consequences on prices expectations of the currency as a unit of account', *Journal of Economic Psychology* 26: 313–25.

Ferris, J. M. 1983. 'Demands for public spending: An attitudinal approach', *Public Choice* 40: 135–54.

1985. 'Interrelationships among public spending preferences: A micro analysis', *Public Choice* 45: 139–53.

Fisher, C. C. 1986. 'The differential impact of inflation on key societal groups and public policy implications', *Journal of Economic Psychology* 7: 371–86.

Font, A. R. 2000. 'Mass tourism and the demand for protected natural areas: A travel cost approach', *Journal of Environmental Economics and Management* 39: 97–116.

Frey, B. S. 1994. 'Direct democracy: Politico-economic lessons from Swiss experience', *American Economic Review (Papers and Proceedings)* 84: 338–42.

Frey, B. S. and Pommerehne, W. W. 1993. 'On the fairness of pricing – an empirical survey among the general population', *Journal of Economic Behavior and Organization* 20: 295–307.

Frey, B. S. and Stutzer, A. 2000. 'Happiness, economy and institutions', *Economic Journal* 110: 918–38.

Frijters, P., Haisken-DeNew, J. P. and Shields, M. A. 2003. *Investigating the pattern and determinants of life satisfaction in Germany following reunification*. Paper delivered at the XXVIII Annual Colloquium on Research in Economic Psychology. Christchurch, 2003.

Funk, C. L. and Garcia-Monet, P. A. 1997. 'The relationship between personal and rational concerns in public perceptions about the economy', *Political Research Quarterly* 50: 317–42.

Galbraith, J. K. (1969). *The Affluent Society*, 2nd edn. London: Hamish Hamilton.

Gemmell, N., Morrissey, O. and Pinar, A. 2004. 'Tax perceptions and preferences over tax structure in the United Kingdom', *Economic Journal* 114: F117–F138.

General Social Survey. 2002. *General Social Survey (United States)*. Downloaded from www.cpanda.org/data/a00079/ddi_cbk.html on 6 March 2006.

Gold, M. E., Siegel, J. E., Russell, L. B. and Weinstein, M. C. (eds.) 1996. *Cost-effectiveness in Health and Medicine*. Oxford: Oxford University Press.

Güth, W., Schmittburger, R. and Schwartz, B. 1982. 'An experimental analysis of ultimatum games', *Journal of Economic Behavior and Organization* 3: 367–88.

Hanley, N. and Spash, C. L. 1993. *Cost–Benefit Analysis and the Environment*. Cheltenham: Edward Elgar.

Harris, R. and Seldon, A. 1979. *Over-ruled on Welfare*. London: Institute of Economic Affairs.

Henrich, J., Boyd, R., Bowles, S., Camerer, C., Fehr, E., Gintis, H., McElreath, R., Alvard, M., Barr, A., Ensminger, J., Smith Henrich, N., Hill, K., Gil-White, F., Gurven, M., Marlowe, F. W., Patton, J. Q. and Tracer, D. 2005. '"Economic man" in cross-cultural perspective: Behavioral experiments in 15 small-scale societies', *Behavioral and Brain Sciences* 28: 795–815.

Heyman, D. and Leijonhufvud, A. 1995. *High Inflation: The Arne Ryde Memorial Lectures*. Oxford: Clarendon.

Heyndels, B. and Smolders, C. 1995. 'Tax complexity and fiscal illusion', *Public Choice* 85: 127–41.

Hockley, G. C. and Harbour, G. 1983. 'Revealed preferences between public expenditures and taxation cuts: Public sector choice', *Journal of Public Economics* 22: 387–99.

Hudson, J. and Jones, P. R. 1994. 'The importance of the "ethical voter": An estimate of "altruism"', *European Journal of Political Economy* 10: 499–509.

Ingberman, D. E. 1985. 'Running against the status quo: Institutions for direct democracy referenda and allocations over time', *Public Choice* 46: 19–43.

Inglehart, R. and Klingemann, H.-D. 2000. 'Genes, culture, democracy, and happiness'. In E. Diener and E. M. Suh (eds.), *Culture and Subjective Well-being*, pp. 165–83. Cambridge, MA: MIT Press.

Irwin, D. A. 2002. *Free Trade Under Fire*. Princeton: Princeton University Press.

Kahneman, D. 2000. 'Experienced utility and objective happiness: A moment-based approach'. In D. Kahneman and A. Tversky (eds.), *Choices, Values and Frames*, pp. 673–92. Cambridge: Cambridge University Press.

Kahneman, D., Ritov, I., Jacowitz, K. E. and Grant, P. 1993. 'Stated willingness to pay for public goods: A psychological perspective', *Psychological Science* 4: 310–15.

Kahneman, D. and Tversky, A. (eds.) 2000. *Choices, Values and Frames*. Cambridge: Cambridge University Press.

Kawachi, I., Bethwaite, P. and Bethwaite, J. 1990. 'The use of quality-adjusted life years (QALYs) in the economic appraisal of health care', *New Zealand Medical Journal* 103(883): 46–8.

Kemp, S. 1987. 'Estimation of past prices', *Journal of Economic Psychology* 8: 181–9.

    1996. 'Preferences for distributing goods in times of shortage', *Journal of Economic Psychology* 17: 615–27.

    1998. 'Rating the values of government and market supplied goods', *Journal of Economic Psychology* 19: 447–61.

    2002. *Public Goods and Private Wants: A Psychological Approach to Government Spending*. Cheltenham: Edward Elgar.

    2003. 'The effect of providing misleading cost information on the perceived value of government services', *Journal of Economic Psychology* 24: 117–28.

    2005. 'Preferences for funding particular government services from different taxes'. Unpublished manuscript.

Kemp, S. and Bolle, F. 1999. 'Preferences in distributing scarce goods', *Journal of Economic Psychology* 20: 105–20.

Kemp, S. and Burt, C. D. B. 2001. 'Estimation of the value and cost of government and market supplied goods', *Public Choice* 107: 235–52.

    2002. 'Altruism in valuing government and market supplied goods', *Journal of Socio-Economics* 31: 167–9.

Kemp, S. and Willetts, K. 1995a. 'Rating the value of government-funded services: Comparison of methods', *Journal of Economic Psychology* 16: 1–21.

    1995b. 'The value of services supplied by the New Zealand government', *Journal of Economic Psychology* 16: 23–37.

Kluegel, J. R. and Smith, E. R. 1986. *Beliefs About Inequality: Americans' Views of What Is and What Ought to Be*. New York: Aldine de Gruyter.

Kristensen, O. P. 1982. 'Voter attitudes and public spending: Is there a relationship?' *European Journal of Political Research* 10: 35–52.

Ledyard, J. O. 1995. 'Public goods: A survey of experimental research'. In J. H. Kagel and A. E. Roth (eds.), *The Handbook of Experimental Economics*, pp. 111–94. Princeton: Princeton University Press.

Lewis, A. and Jackson, D. 1985. 'Voting preferences and attitudes to public expenditure', *Political Studies* 33: 457–66.

Lipscomb, J., Weinstein, W. C. and Torrance, G. W. 1996. 'Time preferences'. In M. E. Gold, J. E. Siegel, L. B. Russell and M. C. Weinstein (eds.), *Cost-effectiveness in Health and Medicine*, pp. 214–46. Oxford: Oxford University Press.

Lucas, R. E., Clark, A. E., Georgellis, Y. and Diener, E. 2004. 'Unemployment alters the set point for life satisfaction', *Psychological Science* 15: 8–13.

Mahoney, M., Kemp, S. and Webley, P. 2005. 'Factors in lay preferences for government or private supply of services', *Journal of Economic Psychology* 26: 73–87.

Mayer, R. N. 1999. 'Consumer protection'. In P. E. Earl and S. Kemp (eds.), *The Elgar Companion to Consumer Research and Economic Psychology*, pp. 121–8. Cheltenham, UK and Northampton, MA: Edward Elgar.

McCaffery, E. J. and Baron, J. 2003. 'The Humpty Dumpty blues: Disaggregation bias in the evaluation of tax systems', *Organizational Behavior and Human Decision Processes* 91: 230–42.

2004a. 'Framing and taxation: Evaluation of tax policies involving household composition', *Journal of Economic Psychology* 25: 679–705.

2004b. 'Heuristics and biases in thinking about tax'. In *Proceedings of the 96th Annual Conference on Taxation (2003)*, pp. 434–43. Washington: National Tax Association.

Meier, K. and Kirchler, E. 1998. 'Social representations of the euro in Austria', *Journal of Economic Psychology* 19: 755–74.

Mill, J. S. 1909. *Principles of Political Economy*, ed. W. J. Ashley. London: Longmans, Green and Co. (Originally published in 1848.)

Misiolek, W. S. and Elder, H. W. 1988. 'Tax structure and the size of government: An empirical analysis of the fiscal illusion and the fiscal stress arguments', *Public Choice* 57: 233–45.

Müller-Peters, A. 1998. 'The significance of national pride and national identity to the attitude toward the single European currency: A Europe-wide comparison', *Journal of Economic Psychology* 19: 701–19.

Mussweiler, T. and Strack, F. 2004. 'The euro in the common European market: A single currency increases the comparability of prices', *Journal of Economic Psychology* 25: 557–63.

Nisbett, R. E. and Wilson, T. D. 1977. 'Telling more than we can know: Verbal reports on mental processes', *Psychological Review* 84: 231–59.

Oswald, A. J. 1997. 'Happiness and economic performance', *Economic Journal* 107: 1815–31.

Pommerehne, W. W. 1990. 'The empirical relevance of comparative institutional analysis', *European Economic Review* 34: 458–69.

Poulton, E. C. 1989. *Bias in Quantifying Judgements*. Hove: Erlbaum.

Price, S. and Sanders, D. 1995. 'Economic expectations and voting intentions in the UK, 1979–1989. A pooled cross-section approach', *Political Studies* 43: 451–71.

Ricardo, D. 1971. *On the Principles of Political Economy, and Taxation*. Harmondsworth: Penguin. (Originally published in 1817.)

Ridley, M. 1997. *The Origins of Virtue: Human Instincts and the Evolution of Cooperation*. New York: Viking.

Roberts, R. 2001. *The Choice: A Fable of Free Trade and Protectionism*. Upper Saddle River, NJ: Prentice-Hall.

Rowley, C. K. 2001. 'The international economy in public choice perspective'. In W. F. Shughart and L. Razzolini (eds.), *The Elgar Companion to Public Choice*, pp. 645–72. Cheltenham, UK: Edward Elgar.

Russell, C. and Megaard, I. (eds.) 1988. *The General Social Survey, 1972–1986: The State of the American People*. New York: Springer.

Samuelson, P. A. 1955. 'Diagrammatic exposition of a theory of public expenditure', *Review of Economics and Statistics* 37: 350–6.

Schwartz-Shea, P. and Simmons, R. T. 1990. 'The layered prisoners' dilemma: Ingroup vs. macro-efficiency', *Public Choice* 65: 61–83.

1991. 'Egoism, parochialism, and universalism', *Rationality and Society* 3: 106–32.

Shabman, L. and Stephenson, K. 1994. 'A critique of the self-interested voter model: The case of a local single issue referendum', *Journal of Economic Issues* 28: 1173–86.

Shamir, J. 1985. 'Consumers' subjective perception of price in times of inflation', *Journal of Economic Psychology* 6: 383–98.

Shughart, W. F. and Razzolini, L. (eds.) 2001. *The Elgar Companion to Public Choice*. Cheltenham, UK: Edward Elgar.

Sloan, F. A. (ed.) 1995. *Valuing Health Care: Costs, Benefits, and Effectiveness of Pharmaceuticals and Other Medical Technologies*. Cambridge: Cambridge University Press.

Smith, R. and Wearing, M. 1987. 'Do Australians want the welfare state?' *Politics* 22(2): 55–65.

Sorensen, R. 1992. 'Fiscal illusions: Nothing but illusions', *European Journal of Political Research* 22: 279–305.

Staquet, M. J., Hays, R. D. and Fayers, P. M. (eds.) 1998. *Quality of Life Assessment in Clinical Trials: Methods and Practice*. Oxford: Oxford University Press.

Stevens, S. S. 1946. 'On the theory of scales of measurement', *Science* 103: 677–80.

Stigler, G. J. 1972. 'Economic competition and political competition', *Public Choice* 12: 91–106.

Stiglitz, J. E. 1988. *Economics of the Public Sector*, 2nd edn. New York: Norton.

Strauss, R. P. and Hughes, G. D. 1976. 'A new approach to the demand for public goods', *Journal of Public Economics* 6: 191–204.

Thompson, L. and Elling, R. C. 2000. 'Mapping patterns of support for privatization in the mass public: The case of Michigan', *Public Administration Review* 60: 338–47.

Tullock, G. 1976. *The Vote Motive*. London: Institute of Economic Affairs.

Ubel, P. 2000. *Pricing Life: Why It's Time for Health Care Rationing*. Cambridge, MA: Bradford.

Van Everdingen, Y. M. and Van Raaij, W. F. 1998. 'The Dutch people and the euro: A structural equations analysis relating national identity and economic expectations to attitude towards the euro', *Journal of Economic Psychology* 19: 721–40.

West, E. G. and Winer, S. L. 1980. 'Optimal fiscal illusion and the choice of government', *Public Choice* 35: 607–22.

Williamson, M. R. and Wearing, A. J. 1996. 'Lay people's cognitive models of the economy', *Journal of Economic Psychology* 17: 3–38.

Zanardi, A. 1996. 'The distribution of benefits of public expenditure programmes: Evidence from Italy from a budget game experiment', *Public Finance* 51: 393–414.

12 How big should government be?

JOHN G. CULLIS AND PHILIP R. JONES

12.1 Introduction

When answering the question 'How big should government be?' the controversial, now deceased, UK Conservative Member of Parliament Enoch Powell argued:

> This is one of those questions which have the appearance of being capable of an experimental or objective answer, but of which, on examination, prove to refer us back to matters of opinion and intent. It is a debating proposition. It is a proposition in a debate which mankind will never conclude and in which the tides and currents will continue to flow back and forth. Those of us who today offer our own answer to the question are borne on those tides and currents and are indicators of their direction. The question is not so much analogous to 'how ought a lunar spaceship be constructed?' as to 'where is human happiness to be found?'   (Powell, 1968: p. 41)

When Enoch Powell offered this response, the UK government sector (combined total of central and local government spending and the capital expenditure on public corporations) was 50.6 per cent of GNP; today it is some 45.5 per cent of GDP at factor cost. In the interim, by 1969, man had landed on the moon but answers to the question regarding the size of government remain as equivocal as ever. Powell's insight was prescient. Where happiness is to be found is an essential consideration, and in recent years analysts have focused on empirical studies of happiness (e.g. Frey and Stutzer, 2002 survey this literature; see also chapter 9 in the current volume by Ahuvia). Layard (2005b) argues: 'In my view the prime purpose of social science should be to discover what helps and hinders happiness' (p. 11).

Neoclassical welfare economics offers normative prescriptions premised on the preferences and capabilities of *Homo economicus*. *Homo economicus* is described as:

(i)   'rational';
(ii) egoistic;
(iii) with egoism predicated on self-interest narrowly defined in terms of income or wealth (Brennan and Lomasky, 1993).

'Rational' behaviour is consistent behaviour. Predictions are made when *Homo economicus* faces new constraints (relative prices, income) but when preferences are assumed to be exogenous and constant (Stigler and Becker, 1977). Smith (1776) demonstrated that competitive markets have the capacity to maximize happiness for *Homo economicus*. In such circumstances, only a minimal role of government is required. However, if there was inequity and market failure, further government intervention might be necessary.

This analysis is sensitive to the 'tides and currents' of academic research. In this chapter the focus is on the extent to which *Homo economicus* might be deemed 'representative' and the implications when considering the question of how big government should be.

A well-established behavioural empirical literature now describes *Homo realitus* as:

(i)   reliant on bounded rationality;
(ii) concerned with more than pure self-interest;
(iii) responsive to reference frames (with endogenous preferences).

This 'dog Latin tag' was coined by Jones and Cullis (2000) to invoke a more realistic actor as the unit of behavioural analysis. In each of the following sections these defining axioms are considered. The role assigned to government, and hence its size, depends on this taxonomy.

12.2 Beliefs about 'rationality': 'individual failure' and the role of government

The neoclassical world is populated by 'rational' *Homo economicus*. Competitive markets have the capacity to maximize happiness for *Homo economicus* (Smith, 1776). On the production/supply side, there should be no exclusion. Freedom of entry and exit invokes perfect competition (except in the case of natural monopoly); the presence of exclusion (barriers to entry) would imply imperfect competition and associated inefficiency. On the consumption/demand side, exclusion is required. With exclusion, markets generally work efficiently (for example, in terms of providing private goods); in the absence of 'appropriate' exclusion, markets fail (for example, in the presence of public goods, club goods, quasi-public goods and common pool goods).

Only 'minimal government' is required when markets succeed. Property rights are necessary to provide the legal specification of an economic actor's ability to own, to transform and to transfer resources to others (as far as possible, property rights should be fully assigned). If property rights are to be defined and transferred, contract laws must define weights and measures and the like (a mechanism must be provided to seek compensation if trade did not do 'what it said on the tin'). Respecting property rights and contract laws involves a form of government and legal system (e.g. parliament, policing agencies, law courts, punishment mechanisms). But when markets fail there is a *prima facie* case for greater intervention by government. Corrective action may be required to deal with decreasing cost industries (natural monopoly), public goods and externalities; governments are required to defend property rights from aggression by other nation states (to prevent their forceful non-sanctioned redistribution).

This, essentially standard, analytical framework is challenged with the arrival of *Homo realitus*, i.e. individuals who: rely on bounded rationality (less than full information); satisfice (rather than optimize); are subject to interrelatedness (i.e. to reference points and framing effects). Anomalies are persistently reported; behaviour differs systematically from predictions of behaviour by 'rational' *Homo economicus* (Thaler 1994 provides an early survey of empirical studies).[1] Economics texts often refer to a subtitle (or subtext), *Economics – the Science of Common Sense*, but behavioural economics calls into question the definition of 'common sense'. Prospect Theory (Kahneman and Tversky, 1979) encompasses many (but not all) anomalies and behaviour can be analysed when (i) probabilities are replaced by decision weights, and (ii) the utility function is replaced with a value function. Anomalous behaviour is systematic. It is possible to make predictions; potentially falsifiable hypotheses are possible. Given that many of the results come from cognitive psychology, it is important that they are commensurate in the sense of having a common unit of analysis with economics, namely, the individual.

Maital (2004: p. 8) reports that Amos Tversky said of himself 'that he merely examined in a scientific way things about behaviour that were already known to advertisers and used-car salesmen'. Frey and Eichenberger (1994) focus on behaviour often attributed to 'advertisers and car salesmen'. They refer to 'trap setting' when producers/sellers attempt to exploit anomalous behaviour, for example by offering:

(i)   'overpriced' insurance at airports, where the *availability bias* of an accident probability can be exploited;

(ii) 'free trials' from book clubs that send you books, so that once you have had them for a period the *endowment effect* sets in and you become reluctant to return them (more willing to buy them);

(iii) film sequels that exploit the *sunk cost effect* (so that once you have seen *Rocky 1*, you are more likely to see *Rocky 2007*, etc.);

(iv) national lotteries that exploit the fact that decision weights exceed probabilities at low probability levels (encouraging purchase) and choosing your own numbers creates the illusion that you have a degree of control over the outcome of the lottery.

---

[1] Some argue that they can be dismissed as 'mistakes' (Wittman, 1989) but such 'mistakes' are not random. They are repeated time after time in experiments and do not 'wash out' of policy analysis.

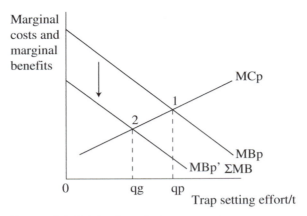

Figure 12.1 Gaining from the 'nanny state'

Trap setting is resisted by 'trap spiking', and trap spiking is more viable when:

(i)   it is possible to perceive more easily that you are acting irrationally (e.g. when you can compare your choices to those of other more educated, or experienced, consumers);
(ii) payoffs to avoid exploitation are greater;
(iii) costs of changing behaviour are lower (i.e. it is not costly to avoid misguiding heuristics, etc.).

Frey and Eichenberger's analysis can be illustrated by figure 12.1. The horizontal axis depicts quantity effort per period allocated to 'trap setting'. The marginal real resource cost to producers/sellers of trap setting is MCp. The marginal benefit to producers/sellers is MBp (here for simplicity envisaged essentially as a transfer from consumers/buyers to producers/sellers). The optimal level of effort from the producer/seller viewpoint is 0-qp where MBp = MCp. As the benefit is viewed as a redistribution (and hence ΣMB is in effect the horizontal axis), the whole of the resources devoted to trap setting is a waste (the social rate of return is unambiguously negative). In this case even 'minimal government' requires more. Government can use legislation to lower, or raise, the marginal benefit of trap setting (and equivalently lower the marginal cost of trap spiking): for example, providing 'watchdog' type information, introducing legislation that allows consumers the option to return unsolicited goods at no cost, providing compulsory 'cooling off' periods for contracts signed in deliberately 'heated up' contexts; the right to have yourself banned from casinos lowers the marginal cost of trap spiking. Compensating individuals for imposing time and trouble costs on them, increasing the cost of 'mail shots' and limiting unsolicited 'contacts' are all steps that a government might take in the 'minimal state' to increase happiness. As illustrated, MBp lowers to MBp' and the optimal effort to trap setting is found at point 2, reducing it to 0-qg. In this instance, the 'nanny state' has increased welfare to the extent of

Table 12.1 *Contrasting views of theory and individuals*

Features	Mainstream neoclassical (Homo economicus) *(1)* Micro-economic theorizing	Behavioural economics (Homo realitus) *(2)* Theorizing
1. Methodology	Deductive	Inductive
2. Results	Prescriptive	Descriptive
3. Breadth of application	Sophisticated minority	Dumb majority
4. Rational thinking errors (individual failure)	Rare and eradicated by experience and learning	Common, systematic and enduring
5. Need for consumer protection	Minimal	Extensive
6. Problem in establishing competitive markets (market failure)	Minimal	Extensive
7. Connection/concern of individuals to the choices or fate of other individuals	Minimal	Extensive

the saved real resources trapezoid qg-2-1-qp. This is a clear benefit that arises where individuals are not as sophisticated as implied by neoclassical theory; 'merit want' goods have a rationale.

This example is just one of many that illustrate the more general proposition of Jones and Cullis (2000). Neoclassical micro-economics focuses on behaviour by *Homo economicus* when there is *market failure*. Behavioural micro-economics focuses on *Homo realitus* when there is *individual failure* (individual failure defined with reference to systematic differences in behaviour and predicted behaviour of 'rational' *Homo economicus*). Jones and Cullis provide a taxonomy of individual failure and prescriptions for action by government.

Table 12.1 summarizes the distinguishing characteristics of neoclassical micro-economics and behavioural micro-economics. Distinctive properties of each approach are compared, as are the implications for analysis of the role of government.

12.3 Beliefs about ego: self-importance or concern for others?

Homo economicus' ego is defined with reference to consumption of goods and services; self-interest is defined in terms of maximization of income and wealth (Brennan and Lomasky, 1993). But egoism can rely on other considerations; it is not at all obvious that individuals are *purely* self-interested.

(a) The determinants of ego   A recent avalanche of research focuses on estimates of happiness. Layard (2005b) reviews this research to emphasize three psychological findings:

(i)   The increase in happiness from additional consumption is far less important than might be assumed; beyond a 'reasonable level', increases in income have very little impact on reported happiness.
(ii) Happiness depends on relative consumption; the motivation is to exceed, or at least match, acquisitions of private goods by others.
(iii) Tastes and preferences are not stable; primarily, happiness obtained from an endowment of goods and services is culturally determined.

Homo economicus derives happiness from consumption of goods and services but estimates of happiness reveal that 'acquisition' of goods and services is an important signal. Ego depends on status within the community and status is signalled by acquisition (as foreshadowed in Veblen's 1934 discussion of 'conspicuous consumption').

An individual's ego depends on position relative to others. Layard (2005a) reports the results of a simple questionnaire administered to Harvard graduates. Respondents were asked to choose between living in two 'worlds' (A or B). In A, each respondent would earn \$50k and others would earn \$25k. In B, the respondent would earn \$100k and others would earn \$250k. Over half chose A.

Ego also depends on signalling position, i.e. that you have exceeded (or at least not fallen behind) a social norm. The result is that individuals are trapped in an 'acquisition race'. Excessive time is allocated to pursuit of income (to acquire goods as symbols of status). The problem can be described in terms of a 'prisoner's dilemma':

(i)   *If others work*, the payoff to a representative individual is greater from working (for otherwise status is in jeopardy).
(ii) *If others do not choose to work as much*, the payoff from work is greater (for there is the opportunity to signal enhanced status – by acquisition of bigger cars and larger houses, etc.).

Regardless of how others behave, the dominant strategy is to expend further effort in an acquisition race. Individuals struggle in an acquisition race, much as nation states often appear locked in an arms race (Frank, 2005). Estimates of happiness reveal that consumption of goods adds only a modest increase beyond reasonable levels; greater happiness is reported for time spent in health-enhancing exercise or in the company of friends.

If behaviour depends on ego (defined in these terms), neoclassical assessment of the 'optimum' size of government is called into question. Neoclassical public finance scholars point to 'deadweight loss' (or 'excess burden') when tax is set to raise revenue. By contrast, Layard (2005a) advocates an income tax to reduce the proportion of time spent in pursuit of income. With ego dependent on acquisition of private goods, such an income tax is 'efficient'. Layard insists: 'This is an externality problem. When someone works an extra unit and increases his consumption by one unit, this affects the average level of consumption faced by other members of society' (p. 155). An income tax need not imply a deadweight loss if it corrects an externality problem.

Layard (2005a: p. 155) advocates an income tax because 'we should force individuals to internalise the externality'; such a tax mitigates the costs created by 'self defeating efforts to out-do each other'. The tax changes the relative return to time spent in pursuit of income to acquire bigger houses, more powerful cars (as compared to time spent in the companionship of friends and other activities that yield greater happiness). Of course this outcome might be achieved by other policies, for example provision of compulsory education that delivers such 'habituated' behaviour.

The definition of ego has implications for assessments of the role that taxation 'should' play. Neoclassical public finance scholars would compare willingness to pay for services provided by government with tax cost plus deadweight loss of taxation (i.e. with the marginal cost of public funds) when assessing how big government should be. If Layard (2005a: p. 158) is correct, then tax is efficient and 'we should not, as in standard theory, augment the cost by the excess burden of taxation which finances it'. When focusing on how big government should be, 'public expenditure is more likely to be justified than appears from the traditional analysis' (p. 158).

(b) *Concern for others*   If the role of government is sensitive to the definition of ego, it also depends on the assumption that only self-interest is relevant. The assumption that individuals are concerned only with consumption of goods and services is far from compelling. There is also evidence that individuals care about the well-being of others. Such concern can be analysed with reference to interdependent utility functions; the utility of individual B might enter the utility function of altruist A (Hochman and Rodgers 1969). In these circumstances, government is required to solve a 'public good' problem; rational altruists may prefer to free ride (Collard, 1978).[2]

Recent behavioural experiments reveal that there is also a private gain from acting altruistically and this has changed perceptions of the role of government. Individuals are also motivated by a 'warm glow' effect (Andreoni, 1988; 2001). Contributions to charities are far greater than predicted with reference to public good analysis. *Homo realitus* reveals concern for others.

If individuals derive happiness from the act of altruism, should government be so large? Payne (1993a and 1993b) doubts the need for a large public sector by combining *Homo economicus* with characteristic (b) of *Homo realitus*. He notes that utility may come from many sources and, in particular, individuals display charitable behaviour. In this way, the size of government implied by *Homo economicus* looks 'Leviathan like'. Payne estimates the cost of the tax

[2] A public good is non-rival in consumption and non-excludable (Buchanan, 1968).

Table 12.2 *Assumptive worlds*

	People have broadly similar abilities and opportunities	People have broadly similar tastes/preferences	Equity motivated role for government
Case 1:	Yes	Yes	Very little
Case 2:	Yes	No	Very little
Case 3:	No	Yes	In-kind redistribution
Case 4:	No	No	Cash redistribution

system in the USA and poses the question: 'Is there a lower cost alternative way of raising public funds?' He provides an estimate of the cost of raising $100 in tax, which is some $65. The items in the calculation are: compliance costs (the cost of reading detailed instructions, filling in forms and having additional records for tax purposes); disincentive costs (reductions in work hours and willingness to invest); uncertainty costs (frequent tax code and law changes make it very difficult to plan the efficient use of capital and labour); enforcement and litigation costs (individuals can appeal against decisions made by tax authorities and this involves expensive court and other legal procedures); evasion and avoidance costs (individuals devote real resources to legally and illegally trying not to pay tax, e.g. using tax havens and doing work for cash in hand); and government costs (expenditures on the various agencies that collect taxes). Whilst there are problems with the precise estimates, it is difficult to escape the conclusion that tax revenue raising, in itself, is an extremely costly business. Can these costs be reduced while public funds are still raised?

Payne's answer is 'yes'. He views charitable giving as zero-cost fund-raising, as workers seek extra hours to contribute to their favourite charity, incur no compliance costs as no records of giving are required and enforcement litigation and avoidance cost also evaporate (as there is no code to enforce or avoid). Relying on the voluntary, or charitable, sector is typically thought sub-optimal as it runs into the 'free rider' problem. Payne argues that this is an over-exaggerated issue and that, historically and currently, the voluntary sector was, and is, thriving. The argument that the voluntary sector can provide funds for non-private activities raises important questions concerning the role of the government.

12.4   Beliefs about preferences

Turning to the third axiom that describes individual behaviour, what is the significance of preferences that are context laden and endogenous?

(a) The importance of beliefs   Neoclassical micro-economics calls for action by government if there is inequity. But what does 'inequity' mean? Analysis of the beliefs that inform preferences offers insight. Table 12.2 describes

different assumptive worlds. Preference for government activity to redistribute and preference for difference forms of inequality reduction prove sensitive to different assumptive worlds.

Two considerations are highlighted. The first is whether the individual believes that people are broadly similar in their abilities and opportunities (especially in relation to the marketplace). The second is whether people have similar tastes or preferences, especially in relation to certain basic commodities. These beliefs are relevant when predicting preference for equity-motivated government intervention. For example:

(i) Case 1 is a world of broadly similar abilities, opportunities and tastes. There would be little observed inequality (work and consumption patterns would be very similar), and therefore little need to direct government sector policy towards it.

(ii) Case 2 also leads to little concern about inequality. The different tastes or preferences of people would mean that they would choose different work and consumption patterns. Therefore, there would be observed inequality but, given broadly equal abilities, it would be within everyone's grasp to achieve what others around them have. The main purpose of any equality-motivated policies would be to establish equality of opportunity. In short, if you believe that individuals have broadly similar basic abilities and opportunities in life, and you are not really concerned with the fate of others, then a low concern for equity-motivated public sector policies is appropriate for you.

(iii) Case 3 provides grounds for strong welfare state policies, especially those provided in an in-kind form. Unequal abilities would mean considerable inequality being observed in the economy and would be a rather intractable problem because, for the individuals doing less well, equality of opportunity is not enough; they are fundamentally disadvantaged. However, because tastes or preferences are similar (to the extent, again, that inequality is thought to be a problem), government in-kind provision is acceptable because there is little efficiency loss from in-kind redistribution where (basic) preferences are not very different and therefore all will tend to choose in the same way.

(iv) Case 4 provides similar concern over observed inequality, but suggests that the efficiency losses from in-kind provision would be large and hence (to the extent inequality is to be tackled) cash transfer payments will invoke less efficiency loss. (Field, 1981, seems broadly to hold this view.)

This analysis illustrates how preference for redistribution activity by government might be predicted with reference to individuals' beliefs. For example, Alesina *et al.* (2001) report that, in the World Values Survey, Americans have much stronger beliefs that poverty is caused by laziness than Europeans; they argue that this might explain the smaller size of the American welfare state.

(b) Preference endogeneity   If preference for government action is context laden, it follows that preference for government activity is endogenous. Consider the following debate concerning the size of government. In his first presidential address to Congress, George W. Bush was scathing of the evils of high taxation that repressed civic concern and reduced voluntary giving to charity (*Independent*, 28 February 2001: p. 17). The proposition might be sustained with reference to the perception that altruism was a public good and additional action by government crowded out private altruism. But as already noted, recent experiments insist that private giving can be explained, amongst other arguments, by the warm glow of acting altruistically.

While there is evidence that government provision of welfare crowds out voluntary giving, estimates of 'crowd out' parameters are far lower than one for one: they are usually 0.1 and very rarely as high as 0.6 (Schiff, 1989; Jones and Posnett, 1993 survey empirical work).[3] One reason is that individuals also enjoy a warm-glow effect from giving. Berman and Davison's (2003: p. 428) statistical analysis of donation leads them to conclude: 'donors are concerned primarily with the donative act'. Perceptions of the intrinsic value of action matter.

Frey (1997) argues that perceptions of the intrinsic value of action are enhanced if the intrinsic value of action is acknowledged; there is evidence that signals that recognize the importance of 'good citizenship' for tax compliance increase compliance. Such analysis is important when explaining why there is also evidence of crowding in (Rose-Ackerman, 1981; Weisbrod, 1988; Khanna *et al.*, 1995). Roy (1998: p. 417) concluded that 'the actions of others seem to serve as cues to guide behaviour rather than . . . as strategies to be counteracted'. Jones *et al.* (1998) note that government action can act as a 'demonstration effect' that acknowledges the intrinsic value of action.

If preference for action is endogenous, the question of 'how big government should be' is far more problematic than implied by neoclassical microeconomics, which relies on exogenous preferences. Perceptions of equity are context laden and action by government is itself part of the context.

12.5 What government activity facilitates happiness?

Two foundational approaches to the question of 'how big government should be' have been discussed and summarized in tables 12.1 and 12.2. Table 12.1 relies on analysis of behaviour set in train by *Homo economicus* (Column

---

[3] Lower values might be explained with reference to pure self-interest. Charitable giving may be a *response to fund-raising*; donors acquire invitations to gala occasions, lottery tickets, etc. (Olson, 1965). Voluntary work may be donated to acquire 'on-the-job' training and personal contacts (Knapp *et al.*, 1994). Social pressure from employers might explain workers' philanthropy (Keating, 1981; Keating *et al.*, 1981). However, it is impossible to dismiss perceptions of the 'consumption gain' derived from action.

(1)), or focuses on the defining characteristics of *Homo realitus* and related implications or consequences (Column (2)). Table 12.2 focuses on the extent of concern for others and assumptions about the commonality of abilities and preferences. In this section, the objective is to try to connect these arguments to the observed size and composition of actual 'public or government sectors' and the effect on human happiness. This section is indicative of lines of thought and is not an exhaustive treatment of all possible connections and statistics. Seldon's (1977) analysis of UK government expenditure provides a convenient starting point.

Table 12.3 describes Seldon's (1977) classification of UK government expenditures as a proportion of 1974 GNP (the overall figure for government expenditure was 56 per cent of GNP). Given the date and the organization that the author worked for, it is not surprising that the analysis is set in terms of a 'Column (1)' type perspective with a traditional market-failure type rationale for government intervention. Seldon was Editorial Director of the liberal/right wing Institute of Economic Affairs and was advocating widespread privatization and the so-called 'roll back' of the welfare state: the case for small government writ large.

By the 1990s Seldon may be forgiven for thinking that 'his ship had come in', as liberal democracies seemed to be 'the' political optimum. Peace dividends were in the offing, public sector inefficiency was apparently everywhere and everyone, it was claimed, should be free to spend their income as they saw fit. In short, 'small government' seemed to be the way forward; 'Column (1)' seemed to reflect the world view (Alter, 2003).

However, experience proved quite different (Seldon's ship seemed to have stayed becalmed out at sea). The day of small government did not dawn. Indeed, Seldon's dark night is forecast to continue as the predicted size of the UK government sector for 2010–11 is 1.4 per cent higher than it was in 2007. The changes in the size and composition of UK public expenditure that have occurred can be assessed with reference to data from 1998. While the way in which data is reported has changed and while government's role has changed (for example, with the advent of an extensive privatization programme), it is still broadly possible to describe 'government' in 1998 in Seldon's terms (where possible, square brackets contain the 1977 equivalent figure):

(i) *Public goods with inseparable benefits (charging impractical or uneconomic)*
     Defence   (6%)
     Public order and safety (4%)
     General public services (6%)
     Overall   (16%)
(ii) *Public goods with some separable benefits (charging partly practicable)*
     Recreation and culture (1%)
     Overall (1%)

Table 12.3 *Seldon's classification of 'UK government'. After Seldon, A. (1977)*

Public expenditure category	Market failure rationale for government action	Expenditures (subcategories) encompassed	Percentage of GNP (1974)
Public goods with inseparable benefits (charging impractical or uneconomic)	Non-rivalness and non-exclusion leading to market failure	Military defence (6%); civil defence; external relations (embassies, missions, EC, etc.) (1%); Parliament and law courts; prisons; public health; land drainage and coast protection; finance and tax collection; other government services	8 per cent
Public goods with some separable benefits (charging partly practicable)	Increasing returns to scale (decreasing cost to industry) leading to an inefficient level of production	Government (central and local) and 'public' corporation current and capital expenditure (3%); roads and public lighting (2%); research; parks, pleasure grounds, etc.; local government services (misc.) (1%); police (1%); fire services; records, registration surveys	8 per cent
Substantially or wholly separable benefits (charging substantially practicable)	Quasi-public goods (significant internalities and externalities) and/or in-kind redistribution leading to an inefficient level of production and/or inequitable allocation	Education (7%); National Health Service (5%); personal social services (1%); school meals, milk and welfare foods; employment service; libraries, museums and art galleries; housing (5%); water, sewage and refuse disposal (1%); transport and communications (3%)	22 per cent
Subsidies, grants, pensions and other (mostly) cash disbursements	Income redistribution, income support mitigating the costs of economic change, macro-stabilization policy	Agriculture, forestry, fishing and food (1%); cash benefits for social insurance, etc. (9%); miscellaneous subsidies, grants, lending, etc. to private/personal sector (2%).	13 per cent
		Interest payments	6 per cent

(iii) *Substantially or wholly separable benefits (charging substantially practicable)*
Education (11% [7%])
National Health Service (16% [5%])
Housing and community 3%
Overall (30% [22%])

(iv) *Subsidies, grants, pensions and other (mostly) cash disbursements*
Other economic affairs 3%
Social security and welfare 34%
Overall (37% [22%])

(v) *Interest on national debt (6%)*

(vi) *Other (2%)*

The level of government expenditure as a proportion of GDP has remained at around 50 per cent. However, it is the case that its composition has changed. Health and education, as noted above, are usually represented as quasi-public goods (offering both large internalities – private benefits – and widespread externalities) and are big gainers. Housing and transport and communications (whilst here recorded in the same overall category) do not exhibit such growth of share. The other glaring observation is that social security and welfare attracts a strongly rising share of total government expenditure. In a sentence, it would appear that the UK electorate were convinced that health, the provision of a social security net (poverty reduction) and education deserved more prominence at the end of the twentieth century. With reference to the old adage that happiness seems to be located in being 'healthy, wealthy and wise', it appears that happiness lies in being 'healthy, at least not poor, and wise'. Seldon may be able to 'rationalize' government in the UK with reference to neoclassical micro-economics (and *Homo economicus*). However, it is quite different to argue that these considerations adequately explain the *motivation* for government in the UK or elsewhere. A closer analysis of behaviour sheds greater insight because, ultimately, changes reflect the nature ascribed to individuals (Column (1) or Column (2) in table 12.1 and Case 1, 2, 3 or 4 in table 12.2) and the way in which collective decisions are made. Further questions arise as to whether this is simply a reflection of democratic processes at work, or whether the processes in themselves are a separate source of happiness.

12.5.1 Government processes and happiness

An important observation is that the change in composition just noted reflects preference for government spending as documented in questionnaire responses. Hills (2002: p. 542) comments: 'One of the best known findings of the BSA (British Survey Attitudes) survey has been the consistent balance respondents have shown since the late 1980s in favour of higher public spending on "health, education and social benefits", even if this means higher taxes.'

The percentage who stated that either health or education was the highest priority of extra government spending was 61% in 1983, 80% in 1989 and 82% in 1996. While there are exceptions, Hills concludes that: 'Overall it is notable that the list of measures where policies have been in line with public attitudes or have come in line with them is much longer than the list of measures where policies have been out of line with public attitudes or appear to have led them' (p. 557). This appears to tie directly into a source of happiness located in political processes.

If the preferences of individuals matter when assessing policy changes, those who see the 'optimum' size of government determined with reference to neoclassical criteria (of efficiency and equity) express concern that spending will be excessive if policies 'come in line' with public attitudes. Voters are less than fully informed (see Kemp's discussion in chapter 11 of this book). Indeed, following an initial contribution by Puviani (1903), there is now an established literature on 'fiscal illusion' that reports systematic underestimation of the tax-price. Wagner (1976) focuses on tax complexity: the more diverse the tax base, the more difficult it is to keep track of the tax-price. Buchanan and Wagner (1977) focus on borrowing: the more the government relies on borrowing, the more voters underestimate the tax-price (Buchanan and Wagner, 1977). Oates (1979) argues that in local jurisdictions the price of locally provided services appears to be subsidized by receipt of a grant from federal governments.

Lewis (1982) surveys the literature on voters' awareness and reports that voters are less than well informed about tax. Sometimes biases are systematic (Cullis and Lewis (1985) reported that British taxpayers were more knowledgeable about income tax than about indirect tax). But overall levels of tax are sometimes overestimated and sometimes underestimated (Gemmell et al., 2003), and when Cullis and Jones (1987) assessed individuals' awareness of both tax and public spending it was far from obvious that preferences for public spending would always be biased in favour of an 'excessive' size of government.

If, for neoclassical micro-economics, the concern is how outcomes deviate from 'optimum' if policy responds to preferences, a new behavioural analysis of 'happiness' suggests that well-being depends on process (as well as on outcome). There is, of course, a very large literature on political/collective decision-making and the properties of decision-making mechanisms. Whilst it is unanimity that corresponds with efficient collective decision-making (in terms of Pareto optimality), some have argued that acceptance of a simple majority voting rule suggests that individuals are satisfied with outcomes that ensue when this rule is applied. In this context, the median voter is in a pivotal position. There are circumstances in which majority voting will result in the preferred outcome of the median voter (Cullis and Jones 1998). In this literature, 'the median voter occupies a position very similar to that of the representative consumer in standard consumer theory' (Hamlin, 1993: p. 82). Pleasing a majority of voters is attractive to politicians and makes voters happy. Indeed Marshall (1963) sees happiness as being connected to civil (constitutional

Table 12.4 *Paths to happiness*

Economic actor	Required political participation	Justified concerns for others	Government size
Neoclassical	Restricted	Restricted	Small
Behavioural	Extensive	Extensive	Large

state) and political rights (democracy) but not social rights (welfare state). His is the theme explored below.

Frey and Stutzer (2005) documented the importance of participation in political processes. They tested the hypothesis that utility derived from the right to participate in the political process supports citizens' perception of subjective well-being. Foreigners are excluded from political participation but not from the outcome of political participation. The authors began by comparing data on levels of satisfaction for citizens and foreigners in Swiss cantons. Differences in well-being between Swiss citizens and foreigners appeared lower in cantons in which participation rights were weak; it appeared to be evident that 'foreigners . . . excluded from this process experience lower levels of happiness than the citizens' (Frey and Stutzer, 2005: pp. 96–7). Closer empirical analysis supported the view that citizens living in cantons with more developed political participation rights enjoyed higher levels of well-being but the positive effect on reported satisfaction was smaller for foreigners (reflecting their exclusion from decision-making processes).

Furthermore, Frey and Stutzer (2005) argue that a subsidiarity principle applies: decentralized political structures (giving decision rights to the lowest possible level of government) also increase happiness. Direct democracies raise happiness because decisions more closely reflect individual preferences and 'procedural utility' is derived from the option to participate politically by voting. However, Switzerland has a very particular constitution and the authors also consider how politics within a given constitutional framework influence individual happiness. Does trust in government matter? Is it the case that different types of expenditure induce happiness in a universal way independent of the way they are secured, for example by social welfare expenditure or private independent provision?

With respect to key ingredients, the results from happiness research seem to suggest a common recipe for happiness internationally. However, the outcome of the political process as regards government size depends on how Column (1) or (2) and Cases 1 to 4 (see tables 12.1 and 12.2) combine to capture the individuals in a given country. With respect to government size, different countries seem to have different paths to happiness (see table 12.4). For example, Column (1) and Case 1 would suggest a small role for the government in the pursuit of happiness for all as individual capabilities are adequate for all to be happy without much intervention by government. In contrast, Column (2) and Cases 3 or 4 provide the basis for 'the healthy, at least not poor, and wise' role for the government, as many individuals do not have the capabilities to secure happiness unaided. Additionally, as noted above, there is a strong case for government to devote real resources to extensive political rights and participation activities as this has a direct and separate influence on happiness.

Countries like the USA do seem to have a different underlying actor motivating government size. Frey and Stutzer (2002) point out how Americans increasingly think that government can only be trusted 'some of the time'. They associate this with democratic ineffectiveness (relative voter powerlessness) and a sense of dissatisfaction with politicians. If actors are narrowly self-interested, unconcerned with the fate of others, and respect market solutions, it is not surprising that these traits will show up in attitudes to, and the size of, government (as mediated through the median voter). Government sizes are both the effect and cause of what individuals are like. They are an effect in the sense just described and a cause in that, as argued above, government sector composition and size, especially in the long run, help shape the nature of individuals. Smaller government size reflects greater emphasis on individualism and self-reliance which, at the same time, forces individuals to take care of themselves and not to look to government for welfare-state type solutions: i.e. domination of a Column (1) type perspective. But does this make them less happy?

12.5.2 Welfare states and happiness

The typical resident of an OECD country in 2002 lived in a country where 36.3% of GDP was collected in total tax receipts. If they were married with two children, the average production worker would have had 86.9% of their gross pay as disposable income. Social expenditure by government would have been 21.2% of GDP (2001). However, these average figures cover wide variation. Focusing on social expenditure as a proxy for 'justified concern for others',[4] table 12.5 provides some selected comparison statistics.

Comparing Sweden with the USA in 2001: 50.2% and 26.4% of GDP was collected in total tax receipts respectively; the 'married with two children average production worker' would have had 79.2% and 88.5% of their gross pay as disposable income respectively, and, as can be seen from table 12.5, enjoyed social expenditure of 28.92% and 14.78% of GDP respectively (data from OECD 2005a). But what of the possible connections of these considerable variations to self-reported happiness?

Veenhoven (2000) has addressed this question with respect to social security expenditure. He set up the paradox that happiness does not appear to be higher and its distribution more equitable in countries where social security

---

[4] Social expenditures as a percentage of GDP are a measure of the extent to which governments assume responsibility for supporting the standard of living of disadvantaged or vulnerable groups. They include cash benefits, direct 'in-kind' provision and tax breaks with social purposes.

Table 12.5 *Table of social expenditure as a percentage of GDP 2001. Reprinted from* OECD Factbook, *Copyright OECD, 2005*

Country	1990	2001	Change
Canada	18.61	17.81	−0.80
France	26.61	28.45	1.84
Germany	22.80	27.39	4.59
Italy	23.27	24.45	1.18
Korea	3.13	6.12	2.99
Mexico	3.84	11.83	7.99
Sweden	**30.78**	**28.92**	**−1.86**
Switzerland	17.92	26.41	8.49
UK	19.55	21.82	2.27
USA	**13.43**	**14.78**	**1.35**

expenditure is higher.[5] The size of the welfare budget comprises expenditure on compulsory insurance for illness, disablement, old age, unemployment, inability to work and child benefit. Happiness is measured by mood (ten survey questions about occurrence of feelings in recent weeks: five positive and five negative feelings, answers (yes/no) summarized in Affect Balance Scale (-5 to $+5$)); satisfaction with life (single survey question: 'All in all, how satisfied are you with your life as a whole? Indicate on a scale from 10 (satisfied) to 1 (dissatisfied)'); and overall happiness (single survey question: 'All in all, are you: very happy (4); fairly happy (3); not very happy (2); or not happy at all (1)?'). All levels of a national variable were measured as average values and inequality of a variable as standard deviations. The data are for a cross-section of countries for the years reported.

Table 12.6 reports the partial correlations (from which the effect of national income is removed) between the levels and changes in social security expenditure as a percentage of GNP per capita and the three happiness measures. Column (i) refers to happiness levels (average scores from the happiness measures). Column (ii) refers to changes in the level of well-being denoted by Δ. Column (iii) refers to the inequality of well-being or reported happiness as measured by the standard deviations of the happiness scores denoted by {SD}. Column (iv) refers to the change of inequality of well-being or reported happiness as measured by the change in standard deviations of the happiness scores denoted by {ΔSD}. Contrary to common expectation, there appears to be no link between the size of welfare states as proxied by social security expenditures and: (a) the levels of reported happiness (column (i)); (b) the inequality or 'spread' of reported happiness levels (column (iii)). Further, there appears to be no link between the change in the size of welfare states as proxied by the ten-year (1980–90) percentage change in social

---

[5] This probably reflects Northern European thinking as many economists would not see this as a paradox, especially those following the public choice school of thought.

Table 12.6 *Size of state welfare and happiness in a cross-section of countries in 1990. Adapted from Veenhoven, R. (2000)*

Happiness measures	Link with social security expenditure as a percentage of GNP per capita and its change (wealth of nation constant partial correlation coefficients [N])			
	Social security expenditure (i)	Percentage rise/fall 1980–90 (ii)	Social security expenditure (iii)	Percentage rise/ fall 1980–90 (iv)
Mood level	0.06 [27]	Δ −0.10 [13]	{SD} 0.07 [28]	{ΔSD} −0.40 [10]
Life satisfaction	−0.24 [29]	Δ 0.35 [18]	{SD} 0.20 [29]	{ΔSD} −0.10 [16]
Overall happiness	0.20 [35]	Δ −0.33 [14]	{SD} **−0.39** [29]	{ΔSD} 0.14 [15]

Note: **bold** = significant at 5% level, all others insignificant

security expenditures and: (c) the change in reported happiness levels (column (ii)); (d) the change in the inequality or 'spread' of reported happiness levels (column (iv)). The only significant coefficient is a deviation from result (b) as it is between the inequality of overall happiness and social security expenditure, which suggests that the inequality of overall happiness decreases as the level of social security spending is increased – social security spending increases do seem to equalize happiness. The partial correlation coefficient is significantly negative, meaning that the standard deviation of this measure of happiness varies inversely with the size of the state welfare budget. However, this result is dismissed by the author as an outlier, as the 'Overall happiness' standard deviation is estimated from only a four-point scale with an uneven distribution of scores, making the value of the standard error dubious and the result therefore questionable. Whilst some econometricians would see the statistical work as somewhat unsophisticated, what does this evidence suggest?

To make matters more concrete, consider that in 1990, using the life satisfaction scale (1–10), Sweden enjoyed a value of 8 and the USA a very similar value at approximately 7.8 (no difference in happiness). However, social security benefits as a percentage of GDP were 32% in Sweden and 10% in the USA (higher in Sweden by a factor of 3). Veenhoven explored whether state intervention causes 'crowding out'. However, as noted above, this is not that significant. Other explanations considered are the possible lower quality of state services, their possible overprovision and possible happiness-reducing side effects, e.g. lower economic growth counterbalancing their happiness-raising quality. The arguments presented here offer a different perspective.

Consider figure 12.2. The axes record other expenditures per period and social security expenditure per period. The straight line 1–2 depicts possible combinations available, say, to Sweden and the USA. As noted above, the USA, seen as a welfare state 'laggard', locates at point 3 with 0-U other expenditure and 0-U' social security expenditure, and achieves iso-happiness curve IH_0. Ironically, Sweden, seen as displaying an 'advanced' welfare state, when it

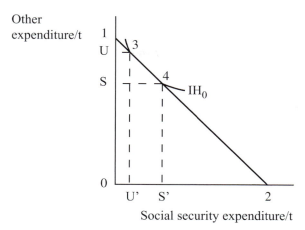

Figure 12.2 Multiple happiness equilibria

locates at point 4 with only 0-S other expenditure but comparatively higher social security expenditure at 0-S', also only achieves the same iso-happiness curve IH_0. The speculation here is that this is because the welfare states are predicated on different underlying actors. The USA, motivated by a Column (1) perspective, chooses a small government size as the path to happiness, and Sweden, motivated by a Column (2) perspective, chooses a large government size as the path to happiness. They are both happy with their choices because over the range 3–4 there are multiple equilibria.

12.6   Conclusions

The objective in this chapter has been to demonstrate that the question of 'how big government should be' is sensitive to insight from an empirical behavioural literature. Neoclassical economics assumes that *Homo economicus* is representative and answers the question with reference to a taxonomy premised on market failure (Bator, 1958). But the answer is sensitive to the perception that *Homo economicus* is representative.

Homo realitus displays anomalous behaviour (individual failure). Defenders of neoclassical theory see conventional predicted behaviour as a close enough approximation to sustain the argument that *Homo economicus* is representative. They argue that anomalous behaviour observed in laboratory testing arises because participants lack a 'correct' understanding and that, in practice, anomalous behaviour is far less than implied in experiments. In short, they see neoclassical theory as being applied in 'evolved' settings, where similar decisions are repeated. However, study after study reports the ubiquity of anomalies. If anomalous behaviour is open to exploitation, the question of how big government should be can also be answered with reference to a taxonomy premised on *individual failure*.

For *Homo economicus* happiness depends on outcome (consumption of goods and services) but the act of acquisition can also yield happiness (by signalling of status). Closer analysis of 'ego' suggests that happiness is far from maximized in today's economies and that only government can correct an 'acquisition race'.

This said, behavioural economics also insists that individuals derive happiness for the warm glow associated with gifts to charities. When altruism is modelled simply as a public good there are prescriptions for further government intervention, but when happiness also depends on action, some question the extent to which government is required given the inherent costs of government intervention (Payne, 1993b).

Neoclassical micro-economics predicts the behaviour of *Homo economicus* when preferences are assumed to be constant. It is clear that preferences are context-laden and, in the case of redistribution, preference for government will differ systematically with respect to beliefs about the distribution of tastes and abilities. But, of course, if preferences are context-laden then preferences are endogenous. Action by government itself informs preferences (Jones *et al.*, 1998) and the question of 'how big government should be' can only be answered when this dimension is addressed.

If neoclassical micro-economics appears to address the question 'how big should government be?', in practice it is addressing the question 'how big should government be *for Homo economicus*?' However, the question cannot be satisfactorily addressed without recognizing that 'tides and currents' of research in behavioural economics have questioned the degree to which *Homo economicus* is representative; 'matters of opinion and intent' and assumptions concerning where human happiness is found have been called in question.

In the empirical section of the chapter, it is suggested that *Homo economicus* is alive and happy and living in the USA whereas *Homo realitus* is alive and happy and living in Sweden. It is surely not the case that the different sizes of the public sector match perfectly the preferences of everyone in these societies. However, the conclusion in this chapter is that government need not always be deemed greater than 'optimal' with reference to analysis of the 'representative' individual found in neoclassical economic theory. There is an alternative. The answer to the question 'how big should government be?' requires answers to at least two further questions: first 'What do you believe about the nature and capabilities of individuals?'; and second 'What will further research tell us about what makes individuals happy?'

12.7 References

Alesina, A., Glaeser, E. L. and Sacerdote, B. 2001. Why doesn't the United States have a European-style welfare state? *Brookings Papers on Economic Activity* 2: 187–254.

Alter, R. 2003. *What Future for Government?* OECD: Public Governance and Territorial Development Directorate.

Andreoni, J. 1988. 'Privately provided goods in a large economy: The limits of altruism', *Journal of Public Economics* 35: 57–73.

  2001. 'The economics of philanthropy', in N. J. Smelser and P. B. Bates (eds.) *International Encyclopaedia of the Social and Behavioural Sciences*. London: Elsevier, pp. 11369–76.

Bator, F. M. 1958. 'The anatomy of market failure', *Quarterly Journal of Economics* 7: 351–79.

Berman, G. and Davison, S. 2003. 'Do donors care? Some Australian evidence', *Voluntas: International Journal of Voluntary and Nonprofit Organizations* 14: 421–9.

Brennan, G. and Lomasky, L. 1993. *Democracy and Decision: The Pure Theory of Electoral Preference*. Cambridge: Cambridge University Press.

Buchanan, J. M. 1968. *The Demand and Supply of Public Goods*. Chicago: Rand McNally.

Buchanan, J. M. and Wagner, R. E. 1977. *Democracy in Deficit: The Political Legacy of Lord Keynes*. New York: Academic Press.

Collard, D. 1978. *Altruism and Economy*. Oxford: Martin Robertson.

Cullis, J. G. and Jones, P. R. 1987. 'Fiscal illusion and excessive budgets: Some indirect evidence', *Public Finance Quarterly* 15: 219–28.

  1998. *Public Finance and Public Choice*, 2nd edn. Oxford: Oxford University Press.

Cullis, J. G. and Lewis, A. 1985. 'Some hypotheses and evidence on the tax knowledge and preferences', *Journal of Economic Psychology* 6: 271–87.

Field, F. 1981. *Inequality in Britain*. London: Fontana.

Frank, R. H. 2005. 'Does absolute income matter?' in L. Bruni and P. L. Porta (eds.) *Economics and Happiness: Framing the Analysis*. Oxford: Oxford University Press, pp. 65–90.

Frey, B. S. 1997. *Not Just for the Money: An Economic Theory of Personal Motivation*. Cheltenham: Edward Elgar.

Frey, B. and Eichenberger, R. 1994. 'Economic incentives transform psychological anomalies', *Journal of Economic Behaviour and Organisation* 23: 215–34.

Frey, B. and Stutzer, A. 2002. *Happiness and Economics: How the Economy and Institutions Affect Well-being*. Princeton: Princeton University Press.

  2005. 'Beyond outcomes: Measuring procedural utility', *Oxford Economic Papers* 57(1): 90–111.

Gemmell, N., Morrissey, O. and Pinar, A. 2003. 'Tax perceptions and the demand for public expenditure: Evidence from UK micro-data', *European Journal of Political Economy* 19: 793–816.

Hamlin, A. 1993. 'Public expenditure and political process', in N. Gemmell (ed.) *The Growth of the Public Sector*. Aldershot: Edward Elgar, pp. 72–85.

Hills, J. 2002. 'Following or leading public opinion: Social security policy and attitudes since 1997', *Fiscal Studies* 23: 539–58.

Hochman, J. M. and Rodgers, J. D. 1969. 'Pareto optimal redistribution', *American Economic Review* 59: 542–57.

Jones, A. M. and Posnett, J. W. 1993. 'The economics of charity', in N. Barr, and D. Whynes (eds.) *Current Issues in the Economics of Welfare*. London: Macmillan, pp. 130–52.

Jones, P. R. and Cullis, J. G. 2000. '"Individual failure" and the analytics of social policy', *Journal of Social Policy* 29: 73–93.

Jones, P. R., Cullis, J. G. and Lewis, A. 1998. 'Public versus private provision of altruism: Can fiscal policy make individuals "better" people?' *Kyklos* 51: 3–24.

Kahneman, D. and Tversky, A. 1979. 'Prospect Theory: An analysis of decision under risk', *Econometrica* 47: 263–91.

Keating, B. 1981. 'United Way contributions: Anomalous philanthropy', *Quarterly Review of Economics and Business* 21: 114–19.

Keating, B., Pitts, R. and Appel, D. 1981. 'United Way contributions: Coercion, charity or economic self-interest?' *Southern Economic Journal* 47: 815–23.

Khanna, J., Posnett, J. and Sandler, T. 1995. 'Charity donations in the UK: New evidence based on panel data', *Journal of Public Economics* 56(2): 257–72.

Knapp, M., Koutsogeorgopoulou, V. and Smith, J. D. 1994. *The Economics of Volunteering: Examining Participation Patterns and Levels in the UK*. Mimeo, University of Kent.

Layard, R. 2005a. 'Rethinking public economics: The implications of rivalry and habit', in L. Bruni and P. L. Porta (eds.) *Economics and Happiness: Framing the Analysis*. Oxford: Oxford University Press, pp. 147–69.

   2005b. *Happiness and Public Policy: A Challenge to the Profession*. Mimeo, London School of Economics.

Lewis, A. 1982. *The Psychology of Taxation*. Oxford: Martin Robertson.

Maital, S. 2004. 'Daniel Kahneman: On redefining rationality', *Journal of Socio-Economics* 33: 1–14.

Marshall, T. H. 1963. *Sociology at the Crossroads and Other Essays*. London: Heinemann.

Oates, W. E. 1979. 'Lump sum intergovernmental grants have price effects', in P. Mieszkowski and W. Oakland (eds.) *Fiscal Federalism and Grants-in-Aid*. Washington, DC: Urban Institute, pp. 22–30.

OECD 2005a. *OECD in Figures*. Paris: OECD.

   2005b. *OECD Factbook*. Paris: OECD.

Olson, M. Jr 1965. *The Logic of Collective Action: Public Goods and the Theory of Groups*. Cambridge, MA: Harvard University Press.

Payne, J. L. 1993a. 'The end of taxation?' *Public Interest* 112: 110–18.

   1993b. *Costly Returns – The Burdens of the US Tax System*. San Francisco: ICS Press.

Powell, J. E. 1968. 'How big should government be?' in P. H. Douglas and J. E. Powell (eds.) *How Big Should Government Be?* Washington, DC: American Enterprise Institute, pp. 41–61.

Puviani, A. 1903. *Teoria dell Illusione Fianziaria*. Milan: Remo Sandon. (Partially translated and edited in J. M. Buchanan, *Public Finance in Democratic Process: Fiscal Institutions and Individual Choice*. Chapel Hill: University of North Carolina Press (1967).)

Rose-Ackerman, S. 1981. 'Do government grants to charity reduce private donations?' in M. White (ed.) *Nonprofit Firms in a Three-Sector Economy*. Washington, DC: Urban Institute, pp. 95–114.

Roy, L. 1998. 'Why we give: Testing economic and social psychology accounts of altruism', *Polity* 30: 383–415.

Schiff, J. 1989. 'Tax policy, charitable giving and the non-profit sector: What do we really know?' in R. Magat (ed.) *Philanthropic Giving*. Oxford: Oxford University Press, pp. 128–42.

Seldon, A. 1977. *Charge*. London: Temple Smith.

Smith, A. 1776/1993. *An Inquiry into the Nature and Causes of the Wealth of Nations*, K. Sutherland (ed.). Oxford: Oxford University Press.

Stigler, G. and Becker, G. 1977. 'De gustibus non est disputandum', *American Economic Review* 67: 76–90.

Thaler, R. H. 1994. *Quasi Rational Economics*. New York: Russell Sage Foundation.

Veblen, T. 1934. *Theory of the Leisure Class*. New York: Modern Library.

Veenhoven, R. 2000. 'Well-being in the welfare state: Level not higher, distribution not more equitable', *Journal of Comparative Policy Analysis: Research and Practice* 2: 91–125.

Wagner, R. E. 1976. 'Revenue structure, fiscal illusion and budgetary choice', *Public Choice* 25: 45–61.

Weisbrod, B. A. 1988. *The Nonprofit Economy*. Cambridge, MA: Harvard University Press.

Wittman, D. A., 1989. 'Why democracies produce efficient results', *Journal of Political Economy* 97: 1395–1424.

13 Integrating explanations of tax evasion and avoidance

VALERIE BRAITHWAITE AND MICHAEL WENZEL

Tax evasion and tax avoidance are forms of economic behaviour that dwell at the margins of scholarship, not because they are uncomplicated activities, but because they have ties to such different and conflicting fields of social action. Added to this uncertainty over where they belong is uncertainty over how they are best approached. The deterrence model has dominated explanations of evasion and avoidance (Allingham and Sandmo, 1972), but the approach has created a quandary for tax researchers, best summed up by the question: If this model is true, why aren't more people evading and avoiding tax? Given that the odds of detection and penalties are so low, it is mostly rational to cheat (Alm, McClelland and Schulze, 1992; Alm, Sanchez and de Juan, 1995). Slemrod's (1992) landmark collection, *Why People Pay Taxes*, produced a paradigm shift, moving attention away from what was proving to be a narrow exploration of why people don't pay tax to a quest for understanding how a much broader base of social science research might explain why they do. This change of direction, pioneered in the early years by Schmölders (1970), Schwartz and Orleans (1967), Lewis (1982), Smith and Kinsey (1987), Weigel, Hessing and Elffers (1987) and Roth, Scholz and Witte (1989) has offered a fusion of economic, psychological and social perspectives on tax evasion and avoidance.

This chapter continues in this tradition, presenting an integrated analysis of how taxpaying can be viewed from a consumer perspective (similar to Smith and Stalans, 1991) and a citizen perspective (Frey, 1997, 2003); and how the consumer–citizen role, while not precluding evasion and avoidance, leaves the individual 'psychologically open' to cooperating with tax authority demands.[1] Following others in the field, tax system design and management is assumed to

---

[1] Two limitations of the approach should be noted. First, the most costly forms of tax evasion and avoidance involve large corporations and the wealthy individuals who control them (Slemrod, 2000; Slemrod and Yitzhaki, 2002). The focus of this chapter is on the average taxpayer, not on these groups. Second, the account of taxpaying provided in this chapter is based on western understandings of the institution of taxation. Not only are non-western considerations omitted from the analysis but so too is consideration of international tax issues that increasingly are shaping the form that national tax systems take. (For discussion of global tax issues, see Avi-Yonah, 2000a, 2000b; Burgess and Stern, 1993; Genser, 2001; Mumford, 2002; Organization for Economic Cooperation and Development, 2001a; Ott, 1999; Stiglitz, 2002; Swank, 2002; Tanzi, 2000, 2001.)

shape the individual's pro- or anti-tax behaviour (Frey and Feld, 2001; Lewis, 1982; Tomkins, Packman, Russell and Colville, 2001), as does the individual's social environment (Smith and Kinsey, 1987). A wheel of social alignments is proposed to show how a pro-taxpaying sentiment hinges on deliberation about assessment of benefits, acceptability of coercion, and perceptions of justice. The nature of the deliberations depends on how the tax system is designed and administered, how significant others interpret and make sense of its operation, and how responsive the system is to these deliberations. Governments and tax authorities must lead the process of pro-tax alignment, but once initiated, a combination of genuine deliberation and mutual responsiveness between community and government is presumed to move the wheel forward toward a sustainable and voluntary taxpaying culture.

13.1 Two different but not necessarily incompatible theoretical positions

Based on Becker's (1968) economic theory of crime, the deterrence model conceives taxpaying as a decision that individuals make through comparing the financial gain of not paying tax with the loss incurred should penalties be imposed. A pro-tax decision might be expected when the loss outweighs the gain. The model has been elaborated many times and in many ways over the years, but has stayed true to its basic economic cost–benefit calculus (see Andreoni, Erard and Feinstein, 1998 for a comprehensive review). Adherence to principles of rational decision-making is at the core of this approach, but the preferences that feed into the decision have proven to be negotiable. While self-interest remains at the heart of decision-making, the self may be satisfying social, psychological or economic needs.

Quite a different tradition of work has emerged from what might be called the socialization theories, socialization in this context meaning that behaviour is shaped by attachment and exposure to others. The explanations of taxpaying that nestle under this label are based on the common assumption that individuals are interdependent beings, with a boundary between self and other that is permeable and negotiable. This means that individuals look to others for a sense of belonging, social approval, self-affirmation and social truth (Allport, 1943; Asch, 1955; Steele, 1988; Tajfel, 1978). Individuals and their social infrastructure are intertwined in determining both identity and behaviour.

From this perspective, individuals may or may not act in their self-interest. They may act on an emotional whim that stems from group attachment that is totally counter to their self-interest (Massey, 2002). But then again, they may behave like rational economic actors, particularly if the social context calls for them to do so. Reconciling tensions between the economic and socialization traditions drives much current tax compliance research.

13.1.1 Defining concepts

In addition to reconciling theoretical approaches, tax compliance research faces the challenge of integrating explanations of tax avoidance and evasion. Much of the research over the past thirty years has had the effect of separating these concepts, spotlighting evasion, while avoidance occupies a dark corner. *Tax evasion* is defined as an illegal act of commission or omission that reduces or prevents tax liability that would otherwise be incurred (Webley, Robben, Elffers and Hessing, 1991). To put some flesh on the term, Tanzi and Shome (1994) offer, as examples, the non-declaration of income to an authority, the under-reporting of income, sales or wealth, the over-reporting of deductible expenses, smuggling activities and black market transactions. These are but a handful of what Tanzi and Shome describe as the 'truly remarkable' array of activities, continually being invented by those looking for ways of not paying tax (p. 328).

For the present purpose, evasion and non-compliance will be used interchangeably. Webley *et al.* (1991), however, note that it has become commonplace to reserve tax evasion for actions that are deliberately designed to circumvent the law, and to use the less stigmatizing term of *non-compliance* to refer to the unintentional failure to pay taxes correctly. The distinction is intuitively appealing, but in practice, it is extremely difficult to differentiate thoughtlessly illegal acts from intentionally illegal acts (Braithwaite, Braithwaite, Gibson and Makkai, 1994; Long and Swingen, 1991). Slippage between the two becomes even greater when law is so complex that accidental evasion is a highly plausible defence for deliberate evasion, and the two are difficult to disentangle even in a court of law (Salter, 2002). Complexity of tax law is an undisputed problem in most developed countries, giving rise to poor understanding of what the law means and widely varying interpretations among experts (Freedman, 2004; James, Lewis and Allison, 1987; Long and Swingen, 1988; Picciotto, 2007).

When attention turns from evasion to avoidance, the practical problems do not disappear. Differentiating accidental or deliberate evasion from legitimate tax minimization is no simple matter. In theory, *tax avoidance* refers to effort within the law to minimize tax payments, whereas tax evasion refers to effort outside the law to minimize tax payments (Seldon, 1979). When tax law is as complex as it is, however, opportunities arise for finding loopholes and ambiguities, so that 'the arrangement of one's affairs, within the law, to reduce one's tax liability' becomes possible (James and Nobes, 2000, p. 300), in circumstances where such action is 'contrary to the spirit of the law and . . . accomplishes the pre-tax objective' (James and Nobes, 2000, p. 100).

Seldon (1979) coined the term 'avoision' to indicate 'the blurring between tax avoidance and evasion that arises from the looser connection between the legal and the moral: . . . practised by the taxpayer who has difficulty equating the legal with the moral and the illegal with the immoral' (p. 4).

Recent legislative changes in some countries that have introduced general anti-avoidance rules (principles) have sought to bring avoision under the control of the legal system (see Braithwaite, 2005; Freedman, 2004; Jones, 1996). These general tax principles make it illegal to act in ways that are counter to the spirit of the law for no other purpose than to minimize tax.

13.2 Moving from an individual to a social frame of reference: the pro-tax imperative

Paying tax to a revenue authority is different from most other economic transactions that we engage in regularly as individuals. As with all economic transactions, money is exchanged for benefits. But we lack choice about how much we pay and for what (van de Braak, 1983); and if we refuse to buy what is on offer, we are punished. The situation would be absurd, if it were not for the fact that we have a social role ascribed to us in the tax system that overlays our individual consumer role. That role involves being a collectively minded and responsible citizen, acting in ways that contribute to keeping the community secure, harmonious and prosperous.[2]

Justifications and reasons are a necessary part of moving our thinking from that of an encapsulated individual to that of a socially interdependent taxpayer. Cullis and Lewis (1997) and Tanzi (2001) have observed the points around which conflicts for individuals are likely to occur as they make this transition: (1) benefits accrued from contributions; (2) coercion to make contributions; and (3) justice in collecting contributions. If a tax system is to be sustainable and honour democratic principles of governance, these conflicts must be resolved by most people most of the time in ways that are sympathetic rather than antagonistic to taxpaying.

First, in order to resolve the benefit conflict, taxpayers must have the ability to downplay the benefits that would be best for them in favour of the benefits that would be best for the community and for the smooth functioning of the democratic system. Presumably, they must also have hope that their turn will come as beneficiaries of democratic decision-making. Without hope, support for taxation seems unlikely.

Second, in order to move past the coercion conflict, taxpayers must be able to forgo personal freedom by submitting to a legal authority, and accepting the obligation to pay tax. They may accept coercion in the background, if obligation is in the foreground. Within a democracy, coercion without adequate justification is unlikely to be sustainable.

Third, in order to resolve the justice conflict, taxpayers must give up their perceived 'right' to have their sense of justice prevail. Tolerance may come with

---

[2] Taxpayers are not always citizens and citizens are not always taxpayers. The sustainability of voluntary taxpaying systems as the degree of overlap in these roles diminishes poses a challenge for governments that rely on cooperation rather than coercion in the collection of taxes.

being part and parcel of a democracy. But if the mismatch between expectations of justice and what is delivered is too extreme, support for taxation is unlikely to be forthcoming. Each of these 'sticking points' for voluntary compliance is reviewed below.

13.2.1 Lack of choice of benefits

When we pay tax, control over what is purchased is at best indirect and is exercised only intermittently by citizens at the ballot box when the democratically elected government puts itself up for re-election on the basis of its record in office and its plans for the future. Taxes support the democratic process and the machinery of government. Some of the decisions and activities of government will meet with our approval, others will not. Issues of contention include the amount of tax that should be spent on public infrastructure, on welfare for those in need, as incentives for big business, and as investments in trading and defence. Paying tax, therefore, is a special kind of economic transaction in that it does not guarantee that we receive anything that we want: paying tax is an expression of hope that the democracy and the government of the day, on balance, will deliver a set of benefits that would be denied without a tax system. Taxpaying challenges us to consider the democratic will, whether it incorporates our private hopes for a better life; and if it does not, whether we will still support it.

Empirical evidence on whether valuing the democratic will protects against evasion and avoidance is at best partial and indirect. Andreoni *et al.* (1998) have reviewed the research on satisfaction with government and conclude that taxpayers who feel that their tax dollars are not spent well may refuse to pay their full tax liability. Richardson and Sawyer (2001) are more circumspect, however, warning against generalizations because of variations in what is meant and measured when considering satisfaction with government. Exacerbating the problem raised by Richardson and Sawyer (2001) is the absence of research that differentiates satisfaction with government expenditure for the common good from satisfaction with government spending for the self.

Western democracies are experiencing high levels of disillusionment with government (Braithwaite, Reinhart, Mearns and Graham, 2001; Dean, Keenan and Kenney, 1980; LaFree, 1998), and some studies have linked this general form of alienation with tax evasion (Webley *et al.*, 1991). Braithwaite, Schneider, Reinhart and Murphy (2003) linked discontent with public goods and services received, and dissatisfaction with government spending more generally, to resistance among taxpayers. However, they were unable to establish a link with evasion through cash economy activity. Mason and Calvin (1984) have disputed the claim that individuals who are dissatisfied with government will engage in tax evasion, but they suggest indirect effects may occur, involving a watering down of the legitimacy of government authority. Ahmed's work on government loans for tertiary education exemplifies how perceptions of unjust government policy can indirectly impinge on tax compliance through generating a 'don't care' attitude (Ahmed and Braithwaite, 2005). In this instance, personal loss brought about through government education policy contributed to strained citizen–state relations in the tax domain. An accompanying study, however, suggested that loss of cooperation was offset in part by commitment to collective values favouring social harmony (Ahmed and Braithwaite, 2007). These findings suggest that individuals can find a way of supporting the democratic will through paying tax, even if, at a particular point in time, they do not see themselves as beneficiaries of government policy.

13.2.2 Coercion to pay

For the average individual, the price of the tax that is paid for governance is not negotiable.[3] The rules determining the amount of tax an individual pays are set down by the legislature and are legally binding on taxpayers (for example, percentage of income). Each individual is expected to accept his or her legal obligation to comply. If a cooperative response is not forthcoming, coercion makes its presence felt through the revenue authority's enforcement powers (legal sanctions, social stigma and/or conscience, see Grasmick and Bursik, 1990). Enforcement regimes are formalized, involving fines and penalties, and less often, legal proceedings and jail terms.

Needless to say, the cost of enforcement can be high, so methods that take away the choice of taxpayers to resist have proven popular. Withholding tax, for example, is used to extract tax payments automatically at source from an employee's salary, so that individuals have no choice as to how much they pay and when they pay it. Loss of freedom and personal agency in the payment of tax is psychologically disempowering for individuals (Brehm and Brehm, 1981; Kirchler, 1999; Taylor, 2003), however, breeding resentment. When freedom can only be achieved through breaking the law, the individual's much-prized world of personal agency is likely to clash with regulatory and legal institutions. Without taking on board taxpaying as a legal obligation, individuals are likely to have difficulty accepting sanctioning as anything other than coercion that infringes on individual rights.

Moving away from models of coercion is normatively desirable in a democracy. Coercion never disappears, however. Within a democratic system, the best that can be hoped for is that citizens consent to government using coercive powers against people (including themselves) who break the law. Within democracies, consent to the policy of law enforcement meets with little resistance. Greater variation surrounds the related construct of taking sanctions seriously.

Fear of sanctioning (particularly being caught) has emerged as a significant predictor of tax compliance in some studies (Braithwaite *et al.*, 2003; Grasmick and Bursik, 1990; Mason and Calvin, 1978; Smith, 1992), but not

---

[3] This may not be the case in transitional economies (Tanzi, 2001), nor in the developed world for the very wealthy (Braithwaite, 2005).

others (Hessing, Elffers, Robben and Webley, 1992). In explaining their non-significant effects for deterrence, Hessing *et al.* (1992) concluded that different taxpayers respond differently to deterrence: some need a little bit of deterrence to keep on the compliance path, others need none at all, and yet others are totally dismissive, perhaps because they don't care or perhaps because they are pre-occupied with how to recover their losses. Wenzel (2004a), Scholz and Pinney (1993, cited in Andreoni *et al.*, 1998), and Slemrod, Blumenthal and Christian (cited in Slemrod and Yitzhaki, 2002), all report findings that show that the effectiveness of deterrence varies depending on how the individual engages with the tax system. Wenzel found deterrence was associated with less tax evasion when personal ethical norms were weak and when social norms were perceived to be supportive of the sanctions.

Field studies suggest that legal sanctions may be less important than anticipated feelings of shame and guilt in containing evasion (Grasmick and Bursik, 1990; Grasmick and Scott, 1982; Porcano and Price, 1993; Schwartz and Orleans, 1967). Orviska and Hudson (2002) distinguish the externally motivated 'I have to contribute' and the internally motivated 'I would like to contribute.' An internally motivated responsibility to contribute is variously referred to in the literature as tax ethics, a personal norm to pay tax, a moral obligation or tax morale. The degree to which individuals espouse this commitment to honesty in meeting a tax obligation, or guilt or shame over not paying tax, has been one of the most consistent predictors of tax evasion (see Andreoni *et al.*, 1998 and Richardson and Sawyer, 2001 for reviews).

When it comes to making a decision about accepting government coercion to pay tax, the key milestones appear to be believing that paying tax is a moral obligation, with acceptance of deterrence in the background as a means of maintaining social order and ensuring that others pay their tax too (Mason and Calvin, 1984; Schwartz and Orleans, 1967). The critical element that is required to bring acceptance and commitment together to produce a pro-taxpaying frame of reference is legitimacy and credibility of the law that ultimately is based on stable and effective democratic governance. Mason and Calvin have pointed out the interdependencies among obligations, sanctions, and legitimate and credible law. They have argued that when compliance norms are allowed to weaken in the society, particularly as a result of perceptions of unfairness, the shared sense of moral obligation and the accompanying guilt feelings also weaken. Coercive efforts to reverse this downward compliance spiral will not necessarily lift moral obligation: they may increase perceptions of unfairness and crowd out feelings of moral obligation (Frey, 1997).

13.2.3 Imposition of justice

The third aspect of the taxpaying role that sets it apart from other individual consumer transactions is the tensions it creates around different expectations and understandings of justice. A pro-taxpaying frame involves interest not only in the justice of paying the same as similar others in exchange for comparable benefits, but also in broader justice issues such as the acceptance of a system that is progressive or regressive. In many western countries, progressivity is widely endorsed: in principle, each should pay according to capacity; in practice, the rich pay more in tax than the poor (Braithwaite *et al.*, 2001; Edlund, 2003). Roberts, Hite and Bradley (1994), however, have observed less support for progressivity when it is contextualized, a finding that has led to a questioning of how deeply held and how stable this preference actually is.

The evidence for the importance of progressivity is historical. Tax systems have had periods of being both regressive and progressive. In the Middle Ages and the early Renaissance, the nobility in England and Europe presided over systems of tax collection that were highly regressive, resulting in a series of uprisings by peasants who were paying the most taxes, and suffering the most. In 1381, the Peasants' Revolt in England led to the burning of buildings that housed tax registers as a protest against the nobility imposing a poll tax (each lay person had to pay the same amount, regardless of their circumstances) to raise money for the Hundred Years War. In Germany, the Peasants' Revolt of 1525 brought together an array of commoners seeking economic justice in response to increasing food prices, falling incomes, heavy burdens of taxation and rents, including the death tax, whereby families were forced to surrender their best horse or cow to the landlord on a peasant's death, leaving widows and children without an inheritance. The French Revolution in 1789 also saw the clergy and nobility living lavishly, as the third estate carried the brunt of the tax burden and struggled to provide basic necessities for themselves and their families. The imposition of excessive taxation by the ruling classes also loomed large in the American Revolution (1775–81) and Australia's far more modest rebellion, the Eureka Stockade in 1852.

In the context of western history, the twentieth century seemed to be oddly out of place in its support for progressivity. In the words of Professor Christopher Hood in 2000, the twentieth century was 'a great century for tax collection by Western governments'.[4] From the perspective of understanding the causes of evasion and avoidance, it is important to recognize that our database tends to be historically narrow, collected at a time when the wealthy paid more tax than the poor and when income redistribution was occurring through the Keynesian welfare state. The twenty-first century may be far less progressive.

Acceptance or rejection of progressivity goes to the heart of a society and engages its core values. Should individuals who are prepared to be single minded in the pursuit of wealth and status be rewarded for their entrepreneurship, unencumbered by obligations to society? Or should those who have prospered be required to pay proportionately more in tax than the poor on the grounds that they have benefited most through what the society has had to

---

[4] This quote was taken from discussions with Professor Hood from Oxford University during a visit to the Research School of Social Sciences at ANU in 2000.

offer? Or should everyone pay the same amount of tax, regardless of the fact that for some a tax contribution is hardly noticeable, while for others it could drive them into poverty and despair? Revenue authorities and governments hear, and respond as best they can to, the multiple voices telling them what constitutes appropriate vertical equity for their tax system.

Less politically contentious than vertical equity is horizontal equity, although horizontal equity poses a different set of problems. The principle underlying horizontal equity is that the same tax is paid by members of groups of comparable taxpaying capacity, both in terms of what the tax designers expect and what the tax authority actually collects (Dean, Keenan and Kenney, 1980; Wenzel, 2003). Complex tax law and weaknesses in tax administration make horizontal equity an ideal that tax authorities strive for rather than something they achieve.

Taxpaying may be private, but its meaning is socially constructed and depends on how we see ourselves in relation to others in the society. When we consider comparisons between self and other, we inevitably consider the fairness of the system, both vertically and horizontally. Taxation, therefore, calls into play notions of both justice as perceived by individuals and justice as imposed by the state, justice as we personally wish to define it and as the state has defined it through the tax system and its administration. As part of a democratic society, individuals assess the magnitude of the mismatch between their views and those of the state. If the mismatch is too great, and they see the system as unfair with no hope of improvement, they may find it difficult to opt for a pro-tax frame of reference.

While there is evidence that injustice is an important correlate of tax evasion at a general level (Smith, 1992; Spicer and Becker, 1980), there is little consistency in the literature on which aspects of injustice precipitate evasion in contemporary western democracies. Empirical findings are mixed on these issues (Andreoni et al., 1998; Richardson and Sawyer, 2001; Wenzel, 2003). Hite (1997) was successful in experimentally demonstrating improved compliance when a vertical equity message was given on the amount of tax the wealthy pay. Wenzel (2005) had similar success with a message that others were paying their fair share of tax. Wenzel (2002), however, has produced evidence that justice concerns are associated with tax compliance only when individuals are able to identify with the broader Australian community. If this collective self is not salient in the taxation context, their concerns remain predominantly self-interested.

Scholz and Lubell's (1998b) work also suggests that the absence of consistent findings may be due to too much contextual variation, and Hite (1997) adds support to this argument, suggesting that attitude salience in the situation is critical. Scholz and Lubell (1998a, 1998b) opt for a measure of trust in tax governance. Their measure covers trust in government and trust in other citizens, and therefore, subsumes both acceptance of the government's notion of a fair tax system and the democratic will on benefits. Scholz and Lubell conclude that the trustworthiness that government earns (called the trust heuristic) is reciprocated by taxpayers when they accept their obligation to pay tax.

13.3 Social alignments and the pro-tax imperative

Consideration of taxpaying benefits, acceptance of coercion and belief in the justice of the system have been identified as separate turning points in the decision to view taxpaying as a worthy investment. A psychological need for cognitive consistency (Festinger, 1957) is likely to push these considerations toward alignment under normal circumstances. The alignment of the three sets of beliefs could be uniformly pro- or anti-tax. The alignment may change depending on the degree to which the designers and managers of the tax system are sensitive to public perceptions of benefits, coercion and justice, and the extent to which others in the community can mount a credible challenge to the tax authority's claims.

Two research studies illustrate how easy it is for tax administrations to fail in the creation of alignments, and instead to become locked onto a collision course with those they seek to regulate. In a study of Chicago immigrant street vendors, Morales (1998) observed the commonly shared belief that paying taxes is a good thing in so far as it provides public infrastructure such as quality schooling. At the same time, these immigrants expressed little hope that their poor neighbourhoods would benefit from their taxpaying: they saw a discrepancy between what they and the government considered a fair allocation of tax dollars. Thus, in order for their children to make good, they chose to evade some tax and put the money away, so that they could move out of their poor neighbourhood into a wealthier one, or pay privately for their children's education.

Crush (1985) provides a fascinating account of how the imposition of a coercive colonial tax system in Swaziland at the beginning of the twentieth century came to be resisted by Swazi peasants, in spite of acceptance initially by their chiefs. The British authorities were intent on forcing the Swazi into wage labour through imposing a tax system on them. The Swazi could not see the benefits. Moreover, the system offended the Swazi's sense of justice and did nothing to elicit a legal obligation to pay. As a result they chose tax evasion with devastating results for the British authority: 'The police were spread too thin on the ground, defaulters invariably elected to serve prison sentences rather than pay fines . . . additional revenue was not collected . . . the new element of naked force led to still greater dissatisfaction in the country, and the assault largely failed . . . [to move] labour migrants out of the country' (p. 186).

How authorities design and collect tax matters to the choices that individuals make regarding their taxpaying (Hite, 1989; Smith and Stalans, 1991). It is therefore ironic that revenue authorities in western democracies have allowed themselves to get into the position of being criticized for being remote and unsympathetic in their relationship with the public (Joint Committee of Public Accounts, 1993; National Commission on Restructuring the Internal Revenue Service, 1997; Senate Economics References Committee, 2002). In the next section, these issues are brought together through adapting Lewin's (1951) notion of life space to construct a wheel of social alignments for the taxpayer.

13.4 The life space of the taxpayer

The purpose in proposing a life space model is to place the focus on how the individual sees his or her taxpaying world. The outer circle of figure 13.1 represents the design of the tax system and its administration. The literature on best practice in design and administration will be reviewed below, but the value of looking at this system through figure 13.1 is to remind us that while the system objectively makes its presence felt on the individual, the system designers have less control over meanings that individuals give to their experience. Moreover, tax authorities cannot control how these meanings become consolidated into narratives that taxpayers share with each other. In the process, significant others become influential actors in shaping the imperatives that the taxpayer sees as operating in his or her life space. Thus, the taxpayer experiences and interprets the demands and operations of the tax authority (the outer circle in figure 13.1), as well as the stories, opinions and actions of significant others that may be in accord with the authority or in opposition to the authority (the inner circle in figure 13.1). The individual may, at this point, blindly follow the lead of the authority or of others, without giving much thought to why these actions should be followed (McAdam and Nadler, 2005; Tajfel, 1978). Alternatively, they may take on the role of a consumer-citizen and reflect on the wisdom of endorsing taxation as a good investment. The middle circle of figure 13.1 represents this reflective process in which individuals decide whether or not to throw their lot in with others in the democracy: to value the benefits offered in the name of the democratic will, to accept sanctions as a legitimate form of coercion to make sure everyone pays, and to endorse the system as one that is sufficiently fair, all things considered. This process, influenced as it is by the outer and inner circle, does not have an end point. It continues, with revisions constantly being made as new information becomes available and new experiences are given meaning. As cognitions, feelings and behaviours associated with taxation bed down over time, a degree of stability is likely. If the overall sensibility is pro-tax and this sentiment is widely shared in the community, tax authorities have a cooperative momentum they can harness to sustain voluntary taxpaying. If the sentiment is overwhelmingly negative across the community, the wheel will be locked, with tax authorities seriously hampered in their efforts to influence the flow of events within a regulatory framework that respects democratic rights. In the next section, we review the design features that are purported

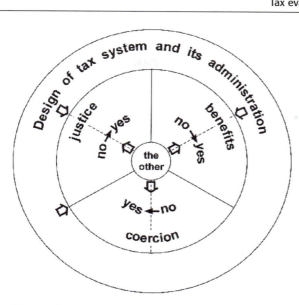

Figure 13.1 The wheel of social alignment of taxpayers

to create sustainable tax systems within western democracies (see Andreoni *et al.*, 1998; Brand, 1996; Forest and Sheffrin, 2002; Organization for Economic Cooperation and Development, 2001a; Tanzi, 2001; Tanzi and Shome, 1994).

13.5 Tax design

Drawing on Adam Smith's four canons of taxation – equity, certainty, convenience and economy – tax experts such as Tanzi (2001), Tanzi and Shome (1994) and Brand (1996) converge in their views on what the gold standards of tax design are and maintain that evasion and avoidance will be lower when good design principles are followed.

Brand (1996) places simplicity at the top of his list. There is intuitive appeal in the argument. People make honest mistakes when they misunderstand what is required, when the forms are too complicated, when they make computational or record-keeping errors, and when they are given incorrect advice (Long and Swingen, 1988). The legal framework for taxation should not be complex and the rules should be clear, without needing the interpretative guidance of experts (Tanzi and Shome, 1994).

But there is another side to this argument. Complexity reflects the highly individualized nature of the tax code and this has been introduced into the system, sometimes to promote certain policies, but often to make the system more palatable to interest groups (Carroll, 1992). Complexity is often the cost of governments pleasing their constituents (Slemrod and Yitzhaki, 2002;

Warskett, Winer and Hettich, 1998), or, to put it more positively, trying to be fair.

While less complexity continues to be hailed as best practice, and for good reasons, it is of note that taxpayers' perceptions of complexity have not always been linked directly with taxpayer non-compliance in empirical research (Forest and Sheffrin, 2002). This is probably not surprising. Perceptions of complexity drive up evasion through taxpayer mistakes and simultaneously drive down evasion through creating opportunity for less risky tax avoidance (Long and Swingen, 1988).

As well as being simple, tax systems should be cost effective, from the perspective of both those who administer them and taxpayers who must comply. Where taxpayer compliance costs are high, compliance is believed to suffer; but Richardson and Sawyer (2001) point to a paucity of hard evidence on this matter. Those who are most concerned about cost appear to find a tax adviser to relieve their burden. In a diary study of how compliance costs affect taxpayers' behaviour, Carroll (1992) observed a willingness to place limits on the amount of time devoted to doing tax; the philosophy was one of cutting corners, not so much to lower tax liability, but rather to save time. Carroll notes that this creates scope for tax evasion.

Compliance costs are generally interpreted to mean loss of time and money. Psychological costs are also relevant, however, including feeling anxious and bothered by one's financial situation. In this respect, prospect theory has attracted some support in the tax domain, showing that non-compliance is more likely when individuals face the prospect of 'paying out' to the revenue authority as opposed to 'claiming back' money that has already been collected through, for example, a withholding system (Hasseldine, 1998; White, Harrison and Harrell, 1993). The explanation offered by prospect theory (Kahneman and Tversky, 1979) is that taxpayers are more likely to take risks when they face loss than when they face gain. Smith and Stalans (1991) have made an interesting contribution to the compliance cost debate through suggesting that a simplified tax system would create more comfort for taxpayers (that is, reduce emotional costs), and in this way serve as a positive incentive for compliance.

The principle of efficiency and equity involves keeping taxes as low as possible and spreading the burden as widely as possible. The evidence on the empirical relationship between tax rates and compliance is mixed (Andreoni *et al.*, 1998; compare Feinstein, 1991 and Clotfelter, 1983), although Besley, Preston and Ridge (1997) took advantage of the relative simplicity of the UK poll tax to show that jurisdictions with higher taxes had larger non-payment problems. This result held up after controlling for attempts at enforcement, economic hardship and the perceived non-compliance of neighbouring jurisdictions, all of which were also significant in predicting evasion.

Finally, the revenue agency must be designed in such a way that it can prove itself as a credible enforcer. The traditional way of interpreting this principle is that penalties should be sufficiently high as to deter potential evaders and avoiders. In the experimental tax literature, the probability of audit and of penalties has been associated with less tax evasion (Andreoni *et al.*, 1998; Slemrod and Yitzhaki, 2002). The effects of audit and penalties from a deterrence perspective are complex, as noted previously, but some basic principles for design appear to merit serious consideration. While penalties must be sufficiently high to signal that non-compliance is unacceptable, they should not be so high that enforcement capability is actually undermined because penalties are applied sparingly by the authority; or because, when they are applied, lengthy appeals ensue that undercut the credibility of the revenue agency as an enforcer (Tanzi and Shome, 1994).

Brand (1996) expresses the design principle of gaining credibility as an enforcer somewhat differently. His argument is that the revenue agency must have 'a presence across the spectrum', being everywhere in the public eye from education through persuasion to sanctioning. There is considerable empirical evidence to support this principle, more often couched in terms of how opportunity to avoid detection encourages non-compliance (Andreoni *et al.*, 1998; Long and Swingen, 1988; Richardson and Sawyer, 2001; Smith, 1992; Taylor and Wenzel, 2001; Wärneryd and Walerud, 1982; Witte and Woodbury, 1985).

13.6 Making tax design work

As Tanzi (2001) points out, the technical design of a tax system is one thing, effective implementation is another. Sometimes the technical design requires human competencies and machine capabilities beyond those available. At other times, administrative realities steer the tax structure in particular directions (Alt, 1983; Slemrod and Yitzhaki, 2002). As model mongering (Braithwaite, 1994) becomes a common feature of a globalized world, it is important to remember that systems, no matter how elegant, rely on people to work, and if the assumptions made about people, either those who work as tax collectors or those who pay taxes, are incorrect, there is no reason for expecting that tax design by the gold standards will achieve the desired outcomes.

The 'people' obstacle to reaping the benefits of an elegant tax system has increasingly been recognized as important. A striking example of a gap emerging in assessments of the gold standard of design between tax experts and taxpayers involves withholding taxes. Few would question the attraction of withholding tax as a highly cost-effective method of tax or loan collection (Tanzi and Shome, 1994). But concerns have been expressed about how this method affects tax behaviour in other parts of the system (Yaniv, 1992). Evasion and avoidance activities move 'sideways', presumably to accommodate individuals' perceptions of what are fair and reasonable expectations of taxpayers. Ahmed's work has extended appreciation of the sideways movement that can accompany withholding systems: individuals whose employers are required by law to extract higher education debt repayments (along with income tax) from salary at source are more likely to overclaim deductions and not report additional sources of income when they lodge their annual tax return (Ahmed and Braithwaite, 2004).

The secret to successful design in practice depends on how individuals construe their life space and the interactions between components. Ultimately, taxpayers peruse the forces that are being exerted on them and ask, 'Is this reasonable? Is this fair?' (Bardach and Kagan, 1982). Forest and Sheffrin (2002) found empirically that fairness overshadowed complexity in the prediction of evasion. Tax design is likely to have to meet the standards of being viewed as fair by taxpayers before it can live up to experts' expectations.

13.7 Hearing the voice of taxpayers

Tax authorities often miss out on valuable information about how the design of a tax system affects taxpaying because they do not hear the voice of taxpayers. Authorities assume (to some extent rightly) that their vastly superior power will enable them to control and manipulate taxpayers into acting appropriately, either through command and control strategies or through the soft sell of product marketing. Being deaf to the voice of taxpayers and refraining from dialogue with community critics and supporters alike on tax issues bears costs, however. Socio-legal scholars (McBarnet, 1992, 2003; Nadler, 2005) have demonstrated that individuals can be highly creative in responding to law that is regarded as unjust or a hindrance. They may flout a host of laws, or they may game play with them where they see opportunity. As Tanzi and Shome (1994) observed, there are always new ideas for evading or avoiding tax. Theoretical frameworks for 'listening' to taxpayers, or rather understanding how they make sense of and engage with the tax system, are among the more recent developments in tax research. In this section two approaches are reviewed that provide insight into how taxpayers express personal agency and send messages to the tax authority about how well they are running the tax system.

The concept of motivational postures describes how individuals voice their discontent with tax authorities (Braithwaite, 1995, 2003b; Braithwaite *et al.*, 1994; Braithwaite, Murphy and Reinhart, 2007). Individuals manipulate the social distance between themselves and a tax authority to reduce the stress they feel as a result of the authority's attention and judgement. If they find the policies, the demeanour or the mission of the tax authority and its officers distasteful, individuals move away psychologically from the authority until they find a motivational posture with which they are comfortable. Five motivational postures have been identified: (a) commitment, involving belief in the tax system and acceptance of responsibility for ensuring that taxes are paid; (b) capitulation, meaning deference to tax office authority and openness to doing what is asked to stay out of trouble; (c) resistance, entailing opposition to the tax authority and lack of confidence in its capacity to use its power wisely or fairly; (d) disengagement, meaning not caring or not bothering about tax office demands or threats; and (e) game playing, involving a sophisticated understanding of the limits of tax authority and enthusiasm for pushing these limits in order to beat the authority at its own game.

This social distancing process, if not noticed or addressed by authority, produces two forms of defiance within motivational posturing theory: resistance and dismissiveness (Braithwaite *et al.*, 2007). Individuals may embrace neither, one or both types. In keeping with the work of Tyler (1990) and his followers, resistant defiance responds favourably to procedural fairness and to evidence that the tax authority can be trusted to serve the public interest. Dismissiveness, on the other hand, is not so easily turned around because it empowers the taxpayer to feel confident and beyond the reach of the system. As such, dismissiveness poses the greatest threat to the tax systems of western democracies.

Dismissiveness in the tax domain has been associated with tax avoidance and evasion, the choice of not valuing public benefits, not accepting the government's view of justice, and rejecting a moral obligation to pay tax (Ahmed and Braithwaite, 2005; Braithwaite, 2004; Braithwaite *et al.*, 2003, 2007). Regulating dismissiveness within a democracy demands a listening response from tax authorities because it signals that, for at least a proportion of the population, well-entrenched institutions are not considered valuable or necessary. The principles of taxation and the design of the tax system require public debate, and criticism met with either a public defence or reform.

As with all aspects of governance, when authority is not listening, individuals assess their situation, accept the realities of their world, and try to do the best they can with what they have. Adaptation to the tax climate is a central driver in how ordinary taxpayers become involved in aggressive tax planning (Braithwaite, 2005). Braithwaite has shown that while the wealthy elite engage in aggressive tax planning with very clever, highly innovative and well-thought-out game plans, ordinary taxpayers experience something that is quite different. Schemes that have met with some success at elite levels are repackaged, often losing the niceties that protect against challenges from tax authorities, and are marketed to an unsuspecting public eager to jump on the next financial planning bandwagon and save tax. Often it is not until the mass-marketing stage that tax authorities feel confident that they have the ammunition to challenge the schemes and act to close them down. By this time, promoters have made their financial killing, and small investors are left to their own devices to fight their case against the tax authority.

This sequence of elite marketing, mass marketing and tax authority challenge means that growth of the aggressive tax planning market comes in cycles, with greatest risk occurring at the end of the cycle when smaller players join the stampede. As schemes acquire acceptability as safe and smart investments, and knowledge of them spreads, people become increasingly attracted to them, often unwittingly. Braithwaite starts with the proposition that markets per se are not the problem, but draws a distinction between markets that promote vice and markets that promote virtue. Governments have responsibility for intervening in markets that threaten the well-being of the community. He therefore has argued for tax authorities making it their business to be informed and warning the public, anticipating stampedes and taking responsibility for flipping the market much earlier in the cycle before ordinary taxpayers become their prey. Principle-based tax law, quicker and more effective enforcement of promoters, and restorative justice processes are proposed as strategies that bring a halt to the stampede and generate dialogue among the parties to build knowledge and understanding of acceptable and unacceptable tax-minimizing strategies. This research highlights how open taxpayers are to social influence from a variety of sources outside the tax authority. If tax authorities will not listen to taxpayers and engage them in regulatory conversations, other players in the marketplace will. And their objective may not be to strengthen pro-tax sensibilities.

13.8   The role of the other

The role of the 'other' is depicted in figure 13.1 as the inner circle. The other in the life space of the taxpayer comprises tax advisers, friends, family, work colleagues, celebrities or newspaper columnists. The other may constitute the taxpayer's reference group in so far as the taxpayer is prepared to listen to them, take advice and model their behaviours. But the other may also represent actors or groups who exercise power over the taxpayer without consent, such as the employer who makes it impossible for an employee to pay tax through operating in the black economy.

The influence of the other may be pro-tax or anti-tax. Most of us most of the time take our cue as to what we should do by watching how others observe rules, a form of behavioural modelling that McAdam and Nadler (2005) refer to as the coordinating function of law. For this reason, while people pay taxes, the predominant role of the other is assumed to be positive. The negative role is nevertheless present. Wenzel (2005) found that tax evasion could be reduced simply through informing participants that their perception of the proportion of people engaging in tax evasion was inflated.

The influence of the other in tax research is most commonly investigated in terms of the role of tax advisers, tax agents or tax practitioners in 'leading' taxpayers into and out of compliance; and of taxpayers demanding aggressive tactics from their agents who then feel pressured into supplying riskier advice than they would otherwise give (see, for example, Klepper and Nagin 1989; Klepper, Mazur and Nagin, 1991). While most taxpayers want a tax adviser who is honest and will keep them out of trouble with the authorities, there is clearly a market in aggressive tax planning. High-risk-takers find tax advisers who specialize in aggressive advice and creative compliance, while cautious, no-fuss taxpayers find advisers who deliver a competent and honest service (Karlinsky and Bankman, 2002; Sakurai and Braithwaite, 2003; Tan, 1999).

Advisers, however, are but one source of influence. Informally, taxpayers are influenced by the groups to which they belong, from intimate social circles of friends and colleagues, to wider interest groups as defined by their profession or income level, and the nation as a whole (Wenzel, 2007). Importantly, taxpaying cultures, or more specifically the norms and beliefs shared within them, do not affect group members uniformly. Psychologists have been particularly interested in self-categorization theory (Turner, Hogg, Oakes, Reicher and Wetherell, 1987) to explain how social identities associated with taxpaying come into being (Sigala, Burgoyne and Webley, 1999; Wenzel, 2002, 2004b). Social identities assume prominence through identification with groups. If identification is weak, the likelihood of the individual assuming the taxpaying identity of that group will be relatively small. Identities change as individuals move into and out of groups with different taxpaying cultures (for example, lawyers may be different from teachers, and both of the taxpaying identities of these occupational groups may be different from that associated with citizens).

The narratives of the other and the extent of identification with the other play an important role in how consumer-citizens deliberate on benefits, legitimacy of coercion and justice (see figure 13.1). Identifying with a certain subgroup of taxpayers (for example, an occupational group) gives rise to perceptions of benefits that differ and are likely to be more 'local' than the benefits that come to mind when we identify with the nation as a whole (Wenzel, 2002, 2007). Peers influence perceptions of formal deterrence; that is, it is through perceptions of the honesty of peers that we can arrive at an understanding of how bad it looks if we are caught for tax evasion (Wenzel, 2004a). Perceptions of justice too are greatly influenced by group identification. A strong identification with a group that is inclusive of all taxpayers (for example, one's nation) is likely to increase taxpayers' concerns for justice for all (Wenzel, 2002). Identification with a more narrowly defined taxpayer group (for example, an occupational group) gives rise to differences in perceptions of whose just treatment is most important (Wenzel, 2004b). The other is thus the indeterminate element in explaining tax evasion and tax avoidance, because the other, if it is an object of identification, can change the alignment of the wheel in figure 13.1 completely.

In principle, there is no limit to the identities that one can adopt as a taxpayer, but in reality, the structure of the system and the discourse and activities one is exposed to place constraints on the options available. Even so, it is impossible to predict in each single case the identity that taxpayers will adopt at a particular moment. In order for a pro-taxpaying identity to be salient, the life space model of taxpaying in figure 13.1 must incorporate a collective social process that enables consumer-citizens to make an informed, thoughtful transition to see benefits, legitimacy in coercion and justice in the tax system. The responsibility for institutionalizing this social process lies with tax authorities and their governments. It is a process designed to demonstrate integrity on the part of government; the presumption is that consumer-citizens respond with pro-tax sentiments and cooperation (Braithwaite, 2003a; Scholz and Lubell, 1998a, 1998b).

13.9   Processes of procedural justice and dialogue

A high-integrity tax system is not only well designed, but is also respectful of and responsive to the democratic will (Braithwaite, 2003a). Empirical support has been found for two approaches to showing respect and responsiveness: (a) treating taxpayers with procedural justice (in practical terms, abiding by taxpayers' charters or bills of rights, see Organization for Economic Cooperation and Development, 2001b), and (b) engaging in dialogue with the public.

Tyler (1990) has pioneered a strong intellectual movement on the importance of authorities ensuring that their processes and, more particularly, the way they deal with people, are transparent, impartial, respectful and inclusive of others' interests and concerns. The important message from this work for tax research is that authorities develop trust and build their legitimacy, not through giving people the outcomes they want, which is often impossible, but rather through observing their right to a fair hearing and respectful treatment.

Kristina Murphy's (2003a, 2003b, 2004, 2005) work with Australians who became caught up in mass-marketed aggressive tax planning schemes has provided a telling story of how law that is complex and like 'Swiss cheese' can cause a political storm when combined with a timid and indecisive tax administration. Investors in these schemes had been claiming tax benefits that the tax office eventually ruled as illegal on grounds that their primary purpose was tax avoidance. Penalties and interest, for several years in some cases, increased the sizeable 'payback' that the tax authority demanded of investors. As the storm clouds brewed, and even after concessions were gained to wipe penalties and interest for supposedly naïve investors, the absence of procedural justice was the factor that continued to fuel anger and resistance.

The importance of procedural justice is linked to another development that has found its way into best practice guidelines (see guidelines provided by the Organization for Economic Cooperation and Development, 2001a), democratic deliberation and consultation (Braithwaite, 2003a; Dryzek, 1990). The democratic voice seems to have been lost, partly because of the complexity of tax systems (Picciotto, 2007), partly because of the common view that people don't want to pay tax (Alm, 1999), and therefore, cannot deliberate on the matter constructively. Loss of hope that authorities will listen and consider different interests has been at the heart of much of the recent loss of legitimacy of governments (Braithwaite, 2004; LaFree, 1998). Cutting the public out of deliberation about the rights and wrongs of tax evasion and avoidance may also be a key factor in escalating what many depict as a cat-and-mouse game of law invention that leads eventually to loss of respect for law (McBarnet, 2003). The US research of Kinsey and Grasmick (1993) and Scholz, McGraw and Steenbergen (1992) on the Tax Reform Act of 1986 provides evidence of how changes to the tax system can create a far better climate of compliance when the changes are championed through deliberative forums. Tax design needs not only to be responsive to administrative capabilities, it also needs the endorsement of the people.

Bruno Frey and his colleagues have shown that in tax jurisdictions where democratic deliberation is regularly practised and inclusive, compliance is likely to be high (Feld and Kirchgässner, 2000; Feld and Frey, 2002, 2005; Frey, 2003; Frey and Feld, 2001; Pommerehne, Hart and Frey, 1994; Torgler, 2003). Using panel data collected from tax authorities that represent twenty-five Swiss cantons, empirical evidence was produced to show that in cantons where direct democracy was strong (citizens voting in referenda on political and economic issues), tax evasion was relatively low (Frey and Feld, 2001).

The theoretical account that frames these findings is that when tax authorities and taxpayers have a psychological contract that communicates mutual respect, loyalty and commitment to the deliberative process, the individual takes on the persona of citizen who is engaged in the democratic process and accepts responsibility for contributing to the collective good (Feld and Frey, 2007). Tolerance for minor infringements is high, but if there is evidence of the psychological contract being broken by a taxpayer, penalties are substantial. The system prioritizes promotion of trust between citizens and the state above a sense of fear.

13.10 Conclusion

Individuals have the right to deliberate on the benefits taxation brings to themselves and their community, the acceptability of coercion to ensure that everyone shares responsibility for paying tax, and the justice of the rules that are put in place for the collection of taxes. Individuals may blindly follow others into compliance, but unthinking compliance on a mass scale does not augur well for democratic governance. The work of Frey and his colleagues provides insight into how the wheel of social alignments can move toward a voluntary taxpaying culture. Sustainable progress is made, not through appeals to self-interest or slick marketing or blind rule following, but rather through deliberation as consumer-citizens. Not all of the people will be satisfied all of the time, but the process of delivering respect through procedural justice and opening the doors to dialogue means that taxpayers are nudged out of the identity of the encapsulated individual and toward the identity of a socially interdependent taxpayer who sees benefits, obligations and justice from a collective perspective. Not all taxpayers will decide to adopt the consumer-citizen frame: encapsulated individuals from time to time will show their defiance through putting a spoke in the wheel. Consumer-citizens may well reserve the right to say to government, 'no, that is not good enough', even when government cannot do better. But the problem this creates for tax administrations does not detract from the more fundamental message: contestation about tax is to be embraced and encouraged as an essential part of building better tax systems and healthier democracies.

13.11 References

Ahmed, Eliza and Valerie Braithwaite (2004) 'When tax collectors become collectors of child support and student loans: Jeopardizing the revenue base' *Kyklos* 57, 303–26.
  (2005) 'A need for emotionally intelligent policy: Linking tax evasion with higher education funding' *Legal and Criminological Psychology* 10, 1–19.
  (2007) 'Higher education loans and tax evasion: A response to perceived unfairness' *Law and Policy* 29(1), 121–36.
Allingham, Michael G. and Agnar Sandmo (1972) 'Income tax evasion: A theoretical analysis' *Journal of Public Economics* 1, 323–62.
Allport, Gordon W. (1943) 'The ego in contemporary psychology' *Psychological Review* 50, 451–78.
Alm, James (1999) 'Tax evasion'. In Joseph J. Cordes, Robert D. Ebel and Jane G. Gravelle (eds.), *The Encyclopedia of Taxation and Tax Policy*. Washington DC: Urban Institute Press (www.urban.org/books/TTP/alm.cfm).
Alm, James, Gary H. McClelland and William D. Schulze (1992) 'Why do people pay taxes?' *Journal of Public Economics* 48, 21–38.
Alm, James, Isobel Sanchez and Ana de Juan (1995) 'Economics and noneconomic factors in tax compliance' *Kyklos* 48, 3–18.
Alt, James (1983) 'The evolution of tax structures' *Public Choice* 41, 181–222.
Andreoni, James, Brian Erard and Jonathan Feinstein (1998) 'Tax compliance' *Journal of Economic Literature* 36, 818–60.
Asch, Solomon E. (1955) 'Opinions and social pressure' *Scientific American* 193, 31–5.
Avi-Yonah, Reuven (2000a) 'World-class tax evasion' *American Prospect* 11 (May 22), 1–4.
  (2000b) 'Globalization, tax competition, and the fiscal crisis of the welfare state' *Harvard Law Review* 113, 1573–1677.
Bardach, Eugene and Robert Kagan (1982) *Going by the Book: The Problem of Regulatory Unreasonableness*. Philadelphia: Temple University Press.
Becker, Gary S. (1968) 'Crime and punishment: An economic approach' *Journal of Political Economy* 76, 169–217.
Besley, Timothy, Ian Preston and Michael Ridge (1997) 'Fiscal anarchy in the UK: Modelling poll tax noncompliance' *Journal of Public Economics* 64, 137–52.

Braithwaite, John (1994) 'A sociology of modeling and the politics of empowerment' *British Journal of Sociology* 45, 443–79.

(2005) *Markets in Vice, Markets in Virtue*. New York and Sydney: Oxford University Press and Federation Press.

Braithwaite, Valerie (1995) 'Games of engagement: Postures within the regulatory community' *Law and Policy* 17, 225–55.

(2003a) 'Tax system integrity and compliance: The democratic management of the tax system'. In Valerie Braithwaite (ed.), *Taxing Democracy: Understanding Tax Avoidance and Evasion* (pp. 271–89). Aldershot: Ashgate.

(2003b) 'Dancing with tax authorities: Motivational postures and non-compliant actions'. In Valerie Braithwaite (ed.), *Taxing Democracy: Understanding Tax Avoidance and Evasion* (pp. 15–39). Aldershot: Ashgate.

(2004) 'The hope process and social inclusion' *Annals of the American Academy of Political and Social Science* 592, 128–51.

Braithwaite, Valerie, John Braithwaite, Diane Gibson and Toni Makkai (1994) 'Regulatory styles, motivational postures and nursing home compliance' *Law and Policy* 16, 363–94.

Braithwaite, Valerie, K. Murphy and M. Reinhart (2007) 'Threat, motivational postures and responsive regulation' *Law and Policy* 29(1), 137–58.

Braithwaite, Valerie, Monika Reinhart, Malcolm Mearns and Rochelle Graham (2001) 'Preliminary findings from the Community Hopes, Fears and Actions Survey'. Centre for Tax System Integrity Working Paper No. 3, Australian National University and Australian Taxation Office, Canberra.

Braithwaite, Valerie, F. Schneider, M. Reinhart and K. Murphy (2003) 'Charting the shoals of the cash economy'. In Valerie Braithwaite (ed.), *Taxing Democracy: Understanding Tax Avoidance and Evasion* (pp. 93–108). Aldershot: Ashgate.

Brand, Phil (1996) 'Compliance: A 21st century approach' *National Tax Journal* 49, 413–19.

Brehm, Sharon S. and Jack W. Brehm (1981) *Psychological Reactance: A Theory of Freedom and Control*. New York: Academic Press.

Burgess, Robin and Nicholas Stern (1993) 'Taxation and development' *Journal of Economic Literature* 31, 762–830.

Carroll, John S. (1992) 'How taxpayers think about their taxes: Frames and values'. In Joel Slemrod (ed.), *Why People Pay Taxes* (pp. 43–63). Ann Arbor: University of Michigan Press.

Clotfelter, Charles T. (1983) 'Tax evasion and tax rates: An analysis of individual returns' *Review of Economics and Statistics* 65, 363–73.

Crush, Jonathon (1985) 'Colonial coercion and the Swazi tax revolt of 1903–1907' *Political Geography Quarterly* 4, 179–90.

Cullis, John G. and Alan Lewis (1997) 'Why people pay taxes: From a conventional economic model to a model of social convention' *Journal of Economic Psychology* 18, 305–21.

Dean, Peter, Tony Keenan and Fiona Kenney (1980) 'Taxpayers' attitudes to income tax evasion: An empirical study' *British Tax Review* 28, 28–44.

Dryzek, John S. (1990) *Discursive Democracy: Politics, Policy, and Political Science*. Cambridge: Cambridge University Press.

Edlund, Jonas (2003) 'Attitudes toward taxation: Ignorant or incoherent?' *Scandinavian Political Studies* 26, 145–67.

Feinstein, Jonathon S. (1991) 'An econometric analysis of income tax evasion and its detection' *Rand Journal of Economics* 22, 14–35.

Feld, Lars and Bruno Frey (2002) 'Trust breeds trust: How taxpayers are treated' *Economics of Governance* 3, 87–99.

(2005) 'Tax compliance as the result of a psychological contract: The role of incentives and responsive regulation'. Centre for Tax System Integrity Working Paper No. 76, Australian National University, Canberra.

(2007) 'Tax compliance as a result of a psychological tax contract: The role of incentives and responsive regulation' *Law and Policy* 29(1), 102–20.

Feld, Lars and Gebhard Kirchgässner (2000) 'Direct democracy, political culture, and the outcome of economic policy: A report on the Swiss experience' *European Journal of Political Economy* 16, 287–306.

Festinger, Leon (1957) *A Theory of Cognitive Dissonance*. Stanford, CA: Stanford University Press.

Forest, Adam and Steven M. Sheffrin (2002) 'Complexity and compliance: An empirical investigation' *National Tax Journal* 55, 75–88.

Freedman, Judith (2004) 'Defining taxpayer responsibility: In support of a general anti-avoidance principle' *British Tax Review* 4, 332–57.

Frey, Bruno S. (1997) *Not Just for the Money: An Economic Theory of Personal Motivation*. Cheltenham: Edward Elgar.

(2003) 'The role of deterrence and tax morale in taxation in the European Union', Jelle Zijlstra Lecture, Netherlands Institute for Advanced Study in the Humanities and Social Sciences (NIAS).

Frey, Bruno S. and Lars P. Feld (2001) 'The tax authority and the taxpayer: An exploratory analysis'. Paper presented at the Second International Conference on Taxation, Centre for Tax System Integrity, Australian National University, Canberra 10–11 December.

Genser, Bernd (2001) 'Corporate income taxation in the European Union: Current state and perspectives'. Centre for Tax System Integrity Working Paper No. 17, Australian National University, Canberra.

Grasmick, Harold G. and Robert J. Bursik Jr (1990) 'Conscience, significant others, and rational choice: Extending the deterrence model' *Law and Society Review* 24, 837–61.

Grasmick, Harold G. and Wilbur J. Scott (1982) 'Tax evasion and mechanisms of social control: A comparison with grand and petty theft' *Journal of Economic Psychology* 2, 213–30.

Hasseldine, John (1998) 'Prospect theory and tax reporting decisions: Implications for tax administrators' *Bulletin for International Fiscal Documentation* 47, 501–5.

Hessing, Dick J., Henk Elffers, Henry S. J. Robben and Paul Webley (1992) 'Does deterrence deter? Measuring the effect of deterrence on tax compliance in field studies and experimental studies'. In Joel Slemrod (ed.), *Why People Pay Taxes* (pp. 291–305). Ann Arbor: University of Michigan Press.

Hite, Peggy A. (1989) 'A positive approach to taxpayer compliance' *Public Finance* 44, 249–62.

(1997) 'Identifying and mitigating taxpayer non-compliance' *Australian Tax Forum* 13, 155–80.

James, Simon, Alan Lewis and Frances Allison (1987) *The Comprehensibility of Taxation: A Study of Taxation and Communications*. Aldershot: Gower Publishing.

James, Simon and Christopher Nobes (2000) *The Economics of Taxation: Principles, Policy and Practice* (7th edn). Harlow, Essex: Prentice-Hall.

Joint Committee of Public Accounts (1993) *An Assessment of Tax: A Report on an Enquiry into the Australian Taxation Office. JCPA Report No. 326*. Canberra: Australian Government Publishing Service.

Jones, J. A. (1996) 'Tax law: Rules or principles?' *Fiscal Studies* 17, 63–89.

Kahneman, Daniel and Amos Tversky (1979) 'Prospect theory: An analysis of decision under risk' *Econometrica* 47, 263–91.

Karlinsky, Stewart and Joseph Bankman (2002) 'Developing a theory of cash businesses tax evasion behavior and the role of their cash preparers'. Paper presented at the Fifth International Conference on Tax Administration, Australian Taxation Studies Program (ATAX), University of New South Wales, 4–5 April.

Kinsey, Karyl A. and Harold G. Grasmick (1993) 'Did the Tax Reform Act of 1986 improve compliance? Three studies of pre- and post-TRA compliance attitudes' *Law and Policy* 15, 293–325.

Kirchler, Erich (1999) 'Reactance to taxation: Employers' attitudes towards taxes' *Journal of Socio-Economics* 28, 131–8.

Klepper, Steven, Mark Mazur and Daniel Nagin (1991) 'Expert intermediaries and legal compliance: The case of tax preparers' *Journal of Law and Economics* 34, 205–29.

Klepper, Steven and Daniel Nagin (1989) 'The role of tax preparers in tax compliance' *Policy Sciences* 22, 167–94.

LaFree, Gary (1998) *Losing Legitimacy: Street Crime and the Decline of Social Institutions in America*. Boulder, CO: Westview Press.

Lewin, Kurt (1951) *Field Theory in Social Science: Selected Theoretical Papers* (D. Cartwright ed.). New York: Harper and Row.

Lewis, Alan (1982) *The Psychology of Taxation*. Oxford: Martin Robertson.

Long, Susan B. and Judyth A. Swingen (1988) 'The role of legal complexity in shaping taxpayer compliance'. In Peter J. van Koppen, Dick J. Hessing and Grat van den Heuvel (eds.), *Lawyers on Psychology and Psychologists on Law* (pp. 127–46). Amsterdam: Swets and Zeitlinger.

(1991) 'The conduct of tax-evasion experiments: Validation, analytic methods, and experimental realism'. In Paul Webley, Henry Robben, Henk Elffers and Dick Hessing, *Tax Evasion: An Experimental Approach* (pp. 128–38). Cambridge: Cambridge University Press.

Mason, Robert and Lyle D. Calvin (1978) 'A study of admitted income tax evasion' *Law and Society* 13, 73–89.

(1984) 'Public confidence and admitted tax evasion' *National Tax Journal* 37, 489–96.

Massey, Douglas S. (2002) 'A brief history of human society: The origin and role of emotion in social life: 2001 Presidential Address' *American Sociological Review* 67, 1–29.

McAdam, Richard H. and Janice Nadler (2005) 'Testing the focal point theory of legal compliance: The effect of third-party expression in an experimental hawk/dove game' *Journal of Empirical Legal Studies* 2, 87–123.

McBarnet, Doreen (1992) 'The construction of compliance and the challenge for control: The limits of non-compliance research'. In Joel Slemrod (ed.), *Why People Pay Taxes* (pp. 332–45). Ann Arbor: University of Michigan Press.

—— (2003) 'When compliance is not the solution but the problem: From changes in law to changes in attitude.' In Valerie Braithwaite (ed.), *Taxing Democracy: Understanding Tax Avoidance and Evasion* (pp. 229–43). Aldershot: Ashgate.

Morales, Alfonso (1998) 'Income tax compliance and alternative views of ethics and human nature'. In Robert W. McGee (ed.), *The Ethics of Tax Evasion* (pp. 242–58). South Orange, NJ: Dumont Institute for Public Policy Research.

Mumford, Ann (2002) *Taxing Culture: Towards a Theory of Tax Collection Law.* Burlington, VT: Ashgate.

Murphy, Kristina (2003a) 'Procedural justice and tax compliance' *Australian Journal of Social Issues* 38, 379–408.

—— (2003b) 'An examination of taxpayers' attitudes towards the Australian tax system: Findings from a survey of tax scheme investors' *Australian Tax Forum* 18, 209–42.

—— (2004) 'The role of trust in nurturing compliance: A study of accused tax avoiders' *Law and Human Behavior* 28, 187–209.

—— (2005) 'Regulating more effectively: The relationship between procedural justice, legitimacy and tax non-compliance' *Journal of Law and Society* 32, 562–89.

Nadler, Janice (2005) 'Flouting the law' *Texas Law Review* 83, 1399–1441.

National Commission on Restructuring the Internal Revenue Service (1997) *A Vision for a New IRS.* Washington, DC: National Commission on Restructuring the Internal Revenue Service.

Organization for Economic Cooperation and Development (2001a) *Principles for Good Tax Administration – Practice Note GAP001*, Centre for Tax Policy and Administration.

—— (2001b) *Taxpayer Rights and Obligations – Practice Note GAP002*, Centre for Tax Policy and Administration.

Orviska, Marta and John Hudson (2002) 'Tax evasion, civic duty and the law abiding citizen' *European Journal of Political Economy* 19, 83–102.

Ott, Katarina (1999) 'Economic policy and the underground economy in transition'. In Edgar L. Feige and Katarina Ott (eds.), *Underground Economies in Transition: Unrecorded Activity, Tax Evasion, Corruption and Organized Crime* (pp. 29–41). Aldershot: Ashgate.

Picciotto, Sol (2007) 'Constructing compliance: Game playing, tax law and the regulatory state' *Law and Policy*, 29(1), 11–30.

Pommerehne, W. W., A. Hart and B. S. Frey (1994) 'Tax morale, tax evasion, and the choice of policy instruments in different political systems' *Public Finance* 49 (Supplement), 52–69.

Porcano, Thomas M. and Charles E. Price (1993) 'The effects of social stigmatization on tax evasion' *Advances in Taxation* 5, 197–217.

Richardson, Maryann and Adrian J. Sawyer (2001) 'A taxonomy of the tax compliance literature: Further findings, problems and prospects' *Australian Taxation Forum* 16, 137–320.

Roberts, Michael L., Peggy A. Hite, and Cassie F. Bradley (1994) 'Understanding attitudes toward progressive taxation' *Public Opinion Quarterly* 58, 165–90.

Roth, Jeffrey A., John T. Scholz and Ann D. Witte (1989) *Taxpayer Compliance: An Agenda for Research*. Philadelphia: University of Philadelphia Press.

Sakurai, Yuka and Valerie Braithwaite (2003) 'Taxpayers' perceptions of practitioners: Finding one who is effective and does the right thing?' *Journal of Business Ethics* 46, 375–87.

Salter, David (2002) 'Some thoughts on fraudulent evasion of income tax' *British Tax Review* 6, 489–505.

Schmölders, Günter (1970) 'Survey research in public finance: A behavioral approach to fiscal theory' *Public Finance* 25, 300–6.

Scholz, John T. and Mark Lubell (1998a) 'Adaptive political attitudes: Duty, trust and fear as monitors of tax policy' *American Journal of Political Science* 42, 903–20.

(1998b) 'Trust and taxpaying: Testing the heuristic approach to collective action' *American Journal of Political Science* 42, 398–417.

Scholz, John T., Kathleen M. McGraw and Marco R. Steenbergen (1992) 'Will taxpayers ever like taxes? Responses to the US Tax Reform Act of 1986' *Journal of Economic Psychology* 13, 625–56.

Schwartz, Richard D. and Sonya Orleans (1967) 'On legal sanctions' *University of Chicago Law Review* 34, 274–300.

Seldon, Arthur (1979) *Tax Avoision*. London: Institute of Public Affairs.

Senate Economics References Committee (2002) *Inquiry into Mass Marketed Tax Effective Schemes and Investor Protection: Final Report*. Canberra: Parliament of Australia.

Sigala, Maria, Carole B. Burgoyne and Paul Webley (1999) 'Tax communication and social influence: Evidence from a British sample' *Journal of Community and Applied Social Psychology* 9, 237–41.

Slemrod, Joel (ed.) (1992) *Why People Pay Taxes*. Ann Arbor: University of Michigan Press

(2000) *Does Atlas Shrug? The Economic Consequences of Taxing the Rich*. New York and Cambridge, MA: Russell Sage Foundation and Harvard University Press.

Slemrod, Joel and Shlomo Yitzhaki (2002) 'Tax avoidance, evasion and administration'. In Alan Auerbach and Martin Feldstein (eds.), *Handbook of Public Economics*, vol. III (pp. 1425–70). Amsterdam: Elsevier Press.

Smith, Kent W. (1992) 'Reciprocity and fairness: Positive incentives for tax compliance'. In Joel Slemrod (ed.), *Why People Pay Taxes* (pp. 223–50). Ann Arbor: University of Michigan Press.

Smith, Kent W. and Karen A. Kinsey (1987) 'Understanding taxpaying behavior: A conceptual framework with implications for research' *Law and Society Review* 21, 639–63.

Smith, Kent W. and Loretta J. Stalans (1991) 'Encouraging tax compliance with positive incentives: A conceptual framework and research directions' *Law and Policy* 13, 35–53.

Spicer, Michael W. and Lee A. Becker (1980) 'Fiscal inequality and tax evasion: An experimental approach' *National Tax Journal* 33, 171–5.

Steele, C. M. (1988) 'The psychology of self-affirmation: Sustaining the integrity of the self'. In L. Berkowitz (ed.), *Advances in Experimental Social Psychology*, vol. XXI (pp. 261–302). New York: Academic Press.

Stiglitz, Joseph (2002) *Globalization and Its Discontents*. New York: W. W. Norton.

Swank, Duane (2002) 'The transformation of tax policy in an era of internationalization: An assessment of a conditional diffusion model'. Paper presented at the Annual Meeting of the American Political Science Association, 29 Aug.–1 Sep., Boston, MA.

Tajfel, Henri (ed.) (1978) *Differentiation Between Social Groups: Studies in the Social Psychology of Intergroup Relations*. London: Academic Press.

Tan, Lin Mei (1999) 'Taxpayers' preference for type of advice from tax practitioner: A preliminary examination' *Journal of Economic Psychology* 20, 431–47.

Tanzi, Vito (2000) *Globalization, Technological Developments and the Work of Fiscal Termites*. Washington, DC: International Monetary Fund WP/00/181.

(2001) 'Creating effective tax administrations: The experience of Russia and Georgia'. In János Kornai, Stephan Haggard and Robert R. Kaufman (eds.), *Reforming the State: Fiscal and Welfare Reform in Post-Socialist Countries* (pp. 53–74). Cambridge: Cambridge University Press.

Tanzi, Vito and Parthasarathi Shome (1994) 'A primer on tax evasion' *International Bureau of Fiscal Documentation* June/July, 328–37.

Taylor, Natalie (2003) 'Understanding taxpayer attitudes through understanding taxpayer identities'. In Valerie Braithwaite (ed.), *Taxing Democracy: Understanding Tax Avoidance and Evasion* (pp. 71–92). Aldershot: Ashgate.

Taylor, Natalie and Michael Wenzel (2001) 'The effects of different letter styles on reported rental income and rental deductions: An experimental approach'. Centre for Tax System Integrity Working Paper No. 11, Australian National University, Canberra.

Tomkins, Cyril, Chris Packman, Sandy Russell and Ian Colville (2001) 'Managing tax regimes: A call for research' *Public Administration* 79, 751–8.

Torgler, Benno (2003) 'Tax morale and institutions'. CREMA Working Paper No. 2003–09, Basel.

Turner, John C., Michael A. Hogg, Penelope J. Oakes, Stephen J. Reicher and Margaret S. Wetherell (1987) *Rediscovering the Social Group: A Self-Categorization Theory*. Oxford: Blackwell.

Tyler, Tom (1990) *Why People Obey the Law*. New Haven, CT: Yale University Press.

van de Braak, Hans (1983) 'Taxation and tax resistance' *Journal of Economic Psychology* 3, 95–111.

Wärneryd, Karl-Erik and Bengt Walerud (1982) 'Taxes and economic behaviour: Some interview data on tax evasion in Sweden' *Journal of Economic Psychology* 2, 187–211.

Warskett, George, Stanley L. Winer and Walter Hettich (1998) 'The complexity of tax structure in competitive political systems' *International Tax and Public Finance* 5, 123–51.

Webley, Paul, Henry Robben, Henk Elffers and Dick Hessing (1991) *Tax Evasion: An Experimental Approach*. Cambridge: Cambridge University Press.

Weigel, Russel H., Dick Hessing and Henk Elffers (1987) 'Tax evasion research: A critical appraisal and a theoretical model' *Journal of Economic Psychology* 8, 215–35.

Wenzel, Michael (2002) 'The impact of outcome orientation and justice concerns on tax compliance: The role of taxpayers' identity' *Journal of Applied Psychology* 87, 629–45.

(2003) 'Tax compliance and the psychology of justice: Mapping the field'. In Valerie Braithwaite (ed.), *Taxing Democracy: Understanding Tax Avoidance and Evasion* (pp. 41–69). Aldershot: Ashgate.

(2004a) 'The social side of sanctions: Personal and social norms as moderators of deterrence' *Law and Human Behavior* 28, 547–67.

(2004b) 'Social identification as a determinant of concerns about individual-, group-, and inclusive-level justice' *Social Psychology Quarterly* 67, 70–87.

(2005) 'Misperceptions of social norms about tax compliance: From theory to intervention' *Journal of Economic Psychology* 26, 862–83.

(2007) 'The multiplicity of taxpayer identities and their implications for tax ethics' *Law and Policy* 29, 31–50.

White, Richard A., Paul D. Harrison and Adrian Harrell (1993) 'The impact of income tax withholding on taxpayer compliance: Further empirical evidence' *Journal of the American Taxation Association* 15, 63–78.

Witte, Ann D. and Diane F. Woodbury (1985) 'The effect of tax laws and tax administration on tax compliance: The case of the US individual income tax' *National Tax Journal* 38, 1–13.

Yaniv, Gideon (1992) 'Collaborated employee–employer tax evasion' *Public Finance* 47, 312–21.

PART V

Environment

14 Sustainable consumption and lifestyle change

TIM JACKSON

14.1 Introduction

Amongst the most firmly held desiderata of modern liberal society is the notion of individual freedom of choice. It seems almost sacrilegious for governments to assume influence over the complex mix of personal preferences, social expectations and cultural norms which, taken together, constitute 'consumer choice'. Yet this is precisely what the new environmental and social agenda of 'sustainable consumption' appears to demand of policy. Perhaps even more striking is that it seems to call for quite radical changes in people's behaviours, attitudes and lifestyles.

The discourse around sustainable consumption is relatively recent. The terminology itself emerged in 1992 at the United Nations Conference on Environment and Development in Rio. Chapter 4 of *Agenda 21* – the voluminous 'blueprint for action' launched at the conference – was entitled 'Changing consumption patterns'. It argued that 'the major cause of the continued deterioration of the global environment is the unsustainable pattern of consumption and production, particularly in industrialized countries' and called for 'new concepts of wealth and prosperity which allow higher standards of living through changed lifestyles and are less dependent on the Earth's finite resources' (UN 1993). In so doing, *Agenda 21* provided a potentially far-reaching mandate for examining, questioning and revising consumption patterns – and, by implication, people's behaviours, expectations and lifestyles.

The intervening years have borne witness to some clear tensions over what exactly sustainable consumption is supposed to mean (Jackson and Michaelis 2003, Jackson 2006a, SDC/NCC 2006). Some people insist that it must involve profound lifestyle changes and clearly entails 'consuming less'. In this camp are those who lament the 'rampant materialism' of modern society and suggest that we could all live better by consuming less. They point to evidence of voluntary 'down-shifting': people who appear to opt for a better work–life balance, more quality time with their families and a low-consumption lifestyle over the conventional model of chasing higher earnings and higher consumer spending (Frank 1999, Etzioni 1998, Hamilton 2004, Kasser 2002, Schor 1998).

In the second camp are those who suggest that consuming less would restrict choice and reduce the quality of people's lives. They maintain just as fervently that consuming less is not an option and argue instead that sustainable consumption involves 'consuming differently' and, in particular, 'consuming efficiently'. They highlight the transformative power of the market to deliver more with less: greater efficiency in industrial processes, cleaner and greener products, more sustainable consumer choices (Defra 2003, PIU 2002, UNEP 2001, 2005).

The argument over whether or not we should be consuming less often skates over the question of what exactly we should be consuming less of. The 'consumption' of material resources is not necessarily the same thing as the 'consumption' of economic goods and services. But the argument often either proceeds as though it were the same, or else it assumes that the one can easily be 'decoupled' from the other.

Those who argue for a simpler life tend to look at the existing structure of consumer society – built on the ever-increasing accumulation and disposal of material possessions – and assume that the only way to stop the damage is to curb the economic system which feeds it. Not surprisingly, this view alarms those responsible for keeping the economy going, as well as those who have an economic interest in the existing system. Those resisting any notion of consuming less have a tendency to level charges of naivety at the down-shifters, and insist that it is possible to reduce environmental and social impacts without compromising economic consumption. Not surprisingly, this view is seen by the 'down-shifters' as a defence of the status quo which is unlikely to deliver the radical changes in consumption that appear to be needed. And so the debate gets increasingly polarized.

After more than a decade of wrangling, two things have become relatively clear. The first is that there is considerable scope for improving the efficiency with which resources are used in delivering human well-being. Reducing resource consumption while increasing economic consumption is certainly possible in principle. It requires us either to reduce the materials needed to deliver a given good or service, or else to shift the balance of people's economic consumption towards goods and services that require fewer material inputs and outputs to start with (Jackson 1996, von Weizsäcker et al. 1997, Defra 2005, SDC/NCC 2006).

The second is that consuming more efficiently simply does not exhaust the scope or remit of the debate (Jackson 2006a). Sustainable consumption must mean consuming less of certain things. To take only one example, it is clear from the scientific evidence that we must burn fewer carbon-intensive fuels (overall) if we are to stabilize atmospheric concentrations at levels that prevent 'dangerous anthropogenic interference' in the climate system. International policy has struggled even to contain this problem. The Kyoto target to reduce emissions from 1990 levels by around 5 per cent is now unlikely to be met even by those countries who have ratified the Protocol. The United States refused to ratify. India, China and a number of other rapidly industrializing nations never had targets under the Protocol. Global carbon emissions in 2012 – the year in which the Kyoto targets were to have been met – will almost certainly exceed those in 1990. The best science now indicates that a reduction in global emissions of around 60 per cent over 1990 levels is essential if the worst impacts of climate change are to be averted (IPCC 2001).

But it is also clear that changes in technology and increases in resource productivity will be insufficient to deliver such targets. The UK Government has recently had to admit that it will fail to meet its much more modest target of a 20 per cent reduction in emissions by 2010 and to acknowledge that shifts in the scale and pattern of consumption are going to be essential if longer-term targets are to be met (Defra 2006). Achieving the latter relies on being able to influence not only the efficiency of industry, the performance of business and the design of products, but also the expectations, choices, behaviours and lifestyles of consumers.

Moreover, meeting such 'deep' reduction targets will require more than slight shifts in people's marginal preferences for energy-efficient light bulbs. Policy will need to influence behaviours and practices in a number of different arenas, including supply tariff choices, purchases of energy-using appliances, energy-consuming practices in the home (personal hygiene, laundry, food preparation, etc.), demands for mobility and access (for both work-related and recreational reasons), food consumption behaviours, engagement in recycling and re-use of products, material product choices, home-buying, patterns of use of domestic space, choice of leisure pursuits, demand for public services, and so on.

In short, it appears that in order to accomplish its own declared environmental and social goals, government now finds itself forced to engage in a terrain which, if the rhetoric of the last two or three decades is to be believed, is not the terrain of government at all. Policy-makers must begin to intervene in and to influence people's everyday behaviours and practices and to find ways to encourage lifestyle change.

The extent of this task is potentially enormous and it is beyond the scope of this chapter to give an exhaustive account of what might be involved here. Rather, the aim of this chapter is to explore the social-psychological and institutional foundations of *unsustainable* consumption, and to tease out some of the implications for governance in pursuit of lifestyle change. In the following sections, I explore briefly what is involved in confronting lifestyles, develop three separate perspectives on the socio-cultural basis of modern lifestyles and tease out the implications of this discussion for sustainable consumption policy.

14.2 Confronting modern lifestyles

Few people would disagree that modern society has changed dramatically in the course of only a few decades. These changes can be characterized in a variety of different ways. We can point, for example, to the growth in disposable incomes, to a massive expansion in the availability of consumer goods and services, to higher levels of personal mobility, increases in leisure expenditure, and a reduction in the time spent in routine domestic tasks.

We might highlight the gains in technological efficiency provided by an increasingly sophisticated knowledge base. Or the rising resource 'footprint' of modern consumption patterns. Or the intensification of trade. Or the decline in traditional rural industries. Or the translocation of manufacturing towards the developing world. Or the emergence of the 'knowledge' economy.

We should certainly point out that these changes have been accompanied, and sometimes facilitated, by changes in the underlying institutional structures: the de-regulation (or re-regulation) of key industries, the liberalization of markets, the easing of international trade restrictions, the rise in consumer debt, and the commoditization of previously non-commercial areas of our lives.

We could also identify some of the social effects that have accompanied these changes: a faster pace of life, rising social expectations, increasing divorce rates, rising levels of violent crime, smaller household sizes, the emergence of a 'cult of celebrity', the escalating 'message-density' of modern living, increasing disparities (in income and time) between the rich and the poor, the emergence of 'post-materialist' values, a loss of trust in the conventional institutions of church, family and state, a more secular society.[1]

It is clear, even from this cursory overview, that no simple overriding 'good' or 'bad' trend emerges from this complexity. Rather modernity is characterized by a variety of trends that often seem to be set (in part at least) in opposition to each other. The identification of a set of 'post-materialist' values in modern society appears at odds with the increased proliferation of consumer goods. People appear to express less concern for material things, and yet have more of them in their lives.

The abundance offered by the liberalization of trade is offset by the environmental damage from transporting these goods across large distances to reach our supermarket shelves. The liberalization of the electricity market has increased the efficiency of generation, reduced the cost of electricity to consumers and at the same time made it more difficult to identify and exploit the opportunities for end-use energy efficiency.

To take another example, the emergence of the knowledge economy has increased the availability and the value of information. Simultaneously, it has intensified the complexity of ordinary decision-making in people's lives. As Nobel laureate Herbert Simon has pointed out, information itself consumes scarce resources. 'What information consumes is rather obvious: it consumes the attention of its recipients. Hence a wealth of information creates a poverty of attention, and a need to allocate that attention efficiently among the

---

[1] For a more detailed discussion of some of these trends see, for example: Dunlap *et al.* 1978, Inglehart 1991, Jackson 2004, Jackson and McBride 2005, Schor 1998, Stern and Dietz 1994.

overabundance of information sources that might consume it' (Simon 1971). This consuming effect of information makes the concept of 'informed choice' at once more important and at the same time more difficult to achieve in modern society.

These examples all serve to illustrate that modern lifestyles are both complex and haunted by paradox. This is certainly one of the reasons why policy-makers have tended to shy away from the whole question of consumer behaviour and lifestyle change. It is clear nonetheless that getting to grips with consumption patterns, understanding the dynamics of lifestyle and influencing people's attitudes and behaviours are all essential if the kinds of deep environmental targets demanded by sustainable development are to be achieved. To this end, it is worth at least attempting to impose some structure on this difficult terrain.

14.3 Lifestyles as 'livelihoods'

At the most basic level, our lifestyles maintain our lives. In order to live we need access to food and shelter. We consume food in order to nourish ourselves, housing and clothes to protect ourselves, medicines to keep ourselves and our families healthy, transport services in order to maintain access to these basic goods. In many less developed countries, the under-consumption of these basic resources is itself a problem. In most developed countries our access to these commodities is so much taken for granted that we sometimes forget how important the structures for securing and providing them are.

Yet, it is clearly not true to say that these basic physical and physiological functions exhaust our personal (or collective) ambitions and goals. Finding a partner, educating our children, developing our friendships, pursuing a full and active life, following our dreams: all of these ambitions and many more characterize modern living. Nor are such goals and dreams confined to modernity. The precise ways in which social and personal ambitions are framed in modern Western society may differ markedly from other times and places. But there are also a number of key similarities between our society and those that have gone before.

Several different kinds of attempts have been made to characterize these 'universal' aspects of the human condition (Jackson *et al.* 2004). Some have employed the language of 'human needs' to suggest that people everywhere experience a common set of material, social and psychological needs: the need for shelter, the need for belonging, the need for autonomy and relatedness, the need for meaning and purpose in our lives, and so on (Maslow 1954, Max-Neef 1991, Kasser 2002, Doyal and Gough 1991). Fearing that the language of needs is too emotive and too open to manipulation, others have preferred to talk in terms of 'capabilities' or 'functionings', suggesting that people everywhere must have a set of capabilities that will allow them to function properly in whichever society they find themselves (Sen 1985, Nussbaum 1998). Other approaches have tended to emphasize the evolutionary, biological nature of our behavioural drives, pointing out how we are all compelled to seek mates, reproduce the species, compete for scarce resources, and so on (Wright 1994, Ridley 1994, Jackson 2002b).

What unites these different frameworks – aside from the attempt to define something that constitutes a common basis for human motivation – is that they each frame human behaviour in terms of some form of goal-orientation. Human behaviour is regarded as purposive rather than random. People are understood as having underlying motivations, as developing life goals, as actively pursuing improvements in their quality of life (Ajzen and Fishbein 1975, Bagozzi *et al.* 2002).

Some of this purposive behaviour is recognized as being influenced by instinctive drives and evolved behavioural patterns. The biological basis for behavioural dispositions is an important reality check on utopian aspirations for radical behaviour change. But even here, in most accounts, humans remain 'reflexive': able to identify and reflect upon their own behaviours and life aspirations and at least partially separate these from unconscious drives and desires.

This view of lifestyles – as the means to achieve a set of purposive goals and ambitions (including basic survival) – is one that has been captured most clearly in recent debates about 'livelihoods' (DfID 2006, Oxfam 2006). Interestingly, this debate has emerged mainly from discussions about poverty reduction in developing countries. But the framework is also useful in thinking about livelihoods in developed nations.

Livelihoods have been defined as: 'the capabilities, assets (including both material and social resources) and activities required for a means of living' (Chambers and Conway 1992). Much of the focus of the debate in international development has been on people having the means to survive physically. But the framework recognizes explicitly that people's goals potentially involve a wide range of desired 'outcomes', including more food, higher incomes, reduced vulnerability to shocks, better working conditions and lower infant mortality.

In other words, this framework captures quite precisely the notion of lifestyles as strategies for living that are aimed at meeting specific goals and purposes. One of the first elements in applying the livelihoods approach at the local level is to elicit from local people what those goals might be. Livelihoods are characterized (figure 14.1) by a set of 'livelihood strategies' aimed at achieving specific goals or aspirations ('livelihood outcomes'). But these strategies are themselves mediated by the policies, institutions and processes within which individual or collective action is framed.

The success of livelihood strategies is also dependent on the assets available to people in any given context. In the livelihoods framework, these assets are characterized in terms of a set of five interrelated forms of capital: human, social, physical, financial and natural. In addition, the sufficiency of this asset

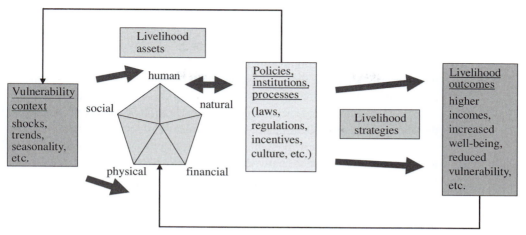

Figure 14.1 A livelihoods framework: assets, strategies and outcomes.
Redrawn from Chambers, R. and Conway, G. *Sustainable rural livelihoods:
practical concepts for the 21st century.* IDS discussion paper 296, 1992, with
permission from the Institute of Development Studies

base in maintaining livelihood strategies is dependent on the 'vulnerability context' within which people operate – the potential shocks, trends or unexpected
eventualities which might disrupt their lives.

One of the important aspects of the Sustainable Livelihoods framework
is the relationship between different forms of 'capital'. Material (financial,
physical, natural) resources are clearly vital in preserving our lifestyles and
pursuing our life goals. But social and human resources are not in any sense
inferior forms of asset. It has been recognized for a long time by anthropologists, for example, that social networks offer a vital form of resilience in
the face of both material and emotional shocks (Douglas 1976, Douglas and
Isherwood 1979, Wright 1994). Finding and keeping a good job, coping with
economic or emotional loss, weathering natural or unnatural storms: all of these
things depend on the strength of our social networks. And this depends in its
turn on our personal ability to negotiate and maintain our place in the social
group.

Obviously, the extent to which social positioning is important depends (at
the individual level) on how strong the rest of our asset base is and (at a broader
cultural level) on what kind of society we live in. Strong, rich people living
in a society where individuality is prized can afford to ignore social norms.
Poorer, weaker people can't. In societies where the group is prized more highly
than the individual, no one can afford to ignore social norms. And somewhere
in the middle of all that, the much-maligned practice of 'keeping up with the
Joneses' becomes an important livelihood strategy in any society where social
position counts.

This framework has been useful in thinking through poverty reduction in developing countries. The high vulnerability of poor rural communities to extreme weather events or to changes in the price of basic commodities, for example, places a premium on understanding the assets they possess, and designing policies and institutions that support the strategies they employ to achieve their desired goals.

In most developed countries, people are not quite so obviously vulnerable to the floods, droughts and crop failures that haunt many poorer nations. But even where markets are relatively stable, assets are secure, unexpected mortality is low and shocks few and far between, one does not need to search far to find an undercurrent of fear about the impact that such vulnerabilities might have on our lives (Berger 1967, Jackson 2006b). Consider, for example, the ferocity of responses to the 'war on terror', or recent 'documentary' examinations of the impacts of sudden unexpected events (global warming, political meltdown, disruptions to the oil and gas markets). When lives, livelihoods and lifestyles are threatened, people tend to react swiftly and sometimes ferociously to try and mitigate the threat (Breakwell 1986).

In summary, what emerges from this discussion is a view of modern lifestyles that links them closely to fundamental underlying motivations to survive, to reproduce, to live well, to conceive and to pursue basic life goals. This view of lifestyles allows us to approach consumer goods (and people's consumption patterns) as critical components in individual and collective livelihood strategies, and to begin to understand processes of lifestyle change – and resistance to change.

14.4 Lifestyles and life-satisfaction

At the heart of the idea of lifestyles as livelihoods lies the notion of well-being or quality of life. Livelihood strategies are, at some broad level, ways of maintaining or increasing (individual or collective) well-being and improving quality of life. Higher incomes, lower infant mortality, improved health, reduced drudgery, stronger social networks, higher resilience to shocks: these are the kinds of things generally reported as desirable livelihood outcomes.

In fact, the idea that the aim of consumer lifestyles is to improve people's well-being lies at the heart of most modern notions of progress. It is cashed out most explicitly in the conventional concept of economic development. Successive governments in most industrialized nations have – at least until recently – taken well-being (or quality of life) to mean more or less the same thing as 'standard of living'. The standard of living in its turn has traditionally been equated with per capita levels of national income – measured conventionally through the gross domestic product (GDP).

The basis for this equation of economic performance with quality of life rests on the idea that (in one formulation at least) the GDP may be regarded as the total of all expenditures made either in consuming finished goods and services or investing money to ensure future consumption possibilities. Since the sum of consumption expenditures is equivalent (under certain conditions) to the value placed by consumers on the goods they consume, then – according to the conventional argument – GDP can be taken as some kind of 'proxy' for the well-being derived from our consumption activities. In a seminal paper in welfare economics, Weitzman (1976) showed that the net domestic product (gross domestic product net of capital depreciation) can be regarded as a proxy for 'sustainable' well-being, since it is formally equivalent to non-declining consumption possibilities.

Since GDP rose more or less consistently over the last fifty years, the comforting logic of this orthodox view suggests that we have been pretty successful in delivering an increasing standard of living and, by proxy, improving the quality of people's lives over recent decades. Furthermore, if our concern is to ensure that quality of life continues to reach new heights, the conventional view provides a ready and familiar formula for achieving this end: namely, to continue to ensure 'high and stable levels of economic growth' (DETR 1999).

But this equation of economic growth with increasing quality of life has come under considerable scrutiny over the last few decades, from a number of different quarters and for a variety of different reasons (Douthwaite 1992, Daly and Cobb 1989, Daly 1996, Jackson and McBride 2005). Not least amongst these is the realization that conventional measures of economic progress fail to account for the depletion of natural resources, and for the environmental and social impacts of consumption and production (Jackson 2002a, 2004). In addition, this conventional view is faced with what is perhaps the most striking ambivalence involved in understanding modern lifestyles: the so-called 'life-satisfaction paradox' (Layard 2005, Jackson 2006c).

This phenomenon is illustrated in figure 14.2. The success of conventional development is illustrated by the rise in GDP. Incomes have almost doubled in the UK since the early 1970s. Yet reported life-satisfaction over the same period has scarcely changed at all. This effect is particularly noticeable in the UK. But it is also observed in a number of other countries. (See, for example, the chapter by Ahuvia in this volume.) Across most developed countries, there is at best a weak correlation between increased income and reported well-being. And for countries with average incomes in excess of $15,000, there is very little correlation at all of increased income with improved happiness (Inglehart and Klingemann 2000).

If rising consumption is supposed to deliver increasing levels of well-being, these data on stagnant 'life-satisfaction' pose a series of uncomfortable questions for modern society. Why is life-satisfaction not improving in line with higher incomes? Is economic growth delivering improved well-being or not? What exactly is the relationship between lifestyle and life-satisfaction?

Explanations for the life-satisfaction paradox have been sought in a variety of different places. Some authors highlight the fact that relative income has a

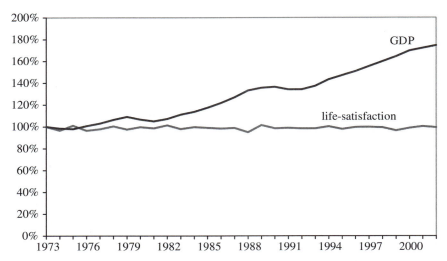

Figure 14.2 UK GDP vs. life-satisfaction 1973–2002. Data on GDP from UK National Accounts. Data on life-satisfaction from Veenhoven, R. World database of happiness: www2.eur.nl/fsw/research/happiness

bigger effect on individual well-being than absolute levels of income (Easterlin 1972). If my income rises relative to those around me I am likely to become happier. If everyone else's income rises at the same rate as my own, I am less likely to report higher life-satisfaction. Moreover, if my increase in income causes envy in those around me, my increased satisfaction is likely to be offset by dissatisfaction in others, so that aggregate life-satisfaction across the nation may not change at all (Layard 2005).

Others point to the impact of 'hedonic adaptation'. As I get richer, I simply become more accustomed to the pleasure of the goods and services my new income affords me. And if I want to maintain the same level of happiness, I must achieve ever higher levels of income in the future just to stay in the same place (Layard 2005, nef 2004).

Humanistic psychologists (and some ecologists and philosophers) have argued that the entire project of income growth rests on a misunderstanding of human nature. Far from making us happier, according to this critique, the pursuit of material things damages us psychologically and socially. Beyond the satisfaction of our basic material needs for housing, clothing and nutrition, the pursuit of material consumption merely serves to entrench us in unproductive status competition, disrupts our work–life balance and distracts us from those things that offer meaning and purpose to our lives (de Boton 2004, Csikszentmihalyi 2000, Kasser 2002, Schor 1998, Wachtel 1983; see also the chapter by Belk in this collection).

Others again have suggested a different – but equally radical – explanation for the life-satisfaction paradox. In a recent attempt to construct an international index of quality of life, *The Economist*'s Intelligence Unit suggested the explanation for the paradox was that 'there are factors associated with modernisation that, in part, offset its positive impact'. They argue that:

> [a] concomitant breakdown of traditional institutions is manifested in the decline of religiosity and of trade unions; a marked rise in various social pathologies (crime, and drug and alcohol addiction); a decline in political participation and of trust in public authority; and the erosion of the institutions of family and marriage.   (*The Economist* 2004)

The point about these changes – which have occurred hand-in-hand with the rise in incomes and the expansion of individual choice – is not that income growth is irrelevant to individual quality of life; all the evidence suggests the contrary. Rather it is that the pursuit of income growth appears to have undermined some of the conditions (family, friendship, community) on which we know that people's long-term well-being depends.

Is this merely a contingent historical coincidence or is it a necessary consequence of income growth? Do we just happen to have inherited an economic system which risks undermining the conditions of well-being or is it a feature of all such systems to operate in this way? Is it or is it not possible to maintain economic growth without the 'concomitant' erosion of some of the other conditions on which well-being depends?

For the sake of sustainable development, we would certainly want to hope that it is. The *Economist* article appears ambivalent on this point. Some critics of modernity have been far less ambivalent, pointing out that modern economies suffer from a structural need for consumerist values in order to sustain consumption growth (Baudrillard 1970, Bauman 1998, Fromm 1976, Illich 1977). The question is clearly a vital one to answer, but it remains beyond the scope of this chapter.

What flows from this discussion is the perhaps surprising insight that lifestyle strategies are not always effective – either because people end up consuming goods that do not contribute to life-satisfaction or because there are other (social or institutional) factors at work that prevent individual consumption choices contributing to collective (and future) well-being. This analysis suggests that it is at least legitimate to ask: is it possible to live better by consuming less (Jackson 2005b)? If some at least of our existing material consumption does not contribute to well-being, can we devise systems of consumption and production which are less resource-intensive but serve our needs better and deliver improved well-being and quality of life?

14.5 Lifestyle as 'social conversation'

This discussion raises an obvious question: why, if material consumption fails to satisfy, do we continue to consume? One answer to this is given by a quite specific view of lifestyles that has emerged in recent sociological writings on consumption and lifestyle (Chaney 1996). Briefly, this idea can be summarized by saying that lifestyles operate partly as 'social conversations': ways of communicating to ourselves and to others what sort of people we are, which kind of groups we belong to, who we like, love and approve of, who we disapprove of, what our social position is, what we hope that it might be, and what our goals, drives and ambitions are. (The use of the term 'social conversation' in this context is not typical of sociological writing. Sociology refers more often to 'social practices' – see next section for details. But it is consistent with the idea that material artefacts constitute what Douglas and Isherwood (1979) call a 'language of goods' and draws strongly from earlier social psychological theories of symbolic interactionism (Blumer 1969, Mead 1934).)

This view of lifestyles relies heavily on one of the most important sociological and anthropological understandings about consumption: namely, that material things embody important symbolic meanings for us. As one observer has remarked: 'the currency of lifestyles is the symbolic meaning of artefacts' (Chaney 1996). We value goods not just for what they can do, but for what they represent to us and to others. Without this almost magical potential to speak for us in some sense, it is doubtful that plain 'stuff' could play such a key role in our lives.

This insight clearly has some resonance with popular psychology about our relationship with material possessions. A child's favourite teddy bear, a woman's wedding dress, a stamp collector's prized first-day cover, the colours of my favourite football team, the brand name of a pair of trainers, the latest BMW sports car: all these examples suggest that there is much more at stake in the possession of material artefacts than simple functional value.

Over the second half of the twentieth century, this popular wisdom was given much more robust and sophisticated footing. The symbolic importance of consumer goods has been underlined by a wide range of intellectual sources. The evidence from social anthropology is perhaps the most convincing. It suggests that societies throughout the ages have used material commodities as symbolic resources to denote a wide variety of different kinds of meanings in an even wider variety of situations and contexts (Appadurai 1986, Csikszentmihalyi and Rochberg-Halton 1981, Dittmar 1992, Douglas 1976, Douglas and Isherwood 1979).

To offer one specific and relevant example, a recent study showed how patterns of lighting design in the home in three different cultures are inextricably linked to underlying social and cultural norms – the way we use space, our emotional attachment to home and hearth, and our sense of propriety in entertaining friends and guests. Lighting isn't solely about being able to see in the dark. Rather it is situated in a complex network of personal and social meanings that must be negotiated in the course of attempting to make domestic lighting patterns more efficient, for example (Wilhite *et al.* 1996).

This symbolic role for material goods is perhaps most obviously put to use in the creation and maintenance of personal identity. I define who I am in part through the symbolic meanings attached to the things that I own, use and display. This has led some sociologists to see modernity quite specifically as characterized by a restless search to define personal identity through one's consumption and lifestyle choices (Giddens 1991, Featherstone 1990, Bauman 2001, 2007, Campbell 2004).

Individual choice, the freedom to create one's identity, the ability to construct an 'authentic' personalized lifestyle: all these are highly prized features of modern society. At the same time, there is an irony inherent in this process. In spite of the high emphasis placed on individuality here, the symbols on which the project of self-identity is built are inherently social in nature. The task of constructing and maintaining symbolic meaning is itself a social one.

Symbols are by their nature socially constructed (Hirschman and Holbrook 1980). The symbolic value attached to material artefacts is neither embodied in the artefacts themselves nor entirely open to personal interpretation. This point was made persuasively by the sociologist Georg Simmel in the early twentieth century (see Simmel 1971). Rather it is a complex mixture of personal experience, historical tradition, societal values and an evolving process of articulating and elaborating social meaning. Symbolic value is constantly negotiated and renegotiated in modern society through social interactions.

Figure 14.3 illustrates something of how this process works. The left-hand side of the diagram represents the process of personal identity formation. As an individual in modern society (according to this view of modern lifestyles), I am continually involved in constructing a narrative about my own life – a personal project of symbolic 'self-completion' (Wicklund and Gollwitzer 1982). I am a forty-something white male, living in the south-east of England. I am married with three children. I live in a particular kind of house, drive a certain kind of car, have this kind of job, wear these kinds of clothes, listen to that kind of music and (like most other parents) agonize over which local school to send my children to. Consciously or subconsciously, I see myself and construct my own sense of identity through these lifestyle 'choices'. To the extent that I can achieve it at all, I know how to make sense of my life and pursue my life goals only through continual reference to this evolving narrative.

In pursuit of this narrative, I have at my disposal two distinct sets of resources. The first set is material: the artefacts and commodities that constitute the range of available goods and services. The second is symbolic: the set of meanings, interpretations and associations with which I am constantly surrounded. A specific, simple example of this dual relationship between 'things' and 'meanings' is the relationship between a product and a brand. The product is essentially a material resource; but the brand operates as a symbolic resource carrying or portraying a set of social meanings about use or ownership of the product.

My 'lived experience' of the material resources and my 'mediated experience' of symbolic resources allows me to construct – at a personal level – a kind

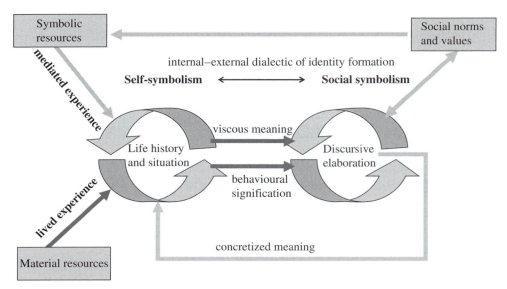

Figure 14.3 The social-symbolic project of identity formation. Adapted by the author from Elliott, R. and Wattanasuwan, K. 1998. 'Brands as resources for the symbolic construction of identity', *International Journal of Advertising* 172, pp. 131–45

of semi-defined or 'viscous' meaning associated with any particular lifestyle choice. It is only through a social process – illustrated on the right-hand side of figure 14.3 – of discussing and elaborating on these social meanings with others that I am able to solidify the specific meaning associated with a particular choice and incorporate it into the narrative of my life.

The implication of this rather complex process is that even personal identity – in this view of modern lifestyles – is bound up irretrievably in social conversations. Individual self-completion is only possible through social interaction with others. Without such social processes I simply have insufficient resources to attribute social value to my life choices and to articulate a meaningful sense of personal identity. In short, the most misanthropic individual is an inherently social creature.

Conversely, of course, the process of discursive elaboration – talking to others about the values attached to material artefacts – is a vehicle for the continual evolution of social meanings. Symbolic meanings of material commodities don't exist in isolation. Brand loyalty, for example, does not emerge spontaneously out of thin air. The relationship between people, meanings and things is the subject of a continually evolving dialogue over which no single individual, interest group or company has absolute control.

This is not to suggest that social meanings are immune from manipulation by powerful interests. On the contrary, an important aspect of this sociological view of lifestyles suggests that modern lifestyles have themselves become the locus for playing out power discourses, articulating class distinctions and reinforcing social inequalities.[2]

Producers, retailers and marketers have a particular interest in vesting their products with social value. The art of marketing is quite precisely the process of attributing social and psychological meanings to individual products. But the history of brand failures (see, for example, Haig 2003) should warn us against any simplistic view of the power of marketers to achieve this end. Rather, lifestyles (and the power discourses played out through them) are the product of a complex 'social logic' that defies absolute control by individuals or individual interest groups – or indeed by well-intentioned government departments.

From the point of view of sustainability, this view of lifestyles offers some interesting insights. In the first place, it positions lifestyles as crucial mediators between resource use, social structure and symbolic meanings. It also points to the importance of being able to understand – both in general and in specific situations – how these relationships are constructed and how they change over time. To attempt to engage in lifestyle change without an awareness of the social-symbolic processes underlying consumer choices is to invite an almost inevitable failure.

In fact, the life-satisfaction paradox does intimate some 'inefficiencies' here. But these inefficiencies are rather complex features of the social organization of lifestyles and we cannot expect many 'easy wins' simply by exhorting people to change or tinkering with incentive structures.

In summary, lifestyles are a way of helping us to create the social world and find a creditable place in it. Modernity is characterized by the increasingly important symbolic role played by material goods in this process. In many cases, existing lifestyle choices and consumption patterns are inextricably linked with people's sense of self, social standing and purpose. Teasing apart consumer demand from these social and psychological processes is going to require a concerted effort to understand social values, renegotiate social norms and offer alternative meaning structures. Without such initiatives, attempts to change lifestyles – as we have already noted – can only expect considerable resistance.

14.6 Consumer 'lock-in'

The modern project of symbolic self-completion – the reflexive construction of personal life-narratives – has sometimes been construed in the literature as an inherently creative project in which the individual has a great deal of freedom in deciding on the outcome. It is precisely this promise of immense, inextinguishable personal opportunity on which the consumer society is built.

---

[2] The most prominent proponent of this view is the French sociologist Pierre Bourdieu (1984). For useful synthetic overviews see Chaney 1996 or Bocock 1993.

Each new consumer purchase is a small piece of this continual reinvention of possibility. Each lifestyle choice opens the door to a brighter and better future: the opportunity to reinvent ourselves, the chance to realize our dreams, the basis for sustaining hope in the face of adversity. Once again, advertising executives have for decades been alive to these ways of investing mundane goods with a sense of hope. It is part of the art of marketing.[3]

The reality of course is something rather different. At the very least, we would have to admit that choice doesn't always appear possible to people. Though I strive continually for control of my life, it often appears to have a momentum and a pattern of its own. This pattern certainly changes over time. But the change sometimes appears to have less to do with my own decisions and desires than it does with the changing demands on my time, the technologies that shape my existence, the sometimes inescapable efforts of others to persuade me to behave and live in particular ways, and the emergence of new social norms and attitudes to which I am expected constantly to adapt if I am to maintain or improve my social standing.

This is one of the most intractable of the paradoxes haunting modern lifestyles. Modern society celebrates choice and personal opportunity; and at the same time we often find ourselves locked into rather predictable patterns of living, working and consuming. The idea that modern society, and consumerism specifically, operates as a kind of 'iron cage' binding us into certain material dependencies and patterns of behaviour has a long pedigree in the social sciences (Weber 1930, Ritzer 2001). Recent work in sociology has revived this traditional theme as a way of better understanding real consumer behaviours.

These sociologists have argued that too much emphasis has been placed on the conspicuous aspects of modern consumer lifestyles and that a great deal of consumption in fact takes place *inconspicuously* as a part of the everyday decision-making of millions of ordinary individuals. 'Ordinary' consumption, argue these authors, is not oriented particularly towards individual display. Rather it is about convenience, habit, practice and individual responses to social norms and institutional contexts over which the individual has little control (Gronow and Warde 2001).

To take one simple and relevant example, the fuel consumption associated with heating our home is determined (amongst other things) by the available fuel supply, the efficiency of the conversion devices, the effectiveness of thermal insulation in the dwelling and the level of thermal comfort programmed into our thermostats. These factors in their turn are constrained by the historical development of the fuel supply and appliance industries, the institutional design of the energy services market, the social norms associated with personal

---

[3] For four interesting and different perspectives on this point see McCracken (1989), Hamilton (2003), Roberts (2004) and Campbell (2003).

convenience and thermal comfort, and our own individual responses to those norms.

The evolution of social and institutional norms is itself complex, often involving incremental changes over long historical periods. Typically, at the point of everyday decision, the ordinary consumer will have little or no control over much of this decision architecture (Guy and Shove 2000, Sanne 2002, Shove 2003).

This message tends to be borne out by empirical studies of consumer attitudes and behaviours. The National Consumer Council, for example, has published a number of studies looking at people's attitudes towards and access to sustainable lifestyle options. They concluded that, for the most part, consumers find their options curtailed by a variety of factors, including time constraints, economic disincentives and the absence or inaccessibility of more sustainable choices (Holdsworth 2003, 2005, Klein 2003). This is particularly true of low income households – for whom restrictions in choice are already onerous (Burningham and Thrush 2000, Brook Lyndhurst 2004).

At the heart of this concept of 'ordinary consumption' lies the issue of habit. The important role that habit plays in our lives has been acknowledged for some time (Bourdieu 1984, Camic 1986, Kahneman 1973, Tversky and Kahneman 1974). Many of our everyday actions appear to take place with little conscious deliberation at all. Rather we relegate routine decisions to the realm of semi-conscious automaticity. At best, we use a variety of mental short-cuts – what the sociologist Anthony Giddens (1984) has called 'practical consciousness' – to simplify routine choice in our lives.

Habit has both good and bad influences on lifestyle choice. On the one hand, it allows us to free up cognitive resources for more important tasks. But, on the other hand, it renders much of our routine decision-making almost invisible, even to ourselves. Changing our behaviour – exercising our ability to choose – becomes more and more difficult as the existing behaviour pattern is repeated.

Resolving the paradox of choice at the heart of modern lifestyles is far from easy. The question of whether consumers are free to make choices about their own actions or whether they are bound by forces outside their control has provoked a long and heated debate in the social sciences. This debate – about the relative influence of human agency and social structure – culminated in the development of Giddens' 'structuration theory' which attempts to show how agency and structure relate to each other (Giddens 1984). Giddens' work provides the basis for a view of lifestyles as a set of *social practices* (figure 14.4) which are influenced, on the one hand, by our lifestyle choices and, on the other, by the institutions and structures of society.

In summary, the message that flows from the evidence reviewed in this section is that – in spite of the conscious attempt to construct personal lifestyle narratives – consumers are often far from being free agents in the execution of lifestyle choice. They do have personal priorities. Their lives are in some broad sense (as we discussed above) goal-oriented. They do exercise deliberative

Actors   Human action   Social practices   Structures

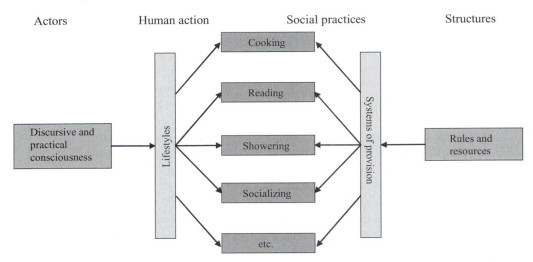

Figure 14.4 Lifestyles and social practices. Adapted from *Environmental Politics*, 9(1), Spaargaren, G. and van Vliet, B. 'Lifestyles, consumption and the environment: the ecological modernization of domestic consumption', pp. 50–77, Copyright 2000, with permission from Taylor & Francis Ltd, www.informaworld.com

decisions. At the same time, many routine decisions are not deliberative. They often find themselves 'locked into' unsustainable patterns of living, by a complex mixture of factors: perverse incentive structures, restrictive social norms, institutional constraints or sheer habit.

14.7   Policies for sustainable consumption

Perhaps unsurprisingly, lifestyle change is fast becoming a kind of 'holy grail' for sustainable consumption policy (Defra 2005, Swedish Ministry of Sustainable Development 2005, UNEP 2005). How can we persuade people to behave in more environmentally and socially responsible ways? How can we shift people's transport modes, appliance choices, eating habits, social drinking, leisure practices, holiday plans, lifestyle expectations (and so on) in such a way as to reduce the damaging impact on the environment and on other people? How can we encourage 'sustainable living' and discourage unsustainable living?

These tasks are enormously complex for a variety of reasons. The previous sections have highlighted some of these reasons. In particular, it is clear that:

- lifestyles are a complex aggregation of social practices the precise nature of which varies widely both within and between population segments;
- lifestyle practices are interwoven with vital social conversations about status, social affiliation and meaning;

- people often find themselves locked into lifestyle 'choices' by a combination of perverse incentives, institutional rules, habit and deeply engrained social and cultural norms.

In spite of these complexities, it is abundantly clear that lifestyles and consumption patterns do change – indeed, have changed – quite radically over relatively short spaces of time. The uptake of mobile phones, 4 × 4s, wide-screen plasma TVs, power showers, standby modes in electronic appliances, domestic air conditioning, patio heaters, cheap short-haul holiday flights: these are all examples of technological and behavioural changes which have occurred in the space of only a decade or so in recent Western development. Much-further-reaching changes have occurred over only slightly longer timescales.

Several things are significant about these sorts of changes. The first is that many of them appear to be in a direction that is moving towards an increase in the energy (and carbon) intensity of lifestyles. They are in fact a part of the reason why achievements in energy efficiency are not matched by overall reductions in the household demand for energy. In this sense, they clearly illustrate how an unconstrained product development market can undermine the best intentions of product-specific policies in one area of that market.

The second interesting point to note is that these kinds of changes represent a kind of 'creeping evolution' of social and technological norms. That is, they occur at a level which is not immediately susceptible to individual control. This is not to deny that individuals sometimes change their behaviours entirely autonomously. Of course they do. This is illustrated, for example, by the emergence of a trend in 'down-shifting' – a spontaneous movement by individuals away from the dominant high-consuming lifestyle and towards voluntary simplicity.

Sometimes, moreover, individual behaviour change can initiate new social trends. This is particularly obvious when the individual in question has some kind of celebrity status. The tendency to 'model' our behaviours closely on influential figures around us is a key lesson from social learning theory (Bandura 1977). But it sometimes also occurs from the margins. New mainstream fashions in both clothing and music (for example) are often gleaned from counter-trends observed at the margins of society. 'Raiding cool' is one of the new corporate marketing strategies (Klein 2001, Kotlowitz 1999).

More often, however, most individuals find themselves responding to societal and technological changes that are initiated elsewhere, at some higher or deeper level. And it is clear from this that we must think of individual behaviour as being 'locked in' not just in a static but also in a dynamic sense. We are locked into behavioural trends as much as, and possibly more than, we are locked into specific behaviours. It is also clear that without policy mechanisms capable of addressing explicitly the underlying trends, it is not going to be a lot of use exhorting individuals to change. Addressing dynamic lock-in is as important as addressing static lock-in.

Conventional responses to issues of behavioural change tend to be based on a particular model of the way that lifestyle choices are made. This 'rational choice' model contends that consumers make decisions by calculating the individual costs and benefits of different courses of action and then choosing the option that maximizes their expected net benefits. If it is cheaper for me to travel from A to B by train than by car, I will usually choose to go by train. If it is more costly and time-consuming for me to recycle my household waste than to throw it in the trash, I will tend to do the latter.

There is a familiar and appealing logic to this model. Faced with two clear choices, different in cost but equal in all other respects, it is in my own self-interest to choose the less expensive one. From this perspective, the role of policy appears to be straightforward, namely to ensure that the market allows people to make efficient choices about their own actions.

For the most part, this has been seen as the need to correct for 'market failures'. These failures occur, for example, if consumers have insufficient information to make proper choices. So, according to this view, policy should seek to improve access to information. In addition, private decisions do not always take account of social costs. So, on this model, policy intervention is needed to 'internalize' these external costs and make them more 'visible' to private choice.

Sadly, the evidence does not support unrestrained optimism in relation to either of these policy options – at least by themselves. In fact, the history of information and advertising campaigns to promote sustainable behavioural change is littered with failures. In one extreme case, a California utility spent more money on advertising the benefits of home insulation than it would have cost to install the insulation itself in the targeted homes.[4]

The fiscal approach has also faced limited success in encouraging long-term pro-environmental behaviour changes. Although there is evidence to suggest that price differentials (for example) are sometimes successful in persuading people to shift between different fuels, there is much less convincing evidence of the success of economic strategies in improving energy efficiency overall or in shifting behaviours more generally.

Some have argued that the failure of conventional policy-making to foster sustainable behaviours is partly the result of a failure to understand the sheer difficulty associated with changing behaviours (Darnton 2004, Jackson 2005a, McKenzie-Mohr 2000). As a review of the residential conservation service – an early energy conservation initiative in the US – once concluded, most such efforts tend to overlook 'the rich mixture of cultural practices, social interactions, and human feelings that influence the behaviour of individuals, social groups and institutions' (Stern and Aronson 1984). The message is certainly borne out by the overview of modern lifestyles presented above.

---

[4] Cited in McKenzie-Mohr 2000.

The conclusion to be drawn from this is not that fiscal incentives and information campaigns are irrelevant or inappropriate as policy options to facilitate lifestyle change. People are sometimes self-interested. They do make economic decisions. Their choices are swayed by cost. Adjusting prices to incorporate negative or positive externalities is therefore a legitimate avenue through which to promote pro-environmental or pro-social behaviour and to discourage anti-social or environmentally damaging behaviour. Providing accessible and appropriate information to facilitate pro-environmental choice is also a key avenue for policy.

But the evidence does suggest very strongly that these measures are insufficient on their own to facilitate pro-environmental behaviour change of the kind and scale required to meet existing environmental challenges. It is clear from the discussions in the earlier sections of this chapter that achieving lifestyle change demands a sophisticated policy approach, responsive to the social complexity of modern lifestyles. Overcoming lock-in and facilitating alternative avenues of social conversation will be vital. A concerted strategy will be needed to make behaviour change easy for people. This must include:

- ensuring that incentive structures and institutional rules favour more sustainable behaviours;
- enabling access to pro-environmental (and pro-social) lifestyle choices;
- engaging people in initiatives to help themselves; and
- exemplifying the desired changes within government's own policies and practices.

Most importantly, the evidence suggests that policy plays a vital role in shaping the social context within which we live and act. Governments influence and co-create the culture of consumption in a variety of ways. In some cases this influence proceeds through specific interventions – such as the imposition of regulatory and fiscal structures. In other cases it proceeds through the absence of such interventions. Most often it is a complex combination of the ways in which government does intervene, and the ways in which it chooses not to intervene.

For example, the way in which the energy market was liberalized offers consumers a remarkable choice of energy suppliers who compete vigorously for custom on the basis of the lowest unit price. The same liberalization process, it could be argued, has actively impeded the development of energy services, by making it difficult (and uncompetitive) for utilities to invest in demand reduction (SDC 2007). At the same time, the UK Government has invested millions of pounds in a communications campaign on climate change, and yet it leaves unregulated the advertising of products that threaten the success of its own carbon emission targets.

To take another example, it has been argued that the long-standing failure of successive UK governments to reduce inequalities in the distribution of incomes has the effect of increasing competitive social pressures, and reducing affiliative, cooperative and social behaviours (Layard 2005, James 1998, 2007).

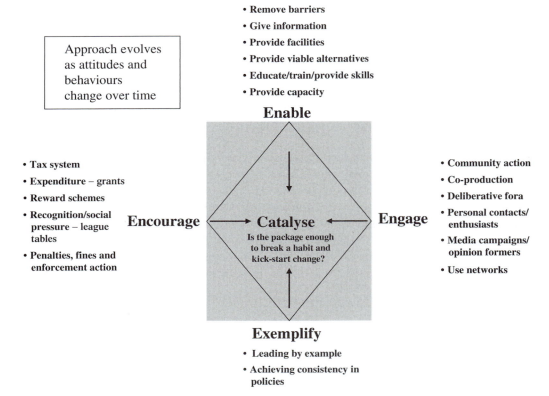

- Remove barriers
- Give information
- Provide facilities
- Provide viable alternatives
- Educate/train/provide skills
- Provide capacity

Approach evolves as attitudes and behaviours change over time

Enable

- Tax system
- Expenditure – grants
- Reward schemes
- Recognition/social pressure – league tables
- Penalties, fines and enforcement action

Encourage

Catalyse
Is the package enough to break a habit and kick-start change?

Engage

- Community action
- Co-production
- Deliberative fora
- Personal contacts/ enthusiasts
- Media campaigns/ opinion formers
- Use networks

Exemplify

- Leading by example
- Achieving consistency in policies

Figure 14.5 A new model for behaviour change policy. Redrawn from *Securing the Future: Delivering UK Sustainable Development Strategy* – Defra 2005 © Crown copyright, material is reproduced with the permission of the Controller of HMSO and Queen's Printer for Scotland

Likewise, successive deregulation of retail and trade has tended to erode the cultural space previously afforded by non-commoditized community-based institutions.

In short, selective policy intervention can have a very significant influence over the institutional and social context of lifestyles. This view of the state – as a continual mediator and 'co-creator' of the social and institutional context – opens out a range of possible avenues for policy intervention in pursuit of behavioural change. The complex terrain of human behaviour, as viewed in a social, psychological and cultural context, is not a place devoid of possibilities for state influence. Rather it is one in which there are numerous possibilities (figure 14.5) at multiple levels for motivating pro-environmental behaviours and encouraging more sustainable lifestyles.[5]

---

[5] For more detailed analyses of the possibilities see: Jackson 2005a, Halpern *et al.* 2003 and Defra 2005, chapter 2. In the wake of the UK Government's 2005 Sustainable Development

14.8 Conclusions

This chapter has summarized the challenge inherent in recent policy debates about sustainable consumption. It has focused in particular on what might be involved in negotiating the kinds of lifestyle changes that are implied by the radical reductions in carbon emissions required to mitigate climate change.

A preliminary overview of lifestyles in modern society portrays modern lifestyles as being haunted by complexity and paradox. The materiality of our lifestyles – the stuff of everyday living – is deeply woven into the social and psychological fabric of our lives. Our enduring attempts at individuality are confounded by inherently social norms and expectations. Our desire for freedom of choice is continually frustrated by institutional lock-in and force of habit. Our relentless pursuit of the good life is undermined by the breakdown of traditional institutions and the erosion of community and trust.

In these circumstances, the idea of lifestyle change in pursuit of social or environmental goals is immensely challenging. The starting point for any such endeavour has got to be a sophisticated engagement with the material and social basis of lifestyles. This recognition already lies at the heart of commercial consumer engagement strategies. For well over half a century, product designers and marketers have approached the topic of lifestyle in a rigorous and scientific manner: relentlessly unpicking the dimensions of human motivation and desire, carefully exploring the detailed make-up of lifestyle sectors, and delving into the dynamics of population segments and social structure.

In one sense, government policy in pursuit of lifestyle change needs to adopt the same rigour. For example, it needs to develop or borrow expertise in lifestyle segmentation analysis and lifestyle sector analysis. It needs to build the capability to map (at national, regional and local levels) the resource and environmental implications of different lifestyle sectors and segments – something which the commercial sector has conspicuously avoided doing. And it also needs to be able to develop an understanding of the broader cultural and institutional dynamics which frame these social and material patterns – something which the commercial sector is simply not positioned to do.

It has also been argued that government needs to engage in a more sophisticated way with the dynamics of behavioural change and lifestyle change. The tendency until now has been to fight shy of this difficult terrain and cling to notions of consumer sovereignty and 'hands-off' governance. The evidence reviewed in this chapter suggests that this strategy is neither an accurate reflection of the role of government in lifestyle choice nor particularly helpful. A more useful (and more accurate) view sees government as a 'co-creator' of the culture of consumption, with an integral part to play in negotiating lifestyle

strategy, behavioural change is now the subject of an ongoing cross-departmental working group in the UK.

change. One thing is clear from all this: simplistic attempts to exhort consumers to change their behaviours and lifestyles, without taking account of the complexity reviewed here, are almost certainly doomed to failure.

14.9 References

Ajzen, I. and M. Fishbein 1975. *Belief, Attitude, Intention and Behavior: An Introduction to Theory and Research*. Reading, MA: Addison-Wesley.

Appadurai, A. 1986. *The Social Life of Things: Commodities in Cultural Perspective*. Cambridge: Cambridge University Press.

Bagozzi, R., Z. Gürnao-Canli and J. Priester 2002. *The Social Psychology of Consumer Behaviour*. Buckingham: Open University Press.

Bandura, A. 1977. *Social Learning Theory*. Englewood Cliffs, NJ: Prentice-Hall.

Baudrillard, J. 1970. *The Consumer Society – Myths and Structures*. London: Sage Publications.

Bauman, Z. 1998. *Work, Consumerism and the New Poor*. Buckingham: Open University Press.

2001. *Liquid Modernity*. Cambridge: Polity Press.

2007. *Consuming Life*. Cambridge: Polity Press.

Berger, P. 1967. *The Sacred Canopy – Elements of a Sociological Theory of Religion*. New York: Anchor Books.

Blumer, H. 1969. *Symbolic Interactionism – Perspective and Method*. Berkeley, CA: University of California Press.

Bocock, R. 1993. *Consumption*. Routledge, London.

Bourdieu, P. 1984. *Distinction – A Social Critique of the Judgement of Taste*. London: Routledge.

Breakwell, G. 1986. *Coping with Threatened Identities*. London: Routledge.

Brook Lyndhurst 2004. *Bad Habits and Hard Choices – In Search of Sustainable Lifestyles*. London: Brook Lyndhurst.

Burningham, K. and D. Thrush 2000. *Rainforests Are a Long Way from Here: Environmental Attitudes in Disadvantaged Communities*. A report to the Joseph Rowntree Foundation. London: JRF.

Camic, C. 1986. 'The matter of habit'. *American Journal of Sociology* 91(5), 1039–87.

Campbell, C. 2004. 'I shop therefore I know that I am: The metaphysical basis of modern consumerism', in K. Ekstrom and H. Brembeck (eds.), *Elusive Consumption: Tracking New Research Perspectives*, pp. 27–44. Oxford: Berg.

Chambers, R. and G. Conway 1992. 'Sustainable rural livelihoods: Practical concepts for the 21st century'. IDS discussion paper No. 296. Brighton: IDS.

Chaney, D. 1996. *Lifestyles*. London: Routledge.

Csikszentmihalyi, M. 2000. 'The costs and benefits of consuming'. *Journal of Consumer Research* 27, 267–72.

Csikszentmihalyi, M. and E. Rochberg-Halton 1981. *The Meaning of Things – Domestic Symbols and the Self*. Cambridge: Cambridge University Press.

Daly, H. 1996. *Beyond Growth – The Economics of Sustainable Development*. Boston: Beacon Press.

Daly, H. and J. Cobb 1989. *For the Common Good*. Washington, DC: Island Press.

Darnton, A. 2004. 'The impact of sustainable development on public behaviour', report 1 of Desk Research commissioned by COI on behalf of Defra, www.sustainable-development.gov.uk/documents/publications/desk-research1.pdf.

de Boton, A. 2004. *Status Anxiety*. Oxford: Oxford University Press.

Defra 2003. *Changing Patterns: The UK Sustainable Consumption and Production Framework*. London: Stationery Office.

   2005. *Securing the Future: Delivering UK Sustainable Development Strategy*. London: Stationery Office.

   2006. *UK Climate Change Programme Review*. Department for Environment, Food and Rural Affairs. London: Stationery Office.

DETR 1999. *Towards a Better Quality of Life*. London: Stationery Office.

DfID 2006. *Sustainable Livelihoods Guidance Sheets*. London: Department for International Development (DfID). Available online at: www.livelihoods.org/info/info_guidancesheets.html (accessed 20 July 2006).

Dittmar, H. 1992. *The Social Psychology of Material Possessions – To Have Is to Be*. New York: St Martin's Press.

Douglas, M. 1976. 'Relative poverty, relative communication', in A. Halsey (ed.), *Traditions of Social Policy*, p. 207. Oxford: Basil Blackwell.

Douglas, M. and B. Isherwood 1979. *The World of Goods – Towards an Anthropology of Consumption*. London: Routledge.

Douthwaite, R. 1992. *The Growth Illusion*. Bideford, Devon: Green Books.

Doyal, L. and I. Gough 1991. *A Theory of Human Needs*. London: Macmillan.

Dunlap, R. and K. van Liere 1978. 'The new environmental paradigm – a proposed measuring instrument and preliminary results'. *Journal of Environmental Education* 9, 10–19.

Easterlin, R. 1972. 'Does economic growth improve the human lot? Some empirical evidence', in D. David and M. Reder (eds.), *Nations and Households in Economic Growth*. Stanford: Stanford University Press.

The Economist 2004. 'The Economist Intelligence Unit's quality of life index', Economist Online, December 2004: www.economist.com/media/pdf/QUALITY_OF_LIFE.pdf.

Elliott, R. and K. Wattanasuwan 1998. 'Brands as resources for the symbolic construction of identity'. *International Journal of Advertising* 172, 131–45.

Etzioni, A. 1998. 'Voluntary simplicity: Characterization, select psychological implications and societal consequences'. *Journal of Economic Psychology* 19, 619–43.

Featherstone, M. 1990. *Consumer Culture and Post-modernism*. London: Sage.

Frank, R. 1999. *Luxury Fever*. Princeton, NJ: Princeton University Press.

Fromm, E. 1976. *To Have or to Be?* London: Jonathan Cape.

Giddens, A. 1984. *The Constitution of Society – Outline of the Theory of Structuration*. Berkeley, CA: University of California Press.

   1991. *Modernity and Self-identity: Self and Society in the Late Modern Age*. Cambridge: Polity Press.

Gronow, J. and A. Warde 2001. *Ordinary Consumption*. London: Routledge.

Guy, S. and E. Shove 2000. *A Sociology of Energy, Buildings and the Environment: Constructing Knowledge, Designing Practice*. London: Routledge.

Haig, M. 2003. *Brand Failures: The Truth about the 100 Biggest Branding Mistakes of All Time*. London: Kogan Page.

Halpern, D., C. Bates and G. Beales 2003. *Personal Responsibility and Behaviour Change, Strategic Audit Paper*. London: Cabinet Office Strategy Unit.

Hamilton, C. 2003. 'Downshifting in Britain – A sea-change in pursuit of happiness'. discussion paper No. 58. Canberra: Australia Institute.

2004. *Growth Fetish*. London: Pluto Press.

Hirschman, E. and M. Holbrook (eds.) 1980. 'Symbolic consumer behaviour, Proceedings of the Conference on Consumer Aesthetics and Symbolic Consumption'. New York: Association for Consumer Research.

Holdsworth, M. 2003. 'Green choice: What choice? Summary of NCC research into consumer attitudes to sustainable consumption'. London: National Consumer Council.

2005. *16 Pain-free Ways to Help Save the Planet*. London: National Consumer Council.

Illich, I. 1977. *Towards a History of Needs*. New York: Pantheon Books.

Inglehart, R. 1991. *Culture Shift in Advanced Modern Society*. Princeton, NJ: Princeton University Press.

Inglehart, R. and H.-D. Klingemann 2000. *Genes, Culture and Happiness*. Boston, MA: MIT Press.

IPCC 2001. *Third Assessment Report of the Intergovernmental Panel on Climate Change*. Oxford: Oxford University Press, vols. I–III.

Jackson, T. 1996. *Material Concerns: Pollution, Profit and Quality of Life*. London: Routledge.

2002a. 'Quality of life, sustainability and economic growth', in T. Fitzpatrick and M. Cahill (eds.), *Environment and Welfare*, pp. 97–116. London: Palgrave Macmillan.

2002b. 'Evolutionary psychology and ecological economics – Consilience, consumption and contentment'. *Ecological Economics* 41(2), 289–303.

2004. *Chasing Progress: Beyond Measuring Economic Growth*. London: New Economics Foundation.

2005a. 'Motivating sustainable consumption – A review of evidence on consumer behaviour and behavioural change'. London: Policy Studies Institute, www.sd-research.org.uk/documents/MotivatingSCfinal.pdf.

2005b. 'Live better by consuming less? Is there a "double dividend" in sustainable consumption?' *Journal of Industrial Ecology* 9(1–2), 19–36.

2006a. *Earthscan Reader in Sustainable Consumption*. London: Earthscan/James & James.

2006b. 'Consuming paradise? Towards a socio-cultural psychology of sustainable consumption', chapter 24 in T. Jackson, *Earthscan Reader in Sustainable Consumption*. London: Earthscan/James & James.

2006c. 'Beyond the wellbeing paradox: Wellbeing, consumption growth and sustainability'. Concept paper prepared for a Defra review of evidence on well-being. London: New Economics Foundation.

Jackson, T., W. Jager and S. Stagl 2004. 'Beyond insatiability – Needs theory and sustainable consumption', chapter 5 in L. Reisch and I. Røpke (eds.), *Consumption – Perspectives from Ecological Economics*. Cheltenham: Edward Elgar.

Jackson, T. and N. McBride 2005. *Measuring Progress? A Review of Alternative Indicators of Economic Progress*. A report to the European Environment Agency. Guildford: University of Surrey.

Jackson, T. and L. Michaelis 2003. *Policies for Sustainable Consumption*. A report to the Sustainable Development Commission. London: Sustainable Development Commission.

James O. 1998. *Britain on the Couch: Why We're Unhappier Compared to 1950 Despite Being Richer*. London: Arrow Books.

2007. *Affluenza*. Oxford: Blackwell.

Kahneman, D. 1973. *Attention and Effort*. Englewood Cliffs, NJ: Prentice-Hall.

Kasser, T. 2002. *The High Price of Materialism*. Cambridge, MA: MIT Press.

Klein, G. 2003. *Life Lines: The NCC's Agenda for Affordable Energy, Water and Telephone Services*. London: National Consumer Council.

Klein, N. 2001. *No Logo*. London: Flamingo.

Kotlowitz, A. 1999. 'False connections', in R. Rosenblatt (ed.), *Consuming Desires – Consumption, Culture and the Pursuit of Happiness*. Washington, DC: Island Press (reproduced as chapter 10 in Jackson 2006a).

Layard, R. 2005. *Happiness – Lessons from a New Science*. London: Allen Lane.

Maslow, A. 1954. *Motivation and Personality*. New York: Harper & Row.

Max-Neef, M. 1991. *Human-Scale Development – Conception, Application and Further Reflection*. London: Apex Press.

McCracken, G. 1989. *The Culture of Consumption*. Bloomington: Indiana University Press.

McKenzie-Mohr, D. 2000. 'Promoting sustainable behavior: An introduction to community-based social marketing'. *Journal of Social Issues* 56(3), 543–54.

Mead, G. 1934. *Mind, Self and Society*. Chicago: University of Chicago Press.

nef 2004: *A Wellbeing Manifesto for a Flourishing Society*. London: New Economics Foundation.

Nussbaum, M. 1998. 'The good as discipline, the good as freedom', in D. Crocker and T. Linden (eds.), *The Ethics of Consumption*, pp. 312–41. New York: Rowman and Littlefield.

Oxfam 2006. *Sustainable Livelihoods – Introduction*. Available online at www.oxfam.org.uk/what_we_do/issues/livelihoods/introduction.htm (accessed 20 July 2006).

PIU 2002. *Resource Productivity – Making More with Less*. London: Performance and Innovation Unit, UK Cabinet Office.

Ridley, M. 1994. *The Red Queen – Sex and the Evolution of Human Nature*. Harmondsworth: Penguin Books.

Ritzer, G. 2001. *Explorations in the Sociology of Consumption*. London: Sage.

Roberts, K. 2004. *Lovemarks: The Future Beyond Brands*. London: Saatchi and Saatchi.

Sanne, C. 2002. 'Willing consumers – Or Locked in? Policies for a sustainable consumption'. *Ecological Economics* 42, 273–87.

Schor, J. 1998. *The Overspent American: Upscaling, Downshifting and the New Consumer*. New York: Basic Books.

SDC/NCC 2006. *I Will if You Will*. Report of the UK Sustainable Consumption Round Table. London: Sustainable Development Commission/National Consumer Council.

SDC 2007. *Lost in Transmission*. A review of the Office of Gas and Electricity Markets. London: Sustainable Development Commission.

Sen, A. 1985. *Commodities and Capabilities*. Amsterdam: Elsevier.

Shove, E. 2003. *Comfort, Cleanliness and Convenience – The Social Organisation of Normality*. London: Routledge.

Simmel, G. 1971. 'The metropolis and mental life', in D. Levine (ed.), *On Individuality and Social Forms: Selected Writings*. Chicago: University of Chicago Press.

Simon, H. 1971. 'Designing organizations for an information-rich world', in M. Greenberger (ed.), *Computers, Communications, and the Public Interest*, pp. 37–72. Baltimore, MD: Johns Hopkins Press.

Spaargaren, G. and B. van Vliet, 2000. 'Lifestyles, consumption and the environment: The ecological modernization of domestic consumption'. *Environmental Politics* 9(1), 50–77.

Stern, P. and E. Aronson 1984. *Energy Use – The Human Dimension*. New York: Freeman.

Stern, P. and T. Dietz 1994. 'The value basis of environmental concern'. *Journal of Social Issues* 50, 65–84.

Swedish Ministry of Sustainable Development 2005. International Task Force on Sustainable Lifestyles. Memorandum, 25 August 2005, Stockholm. Available at www.uneptie.org/pc/sustain/resources/MTF/Sweden%20TF%20Sust. Lifestyles.pdf (accessed 17 July 2006).

Tversky, A. and D. Kahneman 1974. 'Judgement under uncertainty: Heuristics and biases'. *Science* 185, 1124–31.

UN 1993. *Agenda 21: The United Nations Program of Action from Rio*. New York: United Nations.

UNEP 2001. *Consumption Opportunities: Strategies for Change*. Paris: United Nations Environment Programme.

  2005. *Talk the Walk? Advancing Sustainable Lifestyles through Marketing and Communications*. Paris: United Nations Environment Programme.

Veenhoven, R. 2004. 'States of nations, world database of happiness', available at www2.eur.nl/fsw/research/happiness.

von Weizsäcker, E., A. Lovins and L. Hunter Lovins 1997. *Factor Four: Doubling Wealth, Halving Resource Use*. A report to the Club of Rome. London: Earthscan.

Wachtel, P. 1983. *The Poverty of Affluence – A Psychological Portrait of the American Way of Life*. New York: Free Press.

Weber, M. 1930. *The Protestant Ethic and the Spirit of Capitalism*. London: Routledge.

Weitzman, M. 1976. 'On the welfare significance of the national product in a dynamic economy'. *Quarterly Journal of Economics* 90, 156–62.

Wicklund, R. and P. Gollwitzer 1982. *Symbolic Self-Completion*. Hillsdale, NJ: Erlbaum.

Wilhite, H., H. Nakagami, T. Masuda and Y. Yamaga 1996. 'A cross-cultural analysis of household energy use in Japan and Norway'. *Energy Policy* 24(9), 795–803.

Wright, R. 1994. *The Moral Animal – Why We Are the Way We Are: The New Science of Evolutionary Psychology*. London: Abacus.

15 Environmentally significant behavior in the home

PAUL C. STERN

Environmentally significant behavior can be defined either by its *impact* or by its *intent*. Impact is the extent to which a behavior "changes the availability of materials or energy from the environment or alters the structure and dynamics of ecosystems or the biosphere itself" (Stern 2000:408; see also Stern 1997). Behavior may affect the environment directly (e.g., disposing of household waste) or indirectly (e.g., acting to promote pro-environmental public policies). In some cases, behaviors with indirect environmental effects can have greater impact than behaviors that directly change the environment.

Only with the rise of environmental social movements has environmental protection become an important motive for behavior. Environmentally significant behavior can thus "be defined from the actor's standpoint as behavior that is undertaken with the intention to change (normally, to benefit) the environment" (Stern 2000:408). An important way that impact is different from intent is that "environmental intent may fail to result in environmental impact. For example, many people in the United States believe that avoiding the use of spray cans protects the ozone layer, even though ozone-destroying substances have been banned from spray cans for two decades" (Stern 2000:408).

Impact-oriented and intent-oriented definitions are both important for research, but for different purposes. An impact-oriented definition is necessary to make research useful, because it allows researchers to target those behaviors that can make the greatest difference to the environment (Stern and Gardner 1981a). An intent-oriented definition that focuses on people's beliefs, motives, and so forth may be necessary to understand and change the target behaviors.

Second, it is useful to distinguish different types of environmentally significant behavior that may respond to different causal factors. Researchers have not settled on a single best classification scheme, but there is considerable support for distinguishing the following classes of behavior: (a) environmental activism (e.g., active involvement in environmental organizations and demonstrations); (b) non-activist public-sphere behaviors (support for environmental movement goals, for example, by joining or contributing to movement organizations, supporting pro-environmental public policies, expressing willingness to pay higher taxes for environmental protection); (c) various types of private-sphere environmentalism, such as purchases of household goods and services with significant environmental impacts (motor vehicles, heating systems), the use and maintenance of such goods, household waste disposal, and "green" consumerism (purchasing practices that consider the environmental impacts of production, for example purchasing recycled products or organically grown foods); and (d) behaviors that affect the environment by influencing the actions of organizations to which individuals belong, such as their workplaces (Stern 2000). The topic of environmentally significant behavior in the home is normally considered to include only behaviors of class (c) above; accordingly, this review is restricted to a subset of environmentally significant individual behavior.

Such distinctions of types and subtypes of environmentally significant behavior are supported by various studies (e.g., Black, Stern, and Elworth 1985; Dietz, Stern, and Guagnano 1998; Stern, Dietz, Abel, Guagnano, and Kalof 1999). Other researchers, however, have presented evidence that a single underlying factor unites a very wide range of environmentally significant behaviors (e.g., Kaiser 1998). The apparent inconsistency between these lines of research has not yet been resolved empirically, but progress is being made toward a resolution (see, e.g., Thøgerson and Ölander 2006). Distinctions among behavioral classes and even among subclasses of behavior are likely to remain useful, however, for at least three reasons. First, behaviors of the same type tend to have the same patterns of social-psychological and socio-demographic predictors, and these predictors are not the same for all behavioral types (e.g., Black *et al.* 1985; Dietz *et al.* 1998; Bratt 1999; Stern *et al.* 1999; Poortinga *et al.* 2004; Thøgerson and Ölander 2006). Second, the distinctions matter in terms of environmental impact (e.g., equipment purchase decisions typically have greater impact than decisions regarding use of the same equipment, see Stern and Gardner 1981a, 1981b). Third, the distinctions are readily understandable to non-specialists – both in their roles as consumers and in policy processes – so they are likely to be useful in public policy contexts and in designing programs to support behavioral change. It is likely that a great variety of environmentally significant behaviors have certain motives in common and that, at the same time, behavioral types vary systematically in the patterns of factors that influence them (of which personal motives are a subset), as well as in their environmental effects.

15.1   Influences on environmentally significant behavior

Research on environmentally significant behavior in the home focuses on certain private-sphere behaviors of type (c) above: purchases and use of household equipment, goods, and services; the maintenance and use of those goods and services; disposal of wastes, and the like. Personal transportation, though only partly "in the home," also deserves attention (see Gärling and Loukopoulos, chapter 16 in this volume).

Psychologists and economists both study environmentally significant behavior, but tend to begin from different assumptions. The stylized social-psychological approach assumes that the behaviors are expressions of individual values, beliefs, attitudes, and motives; that is, that intent, including individual differences in intent, is a very important determinant of behavior. Other psychologists would add that habit, the willingness and ability to assimilate decision-relevant information, interpersonal influences, and external reinforcements also matter. A stylized economic approach assumes that behavior is rational action in free markets that tends to maximize utility, usually boiled down to money and time (which, as the saying goes, is money). These approaches each illuminate parts of the phenomena of environmentally significant behavior, but neither gives a full picture (Stern 1986).

Even taken together, they do not give a complete picture. Other social scientists point out that environmentally significant behavior in the home is affected by household-level variables and processes, such as income, desires to display household status, the household "life cycle" (Gladhart et al. 1986; Zuiches et al. 1987; Lutzenhiser 1988; Schipper et al. 1989), and beliefs about what makes a "good home" (e.g., Hackett and Lutzenhiser 1991; Shove and Warde 1997). Still others point out the role of actor networks, for example, the combined effects of the actions of developers, builders, planners, mortgage lenders, and contractors on the energy efficiency built into new homes and their appliances (Lutzenhiser et al. 2001). These actions in housing markets have major effects on the environmental impact of living in a home, and determine how much difference individual motives and behavior can make. Individual behavior makes more environmental difference in an energy-inefficient home than in an efficient one, but if a housing market provides energy-efficient homes and appliances, this may make more environmental difference than anything that a population of highly motivated households can do in inefficient homes.

This example illustrates the larger point that the broad context of environmentally significant behavior determines the relative impact of changing different kinds of behavior. In a community with old, energy-inefficient housing, inducing purchase of improvements in the housing stock (e.g., home insulation) can have a major impact, though it is expensive; changing everyday household behavior can also have a major impact, at less financial cost but perhaps requiring significant investments in efforts to induce behavior change. In a community with energy-efficient housing, there may be no room for improvement through financial investment, but some room for improvement through behavior change. In a community with a mixed housing stock, the greatest impact may come from changing different behaviors in different households, depending on the housing stock, the household's ability to invest, and residents' knowledge, skills, and motives.

For understanding the determinants of environmental impact from homes and for inducing change, it is useful to consider four major types of influences on private-sphere behaviors.

15.1.1   Personal motives and beliefs

Psychologists have developed many behavioral theories that focus on the motives (including values, attitudes, and intentions) that may drive individual action. Several such theories have been applied to, or developed for, understanding environmentally significant behavior. The best established of these is probably the Theory of Reasoned Action, now the Theory of Planned Behavior (TPB: Ajzen 1985, 1991). This theory emphasizes the volitional aspects of behavior and specifies a set of variables, including behavior-specific attitudes and perceived behavioral control, which are held to predict behavioral intention and then behavior itself. Evidence consistent with this theory has been provided in numerous studies of environmentally significant behavior (e.g., Kantola, Syme, and Campbell 1982; Jones 1990; Bamberg and Schmidt 1998, 1999, 2003).

Another line of enquiry expands on existing models of altruistic behavior (Schwartz 1973, 1977) and of human values (Schwartz 1994) and has been developed into what is known as the value–belief–norm or VBN theory (Stern and Dietz 1994; Stern, Dietz, Kalof, and Guagnano 1995; Stern *et al.* 1999). This theory treats environmental quality as an emergent attitude object and argues that pro-environmental behavior results when an individual comes to believe that a personal value is threatened and that he or she can relieve that threat by appropriate action. The values and beliefs combine to activate a personal norm, that is, a sense of personal moral obligation to act, that directly affects action (Stern, Dietz, Kalof, and Guagnano 1995, Stern *et al.* 1999). Unlike the Theory of Planned Behavior, which requires an explanatory model for each individual behavior, the value–belief–norm theory postulates a more general factor that can influence a range of behaviors that an individual considers to relieve a particular threat to environmental or altruistic values. Like the TPB, VBN theory includes explanatory variables that affect only specific environmentally relevant behaviors. It holds that personal moral norms are activated when an individual believes that inaction in a particular context would have negative effects on a personal value and when the person sees himself or herself as personally responsible for acting.

Research applying several social-psychological theories in addition to TPB and the VBN theory, including cognitive dissonance theory (e.g., Thøgerson 2004) and Triandis's (1977, 1980) Theory of Interpersonal Behavior (Bamberg and Schmidt 2003), has shown that they can explain variance in specific pro-environmental behaviors. This research has demonstrated that pro-environmental behaviors can be affected by personal commitment and the perceived personal costs and benefits of particular actions (e.g., Katzev and Johnson 1987), as well as by behavior-specific beliefs and personal norms (e.g., Black *et al.* 1985).

Environmentally significant behavior can, of course, also be affected by individuals' non-environmental attitudes and beliefs. For example, purchasers of motor vehicles may consider speed, power, and luggage capacity, all of which increase the environmental impact of using the vehicle. Such considerations may override environmental considerations or push them out of awareness at the time of purchase. Attitudes and beliefs about frugality, luxury, waste, or the importance of spending time with family may also affect environmentally significant behavior in the home. For example, a decision to spend more time as a family may have an environmental impact by reducing separate travel by family members – or by increasing vacation travel together. Acting to reduce household waste out of a motive for frugality has the same environmental effect as doing so out of an environmental protection motive.

Environmentally significant behavior can also be affected by motivational factors at the household level, such as beliefs about what is a "good home" and about the desired presentation of the household to neighbors and guests. Some of these attitudes and beliefs may be culturally conditioned. Thus, some of the observed differences in environmentally significant behavior among different socio-cultural groups, discussed below, may be mediated by different motives, attitudes, and beliefs.

15.1.2   External or contextual forces

A variety of factors outside the individual and household also affect environmentally significant behaviors. These include the monetary or financial incentives and costs associated with behaviors that are the standard focus of economic analyses, as well as: interpersonal influences (e.g., persuasion, modeling); community expectations; advertising; the availability and ease of interpreting information on the environmental and personal consequences of choices; government regulations; other legal and institutional factors (e.g., contract restrictions on occupants of rental housing); the physical difficulty of specific actions; capabilities and constraints provided by technology and the built environment (e.g., building design, availability of bicycle paths, solar energy technology); the availability of public policies to support behavior (e.g., curbside recycling programs); and various other features of the broad social, economic, and political context (e.g., the price of oil, the sensitivity of government to public and interest group pressures, interest rates in financial markets). It is worth noting that a contextual factor may have different effects on people with different attitudes or beliefs. For example, the higher price of "organic" produce may be an economic barrier to purchase for some people, while for others it is a marker of a superior product.

An important aspect of the behavioral context is the role of "actor networks" (Lutzenhiser *et al.* 2001; Lutzenhiser Associates 2004) – the collection of individuals and organizations that affect householders' choices or the choices that are made for them, which shape the environmental impacts of behavior in the home. For example, a study of energy use in new commercial buildings concluded that the key decisions determining energy efficiency were made by developers in their interactions with bankers, and not by building occupants, architects, or builders (Lutzenhiser *et al.* 2001). The parallel actor network determining the energy efficiency of residences has not been carefully examined.

15.1.3 Personal capabilities and constraints

A third type of causal factor includes the knowledge and skills required for particular actions (e.g., mechanical knowledge, for energy-conserving home repairs, or the ability to search the Internet for useful information), the availability of time to act, and more general capabilities, resources, and constraints, such as literacy, money, social status and power, and household size and life cycle. Information processing capacity is an important factor in decision making. It is not only that some people can handle more information than others; at least as important is that few people have sufficient time and attention to assimilate all the available information that is relevant to rational consumer choice (National Research Council 1984; Stern 1986). Consequently, consumers typically follow simple rules, such as maintaining the status quo, copying neighbors, or accepting the recommendations of prominent and trusted sources, rather than considering and evaluating a lot of information. The results may or may not be the same behaviors that would follow from a rational utility calculation.

Socio-demographic variables such as age, educational attainment, race, and income may be meaningful in part as indicators or proxies for personal capabilities. Although these variables have very limited explanatory power for many environmentally significant behaviors (e.g., Dietz *et al.* 1998), they may be important for behaviors that depend strongly on particular capabilities, such as environmental citizenship behaviors and environmental activism, which are positively associated with income and other socio-demographic variables in some studies (e.g., Stern *et al.* 1999). Such findings reflect the fact that the efficacy of environmental citizenship depends on an individual's social and economic resources.

15.1.4 Habit or routine

Much of environmentally significant behavior is habitual. Behavior change often requires breaking old habits and becomes established by creating new ones (Dahlstrand and Biel 1997). Habit, in the form of standard operating procedure, is also a key factor in environmentally significant organizational behavior. The performance characteristics of homes and household equipment, sometimes called embodied energy or consumption, have an effect similar to that of habits, in that whenever someone needs the service provided by a home heating or cooling system or an appliance, the environmental consequences of operation are largely predetermined. The environmental impact of each usage is the same, and is driven by the performance characteristics of the product, such as its energy efficiency or emissions per unit usage. For example, a household can change the overall environmental consequences of keeping warm in winter by turning down the heat or by changing to a heating system with more environmentally beneficial performance characteristics. Thus, choices about the purchase of household equipment have habit-like consequences in that they affect subsequent usage behaviors in a way that is automatic and often outside awareness. The analogue to a change of habit is a change of the equipment.

The evidence suggests that the relative importance of different types of causal variables depends on the behavior (Gardner and Stern 1996; Stern 2000). Expensive behaviors, such as changing home heating systems, are likely to be strongly influenced by monetary factors; behaviors governed by convenience, such as reducing automobile use in the suburbs, are likely to be strongly influenced by public policy supports (e.g., for alternative transport modes); behaviors that require specialized skills are likely to be strongly influenced by those capabilities; and so forth. Such hypotheses, though fairly obvious, do not go without saying. They offer a good starting point for efforts to understand particular environmentally significant behaviors.

15.2   Energy use in homes: what do we know?

Energy use is one of the most important environmentally significant behaviors in homes. It provides an instructive case example of what is known about such behaviors. Much of the variation in energy use among homes is predetermined by the physical features of the housing unit (e.g., its size and type of construction) and the physical and technological attributes of its energy-using equipment, chiefly its heating and cooling systems and major appliances. In one early study, physical features accounted for 54 percent of the variance in energy use in a sample of homes (Sonderegger 1978). This percentage undoubtedly varies across samples, but in most populations of homes, it is probably large (see also Stern and Gardner 1981a). Significant amounts of variance can also be accounted for by non-physical factors: households in homes with similar physical attributes may vary in energy consumption by as much as 3:1 (Hackett and Lutzenhiser 1991; Lutzenhiser 1992, 1993; Schipper *et al.* 1989; Shove *et al.* 1998).

15.2.1   Household characteristics

Variation in energy use is strongly associated with household composition and income. For example, in a study in the US state of California, households with incomes above $100k/yr used 82% more electricity and 66% more gas than households with incomes under $25k/yr. Households with five or more members used 69% more electricity and 51% more gas than single-member households. Old people living alone used 30% more electricity and 88% more gas than young people living alone (Lutzenhiser *et al.* 2005). Such household characteristics undoubtedly affect energy use indirectly, through their effects on both the physical attributes of homes (e.g., larger and more affluent households choose to live in larger homes) and their operation (e.g., older people may experience more discomfort than younger people when the home gets cold or warm).

The connection between household characteristics and energy consumption is mediated in part by households' social and cultural attributes (Schipper *et al.* 1989; Lutzenhiser 1992, 1997). For example, in the California study mentioned above, middle-aged African-American couples with children, living in single-family houses, and with incomes between $100k and $150k/yr used 35% more electricity and 67% more gas than similar Asian-American households (Lutzenhiser *et al.* 2005). Such differences are undoubtedly mediated by some combination of differences in the physical characteristics of homes and differences in ownership, maintenance, and use of appliances and other household equipment.

15.2.2   Interpersonal and psychological factors

It is reasonable to hypothesize that these socioeconomic, demographic, and cultural differences in energy use are mediated by interpersonal and psychological processes within households that directly affect household choices, but surprisingly little research exists on how such processes affect major home technology choices such as those concerning the size of a housing unit or the adoption of home heating and cooling technologies. Most of the behavioral research on energy conservation, as with other environmentally significant behavior in the home, has examined frequently repeated behaviors, mostly in the operation of home equipment. It has examined these behaviors mainly as a function of individuals' values, beliefs, and attitudes. The conclusions from this research seem robust across types of environmentally significant behavior. They are summarized later in this review.

15.3   Interventions to reduce household energy consumption

It is useful to distinguish interventions that rely on communication and diffusion (Kauffmann-Hayoz *et al.* 2001), such as information, education, and the use of interpersonal influences, from the traditional policy instruments of regulation, economic influence, and provision of infrastructure. What is distinctive about communication and diffusion instruments is their primary reliance on language and symbols. Of course, different kinds of instruments can be combined. Psychologists and economists have both considered a range of policy instruments. However, psychologists' comparative advantage in knowledge is about the communication and diffusion instruments, whereas economists' is about the economic and regulatory ones.

15.3.1 Communication and diffusion instruments

A small body of psychological research, mostly dating from the 1970s and 1980s, has directly examined interventions to reduce energy use in homes. Abrahamse *et al.* (2005) recently reviewed studies that appeared in peer-reviewed psychology journals and found thirty-eight, only seven of which were published since 1990. These studies test the effects of interventions, most of them communication and diffusion interventions, that various psychological theories predict would change behavior. Some of the interventions, such as eliciting a personal commitment to cut energy use by a specified percentage or using neighbors as behavioral models, are not readily transferable into policy on a large scale. The review found that providing information about how to save energy increased knowledge, but generic information, such as is offered in mass media campaigns, had little or no effect on behavior or energy consumption. Tailored information, such as that provided by home energy audits, was successful in some studies. Feedback (providing householders with frequent or continuous data on their energy use) had fairly consistent positive effects, with an effect size often amounting to between 0.5 and 1.0 of the standard deviation within experimental groups. More frequent feedback was more effective, and the review concluded that combinations of intervention types were more promising than their components alone. Monetary rewards were found to change behavior, but only temporarily. Most of these studies were small, and many did not quantify effect sizes or measure long-term effects.

Other bodies of research on communication and diffusion instruments, some of them considerably more extensive than that on energy conservation, can offer useful lessons for energy policy. Many of these have been examined in papers commissioned by the Committee on the Human Dimensions of Global Change at the US National Research Council (2002). They include research on health-promoting behavior (Glanz *et al.* 1997; Valente and Schuster 2002), disaster preparedness (Mileti and Peek 2002), social marketing (McKenzie-Mohr and Smith 1999), and environmental education (Ramsey and Hungerford 2002). These lines of research suggest that policy instruments are most likely to be effective when they "provide just what is needed to overcome the barriers to obtaining the [policy] objective" (Stern 2002:201). Thus, communication and diffusion instruments are likely to be most effective when target behaviors are seriously impeded by lack of information, social support, and so forth. Energy informational interventions typically fail when they do not address non-informational barriers to behavioral change (National Research Council 1984; Gardner and Stern 1996; Lutzenhiser 2002).

The various lines of research on communication and diffusion instruments suggest that they are most likely to be effective when they are designed from the audience's perspective, use multiple communication channels, build on direct interpersonal communication, apply psychological principles of message design, set realistic expectations for change, and are modified on the basis of information on how they are working (Stern 2002). The public health research also suggests that, over time, small changes in behavior can be significant in policy terms because they can prime people for larger changes later, as well as because of their aggregate effect (Valente and Schuster 2002).

15.3.2 Economic instruments

Investments in energy efficiency, particularly in the residential sector, are often far less than the levels that would be justified if energy users followed economic principles of cost minimization (Office of Technology Assessment 1982; Hirst *et al*. 1986; Stern *et al*. 1986). There are several likely reasons, including lack of accurate information, lack of time or skills to evaluate available information, distrust of the suppliers of consumer services and information, lack of capability to act on the information and incentive, and inability to observe and assess the benefits of the investments. In addition, cost minimization is only one of the many motives that can affect the consumer choices that shape energy use (National Research Council 1984). For all these reasons, it should not be surprising that financial incentives yield less behavioral change than would be optimal in narrow economic terms.

A review of energy conservation incentive programs from the 1980s (Stern *et al*. 1986), when many incentives were being offered in the United States, still provides useful insights. The review demonstrated that although larger incentives for investments in home energy efficiency increased the proportion of households that made investments, participation varied tremendously depending on how the programs were marketed and implemented. This conclusion was most strongly demonstrated by the results of three natural experiments in which a region-wide incentive program was implemented independently by each of the energy utility companies in the region. In each case, the proportion of eligible homes that took advantage of the incentive varied by a factor of more than ten between the most and least successful utility companies. The more successful incentive programs tended to be operated by trusted organizations and aggressively marketed by word of mouth and other attention-getting methods. The way in which the incentive was provided (grant or loan subsidy) also affected participation independently of the size of the incentive.

The evidence on interventions for energy conservation is entirely consistent with evidence from the study of other environmental interventions at the individual and household level. The effectiveness of interventions depends on the fit between the intervention and the set of barriers to behavioral change in the target population (Gardner and Stern 1996; Stern 2002). Generally, single interventions, such as providing information or financial incentives, are well suited to removing single barriers to change. Because there are typically multiple factors maintaining existing behavioral patterns, studies of single-factor interventions often report low overall effectiveness or great variability across target populations or implementing organizations. The best strategy for behavior change begins with detailed understanding of the target behaviors and households and the factors that impede behavioral change. Interventions should be designed to address all the significant barriers, which often means employing strategies familiar to psychologists and to economists in combination. It may also mean working through the relevant actor networks (e.g., for energy-efficient appliances, manufacturers, home equipment retailers, appliance repair companies, companies offering home-improvement loans, and so forth) to determine what would change the behavior of the various actors in the networks and through that, energy use in homes.

15.4 Conclusions

The many influences on environmentally significant behavior appear to work in different ways and to affect each other. For example, broad environmental values and attitudes may create a general predisposition to act, which may be shaped into specific action largely by personal capabilities and contextual forces. A new context may make old habits untenable and lead a person to construct new ones by paying renewed attention to values and attitudes as a basis for choosing the behaviors that then become new habits (Dahlstrand and Biel 1997). Or, financial incentives may favor behaviors that nevertheless do not occur unless information makes individuals aware that the incentive is available (Stern 1999). In short, research indicates that the causes of environmentally significant behavior are varied – more complex than any single disciplinary analysis focusing only on economic, psychological, or social factors would suggest. The following general conclusions seem to be strongly supported by the evidence:

1. **The influences on environmentally significant behavior are more varied than reflected in most psychological or economic research**. They can be roughly classified as shown in table 15.1.
2. **The pattern of influences – which factors matter most – can vary greatly across behaviors and places**. Thus, one should not expect that the influences found to be strongest in one study generalize across behaviors or across contexts. A key question for research is to find the principles governing generalization – which findings generalize, and to what.
3. **The strongest influences on behavior are often contextual**. These are generally the factors listed at the top of table 15.1 (see over) that are emphasized by engineers, economists, sociologists, political scientists, and policy makers. Psychologists rarely examine more than a few of these strong contextual influences on behavior, and have instead focused their

Table 15.1 *Variables influencing environmentally significant behaviors*

Contextual factors (constraint and facilitation)
- Available technology
- Embodied environmental impact (e.g., energy efficiency of buildings, vehicles; materials in consumer products)
- Legal and regulatory requirements
- Material costs and rewards (payoffs)
- Convenience (e.g., of public transit, recycling)
- Social norms and expectations

Personal capabilities
- Financial resources
- Literacy
- Social status
- Behavior-specific knowledge and skills

Habit and routine

Attitudinal factors
- Personal values
- General environmentalist predisposition (abstract norms)
- Behavior-specific (concrete) norms and beliefs
- Non-environmental attitudes (e.g., about product attributes)
- Perceived costs and benefits of action

---

attention on personal and interpersonal variables toward the bottom of the table. It is no surprise, then, that psychological research has been marginalized in these other, more influential, fields. It will continue to be so until psychology is better integrated into an interdisciplinary field of human-environment science (Stern 1993) that also addresses contextual variables that go beyond the interpersonal context of behavior.

4. **The more a behavior is shaped by technology, infrastructure, regulation, financial cost, convenience, and other contextual factors, the weaker the effect of personal variables** (Black *et al*. 1985; Guagnano *et al*. 1995). To put this another way, the strength of psychological influences varies from moderate to weak to almost non-existent, dependent on the strength of non-psychological factors. Effective laws and regulations, strong financial incentives or penalties, irresistible technology, powerful social norms, and the like can leave little room for personal factors to affect behavior. Control over these strong influences means control over behavior – at least in the short run. This does not mean that individual-level causes do not matter, but that their importance does not always lie where psychologists look for it. For example, the effect of well-delivered information on behavior is often minimal, but it can be dramatic as part of an incentive program (Stern *et al*. 1986). Another example is the

possibility that individuals can change their contexts over time by changing laws, policies, financial incentives, technology, and so on. Thus, psychological factors may affect behavior in the home in interaction with other forces, or indirectly, through their effects on political behavior. The pattern of influences on behavior also implies that psychological variables operate in certain niches. For instance, when contextual influences are weak, the personal factors at the bottom of table 15.1 are likely to include the strongest influences on behavior. When contextual factors cannot be changed, the personal factors may provide the only levers on behavior, even if they only apply in restricted situations. And personal factors are important in certain specific contexts, as noted below.

5. **Although behavioral models typically presume that behavior is chosen, choice models apply only in limited situations**. Much of the determination of environmentally significant individual consumption is embodied in infrastructure or technology. People sometimes choose technology, as when they pick a new home or car, but when they do so, environmental aspects are often not considered or are overwhelmed by more pressing concerns. Environmental impacts are nevertheless embodied in the equipment from that point on. In addition, much of everyday consumption is driven by habit, not conscious choice. The implication is that the favored variables of psychologists and economists are important mainly at the restricted places and times when choice models apply.

6. **Choices, when they are made, are not often carefully considered**. People who want to make the "green" choice or the money-saving choice rarely conduct the full analysis of choices and consequences that an idealized rational actor would. The idea of information economics recognizes this. Psychological research specifies the range of cognitive short-cuts people use, including models provided by neighbors, communications from trusted organizations, and other effort-reducing heuristics. This phenomenon probably accounts for the great importance of marketing and implementation to the effectiveness of incentive programs for home energy efficiency.

7. **The effects of many psychological causal variables on specific behaviors are highly indirect**. However, some of these variables can potentially influence a wide variety of behaviors. Social-psychological research is helping to reveal the workings of the personal factors influencing environmentally significant individual behavior, though strong debates continue in the field about which theoretical model best accounts for the evidence. The model in figure 15.1, which represents concepts from the value–belief–norm (VBN) theory of environmentally significant behavior (Stern *et al.* 1999), has considerable support from the available research and is useful in describing important personal influences and in thinking about influences that bear not only on single environmental behaviors, but also on broader classes of behaviors. It is a partial theory, focusing only on the role of

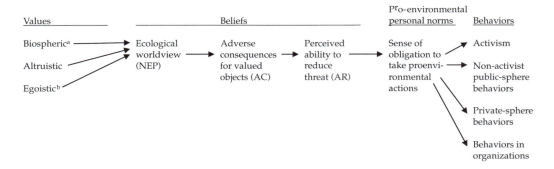

^a Arrows represent postulated direct effects. Direct effects may also be observed on variables more than one level downstream from a causal variable.

^b Empirically, measures of egoistic values have been negatively correlated with indicators of environmentalism.

Figure 15.1 A schematic representation of variables in the value–belief–norm theory of environmentalism. Reprinted from Stern, P. "Toward a coherent theory of environmentally significant behavior," *Journal of Social Issues*, 56, p. 412, Copyright 2000, with permission from Blackwell Publishing

personal influences on behavior. A key element in the model is the notion that individual choice can be driven by personal norms, that is, an internalized sense of obligation to act in a certain way. Personal norms for specific pro-environmental actions (recycling, reducing car use, producing less household waste, etc.) are activated when an individual believes that violating them would have adverse effects on things the individual values (called awareness of consequences, or AC, in the research literature) and when the person believes that by taking action, he or she would bear significant responsibility for those consequences (called ascription of responsibility, or AR, in the literature) (Schwartz 1973, 1977). Research shows that with behaviors that are not strongly constrained by contextual forces, these AC and AR beliefs are associated with a sense of personal obligation and, in turn, with environmentally significant behavior. Although the evidence is weaker for lack of studies, there is evidence that interventions that change AC and AR beliefs also affect behavior. The weaker the contextual influences, the stronger these personal-norm effects are. Table 15.2 presents the VBN model in the context of other influences on behavior (Stern and Oskamp 1987; Gardner and Stern 1996).

This model suggests that it is possible to influence individual behavior, within the limits set by context, habit, personal capability, and the like, by making people aware of the consequences, particularly adverse ones, for things they value, and by showing them that their personal behavior is important enough to make a difference. People who do not see connections between their behavior and such consequences or who believe that their

Table 15.2 *A causal model of environmentally relevant behavior. Adapted from Stern, P. and Oskamp, S. 1987. Managing scarce environmental resources. Vol. II, pp. 1043–88. In D. Stokols (ed.),* Handbook of Environmental Psychology. *Reprinted with permission from John Wiley & Sons, Ltd*

Level of causality	Type of variable	Examples
7	Social background and general personal capabilities	Race, socioeconomic status, financial resources
7	External conditions (incentives and constraints)	Prices, regulations, technology, convenience
7	Social influences	Social norms, advertising
6	*Basic values*	*Egoism, altruism, openness to change, maintaining tradition*
5	*General beliefs and norms*	*Belief that the environment is fragile or resilient; attitude about environmental protection*
4	*Behavior-specific attitudes, beliefs, and personal norms*	*Belief that recycling is good for environment, sense of personal obligation to reduce fossil fuel use; beliefs about the personal and environmental costs and benefits of particular behaviors*
3	Behavior-specific knowledge	Knowing which packaging is biodegradable; which household behaviors emit air pollutants; how to petition legislators
2	Behavioral commitment	Decision to travel by bus
1	Environmentally relevant behavior	Automobile purchase

The parts of the table in italics are those elaborated by the VBN theory.
Variables at higher-numbered levels of causality have the potential for direct influence on variables at each lower-numbered level. Sometimes, the most important effects skip levels of causality. For example, many external conditions (level 7) influence behavior mainly through their direct effects on behavior-specific knowledge and beliefs (level 3).

actions are so insignificant in the scheme of things as not to matter will not be motivated to act by an internalized sense of obligation. It will require external motivations or pressures to get them to change. The VBN model also suggests that calling attention to certain values can influence behavior. References to consequences, responsibility, and broad values are often seen in pro-environmental social marketing campaigns, but systematic research is lacking regarding the effectiveness of such appeals.

The VBN model is incomplete and likely to undergo modification as a result of further research. The point it is cited to illustrate, however, is probably more robust: most of the personal variables of interest to environmental psychologists are likely to have practical importance for environmental consumption behaviors only under very limited conditions. Elaborating psychological theories of environmentally significant behavior is important for basic understanding, but in order to use them to suggest good practical lines of intervention in consumption, such models must be considered within the larger context of influences on individual behavior.

8. **The most important practical applications of psychological interventions to behavior in the home probably lie in niches between powerful contextual variables**. Psychological variables make the most difference when behavior is not strongly constrained by regulation, habit, matters of economic cost and convenience, and the like. To put it another way, the choice models of psychology – the ones that attribute behavior to values, attitudes, norms, beliefs, and the other favorite psychological causal variables – matter more when people make conscious choices (e.g., changing homes, buying cars or major appliances, changing jobs, voting, reconsidering old habits). Even then, choices are more constrained than psychological models typically allow. Thus, it may be that psychological variables matter enough to be of practical use only in very limited situations. But they may be very important nevertheless, because some of the choices made in these situations, particularly the purchases of major household equipment and the establishment of environmentally significant habits, determine the environmental impact of many future behaviors. It follows that interventions based on psychological variables – information, persuasion, social marketing, and the like – are most likely to make a significant environmental difference in those situations.

For example, if people consult their values primarily when they are making difficult choices or when their preferences are unclear (Stern *et al.* 1995; Dietz *et al.* 1998), it may make a lot of difference to make particular values salient at those times. Examples can easily be found in marketing. A recent negative example is an automobile advertisement from the Mazda Corporation that ran on United States television in 2005. A sports car is traveling fast along a winding road into the mountains with a catchy tune in the background and the words, "zoom, zoom, zoom." The ad makes salient the value of stimulation seeking – openness to change, in the terminology of value theory (Schwartz 1994) – at the point of considering the purchase of an automobile. If this sort of value appeal is effective, well-crafted appeals to values may also be effective in promoting more environmentally benign forms of transportation. Similarly, appeals to the consequences of behavior and to personal responsibility that evoke personal norms may also make an environmental difference when they reach people at important times of choice.

9. **The most productive approach to understanding and influencing environmentally significant behavior in the home is an interdisciplinary**

one that seeks to understand the full range of causes of behavior, and their interactions, and to base interventions on that understanding. Such an approach would help overcome the blind spots in disciplinary analysis in both psychology and economics (Stern 1986), build the much-needed interdisciplinary science of human-environment interactions (Stern 1993), and address pressing global environmental concerns.

15.5 References

Abrahamse, W., L. Steg, C. Vlek, and T. Rothengatter 2005. A review of intervention studies aimed at household energy conservation. *Journal of Environmental Psychology*, 25, 273–91.

Ajzen, I. 1985. From intentions to actions: A theory of planned behavior. In J. Kuhl and J. Beckman, eds., *Action-Control: From Cognition to Behavior*, pp. 11–39. Heidelberg: Springer.

1991. The theory of planned behavior. *Organizational Decision and Human Decision Process*, 50, 179–211.

Bamberg, S., and P. Schmidt 1998. Changing travel mode choice as rational choice: Results from a longitudinal intervention study. *Rationality and Society*, 10, 223–52.

1999. Regulating transport: Behavioral changes in the field. *Journal of Consumer Policy*, 22, 479–509.

2003. Incentives, morality, or habit? Predicting students' car use for university routes with the models of Ajzen, Schwartz, and Triandis. *Environment and Behavior*, 35, 264–85.

Black, J. S., P. C. Stern, and J. T. Elworth 1985. Personal and contextual influences on household energy adaptations. *Journal of Applied Psychology*, 70, 3–21.

Bratt, C. 1999. Consumers' environmental behavior: Generalized, sector-based, or compensatory? *Environment and Behavior*, 31, 28–44.

Dahlstrand, U., and A. Biel 1997. Pro-environmental habits: Propensity levels in behavioral change. *Journal of Applied Social Psychology*, 27, 588–601.

Dietz, T., P. C. Stern, and G. Guagnano 1998. Social structural and social psychological determinants of environmental concern. *Environment and Behavior*, 30, 450–71.

Gardner, G. T., and P. C. Stern 1996. *Environmental Problems and Human Behavior*. Needham Heights, MA: Allyn & Bacon.

Gladhart, P. M., B. M. Morrison, and J. J. Zuiches 1986. *Energy and Families: Lifestyles and Energy Consumption in Lansing*. Family Energy Project, Institute for Family and Child Study. Lansing: Michigan State University Press.

Glanz, K., F. M. Lewis, and B. K. Rimer, eds. 1997. *Health Behavior and Health Education*. San Francisco: Jossey-Bass.

Guagnano, G., P. C. Stern, and T. Dietz 1995. Influences on attitude–behavior relationships: A natural experiment with curbside recycling. *Environment and Behavior*, 27, 699–718.

Hackett, B., and L. Lutzenhiser 1991. Social structures and economic conduct: Interpreting variations in household energy consumption. *Sociological Forum*, 6, 449–70.

Hirst, E., J. Clinton, H. Geller, and W. Kroner 1986. *Energy Efficiency in Buildings: Current Status and Future Directions.* Washington, DC: American Council for an Energy-Efficient Economy.

Jones, R. E. 1990. Understanding paper recycling in an institutionally supportive setting: An application of the theory of reasoned action. *Journal of Environmental Systems*, 19, 307–21.

Kaiser, F. G. 1998. A general measure of ecological behavior. *Journal of Applied Social Psychology*, 28, 395–422.

Kantola, S. J., G. J. Syme, and N. A. Campbell 1982. The role of individual differences and external variables in a test of the sufficiency of Fishbein's model to explain behavioral intentions to conserve water. *Journal of Applied Psychology*, 12, 70–83.

Katzev, R. D., and T. R. Johnson 1987. *Promoting Energy Conservation: An Analysis of Behavioral Techniques.* Boulder, CO: Westview Press.

Kauffmann-Hayoz, R., C. Bättig, S. Bruppacher, R. Defila, A. Di Gioilio, U. Friedrich, M. Garbely, H. Gutscher, C. Jäggi, M. Jegen, A. Müller, and N. North 2001. A typology of instruments for the promotion of sustainable development. In R. Kauffmann-Hayoz and H. Gutscher, eds., *Changing Things – Moving People: Strategies for Promoting Sustainable Development at the Local Level.* Basel: Birkhäuser.

Lutzenhiser, L. 1988. Energy, technology and everyday life: A cultural theory of energy use. Ph.D. dissertation, Department of Sociology, University of California, Davis.

1992. A cultural model of household energy consumption. *Energy – The International Journal*, 17, 47–60.

1993. Social and behavioral aspects of energy use. *Annual Review of Energy and the Environment*, 18, 247–89.

1997. Social structure, culture, and technology: Modeling the driving forces of household energy consumption. In National Research Council, *Environmentally Significant Consumption: Research Directions*, pp. 77–91. P. C. Stern, T. Dietz, V. W. Ruttan, R. H. Socolow, and J. L. Sweeney, eds. Washington, DC: National Academy Press.

2002. Marketing household energy conservation: The message and the reality. In National Research Council, *New Tools for Environmental Protection: Education, Information, and Voluntary Measures*, pp. 49–66. Committee on the Human Dimensions of Global Change, T. Dietz and P. C. Stern, eds. Washington, DC: National Academy Press.

Lutzenhiser, L., N. W. Biggart, R. Kunkle, T. D. Beamish, and T. Burr 2001. Market structure and energy efficiency: The case of new commercial buildings. Washington State University. Report to the California Institute for Energy Efficiency.

Lutzenhiser, L., S. Lutzenhiser, and A. Eickman 2005. Looking at lifestyle: The impacts of American ways of life on energy/resource demands and pollution patterns. Unpublished manuscript.

Lutzenhiser Associates 2004. Social science literature review. AB 549 Intervention-relevant work. Prepared for the California Energy Commission. Portland, OR: Author. November 15.

McKenzie-Mohr, D., and W. Smith 1999. *Fostering Sustainable Behavior: An Introduction to Community-Based Social Marketing.* Gabriola Island, British Columbia, Canada: New Society Press.

Mileti, D. S., and L. A. Peek 2002. Understanding individual and social characteristics in the promotion of household disaster preparedness. In National Research Council, *New Tools for Environmental Protection: Education, Information, and Voluntary Measures*, pp. 125–40. Committee on the Human Dimensions of Global Change, T. Dietz and P. C. Stern, eds. Washington, DC: National Academy Press.

National Research Council 1984. *Energy Use: The Human Dimension.* Committee on the Behavioral and Social Aspects of Energy Consumption and Production, P. C. Stern and E. Aronson, eds. New York: Freeman.

2002. *New Tools for Environmental Protection: Education, Information, and Voluntary Measures.* Committee on the Human Dimensions of Global Change, T. Dietz and P. C. Stern, eds. Washington, DC: National Academy Press.

Office of Technology Assessment 1982. *Energy Efficiency in Buildings in Cities.* Washington, DC: Author.

Poortinga, W., L. Steg, and C. Vlek 2004. Values, environmental concern, and environmental behavior: A study into household energy use. *Environment and Behavior*, 36, 70–93.

Ramsey, J., and H. R. Hungerford 2002. Perspectives on environmental education in the United States. In National Research Council, *New Tools for Environmental Protection: Education, Information, and Voluntary Measures*, pp. 147–60. Committee on the Human Dimensions of Global Change, T. Dietz and P. C. Stern, eds. Washington, DC: National Academy Press.

Schipper, L., S. Bartlett, D. Hawk, and E. Vine 1989. Linking lifestyles and energy use: A matter of time. *Annual Review of Energy*, 14, 273–320.

Schwartz, S. H. 1973. Normative explanations of helping behavior: A critique, proposal, and empirical test. *Journal of Experimental Social Psychology*, 9, 349–64.

1977. Normative influences on altruism. In L. Berkowitz, ed., *Advances in Experimental Social Psychology*, vol. X, pp. 221–79.

1994. Are there universal aspects in the structure and contents of human values? *Journal of Social Issues*, 50(4), 19–46.

Shove, E., L. Lutzenhiser, S. Guy, B. Hackett, and H. Wilhite 1998. Energy and social systems. In S. Rayner and E. Malone, eds., *Human Choice and Climate Change*, pp. 201–34. Columbus, OH: Battelle Press.

Shove, E., and A. Warde 1997. Inconspicuous consumption: The sociology of consumption, lifestyles, and the environment. In R Dunlap, F. Buttel, P. Dickens, and A. Gijswijt, eds., *Sociological Theory and the Environment*, pp. 230–51. Lanham, MD: Rowman and Littlefield.

Sonderegger, R. C. 1978. Movers and stayers: The resident's contribution to variation across houses in energy consumption for space heating. In R. H. Socolow, ed., *Saving Energy in the Home: Princeton's Experiments at Twin Rivers*, pp. 207–30. Cambridge, MA: Ballinger Press.

Stern, P. C. 1986. Blind spots in policy analysis: What economics doesn't say about energy use. *Journal of Policy Analysis and Management*, 5, 200–27.

1993. A second environmental science: Human-environment interactions. *Science*, 260, 1897–9.

1997. Toward a working definition of consumption for environmental research and policy. In P. C. Stern, T. Dietz, V. R. Ruttan, R. H. Socolow, and J. L. Sweeney, eds., *Environmentally Significant Consumption: Research Directions*, pp. 12–35. Washington, DC: National Academy Press.

1999. Information, incentives, and proenvironmental consumer behavior. *Journal of Consumer Policy*, 22, 461–78.

2000. Toward a coherent theory of environmentally significant behavior. *Journal of Social Issues*, 56, 407–24.

2002. Changing behavior in households and communities: What have we learned? In National Research Council, *New Tools for Environmental Protection: Education, Information, and Voluntary Measures*, pp. 201–11. Committee on the Human Dimensions of Global Change, T. Dietz and P. C. Stern, eds. Washington, DC: National Academy Press.

Stern, P. C., E. Aronson, J. M. Darley, D. H. Hill, E. Hirst, W. Kempton, and T. J. Wilbanks 1986. The effectiveness of incentives for residential energy conservation. *Evaluation Review*, 10, 147–76.

Stern, P. C., and T. Dietz 1994. The value basis of environmental concern. *Journal of Social Issues*, 50(3), 65–84.

Stern, P. C., T. Dietz, T. Abel, G. A. Guagnano, and L. Kalof 1999. A value-belief-norm theory of support for social movements: The case of environmentalism. *Human Ecology Review*, 6, 81–97.

Stern, P. C., T. Dietz, L. Kalof, and G. Guagnano 1995. Values, beliefs, and proenvironmental action: Attitude formation toward emergent attitude objects. *Journal of Applied Social Psychology*, 25, 1611–36.

Stern, P. C., and G. T. Gardner 1981a. Psychological research and energy policy. *American Psychologist*, 36, 329–42.

1981b. The place of behavior change in managing environmental problems. *Zeitschrift für Umweltpolitik*, 2, 213–39.

Stern, P. C., and S. Oskamp 1987. Managing scarce environmental resources. In D. Stokols, ed., *Handbook of Environmental Psychology*, vol. II, pp. 1043–88. New York: Wiley.

Thøgerson, J. 2004. A cognitive dissonance interpretation of consistencies and inconsistencies in environmentally responsible behavior. *Journal of Environmental Psychology*, 24, 93–103.

Thøgerson, J., and F. Ölander 2006. To what degree are environmentally beneficial choices reflective of a general conservation stance? *Environment and Behavior*, 38, 550–69.

Triandis, H. C. 1977. *Interpersonal Behavior*. Monterey, CA: Brooks-Cole.

1980. Values, attitudes, and interpersonal behavior. In E. Howe and M. M. Page, eds., *Nebraska Symposium on Motivation 1979*, pp. 195–259. Lincoln: University of Nebraska Press.

Valente, T. W., and D. V. Schuster 2002. The public health perspective for communicating environmental issues. In National Research Council, *New Tools for Environmental Protection: Education, Information, and Voluntary Measures*, pp. 105–24. Committee on the Human Dimensions of Global Change, T. Dietz and P. C. Stern, eds. Washington, DC: National Academy Press.

Zuiches, J. J., P. Gladhart, and B. Morrison 1987. *Energy and Families: Lifestyles and Energy Consumption*. Lansing: Michigan State University Press.

16 Economic and psychological determinants of car ownership and use

TOMMY GÄRLING AND PETER LOUKOPOULOS

16.1 Introduction

In this chapter we will try to answer two questions: why are automobiles purchased, and why are automobiles, when they are owned, used to such a great extent? We argue that economic factors (including time savings) play an important role. Yet, psychological factors may play an even more decisive role. Following a brief overview of historical trends in private car ownership and use (section 16.2), determinants of car use will be analysed in a following section (section 16.3).

Substantial environmental and societal costs of private car use, such as congestion, noise, air pollution, and depletion of energy, are expected future consequences of the worldwide increasing trend in car ownership and use (Goodwin, 1996; Greene and Wegener, 1997). In many urban areas, these consequences are already being felt, leading to various policy measures for reducing or changing private car use being placed high on the political agenda. In section 16.4 we describe and classify a number of such policy measures. Following this classification, in section 16.5 we review evidence of these policy measures' effectiveness, public acceptability, and political feasibility.

16.2 Historical trends in car ownership and use

The automobile has drastically altered the development of the world like few other human inventions. Furthermore, even though cars were available at the beginning of the twentieth century, it was only in the years after the Second World War with the subsequent spread of affluence and the acceleration of auto-mobile mass production that ownership was brought within the reach of most households in the industrialized world. Car ownership has been shown to be related to household socio-economic characteristics (e.g., income, household composition, employment status), the characteristics of the transport system

Financial support for the preparation of this chapter was obtained through grants from the Swedish Agency for Innovation Systems (No. 2002–00434) and the Swedish Research Council for Environment, Agricultural Sciences, and Spatial Planning (No. 25.9/2001–1763). We thank our collaborators Satoshi Fujii and Cecilia Jakobsson.

(e.g., car purchase costs, access to public transport), and attributes of residential location (e.g., population density, access to services and amenities) (see, for example, Dargay and Vythoulkas, 1999; Giuliano and Dargay, 2006; Train, 1980). Much research has also documented the trends in ownership and use. For example, Bonsall (2000) provides data showing that car ownership in the UK rose from 30% of households in 1960 to 70% in 1995. Pucher (1999) provides evidence of a similarly large increase for the USA: per capita car ownership increased from 0.31 in 1960 to 0.65 in 1996. Considering only licensed drivers, this trend is particularly alarming, as noted by Southworth (2001), who calculates that an average of more than one vehicle per licensed driver has already been reached. Such a growth in car ownership is not limited to these Anglo-Saxon countries, to which Australia and Canada can be added with increases in cars per capita for the period 1970 to 1992 from 0.31 to 0.45 and 0.31 to 0.49, respectively (Dargay and Gately, 1999). Similar trends were observed for other industrialized countries and, causing most concern, similar and even more extreme trends were observed for countries only just beginning the industrialization process (e.g., China) or which are to some extent industrialized but are beginning to experience income growth and a spread of affluence (e.g., South Korea, Taiwan) (Dargay and Gately, 1999). Indeed, according to Sperling and Claussen (2004), the fastest growth has been observed in Latin America and Asia, with vehicle sales in China, for example, having increased by more than 50% per year in recent years (from 700,000 in 2001 to 1.1 million in 2002, and about 1.7 million in 2003).

The trends with respect to automobile use are equally alarming. Surveying the Swedish domestic context, Vilhelmson (1999, 2005) estimates that almost all daily mobility growth since the 1950s is attributable to an increase in car use. Similar trends are apparent elsewhere in Europe and the industrialized world: Eurostat (2005) estimates that the car accounts for more than 80% of the total daily distance of passenger travel; the corresponding figure for the USA is similar (Pucher, 1999). When automobile use is indexed in terms of number of trips as opposed to distance travelled, the car accounts for 45% of urban trips in Europe but a staggering 90% in the USA (Pucher, 1999).

16.3 Determinants of car use

There are a variety of reasons why the car is such a popular travel mode. Determinants of car use can be broadly classified in terms of whether they are primarily instrumental, economic, or psychological. Each is discussed in turn below. However, prior to doing so, it is important to bear in mind that car ownership (or availability) is an important determinant of car use. If an individual owns or has access to a car, then he or she is likely to use it even though there are equal or better alternatives. Wootton (1999) summarizes clear evidence of this from the UK context: the purchase of a household's first car leads to

(i) a doubling in the total number of journeys made; (ii) roughly half the journeys previously made by public transport transferring to the newly purchased car; and (iii) cycling and walking journeys falling slightly. In other words, accessibility to the car leads to large increases in travel demand; accessibility to additional cars exacerbates such tendencies. Citing UK National Travel Survey data, Wootton (1999) further reports that families without access to a car performed an average of 2.5 journeys per weekday, families with a car an average of 6.4, while families with two or more cars averaged 8.7 journeys per weekday. As another example, Cullinane and Cullinane (2003) showed that the average length driven per car per day in Hong Kong is 35 kilometres. This is despite the fact that Hong Kong is small in size (50 × 40 kilometres), that very few drivers have permits to drive into mainland China, and that public transport accounts for 90 per cent of all motorized journeys. In other words, once a car has been acquired, it quickly becomes considered less of a luxury and more of a necessity and, in turn, car use appears to become habitual. Yet, there are other factors that also influence car use in addition to mere access to a car.

16.3.1 Instrumental factors

Fulfilling biological needs, social obligations, and personal desires requires that people move from one place to another in the environment to perform goal-directed behaviours such as work, maintenance activities (e.g., shopping), and various leisure activities (Gärling and Garvill, 1993). That demand for travel is derived from this requirement constitutes a basic tenet of the activity-based approach to travel behaviour (e.g., Axhausen and Gärling, 1992; Bhat and Koppelman, 1999; Ettema and Timmermans, 1997; Jones et al., 1983; Kitamura, 1988; Recker et al., 1986). It follows that the way a society is spatially organized is an essential determinant of the degree and type of travel demand and that using the car to fulfil such aforementioned needs and desires can be considered an instrumental reason for car use. The versatility of the car has made it the most popular alternative.

This popularity of the car has been stepped up even further by the fact that, from the turn of the twentieth century, a much more extreme spatial separation of activities has evolved. Furthermore, the spread of affluence subsequent to the Second World War made cars affordable to most people so that the rail network ceased to dictate the pattern of development (Crawford, 2000; Maat, 2002). As a result of owning an automobile, people could live further away from their place of work in locations that had previously not been accessible. This gave rise to suburbanization due to preferences for low-density, single-family homes with a garden in a green setting (Garreau, 1991; Maat, 2002; Muller, 1995). Other contributing factors to suburbanization included population growth, as well as the cost of land and construction in city centres vis-à-vis transport costs, which were becoming increasingly cheaper even up to the end of the previous century (Gordon and Richardson, 1997). It was often the case that cheaper land for housing, retail, and industry was available on the outskirts of urban areas and, as a result, suburbanization and urban sprawl gathered momentum.

The spatial separation due to the decentralization of activities means that journeys are often too great to walk or cycle and the dispersion of humans and activities makes it difficult to plan efficient, regular, and effective public transport services. Using Los Angeles as an example, Modarres (2003) illustrates how the city centre area is well served by public transport, as are various work sub-centres located outside the city centre area. However, while the public transport system is good at connecting workplaces, it is poor at connecting employees to their place of work (particularly if it is located outside the city centre). Examining the Norwegian context, Aarhus (2000) found that the suburbanization of jobs was associated with increases in commuting by automobile, presumably because suburbanization is associated with improved access to (free) parking, poorer access to public transport, and a smaller share of employees living near enough to work to be able to walk or cycle.

The versatility of the car is made possible by the advancements made in automobile technology and societies' great investments in road infrastructure. Thus, the car, coupled with associated infrastructure investments, assists people in overcoming the natural limitations to their speed of movement and radius of action. This utilitarian tool-function of automobiles can be extended to include comfort, protection or safety, and autonomy (Stradling, 2002). Cars shield people from direct exposure to the elements and this shielding property also means that direct interactions with humans outside the car are limited and that the driver of the car feels secure (Wright and Egan, 2000). The transportation of goods, the chauffeuring of others, or time and distance constraints also often make the car a most convenient tool.

The increasing complexity of individual and household activity agendas (i.e., the more complex pattern of needs, desires, and obligations) is an additional contributing factor to the use of the car. Current travel demand goes far beyond the home-to-work journey on weekdays (e.g., Hemily, 2004; Levinson and Kumar, 1995). In Levinson and Kumar's (1995) work, for example, household travel surveys from the Washington, DC metropolitan area for the years 1968 and 1988 were compared and analysed. They found significant increases in the linking of work and non-work trips, as well as a shift in the peak of non-work trips such that it coincided with the afternoon peak of work trips (i.e., trip chaining with the afternoon commute home). Such trip chaining, which can be construed as attempts to more efficiently fulfil the ever-growing list of needs, desires, and obligations associated with modern life, is arguably also behind the growth in car travel.

These propositions are summarized in figure 16.1. Degree and type of travel demand depend on activity choice and the spatial organization of the environment. Mediating between travel demand and travel (sometimes referred to as manifest travel demand or, simply, travel demand) is travel choice, which is

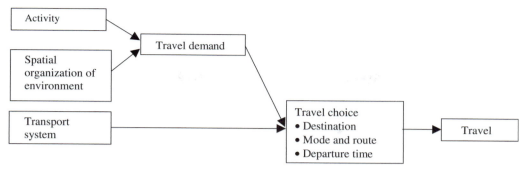

Figure 16.1 Determinants of travel

influenced by attributes of the transportation system such as speed, frequency, reliability, safety, and cost. It is thus implied that some degree of freedom exists (cf. Timmermans *et al.*, 2003) in choosing whether to travel or not, where to travel, how to travel, and when to travel.

16.3.2 Economic factors

Lave (1992) has argued that as affluence and incomes rise, the value placed on time increases such that faster modes of transport are attractive. Indeed, research generally shows income to be related to the value of travel time, with elasticities of around 0.5 having been obtained (e.g., Wardman, 2001). Given the complexity of modern activity agendas, with their tight schedule of activities (e.g., Vilhelmson, 1999), and given the aforementioned pattern of urban development (e.g., Muller, 1995), in most cases the private car is the fastest mode (i.e., the mode yielding smallest total values of time spent travelling). Research by Cullinane (2003) found that it is the preference for a faster mode of transport (car or public transport) that is a major determinant of mode choice in Hong Kong. Despite this and other qualifications (e.g., Priemus *et al.*, 2001), it is nevertheless the case that the spatial separation of activities within the context of mass suburbanization is a major determinant of car use. Schwanen *et al.* (2001) illustrated how decentralization of urban land invariably leads to palpable increases in automobile use and reductions in cycling, walking, and the use of public transport. Thus, in sum, travel time and the value of time is such that in the majority of cases it makes 'economic sense' to use the car.

Car use is also cheaper in the sense that its full external costs are not paid for. As noted by Steg (2003), the costs of accidents, environmental problems (e.g., air and noise pollution, congestion), traffic safety, and infrastructure maintenance are passed from motorists to society as a whole. In the majority of places in the world, motorists are then able to continue driving without in some way paying for these external costs. It is only in a handful of cities that attempts have been made to internalize such costs, the most obvious example being road pricing in its various forms. The idea with most road pricing schemes (e.g., in Singapore) is to raise costs so that the congestion externality is internalized (Emmerink *et al.*, 1995).

16.3.3 Psychological factors

The status and identity associated with being a car owner are one source of attraction to the car that has roots in the very early days of automobilization. Initially, being a car owner was an envied and respected position (Sandqvist, 1997) and ever since the car has continued fulfilling the role of powerful status symbol, albeit with a slightly different emphasis: the ubiquity of the car has led to it being perceived as an everyday tool, much like a refrigerator, and anyone not owning a car is perceived as being less well-off. Indeed, the norm in many parts of the developed world, particularly the USA, is for families to own more than one car; not owning a car is interpreted as a sign of deep poverty (Sandqvist, 1997). Not only does ownership of an automobile communicate status, driving the automobile also allows for the expression of individuality, identity, and personality (Stradling, 2002). More specifically, the type of car owned and the manner in which it is driven are crucial aspects allowing drivers to communicate their personality. Indeed, Stradling (2002) reviews evidence indicating not only that identity and independence are important reasons for driving a car but that the importance of these factors varies with sociodemographic variables: personal identity was particularly important for young drivers and the poor, while driving was particularly important for women over forty because of the sense of independence it conveyed. It should thus come as no surprise that advertisers emphasize different aspects of driving dependent on the demographic group to which they are trying to sell their product. For example, the Mazda Miata roadster advertising campaign from 1989 – 'Before the spouse, the house, the kids, you get one chance . . . You should know how it feels to have the sun on your head and a growl at your back as you flick through five gears with no more baggage than a friend' – emphasized the independence that driving a car can bring to women (Hupfer, 2002).

It may even be argued that the car is an extension of the human body, making people more powerful and energetic, with younger car users in particular seeking enjoyment in the ability to travel at great speed. According to Wright and Egan (2000), this is why car design in recent years has emphasized horizontal lines that proclaim power and speed. While designs have changed over the years (for example, recent designs have given much greater weight to safety because of the increasing number of female drivers), the rationale behind them (i.e., reflecting and communicating personality and as extensions of the human body) has not. Consider, for example, the flamboyant automobile designs of the 1960s complete with shark fins and teeth, as well as the more contemporary designs associated with many of the larger sport-utility vehicles (e.g., the Hummer) with their massive weight, size, and raised bodies (see also Wright and Curtis, 2005, for a review of the history of car design and its implications). Clearly, car consumption is not simply an issue of rational economic choice, but has also to do with aesthetic, emotional, and sensory responses to driving (Sheller, 2004).

The various benefits of the car together with the spatial separation of activities, which in its extreme form requires and assumes that one has access to a car, can in the long term lead to development of a car-use habit (Fujii and Gärling, 2006). An important prerequisite for the development of a habit is that the behaviour is rewarded, repeated under stable circumstances, and that an individual is motivated and able to repeat the earlier behaviour (Ouellette and Wood, 1998): conditions applying to car use. Attitudes and the appeal of the automobile contribute to the instigation of driving, which often acts as its own reward. Furthermore, the urban environment in which people live changes very slowly (in terms of road networks, place of residence, and work) and, as such, the context in which choices of driving occur is stable. Thus, car use is likely to be repeated and, more importantly, the cognitive processing of information that occurred on the initial occasions of driving to various activities is likely to be changed such that the need to participate in an activity automatically activates a script-based choice of the car (Gärling *et al.*, 2001; Verplanken *et al.*, 1997). The resulting limited information processing makes breaking car-use habits difficult and requires some incentive to attend to new information (Garvill *et al.*, 2003). Yet, travel by car is also desired as a goal and not a means. That is, travel is not purely undertaken for the sake of activity participation; it is not purely a derived demand. This is clearly the case when people travel for the sake of travelling or travel to another destination via a more scenic route (Mokhtarian and Salomon, 2001), or when commuters choose public transport in order to work or read for pleasure (Lyons and Urry, 2005). Also, in addition to instrumental motives, Steg (2005) has shown that affective (e.g., enjoyment) and symbolic (e.g., prestige) factors are important for understanding the choice to commute by car in the Netherlands. Complementing these findings, Handy *et al.* (2005) found that excess driving may be due to valuing driving itself, valuing the activities that may be conducted while driving (e.g., talking on the phone), and variety seeking. That is, people may choose to drive because they like it and not only out of habit, poor planning, or poor quality information.

16.4 Policies to reduce or change private car use

There are several conceivable policy measures that may reduce the adverse effects of private car use. Some measures may not require a reduction in car use (e.g., increasing capacity of road infrastructure, improving car technology, or limiting speed) if they are able to decrease the environmental impact per car to a sufficient degree. However, a general assessment of the current state is that measures reducing manifest demand for private car use must be implemented in many urban areas (e.g., OECD, 1996). Furthermore, it is necessary to change private car use with respect to when and where people drive, particularly on major commuter arteries during peak hours and in city centres. The proposed measures are generally referred to as *travel demand management* (TDM) (Kitamura *et al.*, 1997) since they focus on changing or reducing demand. Other terms with similar meanings include, for instance, transport system management (Pendyala *et al.*, 1997) or mobility management (Kristensen and Marshall, 1999).

16.4.1 Classification

Several attempts have been made to classify TDM measures. At a more specific level, Litman (2003) distinguishes five classes: improvements in transport options; provisions of incentives to switch mode; land-use management; policy and planning reforms; and support programmes. A partly overlapping set is proposed by May *et al.* (2003) as land-use policies, infrastructure provision (for modes other than the private car), management and regulation, information provision, attitudinal and behavioural change measures, and pricing. Vlek and Michon (1992) suggest the following classes: physical changes such as, for instance, closing out car traffic or providing alternative transportation; law regulation; economic incentives and disincentives; information, education, and prompts; socialization and social modelling targeted at changing social norms; and institutional and organizational changes such as, for instance, flexible work hours, telecommuting, or 'flexplaces'. Louw *et al.* (1998) note that there are policies encouraging mode switching, destination switching, changing time of travel, linking trips, substitution of trips with technology (e.g., teleworking), and substitution of trips through trip modification (e.g., a single goods delivery in lieu of a series of shoppers' trips). At a more general level, Gatersleben (2003) distinguishes measures aimed at changing behavioural opportunities from measures aimed at changing perceptions, motivations, and norms. In a similar vein, Jones (2003), Steg and Vlek (1997), Stradling *et al.* (2000), and Thorpe *et al.* (2000) distinguish between push and pull measures. Push measures discourage car use by making it less attractive; pull measures encourage the use of alternative modes to the car by making such modes more attractive.

Partly based on these different systems of classification, Loukopoulos *et al.* (2007) proposed that TDM measures may be characterized as varying with respect to *targeting latent vs. manifest travel demand, time scale, spatial scale, coerciveness, top-down vs. bottom-up process,* and *market-based vs. regulatory mechanism.* Brief definitions of each are given in table 16.1 together with assessments on these dimensions of *individualized marketing* (IM), *road pricing* (RP), and *prohibition* (Pn) (examples of each are described in the appendix). Any TDM measure may thus be characterized with respect

Table 16.1 *Proposed system of classifying travel demand management (TDM) measures*

Attribute with definition	IM	RP	Pn
Targeting latent (vs. manifest) demand Changing unobserved (vs. observed) car use	Yes	Partly	No
(Restriction of) time scale Hours of operation	No	Yes	Yes
(Restriction of) spatial scale Area of operation	No	Yes	Yes
Coerciveness Reducing car users' voluntary control	No	Partly	Yes
Bottom-up (vs. top-down) process Empowering car users and increasing voluntary control	Yes	Partly	No
Market-based (vs. regulatory) mechanism Increasing voluntary control at a cost	No	Yes	No

IM = individualized marketing
RP = road pricing
Pn = prohibition

to whether it targets observed or unobserved travel (e.g., measures reducing congestion targeting manifest travel demand vs. measures increasing public transport capacity targeting latent demand), with respect to time and area of operation (e.g., weekday morning peak on major arteries into city centres), and with respect to the degree to which the measure affects voluntary control or freedom of choice. Coercive measures (such as prohibition) target change in manifest travel demand by reducing car users' voluntary control. Other measures are designed to empower car users and to increase voluntary control (e.g., information campaigns aimed at affecting attitudes toward coercive measures) or are designed to make voluntary control costly (e.g., pricing travel). IM is non-coercive, Pn is coercive, whereas RP tends to fall in between the two. It is coercive for those who cannot afford the fees but non-coercive for those who can. As observed in Loukopoulos *et al.* (2005b), these measures also differ with respect to car-users' and non-car-users' attitudes, beliefs, and evaluations.

It is apparent that devising and trusting a TDM measure is in part shaped by the view one holds about determinants of people's behaviour in general and car use in particular. The view associated with theories of neoclassical economics that persons or households act in selfish and rational ways clearly underpins economic interventions. Coupled with this is the view that people have an unlimited capacity to acquire and process information. The proposal of complex road pricing schemes to internalize externalities (Ubbels and Verhoef, 2006) is an example. Yet, in conjunction with the implementation of road pricing schemes, economists realize that people are concerned about their own unfair (or less fair) positions relative to others (Fehr and Schmidt, 1999). Thus, attempts are made to devise fair measures.

Other measures are based on the view that people are concerned about the collective negative effects of excessive car use, in particular environmental effects. Thus, even though this does not preclude concern about economic incentives or disincentives, it is more important to emphasize that the measures will be perceived to be effective. One may still have different beliefs about what the reasons are for people's environmental concern. Stern and Dietz (1994) have identified three value orientations in relation to environmental issues depending on how encompassing the concern is: concern about own health (egocentric), concern about the welfare of people in general (altruistic), or concern about the biosphere (biospheric or ecocentric). What one believes about people's value orientations is also likely to determine a preference for one type of intervention over another.

A view of people founded in modern cognitive research (Reisberg, 2006) underlies the belief that the difficulties people have in changing their behaviour do not solely reflect a lack of motivation but equally an inability to change. This view of people would lead to emphasizing the importance of devising aids for providing journey information in advance or en route (Intelligent Transportation Systems or ITS, see Golledge, 2002; Golob, 2001), devising in-vehicle information systems, for instance, for navigation, petrol usage, and travel time and costs, and devising methods such as individualized marketing to break old habits and build new ones (Fujii and Gärling, 2006).

16.4.2 Effectiveness

Car-use reduction needs to be viewed broadly as an adaptation by car users to changes in travel alternatives that potentially have consequences for their engagement in different activities and the satisfaction they experience from them. A central issue is whether theories of travel choice – and by implication the aforementioned various models of determinants of people's behaviour – that apply in equilibrium are transferable to conditions of change (as is the case when a TDM measure is implemented). As has been noted (Goodwin, 1998), it may take a long time before a new equilibrium is reached. Furthermore, theories of choice in equilibrium may not include factors that are important for understanding change processes. For this reason, several recent attempts have been made to conceptualize the *change process* (Arentze *et al.*, 2004; Cao and Mokhtarian, 2005a, 2005b; Gärling *et al.*, 2002a; Kitamura and Fujii, 1998; Pendyala *et al.*, 1997; Pendyala *et al.*, 1998). In the following, the theoretical framework proposed by Gärling *et al.* (2002a) will be briefly described. This theoretical framework aims at analysing the multifaceted nature of car users' responses to TDM measures.

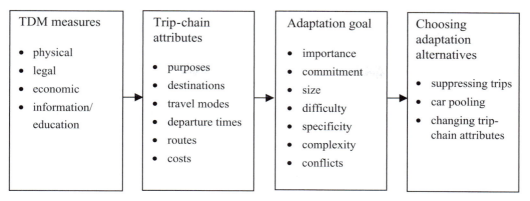

Figure 16.2 Theoretical framework. Adapted from *Transport Policy*, 9, Gärling, T. *et al.* 'A conceptual analysis of the impact of travel demand management on private car use', pp. 59–70, Copyright 2002, with permission from Elsevier

As illustrated in figure 16.2, travel alternatives are defined as bundles of attributes describing trip chains (including purposes, destinations, travel modes, departure times, routes, and costs), with choices of travel alternatives being influenced by these bundles of attributes. Another determinant is the reduction or change goals set by households. Such goals may form a hierarchy from concrete programmes (e.g., cycling to work, walking to the local grocery store) to abstract principles (e.g., reducing car use, being a responsible member of society) functioning as reference values in negative feedback loops regulating ongoing behaviour or changes in behaviour (Carver and Scheier, 1998). That is, if a discrepancy is detected between the present state and the goal which functions as the reference value, then some action is carried out with the aim of minimizing the discrepancy. For instance, after implementing a road pricing scheme, a car-use reduction goal may be set if households experience increased monetary travel costs. On the other hand, if other changes are simultaneously encountered such as shorter travel times (due to less congestion) or concomitant reduced living costs (e.g., children moving out, a salary increase), no such goal may be set. In effect, a simple relationship does not exist between increasing the cost of driving and the setting of car-use reduction goals.

Needs, desires, attitudes, and values influence the goals that people set and strive to attain (Austin and Vancouver, 1996). Sociodemographic factors are frequently used as proxies. Goals vary in content and intensity (Locke and Latham, 1984, 1990). Content is related to (i) size of goal and difficulty of attainment, (ii) specificity of the goal, (iii) complexity of the goal (the number of outcome dimensions), and (iv) the degree of conflict with other goals at the same or higher levels. Intensity refers to perceived importance and degree of commitment. Research on goal setting and attainment (e.g., Lee *et al.*, 1989) has shown that specific and challenging goals increase the likelihood that they are attained, provided they are not too difficult or challenging. Skills, commitment to the goal, and immediate clear feedback about goal attainment are moderating factors.

After having set a car-use reduction goal, households are assumed to form a plan for how to achieve this goal and to make commitments to execute the formed plan. This process has been referred to as formation of implementation intentions (Gärling and Fujii, 2002; Gollwitzer, 1993). The plan that is formed consists of predetermined choices contingent on specified conditions (Hayes-Roth and Hayes-Roth, 1979). In making plans for how to reduce car use, households may consider a wide range of alternatives such as staying at home, suppressing trips and activities, using electronic communication means instead of driving, car pooling, or changing the effective choice set of travel options with respect to purposes, destinations, travel modes, departure times, or costs. Households may possibly also consider longer-term strategic changes such as moving to another residence or changing workplace or work hours.

It is hypothesized that individuals and households seek and select adaptation alternatives that lead to the achievement of their goal. This process is not assumed, however, necessarily to entail a simultaneous optimal choice among all alternatives. Experimental laboratory-based research (Payne et al., 1993) shows that people make sensible tradeoffs between accuracy and (mental and tangible) costs. A crucial difference to microeconomic utility-maximization theories (e.g., McFadden, 2001) is the assumption that people do not invariably invest the same degree of effort. Whether they do or not depends on properties of the goal (e.g., size, importance). As a consequence, if the cost of an effective adaptation is too high, even a small and specific reduction goal to which a household is highly committed may be abandoned or reduced.

Consistent with the notion of bounded rationality (Gigerenzer et al., 1999; Simon, 1990), a second important difference to microeconomic utility-maximization theories is that choices are made sequentially over time. This implies that the change process is prolonged and fails to result instantaneously in outcomes beneficial to society. Furthermore, although both benefits (effectiveness or goal achievement) and costs of chosen alternatives are evaluated, immediately felt costs are likely to be attended to first. Effectiveness is evaluated over time on the basis of negative feedback. If such evaluations indicate a discrepancy with the goal, more costly changes are chosen. Thus, a sequential cost-minimizing principle (Gärling et al., 2002b) may dictate the choices of change or adaptation alternatives. Yet, people may not make appropriate accuracy–cost tradeoffs in real life when making complex travel choices, for instance because car-use habits and related habitual or routine activities cause inertia (Gärling and Axhausen, 2003). Research has also demonstrated that a bias exists such that the current state is overvalued (e.g., Samuelson and Zeckhausen, 1988), thus making changes less attractive. In particular, if the car-use reduction goal is vague, evaluating whether or not a change is effective may possibly be biased toward confirming the expectation that it is (e.g., Einhorn and Hogarth, 1978; Klayman and Ha, 1987). Also, previous research has demonstrated that immediate clear feedback is essential (e.g., Brehmer, 1995).

It is claimed that there are three main reasons why TDM measures may not be effective: (i) TDM measures may fail to make car use less attractive; (ii) TDM measures may fail to activate goals to change car use; and (iii) TDM measures may fail to facilitate the implementation of goals to change car use. Evidence consistent with these claims comes, for example, from analyses of travel diary data reported by Loukopoulos *et al.* (2005a) observing that the number of affected trips varied greatly depending on the temporal and spatial specifications of TDM measures such as prohibition or road pricing. Thus, one cannot assume that such TDM measures make car use less attractive in a given area without first examining existing travel patterns. Furthermore, Loukopoulos *et al.* (2004) demonstrated that individualized marketing may lead to significantly smaller car-use reduction goals being set than either road pricing or prohibition. The same study also revealed that people believed their shopping activities would not be affected because such activities are conducted outside the typical hours of operation of road pricing; that is, car-use reduction goals were not activated in this instance. Finally, Loukopoulos *et al.* (2006) found evidence suggesting that the adaptation to TDM measures took the form of a change hierarchy, which proceeded according to a general cost-minimization principle, with the less costly adaptation alternatives being selected first. The exact nature of the hierarchy varied across different trip purposes, suggesting that less costly alternatives for one trip purpose (e.g., public transport for work trips) are more costly for another (e.g., public transport for shopping trips). The implication is that TDM measures will not be effective if the resulting alternatives are too costly since these alternatives are unlikely to be chosen.

16.4.3 Public acceptability

Car users are opposed to TDM measures if they are perceived to be ineffective and limit their freedom to drive, in particular if they believe that they cannot reduce car use without large sacrifices (Bamberg and Rölle, 2003; Jakobsson *et al.*, 2000). There may also be opposition because the TDM measure is perceived as unfair if some suffer more than others. Yet, prohibition of car use is perceived as fairer (and also more effective) than road pricing, presumably because the latter is believed to allow wealthy people to buy their way out (Jones, 1995, 2003). Another possibility is the belief, perhaps mistaken (Santos and Rojey, 2004), that predominantly poor people will suffer. As shown by social justice research (e.g., Deutsch, 1985), even though minimizing differences in outcomes between groups is the most important goal (referred to as equality), when this goal implies that unprivileged groups will suffer, need may dominate equality as a fairness principle. Finally, Steg (2005) notes that another reason for opposition to TDM measures is their focus on the instrumental motives of car use and not the affective or symbolic motives. She argues that making instrumental reasons salient increases resistance to effective policies aiming to reduce car use.

Other characteristics of a TDM measure such as road pricing include fee level and the allocation of revenues. It has been shown that revenues that benefit the individual car user, for instance by decreasing road or fuel taxes, are more acceptable compared to revenues that benefit society as a whole, such as general public funds (Steg and Schuitema, 2006). Thus, a possible way of increasing the acceptability of economic sanctions is to have revenues compensate for the infringement on freedom and unfairness.

16.4.4 Political feasibility

TDM measures may not be politically feasible because they are not acceptable to the public. Yet, there are also other reasons. In political decision making it is necessary to resolve conflicts between different goals, either because different political parties (ideologies) prioritize different goals or because a TDM measure in itself leads to conflicting goals. In Europe, reducing car traffic is attractive to environmental or green parties but not to social democratic or conservative parties since the latter view it as a threat to economic development and, in the longer term, the welfare of society (Johansson *et al.*, 2003). An additional reason for the conservative opposition is trust in deregulation and free-market solutions. A similar goal conflict exists in political decision making between the municipal and national levels. Although politicians at both levels are sensitive to public opposition, they may be more so at the local, municipal level because of closer ties between politicians and their voters. It may also be the case that public opposition is stronger in a municipality where implementation of the TDM measure is being considered.

A conflict also emanates from the fact that TDM measures have both intended and unintended effects. For instance, road pricing may alleviate congestion if prices are set sufficiently high. At the same time, this may reduce the profits of businesses if their gains from faster transportation due to less congestion fail to offset the increased costs. In a similar vein, poor households may no longer be able to afford leisure travel that they consider highly desirable, at least not without cutting expenditures for other (perhaps essential) goods and services. Prohibition may have even stronger side effects unless exceptions are made for essential road use.

Figure 16.3 illustrates that political feasibility increases with public acceptability but is also affected by the existence of conflicts between different political goals. Given public acceptability of a TDM measure, its implementation is likely only if such goal conflicts can be resolved so that the goal of private car-use reduction is not compromised.

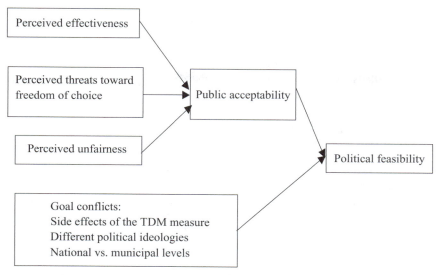

Figure 16.3 Factors assumed to affect political feasibility

16.5 Summary and conclusions

Private car ownership and private car use have many determinants. For instance, owning and using a car is attractive since it makes a desirable lifestyle possible. This is perhaps the most important reason, in conjunction with the spread of affluence, why car ownership and use is increasing so much in developing countries. The increase is a serious threat to human environments on a global scale (Goodwin, 1996; US Department of Energy, 2002). In addition, in Western urban areas the excessive car use has already resulted in many urgent problems. Policies attempting to reduce these problems have been proposed to affect the various determinants of car use. Yet such measures suffer in many cases from a lack of public acceptability because they decrease speed and freedom of travel. They are also objected to because of the strongly held psychological (i.e., non-instrumental) motives associated with car ownership and use. This in turn influences the political feasibility of implementing these policy measures.

Given the versatility of the car, the desirable lifestyles its use makes possible, and the complex multi-determined nature of the implementation of policy measures, the future does not seem bright for any attempts at alleviation of these problems. Are there any ways of designing policy measures that enable the expression of desirable lifestyles and complex activity schedules? If so, these may possibly satisfy many users of the car, but what about the non-instrumental motives? Clearly, the issue is complex, requiring consideration of economic and psychological factors, as well as others. It is also the case that many (lay people, experts, as well as politicians) put faith in future automobile technology. Is a zero-emission, fuel-efficient automobile a last and only hope?

16.6 Appendix

TDM measure	Description
Prohibiting car traffic in city centre (Cambridge, UK) (Cambridgeshire County Council, 2005)	The city of Cambridge is a lively historic city in England. Its streets date from the Middle Ages and are not designed for today's traffic flows. Instead of expanding the road network, Cambridgeshire County Council has chosen another solution. The Council has decided to impose considerable restrictions on private car traffic in the central parts of the city. The policy package is comprised of two parts. First, the area inside the ring road, which is called the Inner Ring Area, has been divided into eight sub-areas. These eight sub-areas have only one entry and exit point to and from the inner-ring road. Second, pedestrian zones have been created in the liveliest business areas and in residential areas. Parking is not permitted in the pedestrian zones twenty-four hours a day, seven days a week. Car traffic is not permitted between the hours of 10 am and 4 pm, Monday to Saturday, except for those vehicles that have a special permit. Time-activated traffic barriers have been designed so as to sink into the ground for cars or buses with a special permit in the form of an electronic ID card. This applies, for example, to taxis.
Road pricing (Singapore) (Foo, 1997, 2000; Goh, 2002)	In Singapore, a city-state with about 3.5 million inhabitants, various forms of road pricing in the city centre have been implemented by the government over the past thirty years. The latest system in Singapore is called ERP (Electronic Road Pricing). This means that drivers have to pay to be able to drive a car within a zone referred to as the 'Restricted Zone', which is about 7 square kilometres in size and has about thirty entry points. All entry points are clearly marked with portals over the road and when the ERP system is in operation, the words 'In Operation' flash on screens situated on the portals. ERP works with the assistance of these portals, an in-vehicle unit which is in every type of vehicle, and a smart card system. There are antennae, cameras, and optical detectors situated on the portals. When a vehicle approaches the portal, the ERP system communicates with the in-vehicle unit, identifies what type of vehicle it

TDM measure	Description
	is (i.e., car, taxi, truck, motorcycle, etc.), deducts the appropriate fee from the card which is loaded with money and, if a transgression is detected (e.g., no in-vehicle unit or insufficient funds on the card, etc.) the vehicle and licence plate are photographed. The prices vary depending on vehicle type and time of entry into the 'Restricted Zone'. For example, the average price for a private car is SGD 1.00. The price levels are reviewed every three months. If the congestion levels are too high then the prices are raised; if the roads are not being sufficiently utilized then the prices are lowered.
Individualized marketing (Perth, Australia) (Department of Transport Western Australia, 1999, 2001)	The city of Perth, Western Australia has a population of approximately 1 million. In an attempt to reduce traffic by 10 per cent, a programme known as 'TravelSmart' has been introduced. In the suburb of South Perth (population 37,000), a part of the TravelSmart programme known as individualized marketing has been introduced. Individual households are contacted. Information is gathered about the type of car users living in the household and whether they are interested in using alternatives to the car. The decision to participate in the programme is left to the household. Those households that are interested in beginning to use alternative modes of transport to the car are provided with information about the various modes in the Perth area (cycle, buses, walking, etc.). They are offered personal advice about their trips. This information consists of personalized timetables, which can be sent by post, received over the phone or by a home visit from a consultant who analyses the household's trips and provides suggestions for alternatives to the car. It has been found that an important reason why people do not refrain from using the car more often is that they believe that the same trip with another transport mode (walking, cycling, public transport) would take twice as long and cost one-third more than is actually the case.

16.7 References

Aarhus, K. (2000). Office location decisions, modal split and the environment: The ineffectiveness of Norwegian land use policy. *Journal of Transport Geography*, 8, 287–94.

Arentze, T., Hofman, F., and Timmermans, H. P. J. (2004). Predicting multi-faceted activity-travel adjustment strategies in response to possible pricing scenarios using an Internet-based stated adaptation experiment. *Transport Policy*, 11, 31–41.

Austin, J. T., and Vancouver, J. B. (1996). Goal constructs in psychology: Structure, process, and content. *Psychological Bulletin*, 80, 286–303.

Axhausen, K., and Gärling, T. (1992). Activity-based approaches to travel analysis: Conceptual frameworks, models, and research problems. *Transport Reviews*, 12, 323–41.

Bamberg, S., and Rölle, D. (2003). Determinants of people's determinants of pricing measures. In J. Schade and B. Schlag (eds.), *Acceptability of Transport Pricing Strategies* (pp. 235–48). Amsterdam: Elsevier.

Bhat, C. R., and Koppelman, F. S. (1999). A retrospective and prospective survey of time-use research. *Transportation*, 26, 119–39.

Bonsall, P. (2000). Legislating for modal shift: Background to the UK's New Transport Act. *Transport Policy*, 7, 179–84.

Brehmer, B. (1995). Feedback delays in complex dynamic decision making. In P. A. Frensch and J. Funke (eds.), *Complex Decision Making: The European Perspective* (pp. 103–30). Hillsdale, NJ: Erlbaum.

Cambridgeshire County Council (2005). *Vehicle Access to Cambridge City Centre*, www.cambridgeshire.gov.uk/transport/around/city_access/. Retrieved 15 November 2005.

Cao, X., and Mokhtarian, P. L. (2005a). How do individuals adapt their personal travel? A conceptual exploration of the consideration of travel-related strategies. *Transport Policy*, 12, 199–206.

(2005b). How do individuals adapt their personal travel? Objective and subjective influences on the consideration of travel-related strategies. *Transport Policy*, 12, 291–302.

Carver, C. S., and Scheier, M. F. (1998). *On the Self-regulation of Behaviour*. Cambridge: Cambridge University Press.

Crawford, J. H. (2000). *Carfree Cities*. Utrecht: International Books.

Cullinane, S. (2003). Hong Kong's low car dependence: Lessons and prospects. *Journal of Transport Geography*, 11, 25–35.

Cullinane, S., and Cullinane, K. (2003). Car dependence in a public transport dominated city: Evidence from Hong Kong. *Transportation Research D*, 8, 129–38.

Dargay, J., and Gately, D. (1999). Income's effect on car and vehicle ownership, worldwide: 1960–2015. *Transportation Research A*, 33, 101–38.

Dargay, J., and Vythoulkas, P. C. (1999). Estimation of a dynamic car ownership model: A pseudo-panel approach. *Journal of Transport Economics and Policy*, 33, 283–302.

Department of Transport Western Australia (1999). *TravelSmart 2010: A 10 Year Plan*. Perth: Transport WA.

(2001). *TravelSmart Individualized Marketing Program for Perth* (brochure). Perth: Transport WA.

Deutsch, M. (1985). *Distributive Justice: A Social Psychological Perspective*. New Haven, CT: Yale University Press.

Einhorn, H. J., and Hogarth, R. M. (1978). Confidence in judgment: Persistence of the illusion of validity. *Psychological Review*, 85, 396–416.

Emmerink, R. H. M., Nijkamp, P., and Rietveld, P. (1995). Is congestion pricing a first-best strategy in transport policy? A critical review of arguments. *Environment and Planning B*, 22, 581–602.

Ettema, D., and Timmermans, H. J. P. (1997). Theories and models of activity patterns. In D. Ettema and H. J. P. Timmermans (eds.), *Activity-based Approaches to Travel Analysis* (pp. 1–36). Oxford: Pergamon.

Eurostat (2005). *Themes/Transport*, http://epp.eurostat.cec.eu.int. Retrieved 7 November 2005.

Fehr, E., and Schmidt, K. M. (1999). A theory of fairness, competition, and cooperation. *Quarterly Journal of Economics*, 114, 817–68.

Foo, T. S. (1997). An effective demand management instrument in urban transport: The Area Licensing Scheme in Singapore. *Cities*, 14, 155–64.

  (2000). An advanced demand management instrument in urban transport. *Cities*, 17, 33–45.

Fujii, S., and Gärling, T. (2006). Role and acquisition of car-use habit. In T. Gärling and L. Steg (eds.), *Threats from Car Traffic to the Quality of Urban Life: Problems, Causes, and Solutions* (pp. 235–50). Amsterdam: Elsevier.

Gärling, T., and Axhausen, K. (2003). Habitual travel choice (introduction to special issue). *Transportation*, 30, 1–11.

Gärling, T., Eek, D., Loukopoulos, P., Fujii, S., Johansson-Stenman, O., Kitamura, R., Pendyala, R., and Vilhelmson, B. (2002a). A conceptual analysis of the impact of travel demand management on private car use. *Transport Policy*, 9, 59–70.

Gärling, T., and Fujii, S. (2002). Structural equation modelling of determinants of implementation intentions. *Scandinavian Journal of Psychology*, 43, 1–8.

Gärling, T., Fujii, S., and Boe, O. (2001). Empirical tests of a model of determinants of script-based driving choice. *Transportation Research F*, 4, 89–102.

Gärling, T., Gärling, A., and Loukopoulos, P. (2002b). Forecasting psychological consequences of car-use reduction: A challenge to an environmental psychology of transportation. *Applied Psychology: An International Review*, 51, 90–106.

Gärling, T., and Garvill, J. (1993). Psychological explanations of participation in everyday activities. In T. Gärling and R. G. Golledge (eds.), *Behaviour and Environment: Psychological and Geographical Approaches* (pp. 270–97). Amsterdam: Elsevier/North-Holland.

Garreau, J. (1991). *Edge City: Life on the New Frontier*. Garden City, NY: Doubleday.

Garvill, J., Marell, A., and Nordlund, A. (2003). Effects of awareness on choice of travel mode. *Transportation*, 30, 63–79.

Gatersleben, B. (2003). On yer bike for a healthy commute. In L. Hendrickx, W. Jager, and L. Steg (eds.), *Human Decision Making and Environmental Perception: Understanding and Assisting Human Decision Making in Real-life Settings* (pp. 161–82). Groningen: University of Groningen.

Gigerenzer, G., Todd, P. M., and the ABC Research Group (eds.) (1999). *Simple Heuristics That Make Us Smart*. Oxford: Oxford University Press.

Giuliano, G., and Dargay, J. (2006). Car ownership, travel and land use: A comparison of the US and Great Britain. *Transportation Research A*, 40, 106–24.

Goh, M. (2002). Congestion management and electronic road pricing in Singapore. *Journal of Transport Geography*, 10, 29–38.

Golledge, R. G. (2002). Dynamics and ITS: Behavioural responses to information available from ATIS. In H. S. Mahmassani (ed.), *Perpetual Motion: Travel Behaviour Research Opportunities and Application Challenges* (pp. 81–126). Amsterdam: Pergamon.

Gollwitzer, P. M. (1993). Goal achievement: The role of intentions. *European Review of Social Psychology*, 4, 141–85.

Golob, T. F. (2001). Travelbehaviour.com: Activity approaches to modelling the effects of information technology on personal travel behaviour. In D. Hensher (ed.), *Travel Behaviour Research: The Leading Edge* (pp. 145–83). Amsterdam: Pergamon.

Goodwin, P. (1996). Simple arithmetic. *Transport Policy*, 3, 79–80.

(1998). The end of equilibrium. In T. Gärling, T. Laitila, and K. Westin (eds.), *Theoretical Foundations of Travel Choice Modelling* (pp. 103–32). Amsterdam: Elsevier.

Gordon, P., and Richardson, H. W. (1997). Are compact cities a desirable planning goal? *Journal of the American Planning Association*, 63, 95–106.

Greene, D. L., and Wegener, M. (1997). Sustainable transport. *Journal of Transport Geography*, 5, 177–90.

Handy, S., Weston, L., and Mokhtarian, P. L. (2005). Driving by choice or necessity. *Transportation Research A*, 39, 183–203.

Hayes-Roth, B., and Hayes-Roth, F. (1979). A cognitive model of planning. *Cognitive Science*, 3, 275–310.

Hemily, B. (2004). *Trends Affecting Public Transit's Effectiveness*, www.apta.com/government_affairs/policy/trends_affecting.cfm#_Toc464706596. Retrieved 14 November 2005.

Hupfer, M. (2002). Communicating with the agentic woman and the communal man: Are stereotypic advertising appeals still relevant? *Academy of Marketing Science Review*, 2002(3), Retrieved 9 January 2005 from www.amsreview.org/articles/hupfer03–2002.pdf.

Jakobsson, C., Fujii, S., and Gärling, T. (2000). Determinants of private car users' acceptance of road pricing. *Transport Policy*, 7, 153–8.

Johansson, L.-O., Gustafsson, M., Falkemark, G., Gärling, T., and Johansson-Stenman, O. (2003). Goal conflicts in political decision making: A survey of municipality politicians' views of road pricing. *Environment and Planning C: Government and Policy*, 21, 615–24.

Jones, P. (1995). Road pricing: The public viewpoint. In B. Johansson and L.-G. Mattsson (eds.), *Road Pricing: Theory, Empirical Assessment and Policy* (pp. 159–79). Dordrecht: Kluwer.

(2003). Acceptability of transport pricing strategies: Meeting the challenge. In J. Schade and B. Schlag (eds.), *Acceptability of Transport Pricing Strategies* (pp. 27–62). Amsterdam: Elsevier.

Jones, P., Dix, M. C., Clarke, M. I., and Heggie, I. G. (1983). *Understanding Travel Behaviour*. Aldershot: Gower.

Kitamura, R. (1988). An evaluation of activity-based travel analysis. *Transportation*, 15, 9–34.

Kitamura, R., and Fujii, S. (1998). Two computational process models of activity-travel choice. In T. Gärling, T. Laitila, and K. Westin (eds.), *Theoretical Foundations of Travel Choice Modelling* (pp. 251–79). Amsterdam: Elsevier.

Kitamura, R., Fujii, S., and Pas, E. I. (1997). Time-use data, analysis and modelling: Toward the next generation of transportation planning methodologies. *Transport Policy*, 4, 225–35.

Klayman, J., and Ha, Y.-W. (1987). Confirmation, disconfirmation, and information in hypothesis testing. *Psychological Review*, 94, 211–28.

Kristensen, J. P., and Marshall, S. (1999). Mobility management to reduce travel: The case of Aalborg. *Built Environment*, 25, 138–50.

Lave, C. A. (1992). Cars and demographic access. *Access*, 1, 4–11.

Lee, T. W., Locke, E. A., and Latham, G. P. (1989). Goal setting theory and performance. In L. A. Pervin (ed.), *Goal Concepts in Personality and Social Psychology* (pp. 291–326). Hillsdale, NJ: Lawrence Erlbaum.

Levinson, D., and Kumar, A. (1995). Activity, travel, and the allocation of time. *Journal of the American Planning Association*, 61, 458–70.

Litman, T. (2003). The online TDM encyclopedia: Mobility management information gateway. *Transport Policy*, 10, 245–9.

Locke, E. A., and Latham, G. P. (1984). *Goal Setting: A Motivational Technique That Works*. Englewood Cliffs, NJ: Prentice-Hall.

  (1990). *A Theory of Goal-setting and Task Performance*. Englewood Cliffs, NJ: Prentice-Hall.

Loukopoulos, P., Gärling, T., Jakobsson, C., and Fujii, S. (2007). A cost-minimization principle of adaptation of private car use in response to road pricing schemes. In C. Jensen-Butler, M. Larsen, B. Madsen, O. A. Nielsen, and B. Sloth (eds.), *Road Pricing, the Economy, and the Environment*. Amsterdam: Elsevier.

Loukopoulos, P., Gärling, T., and Vilhelmson, B. (2005a). Mapping the potential consequences of car-use reduction in urban areas. *Journal of Transport Geography*, 13, 135–50.

Loukopoulos, P., Jakobsson, C., Gärling, T., Meland, S., and Fujii, S. (2006). Understanding of adaptation to car-use reduction goals. *Transportation Research F.*, 115–27.

Loukopoulos, P., Jakobsson, C., Gärling, T., Schneider, C. M., and Fujii, S. (2004). Car user responses to travel demand management measures: Goal setting and choice of adaptation alternatives. *Transportation Research D*, 9, 263–80.

  (2005b). Public attitudes towards policy measures for reducing private car use: Evidence from a study in Sweden. *Environmental Science and Policy*, 8, 57–66.

Louw, E., Maat, K., and Mathers, S. (1998). Strategies and measures to reduce travel by car in European cities. Paper presented at the Eighth World Conference on Transport Research, Antwerp, Belgium, July.

Lyons, G., and Urry, J. (2005). Travel time use in the information age. *Transportation Research A*, 39, 257–76.

Maat, K. (2002). The compact city: Conflict of interest between housing and mobility aims in the Netherlands. In E. Stern, I. Salomon, and P. H. L. Bovy (eds.), *Travel Behaviour: Spatial Patterns, Congestions and Modelling* (pp. 3–19). Cheltenham: Edward Elgar.

May, A. D., Jopson, A. F., and Matthews, B. (2003). Research challenges in urban transport policy. *Transport Policy*, 10, 157–64.

McFadden, D. (2001). Disaggregate behavioural travel demand's RUM side – A 30 years retrospective. In D. A. Hensher (ed.), *Travel Behaviour Research* (pp. 17–63). Amsterdam: Elsevier.

Modarres, A. (2003). Polycentricity and transit service. *Transportation Research A*, 37, 841–64.

Mokhtarian, P. L., and Salomon, I. (2001). How derived is the demand for travel? Some conceptual and measurement considerations. *Transportation Research A*, 35, 695–719.

Muller, P. O. (1995). Transportation and urban form. In S. Hanson (ed.), *The Geography of Urban Transportation* (2nd edn, pp. 26–52). New York: Guilford Press.

OECD (1996). *Towards Sustainable Transportation*. Paris: OECD Publications.

Ouellette, J. A., and Wood, W. (1998). Habit and intention in everyday life: The multiple processes by which past behaviour predicts future behaviour. *Psychological Bulletin*, 124, 54–74.

Payne, J. W., Bettman, J. R., and Johnson, E. J. (1993). *The Adaptive Decision Maker*. New York: Cambridge University Press.

Pendyala, R. M., Kitamura, R., Chen, C., and Pas, E. I. (1997). An activity-based micro-simulation analysis of transportation control measures. *Transport Policy*, 4, 183–92.

Pendyala, R. M., Kitamura, R., and Reddy, D. V. G. P. (1998). Application of an activity-based travel demand model incorporating a rule-based algorithm. *Environment and Planning B*, 25, 753–72.

Priemus, H., Nijkamp, P., and Banister, D. (2001). Mobility and spatial dynamics: An uneasy relationship. *Journal of Transport Geography*, 9, 167–71.

Pucher, J. (1999). Transportation trends, problems, and policies: An international perspective. *Transportation Research A*, 33, 493–503.

Recker, W. W., McNally, M. G., and Roth, G. S. (1986). A model of complex travel behaviour: Theoretical development. *Transportation Research A*, 20, 307–18.

Reisberg, D. (2006). *Cognition*. New York: Norton.

Samuelson, W., and Zeckhausen, R. (1988). Status quo bias in decision making. *Journal of Risk and Uncertainty*, 1, 7–59.

Sandqvist, K. (1997). *The Appeal of Automobiles – Human Desires and the Proliferation of Cars (KFB Report 1997:21)*. Stockholm: Swedish Transport and Communications Research Board.

Santos, G., and Rojey, L. (2004). Distributional impacts of road pricing: The truth behind the myth. *Transportation*, 31, 21–42.

Schwanen, T., Dieleman, F. M., and Dijst, M. (2001). Travel behaviour in Dutch monocentric and polycentric urban systems. *Journal of Transport Geography*, 9, 173–86.

Sheller, M. (2004). Automotive emotions: Feeling the car. *Theory, Culture and Society*, 21, 221–42.

Simon, H. A. (1990). Invariants of human behaviour. *Annual Review of Psychology*, 41, 1–19.

Southworth, F. (2001). On the potential impacts of land use change policies on automobile vehicle miles of travel. *Energy Policy*, 29, 1271–83.

Sperling, D., and Claussen, E. (2004). Motorizing the developing world. *Access*, 24 (Spring), 10–15.

Steg, L. (2003). Can public transport compete with the private car? *IATSS Research*, 27, 27–35.

  (2005). Car use: Lust and must. Instrumental, symbolic and affective motives for car use. *Transportation Research A*, 39, 147–62.

Steg, L., and Schuitema, G. (2006). Behavioural responses to transport pricing: A theoretical analysis. In T. Gärling and L. Steg (eds.), *Threats from Car Traffic to the Quality of Urban Life: Problems, Causes, and Solutions* (pp. 347–66). Amsterdam: Elsevier.

Steg, L., and Vlek, C. (1997). The role of problem awareness in willingness-to-change car use and in evaluating relevant policy measures. In T. Rothengatter and W. Carbonell Vaya (eds.), *Traffic and Transport Psychology. Theory and Application* (pp. 465–75). Amsterdam: Pergamon.

Stern, P. C., and Dietz, T. (1994). The value basis of environmental concern. *Journal of Social Issues*, 50(3), 65–84.

Stradling, S. G. (2002). Transport user needs and marketing public transport. *Municipal Engineer*, 151, 23–8.

Stradling, S. G., Meadows, M. L., and Beatty, S. (2000). Helping drivers out of their cars. Integrating transport policy and social psychology for sustainable change. *Transport Policy*, 7, 207–15.

Thorpe, N., Hills, P., and Jaensirisak, S. (2000). Public attitudes to TDM measures: A comparative study. *Transport Policy*, 7, 243–57.

Timmermans, H. J. P., van der Waerden, P., Alves, M., Polak, J., Ellis, S., Harvey, A. S., Kurose, S., and Zandee, R. (2003). Spatial context and the complexity of daily travel patterns: An international comparison. *Journal of Transport Geography*, 11, 37–46.

Train, K. (1980). A structured logit model of auto ownership and mode choice. *Review of Economic Studies*, 28, 357–70.

Ubbels, B., and Verhoef, E. (2006). The economic theory of transport pricing. In T. Gärling and L. Steg (eds.), *Threats from Car Traffic to the Quality of Urban Life: Problems, Causes, and Solutions* (pp. 325–45). Amsterdam: Elsevier.

US Department of Energy (2002). *Annual Energy Review 2000*. Washington, DC: Energy Information Administrator.

Verplanken, B., Aarts, H., and Van Knippenberg, A. (1997). Habit, information acquisition, and the process of making travel mode choices, *European Journal of Social Psychology*, 27, 539–60.

Vilhelmson, B. (1999). Daily mobility and the use of time for different activities: The case of Sweden. *GeoJournal*, 48, 177–85.

(2005). Urbanisation and everyday mobility. Long-term changes of travel in urban areas of Sweden. *Cybergeo*, 302, 1–13.

Vlek, C., and Michon, J. A. (1992). Why we should and how we could decrease the use of motor vehicles in the near future. *IATSS Research*, 15, 82–93.

Wardman, M. (2001). A review of British evidence on time and service quality valuations. *Transportation Research E*, 37, 107–28.

Wootton, J. (1999). Replacing the private car. *Transport Reviews*, 19, 157–75.

Wright, C., and Curtis, B. (2005). Reshaping the motor car. *Transport Policy*, 12, 11–22.

Wright, C., and Egan, J. (2000). De-marketing the car. *Transport Policy*, 7, 287–94.

17 Environmental morale and motivation

BRUNO S. FREY AND ALOIS STUTZER

17.1 Why is environmental morale important?

Economists are convinced that mankind has the capacity to overcome environmental problems if only the right incentives are in place. The environmental problem is identified to lie in the externalities inducing people to destroy the environment because such action is free of cost. The solution is to establish property rights ensuring that every user of the services provided by the environment must pay an appropriate price. The policy instruments suggested rely on an imitation of markets via tradeable licenses, or environmental taxes and subsidies. The relative price effect (see Becker 1976, Frey 1992a) ensures that an efficient allocation of all resources, produced and natural, is achieved. These instruments alone are sufficient to reach that goal provided they are correctly applied; no other instruments are needed. There is by now a large literature on environmental economics buttressing this view (see, for example, the surveys by Cropper and Oates 1992 and Stavins 2005), and there are impressive examples of the effectiveness of using the price system (e.g. Diekmann and Preisendörfer 2003). A large majority of economists has no doubt that using incentive instruments is far superior to relying on either moralistic behavior, or on commands and controls. Environmental economics has indeed been identified as one of the most successful applications of economic theory (Faulhaber and Baumol 1988).

In contrast to economists, most psychologists take it as a matter of course that in order to address environmental issues successfully people must change their way of thinking and must adopt "environmental values." Economists criticize this approach as having little or no impact on the environment. On the other hand, the use of market incentive instruments is put into doubt by many social scientists and environmental activists. They argue that today's society cannot rightfully sell what it does not own because nature is taken to have rights of its own and also belongs to future generations. Moreover, rationing the scarce environmental resources by prices is often taken to be unfair.

The two approaches take extreme positions; environmental morale is certainly more important than claimed in standard economics. An environmental policy solely using price incentives disregards the useful contribution of environmental morale and motivation to overcome environmental degradation.

The damage to the environment created by the activity of human beings is, to a large extent, due to *public-good or free-riding problems*: while each person values a better state of the environment, conditions are such that it is advantageous for each individual not to contribute to this improvement. In four specific areas, it is possible only to overcome this cooperation problem if the population has a sufficient degree of environmental morale:

(1)   In important areas, economic incentive instruments cannot be applied at all or would be too costly to overcome cooperation problems (see Baumol and Oates 1979). This is the case when the costs of control are extremely high due to many diffuse sources of pollution, or due to a large number of individuals causing environmental damage in small ways (e.g. spitting, throwing away batteries, pieces of paper or used cigarettes). In these cases voluntary contributions must be relied upon in order to prevent negative environmental externalities.

(2)   The provision of environmental public goods has often to be secured by people willing to sanction non-contributors. Sanctioning involves costs over and above individuals' direct voluntary contributions to a public environmental good. Monitoring, complaining, shaming or even punishing at one's own cost involves another public good (a second order public good). For its provision, individuals must have a preference for reciprocal fairness in environmental issues.

(3)   Extensive empirical research shows that controls and punishment are only one factor inducing people to observe existing laws and regulations. The subjective expected utility model used by standard economics is unable to explain in a satisfactory way how people actually behave (Schoemaker 1982). An important factor why people obey the law is the morally based inclination to act legally when the laws are perceived to be "fair" and "legitimate" (Tyler 1990).

(4)   The economic instruments of environmental policy can only be politically applied if the citizens are prepared to support the public good of environmental protection when voting. As no single person can determine the collective decision (it depends on the votes of many thousands or even millions of other citizens) he or she has little or no incentive to cast a vote in favor of the environment especially when his or her private interests are negatively affected. A collective decision for the environment requires that a majority of the voters has an intrinsic motivation to protect the environment, and therefore to support the proposed environmental policy politically.

This contribution discusses the role of environmental morale and environmental motivation in individual behavior from the point of view of economics and psychology. Section 17.2 deals with the fundamental public good problem, and presents empirical (laboratory and field) evidence on how the cooperation problem can be overcome. Four different theoretical approaches are distinguished according to how individuals' underlying environmental motivation is modeled. Section 17.3 looks specifically at the interaction between environmental policy and environmental morale through the lens of cognitive evaluation theory (also known as crowding theory). Section 17.4 concludes.

17.2   The public good problem in the natural environment

17.2.1   Standard prediction versus experimental evidence

Rational, self-interested individuals do not contribute to a public good or the conservation of a common-pool resource. This is the outcome of the n-person prisoner's dilemma game viewed as the canonical representation of the public good problem (Olson 1965, Hardin 1971). The reason for this predicted outcome is the free-rider problem: public goods are defined as goods from which any agent can benefit independently of her or his own contribution (non-exclusion condition). Accordingly, everybody has an incentive to hope that other agents provide the public good. Narrowly self-interested agents contribute only to the extent that their private marginal benefits equal the marginal costs of the public good, whereas it would be optimal for a group if the sum of marginal benefits equates to marginal costs. This tension between individual and collective rationality lies at the heart of many cooperation problems.

This outcome contradicts, however, both laboratory experiments and observations of everyday life. In particular, there is substantial evidence from linear public goods games (or voluntary contribution mechanisms), the games that have probably most often been used to study the incentive to free ride. Such a game can be summarized as follows: "In a typical linear public goods experiment, n people form a group. All group members are endowed with z 'tokens.' Each subject i has to decide independently how many tokens (between 0 and z) to contribute to a common project (the public good). The contributions of the whole group are summed up. The experimenter then multiplies the sum of contributions by $\alpha > 1$ and distributes the resulting amount equally among the four group members" (Gächter 2007: 22). This game has been implemented in many different versions (one-shot versus repeated interaction, with and without identification of fellow agents, with and without a possibility to punish other group members for non-contribution, etc.).

Seven general findings summarize the core results of this experiment and similar others (see Ledyard 1995, Ostrom 2000):

(1)   The contribution by individuals is between 40 and 60 percent of their endowment in one-shot and in the first round of finitely repeated games.

(2)   While in the course of successive rounds the contribution levels fall, they remain above zero.

(3)   If people are grouped in fixed pairs and interact repeatedly with the same "partner," they contribute more than if they interact with a randomly chosen fellow agent (see Keser and van Winden 2000, Andreoni and Croson 2008).

(4)   People can learn to cooperate (strategically) at a moderate level for longer periods of time, in particular with repeated interaction with the same people.

(5)   Individuals who believe that others will contribute to a public good tend to contribute more themselves (see also Frey and Meier 2004, Gächter 2006). This finding suggests that agents' contributions depend on what they expect others to do; or that they behave to some extent as conditional cooperators.

(6)   Individuals are prepared to cooperate much more with face-to-face identification and communication (see also Bohnet and Frey 1999).

(7)   Players are willing to incur costs to punish those who make below average contributions to a public good (see also Fehr and Gächter 2000a).

These experimental results have also been observed in many everyday life contexts. Thus, many people contribute to voluntary associations (Meier 2006), do not cheat on taxes even if they could (Feld and Frey 2002) and vote. These empirical findings have only partly been well integrated into theory. There is still a substantial gap between the (game) theoretic prediction that self-interested individuals do not contribute to a public good and the empirical observation that cooperative behavior is widespread.

17.2.2   Model approaches to environmental morale and motivation

Theoretical research has explored various ways to meet the challenge. Four important approaches can be distinguished to model individuals' underlying motivation to contribute to public environmental goods (or to model moral or norm-based behavior in general):

– altruism,
– social norms and reciprocal fairness,
– internalized norms, and
– intrinsic motivation.

Pure altruism as a type of pro-social preference means in the public goods context that an individual values an increase in the provision of the public good positively because (i) she has private preferences for it, and (ii) additional resources are allocated to a relevant reference agent, i.e. she wants to benefit others (e.g. Andreoni 1988). Pure altruism, however, appears to be counterfactual in most situations as a sole explanation for contributions to a public good; the reason being people's observed reactions in their giving behavior to state subsidies. In the pure altruism model, contributions depend on the utility level achieved by their fellow agents. People contribute more to a public good when the utility level of fellow agents is lower. This also implies that voluntary contributions to a public good are reduced if, for example, the state starts subsidizing or providing the good. In fact, a crowding out euro for euro by state subsidies is predicted. This is the traditional crowding effect (not to be mixed up with motivation crowding introduced in section 17.3). Empirical evidence for people's reactions to state subsidies in the voluntary contributions, however, shows no full crowding out (see Nyborg and Rege 2003 for a brief overview).

An extended model of *impure altruism* has been proposed (Andreoni 1990) in order to reconcile altruistic giving or contributing to a public good with the empirical findings. If people get a positive feeling from contributing itself, no full crowding out is implied. This pro-social preference is called a preference for "warm glow." It is important to note, however, that the later model of altruism can also not account for some of the robust findings about voluntary contributions mentioned above. In particular, altruistic motives are either independent of other people's cooperation behavior or predict lower contributions if others contribute.

Social norms can be understood as socially shared beliefs about how one ought to behave, for example, contributing to a public good. The prescribed behavior is enforced by informal social sanctions. It is argued that social norms can be understood as a reaction by societies to overcome market failure such as in a public good situation (e.g. Arrow 1971). While with impure altruism warm glow is the by-product of contributing, the by-product of following a social norm is social approval or the avoidance of disapproval (e.g. Holländer 1990, Gächter and Fehr 1999). Social norms for "environmentally friendly" behavior can be issue specific (e.g. against littering the street) or refer in general to behavior in a public goods context (Biel *et al.* 1999, Kerr 1995). Probably theoretically more important than the specific content of norms is their enforcement. Thereby, *reciprocal fairness* takes a key role as a norm enforcement device (Fehr and Gächter 2000b). Reciprocal fairness or reciprocity means that an individual responds to an action that is perceived to be kind or fair in a kind matter, and to an action that is perceived as hostile or unfair in a hostile manner. The perceived kindness, fairness or hostility of an action depends on the outcomes, intentions and procedural qualities associated with the action (for a model of reciprocity see, for example, Falk and Fischbacher 2006).

Internalized norms differ from social norms by the nature of rewards and sanctions as a reaction to individual behavior. If a norm is internalized, sanctions are internal and result in feelings of guilt, reduced self-respect and other negative self-evaluations.[1]

---

[1] The relationship between norms, their internalization and the composition of intrinsic motivation is described in Coleman (1990).

Intrinsic motivation with regard to contributing to public goods means that people pursue an activity for the inherent satisfaction of the activity itself (Ryan and Deci 2000). In contrast, extrinsic motivation "refers to the performance of an activity in order to attain some separable outcome" (Ryan and Deci 2000, 71). It might be argued that most environmentally desirable behavior is motivated by the expectation of separable outcomes and thus pro-social behavior in the environmental realm is rarely intrinsic in the narrow meaning of the term. However, the differences are subtle, in particular with regard to internalized norms. With internalized norms, people feel an obligation or a commitment to contribute and non-performance results in negative feelings (e.g. Schwartz 1977). The two approaches converge to the extent that internalized norms are derived from the person's internalized values (Schwartz and Howard 1984, and for the case of pro-environmental action Stern *et al.* 1995, 1999). It is not anticipated guilt or pride then that motivates cooperation but an intrinsic motivation to act according to one's values. The degree of internalization can be understood to determine the extent to which individuals perceive autonomy in their behavior. This might serve as a conceptual link between norm theories and cognitive evaluation theory. Moreover, it indicates the broader application of motivational crowding theory outlined in section 17.3.

17.2.3 Conditions for successful cooperation

It is very difficult to disentangle the different motives and the kind of social interaction in concrete social dilemmas (Manski 2000). Often individual behavior is determined by several motives simultaneously or different motives matter for different people in the same context (Thogersen 2006). The identification of preconditions for successful cooperation is thus a major challenge. Some recent evidence is from laboratory experiments. It is found that cooperation can be sustained even if there is a large fraction of agents with a tendency to free-ride in a group. This is the case if other agents in the group are motivated to contribute voluntarily and in addition to punish free-riders reciprocally at their own cost. Narrowly self-interested agents are then provided incentives to contribute to public goods as well. The composition of groups who have to solve a cooperation problem as well as their possibilities to punish fellow agents can thus become crucial (Gächter 2006).

The management of commons offers interesting field evidence with regard to the environment. In extensive empirical research, Ostrom and co-workers (2000) have been able to identify the conditions under which people are able to organize a scarce resource even though everyone has an incentive not to contribute to its maintenance, examples being a fish pond or a cow pasture (common-pool resource). A successful organization is more likely when:

– the resource users are able to design their own rules;
– the rules are enforced by the local users;

- the sanctions applied are graduated;
- the rights to withdraw from the resources are well defined;
- the collective action and monitoring reinforce each other.

These conditions make clear that environmental morale alone does not suffice. Rather, it is necessary that such morale is embedded in an appropriate institutional setting including sanctions – but such sanctions are most effective when they are voluntarily agreed by the users *before* the environment has been damaged.

17.3 Motivational crowding theory and the interaction between environmental policy and environmental morale

17.3.1 Theoretical issues

Environmental morale can be understood as a conglomerate of internalized norms and intrinsic motivation. It is not given but depends on a great many factors. A crucial question is how intrinsic motivation and internalized norms (here intrinsic motivation for short) are influenced by extrinsic motivation. This is particularly important for environmental policy with its interventions from outside in the form of commands and controls (as in the traditional policy) or in the form of induced price changes (as in the market-based economic approach). These issues have been analyzed in *Motivational Crowding Theory* which stems from social psychology and has been integrated into economics (Frey 1992b, 1997b, Le Grand 2003, Bénabou and Tirole 2003).

Social psychologists have analyzed and empirically measured the "hidden cost of reward" (see, for example, Deci and Ryan 1985, Pittman and Heller 1987) suggesting that an external intervention in the form of a reward may reduce individuals' intrinsic incentives to act. This *crowding-out* effect can be attributed to two major psychological processes:

(1) Self-determination is reduced. When people perceive an external intervention as a restriction to act autonomously, intrinsic motivation is substituted by this external intervention. The locus of control shifts from inside to outside the person (Rotter 1966). The person in question no longer feels responsible but makes the outside intervention responsible instead. However, this shift in the locus of control only takes place when the intervention is considered to be controlling. In contrast, when the intervention is perceived to be supportive, in the sense that it acknowledges one's competence, internal control is strengthened. Intrinsic or extrinsic motivation is raised depending on which aspect is more prominent.

(2) Reciprocity is violated. The implicit contract based on mutual acknowledgment of one's engagement is violated when a task undertaken by intrinsic motivation is rewarded extrinsically (Gouldner 1960, Rousseau 1995).

Conversely, maintaining norms of reciprocity causes a higher willingness to contribute to a public good or prevent over-exploitation of a common-pool resource.

The "hidden cost of reward" has been generalized in economics in three dimensions:

a) *All* outside interventions can affect intrinsic motivation: in addition to *rewards*, the same effect can come about by external *regulations* (commands and controls).

b) External interventions *crowd-out* intrinsic motivation if they are perceived to be *controlling* and they *crowd-in* intrinsic motivation if they are perceived to be *supporting*. Intrinsic motivation is bolstered by the following factors leading to the *crowding-in* effect: *(i) Personal relationships foster intrinsic motivation*. Mutual acknowledgment of one's obligations and responsibilities is appreciated among friends, colleagues and family members. Thus, team-based or community-based structures provide motivational benefits (Grant 1996, 118). *(ii) Principals and agents communicate with each other*. Communication is a precondition for reciprocity via learning about, and acknowledging the duties and responsibilities of, other people. Experiments show that communication systematically raises the intrinsic motivation to cooperate (e.g. Dawes, van de Kragt and Orbell 1988, Frey and Bohnet 1995). *(iii) Citizens participate in decision making*. The greater the possibility to codetermine, the more the citizens would adopt decisions as their own. Participation thus raises self-determination and is a precondition for reciprocity.

c) Motivational crowding effects must be considered simultaneously with the relative price effect (psychologists considered the first effect in isolation, while economists were aware of only the second effect).

The three dimensions are best analyzed in a principal–agent setting.

A (representative) agent adjusts his or her performance considering the benefits B and the cost C induced. Both benefits and costs increase in performance P, i.e. $\delta B/\delta P \equiv B_P > 0$, and $\delta C/\delta P \equiv C_P > 0$. Higher performance exhibits diminishing marginal returns ($B_{PP} < 0$) and has increasing marginal cost ($C_{PP} > 0$). Benefits and cost are also influenced by the principal's external intervention E

$$B = B(P, E); B_P > 0, B_{PP} < 0; \tag{1}$$
$$C = C(P, E); C_P > 0, C_{PP} < 0. \tag{2}$$

A rational agent chooses that level of performance P* that maximizes net benefits (B − C) which yields the first-order condition

$$B_P = C_P. \tag{3}$$

Differentiating this utility maximizing condition with respect to E shows how the agent's optimal performance P* is affected when the principal changes the extent of external intervention

$$B_{PE} + B_{PP}\, dP^*/dE = C_{PE} + C_{PP}\, dP^*/dE, \text{ or}$$

$$\frac{dP^*}{dE} = \frac{B_{PE} - C_{PE}}{C_{PP} - B_{PP}} \lessgtr 0. \tag{4}$$

Following standard principal–agent theory (e.g. Alchian and Demsetz 1972, Fama and Jensen 1983), external intervention raises performance by imposing higher marginal cost on shirking or, equivalently, by lowering the marginal cost of performing, $C_{PE} < 0$. This is the *relative price effect* of external intervention. As the crowding effect is neglected, a change in external intervention does not affect the marginal utility of performing ($B_{PE} = 0$), the orthodox economic theory predicts that external intervention raises performance ($dP^*/dE > 0$).

This positive effect is strengthened if the external intervention bolsters intrinsic motivation (*crowding-in effect*, $B_{PE} > 0$). On the other hand, the *crowding-out effect* ($B_{PE} < 0$) and the relative price effect ($C_{PE} < 0$) of an external intervention work in opposite directions, so that the outcome dP^*/dE depends on the relative size of C_{PE} and B_{PE}.

External interventions may moreover have an *indirect* damaging effect on intrinsic motivation. The crowding-out effect may spread to further areas, even into those where the external intervention has not been applied. If intrinsic motivation is crowded out in areas where it is a major (or even the only) behavioral incentive, the overall outcome of an external intervention tends to be even more strongly against the principal's interest. There may thus be an indirect *motivational spill-over effect* to be added to the direct crowding-out effect. A possible scenario can be based on policy instruments such as effluent charges or tradeable permits. They work efficiently where they are applied, but an induced substitution of environmental morale by monetary incentives may well lead people to protect the environment less in areas where no external incentives exist. This undesired spill-over effect is a possibility not only with monetary incentives but also with rules and regulations.

17.3.2 Empirical evidence

Crowding theory has been the subject of such a large number of *laboratory experiments* that it is impossible to summarize their results here. Fortunately, there have already been no fewer than five formal meta-analytical studies relating to crowding theory.

Rummel and Feinberg (1988) used forty-five experimental studies covering the period 1971–85; Wiersma (1992) twenty studies covering 1971–90; and Tang and Hall (1995) fifty studies from 1972 to 1992. These meta-analyses essentially support the cognitive evaluation theory developed by Deci and his co-workers where intrinsic motivation is undermined if the externally applied rewards are perceived to be controlling by the recipients. This by now "conventional" view was challenged by Cameron and Pierce (1994) and Eisenberger and Cameron (1996) who, on the basis of their own meta-analysis covering studies published in the period 1971–91 (the two studies are based on a virtually identical set of studies), concluded that the undermining effect is largely "a myth" and that cognitive evaluation theory should therefore be abandoned. These studies attracted a great deal of attention, and many scholars on that basis seem to have concluded that no such thing as a crowding-out effect exists. Deci, Koestner and Ryan (1998), in a very extensive study, were able to show that these conclusions are unwarranted and that the crowding-out effect is a robust phenomenon of significant size under the conditions identified. This most recent meta-analysis includes all the studies considered by Cameron, Pierce and Eisenberger as well as several studies which have appeared since then. The sixty-eight experiments reported in fifty-nine articles span the period 1971–97, and refer to ninety-seven experimental effects. It turns out that tangible rewards undermine intrinsic motivation for interesting tasks (i.e. tasks for which the experimental subjects show an intrinsic interest) in a highly significant and very reliable way, and that the effect is moderately large. Tangible rewards, in particular monetary compensations, are obviously perceived to be controlling by the experimental subjects and therefore tend to crowd out intrinsic motivation. It is important to see that the experimental studies look at the net effect of a reward while we argue that the conventional relative price effect should be separated from the crowding-out effect, and that it is important to consider their relative size under various conditions.

Crowding theory has also received strong support in *field studies*. A case study refers, for example, to the so-called "token economies" where people living in homes for the elderly were induced to undertake certain tasks (such as making their bed) in exchange for vouchers. As a consequence, after some time, these people were only willing to do anything at all if they received a compensation. The intended activation of the aged proved to be a failure (Kazdin 1982). Crowding out has also been the subject of econometric studies. For example, in an econometric study of 116 managers in medium-sized Dutch firms, Barkema (1995) found that the number of hours worked in the company decreased with the intensity of personal control effected by the superiors.

Another meta-analysis of 19 studies and 115 effect sizes for the period 1975–95 devoted to the effects of organizational behavior modification on task performance (Stajkovic and Luthans 1997: 1141) also identifies a crowding-out effect. When a financial reward is used in combination with non-financial interventions, the monetary payment has been observed to diminish the effect of the total intervention.

The crowding-in effect is also well supported by experimental (see again Deci, Koestner and Ryan 1998) as well as field evidence. For example, an econometric analysis documents the positive effect of political participation possibilities on intrinsic motivation in the form of civic virtue (Frey 1997b): keeping many other influences constant, the citizens in those cantons of Switzerland with more developed institutions of direct democracy have a higher level of civic virtue resulting in a lower level of tax cheating.

17.3.3 Crowding effects in environmental policy

Individuals as consumers are of great importance for the preservation of the natural environment (see Ölander and Thogersen 1995). Firms and other private organizations, as well as the government sector, also play a major role in the protection and preservation of the environment. Their behavior when subjected to environmental policy can also be analyzed using crowding theory but care must be taken to aggregate the behaviour of individual decision makers to the reactions of the units themselves.

The *crowding-out effect* can only take place if individuals have a substantial amount of environmental morale before the external intervention occurs. It undermines environmental morale in the area where the policy intervention takes place, and/or in a related area (spill-over effect). There exists abundant evidence that people are prepared to follow their environmental conscience provided the cost of doing so is not too high (particularly in low-cost situations, see Kliemt 1986, Kirchgässner 1992, Diekmann and Preisendörfer 2003). Examples are the separation of types of refuse, non-littering in public places, and the boycott of firms which damage the environment, such as choosing a rival petrol station over Shell in the case of the Brent Spar incident (see Thogersen 1994 for many further examples).

The following propositions are formulated to work out as clearly as possible the expected consequences of applying the various instruments of environmental policy. The first proposition deals with direct governmental interventions as employed in wide areas of environmental policy.

Proposition 1: An environmental policy via controls and commands
              (regulations) undermines environmental morale.

When government intervenes via regulations, it often prescribes in great detail a particular behavior, and threatens punishments. This shifts the locus of control away from individuals. Consumers' self-determination is reduced and they feel that to exercise high environmental morale is superfluous. On the other hand, the use of the legal system to influence behavior has an *expressive* function. The citizens are clearly informed that an environmentally friendly behavior is expected of them. Such affirmation tends to reinforce existing environmental morale.

In order to see the outcome on behavior in the case of an intervention that is perceived as controlling, it is necessary to compare the crowding-out effect to the countervailing relative price effect. The latter is induced by an expected cost of punishment if environmental regulations are violated. Individuals are punished only if their deviant behavior is detected, if they are convicted and if they are actually punished with a fine or imprisonment. Thus, many steps have to be taken, and there are many interventions possible in the form of outright bribes or calling upon political conveniences before a punishment is really effected. Especially with regard to the environment, it is often difficult to prove that a regulation has been violated so that punishments tend to be of small magnitude and delayed. It is, moreover, well known that individuals find it difficult to deal rationally with the probabilities involved (Kahneman, Slovic and Tversky 1982, Dawes 1988, Thaler 1992) so that the underlying calculus of expected punishment leads to uncertain behavioral consequences (Schoemaker 1982). It follows that the implicit relative price effect induced by controls and commands is in general rather limited.

The relative size of the countervailing effects of crowding out environmental morale and regulations depends on the specific situation. The more strongly induced environmentally friendly behavior is, and the more the expressive function of the law strengthens existing environmental morale, the less regulations reduce individuals' discretionary room, and the more consistently obvious violators are punished. This is best achieved with a few, easy to understand regulations where punishments fit the damage done to nature. A large number of complex, abstract and opaque regulations, on the other hand, are unlikely to improve the environment as environmental morale will be strongly crowded out while threatened punishments are easier to evade.

The next two propositions deal with environmental instruments preferred by economists because they explicitly affect the monetary incentives faced by consumers (see, for example, Stavins 1998).

Proposition 2: Tradeable emission rights tend to strongly crowd out environmental morale.

Tradeable emission rights fix the quantity of pollution (see, for example, Tietenberg 1985). The environment may thus be burdened only insofar as the emitter is licensed to do so by the emission rights in his or her possession. The trade between prospective polluters results in a price for the pollution rights. While this instrument has been devised for, and so far has been applied to, firms, it may also be used to curb the pollution caused by private households. The basic idea is that the property rights to nature belong to society as a whole (and are administered by the government), and that its use is no longer free of charge but that a price has to be paid. The scheme thus effects a change in relative prices and induces a change in behavior based on extrinsic motivation.

Payment for being able to undertake an undesired activity – the pollution of the natural environment – can be compared with indulgences sold in the Middle Ages (Goodin 1994). Such trades foster a cynical attitude, conveying the notion that it is acceptable to sin, provided you pay for it. The sense of punishment for sinning is at least partly lost. The exchange and bargaining process between the buyers and sellers of emission rights focuses the attention on the possibilities to pollute thereby acquired. In this particular sense, the polluter has been conferred a "license to pollute" (see Kelman 1981). The use of the price system is accompanied by a process whose expressive connotations suggest that owners of these rights can legitimately pollute the environment (Blinder 1987). Conversely, to refrain from damaging the environment for a moral reason plays no role, or is even taken to be irrational or naive. These are the reasons why the use of tradeable emission rights is expected to lead to a strong crowding out of environmental morale.

The relative price and the crowding-out effect work in opposite directions. Emission rights tend to reduce pollution because they make violation costly but at the same time the exact mechanism producing this result tends markedly to destroy the intrinsic motivation to safeguard the environment.

This negative effect on environmental morale is also expected in the case of a second instrument preferred by economists, environmental taxes.

Proposition 3: Environmental taxes (emission charges) tend to crowd out environmental morale but the effect is smaller than in the case of tradeable emission rights.

Environmental taxes fix the cost of polluting by government decree. Unlike tradeable emission rights, this instrument directly imposes charges on those consumers (and firms) damaging nature. While the mechanism for calculating a particular price differs, the extrinsically induced change of behavior is identical. But the expressive connotation is quite different. To charge for the use of the environment makes it clear that it is an undesired activity better not to be undertaken. There is still a crowding-out effect to be expected because the government's intervention reduces the extent of individuals' self-determination. The locus of control is shifted to the government, and consumers are induced to feel that they are no longer responsible for protecting nature. The expressive connotation in the case of environmental taxes is clearly less destructive to environmental morale than are tradeable emission rights. As the relative price effect is of the same magnitude with both instruments (given that the same cost for polluting is imposed), but crowding out is expected to be less marked, emission taxes are in general more effective in protecting the environment than are tradeable emission rights. The exact size of the crowding-out effect connected with environmental taxes depends on a variety of circumstances. On the basis of the considerations just discussed, it is, however, possible to advance a proposition comparing the effect of different tax rates.

Proposition 4: Either "low" or "high" environmental tax rates are more effective than "intermediate" tax rates.

Low environmental taxes work because they have a clear expressive function which supports environmental morale. Because taxes are low, consumers do not feel they are strongly controlled by this instrument so that the crowding-out effect is small or may even turn into a crowding-in effect due to the expressive aspects of the tax (but the relative price effect is, of course, also low). There exists empirical evidence suggesting that low environmental taxes work well under these conditions (see, for example, Thogersen 2003 for small differentiated garbage fees).

High environmental taxes work because a strong relative price effect is induced: it becomes very costly to pollute nature. This effect is likely to dominate the crowding-out effect of taxation, especially when environmental morale is low from the very beginning.

An intermediate-sized environmental tax induces undesirable effects on both accounts. Environmental morale is crowded out as individuals' self-determination becomes noticeably impaired but the tax rates are insufficient to induce much reduction in pollution due to extrinsic motivation. This proposition has been empirically supported for the case of positive incentives in an article with the suggestive title "Pay Enough or Don't Pay at All" (Gneezy and Rustichini 2000). The study is about day-care centers confronted with the problem that parents sometimes arrive late to pick up their children, which forces teachers to stay after the official closing time. A typical economic approach would suggest introducing a fine for collecting children late. Such a punishment is expected to induce parents to reduce the occurrence of belatedly picking up their children. In the study, they first recorded the number of late-coming parents over a particular period of time. In a second period extending over twelve weeks, a significant monetary fine for collecting children late was introduced. After an initial learning phase, the number of late-coming parents *increased* substantially, which is consistent with the crowding-out effect. The introduction of a monetary fine transformed the relationship between parents and teachers from a non-monetary into a monetary one. As a result, the parents' intrinsic motivation to keep to the time schedules was reduced or was crowded out altogether; the feeling now was that the teachers are "paid" for the disamenity of having to stay longer. That parents' intrinsic motivation was crowded out for good by the introduction of a penalty system is supported by the fact that the number of late-coming parents remained stable at the level prevailing even after the fine was cancelled in a third phase.

The following two propositions show how various policy instruments produce a *crowding-in effect* to preserve nature.

Proposition 5: Environmental morale is supported in the short term by
                appeals and participation, and in the long term by education.

These outside interventions strengthen consumers' self-determination. The locus of control remains with the individuals as these measures – at least if well done – emphasize their own responsibility. This crowding-in effect may be restricted to a particular area addressed by an intervention, but is likely to extend beyond that if individuals perceive a substantial degree of similarity of issue and content.

There exists substantial empirical evidence that these short-and long-run interventions do indeed motivate consumers to change their behavior. Examples are appeals to save water in times of drought (e.g. Baumol and Oates 1979: 296–9) or recycling (e.g. De Young 1986, Hopper and Nielsen 1991, see more generally Thogersen 1994).

To undertake an environmental policy based on the respective intrinsic motivation has strong limitations. There are two major aspects to be considered:

(1)   Environmental morale can only be evoked and targeted to reach a specific goal if the contributions expected by the consumers are easy to comprehend and correspond to common sense. This is true for some environmental problems but certainly not for all. Often, the damage done to the environment by a good or service is hidden and occurs at earlier stages of production not visible in the commodity itself (for example, a good which looks environmentally clean may cause heavy pollution because of the way it is transported to the stores).

(2)   Environmental morale may be unreliable and unsustainable. It may, in particular, suddenly drop when consumers realize that other persons take advantage of their environmentally responsible behavior. This "sucker" effect corresponds to everyday observations and has been well documented in prisoner's dilemma experiments (e.g. Dawes, McTavish and Shaklee 1977, Ledyard 1995). There is also strong empirical evidence (Diekmann and Preisendörfer 2003) that individuals consistently follow their intrinsic motivation only as long as the cost is not substantial (for so-called "low-cost decisions" see Kliemt 1986, Kirchgässner 1992 and, especially for the environment, Frey 1997a). A typical low-cost decision is voting – where, as stated in the introduction, environmental morale is crucial to having the government's respective policies sanctioned.

It follows that an environmental policy solely based on people's intrinsic motivation would be misguided and ineffective. Environmental morale is, however, an indispensable element needed in an overall policy effort, and in particular to accompany the application of market-based instruments.

Proposition 6: Environmental morale is supported and raised by the expressive function of legal regulations.

Such regulations differ strongly from the control-and-command type of legal interventions. Punishment for non-observers is sometimes not even mentioned, or plays a small role (for example, it is irrelevant whether there is a good chance of being able to apply a punishment). The main function of the law in this case is to emphasize a certain direction – for desired behavior to protect the environment – and to express it officially. While orthodox economists have disregarded this function, lawyers have always been aware of its importance (among adherents of the law and economics movement: e.g. Cooter 1984, 1994, Sunstein 1997).

The final proposition remains open with regard to the effect on intrinsic motivation.

Proposition 7: Government subsidies have an ambiguous effect on environmental morale.

On the one hand, environmental morale might be supported by government subsidies. This is the case if subsidies for activities reducing pollution serve an expressive function. Government policy indicates what is considered desirable behavior. The monetary transfers as such corroborate the change in behavior due to the change in relative prices. The relative price and the crowding effect work in the same direction.

For various other reasons, environmental subsidies are, however, no ideal policy instrument. To mention only a few problems: (i) Subsidies are often handed out independent of the reduction of pollution so that there is no marginal extrinsic incentive effect. In this case, the beneficial effect must come solely from crowding in environmental morale. But as the subsidy is not targeted, and money as such does not talk, the expressive effect is likely to be minor. (ii) Subsidies effecting a change in relative prices provide an incentive to increase pollution before their introduction so that the recipients can benefit even more from the subsidy. (iii) Subsidies are a drain on government revenues. The good achieved by the inducements must be compared to the costs imposed on individuals by the necessary taxation. The size of these "dead weight costs" depends on a number of conditions but some studies have calculated a rather high burden (e.g. Stuart 1984) so that this aspect cannot be treated lightly.

On the other hand, government subsidies are expected to undermine environmental morale if they are perceived as (controlling) bribes. A case in point is compensation offered to host so-called locally unwanted projects (Frey and Oberholzer-Gee 1997). This siting problem is known as the "not in my backyard" or NIMBY problem. For many different projects and major capital investments, a wide consensus exists that they are worth being undertaken. But no community is prepared to tolerate their vicinity. Such "nimbyistic" behavior is well documented in cases where communities object to the siting of, for example, hazardous waste disposal facilities or the construction of freeways.

Economists have a handy tool to deal with such a situation. As the aggregate net benefits of undertaking the project are positive, one must simply redistribute them in an appropriate way. The communities which are prepared to accept the undesired project within their borders must be *compensated* in such a way as to make their net benefits positive (O'Hare 1977, Kunreuther and Kleindorfer 1986). This policy recommendation underestimates the true costs of price incentives in that it fails to take into account the detrimental effects of motivation crowding out.

The hypothesis that external incentives crowd out civic duty or intrinsic motivation and therefore the willingness to accept the locally undesired project was tested by analyzing the reaction to monetary compensation offered for a nuclear waste repository (Frey and Oberholzer-Gee 1997). A survey was undertaken in the spring of 1993 among the population of a region in Switzerland that was found to be ideal for hosting a NIMBY-type project. All respondents were asked if they were willing to permit the construction of a nuclear waste repository on the grounds of their community.

More than half of the respondents (50.8%) agreed to have the nuclear waste repository built in their community, 44.9% opposed the siting and 4.3% did not care where the facility was built. Thus, this unfavorable siting decision was widely accepted in spite of the fact that a nuclear waste repository is mostly seen as a heavy burden for the residents of the host community. In a next step, the level of external compensation was varied. To this end the respondents were asked the same questions whether they were willing to accept the construction of a nuclear waste repository. This time, however, it was added that the Swiss parliament had decided to compensate all residents of the host community. The amount offered was varied from CHF 2,500 per individual and year (N = 117), to CHF 5,000 (N = 102) and CHF 7,500 (N = 86).[2] While 50.8% of the respondents agreed to accept the nuclear waste repository without compensation, *the level of acceptance dropped to 24.6%* when compensation was offered. The amount of compensation had no significant effect on the level of acceptance. About one-quarter of the respondents seemed to reject the facility simply because financial compensation was attached to it.

Compensation fundamentally alters the perceived nature of a siting procedure. What was observed in the analysis of verbal behavior represents precisely the type of mechanism postulated by motivation crowding theory. While external intervention, i.e. offering compensation, manages to address concerns regarding the costs of a noxious facility, it reduces the intrinsic motivation to permit the construction of such a facility. In the case studied, this latter effect even outweighs the benefits of external intervention, thereby reducing overall acceptance.

17.4 Concluding remarks

Environmental morale and motivation affect individuals' behavior as potential polluters, users of common-pool resources, consumers of environmentally friendly products, workers, investors, environmental activists, donors or volunteers of environmental organizations, voters on environmental issues and fellow citizens monitoring and sanctioning other polluters. Two kinds of behavioral effects are expected. First, environmental morale is often associated with pro-environmental attitudes or preferences that increase the demand for a clean environment. The result is a common demand effect for *private* environmental

---

[2] The compensation offered here was quite substantial. Median household income for the respondents was CHF 5,250 per month.

goods and is reflected in market prices. There is substantial evidence for the willingness to pay for a clean environment from hedonic market studies on the housing and labor markets. Second, and probably more important, environmental morale helps to overcome the free-rider problem that is pervasive with the provision of a clean environment. Intrinsically motivated people voluntarily contribute to public environmental goods, at least if others contribute too, and are willing to bear costs to punish fellow citizens who do not cooperate. The latter points to the importance of social interaction or social capital in the provision of local environmental goods (see, for example, Pretty and Ward 2001).

We briefly mention two directions for future interdisciplinary research on environmental morale that seem most interesting to us:

First, while there is a theoretical basis and preliminary evidence for the important interaction of environmental policy and individuals' environmental morale, we are still far away from a robust understanding of motivational interactions. Much additional empirical evidence is needed. For example how do deposits or their abolishment affect recycling? What is the effect of "green" gasoline taxes on recreational traffic beyond the price effect?, to mention just two areas of potential enquiry.

Second, under what conditions do firms' managers make environmentally friendly decisions? There are, of course, reputation and other economic arguments. For example, firms are willing to bear costs to reduce environmental externalities if they can avoid consumer boycotts. The latter are more likely in a competitive market. With competition, consumers can easily switch to alternative suppliers at a low cost to themselves. In addition to this indirect effect of consumers' environmental morale, there might, however, also be direct consequences of managers' motivation on business decisions. So far, any links between environmental morale and corporate environmental responsibility are not well understood but they might well rely on similar aspects of discourse as on the community level (see Scherer and Palazzo 2007 for corporate social responsibility in general).

Overall, environmental morale and motivation are found to be necessary for the successful solution of cooperation problems in the environmental realm. In institutional and policy design, this has to be taken actively into account as environmental morale cannot be understood as an invariant individual preference. It follows that institutions have to be designed so that environmental morale is sustained or strengthened rather than made superfluous and crowded out. Environmental morale and motivation thus have to remain high on the research agenda of interdisciplinary social scientists.

17.5 References

Alchian, Armen A. and Harold Demsetz (1972). Production, Information Costs and Economic Organization. *American Economic Review* 62(5): 777–95.

Andreoni, James (1988). Privately Provided Public-Goods in a Large Economy – the Limits of Altruism. *Journal of Public Economics* 35(1): 57–73.

(1990). Impure Altruism and Donations to Public-Goods – a Theory of Warm-Glow Giving. *Economic Journal* 100(401): 464–77.

Andreoni, James and Rachel Croson (2008). Partners versus Strangers: Random Rematching in Public Goods Experiments. Forthcoming in: Charles R. Plott and Vernon L. Smith (eds.), *Handbook of Experimental Economic Results*. Amsterdam: North Holland.

Arrow, Kenneth J. (1971). Political and Economic Evaluation of Social Effects and Externalities. In: Michael D. Intriligator (ed.), *Frontiers of Quantitative Economics*, vol. I. Amsterdam: North Holland: 3–25.

Barkema, Harry G. (1995). Do Executives Work Harder when They Are Monitored? *Kyklos* 48(1): 19–42.

Baumol, William J. and Wallace E. Oates (1979). *Economics, Environmental Policy, and the Quality of Life*. Englewood Cliffs, NJ: Prentice-Hall.

Becker, Gary S. (1976). *The Economic Approach to Human Behavior*. Chicago: Chicago University Press.

Bénabou, Roland and Jean Tirole (2003). Intrinsic and Extrinsic Motivation. *Review of Economic Studies* 70(3): 489–520.

Biel, Anders, Chris von Borgstede and Ulf Dahlstrand (1999). Norm Perception and Cooperation in Large-Scale Social Dilemmas. In: Margaret Foddy *et al.* (eds.), *Resolving Social Dilemmas: Dynamic, Structural, and Intergroup Aspects*. London: Psychology Press: 245–52.

Blinder, Alan S. (1987). *Hard Heads, Soft Hearts*. Reading, MA: Addison-Wesley.

Bohnet, Iris and Bruno S. Frey (1999). The Sound of Silence in Prisoner's Dilemma and Dictator Games. *Journal of Economic Behavior and Organization* 38(1): 43–57.

Cameron, Judy and W. David Pierce (1994). Reinforcement, Reward, and Intrinsic Motivation: A Meta-Analysis. *Review of Educational Research* 64 (Fall): 363–423.

Coleman, James S. (1990). *Foundations of Social Theory*. Cambridge, MA: Belknap Press of Harvard University Press.

Cooter, Robert D. (1984). Prices and Sanctions. *Columbia Law Review* 84: 1523–60.

(1994). Laws and Prices: How Economics Contributed to Law by Misunderstanding Morality. Working Paper No. 94–2, Program in Law and Economics, University of California at Berkeley.

Cropper, Maureen L. and Wallace E. Oates (1992). Environmental Economics: A Survey. *Journal of Economic Literature* 30 (June): 675–740.

Dawes, Robyn M. (1988). *Rational Choice in an Uncertain World*. San Diego: Harcourt, Brace, Yovanovich.

Dawes, Robyn M., Jeanne McTavish and Harriet Shaklee (1977). Behavior, Communication, and Assumptions about Other People's Behavior in a Commons Dilemma Situation. *Journal of Personality and Social Psychology* 35: 1–11.

Dawes, Robyn M., Alphons J. C. van de Kragt and John M. Orbell (1988). Not Me or Thee but WE: The Importance of Group Identity in Eliciting Cooperation in Dilemma Situations – Experimental Manipulations. *Acta Psychologica* 68: 83–97.

De Young, R. (1986). Encouraging Environmentally Appropriate Behavior: The Role of Intrinsic Motivation. *Journal of Environmental Systems* 15(4): 281–92.

Deci, Edward L., Richard Koestner and Richard M. Ryan (1998). *Extrinsic Rewards and Intrinsic Motivation: A Clear and Consistent Picture After All*. Mimeo, Department of Psychology, University of Rochester.

Deci, Edward L. and Richard M. Ryan (1985). *Intrinsic Motivation and Self-Determination in Human Behaviour*. New York: Plenum Press.

Diekmann, Andreas and Peter Preisendörfer (2003). Green and Greenback: The Behavioral Effects of Environmental Attitudes in Low-Cost and High-Cost Situations. *Rationality and Society* 15(4): 441–72.

Eisenberger, Robert and Judy Cameron (1996). Detrimental Effects of Reward. Reality of Myth? *American Psychologist* 51 (Nov.): 1153–66.

Falk, Armin and Urs Fischbacher (2006). A Theory of Reciprocity. *Games and Economic Behavior* 54(2): 293–315.

Fama, Eugene F. and Michael C. Jensen (1983). Separation of Ownership and Control. *Journal of Law and Economics* 26: 301–51.

Faulhaber, Gerald R. and William J. Baumol (1988). Economists as Innovators. *Journal of Economic Literature* 26(2): 577–600.

Fehr, Ernst and Simon Gächter (2000a). Cooperation and Punishment in Public Goods Experiments. *American Economic Review* 90(4): 980–94.

(2000b). Fairness and Retaliation: The Economics of Reciprocity. *Journal of Economic Perspectives* 14(3): 159–81.

Feld, Lars P. and Bruno S. Frey (2002). Trust Breeds Trust: How Taxpayers Are Treated. *Economics of Governance* 3(3): 87–99.

Frey, Bruno S. (1992a). *Economics as a Science of Human Behaviour*. Boston: Kluwer.

(1992b). Tertium Datur: Pricing, Regulating and Intrinsic Motivation. *Kyklos* 45(2): 161–84.

(1997a). A Constitution for Knaves Crowds Out Civic Virtues. *Economic Journal* 107 (July): 1043–53.

(1997b). *Not Just for the Money. An Economic Theory of Personal Motivation*. Cheltenham: Edward Elgar.

Frey, Bruno S. and Iris Bohnet (1995). Institutions Affect Fairness: Experimental Investigations. *Journal of Institutional and Theoretical Economics* 151 (June): 286–303.

Frey, Bruno S. and Stephan Meier (2004). Social Comparisons and Pro-Social Behavior: Testing "Conditional Cooperation" in a Field Experiment. *American Economic Review* 94(5): 1717–22.

Frey, Bruno S. and Felix Oberholzer-Gee (1997). The Cost of Price Incentives: An Empirical Analysis of Motivation Crowding-Out. *American Economic Review* 87(4): 746–55.

Gächter, Simon (2007). Conditional Cooperation: Behavioral Regularities from the Lab and the Field and Their Policy Implications. In: Bruno S. Frey and Alois Stutzer (eds.), *Economics and Psychology. A Promising New Cross-Disciplinary Field*. Cambridge, MA: MIT Press: 19–50.

Gächter, Simon and Ernst Fehr (1999). Collective Action as a Social Exchange. *Journal of Economic Behavior and Organization* 39(4): 341–69.

Gneezy, Uri and Aldo Rustichini (2000). Pay Enough or Don't Pay at All. *Quarterly Journal of Economics* 115: 791–810.

Goodin, Robert E. (1994). Selling Environmental Indulgences. *Kyklos* 47: 573–96.

Gouldner, Alvin Ward (1960). The Norm of Reciprocity: A Preliminary Statement. *American Sociological Review* 25: 161–78.

Grant, R. M. (1996). Toward a Knowledge-based Theory of the Firm. *Strategic Management Journal* 17 (Winter Special Issue): 109–22.

Hardin, Russell (1971). Collective Action as an Agreeable n-Prisoners' Dilemma. *Behavioral Science* 16(5): 472–81.

Holländer, Heinz (1990). A Social Exchange Approach to Voluntary Cooperation. *American Economic Review* 80(5): 1157–67.

Hopper, J. R. and J. M. Nielsen (1991). Recycling as Altruistic Behavior. Normative and Behavioral Strategies to Expand Participation in a Community Recycling Program. *Environment and Behavior* 23: 195–220.

Kahneman, Daniel, Paul Slovic and Amos Tversky (eds.) (1982). *Judgement under Uncertainty: Heuristics and Biases*. Cambridge: Cambridge University Press.

Kazdin, Alan E. (1982). The Token Economy: A Decade Later. *Journal of Applied Behavioural Analysis* 15: 431–45.

Kelman, Steven (1981). *What Price Incentives? Economists and the Environment*. Boston: Auburn.

Kerr, Norbert L. (1995). Norms in Social Dilemmas. In: David A. Schroeder (ed.), *Social Dilemmas: Perspectives on Individuals and Groups*. Westport, CT: Praeger: 36–41.

Keser, Claudia and Frans van Winden (2000). Conditional Cooperation and Voluntary Contributions to Public Goods. *Scandinavian Journal of Economics* 102(2): 23–39.

Kirchgässner, Gebhard (1992). Towards a Theory of Low-Cost Decisions. *European Journal of Political Economy* 8: 305–20.

Kliemt, Hartmut (1986). The Veil of Insignificance. *European Journal of Political Economy* 2/3: 333–44.

Kunreuther, Howard and Paul R. Kleindorfer (1986). A Sealed-bid Auction Mechanism for Siting Noxious Facilities. *American Economic Review* 76(2): 295–9.

Le Grand, Julian (2003). *Motivation, Agency and Public Policy: Of Knights and Knaves, Pawns and Queens*. Oxford: Oxford University Press.

Ledyard, John O. (1995). Public Goods: A Survey of Experimental Research. In: John Kagel and Alvin E. Roth (eds.), *Handbook of Experimental Economics*. Princeton: Princeton University Press: 111–94.

Manski, Charles F. (2000). Economic Analysis of Social Interactions. *Journal of Economic Perspectives* 14(3): 115–36.

Meier, Stephan (2006). *The Economics of Non-Selfish Behaviour: Decisions to Contribute Money to Public Goods*. Cheltenham: Edward Elgar.

Nyborg, Karine and Mari Rege (2003). Does Public Policy Crowd Out Private Contributions to Public Goods? *Public Choice* 115(3–4): 397–418.

O'Hare, Michael (1977). Not On My Block You Don't: Facility Siting and the Strategic Importance of Compensation. *Public Policy* 25: 409–58.

Ölander, Folke and John Thogersen (1995). Understanding of Consumer Behaviour as a Prerequisite for Environmental Protection. *Journal of Consumer Policy* 18: 345–85.

Olson, Mancur (1965). *The Logic of Collective Action: Public Goods and the Theory of Groups*. Cambridge, MA: Harvard University Press.

Ostrom, Elinor (2000). Collective Action and the Evolution of Social Norms. *Journal of Economic Perspectives* 14(3): 137–58.

Pittman, Thane S. and Jack F. Heller (1987). Social Motivation. *Annual Review of Psychology* 38: 461–89.

Pretty, Jules N. and Hugh Ward (2001). Social Capital and the Environment. *World Development* 29(2): 209–27.

Rotter, Julian B. (1966). Generalized Expectancies for Internal versus External Control of Reinforcement. *Psychological Monographs* 80 (1, Whole No. 609).

Rousseau, D. M. (1995). *Psychological Contracts in Organizations. Understanding Written and Unwritten Agreements*. Thousand Oaks: Sage.

Rummel, A. and R. Feinberg (1988). Cognitive Evaluation Theory: A Meta-analytic Review of the Literature. *Social Behavior and Personality* 16: 147–64.

Ryan, Richard M. and Edward L. Deci (2000). Self-determination Theory and the Facilitation of Intrinsic Motivation, Social Development, and Well-being. *American Psychologist* 55(1): 68–78.

Scherer, Andreas G. and Guido Palazzo (2007). Toward a Political Conception of Corporate Responsibility. Business and Society seen from a Habermasian Perspective. *Academy of Management Review* 32(4) (forthcoming).

Schoemaker, Paul J. (1982). The Expected Utility Model: Its Variants, Purposes, Evidence and Limitations. *Journal of Economic Literature* 20 (June): 529–63.

Schwartz, Shalom H. (1977). *Normative Influences on Altruism*. New York: Academic Press.

Schwartz, Shalom H. and Judith A. Howard (1984). Internalized Values as Motivators of Altruism. In: Ervin Staub, Daniel Bar-Tal, Jerzy Karylowski and Janusz Reykowski (eds.), *Development and Maintenance of Prosocial Behavior*. New York: Plenum: 229–55.

Stajkovic, Alexander D. and Fred Luthans (1997). A Meta-analysis of the Effects of Organizational Behavior Modification on Task Performance, 1975–95. *Academy of Management Journal* 40: 1122–49.

Stavins, Robert N. (1998). Economic Incentives for Environmental Regulation. In: Peter Newman (ed.), *The New Palgrave Dictionary of Economics and the Law*, vol. II. London: Macmillan: 6–13.

Stavins, Robert N. (ed.) (2005). *Economics of the Environment: Selected Readings*, 5th edn. New York: W. W. Norton.

Stern, Paul C., Thomas Dietz, Troy Able, Gregory A. Guagnano and Linda Kalof (1999). A Value Belief Norm Theory of Support for Social Movements: The Case of Environmentalism. *Human Ecology Review* 6(2): 81–97.

Stern, Paul C., Thomas Dietz, Linda Kalof and Gregory A. Guagnano (1995). Values, Beliefs, and Proenvironmental Action – Attitude Formation toward Emergent Attitude Objects. *Journal of Applied Social Psychology* 25(18): 1611–36.

Stuart, Charles E. (1984). Welfare Costs per Dollar of Additional Tax Revenue in the United States. *American Economic Review* 74(3): 352–62.

Sunstein, Cass R. (1997). *Free Markets and Social Justice*. New York: Oxford University Press.

Tang, S.-H. and V. C. Hall (1995). The Overjustification Effect: A Meta-analysis. *Applied Cognitive Psychology* 9: 365–404.

Thaler, Richard H. (1992). *The Winner's Curse. Paradoxes and Anomalies of Economic Life*. New York: Free Press.

Thogersen, John (1994). Monetary Incentives and Environmental Concern. Effects of a Differentiated Garbage Fee. *Journal of Consumer Policy* 17: 407–42.

(2003). Monetary Incentives and Recycling: Behavioural and Psychological Reactions to a Performance-Dependent Garbage Fee. *Journal of Consumer Policy* 26(2): 197–228.

(2006). *Norms for Environmentally Responsible Behaviour: An Extended Taxonomy and a Preliminary Assessment*. Mimeo, Aarhus School of Business, Aarhus, Denmark.

Tietenberg, Tom (1985). *Emissions Trading: An Exercise in Reforming Pollution Policy*. Washington, DC: Resources for the Future.

Tyler, T. R. (1990). *Why People Obey the Law*. New Haven: Yale University Press.

Wiersma, Uco J. (1992). The Effects of Extrinsic Rewards on Intrinsic Motivation: A Meta-analysis. *Journal of Occupational and Organizational Psychology* 65: 101–14.

18 Contingent valuation as a research method: environmental values and human behaviour

CLIVE L. SPASH

18.1 Introduction

The contingent valuation method (CVM) is a controversial approach by which economists have attempted to place a value upon environmental changes. The basic method involves a questionnaire which asks a respondent their willingness to pay (WTP) for an environmental improvement or their willingness to accept (WTA) compensation for a loss or degradation of environmental assets or quality. The resulting stated preference is most commonly used as a mean value of the change and then aggregated across the relevant population and discounted for time. The original justification was the need to include the resulting monetary value as part of a cost–benefit analysis to aid project appraisal. The theoretical basis for such an approach relies upon micro-economic welfare theory where individuals maximize their utility subject to an income constraint, or minimize their expenditure subject to a utility constraint (see Hanley and Spash, 1993).

The CVM has proven the most popular of the available methods for monetary valuation of the environment. There are three main reasons. First, the technique has the air of simplicity, and indeed early surveys contained very little beyond a direct question on WTP or WTA and a few socioeconomic details. Second, the range of applications has seemed unlimited because such questions could apparently be asked concerning provision of any environmental 'good or service'. That is, the CVM provided freedom from being restricted by available economic data which had limited all previous approaches to secondary data. Third, the range of 'economic values' was expanded to categories previously outside the economists' grasp so that the CVM introduced measurement of option, existence and bequest values. These new categories have been termed passive or indirect use values.[1] However, all three supposed advantages have proven controversial. Critiques of the first and third advantages have involved psychological perspectives, including concerns that preferences are labile and constructed with susceptibility to framing effects and variations in context and elicitation procedures rather than stable, complete

---

This is the work of an Australian Government employee and is protected by Crown Copyright.

[1] Texts which call these values 'non-use' are misleading as all economic values are preference utilitarian and therefore must provide utility or be useful to an individual.

and transitive (Fischhoff, 1991; Kahneman *et al.*, 1993; Schkade and Payne, 1994).

Vatn (2004) has identified two camps amongst economists concerning environmental valuation. First are those who regard all anomalies as 'measurement bias' to be removed by careful design and data censoring. Second are those who dismiss the whole valuation exercise, and CVM in particular, due to inconsistency with neoclassical theory. This chapter explores the development of these positions while focusing upon the specific role psychology has and can play in aiding the debate. In doing so, the argument is developed that understanding the motives behind responses to CVM surveys is important for improving choice theory. This is in accord with what Vatn (2004) has termed a third way where neither of the existing alternative camps holds sway.

In the next section a brief review is conducted of how the CVM interacted with psychology while moving from an experimental technique to a high-profile internationally recognized method of environmental valuation. This leads to a discussion of the extensive attempts which have been made to address controversy via dictating survey design. The topic of bias is introduced and the specific areas covered include strategic behaviour, hypothetical bias, WTP vs. WTA, and information bias. The findings suggest the need for work on individual motivation for survey responses. This is investigated in terms of pro-social attitude measures and attitude–behaviour models. Ethical beliefs are noted as an often neglected aspect of motivation for CVM responses, but shown to be important factors on the basis of existing empirical results. The chapter closes by drawing some conclusions on future research directions and on the use of the CVM in decision-making processes.

18.2   CVM development and the psychological perspective

The development of CVM took place in the United States and especially amongst researchers at the University of Wyoming in the late 1970s and early to mid-1980s: e.g. Ralph d'Arge, David Brookshire, Bill Schulze and Betsy Hoffman. There was an early interest in behavioural theories associated with this work and explorations of experimental economics using student subjects. Hanemann (1994: 21) has claimed the link with psychology took place at a workshop conducted to review the CVM which was summarized by Cummings, Brookshire and Schulze (1986), hereafter CBS. However, there was already awareness within this North American environmental economics community of a range of psychological ideas,[2] and the CBS volume was merely the first time this became more readily apparent. Indeed, the connection had been made decades earlier by Ciriacy-Wantrup, of whom d'Arge had been a student.

---

[2] For example, Hoffman held PhDs in both economics and psychology.

As an early advocate of 'interrogating' social groups as to their WTP for collective extra-market (i.e. public) goods, Ciriacy-Wantrup argued that:

> Interrogating and voting can be used for quantitative determination as well as for ranking of values. Considerable progress has been made recently in designing and evaluating group interrogations by questionnaire and interview. Economists, so far, have made little use of this progress in the field of individual and social psychology. Welfare economics could be put on a more realistic foundation if a closer cooperation between economics and certain branches of applied psychology could be established.
>
> (Ciriacy-Wantrup, 1947: 1190)

Yet, despite this early signpost, various attempts at establishing more formal links with social psychology and behavioural theories have proven far from easy. Participants at the CBS workshop who were advocating the use of attitude–behaviour models from social psychology were extremely critical of their reception: 'We certainly underestimated the barriers to interdisciplinary communication. Our proposal that economists consider the attitudes–behaviour literature has met with indifference or hostility. CBS are no exception' (Bishop and Heberlein, 1986: 141).

Another attendee at the CBS workshop was the psychologist Daniel Kahneman whose work has shown many of the flaws in economic models of human behaviour, with the risk-related research earning him a Nobel Prize in economics. However, his CVM research with Jack Knetsch (a pioneer of travel cost and hedonic pricing) provoked strong and defensive reactions, especially the paper on embedding (Kahneman and Knetsch, 1992b).[3] Kahneman and Knetsch (1992b) describe WTP under the CVM as the purchase of moral satisfaction rather than an exchange value. This has been linked to a contribution model claiming that, while economists interpret WTP as purchasing a public good, respondents are stating charitable contributions reflecting their attitudinal concerns. Kahneman *et al.* (1993: 314) then argue that, if the only objective of measurement is to rank-order issues, WTP is 'not the preferred way of doing so because it is psychometrically inferior to other measures of the same attitude'.

Critical work on the CVM funded by Exxon corporation also employed psychological approaches (Hausman, 1993). Exxon was concerned by the use of the CVM as legal evidence indicating multi-billion dollar environmental damages arising from the *Exxon Valdez* tanker oil spill in Alaska. In particular, psychologists Schkade and Payne (1993; 1994) cited cognitive and decision-making theories to establish their case for the use of verbal protocol analysis. They found that CVM responses were consistent with the construction of preferences, and reflected moral satisfaction and symbolic values. Hanemann

---

[3] This underwent a protracted review process before finally appearing and then rather unusually simultaneously with a critique (Smith, 1992) and reply by the authors (Kahneman and Knetsch, 1992a). When a second critique was published, the editor (Ron Cummings) refused the authors an opportunity to reply despite their concerns that they be allowed to defend their work. Jack Knetsch, personal communication, June 2004 and January 2006.

blamed the results upon the open-ended format employed and argued for the need to 'work on the instrument until you get a tighter response' (see Hausman, 1993: 297–9). Indeed, a standard response of CVM experts is to argue for improvement in the techniques employed rather than to question the underlying theory.

Following such reasoning, the National Oceanic and Atmospheric Administration (NOAA) hired a group of experts to produce a report on the CVM which amounted to a list of guidelines. The CBS workshop had produced shorter and more general guidelines. The approach of the NOAA Panel included such extensive recommendations that no survey was ever likely to meet them all and still remain within the bounds of what the general public might reasonably be expected to respond to (a typical CVM interview lasts about twenty minutes). The increased technical complexity, in-house interviews and larger samples required for the recommended dichotomous choice model, along with attempts to achieve the elusive goal of perfect random sampling, all added to the expense for CVM surveys. The surveys done for the *Exxon Valdez* case are cited as costing several million dollars by aiming for random sampling; these might have been conducted at a fraction of the cost by using convenience samples to create behavioural models for prediction of population responses on the basis of average population information (Harrison and Lesley, 1996).

The technique had moved in a decade from an obscure experimental approach to a high-profile legally endorsed policy tool. Throughout the 1970s CVM studies had remained US-based and largely of academic interest. In the 1980s and 1990s studies took place first in Europe and then in less developed economies, and became increasingly connected to government decision processes. This fitted well with pro-market governments in Europe and the USA. In the USA cost–benefit analysis returned to the public policy arena with President Reagan's executive order 12291 in 1981, and five years later the CVM was incorporated into regulations for measuring the damages associated with oil spills and hazardous wastes (Department of the Interior, 1986). US Superfund legislation, aimed at hazardous waste site clean-up, then also involved cases where the CVM was employed. In the UK the government's emphasis on monetary valuation increased and by 1988 the Department of the Environment was sponsoring work by environmental economists and soon recommending the use of CVM for both project and policy appraisal (Department of the Environment, 1991). A further boost to the general ease of applying CVM surveys was given by Mitchell and Carson (1989) who provided a widely used manual for those wishing to avoid various pitfalls. A bibliography in 1994 listed almost 1,000 CVM studies and papers worldwide (Carson *et al.*, 1994). The *Exxon* case which led to the NOAA Panel report merely provided further endorsement for advocates because two Nobel laureates could now be cited amongst those approving the CVM. Of course, the proviso was that the method be conducted in very specific ways in order to address all the problems which had become apparent.

18.3   Refining survey design

Many studies under the CVM, and especially earlier studies, were conducted for research purposes using small, non-representative, convenience samples (e.g. undergraduate students) and were performed by untrained interviewers (e.g. postgraduate economics students) without any quality control. There are key areas where such studies can be shown to be inadequate. Several lessons should now have been learnt.

(i)   Survey design should involve easily understood and pre-tested language, taking onboard all feedback from focus groups, not just that which is convenient;

(ii)   Data collection requires attention to sample size, collection methods, sample representation of the general population and randomized selection;

(iii)   Interpreting the values obtained as market prices requires knowledge of and respect for the restrictions imposed by the theoretical economic model;

(iv)   Empirical analysis requires the correct statistical tests;

(v)   Reliability and validity tests need to be conducted with the presentation of regression results explaining bids (WTP/WTA) as a function of relevant factors;

(vi)   Where this has been done, the explanatory power has often proven very low, but this then requires explanation and attention.

This would seem to argue in favour of best practice guidance for economists. However, survey design seems to be more of an art than a science, at least beyond following some basic common sense as to general social science practice. In addition, there seems to be some difficulty in separating out scientific requirements of good practice from politically motivated desires, and this applies to the still dominant set of guidelines, i.e. those of the NOAA Panel.

The NOAA Panel was set within a struggle between competing parties, as evidenced by the inclusion of two Nobel laureates from different camps in the *Exxon Valdez* legal battle: Kenneth Arrow (Exxon consultant) and Robert Solow (State of Alaska consultant). Their recommendation of 'conservative' design to achieve low value estimates appears to be aimed at meeting civil service/political desires and avoiding the embarrassment of excessively large numbers overturning policies or pet projects and annoying lobby groups. This conservative design argument has since been transferred to the UK and most prominently for a CVM survey employed to support a tax on aggregates extraction (Department of the Environment, Transport and the Regions, 1999); in this case numbers were significantly and explicitly reduced by survey design and the use of a 25 per cent discount rate. Conservative design seems theoretically unjustifiable (Knetsch, 1994).

Indeed, several NOAA recommendations are questionable. The exclusive use of WTP formats reduces the size of numbers produced and ignores the beliefs held about rights in society as opposed to what is legally defined (Knetsch, 2005). The exclusion of open-ended formats has been used to ignore results showing anomalies, although the alternative close-ended formats (e.g. dichotomous choice) have increasingly recognized problems of their own. More than a decade ago Willis (1995) noted the culturally specific context of the NOAA Panel recommendations and that, for example, voting on hypothecated taxes is totally outside UK experience. Even within the USA, Hanemann (1994: 20) has admitted that 'there are few cases where local governments actually set environmental quality'. This argues against the approach of a referendum format on taxes as being realistic and familiar to 'the public', although this has not prevented Hanemann advocating that approach. Despite, or perhaps because of, the drawbacks, the guidelines have proven popular with practitioners and the search for 'a manual' has been emulated elsewhere, for example in the UK by the Department of the Environment, Transport and the Regions (Bateman *et al.*, 2002).

The fundamental drive for those economists trying to refine the method in this way has been to find the Holy Grail survey which can access 'true values' as expressed by preferences. This encapsulates the concept of an ideal design to replicate a hypothetical market situation, including the incentive structures. The aim is to measure individual preferences on the basis that they are preformed. The survey instrument should then be 'neutral' and any information provided merely informs those preferences rather than forming them.

CVM economists have then developed various concepts of 'bias' which are believed to obscure 'true values'.[4] The concerns have changed over time, even though older problems remain unresolved. Key issues in the more recent literature have been to avoid hypothetical bias, information bias, scope/scale insensitivity and the embedding effect, and bid elicitation under dichotomous choice formats. Issues given much less frequent explicit coverage include the role of ethics and attitudes, the formation of preferences within the survey administration process, and the treatment of bid item non-response. In the remainder of this section, several key 'bias' problems are reviewed, while the next section probes into some of the less commonly addressed issues and links these to theories from social psychology.

18.3.1 Strategic bias

A repeatedly referenced concern of economists is the potential for individuals to mislead others in order to gain some advantage for themselves. This is

---

[4] Examples include: non-response, starting point for bids and design of payment cards, payment vehicle, respondents acting strategically, quantity and quality of information supplied, interviewer approach for in-house and telephone delivery.

termed strategic behaviour and free riding. In the neoclassical economic model there are no social rules or norms for behaviour and the only ethical guide is individual preference satisfaction. Sen pointed out the problems with such an approach some time ago (Sen, 1977), i.e. that such a world would soon fall apart due to the selfish interested parties' actions, unbounded by the norms of social behaviour and institutions. Still the issue of strategic behaviour is prominent as an explanation for anomalies in data.

In CVM this usually arises where there are 'outlier' bids of a very large amount which have a strong influence on the mean. This should only be regarded as a problem when the bid is unlikely to occur because the individual lacks the income to pay or would actually accept a much lower amount as compensation. However, the justification of strategic bias is used to implement a simple censoring (e.g. 5 per cent trimming) without much attention to the actual intention of respondents making these bids. The NOAA Panel 'conservative' design recommendation is further used to support this blanket trimming approach. Free riding is usually described as underbidding on the basis that the public good will be provided in any case, and this has then been linked to hypothetical bias (i.e. overbidding in WTP surveys and then reducing the bid when actual payment is requested). The solution offered is to choose 'incentive compatible' designs to make individuals avoid such behaviour, although there is also recognition that all designs have their problems and can merely result in different strategies of under- or overbidding (Carson, Flores and Meade, 2001).

The preoccupation of economists with strategic behaviour seems to lack a good empirical basis in CVM results. For example, an extensive review of CVM studies in the health-care literature found no instances of strategic bias (Klose, 1999). Indeed reviews of CVM often make reference to strategic behaviour without citing any empirical case studies and merely take its existence as given; instead, they concentrate on the implications and alternative 'incentive compatible' bid designs (e.g. Carson, Flores and Meade, 2001; Hanley and Shogren, 2005).[5] The evidence which is sometimes offered concerns the divergence between hypothetical requests and actual requests which would appear to be an issue with other potential dimensions.

18.3.2 Hypothetical bias

Economists typically use secondary data in their work, which makes the CVM an unusual foray into the world of direct contact with people. One aspect of early and persistent criticism has then been that the survey is hypothetical rather than an actual market and therefore cannot be trusted to produce realistic

---

[5] An anecdote told by Ralph d'Arge concerned a test of strategic bias and free riding carried out on a group of experts from different disciplines. The only person to exhibit such behaviour was the economist.

results. Hypothetical bias is where individuals fail to answer as if they were in an actual market trade-off situation so that when they are asked for an actual payment, or given compensation, they reject this or their answers diverge significantly in amount.

Typically, WTP is cited as being overestimated by CVM surveys. However, the evidence appears somewhat mixed, with most work being experimental and the relationship of this to environmental scenarios in CVM surveys then being unclear. There have been reviews addressing the issue. For example, Carson *et al.* (1996) compared eighty-three studies involving stated versus revealed preferences and found slight underestimation in the CVM results compared to actual payments. Such meta-studies imply no generalized rule can be applied for 'calibration'. At the level of an aggregated bid from a given study, there may be no difference between a modern CVM survey and actual payments with real goods, but at the individual bid level there can be considerable variation (see study by Bhatia and Fox-Rushby, 2003). Recent experimental results corroborate this finding, and add that individuals giving low bids may underestimate their WTP while those giving high ones overestimate (Camacho-Cuena *et al.*, 2004). However, the results would seem to depend upon the type of 'commodity' under consideration and the specific context being put forward. Variations in design and circumstance make generalized results difficult to discern. For example, there are major differences between asking populations at risk from malaria about their WTP for a mosquito net (e.g. Bhatia and Fox-Rushby, 2003), which has known benefits, and asking those in urban areas about their WTP for saving an endangered species of, say, elephant (e.g. Bandara and Tisdell, 2004).

As mentioned above, hypothetical bias has been linked to strategic behaviour, but without adequately testing why people respond the way they do. When interviewed after a CVM survey, there is good evidence for respondents having a very different understanding of what they are doing than that attributed to them by economists (Burgess, Clark and Harrison, 1998). Participants challenge claims that the CVM is a democratic process for ensuring that public values are incorporated in policy decisions, and argue for a decision-making institution where local people can contribute to environmental policy decisions through dialogue with scientists and policy-makers (Clark, Burgess and Harrison, 2000). Such evidence suggests the CVM process can be viewed as a technique of 'dialogue-at-a-distance' between researchers and respondents which involves encoding and decoding of the 'good'. Incomplete specification of the environmental change, which would seem normal, means respondents are able to bring their own readings to their interpretation of the scenario so that researchers cannot know precisely what 'good' respondents were attempting to 'value' (Burgess, Clark and Harrison, 2000). Respondents may also show: difficulties in contextualizing a scenario and how much it might be worth in both monetary and non-monetary terms; an inability to work out a value for one scheme in isolation from others; and feelings that values are incommensurable, i.e. money vs. Nature (Clark, Burgess and Harrison, 2000).

In order to know why people give the answer they do, some probing of motivations would seem necessary, rather than just drawing inferences. The divergence between stated and revealed preferences might then be paralleled to the Fishbein and Ajzen (1975) attitude–behaviour model and the difference between stated and actual behaviour. In this case motivations might be based upon attitudes, social norms and perceived behavioural control. Extending the economic research in this direction might then enable better understanding of the reasons for the stated WTP prior to researching the link of stated to revealed WTP (Spash, 1998).

One application in this direction does exist on the subject of hypothetical bias. Picking up on the idea of Cummings and Taylor (1999), that entreaties to avoid regarding the CVM survey as hypothetical can remove that bias, Ajzen, Brown and Carvajal (2004) have tested for motivations using the Theory of Planned Behaviour (discussed further in the next section). The predictive power of the model is improved by the entreaties. They argue that norms are activated by the entreaties and that these are already operative in an actual payment scenario. The scenario of WTP towards a college fund amongst 169 students is far removed from environmental applications of the CVM, and the authors qualify their results against generalization to other contexts and populations. The use of entreaties in the above studies was conducted on a single-bid referendum while when a payment range is used only those at the high end are affected (Brown, Ajzen and Hrubes, 2003; Murphy, Stevens and Weatherhead, 2005). In contrast, Aadland and Caplan (2003) find a short entreaty exacerbates the bias. Overall the role of these entreaties and whether they are a form of persuasion to get conformity to the economists' prior expectation remains rather unclear. However, this move seems to reinforce the need for motivational research and collaboration with social psychologists and others.

18.3.3 WTP versus WTA

A persistent difference has been found between WTP and WTA, with the latter typically four to five times greater than the former. This was noted early on in the development of the technique and was a major concern (Thayer, 1981; Knetsch and Sinden, 1984). Empirical studies since then, including those involving actual goods in experimental situations, have found people systematically value losses, measured by WTA, two to four times more than otherwise commensurate gains, measured by WTP (Knetsch, 2005: 96). Attempts at explaining the difference within a neoclassical economic framework have included income effects, strategic behaviour and goods having imperfect substitutes (Hanemann, 1991; Shogren et al., 1994). However, these fail to account for the large and consistent variations in CVM surveys, and generally cannot explain divergence where the conditions required by standard theoretical explanations are violated (Knetsch, 2005).

An alternative explanation is the psychological impact of 'ownership' of a good actually changing the demand function and indeed causing it to become kinked. This has been termed by economists an 'endowment effect' (Thaler, 1980; Knetsch and Sinden, 1984), with the associated psychological explanation being loss aversion (Kahneman, Knetsch and Thaler, 1991). Experimental results show the large differences between people's valuations of gains and losses, and are inconsistent with the axioms of completeness, transitivity and dominance. That is, economic analyses and predictions of consumer behaviour are largely based on theories inconsistent with actual choices (Knetsch, 1995). The repeatedly found differences in the valuation placed on goods and money, depending on whether entitlements are being acquired or given up, provide direct evidence of preference assumption violations.

In this light the NOAA Panel recommendation of using only WTP formats takes on a different form. In effect a troublesome aspect of behavioural findings has been largely excluded by the CVM community from further consideration. Indeed the argument has been put forward that WTP is less problematic, preferred by business, causes less protesting and, therefore, can be substituted for WTA (Hanley and Shogren, 2005). Recent US EPA (2000) guidelines perpetuate this substitution mistake (see critical review by Knetsch, 2005).

As Knetsch has noted, the choice of welfare measure depends upon the reference state which people associate with a given environmental change (Knetsch, 1994), and their feeling of psychological ownership rather than legal entitlements (Knetsch, 2005). Property rights may be contested so that the general public, as in the case of environmental damages, must assert their position, but in CVM these decisions are made behind closed doors. Hanley and Shogren (2005: 16–17) seem to regard a UK policy case where WTA was thrown out for WTP as a success, although the process they describe involved a complaint by the industrial polluter against the WTA study, the government commissioning a new study, and the newly commissioned experts adopting WTP and producing far smaller damage estimates.[6] Some might question the credibility of such a process, let alone its standing as scientific analysis.

In the expert discussions of design for the same study, Hanemann argued that people are unfamiliar with the WTA format. This idea is strange in light of the fact that every payment by a purchasing agent is matched by an acceptance of monetary compensation on the part of the selling agent. So every market transaction involves a WTA and a WTP simultaneously. Some studies have even explored this (Macmillan, Duff and Elston, 2001; Amigues et al., 2002),

---

[6] They neglect to note that the use of a 25 per cent discount rate also substantially reduced the damage estimates. Hanley was one of the paid experts on the second study. I myself consulted on both studies, although my concerns over the second study apparently had little impact.

with one scenario showing WTA to achieve environmental change can be more familiar to a given group, for example farmers, than WTP is for another, for example the public (Bateman *et al.*, 1996).

The importance of context within which exchange occurs should then be noted. For example, there is no reason to expect WTP to diverge from WTA under the loss aversion theory if there is no aversion to loss, such as when the person accepting payment is in the business of selling and that is indeed their goal. This unfortunately leads some to the tortuous tautological argument that if only people were educated in the ways of the market and given the right incentives (carrots and sticks), then they would conform and produce the required results consistent with market theory (List, 2003); after all 'evidence exists suggesting that people can learn to act rationally' (Hanley and Shogren, 2005: 29). The language used in these justifications also has unfortunate connotations, with the problem apparently being that behaviour goes 'unpunished by market discipline' (Shogren and Hayes, 1997: 243). The theory requires people to behave in a certain way and they can be made to do so; this ability to reify economic theory is then meant to be comforting.

Before leaving the topic, I will note two other related issues. First, Knetsch (2005) notes that behavioural findings show people value future losses more than future gains, which implies different discount rates. Others have found negative discount rates for gains (see Lowenstein, 1987; Lowenstein and Prelec, 1991), and other behaviour inconsistent with economists' claims (Lowenstein and Prelec, 1992). Second, economists ignore the moral considerations which people take into account when considering environmental damages. This is important for understanding intergenerational issues (Spash, 2002a), and has also been related to the WTP–WTA divergence under environmental scenarios with motivations including feelings of responsibility for harm, dissociation of entities or changes from the marketplace and trade-offs, and the activation of social norms (see the review by Brown and Gregory, 1999).

18.3.4 Information bias

In environmental valuation, information has largely been discussed in terms of whether providing more information on an issue is likely to increase WTP. The assumption is that objective information relevant to the valuation of an entity can be provided by the interviewer in different quantities. Due to the sensitivity of responses to the information supplied, the pre-testing of the survey, and more recently focus groups, have become of increasing importance. The NOAA Panel recommended CVM aim for a level of information provision 'at least as high as that which the average voter brings to a real referendum on the provision of a specific public good', and make use of 'follow-up questions' on understanding (Arrow *et al.*, 1993: 4607). Their guidelines recommend that: 'Adequate information must be provided to respondents about the environmental program that is offered. It must be defined in a way that is relevant to damage assessment' (Arrow *et al.*, 1993: 4608). However, the meaning of being 'adequately' informed with 'relevant' information is vague and the methods by which individuals assimilate and process information unexplained. Those economists trying to understand human valuation of environmental entities need to know how individuals form their preferences, the key factors which change preferences and their stability.

Acceptance that any presentation of information must be moulded and environmental issues explained within a given frame means the information issue is often conceptualized in terms of a 'framing' problem (e.g. Boyle, 1989). A separation is then attempted between the substance of information (objective data) and the way in which information is supplied or questions asked (framing). Changes in the former are expected to impact perceptions and valuations, while if the latter do so this is regarded as a bias. Objective data are meant to describe the 'commodity' to be valued while the framing is merely the method of obtaining a WTP or WTA measure.

Only if an actual environmental change can be defined 'objectively' can the aim of bringing all individuals to a common understanding of that change have a certain logic. This may be questionable even for a common market commodity (e.g. a house). Certainly a set of physical attributes might be defined. Yet, there are often disagreements between different individuals over the condition of the commodity (e.g. the property with 'much potential') and definition of attributes (e.g. whether a small room is a single bedroom or a store room). A divergence between actual and perceived conditions then becomes harder to define and reliance falls upon subjective perception. The problem is compounded for complex environmental issues. The situation is one where 'the CVM practitioner has no practical anchor for accuracy' and 'must then rely upon individual perceptions of environmental change-related effects', which means 'variations across individuals of CVM values *may* reflect differences in perceptions of the hypothesized commodity' (Cummings, Brookshire and Schulze, 1986: 57–8).

In addition, disagreement has existed over what exactly constitutes a framing problem as opposed to defining attributes of the 'commodity'. In particular, unresolved issues surround whether the payment mechanism (e.g. income tax, trust fund) or institutional arrangements (government, charity) are to be included as framing issues. The difference in treatment means such factors are either a cause of bias to be avoided or individuals should be regarded as valuing 'different' commodities constituted of various attributes which are then widely defined. The bias position implies qualification of the results as an under- or overestimate of some 'true' value, while the commodity change position limits any generalization of values outside the specific context described, making every CVM result specific to a unique 'commodity' (Spash, 2002b).

One thing seems clear, the role of the analyst or survey design team remains central to bounding the information set. Which issues need to be presented, in what format and detail are matters where differences of opinion will result and the outcome can be expected to influence people's perception of the valuation question. However, the analyst may conceive of information and its interpretation by respondents in one way, while respondents interpret that same information in unexpected ways as far as the analyst is concerned, i.e. what Burgess, Clark and Harrison (2000) term encoding and decoding. One aspect of this divergence in understanding arises because environmental issues concern value conflicts. These may, for example, relate to fundamental disagreements over the role of markets and how environmental issues should be addressed. Environmentalists might then be expected to see concerns of justice and rights as central aspects while economists always look for the implicit trade-off. The former may reject the very commensurability which the latter take as given and design into their surveys.

The information presented about an environmental good or service has been connected to the motive to process information (Ajzen, Brown and Rosenthal, 1996). This motive is determined by an individual's ability to understand the issue and their perception of the personal relevance of the issue to them. If their motivation is high, then they enter central processing mode and scrutinize and evaluate information with regard to the substance of the argument. This allows WTP to be increased by favourable reporting of the benefits. Alternatively, a low motivation means peripheral processing mode is entered and moods and subtle cues become determining factors in responses. This leads to the argument that the WTP for a public good is affected more by stimulating a moral perspective when individuals are in peripheral processing mode (Ajzen et al., 1996).

Spash (2002b) offers a different model for the role of ethical beliefs. In an environmental CVM survey, any concerns which an individual holds as ethical beliefs, such as utilitarianism or rights, might come into play directly. That is, rather than being 'peripheral' to the description of environmental changes, these are likely to be key issues. Along with environmental attitudes and social norms, such ethical beliefs would feed into the reasoning over whether to make a monetary trade-off. The empirical results presented by Spash (2002b) show that the same information influences individuals differently so that some individuals find they are being informed while others feel their preferences are being formed, during an identical CVM exercise. This impact on the formation of preferences during a CVM survey influences the bid. Thus the idea of a neutral or objective set of data on an environmental change is challenged and the meaning of information bias brought into question. In addition, rather than finding fundamental ethical beliefs to be peripheral matters which can be cued to distort valuation processes, such beliefs are found to be key determinants of the values expressed. While ethical beliefs are strongly related to the way in which information is processed, the evidence counters the proposal of Ajzen et al. (1996), and instead supports a model where those in central processing mode call upon ethical positions to value environmental changes.

18.4   Attitudes, behaviour and ethical beliefs

Attitudes are not entirely absent from CVM debates. Indeed, the edited volume on the CVM by Bateman and Willis (1999) has a chapter dedicated to psychological issues (Green and Tunstall, 1999) which highlights the topic of attitude–behaviour research, but there is little sign elsewhere in the volume of anyone paying attention to the points raised. A multiple authored volume on the CVM appearing a few years later (Bateman *et al.*, 2002), as a 'manual' for the UK government, has many of the same authors and, while excluding Green and Tunstall and their topic area, has several references to attitudes and at one point even replicates the Theory of Reasoned Action. However, attitudes are recommended as 'warm-up' questions which should appear straight after introductory remarks in a CVM survey (Bateman *et al.*, 2002: 148–50). Besides marginalizing their potential importance, such a use would preload any WTP measured afterwards by placing specific pro- or anti-environmental perspectives foremost in the respondents' minds and inflating or deflating the resulting payment (Pouta, 2004).

In general, the work done by economists in CVM surveys largely fails to pay attention to attitudes or measure attitudes as conceived by social psychologists. Motivation has also been a largely dismissed area of concern for economists because they rely upon the expression of individual preferences for the derivation of value irrespective of the origin of those preferences. In this regard, the CVM is an unwelcome visitor questioning the political economy of mainstream economics in which consumer opinion is supposed to rule supreme and remain unquestioned as long as it meets the basic axioms of choice (complete, transitive, reflexive preferences). The preceding section suggests that motivation needs to be taken more seriously as an issue for CVM research and economics more generally. In this case, research combining social psychology with the CVM seems to have two potential directions: (i) Fishbein and Ajzen attitude–behaviour models, (ii) psychometric scales on pro-social environmental attitudes.

18.4.1   Attitude–behaviour models

An important line of work here is that going back to Fishbein and Ajzen (1975) and their Theory of Reasoned Action (TRA). As the theory has developed, key motivators for explaining a stated intention to act have been identified, including: beliefs, attitudes, social or subjective norms and perceived behavioural control (PBC). The inclusion of the latter led to the model being renamed the Theory of Planned Behaviour (TPB). These models emphasize the importance of differentiating between intentions and actual behaviour. This can be seen as paralleling the difference between stated (intentional) and observed (actual) preferences in economics.

One divergence from the approach in social psychology and that in CVM is the measurement of behaviour. WTP or WTA in contingent valuation are single stated preferences or, under the above model, intentions to act. Individuals may refuse a single requested action at a given time despite being favourably disposed towards that action, and focusing upon that single action may therefore be misleading when trying to analyse the relationship to motives such as attitudes. Instead a set of behaviours over time is regarded as best at revealing the disposition of a person, which in social psychology would be measured by a behavioural index of observations on a range of actions. An attitude then implies a predisposition to a set of consistent behaviours with respect to an object.

Fishbein and Ajzen (1975) suggest prediction of single acts requires that attitudinal measures correspond to the behaviour being analysed in terms of four distinct elements. These elements are the action, target, context and timing. In order to predict behaviour on the basis of attitudes, these elements should be in correspondence, i.e. the measure of attitude should correspond to the behaviour. More generally, this 'correspondence principle' means that for any attitudinal scale to be a good predictor of behaviour requires that the scale should match the type and level of behaviour: for example, general environmental attitudes would predict broadly defined behaviours while specific attitudes towards a particular object are best used to predict behaviours relating to that object. While this may seem intuitive, the earlier failure of attitudes as predictors of behavioural variation in social psychology has been attributed to a lack of such correspondence (Hill, 1981).

A key concept in behavioural prediction under the TRA and TPB is belief, which is used in two contexts by Fishbein and Ajzen (1975).[7] First are beliefs about the probabilistic judgement concerning the consequences of a behaviour, i.e. the relationship between an object and some attribute it may be believed to possess. This type of belief informs attitudes. Ajzen (1991: 191) defines the attitude towards a behaviour as the degree to which performance of the behaviour is positively or negatively valued. Specifically, the outcome's subjective value contributes to the attitude in direct proportion to the strength of the belief, i.e. the subjective probability that the behaviour will produce the outcome in question. Second are beliefs informing personal norms which are adopted on the basis of considering the opinion of reference groups, e.g. people at work, those with whom one socializes and family. In the TPB this is referred to as a subjective norm because of the reliance upon the individual's perception of the opinion of the referent and their importance to the individual. Such beliefs have a social normative aspect while the personal attitudinal position is based upon expectations about behaviour.

---

[7] Primary beliefs are also referred to by Fishbein and Ajzen as key predictors of behavioural intentions. They argue that where the aim is to change behaviour, identifying primary beliefs is of central importance.

Perception of behavioural control is assumed to reflect past experience as well as anticipated impediments and obstacles. 'The more resources and opportunities individuals believe they possess, and the fewer the obstacles or impediments they anticipate, the greater should be their control over the behavior' (Ajzen, 1991: 196). As a general rule, the more favourable are attitudes towards a behaviour and subjective norms and the stronger the PBC with respect to a specified behaviour then the stronger should be an individual's intention to perform the behaviour (Ajzen, 1991: 188).

Environmental applications of these ideas within the CVM context have been limited. The only application of the TRA in this context is Moisseinen (1999) which takes a simplified approach and is best regarded as an indicative pre-test. Attitudes are concluded to resemble socio-economic variables in ability to explain WTP, although the basis is rather thin for generalization. The strength of the results does however indicate some potential for a more refined approach and extension to the TPB.

However, care must be taken over CVM studies which appear to apply the TPB to environmental problems. For example, Connelly, *et al.* (2002) discuss the TPB and claim to show that it outperforms standard socio-demographic variables in explaining WTP for river ecosystem restoration, with the latter proving non-significant in regression analysis. However, rather than applying the TPB, they actually measure only attitudes using an adaptation of the New Environmental Paradigm (NEP) as developed by Dunlap and Van Liere (1978; Dunlap *et al.*, 2000). What they do find is that attitudinal scales (on the concern for the environment, the importance of considering the value of Nature and environmental activism) are better predictors than the socio-demographic variables. Some other studies also cite the relevance of TRA or TPB for understanding CVM results but then employ only a type of attitude measure rather than addressing the complete model with its nuances (e.g. Kerr and Cullen, 1995; Pouta *et al.*, 2000).

Meyerhoff (2002) is one of the few environmental CVM studies which applies a complete version of the TPB; he also measures the NEP (in reduced form). He does not measure salient beliefs and evaluation of the specific belief attribute separately but combines them as a single item and then uses two such items each for attitudes and norms and one for behavioural control. This is what Ajzen, Brown and Carvajal (2004) term 'direct' measures as opposed to belief-based measures. He also interjects a variable on the intention to perform the behaviour between these factors and WTP, although stated WTP is regarded by others as an intended behaviour itself (Spash, 1998; Pouta *et al.*, 2000), and Ajzen *et al.* (2004) have found intentions almost identical to stated WTP. Meyerhoff's findings show that stated WTP is not related directly to the NEP and behavioural control is weak, but attitudes and norms are significantly related to the intention which is in turn related to stated WTP.

Another well-informed study in terms of TPB arises from the doctoral dissertation by Pouta (2003) which combines published papers and unpublished work focused upon attitude–behaviour research within the context of the CVM and forestry. One of the published papers tests the complete TPB model, including: direct and belief-based attitudes, direct norms and PBC (Pouta and Rekola, 2001). The TPB results show WTP related to both direct attitudes and PBC. PBC, measured as a budget constraint, was the most important factor in terms of coefficient and significance. Norms proved non-significant and related to attitudes. Belief-based attitudes related to direct attitudes and were used to show relevant aspects of belief which could be used to inform land use policy.

A complete version of the TPB is also included in the work by Spash *et al.* (2004; 2008). This employed measures of belief-based attitudes and norms, and direct PBC with two target behaviours, one related to biodiversity improvement and the other paying via electricity bills. TPB performed very well at explaining WTP in regression analysis. Ethical categories for identifying consequentialist versus rights-based motives showed 43 per cent of those who bid positively did so on the basis of non-economic reasoning. The ethical model was as strong as the standard socio-economic variables. In a combined model, with exclusion of non-significant factors, the strongest explanatory power came from attitudes, norms, PBC concerning electricity bills, strong rights and consequentialism favouring animals (in that order). Attitudes were by far the strongest factor in explaining variation.

18.4.2 Pro-social environmental attitudes

Stern and his psychologist colleagues have conducted studies which directly measure attitudes in order to understand WTP (Stern, Dietz and Kalof, 1993; Guagnano, Dietz and Stern, 1994; Stern, Dietz and Guagnano, 1995). The economic model has then been hypothesized to favour motivation by egoistic and selfish altruistic motives as opposed to a biospheric orientation. Yet, their studies give conflicting results, with egoistic motives proving significant in one study but non-significant in another, while biospheric beliefs appear to be more consistently significant. Across these studies the environmental attitudinal scales seem to produce rather weak explanatory variables for WTP. However, this empirical work by social psychologists fails to measure WTP as conceived by economists and instead requests payments for very general entities, good causes and environmental schemes, which would mean even strong, significant and persistent results would be questionable in terms of their relevance to the CVM (see Spash, 2000). This has been rectified by economists conducting CVM studies in combination with pro-environmental attitude measures.

Kotchen and Reiling (2000) employed the NEP and applied this to WTP data collected by mail survey from Maine residents in the USA. The results focus exclusively on non-users and also exclude all protest bids. Specific motive questions were used to cover belief in: option value, altruism, bequest

value, existence value and rights-based beliefs. They found the most important motive to be agreement with a rights-based belief, and that those with
pro-environmental attitudes are more likely to bid higher and hold such beliefs.

Cooper, Poe and Bateman (2004), hereafter CPB, built on Kotchen and
Reiling but attempted a more structured approach. A key aim of CPB was
to show that non-economic motives cannot be separated from economic ones
and therefore WTP reflects all such underlying motives and 'total economic
value' is therefore a valid expression of preference utilitarianism. They put
forward a model including: (i) pro-environmental attitudes measured by the
NEP; (ii) specific motives taken from Kotchen and Reiling but adding three
items, with one on use and the others on obligation and responsibility; (iii) a
psychometric scale stated variously to measure 'altruism' or 'prosocial attitudes' which involves ascribed responsibility, personal norms and awareness
of consequences. A convenience sample, students at the University of East
Anglia, UK, provided the data which CPB censored for protest responses. In
terms of explaining WTP via regression, the factors under (i) and (iii) were
analysed together, while those under (ii) were treated separately after having
been reclassified into scales on human value, natural value, responsibility and
obligation. The attitudinal scale, under (ii), was found to be unrelated to WTP
but also noted to be internally weak, while the NEP was also found to lack any
significant positive relationship with WTP. The NEP score was strongly associated with those classified in the natural value group who paid more, and with
existence and bequest motives and rights beliefs. Existence-related motives
for paying were found to be significantly more important than use-related
motives. CPB state that ethically based motives were of 'substantially different importance' and the rights beliefs (termed intrinsic value) amongst the most
important. However, they reject any separability of such beliefs because these
can be linked to the natural value category which was a significant explanatory
variable of WTP. CPB note that the distribution of bid categories was unrelated
to pro-environmental attitudes (i.e. the NEP).

These studies show a relationship between WTP and statements of beliefs
in rights and that underlying motives for WTP are complex, arising from
motives related to economic use and natural value orientations. Yet they provide
contradictory results in terms of the role played by attitudes and whether they
are indeed relevant for understanding WTP. The studies also fail to delineate
clearly the rights position and confuse this with statements about intrinsic and
existence values in their analysis. In order to correct this, the categorization of
ethical positions needs to be explicitly addressed. CPB also state as their final
conclusion that 'a more reliable measure of prosocial attitude could provide
insights to motivation akin to those achieved with the NEP scale'.

Spash (1998; 2006) goes some way to addressing these concerns by combining awareness of consequences scales with CVM in the context of wetland
re-creation. Factor analysis in the more recent work gave two value orientations, egoistic and biospheric, both of which related to altruism. The two-factor

structure is consistent with Stern *et al.* (1995). Positive environmental attitudes are associated with protest bids but they reduce the occurrence rather than increase it. This supports previous findings that censoring protest bids can bias the sample and in this study would reduce the presence of non-rights-based individuals. The egoistic–altruistic attitudes scale proved highly significant and explained more of the variance in WTP than any other variable. The social–biospheric scale explained little of the variance beyond that covered by egoistic–altruistic attitudes and rights-based beliefs (positively related to WTP). At the same time the idea that stated WTP in CVM is merely an attitude fails to find support given an explanatory power of 11 per cent for egoistic–altruistic attitudes. Overall the results support the finding that egoistic and selfish altruistic motives are important determinants of WTP. However, this is not to the exclusion of other motives such as the biospheric which were expressed directly as ethical beliefs in species rights. In addition, the egoistic values being expressed in this study failed to be associated with consequential ethical positions, which means the results failed to support the standard economic model.

18.5 Conclusions

The CVM has proven a controversial technique of environmental valuation, but rather than dismiss the extensive primary data collected, this chapter suggests economists learn from the empirical evidence. Attempts to remove all 'anomalies' via survey design have proven flawed. Certainly some aspects of early work were poor in terms of social science research approaches and there is still room for improvement, but many results cannot be merely explained away on that account and many have been corroborated via experimental evidence. Design of a perfect single survey to reveal true preferences is a misguided ideal. Worse is the attempt to force behavioural conformity to the expectations of the economic analyst to achieve 'market discipline'. Indeed anomalies show the richness and variety of human motivation and behaviour and as a result the need for learning across disciplines.

One problem with the approach of searching for the perfect survey instrument and set of guidelines is how this then restricts future research. CVM surveys are conducted for different reasons with different requirements. These are mainly as follows:

(i)   as research exercises, including work by students to get degree qualifications;
(ii) as theoretical and experimental research tools by academics;
(iii) as aids to project appraisal;
(iv) as evidence in litigation for damages, apparently solely in the USA;
(v)   as part of public policy debates, including advocacy by vested interest groups and government agencies.

The failure of the CVM community is to recognize these different roles and their different requirements and institutional contexts. This is particularly important in light of a decade of dominant reference to the NOAA Panel guidelines as the ultimate authority on how to conduct a valid CVM survey.

Turning to motivation means paying attention to the work done in social psychology. Studies have started to be conducted using measures of pro-social attitudes and using the TPB. These indicate the importance of attitudes in understanding WTP. However, they also show that attitudes and stated WTP are far from identical. Indeed social norms and perceived behavioural control both appear relevant, although results for environmental change are mixed across the few existing studies. Ethical positions are also found to be consistently important.

There seems to be a role for personal normative beliefs based upon deeper moral reflections as to how one should live, for example, religious convictions, an environmental ethic or belief in social justice. These ethical norms have been largely ignored by the TRA and TPB. There is evidently room for overlap between subjective and ethical norms as inputs to the formation and reinforcement of fundamental beliefs, for example choice of friends on the basis of their moral beliefs, or adopting the religious convictions of parents. Alternatively there may be conflict where personal ethical beliefs diverge from those of social groups. This can lead to moral dilemmas where upholding principles conflicts with the expectations of society.

The evidence supporting the role of ethical positions in explaining WTP is growing in the area of environmental valuation. Such a relationship may not generalize outside environmental behaviours. However, in this context, the divergence between beliefs in rights and consequentialism appears fundamental to understanding stated bids under the CVM.

Overall the CVM can be seen as a means of expanding the economists' conception of human psychology and behaviour. Philosophical concepts such as incommensurability and rights, of which economists tend to be either ignorant or scornful, cannot be dismissed. The empirical evidence is showing the importance of understanding the motives for human behaviour and the existence of plural values in society.

18.6 References

Aadland, D. and A. J. Caplan (2003) Cheap talk reconsidered: New evidence from CVM. Discussion paper, Department of Economics, Utah State University.

Ajzen, I. (1991) The theory of planned behaviour. *Organisational Behaviour and Human Decision Processes* 50: 179–211.

Ajzen, I., T. C. Brown and F. Carvajal (2004) Explaining the discrepancy between intentions and actions: The case of hypothetical bias in contingent valuation. *Personality and Social Psychology Bulletin* 30(9): 1108–21.

Ajzen, I., T. C. Brown and L. H. Rosenthal (1996) Information bias in contingent valuation: Effects of personal relevance, quality of information and motivational orientation. *Journal of Environmental Economics and Management* 30(1): 43–57.

Amigues, J. P., C. Boulatoff, B. Desaigues, C. Gauthier and J. E. Keith (2002) The benefits and costs of riparian analysis habitat preservation: A willingness to accept/willingness to pay contingent valuation approach. *Ecological Economics* 43(1): 17–31.

Arrow, K., R. Solow, P. R. Portney, E. Leamer, R. Radner and H. Schuman (1993) Natural resource damage assessment under the Oil Pollution Act of 1990. *Federal Register* 58(10): 4601–14.

Bandara, R. and C. Tisdell (2004) The net benefit of saving the Asian elephant: A policy and contingent valuation study. *Ecological Economics* 48(1): 93–107.

Bateman, I. J., R. T. Carson, B. Day, M. Hanemann, N. Hanley, T. Hett, M. Jones-Lee, G. Loomes, S. Mourato, E. Ozdemioglu, D. W. Pearce, R. Sugden and J. Swanson, eds. (2002) *Economic Valuation with Stated Preference Techniques: A Manual.* Cheltenham: Edward Elgar.

Bateman, I. J., E. Diamand, I. H. Langford and A. Jones (1996) Household willingness to pay and farmers' willingness to accept compensation for establishing a recreational woodland. *Journal of Environmental Planning and Management* 39(1): 21–44.

Bateman, I. J. and K. G. Willis, eds. (1999) *Valuing Environmental Preferences: Theory and Practice of the Contingent Valuation Method in the US, EU and Developing Countries.* Oxford: Oxford University Press.

Bhatia, M. R. and J. A. Fox-Rushby (2003) Validity of willingness to pay: Hypothetical versus actual payment. *Applied Economics Letters* 10(12): 737–40.

Bishop, R. C. and T. A. Heberlein (1986) Does contingent valuation work? *Valuing Environmental Goods: An Assessment of the Contingent Valuation Method.* R. G. Cummings, D. S. Brookshire and W. D. Schulze, eds. Totowa, NJ: Rowman & Allanheld: 123–47.

Boyle, K. (1989) Commodity specification and the framing of contingent valuation questions. *Land Economics* 65: 57–63.

Brown, T. C., I. Ajzen and D. Hrubes (2003) Further tests of entreaties to avoid hypothetical bias in referendum contingent valuation. *Journal of Environmental Economics and Management* 46(2): 353–61.

Brown, T. C. and R. Gregory (1999) Why the WTA–WTP disparity matters. *Ecological Economics* 28(3): 323–35.

Burgess, J., J. Clark and C. M. Harrison (1998) Respondents' evaluations of a CV survey: A case study based on an economic valuation of the wildlife enhancement scheme, Pevensey levels in East Sussex. *Area* 30(1): 19–27.

(2000) Culture, communication, and the information problem in contingent valuation surveys: A case study of a wildlife enhancement scheme. *Environment and Planning C: Government and Policy* 18(5): 505–24.

Camacho-Cuena, E., A. Garcia-Gallego, N. Georgantzis and G. Sabater-Grande (2004) An experimental validation of hypothetical WTP for a recyclable product. *Environmental and Resource Economics* 27(3): 313–35.

Carson, R. T., N. E. Flores, K. M. Martin and J. L. Wright (1996) Contingent valuation and revealed preference methodologies: Comparing the estimates for quasi-public goods. *Land Economics* 72(1): 80–99.

Carson, R. T., N. E. Flores and N. F. Meade (2001) Contingent valuation: Controversies and evidence. *Environmental and Resource Economics* 19(2): 173–210.

Carson, R. T., J. Wright, A. Alberini, N. Carson and N. Flores (1994) *A Bibliography of Contingent Valuation Studies and Papers.* La Jolla, CA: Natural Resource Damage Assessment, Inc.

Ciriacy-Wantrup, S. (1947) Capital returns from soil conservation practices. *Journal of Farm Economics* 29: 1188–90.

Clark, J., J. Burgess and C. M. Harrison (2000) 'I struggled with this money business': Respondents' perspectives on contingent valuation. *Ecological Economics* 33(1): 45–62.

Connelly, N. A., B. A. Knuth and D. L. Kay (2002) Public support for ecosystem restoration in the Hudson River Valley, USA. *Environmental Management* 29(4): 467–76.

Cooper, P., G. L. Poe and I. J. Bateman (2004) The structure of motivation for contingent values: A case study of lake water quality. *Ecological Economics* 50: 69–82.

Cummings, R. G., D. S. Brookshire and W. D. Schulze, eds. (1986) *Valuing Environmental Goods: An Assessment of the Contingent Valuation Method.* Totowa, NJ: Rowman & Allanheld.

Cummings, R. G. and L. O. Taylor (1999) Unbiased value estimates for environmental goods: A cheap talk design for the contingent valuation method. *American Economic Review* 89(3): 649–65.

Department of the Environment (1991) *Policy Appraisal and the Environment: A Guide for Government Departments.* London: Her Majesty's Stationery Office.

Department of the Environment, Transport and the Regions (1999) The environmental costs and benefits of the supply of aggregates: Phase 2. London: Department of the Environment, Transport and the Regions.

Department of the Interior (1986) Final rule for natural resource damage assessments under the Comprehensive Environmental Response, Compensation, and Liability Act of 1980 (CERCLA). *Federal Register* 51(148): 27674–753.

Dunlap, R. E. and K. D. Van Liere (1978) The 'New Environmental Paradigm'. *Journal of Environmental Education* 9(4): 10–19.

Dunlap, R. E., K. D. Van Liere, A. G. Mertig and R. E. Jones (2000) Measuring endorsement of the new ecological paradigm: A revised NEP scale. *Journal of Social Issues* 56(3): 425–42.

Fischhoff, B. (1991) Value elicitation: Is there anything in there? *American Psychologist* 46: 835–47.

Fishbein, M. and I. Ajzen (1975) *Belief, Attitude, Intention and Behavior: An Introduction to Theory and Research.* Reading, MA: Addison-Wesley.

Green, C. and S. Tunstall (1999) A psychological perspective. *Valuing Environmental Preferences: Theory and Practice of the Contingent Valuation Method in the US, EU and Developing Countries.* I. Bateman and K. Willis, eds. Oxford: Oxford University Press: 207–57.

Guagnano, G. A., T. Dietz and P. C. Stern (1994) Willingness to pay for public goods: A test of the contribution model. *Psychological Science* 5(6): 411–15.

Hanemann, W. M. (1991) Willingness to pay and willingness to accept: How much can they differ? *American Economic Review* 81(3): 635–47.

(1994) Valuing the environment through contingent valuation. *Journal of Economic Perspectives* 8(4): 19–43.

Hanley, N. and J. F. Shogren (2005) Is cost–benefit analysis anomaly-proof? *Environmental and Resource Economics* 32(1): 13–34.

Hanley, N. and C. L. Spash (1993) *Cost–Benefit Analysis and the Environment.* Aldershot: Edward Elgar.

Harrison, G. W. and J. C. Lesley (1996) Must contingent valuation surveys cost so much? *Journal of Environmental Economics and Management* 31(1): 79–95.

Hausman, J. A., ed. (1993) *Contingent Valuation: A Critical Assessment.* Amsterdam: North-Holland.

Hill, R. J. (1981) Attitudes and behaviour. *Social Psychology: Sociological Perspectives.* M. Rosenberg and R. Turner, eds. New York: Basic Books: 347–77.

Kahneman, D. and J. L. Knetsch (1992a) Contingent valuation and the value of public-goods: Reply. *Journal of Environmental Economics and Management* 22(1): 90–4.

(1992b) Valuing public goods: The purchase of moral satisfaction. *Journal of Environmental Economics and Management* 22(1): 57–70.

Kahneman, D., J. L. Knetsch and R. H. Thaler (1991) Anomalies: The endowment effect, loss aversion, and status-quo bias. *Journal of Economic Perspectives* 5(1): 193–206.

Kahneman, D., I. Ritov, K. E. Jacowitz and P. Grant (1993) Stated willingness to pay for public goods: A psychological perspective. *Psychological Science* 4(5): 310–15.

Kerr, G. N. and R. Cullen (1995) Public preferences and efficient allocation of a possum control budget. *Journal of Environmental Management* 43(1): 1–15.

Klose, T. (1999) The contingent valuation method in health care. *Health Policy* 47(2): 97–123.

Knetsch, J. L. (1994) Environmental valuation: Some problems of wrong questions and misleading answers. *Environmental Values* 3(4): 351–68.

(1995) Asymmetric valuation of gains and losses and preference order assumptions. *Economic Inquiry* 33(1): 134–41.

(2005) Gains, losses, and the US EPA economic analyses guidelines: A hazardous product? *Environmental and Resource Economics* 32(1): 91–112.

Knetsch, J. L. and J. A. Sinden (1984) Willingness to pay and compensation demanded: Experimental evidence of an unexpected disparity in measures of value. *Quarterly Journal of Economics* 99(3): 507–21.

Kotchen, M. J. and S. D. Reiling (2000) Environmental attitudes, motivations, and contingent valuation of nonuse values: A case study involving endangered species. *Ecological Economics* 32(1): 93–107.

List, J. A. (2003) Does market experience eliminate market anomalies? *Quarterly Journal of Economics* 118(1): 41–71.

Lowenstein, G. (1987) Anticipation and the valuation of delayed consumption. *Economic Journal* 97: 666–84.

Lowenstein, G. and D. Prelec (1991) Negative time preference. *American Economic Review* 81: 347–52.

(1992) Anomalies in intertemporal choice: Evidence and an interpretation. *Quarterly Journal of Economics* 107: 573–97.

Macmillan, D. C., E. I. Duff and D. A. Elston (2001) Modelling the non-market environmental costs and benefits of biodiversity projects using contingent valuation data. *Environmental and Resource Economics* 18(4): 391–410.

Meyerhoff, J. (2002) The influence of general and specific attitudes on stated willingness to pay: A composite attitude–behaviour model. *CSERGE Working Paper*. Norwich: University of East Anglia: 30.

Mitchell, R. C. and R. T. Carson (1989) *Using Surveys to Value Public Goods: The Contigent Valuation Method*. Washington, DC: Resources for the Future.

Moisseinen, E. (1999) On behavioural intentions in the case of the Saimaa Seal: Comparing the contingent valuation approach and attitude–behaviour research. *Valuation and the Environment: Theory, Method and Practice*. M. O'Connor and C. L. Spash, eds. Cheltenham: Edward Elgar: 183–204.

Murphy, J. J., T. H. Stevens and D. Weatherhead (2005) Is cheap talk effective at eliminating hypothetical bias in a provision point mechanism? *Environmental and Resource Economics* 30(3): 327–43.

Pouta, E. (2003) Attitude–behaviour framework in contingent valuation of forest conservation. Department of Forest Economics, Helsinki, University of Helsinki: 57.

(2004) Attitude and belief questions as a source of context effect in a contingent valuation survey. *Journal of Economic Psychology* 25(2): 229–42.

Pouta, E. and M. Rekola (2001) The theory of planned behavior in predicting willingness to pay for abatement of forest regeneration. *Society and Natural Resources* 14(2): 93–106.

Pouta, E., M. Rekola, J. Kuuluvainen, O. Tahvonen and C. Z. Li (2000) Contingent valuation of the Natura 2000 nature conservation programme in Finland. *Forestry* 73(2): 119–28.

Schkade, D. A. and J. W. Payne (1993) Where do the numbers come from? How people respond to contingent valuation questions. *Contingent Valuation: A Critical Assessment*. J. A. Hausman, ed. Amsterdam: North-Holland: 271–93.

(1994) How people respond to contingent valuation questions: A verbal protocol analysis of willingness to pay for an environmental regulation. *Journal of Environmental Economics and Management* 26(1): 88–109.

Sen, A. (1977) Rational fools: A critique of the behavioral foundations of economic theory. *Philosophy and Public Affairs* 6: 317–44.

Shogren, J. F. and D. J. Hayes (1997) Resolving differences in willingness to pay and willingness to accept: Reply. *American Economic Review* 87(1): 241–4.

Shogren, J. F., S. Y. Shin, D. J. Hayes and J. B. Kliebenstein (1994) Resolving differences in willingness to pay and willingness to accept. *American Economic Review* 84(1): 255–70.

Smith, V. K. (1992) Arbitrary values, good causes, and premature verdicts. *Journal of Environmental Economics and Management* 22(1): 71–89.

Spash, C. L. (1998) *Environmental Values and Wetland Ecosystems: CVM, Ethics and Attitudes*. Cambridge: Cambridge Research for the Environment, Department of Land Economy, University of Cambridge: 111.

(2000) Ethical motives and charitable contributions in contingent valuation: Empirical evidence from social psychology and economics. *Environmental Values* 9(4): 453–79.

(2002a) Dividing time and discounting the future. *Greenhouse Economics: Value and Ethics*. C. L. Spash, ed. London: Routledge: 201–20.

(2002b) Informing and forming preferences in environmental valuation: Coral reef biodiversity. *Journal of Economic Psychology* 23(5): 665–87.

(2006) Non-economic motivation for contingent values: Rights and attitudinal beliefs in the willingness to pay for environmental improvements. *Land Economics* 82(4): 602–22.

Spash, C. L., K. C. Urama, R. Burton, W. Kenyon, P. Shannon and G. Hill (2004) *Understanding the Value of Biodiversity in Water Ecosystems: Economics, Ethics and Social Psychology*. Aberdeen: University of Aberdeen: 31.

(2008) Motives behind willingness to pay for improving biodiversity in a water ecosystem: Economics, ethics and social psychology. *Ecological Economics*: forthcoming.

Stern, P. C., T. Dietz and G. A. Guagnano (1995) The New Ecological Paradigm in social-psychological context. *Environment and Behavior* 27(6): 723–43.

Stern, P. C., T. Dietz and L. Kalof (1993) Value orientation, gender and environmental concern. *Environment and Behavior* 25(3): 322–48.

Stern, P. C., T. Dietz, L. Kalof and G. A. Guagnano (1995) Values, beliefs and pro-environmental action: Attitude formation toward emergent attitude objects. *Journal of Applied Social Psychology* 25(18): 1611–36.

Thaler, R. (1980) Toward a positive theory of consumer choice. *Journal of Economic Behavior and Organization* 1(1): 39–60.

Thayer, M. A. (1981) Contingent valuation techniques for assessing environmental impacts: Further evidence. *Journal of Environmental Economics and Management* 8: 27–44.

US Environmental Protection Agency (EPA) (2000) *Guidelines for Preparing Economic Analyses*. Washington, DC: United States Environmental Protection Agency.

Vatn, A. (2004) Environmental valuation and rationality. *Land Economics* 80(1): 1–18.

Willis, K. (1995) Contingent valuation in a policy context: The National Oceanic and Atmospheric Administration report and its implications for the use of contingent valuation methods in policy analysis in Britain. *Environmental Valuation: New Perspectives*. K. G. Willis and J. T. Corkindale, eds. Wallingford: CAB International: 118–43.

PART VI

Biological perspectives

19 Neuroeconomics: what neuroscience can learn from economics

TERRY LOHRENZ AND P. READ MONTAGUE

Economics is about the allocation of scarce resources, and hence is focused on decision-making. All organisms constantly make life-or-death choices about the allocation of scarce resources. In higher organisms these choices are made in brains. Neuroeconomics is broadly the study of how these choices are made in the brain. How one defines and regards neuroeconomics depends on where one sits. Some economists have been attracted to neuroeconomics because they see the study of the actual economic agent as a good thing, and studying the brain is a natural extension of this impulse. The hope is that studying the brain will give biological underpinnings and constraints to economic theorizing. What about the other direction? In a recent review of neuroeconomics from an economics perspective (Camerer *et al.*, 2005), the authors state "although we focused solely on applications of neuroscience to economics, intellectual trade could also flow in the opposite direction." In this chapter we examine this "flow in the opposite direction" and see how economics is informing neuroscience. The intellectual flow from economics to neuroscience naturally breaks into two branches which we will call Neuroeconomics I and Neuroeconomics II.

Neuroeconomics I deals with the construction and organization of neural tissue from an economics perspective: organisms are constrained by the need to replenish energy stores and allocate scarce energy resources. Through the inherently economic mechanism of evolution, efficiency is built into the brain. Current commercially available silicon-based computers are extremely fast, accurate, and communicate internally at high rates of speed. As anyone with a laptop knows, they also generate a tremendous amount of heat. Clearly, current computers are not very efficient. In general, computer designers and programmers have simply not had to really worry about power (except to keep the circuit from burning up). This is not true for organisms: living creatures have never had the luxury of essentially unlimited power supplies. They have had to develop competitive foraging strategies to replenish energy supplies from the environment. As a result, neural computations are extremely efficient. (The human brain runs on 20–5 watts of power. In contrast, Blue Gene, an IBM supercomputer that is the direct descendant of Deep Blue, the computer which defeated the chess champion Gary Kasparov, runs on 40 kW (peak), and requires 13 tons of air-conditioning. (Specifications based on a one-rack configuration of 1,026 compute nodes per rack. IBM, 2006.) Biological computing devices must at least implicitly keep track of the risks and returns

457

of investments in neural tissue. This point of view is supported by numerous studies that have demonstrated optimal matching between neural tissue and the physics problem the tissue was designed to solve. Neuroeconomics I is devoted to understanding biological computation devices in terms of the fundamental economic organizing principle of efficiency.

Neuroeconomics II is concerned with higher level functions, including decision-making and social cognition. Neuroeconomics II exists largely because of (1) behavioral economics/finance and experimental economics, and (2) the emergence of functional magnetic resonance imaging (fMRI). Behavioral economics and experimental economics (Camerer, 2003; Kagel and Roth, 1995) is concerned with the actual behavior of economic agents: it is empirical, and not at heart prescriptive. Indeed a large amount of the work in this field has been to study deviations from standard normative economics. The field has provided a rich collection of economically inspired tasks for probing the neural correlates of choice behavior. Prior to the mid-1990s, evidence about the neural processes in humans came from electroencephalograms (EEG), magnetoencephalography (MEG), positron emission tomography (PET), lesion studies, and from recordings of small groups of neurons in rodents and monkeys. Each of these methods has its own shortcomings: EEG and MEG suffer from the non-uniqueness of the inverse problem (going from extra-cranial signals to source signals, Huettel *et al.*, 2004). PET has poor temporal resolution. Lesion studies are obviously constrained, and electrodes cannot be widely implanted in humans due to ethical constraints. Functional magnetic resonance imaging (see Huettel *et al.*, 2004 for a comprehensive introduction) became a viable human imaging modality in the mid-nineties, and has enabled scientists to peer inside the "black box" of the human brain. fMRI detects signals from individual volume elements ("voxels") of the brain with a spatial resolution of approximately 3 mm^3 and a temporal resolution of about .5 Hz. fMRI thus has reasonable resolution in both the spatial and temporal domains for investigating human behavior. It is therefore quite natural for experimental economists to start to ask questions about brain function, and to use fMRI to explore them.

On the other hand, economics married to fMRI can provide neuroscience with a powerful set of tools to probe the mesoscale structures in the brain recruited in decision-making (figure 19.1). Indeed, an increasing number of imaging experiments in humans (and single-unit recording experiments in non-human primates) have been informed by principles from economics. As outlined above, the efficient harvesting of rewards from the environment is central to the survival of any organism. Given these observations, we first review recent work centering on reward representation, and, more generally, the neural representation of quantities central to models of choice. We start with the static theory of choice under risk and ambiguity, and then turn our attention to neural representations of inter-temporal decisions, including dynamic sequential decision-making. While this first group of studies focuses on studies involving single agents making choices essentially against "nature," we discuss a second group of studies investigating the neuroscience of social interaction between

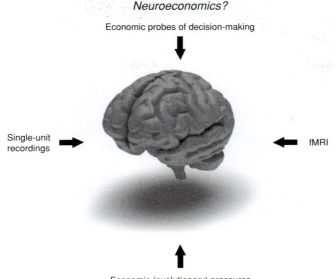

Figure 19.1 Diagram of forces and influences forging neuroeconomics

intelligent agents. The strategic element introduced by social interactions, as well as complex cultural constructs such as trust and fairness, pose a rich set of challenges for the promising interaction of economics and neuroscience.

19.1 Reward

No matter what biologically based theory of choice develops, a neural representation of experienced reward or utility will be a part of it. Any algorithm used to make choices will need a report of the immediate outcome of a choice. It is important to distinguish between reward and value. Reward is the immediate payoff from taking an action. Value refers to the discounted sum of the current reward and *all* future rewards (a concept important in multi-period choice tasks discussed below and in appendix A). A related term, preference, is a derivative concept of value. One state, or more precisely, state–action pair, is preferred to another if the (estimated) value of one state–action pair is greater than the value of the other state–action pair. Numerous fMRI experiments have explored reward representation across a diverse selection of reward categories (for reviews see O'Doherty, 2004 and Montague *et al.*, 2006), including money (Breiter *et al.*, 2001; Elliot *et al.*, 2003; Knutson *et al.*, 2003), art (Erk *et al.*, 2002; Kawabata and Zeki, 2004), physical beauty (Aharon *et al.*, 2001), and even love (Bartels and Zeki, 2000, 2004). Indeed, in a recent study, McClure *et al.* (2004) have even connected activity in the ventromedial prefrontal cortex (VMPFC) with preference for Coca Cola (figure 19.2). These experiments consistently demonstrate activations in response to a diverse spectrum of rewards in the ventral striatum, orbitofrontal cortex (OFC) (see appendix B for

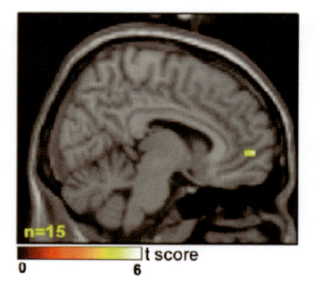

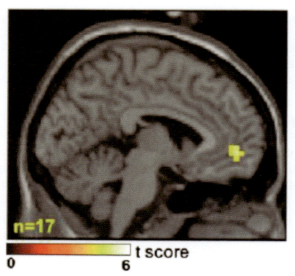

Figure 19.2 Area of VMPFC whose activity scales linearly with subjects' preference for Coke as revealed in an anonymous taste test. Reprinted from *Neuron* 44, McClure, S. M., Li, J., Tomlin, D., Cypert, K. S., Montague, L. S., Montague, P. R., "Neural correlates of behavioral preference for culturally familiar drinks," Copyright 2004, pp. 379–87, with permission from Elsevier

a brief overview of neuroanatomy related to choice behavior), and VMPFC. While the representation and response to rewarding or aversive stimuli is clearly an important component of any organism's valuation machinery, the story certainly does not end there. Economics and machine learning provide conceptual tools for understanding the links between reward, value, and choice. We turn to one of the most basic of conceptual tools from economics next.

19.2 Expected utility

Expected utility (see appendix A) is a cornerstone of normative economic theory. Considerable effort has therefore gone into "finding it" in the brain in both humans and non-human primates. For example, Platt and Glimcher (1999) explored decision-making in macaque monkeys, with a goal of locating the calculation of expected value (EV) (assuming a linear utility function) in the lateral intra-parietal (LIP) region. Indeed, the authors found that LIP neurons modulated their firing rates during a cued saccade (directed eye movement from one fixation point to a target) task according to both expected gain and probability of juice reward delivery. In a similar vein, Sugrue *et al.* (2004) studied the firing rates of LIP neurons in rhesus monkeys in a dynamic reward task. In this task, the monkeys eye-tracked colored dots on a screen, and were rewarded with juice squirts according to a probabilistic schedule (Poisson distribution with reward remaining until taken) which changed periodically. According to the matching law (Herrnstein, 1961), the fraction of choices allocated to a color should be proportional to the total income received from the color. In this study the authors constructed a "leaky integrator" model of total reward to create a local measure of fractional income. The model had a single parameter τ which controlled the decay rate of the integrator. τ was optimized in computer simulations of the reward environment used in the experiment. The τ's fit to the monkeys' behavior was close to the optimal values from the simulation, and furthermore the firing rates of LIP neurons correlated with local fractional income. Corrado *et al.* (2005) extend this model to include a non-linear transformation of local income, while Lau and Glimcher (2005) report similar results, but also find that both previous rewards and previous choices are needed in their model.

A recent series of papers (alluded to above) used fMRI in humans to explore various aspects of the anticipation and receipt of reward (see also Montague *et al.*, 2006). Recently, Knutson and Peterson (2005) examined the representation of anticipated gain and loss, and actual gain and loss outcomes in humans using fMRI. They reported that a region of the ventral striatum, the nucleus accumbens (NAcc), is active in anticipation of gains, while a region of prefrontal cortex, VMPFC, is active during the positive outcome phase. This work suggests that NAcc may encode the value of a positive outcome, whereas VMPFC, as discussed above, encodes actual positive outcomes. The

NAcc did not respond to negative outcomes. This work, however, did not probe the representation of probability of outcome. Knutson *et al.* (2005) included the probabilistic component to investigate all of the pieces of EV in humans using fMRI. Their main result was that the NAcc encodes the outcome size, while the VMPFC encodes reward probability. Another recent paper (Yacubian *et al.*, 2006) investigated the asymmetry between gains and losses explicitly within the framework of expected utility theory (EUT). In this study subjects faced independent reward trials with either high or low probability of gain of a smaller (1 euro) or larger (5 euros) amount of money. Subjects made a motor action to lodge a choice but trials were independent and so no learning was necessary. The trials were divided into an anticipation period and an outcome period. Expected value in this case can be split into two terms:

$$EV = EV_+ + EV_-$$
$$= p_+ V + (1 - p_+) \cdot (-V)$$

where p_+ is the probability of a winning outcome, and V is the value at stake (either 1 or 5 euros). The authors looked for neural correlates of EV_+ and EV_- during the anticipation stage, and correlates of a prediction error ($V - EV_{+/-}$). Their main finding (figure 19.3) is that the ventral striatum encodes EV_+ and the prediction error for positive outcomes, while the amygdala encodes EV_- and the prediction error in the negative outcome case.

These results taken together point to a fundamental issue in neuroeconomics: the asymmetry between losses and gains. Kahneman and Tversky (1979) laid out the systematic violations of EUT in human choice behavior, and developed prospect theory to explain these violations. In this theory the value function for losses is twice as steep at the origin as it is for gains. Numerous fMRI experiments (as noted above) have seen differential effects of losses and gains, but at present there is not a clear link to Kahneman and Tversky's results, nor is there a clear theoretical explanation of the behavioral results (but see Trepel *et al.*, 2005).

The above experiment (Knutson *et al.*, 2005) on expected utility made an assumption about the risk preferences of the subjects. Specifically, they examined expected value (which coincides with expected utility when subjects are "risk neutral," i.e. the utility function is linear: see appendix A). In a recent paper Preuschoff *et al.* (2005) examine the neural correlates of when utility is represented by mean variance analysis (see appendix A) which explicitly parameterizes a subject's risk aversion using the variance of the outcome. In this paradigm the subject picks between two random cards (chosen without replacement from a deck of cards numbered 1 through 10), and wagers $1 on that card. After a pause the second card is turned over and if the chosen card has the higher value the subject wins $1, and otherwise loses the bet. The expected value of the wager is linear in the probability of reward, and the risk is quadratic in the probability of reward, both quantities of which are known when the first card is flipped over. The authors hypothesized that expected

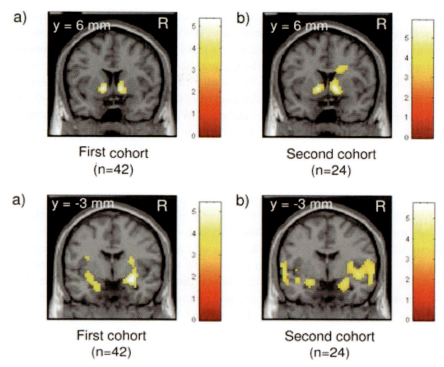

Figure 19.3 Neural activity correlating with expected value and prediction error. Top row: activity in ventral striatum correlated with EV$_+$ and prediction error in positive case. Bottom row: activity in amygdala correlated with EV$_-$ and prediction error in negative case. From Yacubian, J., Gläscher, J., Schroeder, K., Sommer, T., Braus, D. F., and Büchel, C. (2006). Dissociable systems for gain- and loss-related value predictions and error of prediction in the human brain. Reproduced from *Journal of Neuroscience* 26, pp. 9530–7 Copyright 2006 by the Society for Neuroscience

value would be represented immediately in the striatum, whereas risk would be represented later in the course of activity (based on Fiorello *et al.*, 2003). Indeed this is what they found: activation linear in probability of win in the putamen/ventral striatum, and quadratic in probability in the ventral striatum, midbrain, and mediodorsal thalamic nucleus. This result is significant because it adds a new layer of conceptual complexity to the function of the striatum, with which neuroscientists will have to grapple as they put together models of these systems. Below we will see another layer of complexity when we consider learning.

19.3 Decisions under ambiguity

In most of the experiments above, while the outcome of a trial was uncertain the probabilities of gain or loss were known. Usually this is referred to as decision under risk. If, on the other hand, the probabilities are not known, the situation is referred to as decision under ambiguity. The distinction is made clear in the famous Ellsberg paradox (Ellsberg, 1961). Imagine two decks of cards (here we follow Hsu *et al.*, 2005). The first deck contains ten red cards and ten blue cards. The second deck contains twenty red or blue cards. Consider two gambles. In the first you get $10 if a red card is chosen from the first deck. In the second you get $10 if red is chosen from the second deck. Which gamble would you prefer? Most people would choose the first gamble. Most would make a similar choice for the same choice involving the blue cards. Together (using expected value) this would imply that for the ambiguous deck P(RED) + P(BLUE) < 1, which is absurd. Hsu *et al.* (2005) sought to explore the neural basis of this paradox using fMRI. In their design subjects made repeated choices between certain amounts of money, and risky or ambiguous gambles involving the decks of cards mentioned above. Their main analysis looked for parts of the brain that were differentially activated in the risky and ambiguous trials. Two regions of the brain were more active in response to ambiguity than in response to risk: the bilateral amygdala and the bilateral (lateral) orbitofrontal cortex. The dorsal striatum (as well as precuneus and premotor cortex) was more active in the risky versus ambiguous case. The authors also conducted the experiment behaviorally with a group of lesion patients (n = 12). The group was divided into two subgroups. The first subgroup (n = 5) had lesions that overlapped with the OFC activation areas identified above. The second (n = 7) had lesions that did not intersect any of the areas of interest identified by fMRI. The choices of the subjects were analyzed with a model containing a parameter measuring risk preference, and a parameter measuring ambiguity preference. The control group had clustered parameters that clearly indicated risk and ambiguity aversion, while the patients with OFC damage were risk and ambiguity seeking.

Huettel *et al.* (2006) also investigated the neural correlates of ambiguity. In this study subjects made repeated choices between two gambles which were either risky (probabilities known), certain, or ambiguous. The authors found that a region of lateral prefrontal cortex, the inferior frontal sulcus (IFS), was more active in choices involving an ambiguous alternative. Furthermore the degree of activation associated with ambiguous minus risky trials was significantly correlated with a behavioral measure of ambiguity preference (obtained by modeling the subject' choices as in Hsu *et al.* [2005] above). The degree of activation associated with risky minus ambiguous trials was correlated negatively with risk preference. Remarkably, the authors also found a significant negative correlation between scores on a psychometric test of impulsivity and activation in the IFS in the ambiguous minus risky condition. This result is consistent with the assumption that less impulsive people consider more possibilities in ambiguous cases, and this is reflected in activity in the IFS, a region previously thought to be involved in behavioral control (Miller, 2000).

While these two experiments come to different conclusions regarding the regions of activation associated with ambiguity versus risk, they provide an excellent example of how economics can inform neuroscience. Using a

well-defined (quantitative) concept in economics, the authors designed a probe
to find the neural correlates of the quantity. Finding the associated areas can
then inform further theorizing about mesoscale structures and algorithms, in
turn leading to more refined experiments.

19.4 Neural representations of temporal discounting

Would you prefer $100 today to $110 in a week? How about $100 in a year and
$110 in a year and a week? If you chose $100 in the first instance and $110 in
the second, this is a temporal preference reversal. Standard economic theory
assumes exponential discounting, which avoids such reversals, but experiments
have shown that people do not generally behave in this way (Frederick *et al.*,
2002; see also Appendix A). Most people's answer to the introductory question entails a violation of the precept of exponential discounting. McClure
et al. (2004) used fMRI to investigate the hypothesis that there are two neural
systems involved in constructing the discount function: an impulsive system
(the β system) localized in the limbic system, and a "patient," rational system
(the δ system) localized in the prefrontal cortex. The β and δ refer to parameters
in a quasi-hyperbolic discounting function (Phelps and Pollak, 1968; Elster,
1979; Laibson, 1997) (see appendix A). In the McClure *et al.* experiment,
subjects made choices between earlier and later rewards. In some cases the
rewards were available immediately (defined as available right after the scanning session, the "immediate" trials), and in other trials the earliest reward was
only available later ($\sim$ weeks, the delayed trials). Brain areas activated during
the immediate trials decision epoch were declared β areas (figure 19.4), and
included the ventral striatum, medial orbitofrontal cortex, medial prefrontal
cortex, posterior cingulate cortex, and left posterior hippocampus. Generically, the decision epoch activated (modulo "non-decision-related aspects of
task performance": McClure *et al.*, 2004) dorsolateral prefrontal cortex, right
ventrolateral prefrontal cortex, and right lateral orbitofrontal cortex. These
results support the hypothesis that there are two distinct systems involved in
discounting future rewards. The areas activated by the immediate rewards are
in fact limbic structures receiving projections from midbrain dopamine neurons. The areas activated by the "all decisions" variable (areas expected to be
related to δ, since δ appears in the discount calculation for all decisions) are
areas that have previously been implicated in executive control (Smith and
Jonides, 1999; Miller and Cohen, 2001).

19.5 Dynamic choice

In the above experiments the subjects were typically over-trained on the task,
i.e. when measurements started being taken all of the learning had already taken
place, or in fact there was no learning at all. In essence, the expected utility
framework is static: there is no learning. Two important questions immediately

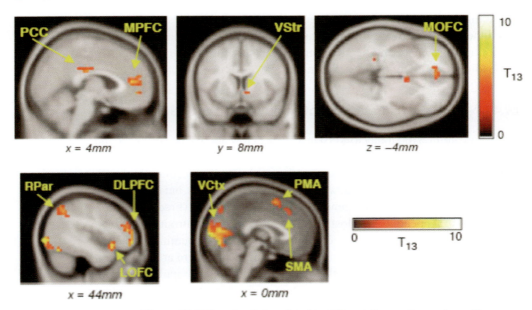

Figure 19.4 Neural activity related to different discounting systems. Top row: areas preferentially activated by immediate gains (β system). Bottom row: areas that activated equally in response to all delays (δ system). Subsequent analysis showed that pre-motor and supplementary motor cortex were not modulated by task difficulty, and hence unlikely to be involved in the decision process. From McClure, S. M., Laibson, D., Loewenstein, G., Cohen, J. D. (2004). "Separate neural systems value immediate and delayed monetary awards," *Science* 306, pp. 503–7. Reprinted with permission from AAAS

emerge: (1) how do organisms, in particular humans, go about learning reward contingencies? and (2) what are the neural mechanisms behind it? The mid-1990s saw the introduction of formal, computer-science-inspired models of learning to explain the patterns of single-unit recordings from the dopamine neurons of monkeys engaged in a Pavlovian conditioning task (Montague *et al.*, 1996; Schultz *et al.*, 1997). These models, "TD-learning" models (see appendix A for details), predict signals that have been found in the ventral and dorsal striatum using fMRI in humans, and electro-physiology in non-human primates. McClure *et al.* (2003a) and O'Doherty *et al.* (2003) provide clear evidence for a temporal difference (TD) error signal in the striatum in the context of Pavlovian conditioning. McClure *et al.* varied the time of reward delivery, while leaving reward amount and reward type the same. More specifically they trained subjects to expect a fixed amount of juice at a specific time interval after a light cue. After training, "catch trials" were inserted where juice was not delivered at the expected time, but rather four seconds later. Two fMRI contrasts were examined: activity at the (later) unexpected delivery of juice versus the expected delivery of juice, and activity at the expected time of juice delivery when the juice was *not* delivered versus the activity four

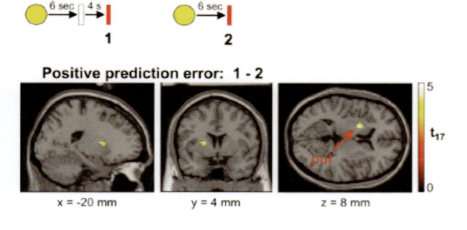

Positive prediction error: 1 - 2

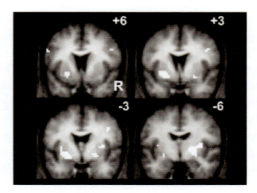

x = -20 mm   y = 4 mm   z = 8 mm

Figure 19.5 fMRI evidence for TD-error signal in ventral striatum. Top: increased activity in ventral striatum in contrast of unexpected juice delivery versus expected juice delivery. Reprinted from *Neuron* 38, McClure *et al.*, "Temporal prediction errors in a passive learning task activate human striatum," pp. 339–46, Copyright 2003, with permission from Elsevier.

Bottom: activity in ventral striatum correlated with TD regressor. Reprinted from *Neuron* 38, O'Doherty *et al.*, "Temporal difference models and reward-related learning in the human brain," Copyright 2003, pp. 329–37, with permission from Elsevier

seconds after actual delivery of juice. In the former case as expected from a TD-error signal there was increased activity in the ventral striatum (the putamen), while in the latter case, as expected, there was decreased activity in the same region (figure 19.5). O'Doherty *et al.* used a related Pavlovian conditioning paradigm using juice squirts to test for brain areas encoding a TD-error signal. Subjects inside the scanner were shown three different visual cues (CS_+, CS_{neut}, CS_-), which were paired with a squirt of glucose, a squirt of neutral liquid ("containing the main ionic components of saliva"), and a squirt of no-taste liquid (presumably water), respectively. After training, on some cued pleasant trials the unconditional stimulus was omitted, and on some cued unpleasant trials a pleasant reward was substituted for the unpleasant stimulus. For analysis, the authors used a model for the TD-error signal based on Schultz *et al.* (1997), and looked for areas in the brain that correlated with this signal at both the cue and reward times. They also found significant (figure 19.5) activity in the ventral striatum, as well as the orbitofrontal cortex (OFC), and the cerebellum.

One shortcoming of these two studies is that while they showed how TD learning could relate to brain activity in a Pavlovian task, no decisions were actually made. O'Doherty *et al.* (2004) explored the role of the striatum in an instrumental conditioning task, where subjects actually made choices. Previous lesion studies had suggested dissociable roles for the dorsal and ventral striatum (O'Doherty, 2004). The ventral striatum was thought to encode reward associations, while the dorsal striatum was thought to be involved in "motor and cognitive control." This split corresponds nicely to a machine learning architecture called the actor–critic learning (Sutton and Barto, 1998; McClure *et al.*, 2003b). In actor–critic learning, the critic keeps track of estimates of the values of states, and a TD-error signal updates these estimates. An actor is in charge of a policy, and the same TD-error signal criticizes (updates) this policy. O'Doherty used a close relative of the basic actor–critic architecture called advantage learning (Baird, 1993; Dayan and Balleine, 2002). In advantage learning the learner tracks the difference between the expected value of an available action in a state (the Q value, see appendix A), and the expected value of that state; this algorithm has an error signal analogous to the TD-error signal. In this paradigm O'Doherty imbedded a Pavlovian conditioning experiment inside an instrumental task to test the hypothesis that the roles of the dorsal and ventral striatum were dissociable according to the actor and critic. More precisely, in the instrumental task, the TD error would be expected to cause activation in the dorsal and ventral striatum, while in the imbedded Pavlovian task, the error signal should only appear in the ventral striatum. Indeed, this is what they found (figure 19.6).

The fMRI evidence of TD-error signals carried by the phasic firing midbrain dopamine neurons has been complemented by further single-unit recording work. In a recent paper Bayer and Glimcher (2005) report on recordings of dopamine neurons in non-human primates. In this study the authors recorded spikes from dopamine neurons in the ventral tegmental area (VTA) and the substantia nigra pars compacta (SNc) of the midbrain while the monkeys performed a free choice task. The monkeys learned to time saccades into a visual target in order to receive juice rewards. The baseline firing rate of these neurons was modulated at two times during the task: first, at the tone which announced that a new trial was to begin – this modulation did not depend on any of the task variables; second, at the time after the reward (or when the reward should have been received). The authors fitted a model of the firing rate during this period as a linear function of the current and previous rewards:

$$FR = \beta_0 \cdot R_t + \beta_1 \cdot R_{t-1} + \beta_2 \cdot R_{t-2} + \ldots + \beta_{10} \cdot R_{t-10}$$

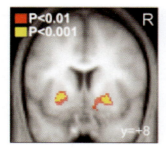
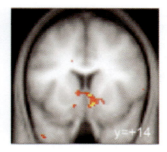

A   Instrumental task   Pavlovian task

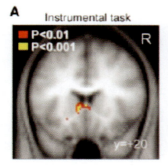
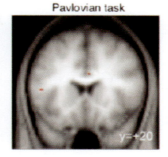

Figure 19.6 Dissociable roles for dorsal and ventral striatum in an instrumental conditioning task. Top: areas of ventral striatum correlated with prediction error signal in Pavlovian (left) and instrumental task (right). Bottom: areas of dorsal striatum correlated with prediction error signal in instrumental task (left), and in Pavlovian task (right). From O'Doherty, J. P., Dayan, P., Schultz, J., Deichmann, R., Friston, K., Dolan, R. (2004). "Dissociable roles of dorsal and ventral striatum in instrumental conditioning," *Science* 304, pp. 452–4. Reprinted with permission from AAAS

and found that (normalizing to the positive non-zero coefficient of R_t) the coefficients of R_{t-1} and later lagged rewards were negative and much smaller in absolute value than β_0 (figure 19.7). This development is compatible with the TD-error picture. If one uses the update equation: $V_t = V_{t-1} + \alpha (R_t - V_{t-1})$ starting from an arbitrary initial value, then the reward prediction error $R_t - V_{t-1}$ will have the form of the fits obtained in the experiment.

One troublesome feature of the data is shown in the right-hand column of figure 19.7. Here firing rate is plotted against the fitted weighted reward value. If the model were perfect, it would show a straight line of slope one. Note however the breakdown of the regression towards negative weighted rewards. The firing rate does not decline as much as it should. Indeed this is a problem alluded to above in Yacubian *et al.* (2006), although the issue is really a bit different: the supposed difficulty of the dopamine neurons representing a negative prediction error is separate from the issue of dissociable representations of positive and negative expected values and the prediction error in those cases. In this case

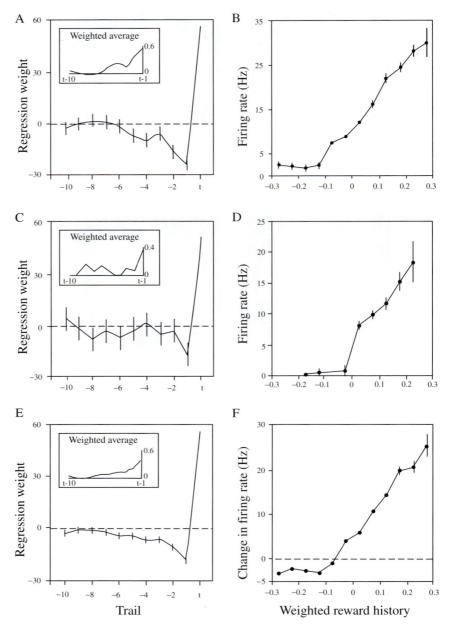

Figure 19.7 Regressions of firing rate of dopamine neurons versus reward history. LHS: graphs of weights of regression from three different monkeys. Inset shows normalized (to weight of current reward) of lagged rewards (signs flipped). RHS: plot of firing rate versus fitted weighted reward. Perfect fit would be line of slope one. Note breakdown for negative firing rates. Reprinted from *Neuron* 47, Bayer, H. M., and Glimcher, P. W., "Midbrain dopamine signals encode a quantitative reward prediction error signal," Copyright 2005, pp. 129–41, with permission from Elsevier

it may be that a different binning of the data, or representing the negative prediction errors as pauses in firing, may clear up the issue (Glimcher, personal communication). Nonetheless, the issues of encoding gains and losses, and negative prediction errors, are an active area of research (Daw *et al.*, 2002), and at some point will need to make contact with the behavioral results of Kahneman and Tversky (1979).

Recently another study of single-unit recordings of midbrain (SNc) dopamine neurons in monkeys has cast a shadow of doubt on the actor–critic interpretation discussed above (Morris *et al.*, 2006; well summarized by Niv *et al.*, 2006). Morris *et al.* repeatedly presented their monkeys with a choice between two icons. Each icon represented a probability of reward taken from the set (.25, .50, .75, 1). After the monkey made a choice it was rewarded with juice according to the reward probability. The choice trials were interspersed within passive reference trials in which the monkeys were presented with a single icon, and then were rewarded with juice according to the probability assigned to the icon. The data in the experiment were taken after the monkeys were well trained in the reward probabilities. Several points are worth noting (here we follow Niv *et al.* 2006 closely). In the reference trials the dopamine neurons fired according to the value of the icon, as expected by the TD model. Behaviorally the monkeys obeyed the matching law as in the Sugrue task discussed above. In the choice trials the dopamine neurons fired immediately after the presentation of the conditioned stimulus at a rate that represented the value of the choice that they *were going* to make. This finding suggests that the actual choice is being made somewhere else and the decision is being relayed by the dopamine neurons. This fact effectively selects among three closely related, but distinct, versions of TD learning. At the presentation of the cue, straight TD learning of the value function would report the expected value of the reward, Q learning would report the maximum of the possible rewards, and a variant of Q learning, SARSA (Sutton and Barto, 1998), would report the value of the actual choice. The third alternative is what the data actually support. This finding casts doubt on the plausibility of an actor–critic architecture or the advantage learning variant reported above (O'Doherty *et al.*, 2004), since in the standard actor–critic architecture the passive critic relays the TD-error signal based only on state-values, and in advantage learning the error signal requires the TD-error signal, and is in this case identical to it. It is known that the dopamine neurons from the VTA and SNc have different projection properties (Gerfen *et al.*, 1987; Fallon, 1981). It is certainly conceivable that the SNc and VTA have dissociable computational roles, although it is not clear why one would need to compute a Q value and a TD-error signal. More research will have to be done, perhaps with multiple recording sites.

While the full story of TD-error signals encoded by the dopamine system has certainly not yet been told, it is clear that the depth and sophistication of this detailed neuroscience approach to decision-making in the brain is increasing rapidly. Additionally, some fMRI paradigms have become more realistic in the type of decisions studied. For example, in Kuhnen and Knutson (2005) the authors studied the neuro-correlates of decision-making in a context much like that of asset allocation decisions made by investors. More precisely, in their experiment subjects in the scanner repeatedly made choices between a "good stock" (represented by a symbol on the screen), a "bad stock," and a "safe bond." The "good stock" had a more favorable outcome distribution than the "bad stock," while the "safe bond" always paid out a certain amount. The subjects did not know which symbol represented which stock; this was something that they had to learn (the learning element distinguishes this paradigm from the non-human primate one discussed above). Their main result was that activation in the insula helped predict risky choices (switch from the stock to bond) or risky errors (choosing a stock when the bond would have been optimal), and that activity in the striatum helped predict aggressive choices (switch from bond to stock) or aggressive errors (choosing a stock when a bond would have been optimal).

The results in Preuschoff *et al.* (2006) suggest that the insula encodes not only risk, but also a new type of prediction error, a risk prediction error. In the fMRI paradigm discussed previously (Preuschoff *et al.*, 2005), the authors modeled prediction risk as the expected squared error of reward prediction, and prediction risk error as the difference between the actual squared prediction error and the expected risk prediction error. They found spatially and temporally dissociable signals in the insula correlated to these regressors. These studies, combined with the results on uncertainty above, suggest a new central role for the insula in decision-making.

In another recent paper in this computational vein, Daw *et al.* (2006) examined the neural correlates of exploration in a "four-armed bandit" problem. Bandit problems have been a staple of decision-making research (Gittins and Jones, 1974; Gittins, 1979) and get to the heart of the exploration – exploitation dilemma (Kaebling *et al.*, 1998; Sutton and Barto, 1998). For example, in the two-armed case, a subject makes repeated choices between two levers, which offer rewards with different probabilities. Once there is evidence that an arm offers better rewards, one might be tempted to stick with it (exploiting). Alternatively, choosing the other arm (exploring) might provide information that would secure better rewards in the future. In this paradigm, subjects are given the choice from among four choices depicted by slot machines on a screen. Each slot has a different (and changing) reward distribution (diffuse and drift). Daw *et al.* modeled the choices of the subjects using a Kalman filter (Anderson and Moore, 2005) and a soft-max decision rule. The Kalman filter produced a mean reward for each slot and then the probability of choice $i = 1, 2, 3, 4$ was given by

$$P_{i,t} = \frac{e^{\beta \mu_{i,t}}}{\sum_{j=1}^{4} e^{\beta \mu_{j,t}}}.$$

The novel result of this paper was the identification of neural correlates of exploratory behavior (i.e. when a lower value action was selected). They found

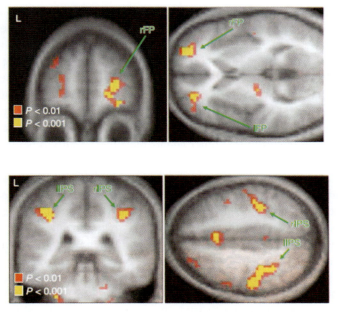

Figure 19.8 Brain regions active in exploratory trials as determined by computational model of behavior. Top: bilateral frontal-polar cortex. Bottom: intra-parietal cortex. Reprinted by permission from Macmillan Publishers Ltd: *Nature* 441, pp. 876–9. Daw, N. D., O'Doherty, J. P., Dayan, P., Seymour, B., and Dolan, R. J., "Cortical substrates for exploratory decisions in humans," copyright 2006

significant activity in exploration trials versus exploitative trials in bilateral frontal-polar cortex and bilateral intra-parietal cortex (figure 19.8).

19.6 Game theory

A qualitatively different level of complexity is given by the (realistic) case where the landscape is no longer stationary but rather consists of intelligent, learning opponents and/or partners. Here the questions become: (1) how does an agent encode the features of the "reward landscape" (social cognition: Adolphs, 2003; Lieberman, 2007)? and (2) how does the agent learn from experience in this setting? A vast amount of work has been done in the machine-learning community in an attempt to create algorithms that can compete with other such algorithms (see Shoham *et al.*, 2007 for an interesting perspective). Game theory (Von Neumann and Morgenstern, 1944) is a vast, highly sophisticated field of economics that considers multi-agent strategic interactions, most often from the point of view of defining and finding equilibrium solutions (Fudenberg and Levine, 1998).

The above experiments involve the interaction of a single agent with an environment that, if not stationary, has a nature independent of the actions of the agent. Social exchange is decidedly not like this. Social interactions of humans (or other social species) involve learning, intelligent agents whose behaviors influence and are influenced by the other agents. Generally speaking, a mode of analysis that posits a single agent interacting with another agent whose actions are not influenced by the single agent's actions is incomplete. Game theory (see appendix A) is the branch of economics and applied mathematics that analyzes the strategic interaction of agents. Typically in game theory, agents are assumed to be " . . . hyper-rational. They know the utility functions of other agents (or the probability that other agents have these utility functions), they are fully aware of the process they are embedded in, they make optimum long run plans based on the assumption that everyone else is making long run plans, and so forth" (Young, 1998). The major aim and effort of game theory has been to establish and study the Nash equilibria of these games. More recently, however, some economists have begun to study experimentally how humans actually interact in these games (Fudenberg and Levine, 1998), both in "one-shot" games (one play of the basic stage game only) and in repeated games. In computer science increasing attention has been paid recently (Shoham *et al.*, 2007) to multi-agent reinforcement learning, or multi-agent learning (MAL). Neuroscience has also begun to study the neural basis of social interaction through neuroimaging. We consider in more depth (1) the repeated trust game, and (2) the one-shot ultimatum game, two particularly rich games that have been studied both behaviorally and with fMRI.

19.7 The repeated trust game

The trust game has been important for studying social interaction in the laboratory, and has recently been studied in the scanner (e.g. Camerer and Weigelt, 1988; Berg *et al.*, 1995; McCabe *et al.*, 2001; King-Casas *et al.*, 2005; Delgado *et al.*, 2005; Tomlin *et al.*, 2006). In the trust game there are two participants, the investor and the trustee. The investor is endowed with an amount of money, say 20 dollars, and must decide how much to entrust with the trustee. The investor keeps whatever amount she doesn't send, while the amount she does send is tripled and given to the trustee. The trustee must then decide how much he wants to keep of the tripled amount. The remainder he sends back to the investor. Standard economic theory tells us to "roll back" from the last round to predict behavior. In the last round the trustee, not having to worry about any more rounds, will keep whatever he was given. Anticipating this outcome, the investor in the last round will not invest anything. Anticipating that the investor will not invest in the last round, the trustee will keep everything in the next-to-last round, and so on, leading to the conclusion that the investor will never invest. This is not, however, what typically happens. King-Casas *et al.* (2005) used fMRI to investigate the neural correlates of trust in a repeated trust game in which each basic stage game described above was repeated ten

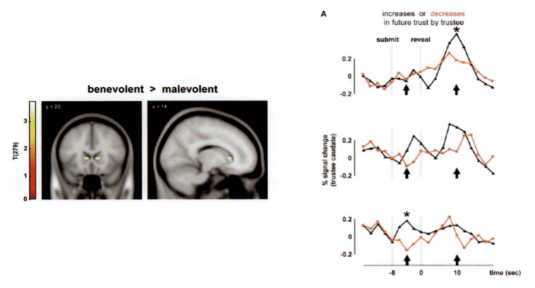

Figure 19.9 Results from the repeated trust game. Left: fMRI contrast image benevolent > malevolent reciprocity. Right: Caudate ROI analysis. Intent to trust signal shifts backward from revelation of result to investor decision time. From King-Casas, B., Tomlin, D., Anen, C., Camerer, C. F., Quartz, S. R., and Montague, P. R. (2005). "Getting to know you: reputation and trust in a two-person economic exchange," *Science* 308, pp. 78–83. Reprinted with permission from AAAS

times. In fact investors do trust the trustees, and the trustees tend to be "fair" (King-Casas *et al.*, 2005, supplementary online material). The main finding of this paper is that there is a signal in the trustee's caudate nucleus that behaves like a TD-learning signal. More precisely, King-Casas *et al.* identified investor reciprocity, defined as the change in investment minus the change in trustee return, as a key variable in the exchange. Indeed, investor reciprocity was the best predictor of change in trustee return. Reciprocity was used to categorize trials into "benevolent," "neutral," and "malevolent," according to whether investor reciprocity was positive, neutral, or negative. An fMRI contrast of the benevolent versus the malevolent condition showed significant activation in the caudate nucleus (figure 19.9). This finding suggests that abstract social rewards (e.g., reciprocity in a social exchange) can engage the same reward system that is activated by primary rewards such as food, drink, rock-and-roll, and sex.

Remarkably, this signal in the caudate shares the temporal characteristics of the TD-error signal seen in a simple Pavlovian conditioning task. Specifically, the authors split the trials into ones in which the trustee significantly increased the share given back to the investor and ones in which the returned share significantly decreased. Furthermore, the rounds were divided into early, middle, and late rounds. In the early rounds the haemodynamic response for the caudate region defined above in the increasing return condition peaked after the investment of the investor was revealed (figure 19.9). In addition, the response in the increasing case was significantly bigger than in the decreasing case. Moreover, as the rounds went by the peak in the signal moved backwards in time, until, in the later rounds, the signal peaked slightly before the investor even submitted her investment. This behavior of the caudate signal is consistent with the interpretation of reciprocity as a reward and the investor submit (or, more precisely, the beginning of the round) as a cue. Furthermore, one can view the temporal transfer of the reward signal back to the cue as a result of the trustee encoding a model of the investor, as in TD learning. Just as a visual cue comes to predict a squirt of juice as a result of modeling the temporal characteristics of the reward landscape, the beginning of a trial comes to predict reciprocity as a result of modeling a more complicated reward landscape.

This social modeling aspect of the repeated trust game is further elucidated in Tomlin *et al.* (2006). In this paper the authors report on a social agency map laid out topographically across the cingulate cortex. Specifically, the middle of cingulate cortex showed activation after the submission of a decision, while the anterior and posterior extremities of the cingulate were activated after the revelation of the partner's decision. Moreover, these activations rose and fell in a continuous fashion across the cingulate, i.e. in the partner-reveal stage activation was highest at the ends of the cingulate and declined continuously as one moved in towards the middle cingulate. Importantly, this pattern was invariant across a broad range of conditions (figure 19.10) – for example, investor, trustee, male, female, reciprocity – strengthening the argument that these activations are in fact an agency map. Certainly a primary modeling concern of any agent engaged in social exchange is credit attribution: who is responsible for what. A general feature of many multiple-agent reinforcement learning (MARL) models is that somehow one constructs and maintains a model of the other agent(s) (which may include a model of how the other agent models the first agent), and how the first agent's actions change the possible behaviors of the other agents. Clearly, in order to assess the impact of various actions and outcomes, an agent must first assign credit for the actions and outcomes to the proper actors. It remains to be seen how these features of MARL, modeling of other agents combined with the use of the DA system in a manner consistent with a TD-error signal, can be put together in a more comprehensive model of the neuroeconomics of repeated social exchange.

19.8 One-shot social interactions

One-shot social interactions, games played without the possibility of repeat encounters, have recently been a subject of intense study. This intense interest in one-shot games derives from the fact that one-shot games bring into sharp

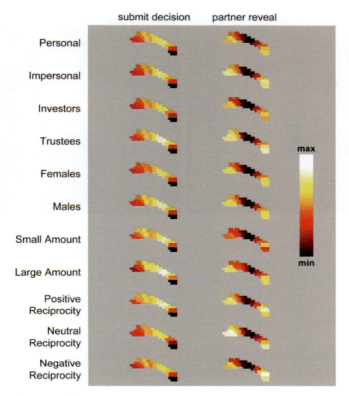

Figure 19.10 "Tequila worm" figures of agency map across various conditions. Left column shows activation across cingulate cortex after the subject's own decision. Right column shows activation across cingulate cortex after the partner's decision. From Tomlin, D., Kayali, M. A., King-Casas, B., Anen, C., Camerer, C. F., Quartz, S. R, and Montague, P. R. (2006), "Agent-specific responses in the cingulate cortex during economic exchanges," *Science* 312, pp. 1047–50. Reprinted with permission from AAAS

relief two very different ways of looking at the ultimate sources of human behavior. Before delving into this conflict, we examine the results.

The ultimatum game is perhaps the most well-known example of a one-shot social interaction. In the ultimatum game there are two players: the proposer and the responder. The proposer is endowed with a sum of money, say $10. She then decides on a split of the money, $10 − x for her, and $x for the responder. The responder, after receiving the offer of $x, must decide whether to accept or reject the offer. If he rejects the offer, the proposer and responder both get $0, otherwise the responder keeps the $10 − x, and the responder gets the $x. Standard economic theory would predict that the responder would accept any offer $x > 0, since something is better than nothing. Anticipating this, the proposer would then offer the smallest amount allowed by the design of the game. Like the trust game, actual humans do not behave like standard economics says

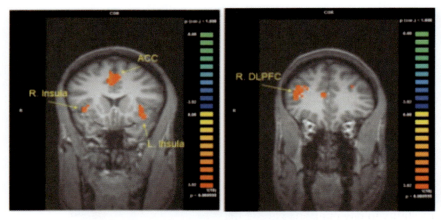

Figure 19.11 Activation in the one-shot ultimatum game. Bilateral insula, anterior cingulate cortex (ACC), and dorsolateral prefrontal cortex (DLPFC) are activated in the responder's brain more in the case of unfair offers than fair offers. From Sanfey, A. G., Rilling J. K., Aronson, J. K., Nystrom, L. E., and Cohen, J. D. (2003), "The neural basis of economic decision-making in the ultimatum game," *Science* 300, pp. 1755–8. Reprinted with permission from AAAS

they should. Modal offers are approximately 50%, and responders reject unfair offers (under 20%) about 50% of the time (Sanfey *et al.*, 2003). The ultimatum game has been played around the world (Henrich *et al.*, 2004), and while the distribution of offers and acceptance rates vary with culture, virtually nobody plays the way prescribed by standard economics. Explanations of this puzzling behavior have generally been attempted using some form of social preference to modify players' utility functions (see Camerer, 2003 for an excellent and thorough exposition). For example, Fehr and Schmidt (1999) examine a form of inequality aversion in which players dislike both getting much more than the other player (guilt), or getting much less (envy). For payoffs $X = \{x_1, x_2\}$ in a two-person game, the modified utility function looks like:

$$U_i(X) = x_i - \alpha \ \max(x_i - x_j, 0) - \beta \ \max(x_j - x_i, 0).$$

The first max term gives the disutility of guilt, whereas the second term gives the disutility of envy. Using this utility function, Fehr and Schmidt were able to fit the data for several games (Camerer, 2003).

Sanfey *et al.* (2003) investigated the neural correlates of fairness in an fMRI version of the ultimatum game. Nineteen subjects played the role of responder against ten confederates in the role of proposer. Each subject saw five "fair" splits ($5, $5), and five "unfair" splits: two of $9, $1, two at $8, $2, and one at $7, $3. The subjects also played ten rounds against a computer (they were told this), and ten rounds of a control condition where they just pressed a button for money. The activity contrast "unfair–fair" showed significant activation (figure 19.11) in bilateral insula, an area that has previously been associated with the emotion of disgust (Phillips *et al.*, 1997), and right dorsolateral prefrontal cortex (DLPFC). The activation was larger in the case of human subjects than in the case of a computer partner. Intriguingly, the activation in the insula correlated negatively with rejection rates while the activation in DLPFC did not.

In the ultimatum game the rejection of an unfair offer can be seen as an act of punishment. However, the game does not explicitly frame the decision this way. Altruistic punishment, punishment dealt to "social norm" violators at the explicit expense of the punisher, is posited to be an important element of the establishment and maintenance of cooperation (Fehr and Gächter, 2002). De Quervain *et al.* (2004) investigated the neural basis of altruistic punishment using a one-shot version of the trust game and PET scanning. In this paradigm the investor, after the trustee's decision was revealed, was sometimes given the ability to buy punishment points to punish the trustee if they had behaved badly. Investors actually experienced four conditions: IC, in which the trustee decision was intentional, and it cost money to punish; IF, in which the trustee decision was intentional, but punishment was free; IS, in which the trustee decision was intentional, but the punishment was merely symbolic; finally NC, in which the trustee decision was actually made by a computer (and the investor knew this), and punishment was costly. Investors were scanned for one minute after the trustee had betrayed them and before they made a decision to punish or not. There were two main findings. The first concerned the activation contrast (IC+IF) − (IS+NC), the contrast of the average of the conditions where punishment is expected, versus the average of the conditions where punishment is not expected (figure 19.12). This contrast showed significant activation in the caudate nucleus, an area we previously noted as

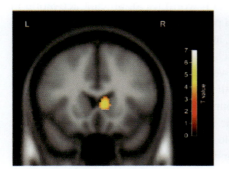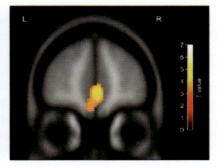

Figure 19.12 Activation in the investor's brain after unfair trustee responses. Left: activation in the caudate is greater when investors desire to punish and can do so effectively, relative to the case where there is no punishment available or punishment is not desired. Right: activation in investor ventromedial prefrontal cortex (VMPFC) is greater in the cases when the investor wishes to punish, but punishment is costly relative to the case where punishment is desired, but free. From De Quervain, D. J. F., Fischbacher, U., Treyer, V., Schellhammer, M., Schnyder, U., Buck, A., and Fehr, E. (2004), "The neural basis of altruistic punishment," *Science* 305, pp. 1254–8. Reprinted with permission from AAAS

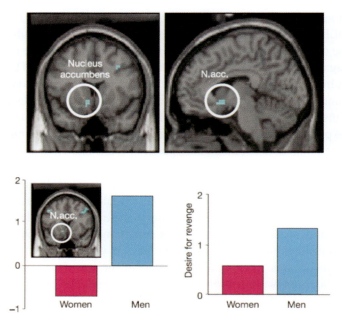

Figure 19.13 Activation in nucleus accumbens for the unfair–fair contrast in the painful condition for males only. Reprinted by permission from Macmillan Publishers Ltd: *Nature*, Singer *et al.*, "Empathetic neural responses are modulated by the perceived fairness of others," 439, pp. 466–9, copyright 2006

being involved in reward processing. The second finding concerned the contrast (IC − IF) (figure 19.12). In both cases one expects there to be a desire to punish, but in one case there is a cost. Is it worth it? Significant activation in this case was found in the ventromedial prefrontal cortex (VMPFC), as well as the medial orbitofrontal cortex (MOF), areas that have previously been shown to be involved in decision-making (Bechara *et al.*, 1994, 2000).

In each of these games the players were told, and presumably understood, that the games were one-shot, and yet they gave up money to punish, presumably to enforce a social norm. Singer pursued this direction directly. In Singer *et al.* (2006) the subject first played the trust game with confederates outside the scanner. The subject played the role of investor, but the game was rigged so that the trustee was sometimes fair and sometimes unfair. The observer then watched in the scanner as the trustees were given mild electric shocks. Both male and female observers showed activity in pain-related areas while observing the shocks, but in men the activity was reduced for the unfair players. Indeed the men showed *greater* activation in the striatum when the trustee receiving the shock had been unfair versus the case of a fair trustee (figure 19.13).

The neural correlates discovered in these one-shot paradigms suggest that social norms (Fehr and Fischbacher, 2004) such as fairness have gained access to our reward circuitry, and assumed value like a primary reward, or trigger disgust like a putrid odor. Others have a different interpretation. Trivers (2004) suggests that if we take seriously the idea that we are social creatures with fine-tuned social instincts, then it should be of little surprise that even in well-advertised one-shot games we might get reactions that are in fact signals from systems "built" to handle repeated interactions. Essentially there are two opposing camps: the self-interest camp and the fairness camp. The former seeks the explanations in the individual and so-called selfish genes, while the latter approaches the problem from the point of view of society. There seems little doubt that behavior justifiably called fairness exists, but teasing out the ultimate basis for these behaviors is a difficult task that exposes deep fault lines in our conceptions of human nature. Imaging experiments, while revealing tantalizing connections between basic reward processes and social interaction, have not yet reached the level of sophistication that would allow us to distinguish between the two camps.

19.9 Conclusion

Neuroeconomics, despite being a young field, is already an expansive one, spanning representation of reward, to sequential learning, and on to multi-agent reinforcement learning and social interaction. A reasonable question is "what is this buying us?" From the top down, from the economics direction, it buys us grounding. Real-life humans are not really like *Homo economicus* in the textbooks, and sometimes this can have real-life consequences (Shleifer, 2000). Studying the neural underpinnings of *Homo realitus* can help us bound the model agents in our economy. From the bottom up, economics has injected a unifying principle into neuroscience. On a small scale the brain is an economic marvel, an extraordinarily efficient computational engine. At a larger scale, through evolution by natural selection, the brain and the algorithms it supports must be finely tuned to its natural decision/reward landscape, and hence using economic probes has been and will continue to be a fruitful way to gain understanding of neural function. Additionally, the natural reward landscape is in fact a social one, and hence neuroscience should be deeply interested in social interaction. Neuroeconomics therefore can provide a conceptual structure for neuroscience as it attempts to integrate the fantastic discoveries it has made at the molecular level into a coherent theory of neural activity at the level of an economic agent embedded in society.

19.10 Appendix A   Background on choice models

In this appendix we briefly introduce some background concepts from economics and computer science that are related to recent experiments in neuroeconomics.

19.10.1 Expected utility

The canonical theory of choice in economics is expected utility theory (EUT) (Von Neumann and Morgenstern, 1944). In EUT (we follow Gollier, 2001), a single agent faces a choice among *lotteries*. First, assume a set of outcomes $X = \{x_i\}$, $i = 1 \ldots N$. A lottery l is then probability distribution $\{p_i\} i = 1 \ldots N$, $\sum_{i=1}^{N} p_i = 1$, on X (which just means in this lottery l you have a probability p_i of getting prize x_i). A preference relation $\succ$ on the set L of lotteries on X is a binary relation on L that satisfies two intuitive conditions: (1) that small changes in probabilities do not change preferences (continuity); (2) if $L_1 \succ L_2$ then mixing in a third lottery L_3 will not change my preferences (i.e., $\alpha L_1 + (1 - \alpha) L_3 \succ \alpha L_2 + (1 - \alpha) L_3$, independence).

Von Neumann and Morgenstern (1944) proved that such a preference relation over lotteries could be given an expected utility representation: i.e., given a preference relation L over lotteries as above, there must exist a function $u : X \rightarrow \mathcal{R}$ (the utility function) such that

$$L_1 \succ L_2 \Leftrightarrow \sum_{i=1}^{N} p_i u(x_i) > \sum_{i=1}^{N} p'_i u(x_i).$$

When the outcome space is continuous, for example the real $\mathcal{R}$, the expected utility is represented by an integral of a real-valued function on $\mathcal{R}$ (the utility function $u(x)$) against the probability distribution of outcomes. The function u has various properties that reflect the risk preferences of the individual. For example, if u is concave down, the individual is risk-averse. If u is concave up, they are risk-seeking. If u is a line of slope one through the origin, the person is said to be risk neutral and expected utility coincides with expected value. Expected utility may be approximated by expanding the utility function in a Taylor series (Levy and Markowitz, 1979) to give

$$U(\mu, \sigma) \sim \mu - \frac{\lambda}{2} \sigma^2$$

where λ is a measure of risk tolerance of the individual, μ is the expected value of the outcome, and σ is its standard deviation. This is an example of a mean variance model (Markowitz, 1952) referred to in the main text.

The natural question then is "Is this how people actually behave?" The short answer is "No." In work eventually culminating in a Nobel Prize, Kahneman and Tversky (1979) showed that people violate the expected utility prescription of choice in systematic ways. Their work led to a surge of interest and research in how people actually behave, creating two new fields, behavioral economics (Thaler, 1992; Shleifer, 2000), the field study of human economic choice, and experimental economics (Kagel and Roth, 1995), the laboratory study of human choice.

19.10.2   Inter-temporal choice

One important question left unanswered is how to compare an outcome now versus an outcome in the future. An economist would probably insist on temporal consistency: if you prefer a dollar now versus two dollars in a week, then you should have the same preference if the reference time were not now, but rather in a year (see Frederick *et al.*, 2002, for a comprehensive review; also see Ainslie, 1975, and Loewenstein *et al.*, 2003). A consistent theory of intertemporal choice can be based on using an exponential discount factor, $0 < \delta < 1$ (Samuelson, 1937; Strotz, 1955–6). For example, \$1 five units in the future is taken to be equivalent to $\$1 \cdot \delta^5$ now. Unfortunately for the normative theory, people do not actually display these preferences. For example, a majority of people would probably prefer \$100 today to \$110 in a week. But few people would likely prefer \$100 in a year to \$110 in a year and a week. Experimental results in humans confirm this intuition (Thaler, 1981; Kirby and Herrnstein, 1995; Kirby and Marakovic, 1996; Kirby, 1997). A hyperbolic discount function (Chung and Herrnstein, 1967) can account for these reversals in preference and is given most generally by $d_t = (1 + \alpha \cdot t)^{-\frac{\beta}{\alpha}}$ (Loewenstein and Prelec, 1992). A more convenient analytical form is given by the so-called quasi-hyperbolic discount function (Phelps and Pollak, 1968; Elster, 1979; Laibson, 1997). This discount function gives the present value of a reward u at time t by: u if $t = 0$, and $\beta \cdot \delta^t \cdot u$ where β and δ are parameters satisfying $0 < \beta, \delta < 1$.

19.10.3   Multi-period choice under uncertainty

What if my choice now affects my opportunities later? What if I learn about the environment as I make choices? How does the knowledge and my ability to learn affect my choices now? These are problems that are faced, for example, by money managers who are attempting to construct optimal portfolios. Incorporating parameter uncertainty and learning into portfolio selection has been an active research topic in finance recently (Barberis, 2000; Xia, 2001). Techniques from artificial intelligence (see Markov decision problems below) that have been imported into neuroscience to study learning have been studied as techniques for portfolio selection (Neuneier, 1996). These are problems that have been studied intensively in computer science and are formalized multi-period choice problems (Sutton and Barto, 1998). More formally (we closely follow Sutton and Barto, 1998), a Markov decision problem (MDP) is described by a set of states $S = \{s_i\}\, i = 1, \ldots, N$, a set of actions available in each state $A = \{a_i\}\, i = 1, \ldots, M$, state–action transition functions $P_{ss'}^a$ (the probability of transitioning from state $s \to s'$ given action a), and expected rewards $R_{ss'}^a$ (the expected reward obtained from choosing a and transitioning from $s \to s'$). A policy $\pi : S \to A$ is a rule giving an action in every state s. The value of a policy π in a state s is the sum of the discounted rewards starting from state s and following policy π:

$$V^\pi(s) = E_\pi\left[\sum_{i=1}^{\infty} \gamma^i r_i | s_0 = s\right].$$

Often it is more convenient to consider the value of a state action pair (s, a) under policy π:

$$Q^\pi(s, a) = E_\pi\left[r + \gamma \sum_{s'} P_{ss'}^a V^\pi(s') | s_0 = s, a_0 = a\right],$$

in other words, the discounted expected value of taking action a and the following policy π. The goal is to find an optimal policy π^*. One particularly useful algorithm for finding an optimal policy is called Q learning (Watkins, 1989; Watkins and Dayan, 1992). After taking an action a in state s, an agent updates their state–action value function according to the rule:

$$\tilde{Q}(s_t, a) \leftarrow \tilde{Q}(s_t, a_t) + \alpha\left[r_t + \gamma \max_{\tilde{a} \in A} Q(s_{t+1}, \tilde{a}) - Q(s_t, a_t)\right].$$

α is the learning-rate, and γ is the discount factor. The term in the square brackets is called the temporal difference (TD) error term. The above rule essentially says that after taking an action and collecting a reward, estimate the value of an action as the sum of the reward and the current estimate of the best action of the new state, then update the old estimate by a fraction of the difference between the old and new estimate. This algorithm can be shown to converge to the optimal Q function under certain reasonable conditions on α. Note that an agent need not know the reward landscape (the transition probabilities and the expected rewards) in order to learn the optimal Q function. The Q values can be used to determine a policy according to:

$$P(s, a) = \frac{e^{\lambda Q(s,a)}}{\sum_{s'} e^{\lambda Q(s',a)}},$$

where $P(s, a)$ is the probability of choosing action a in state s, and λ is a free parameter that is analogous to inverse temperature in statistical mechanics. Q learning is an appealing candidate for an actual model of learning in organisms since it does not rely on a complicated representation of the reward landscape, and can be learned as you go (on-line).

19.10.4 Game theory

Up to this point we have been discussing the interaction of a single human with a fixed if probabilistic "nature" (strictly speaking, this is not true for a market, but to first approximation we can assume an agent is playing against an opponent that is not affected by his choices). Game theory is the theory of strategic choice: intelligent learning agents playing against (or with) each other. In game theory the notion of a solution is slightly different from that of expected utility theory. In expected utility theory, an agent essentially computes a maximum. In game theory the standard solution concept, *Nash equilibrium*, is subtler. In general consider a game with N agents, and suppose that each agent can choose from M actions $a_i \in A, i = 1, \ldots M$. A set of choices by the agents $\vec{a} = (a_1, a_2, \ldots, a_M)$ gives rise to a payoff $R(\vec{a})$. $\vec{a}$ is called a Nash equilibrium if

$$\forall i \quad R(a_1, a_2, \ldots, a_i, \ldots, a_N) \geq R(a_1, a_2, \ldots, \tilde{a}_i, \ldots, a_N) \forall \tilde{a}_i \in A.$$

In words, in Nash equilibrium no agent has an incentive to alter his choice, given that nobody else alters their choice. A great deal of effort is spent by game theorists characterizing equilibria. The question again arises as to whether people actually play at Nash equilibrium, or, if there are multiple equilibria, which equilibrium do they play? If the game is repeated, do the players approach the equilibrium of the stage game (the basic game that is repeated)? How do they reach that equilibrium? (Camerer *et al.*, 2002). In this brief appendix we can only begin to scratch the surface of this complex topic. For a detailed treatment of these issues, see Camerer, 2003; Fudenberg and Levine, 1998; Young, 1998.

19.11 Appendix B Neuroanatomy

The purpose of this appendix is to provide a quick reference to the neural structures mentioned in the text. For a comprehensive treatment, see Afifi and Bergman, 1998. Figures 19.14 and 19.15 locate these structures in the brain.

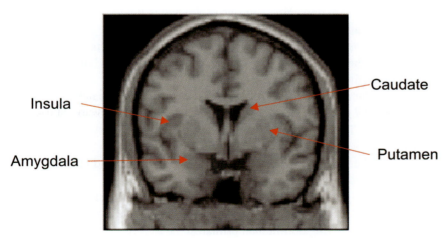

Figure 19.14 Coronal slice of MNI single-subject brain used in SPM2, $y = 2.17$

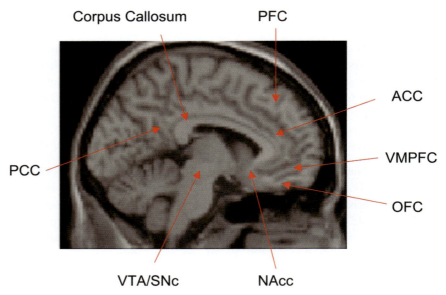

Figure 19.15 Sagittal slice of MNI single-subject brain used in SPM2, $x = -5.25$ SNc at $x = -6.87$

Amygdala – group of nuclei tucked deep beneath the temporal lobe. Thought to be involved in emotional processing, especially fear, although its function in reward processing is still far from understood.

Anterior cingulate cortex (ACC) – anterior portion of the cingulate. Thought to play a role in conflict response, theory of mind, and more recently (see text) in social role in social interactions.

Caudate – part of the dorsal striatum. Structure receives projections (afferents) from midbrain dopamine neurons (SNc) and is thought to play a role in motor control and planning.

Cingulate cortex – large crescent-shaped structure on the medial banks of the cerebral hemispheres just above the corpus callosum, the bundle of white matter connecting the hemispheres. See ACC.

Dorsal striatum – upper (dorsal) part of the striatum. See caudate.

Dorsolateral prefrontal cortex (DLPFC) – upper, lateral portion of the prefrontal cortex. Thought to be involved with working memory and executive control.

Insula – bilateral areas of cortex associated with disgust and fear, and more recently with risk.

Lateral intra-parietal (LIP) region – bilateral region of posterior neocortex involved in eye movements (saccades) thought to encode expected utility in choice games involving non-human primates.

Nucleus accumbens (NAcc) – a nucleus of the ventral striatum. Receives projections from midbrain dopamine neurons. Involved in reward processing.

Orbitofrontal cortex (OFC) – the underbelly of the PFC. Intimately involved in representation of reward and decision-making.

Prefrontal cortex (PFC) – large region in the front of the brain extending from the bottom of the cerebrum to the top, and from the very front tip to a line running approximately from the edge of the ACC straight up. The PFC hosts a large number of functions (see OFC, VMPFC, and DLPFC).

Putamen – part of the ventral striatum. Thought to play a role in motor control and value representation. Receives dopamine projections from the VTA.

Striatum – midbrain structure comprised of the caudate, putamen, and globus pallidus.

Substantia nigra pars compacta (SNc) – a nucleus of the midbrain containing dopamine neurons that project (among other places) to the caudate.

Ventral striatum – lower part of the striatum midbrain composed mainly of the putamen. Involved intimately in reward processing. It receives afferents from dopamine neurons in the VTA.

Ventral tegmental area (VTA) – midbrain region containing dopamine neurons which project to the striatum and the VMPFC.

Ventromedial prefrontal cortex (VMPFC) – literally the middle lower part of the PFC. Thought to be involved in reward and value representation.

The brain image for the neuroanatomy figure is rendered by a program called SPMZ (Wellcome Department of Imaging Neuroscience, University College London). The brain image shown is a standard template (single_subj_tl.mni) found in SPMZ, and obtained from Montreal Neurological Institute.

19.12 References

Adolphs, R. (2003). Cognitive neuroscience of human social behaviour. *Nature Reviews Neuroscience* 4, 165–78.

Afifi, A. K., and Bergman, R. A. (1998). *Functional Neuroanatomy: Text and Atlas* (New York: McGraw-Hill).

Aharon, I., Etcoff, N., Ariely, D., Chabris, C. F., O'Conner, E., and Breiter, H. C. (2001). Beautiful faces have variable reward value: fMRI and behavioral evidence. *Neuron* 32, 537–51.

Ainslie, G. (1975). Specious reward: A behavioural theory of impulsiveness and impulse control. *Psychological Bulletin* 82, 463–96.

(1983). Derivation of "rational" behavior from hyperbolic discount curves. *American Economic Review* 81, 334–40.

Anderson, B. D. O., and Moore, J. B. (2005). *Optimal Filtering* (Mineola, NY: Dover Publications).

Baird, L. C. (1993). Advantage updating Report No. WL-TR-93-1146 (Wright Patterson Air Force Base, Dayton, OH).

Barberis, N. (2000). Investing for the long run when returns are predictable. *Journal of Finance* 55, 225–64.

Bartels, A., and Zeki, S. (2000). The neural basis of romantic love. *Neuroreport* 11, 3824–9.

(2004). The neural correlates of maternal and romantic love. *Neuroimage* 21, 1155–66.

Bayer, H. M., and Glimcher, P. W. (2005). Midbrain dopamine signals encode a quantitative reward prediction error signal. *Neuron* 47, 129–41.

Bechara, A., Damasio, A. R., Damasio, H., and Anderson, S. W. (1994). Insensitivity to future consequences following damage to human prefrontal cortex. *Cognition* 50, 7–15.

Bechara, A., Damasio, H., and Damasio, A. R. (2000). Emotion, decision making and the orbitofrontal cortex. *Cerebral Cortex* 110, 295–307.

Berg, J., Dickhaut, J., and McCabe, K. (1995). Trust, reciprocity, and social history. *Games and Economic Behavior* 10, 122–42.

Breiter, H. C., Aharon, I., Kahneman, D., Dale, A., Shizgal, P. (2001). Functional imaging of neural responses to expectancy and experience of monetary gains and losses. *Neuron* 30, 619–39.

Camerer, C. F. (2003). *Behavioral Game Theory* (Princeton, NJ: Princeton University Press).

Camerer, C. F., Ho, T. H., and Chong, J. K. (2002). Sophisticated experience – weighed attraction learning and strategic teaching in repeated games. *Journal of Economic Theory* 104, 137–88.

Camerer, C. F., Loewenstein, G., and Pralec, D. (2005). Neuroeconomics: How neuroscience can inform economics. *Journal of Economic Literature* 43, 9–64.

Camerer, C. F., and Weigelt, K. (1988). Experimental tests of a sequential equilibrium reputation model. *Econometrica* 56, 1–36.

Chung, S. H., and Herrnstein, R. J. (1967). Choice and delay of reinforcement. *Journal of the Experimental Analysis of Behavior* 10, 67–74.

Corrado, G. S., Sugrue, L. P., Seung, H. S., and Newsome, W. T. (2005). Linear–nonlinear Poisson models of primate choice dynamics. *Journal of the Experimental Analysis of Behavior* 84, 581–617.

Daw, N., Kakade, S., and Dayan, P. (2002). Opponent interactions between serotonin and dopamine. *Neural Networks* 15, 603–16.

Daw, N. D., O'Doherty, J. P., Dayan, P., Seymour, B., and Dolan, R. J. (2006). Cortical substrates for exploratory decisions in humans. *Nature* 441, 876–9.

Dayan, P., and Balleine, B. W. (2002). Reward, motivation, and reinforcement learning. *Neuron* 36, 285–98.

De Quervain, D. J. F., Fischbacher, U., Treyer, V., Schellhammer, M., Schnyder, U., Buck, A., and Fehr, E. (2004). The neural basis of altruistic punishment. *Science* 305, 1254–8.

Delgado, M. R., Frank, R. H., and Phelps, E. A. (2005). Perceptions of moral character modulate the neural systems of reward during the trust game. *Nature Neuroscience* 8, 1611–18. Epub. 2005. Oct. 16.

Elliot, R., Newman, J. L., Longe, O. A., and Deakin, J. F. (2003). Differential response patterns in the striatum and orbitofrontal cortex to financial rewards in humans: A parametric functional magnetic imaging study. *Journal of Neuroscience* 23, 303–7.

Ellsberg, D. (1961). Risk, ambiguity, and the Savage axioms. *Quarterly Journal of Economics* 75, 643–69.

Elster, J. (1979). *Ulysses and the Sirens: Studies in Rationality and Irrationality* (Cambridge: Cambridge University Press).

Erk, S., Spitzer, M., Wunderlich, A. P., Galley, L., and Walter, H. (2002). Cultural objects modulate reward circuitry. *Neuroreport* 13, 2499–503.

Fallon, J. H. (1981). Collateralization of monoamine neurons: Mesotelencephalic dopamine projections to caudate, septum, and frontal cortex. *Journal of Neuroscience* 1, 1361–8.

Fehr, E., and Fischbacher, U. (2004). Third-party punishment and social norms. *Evolution and Human Behavior* 25, 63–87.

Fehr, E., and Gächter, S. (2002). Altruistic punishment in humans. *Nature* 415, 137–40.

Fehr, E., and Schmidt, K. M. (1999). A theory of fairness, competition, and cooperation. *Quarterly Journal of Economics* 114(3), 817–68.

Fiorello, C. D., Tobler, P. N., and Schultz, W. (2003). Discrete coding of reward probability and uncertainty by dopamine neurons. *Science* 299, 1898–1902.

Frederick, S., Loewenstein, G., and O'Donoghue, T. (2002). Time discounting and time preferences: A critical review. *Journal of Economic Literature* 40, 351–401.

Fudenberg, D., and Levine, D. K. (1988). *The Theory of Learning in Games* (Cambridge, MA: MIT Press).

Gerfen, C. R., Herkenham, M., and Thibault, J. (1987). The neostriatal mosaic: II patch- and matrix-directed dopaminergic and non-dopaminergic systems. *Journal of Neuroscience* 7, 3915–34.

Gittins, J. C. (1979). Bandit processes and dynamic allocation indices. *Journal of the Royal Statistical Society* 41, 148–77.

Gittins, J. C., and Jones, D. M. (1974). A dynamic allocation index for the sequential design of experiments. In *Progress in Statistics, European Meeting of Statisticians 1972*, vol. I (Gani, J., Sarkadi, K., and Vince, I., eds.), pp. 241–66 (Amsterdam: North-Holland).

Gollier, C. (2001). *The Economics of Risk and Time* (Cambridge, MA: MIT Press).

Henrich, J., Boyd, R., Bowles, S., Camerer, C., Fehr, E., and Gintis, H. (eds.) (2004). *Foundations of Human Sociality: Economic Experiments and Ethnographic Evidence from Fifteen Small-scale Societies* (Oxford: Oxford University Press).

Herrnstein, R. J. (1961). Relative and absolute strength of response as a function of frequency of reinforcement. *Journal of the Experimental Analysis of Behavior* 4, 267–72.

Hsu, M., Bhatt, M., Adolphs, R., Tranel, D., and Camerer, C. F. Neural systems responding to degrees of uncertainty in human decision-making. *Science* 310, 1680–3.

Huettel, S. A., Song, A. W., and McCarthy, G. (2004). *Functional Magnetic Resonance Imaging* (Sunderland, MA: Sinauer Associates).

Huettel, S. A., Stowe, C. J., Gordon, E. M., Warner, B. T., and Platt, M. L. (2006). Neural signatures of economic preferences for risk and ambiguity. *Neuron* 49, 765–75.

Kaebling, L. P., Littman, M. L., and Moore, A. W. (1998). Reinforcement learning: A survey. *Journal of Intelligence Research* 4, 237–85.

Kagel, J., and Roth, A., eds. (1995). *The Handbook of Experimental Economics* (Princeton, NJ: Princeton University Press).

Kahneman, D., and Tversky, A. (1979). Prospect Theory: An analysis of decision under risk. *Econometrica* 47, 263–92.

Kawabata, H., and Zeki, S. (2004). Neural correlates of beauty. *Journal of Neurophysiology* 91, 1699–1705.

King-Casas, B., Tomlin, D., Anen, C., Camerer, C. F., Quartz, S. R., and Montague, P. R. (2005). Getting to know you: Reputation and trust in a two-person economic exchange. *Science* 308, 78–83.

Kirby, K. (1997). Bidding on the future: Evidence against normative discounting of delayed rewards. *Journal of Experimental Psychology: General*, 126(1), 54–70.

Kirby, K., and Herrnstein, R. J. (1995). Preference reversals due to myopic discounting of delayed reward. *Psychological Science*, 6(2), 83–9.

Kirby, K., and Marakovic, N. N. (1996). Delay-discounting probabistic rewards: Rates decrease as amounts increase. *Psychonomic Bulletin and Review* 3(1), 100–4.

Knutson, B., Fong, G. W., Bennett, S. M., Adams, C. M., and Hommer, D. (2003). A region of mesial prefrontal cortex tracks monetarily rewarding outcomes: Characterization with rapid event-related fMRI. *Neuroimage* 18, 263–72.

Knutson, B., and Peterson, R. (2005). Reconstructing expected utility. *Games and Economic Behavior* 52, 305–15.

Knutson, B., Taylor, J., Kaufman, M., Peterson, R., and Glover, G. (2005). Distributed neural representation of expected value. *Journal of Neuroscience* 25, 4806–12.

Kuhnen, C. M., and Knutson, B. (2005). The neural basis of financial risk taking. *Neuron* 47, 763–70.

Laibson, D. (1997). Golden eggs and hyperbolic discounting. *Quarterly Journal of Economics* 62, 443–77.

Lau, B., and Glimcher, P. W. (2005). Dynamic response-by-response models of matching behavior in rhesus monkeys. *Journal of the Experimental Analysis of Behavior* 84, 555–79.

Levy, H., and Markowitz, H. M. (1979). Approximating expected utility by a function of mean and variance. *American Economic Review* 69, 308–17.

Lieberman, M. D. (2007). Social cognitive neuroscience: A review of core processes. *Annual Review of Psychology* 58, 259–89.

Loewenstein, G. (1996). Out of control: Visceral influences on behavior. *Organizational Behavior and Human Decision Processes* 65, 272–92.

Loewenstein, G., and Prelec, D. (1992). Anomalies in intertemporal choice: Evidence and an interpretation. *Quarterly Journal of Economics* 10, 573–97.

Loewenstein, G., Read, D., and Baumeister, R. F., eds. (2003). *Time and Decision* (New York: Russell Sage Foundation).

Markowitz, H. M. (1952). Portfolio selection. *Journal of Finance* 7, 77–91.

McCabe, K., Houser, D., Ryan, L., Smith, V., and Trouard, T. (2001). A functional imaging study of cooperation in two-person reciprocal exchange. *Proceedings of the National Academy of Science USA* 98, 11832–5.

McClure, S. M., Berns, G. S., and Montague, P. R. (2003a). Temporal prediction errors in a passive learning task activate human striatum. *Neuron* 38, 339–46.

McClure, S. M., Daw, N. D., and Montague, P. R. (2003b). A computational substrate for incentive salience. *TRENDS in Neurosciences* 26, 423–8.

McClure, S. M., Laibson, D., Loewenstein, G., and Cohen, J. D. (2004). Separate neural systems value immediate and delayed monetary awards. *Science* 306, 503–7.

McClure, S. M., Li, J., Tomlin, D., Cypert, K. S., Montague, L. S., and Montague, P. R. (2004). Neural correlates of behavioral preference for culturally familiar drinks. *Neuron* 44, 379–87.

Metcalfe, J., and Mischel, W. (1999). A hot/cool system analysis of delay gratification: Dynamics of willpower. *Psychological Review* 106, 3–19.

Miller, E. K. (2000). The prefrontal cortex and cognitive control. *Nature Reviews Neuroscience* 1, 59–65.

Miller, E. K., and Cohen, J. D. (2001). An integrative theory of prefrontal cortex function. *Annual Review of Neuroscience* 24, 167–202.

Montague, P. R., Dayan, P., and Sejnowski, T. J. (1996). A framework for mesencephalic dopamine systems based on predictive Hebbian learning. *Journal of Neuroscience* 16(5), 1936–47.

Montague, P. R., King-Casas, B., and Cohen, J. D. (2006). Imaging valuation models in human choice. *Annual Review of Neuroscience* 29, 417–48.

Morris, G., Nevet, A., Arkadir, D., Vaadia, E., and Bergman, H. (2006). Midbrain dopamine neurons encode decisions for future actions. *Nature Neuroscience* 9, 1057–63.

Neuneier, R. (1996). Optimal asset allocation using adaptive dynamic programming. In *Proceedings of Advances in Neural Information Processing* 8, 952–8, eds. D. S. Toutretzky, M. C. Mozer, and M. E. Hasselmo (Cambridge, MA: MIT Press).

Niv, Y., Daw, N. D., and Dayan, P. (2006). Choice values. *Nature Neuroscience* 9, 987–8.

O'Doherty, J. (2004). Reward representations and reward-related learning in the human brain: Insights from neuroimaging. *Current Opinion in Neurobiology* 14, 769–76.

O'Doherty, J., Dayan, P., Friston, K., Critchley, H., and Dolan, R. J. (2003). Temporal difference models and reward-related learning in the human brain. *Neuron* 38, 329–37.

O'Doherty, J. P., Dayan, P., Schultz, J., Deichmann, R., Friston, K., and Dolan, R. (2004). Dissociable roles of dorsal and ventral striatum in instrumental conditioning. *Science* 304, 452–4.

Phelps, E. S., and Pollak, R. A. (1968). On second-best national savings and game-equilibrium growth. *Review of Economic Studies* 35, 201–8.

Phillips, M. L., Young, A. W., Senior, C., *et al.* (1997). A specific neural substrate for perceiving the facial expressions of disgust. *Nature* 389, 495–8.

Platt, M. L., and Glimcher, P. W. (1999). Neural correlates of decision variables in parietal cortex. *Nature* 400, 233–8.

Preuschoff, K., Quartz, S., and Bossaerts, P. (2005). Neural differentiation of expected reward and risk in human subcortical structures. *Neuron* 51, 381–90.

(2006). Human insula activation reflects risk prediction error as well as risk. Manuscript.

Samuelson, P. (1937). A note on measurement of utility. *Review of Economic Studies* 4, 155–61.

Sanfey, A. G., Rilling, J. K., Aronson, J. K., Nystrom, L. E., and Cohen, J. D. (2003). The neural basis of economic decision-making in the ultimatum game. *Science* 300, 1755–8.

Schultz, W., Dayan, P., and Montague, P. R. (1997). A neural substrate of prediction and reward. *Science* 275, 1593–9.

Shleifer, A. (2000). *Inefficient Markets: An Introduction to Behavioral Finance* (Oxford: Oxford University Press).

Shoham, Y., Powers, R., and Grenager, T. (2007). If multi-agent learning is the answer, what is the question? *Artificial Intelligence* 171, 365–77.

Singer, T., Seymour, B., O'Doherty, J. P., Stephan, K. E., Dolan, R. J., and Frith, C. (2006). Empathetic neural responses are modulated by the perceived fairness of others. *Nature* 439, 466–9.

Smith, E. E., and Jonides, J. (1999). Storage and executive processes in the frontal lobes. *Science* 283, 1657–61.

Strotz, R. H. (1955–6). Myopia and inconsistency in dynamic utility optimization. *Review of Economic Studies* 23, 165–80.

Sugrue, L. P., Corrado, G. S., and Newsome, W. T. (2004). Matching behavior and the representation of value in the parietal cortex. *Science* 304, 1782–7.

Sutton, R. S., and Barto, A. G. (1998). *Reinforcement Learning* (Cambridge: MIT Press).

Thaler, R. H. (1981). Some empirical evidence on dynamic inconsistency. *Economic Letters* 8, 201–7.

Thaler, R. (1992). *The Winner's Curse Paradoxes and Anomalies of Economic Life* (Princeton, NJ: Princeton University Press).

Thaler, R. H. and Shefrin H. M. (1981). An economic theory of self control. *Journal of Political Economy* 89, 392–406.

Tomlin, D., Kayali, M. A., King-Casas, B., Anen, C., Camerer, C. F., Quartz, S. R., and Montague, P. R. (2006). Agent-specific responses in the cingulate cortex during economic exchanges. *Science* 312, 1047–50.

Trepel, C., Fox, C. R., and Poldrack, R. A. (2005). Prospect theory on the brain? Toward a cognitive neuroscience of decision under risk. *Cognitive Brain Research* 23, 34–50.

Trivers, R. (2004). Mutual benefits at all levels of life (book review of *Genetic and Cultural Evolution of Cooperation*, Peter Hammerstein, ed., MIT Press, Cambridge, MA, 2003). *Nature* 304, 964–5.

Von Neumann, J., and Morgenstern, O. (1944). *Theory of Games and Economic Behavior* (Princeton, NJ: Princeton University Press).

Watkins, C. J. C. H. (1989). Learning from delayed rewards. Ph.D. thesis. University of Cambridge, England.

Watkins, C. J. C. H., and Dayan, P. (1992). Technical note: Q-learning. *Machine Learning* 8, 279–92.

Xia, Y. (2001). Learning about predictability: The effects of parameter uncertainty on dynamic asset allocation. *Journal of Finance* 56, 205–46.

Yacubian, J., Gläscher, J., Schroeder, K., Sommer, T., Braus, D. F., and Büchel, C. (2006). Dissociable systems for gain- and loss-related value predictions and error of prediction in the human brain. *Journal of Neuroscience* 26, 9530–7.

Young, H. P. (1998). *Individual Strategy and Social Structure* (Princeton: Princeton University Press).

20 Evolutionary economics and psychology

ULRICH WITT

20.1 Introduction

Evolutionary economics focuses on the transformation of the economy over time and the consequences this has for the current conditions of production and consumption. The sources of the transformation process are human learning, problem solving, and the accumulation of knowledge and capital. The diversity of individual efforts and capabilities with respect to both learning and innovation results at any time in the generation and diffusion of a variety of innovative technologies, institutions, and commercial activities that compete with each other. The competition between them, and the economic and social adaptations triggered by that competition, fuel the process of transformation from within the economy (see Nelson 1995, Foster and Metcalfe 2001, Fagerberg 2003, Witt 2008 for recent surveys).

The concept of evolution thus has a meaning in evolutionary economics that differs from the one in evolutionary psychology. In the latter, "evolution" – in the sense of the Darwinian theory (see Mayr 1991, chap. 4) – is part of the explanans. It provides the meta-hypothesis on the basis of which capabilities and constraints of the human brain – and the corresponding features of the cognition and choice – are reconstructed as, it is assumed, natural selection has created them at times when early humans were under fierce selection pressure (see Lea, chapter 21 in this volume). In evolutionary economics, in contrast, "evolution" is a synonym for the economic transformation process and, hence, part of the explanandum. However, because of the causal reduction of endogenous economic change to human learning, creativity, and innovative action, there is a basis and a need for engaging in a dialogue with psychological theories on these dynamic aspects of human behavior.

In order to explain the economic transformation process and the results it is generating, it is necessary, thus, to go beyond static decision-making theories. These are theories of choice that take alternatives as given. In some cases, as in evolutionary psychology, they focus on how framing effects bias the perception of the alternatives and how choices follow simple decision heuristics (see Gigerenzer and Goldstein 1996). In evolutionary economics, in contrast, the role of choice alternatives that newly emerge is crucial (see Witt 2003). Accordingly, the focus is on what motivations drive learning and innovativeness from which the newly perceived options arise. How are new insights and actions created, and what behavioral adaptations do they trigger? Obviously, these questions transcend a mode of reasoning often to be found in contemporary economic theorizing which is preoccupied with the characteristics and implications of equilibrium states of the economy. In that mode of reasoning, the complexities of human behavior and its adaptative potential are not considered. The present reflections on the adaptations in economic behavior and their driving forces may therefore be seen as an attempt to broaden the foundation of the theory of economic behavior more generally.

The argumentation in this chapter proceeds as follows. Adaptations in human behavior can be distinguished by the different time scales in which they occur. In rough approximation, three levels can be identified. One level is that of the genes that code certain forms of behavior. Another level is that of innate, non-cognitive learning mechanisms that govern instrumental conditioning and conditioned reinforcement. Last, but not least, there is the level of cognitive reflection, insight, and observational learning. As argued in section 20.2, adaptations at the genetic level – for which the Darwinian theory of evolution would be relevant – need many generations to appear. Given that, in the economic domain, the bulk of change occurs within single generations, the pace of that kind of behavioral adaptation seems too slow to matter for economic evolution. Moreover, systematic behavior adaptations of the kind explained by sociobiology only occur under sufficient natural selection pressure – an assumption that is controversial as far as modern humans are concerned. The facts notwithstanding, it will be argued that, for similar reasons as in evolutionary psychology, the Darwinian theory of evolution in general, and sociobiology in particular, can be considered a relevant meta-hypothesis for evolutionary economics too.

In elaborating this argument, section 20.3 explores the influence of the innate, non-cognitive learning mechanisms on behavior adaptations as they occur in the course of the economic transformation process. To account for these influences within the utilitarian model of economic behavior, a connection to the concepts of utility functions and their logical equivalent, individual preference orderings, needs to be made. These concepts, central to microeconomic theorizing, play no similar role in psychology. In economics the questions of what generates utility and how are left open, as, for that matter, are questions of what becomes the object of preference orders and why. However, as will be explained, it is precisely in answering these questions that the influences of innate dispositions and non-cognitive learning mechanisms are relevant. Section 20.4 turns to the cognitive influences on economic behavior and the systematic changes they are responsible for in interaction with the non-cognitive learning processes. In a short digression, the section also discusses what motivations drive innovativeness from which new choice alternatives emerge. Section 20.5 elaborates in an exemplary fashion on the implications of the theory presented in the previous sections for explaining the economic transformation process. The example chosen is the apparently incessant growth and structural change of consumption. Section 20.6 briefly concludes.

20.2   Setting the frame: the role of the human genetic endowment

When economic evolution is identified with the ongoing transformation processes of the economy, what relevance does the Darwinian theory of evolution then have for evolutionary economics? Opinions on this point are split. If a Darwinian world-view is accepted as a unifying frame for scientific inquiry (see Wilson 1998), a straightforward answer would be to interpret the Darwinian theory as a meta-hypothesis from which the initial conditions and some of the underlying constraints of the historical process of economic change in the long run can be derived. Influenced by the Darwinian revolution of his time, this position had already been suggested by Veblen (1898) – who also introduced the label "evolutionary" economics. But his position was not pursued further in the school he founded (see Hodgson 2004). The discussion on the relevance of the Darwinian world-view for evolutionary economics and on what it implies has therefore only recently reappeared on the agenda of evolutionary economics.[1]

Another way of making use of Darwinian thought in evolutionary economics is a purely heuristic one. Negating the idea of a common ontology of the sciences, this approach borrows key notions and models from evolutionary biology to conveniently conceptualize the economic evolutionary process on the basis of analogy constructions. Analogy constructions to natural selection and recourse to models of population dynamics are characteristic, in particular, of the neo-Schumpeterian branch of evolutionary economics initiated by the work of Nelson and Winter (1982).[2] Yet, population thinking and analogy constructions can be more of a hindrance than a help when it comes to explaining the causal role that behavior adaptations play in economic change. Nelson and Winter (1982, chap. 5) assume that, because of their bounded rationality, economic agents operate on the basis of behavioral routines. When different agents follow different routines this usually means that a variety of more or less successful behaviors emerge. Analogously to the principle of natural selection, selection forces implied by market competition are argued to erode that variety and, thus, to produce adaptations in average behavior. Hence, what is considered to improve average performance is not individual behavior adaption, for

---

[1] See Witt (1996), Vromen (2001), Hodgson (2002), Witt (2003, chap. 1); see also the special issue of the *Journal of Evolutionary Economics*, vol. 16, no. 5, 2006 on "Evolutionary Concepts in Economics and Biology."

[2] See Metcalfe (1998), Nelson and Winter (2002), Fagerberg (2003). In his seminal work on the self-transformation of the economy, Schumpeter (1934) had avoided the term "evolution." He considered it a Darwinian concept and, as such, irrelevant for the social sciences. He also opposed the use of biological analogies.

example through learning and problem solving, and the corresponding motivations, but the changing relative frequencies in a population of behavioral
routines that are themselves unchanging.

In order to be able to account for the impact of individual behavior adaptations on the economic transformation process – the focal point of the present
chapter – the neo-Schumpeterian approach will therefore not be adopted here.
The Darwinian theory will not be used as a source for constructing analogies
but as a meta-theory that, though not directly relevant for the economic transformation process, can shed light on the behavioral foundations of this process.
Not unlike in evolutionary psychology, it can be used to reconstruct the genetic
influences on behavior, deriving from times when early humans were under
fierce selection pressure. The consequences of these influences can be put in
perspective with culturally acquired forms of economic behavior.

As far as animals are concerned, there is little doubt that important parts
of their behavioral repertoire are innate, i.e. develop as an expression of their
genes. Cases in point are elementary behavior dispositions and adaptation patterns like instrumental conditioning and conditioned reinforcement (Dugatkin
2003, chap. 4). With their direct or indirect effect on reproductive success,
innate dispositions and adaptation patterns are likely to have been shaped by
natural selection in a way that enhances individual fitness of the organisms
carrying the corresponding behavior genes. In sociobiology, this hypothesis is
extended to the animals' behavior in social interactions (Wilson 1975). Prominent examples are rearing offspring, the joint stalking of prey, food sharing, support of mating and breeding activities of other animals, and – most puzzling –
"altruistic" forms of behavior, for example in self-sacrifices that increase the
survival chances of others. These and other social forms of behavior are expli-
cable in terms of the theory of natural selection by substituting the concept
of "inclusive fitness" (Hamilton 1964) for the concept of individual genetic
fitness.[3]

Some basic behavioral dispositions and adaptation patterns seem to be innate
also in humans. The question of whether the sociobiological approach can be
extended to explaining human social behavior is, however, highly controversial
(see Caplan 1978). Particularly in the context of early (and of still living, primitive) human societies, the problems of coordination of joint activities, mutual
support, reciprocity, and "altruism" seem to present themselves somewhat similarly to those in higher animal societies. Competition for scarce resources –
food, habitat space, access to mating partners, etc. – is a basic condition of life.
Yet, even in primitive societies, this does not imply that human social behavior is limited to genetically coded forms. There are culturally conditioned

---

[3] Inclusive fitness means to account for the genetic commonalities between kin in calculating
the fitness value of a particular genetically coded social behavior. Behaving altruistically may
lower their chances of reproducing their own genes. On the other hand, depending on the
degree of relationship, the reproductive disadvantage may be over-compensated by increased
reproduction chances of the same genes in kin who benefit from the social behavior.

and intelligently created forms of behavior. They are the major reason why many primitive (but even more so, the economically highly developed modern) societies are capable of mastering their environment so successfully that the selection pressure on their social and economic behavior has decreased dramatically.

Evidence for this finding is provided by the fading correlation between the amount of resources commanded on the one hand and reproductive success on the other. While the amount of scarce resources an animal can command is positively correlated with its reproductive success, in the developed, human societies average real income increases and population growth are negatively correlated.[4] The fact that such inconsequential reproductive behavior is not wiped out indicates that pressure from natural selection does not suffice any more to cut back on an increasing variety of idiosyncratic behaviors with little or no adaptive value in terms of reproductive success. The question then is how the increasing variety of idiosyncratic behaviors comes about, and what determines which behavior is actually displayed.

As will be explained in the next sections, besides the impact of cognitive reasoning and beliefs, some elementary, innate, behavioral dispositions and adaptation mechanisms do have an influence here, albeit an indirect one. (And, precisely because natural selection is no longer a source of rapid systematic change in the human species, these elementary, innate features are likely to be basically the same as those shaped under selection pressure in the earlier phases of human phylogeny.) The indirect influence affects, it will be argued, the individual's utility or preferences and the way in which they change over time.

20.3 Explaining motivation: utility, preferences, and their inherent dynamics

A person's motivation to act and the reflections about possible actions belong to the inner sphere of that person which cannot be observed in the same way as the action actually taken. This simple fact is the crux of a long philosophical debate. Its repercussions have triggered different responses in economic and psychological theorizing. Starting from Bentham's (1789) sensory utilitarianism – guided by a good psychological intuition but a naive attitude towards measurement – economics has over the past two centuries turned first to a theory of subjective utility (lacking any idea of measurability) and then to subjective preference theory. Initially motivated by the desire to give utility theory a proper mathematical expression (Warke 2000), the conversion into

---

[4] See Maddison (2001, chap. 1), who shows in a cross-country comparison that the more per capita income in real terms increased from 1820 to 1998, the more both birth rates and population growth went down. In pre-industrial societies, in contrast, there is evidence for a positive correlation: see, e.g., Chagnon and Irons (1979).

preference theory followed a different path. Strikingly similar to the positivist attitude underlying behaviorism in psychology, the goal was to eliminate all speculations about unobservable inner states of a person from the foundations of microeconomics (see Samuelson 1947, chaps. I and V).

The few empirical implications of subjective utility theory all rest on the – unknown – shape of a person's utility function (usually defined over quantities of n commodities, $x_1, x_2, \ldots, x_n$). However, if certain conditions are satisfied, such a utility function is logically equivalent to an ordering over alternative bundles of the n commodities. For any two bundles $\mathbf{x} = x_1, x_2, \ldots, x_n$ and $\mathbf{y} = y_1, y_2, \ldots, y_n$ such an ordering implies that either "$\mathbf{x}$ is preferred to $\mathbf{y}$" or "$\mathbf{y}$ is preferred to $\mathbf{x}$" or "$\mathbf{x}$ and $\mathbf{y}$ are equally preferred" (indifference). Which of these preferences a person has was, under controlled conditions, expected to be observable by the quantities a person chooses when prices vary (provided the person acts consistently – a version of the rationality assumption whose validity cannot simultaneously be observed). However, such "revealed preference" experiments were rarely carried out. The theory was factually used as a platform logically to deduce "operational" hypotheses about demand behavior, formulated exclusively in terms of observable prices and quantities. As a consequence, individual utility functions and preference orderings now populate economic textbooks, yet with reference to their subjective nature it is left unexplained what the arguments in the functions stand for, or what it is that people have preferences for.

Psychological theorizing took a different route. The concepts of utility and preferences can hardly be found in the psychological literature. However, with respect to the observability problem, radical behaviorism had a similar positivist stance – with one major difference. While revealed preferences theory was oriented towards deriving abstract logical inferences about demand functions, behavioral psychology focused on explaining observable behavior itself – human and non-human. With a minimalist theory, in hundreds of experiments a narrowly limited number of primary reinforcers were identified – findings that invited reflections about the underlying motivation to act. These reinforcers are shared, with some variance, by all humans and by many other species (Herrnstein 1990). This fact and the physiological mechanisms underlying reinforcement that were later discovered in molecular biology point to a genetic basis. By understanding the physiological foundations, the short-term dynamics of deprivation and satiation and their motivational potential can easily be explained. The behaviorists' genuinely dynamic approach to motivation was complemented by the theory of conditioned reinforcement. That theory postulates a primitive, innate mechanism by which associations are learned between stimuli and by which secondary reinforcers emerge on the basis of conditioning learning.

In economics, Bentham's hedonic interpretation of utility as a sensory perception which is observable and even measurable has recently been rehabilitated (see Kahneman, Wakker and Sarin 1997). However, his question of what generates utility and, thus, motivates people to act still needs to be revived. It is particularly important for evolutionary economics, because without being able to explain what motivates a person to act it is impossible, *a fortiori*, to explain how that motivation changes in the short run, and how it can possibly evolve in systematic ways in the longer run. Contrary to what many economists hold, the subjectivity of individual utility and preferences does not prevent one being specific about their causes and contingencies. In fact, the just-mentioned findings in behavioral psychology are directly relevant here. The innate motivational dispositions and the adaptation mechanism expressed respectively in primary reinforcing events and processes of instrumental conditioning and conditioned reinforcement suggest the following hypothesis: A person derives utility from actions depending on (or prefers them according to) their current potential to induce a rewarding sensory experience either by reducing deprivation with respect to primary reinforcers directly or through conditioned secondary reinforcers.[5]

Thus, at least some of the arguments of a person's utility function (if defined over actions rather than commodities) can be connected with the sensory experiences of reinforcers. First, there are experiences with the limited number of innate primary reinforcers shared, with the usual genetic variance, by all humans. Among them are the removal or reduction of aversive stimuli like pain, fear, etc. Furthermore, in numerous experiments the removal or reduction of deprivation from, among others, air, aqueous solutions, sleeping, food, body heat, sensory arousal of certain kind and strength, social status recognition, sex, care, and affection have been identified as primary reinforcing instances.[6] Following the argument above, actions – usually involving goods and services that are purchased in the markets – that are capable of removing or reducing deprivation in these dimensions thus are what generate utility (or, for that matter, are the objects of preference orderings). Correspondingly, the short-run dynamics of the probabilities for certain actions being chosen reflect the variations in the relative degree of deprivation felt in the respective dimensions.

Based on such innate primary reinforcers, a potentially very long chain of secondary reinforcers emerges over the history of conditioned reinforcement a person goes through. The arguments of the individual utility function therefore represent, second, the varying structure of individually acquired secondary reinforcers. Unlike the widely shared primary reinforcers, this structure is of highly idiosyncratic nature, except perhaps for some cultural commonalities in similarly socialized groups. Given their idiosyncrasy and enormous variety, there would be little sense in trying to produce a list of secondary reinforcers. (It is mainly because of these features that it can rightly be claimed that no

---

[5] As the biologists Pulliam and Dunford (1980, 11–44) have shown, this hypothesis can also be given an interpretation in terms of sensory experiences that are based on hard-wired (genetically coded) neurological processes in higher organisms.

[6] See Millenson (1967, p. 368). The survival value of the primary reinforcers is obvious.

two individual utility functions or preferences are alike.) Furthermore, unlike the primary reinforcers allowing for individual malleability in behavior only through instrumental conditioning, the emergence of a structure of individual secondary reinforcers implies a rich dynamic potential for utility functions and preferences to evolve over both individual lifetimes and cultural epochs.

A recourse to elementary innate behavior dispositions and adaptation mechanisms has been suggested here to provide a behavioral foundation for the concepts of utility, preferences, and their inherent dynamics. This suggestion is not meant to imply that the discussion should be confined to the behavioral level. In the economic context, important motivational influences on human behavior, particularly on intentional choices, are likely to emanate also from the cognitive level. These influences are to be discussed next.

20.4   Acknowledging the role of cognition: attention and unfolding action knowledge

Evolution has endowed humans with an exceptional intelligence. Reflection, intuitive insight, intentionality, and logical inference – unique capacities of our cognitive system – play a constitutive role for many economic actions. This means that, in addition to the elementary, innate behavior dispositions and adaptation mechanisms, a set of further causal factors has to be accounted for. The corresponding hypotheses on cognitive influences have to be merged in a more comprehensive theory of economic behavior and its dynamics.

Subjective perception and interpretation can intervene in stimulus–response reaction patterns. Depending on how perceptions are associated with intentions and other existing memory content to form a more or less reflected action plan, reaction patterns can systematically change. Intentional behavior is selectively controlled for goal achievement, and goals may be adjusted as a result of observing the behavior of others. Success or failure in goal achievement can be reflected in terms of subjective cause-and-effect relationships and, by inference, expectations and/or aspirations can be revised. In any case, in addition to learning in the sense of instrumental conditioning and conditioned reinforcement, cognitive learning through insight and observation of others comes into play in a way that moderates the individual dependence on innate behavior dispositions and adaptation mechanisms (Bandura 1986).

As attribution theory has shown, the intervening cognitive activities are not only rather complex but also somewhat arbitrary with respect to their outcome (see van Raaij 1985). However, whether intervening cognitive activities occur, and which ones these are, hinges on the information input. What information is perceived and processed through personal experience or by observation of, and/or communication with, others is contingent, in turn, on certain constraints in human information processing and, thus, knowledge acquisition. These constraints are also part of the human biological inheritance. Since it may be easier to derive hypotheses on the effects of cognitive intervention on economic behavior from constraints on the information input than from the complex internal cognitive processes, these constraints deserve a closer inspection.

In human perception a limited number of sensory stimuli, such as visual and acoustic signals, can spontaneously be processed in parallel into respective stores and be recognized.[7] Unless attention is quickly paid to any such message it will, however, be lost from memory. If, as often, stimuli are offered in abundance to the sensory system, attention must selectively be allocated to competing processing demands. This means that in the brain's processing capacity there is a bottleneck. Of the information coming in at any given point in time, spontaneous selective attention processes must filter out that information that will be processed further in the working memory. There the selected information is maintained by rehearsal, but the amount of information that can be rehearsed at one point in time is also narrowly limited.

What pieces of incoming information grab attention depends on both their physically based attributes[8] and their meaning-based attributes. Meaning is identified through tracing information from long-term memory (the other source of information entering the working memory). In long-term memory, knowledge is stored that has previously been accumulated. In order for elements of long-term memory to be made available, they have to be activated selectively through cognitive cues contained in messages. Only messages containing cues for which there is an associative basis in long-term memory can have a meaningful interpretation and, by means of this, attract attention. Since only what is gaining attention has a chance of being rehearsed in memory and, thus, of being added to an individual's knowledge, the change of individual knowledge hinges on the already acquired knowledge.

The meaning associated with a particular piece of information often has affective connotations of liking or disliking. These reflect previous rewarding or aversive experiences ultimately based on reinforcing instances as discussed in the previous section. In the terminology chosen here, the affective connotations therefore relate to a person's preferences or utility function. More specifically, this means that the more a person has developed a preference (or an aversion) for a particular item or event, the more affective weight is attributed to its meaning. Accordingly, it is more likely that attention is allocated to incoming information relating to that item or event. Concomitantly, there is also an effect on individual knowledge: if information related to a particular item or event attracts more attention, then that information also tends

---

[7] See, e.g., Anderson (2000, chaps. 3, 6 and 7) for the following.
[8] Sensory arousal elicited by a stimulus in general depends on two attributes of the stimulus: frequency and relative strength (Helson 1964). Applied to the present context of allocating attention to the information carried by a sensory stimulus, these two factors may be identified with the frequency of exposure to that particular information and the intensity with which the stimulus is felt.

to be more frequently attended and rehearsed in thinking and, hence, to be better cognitively represented in action knowledge in the long-term memory. Thus, two mutually reinforcing effects interact. One effect is the affection-driven impact of the current preferences on the selective allocation of attention and the incremental change of knowledge. The other effect is that of selective attention and gradually changing knowledge on the formation of individual preferences. The more something is valued, the more it is also able to attract attention, to be rehearsed, and to be retrieved in long-term memory. Conversely, what is more often and persistently recognized as a positive stimulus, or as being related to one, tends, in turn, to be preferred increasingly (provided that a positively conditioning setting is maintained).

The flip side of the coin in this process with self-augmenting features is the relative neglect of, and the rising ignorance with respect to, other information. The capacity of the working memory required to lay out traces to what has earlier been stored in long-term memory is narrowly confined. For this reason, traces that allow retrieval of a particular piece of information can only be established and maintained at the expense of memory traces to other pieces of information. Therefore, the frequency of practicing particular memory traces and the affective value of the stored information are once more decisive factors – this time, however, with regard to the probability and intensity of recalling information. To put it differently: the less frequently and the less intensively a piece of information has been recalled in the past the more likely it is lost from long-term memory, i.e. from current knowledge.

The implications of these specificities of the human information processing system for economic behavior in general and the transformation processes going on in the economy in particular will be highlighted in the next section. Before that, however, a brief digression may be in order into a problem that is of great importance for the explanatory program of evolutionary economics. The problem – also arising at the cognitive level – is how to explain individual innovativeness, i.e. the creation of new choice alternatives and the motivation to do so. Two different questions are involved: first, how is novelty produced? and second, why? Regarding the first question, the key seems to be the brain's continually ongoing recombination activities of already known cognitive components (Koestler 1964, Campbell 1987). For the processes involved in both the recombination and the attribution of meaning, individual creative skills certainly play a crucial role (Sternberg 1988). How these processes work is, however, still little understood. Moreover, the inquiry into these issues is complicated by intricate epistemological problems. One hypothesis that has been suggested is that the meaning of newly produced recombinations is identified through switches in the underlying interpretative *Gestalt* patterns.[9]

---

[9] See Schlicht (1997); these patterns represent highly idiosyncratic, subjective mental states depending on individual experience and current knowledge. For a reconstruction of the brain's recombinatory activity as an act of "conceptual blending" see Fauconnier and Turner (2002).

The second question – why, and under what conditions, a person is motivated to search for novelty – is epistemologically less problematic and therefore easier to answer. Since neither the outcome of the search endeavor nor the time and effort it will need are known in advance, the search cannot be motivated by the expectation of specific outcomes (as implicitly assumed in optimal search models in economics). Search for novelty is motivated in a different way. In fact, there seem to be different forms of motivation corresponding with different forms of searching.

One form is covered by the "satisficing" hypothesis (Siegel 1957, March and Simon 1958, pp. 47–52). According to this hypothesis, the search motivation is dissatisfaction with the status quo. A person experiences a situation that falls short of the current aspiration level of that person, i.e. the level that reflects a balance of the person's earlier successes and failures. Imagine, to give an example, a producer who has a competitor. If the competitor comes up with an innovative move that causes the producer's revenues to fall whatever feasible reaction she can choose, then such a situation is likely to violate the person's current aspiration level. According to the satisficing hypothesis, a motivation to search for not yet known, better alternatives is triggered, notwithstanding the fact that it is unknown whether the search will indeed lead to better alternatives. The search motivation sooner or later vanishes, however, as the search goes on without generating better options. The person's aspiration level gradually declines and when it eventually converges to the best option presently known, the motivation to search vanishes.

A different motivation to search for novelty, and another form of searching, is highlighted by the taste-for-novelty hypothesis. This hypothesis assumes that humans find the experience of certain kinds of novelty a rewarding experience and deprivation from such sensory arousal an aversive experience (Scitovsky 1976). Hence, the more boring a life becomes, i.e. the more deprivation rises in this dimension, the stronger the motivation either to consume (try) a new source of sensory arousal, if available, or to search actively for, and generate the experience of, novelty. Obviously, the two motivational hypotheses refer to different causal contexts and search contexts so that they may be considered complementary hypotheses. The satisficing hypothesis suggests that search for novelty is typically motivated by, and more frequently triggered in, situations of challenge or crisis (where these may be anticipated crises). The taste-for-novelty hypothesis predicts a short-term fluctuation of the search motivation between deprivation and satiation so that, on average, novelty is sought with a, perhaps rather low but constant, basic rate.

20.5 Pulling things together: the example of consumption evolving

Because of space constraints, what follows from the evolutionary approach to economic behavior laid out in the previous sections can only be discussed here in an exemplary fashion. The case to be chosen is that of the growth and structural change of consumption in the developed countries over the past century, i.e. the explanation of what goes on at the demand side of the economy in the historical transformation process. The underlying facts are as follows: per capita income has risen three to six times in the different countries in real terms (Maddison 2001, chap. 1). Consumer spending has grown by a similar magnitude (Lebergott 1993). The enormous expansion of consumer spending was not equally distributed over all consumption categories. To the contrary, over the century there were massive changes in the compositions of goods and services consumed. As empirical research over the past decades has consistently shown, income elasticities of the demand for the different goods and services not only differ but also change over time, resulting in an unequal growth of consumption expenditures across different consumption categories.[10] Moreover, within each of the consumption categories the quality of existing goods and services has constantly been varied and differentiated. An increasing variety of new goods and services has been introduced to the markets.

How can all these observations be explained? How can consumer spending grow so dramatically with rising income without reaching a level of satiation? What role do satiation phenomena play at least in some consumption categories (as they may indeed be conjectured to express themselves in the differing income elasticities)? It is sometimes argued that vicarious entrepreneurs at the supply side of the markets have found ways to offer new or better products appealing to consumer preferences for which there have previously been no suitable offers. Hence the continuously upheld motivation among the consumers to expand expenditures. However, this argument is difficult to accept or refute as long as it is left unspecified what preferences consumers actually have. The discussion in the previous sections provides a basis for making progress.[11]

To recapitulate, some sources of utility – and the corresponding motivation to act – have been identified above with the removal or reduction of deprivation in physiologically determined activities like breathing air, drinking aqueous solutions, eating food, or pain relief. The motivation to consume the corresponding items – air, water, food, medicine – is easy to understand. It is "consumption" in the literal sense of eating up. A significant feature of that kind of consumption is that it is subject to temporary physical satiation that constrains the amount consumed per unit of time. The motivation for additional consumption vanishes as the satiation level is approached, but it reemerges as the organism's

---

[10] See Stone (1954), Houthakker and Taylor (1966), Deaton and Muellbauer (1980), Lebergott (1993). Let I and x denote income and the amount spent on a consumption good respectively. Assuming that a differentiable function $x = x(I)$ exists, the definition of the income elasticity of demand η for that good is $\eta = (dx/dI) / (x/I)$. The good is said to be income inferior if $\eta < 0$, a "normal" good if $0 < \eta \leq 1$, and income superior if $\eta > 1$. This means that, with a marginal increase in disposable income, the percentage change in spending on that good can be smaller (larger) than the percentage change of income.

[11] For a more detailed discussion see Witt (2001).

metabolism gradually uses up what was consumed. As real income increases, consumption can sooner or later be expanded to the average satiation level. Unless people expand their consumption beyond that level ("consumption" in the sense of purchasing items without "consuming" them in the literal sense any more), the absolute per capita consumption of these inputs per unit of time should therefore be expected to face an upper bound.[12] Yet, this is not what can be observed.

Food is an obvious example and some of its forms are therefore preferred candidates for demonstrating statistically that there are income-inferior goods (see Lebergott 1993, part II). However, the food industry has been battling with the satiation problem for decades and there have been ways of circumventing it so far. Household expenditure surveys show that per capita consumption even of many "normal" goods is continuing to grow in absolute terms. The first reason seems to be that with rising income the kind and quality of the diet changes in the direction of more complex and more expensive ingredients with more refined sensory quality. A second reason is that producers have developed new products by which the sensory perception of a rewarding consumption experience can be enjoyed without rapidly approaching physiological satiation. A prominent case is that of foodstuffs made with artificial sweeteners which allow consumers to increase their intake, and thus their expenditure, to a much higher level than the satiation level for similar products made with sugar (see Ruprecht 2005). A typical example is the introduction of Diet Coke. A similar role is played by spices and, more recently, artificial aromas which can be used as low-calorie substitutes for traditional flavoring ingredients with higher calorific content.

For consumption items other than those directly eaten up, the explanation of the change in consumer behavior is more involved. For example, consumption items such as beds or air conditioning facilities serve as means or "tools" in relation to physiologically determined needs such as getting sleep or maintaining body temperature. A television set, to give another example, is one tool among many other options that serve the rewarding experience of a pleasant sensory arousal through entertainment. (In itself, a television set is fairly useless, if it cannot be turned on to emit the entertaining services in the form of a flow of visual and acoustic information.) Being deprived in the dimension of, say, sleep, body heat, or sensory arousal can thus motivate the expenditure on a consumption item able to provide the proper service like beds, clothes, air conditioning, television sets, etc.

The significant feature here is that not the "tools" purchased, but the services they provide contribute to removing or reducing deprivation. This means that

---

[12] The ambiguity of the term "consumption" reflects the etymology of a word that has been used for an increasingly broader set of phenomena after the organization of the economy evolved from the subsistence economy of self-supporting households to an increasingly differentiated division of labor. The extensive market exchange activities related to the latter imply purchasing acts of the households now usually associated with the term consumption ("consumption expenditures").

a temporary satiation level (defined per unit of time) that stifles the motivation to consume can be reached with respect to the *services*. In using them one may feel warm enough, may have had enough sleep, or enough entertainment. But the motivation to utilize the services of the "tools" one possesses and the motivation to purchase the "tools" in the first place are distinct features. The latter motivation depends on how the instrumental relationship of the tools and their services (means and ends) is perceived and is not necessarily affected by satiation in the services. Other reasons than the relative degree of deprivation in their services may influence the motivation to purchase tools. These reasons are likely to emerge from cognitive reflections (e.g., concerning securing a redundant supply, multiple availability for different purposes or at different places, etc.) and subsequent conditioned reinforcement building up secondary reinforcing instances.

People usually reflect and learn about how to instrumentalize consumption items with tool function – most of them belonging to the category of durables (appliances, equipments, etc.) – before a purchasing decision is made. Often rather elaborate knowledge about the consumption technology is necessary and needs to be built up. This knowledge is obtained not only through personal experimentation, but also through communication and observation and imitation of other consumers. Not least, knowledge of the consumption technology is offered by the producers of consumption items – an important function of their advertising. Given the selective nature of individual information processing discussed in the previous section, attention processes tend to shift from information less frequently and less intensely recognized towards information recognized more often and more intensely. At the same time, the perception and, in the longer run, consumption knowledge of items which continue to attract attention tend to become more detailed (refinement effect). By repeated experience a conditioned reinforcement is likely to build up that creates secondary reinforcement instances. Individual preferences extend to ever more details and attributes – attracting more attention in the same direction.

Because of the limitations of the individual information processing capacity, the already mentioned consequence of this process is specialization in consumption. One person may develop into a true motor sport fan following up, with an increasing preference and growing expertise, the most recent technical achievements of the motor car industry. Another person may develop into a similarly attentive opera fan with highly differentiated perception of, and preferences for, the qualitative differences in the music performance. Some people may develop into knowledgeable motor sport and opera fans simultaneously, but nobody can be a fan with differentiated perceptions of, and preferences for, everything. The upshot of specialization and the simultaneous refinement of perception, knowledge, and preferences is that additional reasons can arise for a consumer to purchase, several times over, consumption items with tool functions. These reasons may override the fact that the items provide one and the same service (or very similar ones) and that, with respect to that service, the satiation level is close to being reached or is already reached. (The extreme case is that of collectibles.)

If there is a satiation level with regard to the services in some deprivation dimension, and if multiple purchases of the same "tool" or similar ones exceed the number technically necessary to furnish the satiation level in the services, this simply results in a decreasing average rate of using the services provided by each single tool. For example, since only one pair of shoes (a "tool" providing pain protection and body warmth as "services") can be worn at the same time, purchasing several pairs of shoes means that on average each single pair of shoes is used less intensely. However, although this may induce some dissonant feeling, seeing things being utilized less intensely is likely not to curb the motivation to consume (purchase) as much as the physiological experience of satiation would do.

Another, but related, cause for expanding consumption irrespective of satiation levels being reached can occur when a consumption good is capable of removing or reducing deprivation in several dimensions simultaneously. Such "combination goods" are often deliberately created by product differentiation and product innovations. If, with rising income, consumption of these goods is growing, satiation levels are usually not reached in all dimensions at the same time. In that case, a sufficient motivation to further expand consumption of the good or service may be upheld in those dimensions not yet satiated. For obtaining additional satisfaction from such "combination goods" in some dimensions, consumption in other dimensions is extended beyond the satiation level. The possibility to create new combinations is strongly supported by the refinement effect just mentioned.

The questions addressed in this section are why and in what way consumer spending has been expanding tremendously in real terms with rising income over the past century and how the unequal growth of consumption expenditures across different consumption categories (the differences in the income elasticities of the goods and services) can be explained. For the consumption categories discussed so far, the answers were based on the assumption that the growth of income and consumption would in principle make a reduction or removal of average deprivation feasible. In some consumption categories, however, the satiation level may not, or not easily, be reached by increasing expenditures.

Consider, for example, the primary reinforcing instance of social status recognition. Consumption items with tool function whose services are able to signal the desired status by distinguishing oneself from others may remove or reduce deprivation in this dimension. Yet, with rising average income, lower income groups may also be able to acquire such consumption items. As a consequence, the status-distinguishing character of the corresponding consumption items is lost and deprivation in this dimension returns. To continue to be able to signal the desired social status differences by one's own consumption, other, and usually more expensive, goods need to be consumed. A level of satiation can, if at all, only be upheld by continuously rising expenditures on status goods (see Hirsch 1978) – an unstable condition like in a weapons race.

Another case in which satiation is difficult to attain and consumption can therefore expand without reducing deprivation significantly is the primary reinforcing instance of sensory arousal. As argued by Scitovsky (1976), the reason is again an instability in the deprivation–satiation mechanism, albeit one that is caused in a different way. This time it arises from a kind of sensory stupefaction effect that calls for ever stronger stimuli to reduce deprivation. With growing consumption, the satiation level is continually rising here. The instability can be conjectured to be visible in modern consumption patterns in the expenditures on entertainment, tourism, and the media that have been growing much faster with rising income than average consumption expenditures and are likely to continue to do so.

20.6 Conclusions

Human economic activity and the human economy have changed dramatically over time. Evolutionary economics has been proposed as a paradigm for analyzing the historical process of change. However, evolutionary economics, as much as economics more generally, requires a foundation in the form of a concise theory of economic behavior. Both the historical changes in economic behavior and the behavioral dispositions on the basis of which they could develop can probably be rationalized, but not explained, by the static (and latently normative) theory of constrained maximization. In this chapter the foundations of an evolutionary approach to economic behavior have been laid out. It has been argued that the historical malleability of economic behavior is based on the interactions between elementary, innate behavior dispositions and adaptation mechanisms on the one hand and the limited, and always selective, cognitive and observational learning that contributes to an ever more extended and differentiated action knowledge. The implications of this interpretation have briefly been outlined in an exemplary fashion for the explanation of the evolution and growth of consumption.

The fact that, as a characteristic of the evolutionary economic transformation process, consumption is continually growing has been attributed to several causes. As a consequence of "nature's parsimony" (as Ricardo put it), i.e. of a minimal real per capita income, humans have throughout their history been confronted by a situation of deprivation with respect to many of their needs. Simply as a reaction to that situation of deprivation, consumption expenditures could therefore be expected to rise from their extremely low value, when per capita income in the developed countries started to rise in the early twentieth century. However, as it turned out, a more detailed investigation of this reaction begs the question of what precisely causes deprivation and whether and when, with further rising income, satiation can remove that consumption motivation.

The hypotheses suggested here to answer the question have emphasized the genetically fixed, physiological, and psychological dimensions of deprivation in which a reduction of deprivation is a rewarding experience. In some of these dimensions it may, for different reasons, be difficult to reach satiation even at very high levels of income. Two examples are often mentioned: social or status recognition, sensory or cognitive arousal. In these few dimensions the simple logic of increasing consumption to reduce deprivation seems to induce a long-lasting, if not unbounded, growth of demand and, hence, a rising share of these consumption categories in overall consumption expenditures. Even though this is a selective effect, it does contribute to consumption further expanding even in the richest countries.

Beyond the motivational mechanism of deprivation and satiation, other parts of the human biological inheritance have been claimed also to play a crucial role for economic behavior and its impact on the economic transformation process. These parts are conditioned learning and the intelligent recognition of means–ends or tool–service relationships from which additional motives to expand consumption emerge. As a result of contingent reinforcement, preferences for goods and services can develop where there have been no such preferences before. With disposable income rising, consumers literally learn to appreciate previously unknown consumption opportunities, to develop refined tastes, and to "specialize" in certain consumption activities.

Furthermore, it has been contended that with rising income the opportunities for purchasing consumption goods with "tool" functions increase, provided the consumers command the corresponding consumption knowledge. The information from which this knowledge arises is not least furnished by commercial advertisements, and its impact is often reinforced by socially contingent opinion formation processes and agenda-setting effects. These are the sources that provide all sorts of plausible reasons for why "tools" should be purchased. At the level of cognitively motivated consumption expenditures they may induce expenses, even when satiation with respect to some of the service dimensions of the tools is already reached. The consequence is a decreasing average rate of using the services of the tools. A special case of this phenomenon is that of "combination goods" nowadays representing a substantial share of the consumer goods.

20.7 References

Anderson, J. R. 2000. *Cognitive Psychology and Its Implications*, 5th edn, New York: Worth.

Bandura, A. 1986. *Social Foundations of Thought and Action – A Social Cognitive Theory*. Englewood Cliffs, NJ: Prentice-Hall.

Bentham, J. 1789. *An Introduction to the Principles of Morals and Legislation*. London: T. Payne.

Campbell, D. T. 1987. "Blind Variation and Selective Retention in Creative Thought as in Other Knowledge Processes," in G. Radnitzky and W. W. Bartley II (eds.), *Evolutionary Epistemology, Theory of Rationality, and the Sociology of Knowledge*. La Salle: Open Court, pp. 91–114.

Caplan, A. L. (ed.) 1978. *The Sociobiology Debate*. New York: Harper.

Chagnon, N. A. and Irons, W. (eds.) 1979. *Evolutionary Biology and Human Social Behavior – An Anthropological Perspective*. North Scituate, RI: Duxbury Press.

Deaton, A. and Muellbauer, J. 1980. *Economics and Consumer Behavior*. Cambridge: Cambridge University Press.

Dugatkin, L. A. 2003. *Principles of Animal Behavior*. New York: Norton.

Fagerberg, J. 2003. "Schumpeter and the Revival of Evolutionary Economics," *Journal of Evolutionary Economics* 13: 125–59.

Fauconnier, G. and Turner, M. 2002. *The Way We Think – Conceptual Blending and the Mind's Hidden Complexities*. New York: Basic Books.

Foster, J. and Metcalfe, J. S. 2001. "Modern Evolutionary Perspectives: An Overview," in J. Foster and J. S. Metcalfe (eds.), *Frontiers of Evolutionary Economics*. Cheltenham: Edward Elgar, pp. 1–16.

Gigerenzer, G. and Goldstein, D. G. 1996. "Reasoning the Fast and Frugal Way: Models of Bounded Rationality," *Psychological Review* 103: 650–69.

Hamilton, W. D. 1964. "The Genetical Evolution of Social Behavior I," *Journal of Theoretical Biology* 7: 1–16.

Helson, H. 1964. *Adaptation Level Theory*. New York: Harper & Row.

Herrnstein, R. J. 1990. "Behavior, Reinforcement, and Utility," *Psychological Sciences* 4: 217–21.

Hirsch, F. 1978. *Social Limits to Growth*. Cambridge, MA: Harvard University Press.

Hodgson, G. M. 2002. "Darwinism in Economics: From Analogy to Ontology," *Journal of Evolutionary Economics* 12: 259–81.

　　2004. *The Evolution of Institutional Economics*. London: Routledge.

Houthakker, H. S. and Taylor, L. D. 1966. *Consumer Demand in the United States 1929–1970*. Cambridge, MA: Harvard University Press.

Kahneman, D., Wakker, P., and Sarin, R. 1997. "Back to Bentham? Explorations of Experienced Utility," *Quarterly Journal of Economics* 112: 375–405.

Koestler, A. 1964. *The Act of Creation*. London: Penguin Books.

Lebergott, S. 1993. *Pursuing Happiness – American Consumers in the Twentieth Century*. Princeton: Princeton University Press.

Maddison, A. 2001. *The World Economy: A Millennium Perspective*. Paris: OECD.

March, J. G. and Simon, H. A. 1958. *Organizations*. New York: Wiley.

Mayr, E. 1991. *One Long Argument*. Cambridge, MA: Harvard University Press.

Metcalfe, J. S. 1998. *Evolutionary Economics and Creative Destruction*. London: Routledge.

Millenson, J. R. 1967. *Principles of Behavioral Analysis*. New York: Macmillan.

Nelson, R. R. 1995. "Recent Evolutionary Theorizing about Economic Change," *Journal of Economic Literature* 33: 48–90.

Nelson, R. R. and Winter, S. G. 1982. *An Evolutionary Theory of Economic Change*. Cambridge, MA: Harvard University Press.

　　2002. "Evolutionary Theorizing in Economics," *Journal of Economic Perspectives* 16: 23–46.

Pulliam, H. R. and Dunford, C. 1980. *Programmed to Learn: An Essay on the Evolution of Culture*. New York: Columbia University Press.

Ruprecht, W. 2005. "The Historical Development of the Consumption of Sweeteners – A Learning Approach," *Journal of Evolutionary Economics* 15: 247–72.

Samuelson, P. A. 1947. *Foundations of Economic Analysis*. Cambridge, MA: Harvard University Press.

Schlicht, E. 1997. "Patterned Variation – The Role of Psychological Dispositions in Social and Institutional Evolution," *Journal of Institutional and Theoretical Economics* 153: 722–36.

Schumpeter, J. A. 1934. *Theory of Economic Development*. Cambridge, MA: Harvard University Press.

Scitovsky, T. 1976. *The Joyless Economy*. Oxford: Oxford University Press.

Siegel, S. 1957. "Level of Aspiration and Decision Making," *Psychological Review* 64: 253–62.

Sternberg, R. J. 1988. *The Nature of Creativity*. Cambridge: Cambridge University Press.

Stone, J. R. N. 1954. *Measurement of Consumer Expenditures and Behavior in the United Kingdom*, vol. I. Cambridge: Cambridge University Press.

van Raaij, W. F. 1985. "Attribution of Causality to Economic Actions and Events," *Kyklos* 38: 3–19.

Veblen, T. 1898. "Why Is Economics Not an Evolutionary Science?" *Quarterly Journal of Economics* 12: 373–97.

Vromen, J. J. 2001. "The Human Agent in Evolutionary Economics," in J. Laurent and J. Nightingale (eds.), *Darwinism and Evolutionary Economics*. Cheltenham: Edward Elgar, pp. 184–208.

Warke, T. 2000. "Mathematical Fitness in the Evolution of the Utility Concept from Bentham to Jevons to Marshall," *Journal of History of Economic Thought* 22: 3–23.

Wilson, E. O. 1975. *Sociobiology – The New Synthesis*. Cambridge, MA: Belknap Press.

1998. *Consilience – The Unity of Knowledge*. New York: Knopf.

Witt, U. 1996. "A Darwinian Revolution in Economics?" *Journal of Institutional and Theoretical Economics* 152: 707–15.

2001. "Learning to Consume – A Theory of Wants and the Growth of Demand," *Journal of Evolutionary Economics* 11: 23–36.

2003. *The Evolving Economy*. Cheltenham: Edward Elgar.

2008. "Evolutionary Economics," in S. N. Durlauf and L. E. Blume (eds.), *The New Palgrave Dictionary of Economics*. New York: Palgrave Macmillan, forthcoming.

21 Evolutionary psychology and economic psychology

STEPHEN E. G. LEA

21.1 What is evolutionary psychology?

In the period during which modern economic psychology has been developing, effectively since the work of Katona and his colleagues shortly after the Second World War (summarized by Katona, 1964), psychology has become an increasingly theory-free zone. Early textbooks of economic psychology from this modern period, such as that of Reynaud (1974/1981), still found it desirable to work through some of the major schools of psychology and consider what each has had to say about economic behaviour. But within psychology the 'grand theories of everything' were in retreat throughout that period, and the dominant approach to psychology was firmly bottom-up, empirically driven, constructing small-scale theories on the basis of established experimental or observational trends. This has created an asymmetry between psychology and economics. Whereas it is not hard to identify 'the economic approach' to a particular phenomenon or even 'the economic theory' about it, there is no way of finding 'the psychological approach' or 'the psychological theory'. Instead, there are a multitude of different possible psychological theories, depending on the standpoint of the theorist or the context the problem is placed into. Indeed, so strong has this tendency been that it can be argued that it has made it more difficult for economists and psychologists to work together (see Lea, 1994a; 2006).

More recently, however, a new grand theory of everything has taken shape within psychology, namely evolutionary psychology. This theory has grown out of recent findings in population biology, and recent developments in Darwinian theory. The process of its formation began with the first attempts to make these developments available to a wider audience, through large-scale technical treatments like that of E. O. Wilson (1975) and the more popular, polemical approach of R. Dawkins (1976). In particular, the deliberate application of sociobiological theory to human behaviour by E. O. Wilson (1978) sparked a widespread debate within the social sciences, with many authors vehemently opposed to the attempt to provide general explanations of human behavioural trends in terms of universal evolutionary principles (e.g. Sahlins, 1977). The sociobiologists were convinced that there is such a thing as human nature – a set of motivational and behavioural tendencies which all human beings share, by virtue of being human. Many social scientists have preferred the contrary view, that human behaviour is infinitely plastic, and can only be understood in terms of the cultural influences that shape it. On this view, the only contribution biology can make to an understanding of human behaviour is to explain how it is that humans come to be cultural beings.

Most early sociobiological writings about human nature were concerned with motivational issues, such as differences between sexual and parental motivations between the sexes, and the origins of conflicts between sexual partners or parents and offspring. It is relatively easy to believe that such visceral motives might have something in common between humans and other animals, because humans like other animals depend on them for our survival. But from the publication of the landmark book *The Adapted Mind* (Barkow, Cosmides and Tooby, 1992), a new and less-likely-seeming alliance emerged, between Darwinism and cognitive psychology. It is the fusion of ideas from these two fields that has generally taken the name 'evolutionary psychology'. From one perspective, this was an unexpected combination. Human cognition does seem to be very different from cognition in any other animals, and cognitive psychology has generally been hostile to more biological approaches to the discipline, a legacy of its struggles to free itself from the behaviourist hegemony of the earlier twentieth century. However, the explicit nativism of some influential cognitive theorists, especially the psycholinguist Chomsky (1968), perhaps prepared the way for some such synthesis – though leading figures within the evolutionary psychology of language, such as Pinker (1994), naturally reject Chomsky's claim that language could not have emerged through natural selection.

As Buller (2005, pp. 8ff.) has noted, there is a broad and a narrow sense in which the term 'evolutionary psychology' can be construed. In the broad sense, it means the general attempt to find explanations for modern human behaviour and mental life within the modern Darwinian account of the origin of species by evolution through natural selection. Buller argues that this should be considered as a field of study rather than a body of theory. In effect he is saying that this general attempt is uncontentious. However, this is not quite true. Some social psychologists continue to argue that evolutionary explanation has no role in human psychology, and of course there is a large swathe of public opinion, if not academic argument, which holds that humans are not products of evolution in any case. Thus even in this broad sense, evolutionary psychology must be recognized as a theoretical position.

Buller's narrow sense of 'evolutionary psychology' (which he refers to as 'Evolutionary Psychology', capitalizing to emphasize its distinctiveness) is much more specific. It implies an adherence to a particular theoretical position taken up by authors such as Tooby and Cosmides (1992), Pinker (1994) and Buss (2003). These authors put forward a set of hypotheses about how evolutionary history is reflected in the psychology of modern humans, and then derive an important methodological proposition from them. The key propositions of evolutionary psychology in this narrow sense include:

1. All important adaptive changes to the human brain took place during the Pleistocene era, when humans were living a hunter-gatherer way of life. Our minds thus reflect Stone Age selective pressures. The Pleistocene environment is often referred to as the Environment of Ecological Adaptation, or EEA.
2. To cope with the numerous demands of Stone Age existence, humans evolved a large number (many thousands) of distinct genetically specified brain structures, which are reflected in largely separable mental abilities. These are usually referred to as 'mental organs' or 'modules'.
3. The collectivity of these modules defines a distinctive and unchanging 'human nature', and evidence for it can be found regardless of the culture in which people live.
4. Methodologically, to understand how these modules work, we have to 'reverse engineer' them by understanding what problems Stone Age humans faced and working out what mental organs would have been needed to solve them. We cannot understand them by considering what is adaptive in the conditions of modern life, because these are not the same as the conditions of the EEA.

This distinction between broad and narrow views of evolutionary psychology is crucial for the present chapter. Clearly there are many possible theoretical positions and empirical investigations that would be within evolutionary psychology in the broad sense but would be opposed or irrelevant to evolutionary psychology in this more narrow sense. Despite the current fashion for the narrow sense of evolutionary psychology, the present chapter is concerned with the idea in its broader sense. Because the focus of so much of the literature is on the narrow sense of evolutionary psychology, we will need to focus on it from time to time, but it should be regarded as only one among many possible positions within evolutionary psychology as we conceive it.

There are two reasons for broadening the focus in this way. First, the idea that modern human behaviour is influenced by our evolutionary past is too important to allow it to be hijacked by any one theoretical school. Secondly, regardless of the eventual fate of the theoretical system adopted by evolutionary psychologists in the narrow sense, we have to solve the problem of the evolutionary origins of economic behaviour. Our construction of large-scale economies is one of the ways in which our species most obviously differs from the other apes and our primate relatives in general, and like other kinds of human uniqueness, this requires an evolutionary explanation (see Lea, 1994b).

Although it will not take the usual narrow view of evolutionary psychology, this chapter will take a particular point of view about human evolution, one that is not inherent in the usual narrow sense of 'evolutionary psychology'. Humans are unique in having evolved, through ordinary genetic adaptation and selection, a brain, perceptual apparatus and a social system which between them can rival genetic inheritance as a mechanism for one generation's experiences to influence the behaviour of the next: we have evolved the capacity for culture. As sociobiologists at least since R. Dawkins (1976, chapter 11) have recognized, human evolution at least involves dual evolutionary processes, both genetic evolution and cultural evolution. More probably it involves co-evolution between genetic and cultural structures (Richerson and Boyd, 2005), that is, each adapts to the other. Recognizing this dual or interacting aspect of human evolution is crucial for two reasons. First, to ignore cultural evolution would be to miss a vital component of human evolution (and, if the narrow-sense evolutionary psychologists are right, the only one with the capacity to have changed things since the Stone Age). Second, it enables us to bypass the stifling and sterile 'nature–nurture' debate, and talk about the evolutionary origins of modern behaviour without having to consider whether it is genetically or culturally determined: a co-evolutionary or even a dual-evolutionary stance recognizes without further ado that all behaviours are affected by both our cultural and our genetic history, and there is no meaning in trying to assign percentages to the two influences.

We have stressed the importance of the difference between the broad and narrow sense of evolutionary psychology, and the vital importance of culture in the unique process of human evolution. But despite these differences, there are important characteristics that apply to any evolutionary psychology, whether it is broad or narrow, and whatever role it assigns to cultural evolution has one important characteristic. Any evolutionary approach to behaviour treats current behaviour as though it has a history, and it treats that history as important. This puts it in conflict with much (though not all) modern thinking in economics, which builds a theory of economic behaviour from choices that are both disembodied and decontextualized.

21.2 The role of evolutionary explanation in economic psychology

From one point of view, one might expect evolutionary explanations to have little to contribute to economic psychology. Arguably, the economy is the aspect of human life that has changed most in the transition from the Stone Age Environment of Ecological Adaptation to the present. We conventionally define the major stages of human cultural development since Stone Age times in terms of the technological and economic advances that ushered them in, using descriptions like the Bronze Age, the Agricultural Era or the Machine Age. An important precept of economic psychology is that economic systems influence human behaviour and mental life – in a range of ways that go beyond the economic (see Lea, Tarpy and Webley, 1987, pp. 291–2). Surely little can be predicted about behaviour in the modern economy from a human nature that must, even if one rejects the narrow approach to evolutionary psychology, owe much to the conditions of the Stone Age, not to mention the environments in which our hominid and pre-hominid ancestors lived?

This argument is defective in two ways. First, it has often been the role of economic psychology and behavioural economics to point out ways in which modern human behaviour is maladaptive, or as it is often put, irrational or anomalous (Thaler, 1991). Searching for such irrationalities is probably not the ideal research programme for economic psychology (see Lea, 1994a), but their existence is not in doubt, and an obvious way of explaining them is to say that we are bringing Stone Age brains to modern economic problems. Secondly, however, it is not so obvious that from the point of view of the individual and the psychological processes he or she has to deploy, coping with a modern economy is so very different from coping with a hunter-gatherer environment. It is no accident that the words 'ecology' and 'economy' are similar, and if a coal tit can be considered as a careful shopper (Tullock, 1971), it may not be so unreasonable to consider a shopper as an optimal forager. Lea (2006) has discussed the three-way relationship between psychology, ecology and economics in detail, arguing that psychology relates to the other two disciplines in much the same way because they have important characteristics and theoretical orientations in common.

Lea and Newson (2005) argued that it is timely to consider the role of evolutionary explanations in economic psychology, for several reasons. First of course is the current prominence of evolutionary explanation within psychology generally, as has already been discussed. In addition, however, there is currently a new impetus in evolutionary economics (see the chapter by Witt, this volume), and it tends to be linked to the more behavioural, empirical approaches to economics for which economic psychology has a natural affinity. In addition to the points made by Lea and Newson, we should note that the new field of neuroeconomics is developing with extraordinary speed (see the chapter by Lohrenz and Montague in this volume), and much neuroeconomic discourse makes explicit reference to evolutionary concepts (see, for example, Cory, 2006; Levine, 2006).

We will now consider a few exemplary cases where evolutionary explanations have been deployed in economic psychology. Following the general approach to economic psychology taken by Lea *et al.* (1987), they are grouped under two headings: explanations of individuals' economic behaviours, which according to conventional microeconomic theory and the dogma of consumer sovereignty, are what determine the behaviour of the economy as a whole; and explanations of the impacts of economic events and systems on individuals.

21.3   Evolutionary psychology and economic behaviour: two examples

First, therefore, we turn to two examples of evolutionary explanations of individual economic behaviours.

The first comes from the area where economics and psychology most obviously meet, the study of choice and decision. Both psychology and economics were extensively influenced in their early development by the ideas of utilitarian philosophers such as Bentham (1789/1996), and the idea that individuals would make choices that would maximize their happiness or utility. Although in the twentieth century economics sought to purge away all psychology from its theory of choice, the lack of psychological realism in that theory has remained as both a link and a point of contention between the two disciplines. The two most recognizably psychological winners of the Nobel Prize in economics in the period since the Second World War have both been awarded it for research documenting the empirical limitations of the conventional economic theory of choice (Simon, 1955; Kahneman, 2003).

Standard microeconomic theory assumes that economic behaviour can be understood by assuming that each individual acts so as to maximize his or her utility. It is common ground among many decision theorists that this model of ideal rational choice has to be modified by an understanding of the cognitive limitations of the actual human decision maker. Any such position makes an implicit appeal to a distinctive human nature, because it is from human nature that the cognitive limitations come. Different theorists have taken different approaches to specifying the limitations of human decision making, The most interesting from the point of view of the present chapter is the approach that has been taken by Gigerenzer (e.g. Gigerenzer and Goldstein, 1996; Gigerenzer, Todd *et al.* 1999).

Gigerenzer's theory is interesting for this chapter because it is explicitly cast within the framework of evolutionary psychology – evolutionary psychology, indeed, in the narrow sense. But it has the additional advantage of presenting deviations from ideal rational choice as benefits rather than limitations. He thus rejects the view, often referred to as 'bounded rationality' (e.g. Sargent, 1993) or 'the economics of information' (Stigler, 1961), that deviations from ideal decision making can be understood by taking into account the limitations that search time and human processing power place on decision making, and that the decision maker should respond to these constraints by allocating the optimal amount of time and effort to each decision-making problem. This, Gigerenzer argues, leads to an infinite regress: trying to compute how much optimization one has time to do would be even more time-consuming than carrying out a full optimization. Similarly, assessing human decisions for their rationality against criteria of logical coherence, or noting the use of heuristics and the presence of biases that violate such criteria, in the style of Kahneman and Tversky (e.g. 1979), presents real human choice as merely a hobbled version of ideally rational choice. Instead Gigerenzer argues for the use of a different criterion for assessing actual decision making, which he calls the correspondence criterion: how accurately does the process enable us to predict important facts about the environment?

The correspondence criterion leads naturally to an evolutionary approach, since it is of the essence of natural selection that it assesses everything by its results. Indeed, an evolutionary approach demands that we adopt a correspondence criterion, because natural selection is only interested in outcomes, not in mechanisms. It is outcomes that confer adaptive advantage, and are thus subject to natural selection; mechanisms are only selected indirectly, through the outcomes they produce. Gigerenzer explicitly links his idea of 'fast and frugal' choice heuristics (which are also robust and accurate) with Tooby and Cosmides' (1992) idea of the 'adaptive toolbox', the set of evolved psychological mechanisms that enabled humans to survive in the EEA. Furthermore he shows by a number of distinct approaches that such heuristics can do at least as well as, and sometimes better than, much more complex decision rules that are meant to provide the ideally rational solution to problems. Gigerenzer *et al.* (1999) then proceed to apply these ideas to many of the choice problems that have been analysed by Evolutionary Psychologists (in the narrow sense), such as recognizing the social intentions of another individual, choosing a mate or deciding how much effort to put into parenting.

In almost any practical situation, it should not be surprising that many approaches can do nearly as well as a truly optimal decision rule: this is an inherent consequence of the idea of an optimum. If individuals can vary in their behaviour, and the outcome is some kind of function of that behaviour, we expect to observe the behaviour for which the outcome is a maximum. But the maximum of any function is what mathematicians call a stationary value: in the region of the maximum, minor changes in the independent variable produce little or no change in the dependent variable. It follows that behaviour that is functionally indistinguishable from the 'rational' (in the sense of optimal) may be produced from mechanisms that are far from 'rational' (in the sense of involving reasoning out the best solution). Gigerenzer and his colleagues have demonstrated that this is in fact the case for their fast and frugal heuristics: they do as well as, sometimes better than, the optimal decision algorithm.

It follows that apparently rational behaviour may be produced by creatures that have no power of reason at all, and that even in creatures that do have the power of reason, such as human beings, a rational outcome does not necessarily imply a rational process. It is an entirely reasonable guess, in fact, that much of our economic behaviour relies on processes that we share with other animals. Some anthropologists have studied hunter-gatherer people using the same kind of methodology that primatologists use for studying how monkeys and apes spend their time. Their results reveal that, with the important exception of their social relationships, these humans' allocation of time and patterns of behaviour look remarkably like those of other primates occupying similar ecological niches (Bailey and Aunger, 1990). Conversely, using the common tools of the operant psychology laboratory, it is possible to construct schedules of reinforcement in the Skinner box that are close analogues of the price changes that occur in a complex modern economy. In such experiments, animals such as rats and pigeons respond to price changes in ways that are consistent both with microeconomic theory and with human econometric data

(Lea and Roper, 1977; Lea, 1978; Battalio, Green and Kagel, 1981; Battalio, Kagel, Rachlin and Green, 1981). The analogy is so close that techniques based on economic concepts such as demand curves have become standard in the assessment of animal welfare: demand analysis is now commonly used to determine how valuable different kinds of resources are to animals being kept under agricultural conditions (see M. S. Dawkins, 1990, and examples such as Matthews and Ladewig, 1994; Jezierski, Schefflerb, Bessei and Schumacher 2005). This analogy is part of the evidence that Lea and Newson (2006) have used to argue for an evolutionary account not just of choice and decision, but of the buying and shopping behaviour which, according to microeconomic theory, should flow from it.

In summary, therefore, the boundedness of human rationality requires an evolutionary explanation if it is not to be empty or regressive. Evolutionary considerations have the potential to explain, not just why rationality has to be bounded, but also why people respond in the way they do in situations where formulating an optimal response is impossible.

Our first example came from the heartland of economic psychology, the theory of choice. Our second comes from the heartland of modern Darwinism, the study of altruism. Superficially, altruism is a problem for the theory of natural selection: how can a tendency to do things that benefit others at your own cost survive from generation to generation? Surely altruists, who by definition reduce their own fitness to increase the fitness of others, should always be removed from the population, and hence any gene that favoured altruism should be removed from the gene pool? And yet altruism manifestly exists in many parts of the animal kingdom – most notably in the eusocial insects such as ants, bees, wasps and termites, but also in smaller but no less undeniable ways, such as the tendency of many young birds to stay and help their parents rear the next brood of young, or the way that many group-living animals will give alarm calls when a predator approaches, despite the risk that this will draw the predator's attention to them as individuals. And this is without considering distinctively human forms of altruism such as anonymous gifts to charity.

Sociobiology sprang to prominence within biology, psychology and public discourse precisely because it provided a means of explaining the existence of altruistic behaviour within the context of a strict Darwinism, without invoking the kinds of ideas that had been deployed by earlier ecologists, for example, Wynne-Edwards (1962). These arguments invoked the process of group selection: it was argued that altruistic behaviour emerged because it helped groups to survive, even if it damaged the survival chances of the altruistic individuals. But, as E. O. Wilson (1975) shows, this mechanism cannot work unless groups are more vulnerable to dying out than individuals are – a condition unlikely to be met in any advanced animal. Instead, sociobiology was built on the twin theories of kin altruism, as developed by Hamilton (1963), and reciprocal altruism, as developed by Trivers (1971). In kin altruism, the altruist acts to increase the fitness of related individuals; since those individuals bear the same genes as the altruist, under the right conditions altruism-inducing genes can be passed into the next generation even if the altruist's own individual fitness is reduced. In reciprocal altruism, the altruist acts to increase the fitness of individuals who have an above-chance probability of returning the favour in the future; again, under the right conditions, this can increase the representation of any altruism-inducing genes in the next generation. Armed with these mechanisms, sociobiology was able to explain how altruistic behaviour could emerge at the level of the organism even while the genes remained resolutely, as R. Dawkins (1976) memorably put it, selfish.

When we come to consider human altruistic behaviour, we can see that much of it is inherently economic, whether it involves giving to individuals (which either alienates earned money directly, or involves consumer behaviour through the purchase of gifts) or more or less anonymous donations to charity. Traditionally such behaviour has been seen as challenging the axiom of greed that is an important element of the microeconomic theory of choice. There are ways of circumventing that argument (see Lea *et al.*, 1987, chapter 9) by treating others' benefit as a source of utility for the individual consumer, but considered from the point of view of evolutionary explanation, this simply makes matters worse. First, it simply places the unsolved problem of altruism within the context of a larger unsolved problem of tastes: because most modern economics denies the body (Gagnier and Dupré, 1999), it is unable to do anything to explain why people like what they do (Stigler and Becker, 1977). Furthermore altruism, considered as a taste, remains mysterious relative to other tastes, particularly when it takes the form of anonymous charity (see Khalil, 2004).

Worthwhile explanations of altruism in economic behaviour have to be evolutionary, in the sense of explaining how the behaviour can persist despite its apparent selective disadvantages. An example is Bolle's (1992) demonstration that it might be adaptive to offer disinterested love to a sufficiently powerful enemy. But the evolutionary theory used needs to be a sophisticated one. Without Hamilton's and Trivers' modifications, individual selection theory cannot explain the persistence of any altruism. Sober and Wilson (1998) argue that in fact those modifications amounted to a rehabilitation of group selection. They attempt to make such a rehabilitation explicit through the concept of multi-level selection, in which selection is simultaneously effective at different levels (e.g. both the individual and the group), and thereby to come to an evolutionary explanation of modern altruism. That attempt remains deeply controversial within evolutionary psychology and biology, but what is not controversial is that there are multiple kinds of selection going on in the determination of human behaviour. As we noted above, human evolution inevitably involves cultural as well as genetic evolution. Once we recognize the significance of gene-culture co-evolution (Boyd and Richerson, 1985), group selection even by the exacting standards of E. O. Wilson (1975) becomes a possibility for two reasons. First, cultural groups can be short-lived relative to individuals, the key requirement for group selection. Secondly, cultural inheritance can be Lamarckian rather than Mendelian: that is, acquired characteristics can be passed from one individual to another, rather than transmission depending on genetic change and therefore only occurring by slow processes of mutation and selection. Instead, groups can seek to enforce or at least encourage behaviours like altruism through social rules such as moral or religious norms. People are frequently, perhaps always, motivated to follow or appear to follow such norms, and this can have a direct effect on altruistic behaviour; for example, Fehr and Gächter (1999) have shown experimentally that publishing people's contributions to a common good will enhance the contribution level. On the basis of these and related experimental results, Gintis, Bowles, Boyd and Fehr (2003) have argued that what they call 'strong reciprocity', a form of altruism distinct from kin and reciprocal altruism, can be an evolutionary stable strategy. But it is stable only in the context of cultural processes, social norms and multilevel selection.

21.4 Money as an example of the evolutionary psychology of economic impacts on individual behaviour

Our final example of evolutionary explanation in economic psychology is primarily concerned with the impact of the economy as a whole on the individual. One of the most striking ways in which modern economies differ from those of the Environment of Ecological Adaptation is in the presence and role of money – a huge fact of economic life to which we all have to adapt in the course of our individual development.

Evolutionarily speaking, money is not old. While there is dispute about the first institution that can properly be called money, we can be sure that it goes back no more than 3,000 years (Grierson, 1978; Seaford, 2004). This is far too little time for there to have been any genetic adaptation to its existence, so we must deal with money with brains that evolved long before it existed. Yet we behave towards it in much the same way as we do towards commodities like food, or activities like sex, which have been part of our evolutionary heritage for hundreds of millions of years. And our behaviour towards money is so efficient that it seems perfectly natural, and it requires a stretch of the imagination even to recognize that it requires a psychological explanation, and that such an explanation may not be easy to come by.

Many authors have argued that the invention of money profoundly changed the nature of human society and even human psychology. For example, Seaford (2004) suggests that it was the invention of abstract money that enabled the early Greek philosophers to develop a kind of abstract thought that was previously unknown. But the most obvious change is that modern humans are motivated to obtain money – all kinds of money – in ways that people in non-monetized societies were not. Economic theory treats this fact as unproblematic, and psychologists have generally followed them in this, assuming that money is simply instrumental in obtaining valued goods. Many sociologists and political scientists, however, have recognized that it requires explanation. Classically, for example, Marx (1867/1932, volume I chapter 3) saw employment, the conversion of labour into money, as involving a double transformation of the kind he described as 'commodity fetishism', in which a compelling image can come to eclipse the objects it portrays, and the products of human labour can appear as 'independent beings endowed with life' (chapter 1). While bare of technical psychology, Marx's account represents the motivation for money as involving a complex psychological process.

Lea and Webley (2006) have classified the different psychological accounts of money motivation (including those that come from other social sciences, and not from psychology itself) as 'Tool theories' or 'Drug theories'. Tool theories are those that assume that the instrumental value of money is sufficient to explain all human behaviour towards it: money is nothing but a means to an end, and the psychology of means and ends is all we need to account for it. Drug theories, on the other hand, suppose that money is to some extent parasitic on more ancient motivational systems, so that we desire it for more than it can deliver.

Over recent decades, there has been substantial empirical work on the psychology of money, much of which is hard to accommodate within a Tool theory. There are oddities about the perception of money tokens such as coins and notes (Bruner and Goodman, 1947; Lea, 1981; Brysbaert and d'Ydewalle, 1989). In times of inflation, people are frequently influenced by the nominal rather than the real value of money, a phenomenon Fisher (1928) called money illusion; though long rejected as impossible by economic theorists, its existence has now been convincingly demonstrated in surveys (e.g. Shafir, Diamond and Tversky, 1997) and economic experiments (Fehr and Tyran, 2001). People frequently reject new forms of money such as dollar coins in the US (see Caskey and St Laurent, 1994) or the euro in the UK (Routh and Burgoyne, 1998). Psychometric work on attitudes to money reveals multiple dimensions, with a distinction between cognitive (instrumental) and affective (emotional) responses (e.g. Yamauchi and Templer, 1982; Furnham, 1984; Tang, 1995). Money, which instrumentally should be the perfect medium of exchange, is not socially acceptable in a number of contexts, for example as a gift in some relationships (Webley, Lea and Portalska 1983) or in exchange for sex (Zelizer, 1996), resulting in elaborate ways of disguising such 'taboo' exchanges.

On the basis of this and other evidence, Lea and Webley (2006) conclude that the Tool theory of money is incomplete, and needs to be supplemented with some kind of Drug theory – whose scope may well be wider than the mere explanation of marginal anomalies. They therefore consider what more ancient motivations it might parasitize, and focus attention on two. The first is the instinct for reciprocal altruism, which is a distinctive feature of human evolution, and has often been invoked in discussions of the origins of trade and other economic relationships (Lea, 1994b). The second, bearing in mind that until very recently money has always taken highly tangible forms, is the instinct for object play.

21.5 Envoi

The importance of gene–culture co-evolution in evolutionary understanding of human behaviour drives us towards systems accounts, involving multiple circular patterns of causation. As we saw in our discussion of altruism, it is only by recognizing social processes such as norm-enforcement that we can make an evolutionary account of strong reciprocity work. Within such a systems approach, a rigid division of economic psychology into the economic behaviours of individuals and the economy's impacts on individuals would be artificial. As Lea (2006) emphasizes, these two kinds of process are necessarily integrated – and integrated, furthermore, into a system in which political actors deliberately intervene. In a complete economic psychology, individual-driven and economy-driven causation must be recognized as two sides of the same coin.

What this chapter has demonstrated is that the impact of human evolution can be seen on both sides of that coin. That is no surprise: no field of human science can avoid the question of evolution, and economic psychology is no exception. We humans are what we are because of a 3-billion-year history of evolution, all but the past 5 million years or so shared with other extant species. The economy is not an abstract force but a human creation, and our behaviour within it, and our reactions to it, are consequences of our human nature in the same way as any other kind of behaviour or our responses to any other aspect of our environment. Modern economic psychology, however, largely derived from two fields that have paid little attention to evolutionary hypotheses – decision theory, which has focused on abstractions like the ideally rational decision maker, and social psychology, which has been almost abiological out of a fear of contamination by biological determinism. It is only the over-whelming importance of evolutionary hypotheses in modern intellectual life, brought about by the sociobiological revolution and the different reactions to it in anthropology, cognitive science, economics and psychology, that has led to the development of evolutionary hypotheses within economic psychology. Nonetheless a start has now been made.

21.6 References

Bailey, R. C., and Aunger, R. (1990). Humans as primates: The social relationships of Efe pygmy men in comparative perspective. *International Journal of Primatology*, 11, 127–46.

Barkow, J., Cosmides, L., and Tooby, J. (1992). *The Adapted Mind: Evolutionary Psychology and the Generation of Culture*. Oxford: Oxford University Press.

Battalio, R. C., Green, L., and Kagel, J. H. (1981). Income–leisure tradeoffs of animal workers. *American Economic Review*, 71, 621–32.

Battalio, R. C., Kagel, J. H., Rachlin, H., and Green, L. (1981). Commodity-choice behavior with pigeons as subjects. *Journal of Political Economy*, 89, 67–91.

Bentham, J. (1996). *An Introduction to the Principles of Morals and Legislation*, edited by J. H. Burns and H. L. A. Hart. Oxford: Clarendon. (Originally published, 1789.)

Bolle, F. (1992). Why and when to love your enemy. *Journal of Economic Psychology*, 13, 509–14.

Boyd, R., and Richerson, P. J. (1985). *Culture and the Evolutionary Process*. Chicago: University of Chicago Press.

Bruner, J. S., and Goodman, C. C. (1947). Value and need as organising factors in perception. *Journal of Abnormal and Social Psychology*, 42, 33–44.

Brysbaert, M., and d'Ydewalle, G. (1989). Why Belgian coins grow smaller. *Psychologica Belgica*, 29, 109–18.

Buller, D. J. (2005). *Adapting Minds*. Cambridge, MA: MIT Press.

Buss, D. M. (2003). *Evolutionary Psychology: The New Science of the Mind*. Boston: Allyn and Bacon.

Caskey, J. P., and St Laurent, S. (1994). The Susan B. Anthony dollar and the theory of coin/note substitutions. *Journal of Money, Credit and Banking*, 26, 495–510.

Chomsky, N. (1968). *Language and Mind*. New York: Harcourt Brace & World.

Cory, J. G. A. (2006). A behavioral model of the dual motive approach to behavioral economics and social exchange. *Journal of Socio-Economics*, 35, 592–612.

Dawkins, M. S. (1990). From an animal's point of view: Motivation, fitness, and animal-welfare. *Behavioral and Brain Sciences*, 13, 1–61.

Dawkins, R. (1976). *The Selfish Gene*. Oxford: Oxford University Press.

Fehr, E., and Gächter, S. (1999). Collective action as a social exchange. *Journal of Economic Behavior and Organization*, 39, 341–69.

Fehr, E., and Tyran, J.-R. (2001). Does money illusion matter? *American Economic Review*, 91, 1239–62.

Fisher, I. (1928). *The Money Illusion*. New York: Adelphi.

Furnham, A. (1984). Many sides of the coin: The psychology of money usage. *Personality and Individual Differences*, 5, 501–9.

Gagnier, R., and Dupré, J. (1999). Reply to Amariglio and Ruccio 'literary/cultural "economies", economic discourse, and the question of marxism'. In M. Woodmansee and M. Osteen (eds.), *New Economic Criticism*, pp. 401–7. London: Routledge.

Gigerenzer, G., and Goldstein, D. G. (1996). Reasoning the fast and frugal way: Models of bounded rationality. *Psychological Review*, 103, 650–69.

Gigerenzer, G., Todd, P. M., *et al.* (1999). *Simple Heuristics That Make Us Smart*. New York: Oxford University Press.

Gintis, H., Bowles, S., Boyd, R., and Fehr, E. (2003). Explaining altruistic behavior in humans. *Evolution and Human Behavior*, 24, 153–72.

Grierson, P. (1978). The origins of money. *Research in Economic Anthropology*, 1, 1–35.

Hamilton, W. D. (1963). The evolution of altruistic behavior. *American Naturalist*, 97, 354–6.

Jezierski, T., Schefflerb, N., Bessei, W., and Schumacher, E. (2005). Demand functions for cage size in rabbits selectively bred for high and low activity in open-field. *Applied Animal Behaviour Science*, 93, 323–39.

Kahneman, D. (2003). Maps of bounded rationality: A perspective on intuitive judgment and choice. *American Economic Review*, 93, 1449–75.

Kahneman, D., and Tversky, A. (1979). Prospect theory: An analysis of decision under risk. *Econometrica*, 47, 263–91.

Katona, G. (1964). *The Mass Consumption Society*. New York: McGraw-Hill.

Khalil, E. L. (2004). What is altruism? *Journal of Economic Psychology*, 25, 97–123.

Lea, S. E. G. (1978). The psychology and economics of demand. *Psychological Bulletin*, 85, 441–66.

(1981). Inflation, decimalization and the estimated size of coins. *Journal of Economic Psychology*, 1, 79–81.

(1994a). Rationality: The formalist view. In H. Brandstätter and W. Güth (eds.), *Essays in Economic Psychology*, pp. 71–89. Berlin: Springer-Verlag.

(1994b). The evolutionary biology of economic behavior. In H. Brandstätter and W. Güth (eds.), *Essays in Economic Psychology*, pp. 53–69. Berlin: Springer-Verlag.

(2006). How to do as well as you can: The psychology of economic behaviour and behavioural ecology. In M. Altman (ed.), *Handbook of Contemporary Behavioral Economics*, pp. 277–96. Armonk, NY: Sharpe.

Lea, S. E. G., and Newson, L. (2005). Evolutionary economic psychology. Paper read at the conference of the International Association for Research on Economic Psychology, Prague, September.

(2006). Antelopes, Berries and Children: The ABC of behaving in a consumer culture with a Stone Age brain. Paper read at the conference of the International Association for Research on Economic Psychology, Paris, July.

Lea, S. E. G., and Roper, T. J. (1977). Demand for food on fixed-ratio schedules of reinforcement as a function of the quality of concurrently available reinforcement. *Journal of the Experimental Analysis of Behavior*, 27, 371–80.

Lea, S. E. G., Tarpy, R. M., and Webley, P. (1987). *The Individual in the Economy*. Cambridge: Cambridge University Press.

Lea, S. E. G., and Webley, P. (2006). Money as tool, money as drug: The biological psychology of a strong incentive. *Behavioral and Brain Sciences*, 29, 161–209.

Levine, D. S. (2006). Neural modeling of the dual motive theory of economics. *Journal of Socio-Economics*, 35, 613–25.

Marx, K. (1932). *Capital*. London: Dent. (Originally published, 1867.)

Matthews, L. R., and Ladewig, J. (1994). Environmental requirements of pigs measured by behavioral demand functions. *Animal Behaviour*, 47, 713–19.

Pinker, S. (1994). *The Language Instinct*. New York: Morrow.

Reynaud, P.-L. (1981). *Economic Psychology*. New York: Praeger. (Originally published, 1974.)

Richerson, P. J., and Boyd, R. (2005). *Not by Genes Alone: How Culture Transformed Human Evolution*. Chicago: University of Chicago Press.

Routh, D. A., and Burgoyne, C. B. (1998). Being in two minds about a single currency: A UK perspective on the euro. *Journal of Economic Psychology*, 19, 741–54.

Sahlins, M. (1977). *The Use and Abuse of Biology: An Anthropological Critique of Sociobiology*. London: Tavistock.

Sargent, T. J. (1993). *Bounded Rationality in Macroeconomics*. Oxford: Clarendon.

Seaford, R. (2004). *Money and the Early Greek Mind*. Cambridge: Cambridge University Press.

Shafir, E., Diamond, P., and Tversky, A. (1997). Money illusion. *Quarterly Journal of Economics*, 112, 341–74.

Simon, H. A. (1955). A behavioral model of rational choice. *Quarterly Journal of Economics*, 64, 99–118.

Sober, E., and Wilson, D. S. (1998). *Unto Others: The Evolution and Psychology of Unselfish Behavior*. Cambridge, MA: Harvard University Press.

Stigler, G. (1961). The economics of information. *Journal of Political Economy,* 69, 213–25.

Stigler, G., and Becker, G. (1977). De gustibus non est disputandum. *American Economic Review*, 67, 76–90.

Tang, T. L. P. (1995). The development of a short money ethic scale: Attitudes toward money and pay satisfaction revisited. *Personality and Individual Differences*, 19, 809–16.

Thaler, R. H. (1991). *The Winner's Curse*. New York: Free Press.

Tooby, J., and Cosmides, L. (1992). The psychological foundations of culture. In J. Barkow, L. Cosmides and J. Tooby (eds.), *The Adapted Mind*, pp. 19–136. New York: Oxford University Press.

Trivers, R. L. (1971). The evolution of reciprocal altruism. *Quarterly Review of Biology*, 46, 35–57.

Tullock, G. (1971). The coal tit as a careful shopper. *American Naturalist*, 105, 77–80.

Webley, P., Lea, S. E. G., and Portalska, R. (1983). The unacceptability of money as a gift. *Journal of Economic Psychology*, 4, 223–38.

Wilson, E. O. (1975). *Sociobiology*. Cambridge, MA: Harvard University Press.
   (1978). *On Human Nature*. Cambridge, MA: Harvard University Press.

Wynne-Edwards, V. C. (1962). *Animal Dispersion in Relation to Social Behaviour*. Edinburgh: Oliver and Boyd.

Yamauchi, K. T., and Templer, D. I. (1982). The development of a Money Attitudes Scale. *Journal of Personality Assessment*, 46, 522–8.

Zelizer, V. A. (1996). Payments and social ties. *Sociological Forum*, 11, 481–95.

Index

to test theory 23, 24
see also quasi-experimental method
experimental psychology 4
expert knowledge, of professional investors 159
explanation 40
   across two levels 17–20
   the autonomy of levels of 19
   cross-level 17
   'deep' 22
   depth of 9–24, 32
   in evolutionary economics 502
   hierarchical model 14
   instrumentalism vs. realism in explanation 12
   kinds of 13–17
   levels of 9–17, 32
   prediction and control 14, 26
   the role of evolutionary in economic psychology 515–16
   'shallow' of behaviourism 22, 23
   within-level 16
   see also cognitive explanation; contrastive explanation; generative explanation
exploratory behaviour, brain regions in 473, 473 (fig. 19.8)
exponential discounting 109, 465
exposure avoidance 112
externalities, and the environmental problem 406, 407
externality problem 287
extrapolative expectations 42, 44, 76, 84, 170
extrinsic motivation 411
   influence on intrinsic motivation 412, 417
Exxon, use of contingent valuation method 431

Faber, R.J. 114, 187
'face work' 186
fairness 273
   gender differences in neural correlates 480, 481 (fig. 19.13)
   neuroscience of 459, 478, 480
   perceptions of the tax system 312, 318
   perceptions of travel demand management 395
   reciprocal in environmental issues 407, 410
   or self-interest 481
Fama, E.F. 48, 64, 66, 68, 70
familiarity bias 76
family
   alternative forms of 134, 149
   financial practices within 133
   generational transfer of saving behaviour 125
   influence on consumer behaviour 122, 126
   lone parent 132
   'reconstituted' 142
   rights and responsibilities in 149

   the traditional 133, 135–45
   see also household
fashions 353
Fechner, G. 241
Fedorikhin, A. 114, 244
feelings, and investment in the stock market 52–3
Fehr, E. 5, 18, 19, 21, 22, 31, 478, 521
Feinberg, R. 414
Fenton-O'Creevy, M. 52
Ferrari, L. 266
Ferris, J.M. 263, 263 (table 11.1)
Festinger, L. 24, 25, 209
fiduciary duty 164
   and long-term responsible investment (LTRI) 164–5
Fiedler, K. 46, 47
field studies, crowding theory 415
Figlewski, S. 77, 78
finance 5, 39–60, 64–90, 105–27, 132–50, 155–74
   modern 64, 65
financial decisions in the household 5, 132–50
   relative earning power and 148
financial markets
   economic theory of 39
   the individual investor and 39
   myopic behaviour in 170
   use of psychology in study of 40
fiscal approach, to promote sustainable behaviour change 354
fiscal illusion 268, 294
fiscal policy, benefits, justice and fairness of 6
Fischbacher, U. 5, 18
Fischhoff, B. 49, 50
Fishbein, M. 17, 437, 442–5
Fishburn, P.C. 106
Fisher, I. 121, 522
Fisher, S. 67, 70
fitness 496
   'inclusive' 496
   individual genetic 496
   in kin altruism 519
Fleming, R. 143
focalism 55
food industry, satiation problem 505
Forbes, W. 88
forecasting
   analyst, management and time-series 87–9
   biases and errors in 74, 75, 88
   group mean (consensus) 75
   individual 75
   miscalculation in 75, 84, 88
   self-fulfilling 56
   statistical factors in 81
   see also affective forecasting